UNITED STATES ARMY IN WORLD WAR II

The European Theater of Operations

CROSS-CHANNEL ATTACK

by

Gordon A. Harrison

MILITARY INSTRVCTION

BARNES
&NOBLE
BOOKS
NEW YORK

This edition published by Barnes & Noble, Inc.
by arrangement with W. S. Konecky Associates, Inc.

1995 Barnes & Noble Books

First printed in 1951 by the Center of Military History
United States Army, Washington, D. C.

Printed and bound in the United States

ISBN: 1-56619-877-1

M 10 9 8 7 6 5 4 3 2 1

UNITED STATES ARMY IN WORLD WAR II
Kent Roberts Greenfield, General Editor

Advisory Committee

James P. Baxter	William T. Hutchinson
President, Williams College	University of Chicago
Henry S. Commager	S. L. A. Marshall
Columbia University	Detroit News
Douglas S. Freeman	E. Dwight Salmon
Richmond News Leader	Amherst College
Pendleton Herring	Col. Thomas D. Stamps
Social Science Research Council	United States Military Academy
John D. Hicks	Charles H. Taylor
University of California	Harvard University

*Historical Division, SSUSA**
Maj. Gen. Orlando Ward, Chief

Chief Historian	Kent Roberts Greenfield
Chief, World War II Group	Col. Allison R. Hartman**
Editor-in-Chief	Hugh Corbett
Chief Cartographer	Wsevolod Aglaimoff

*Redesignated Office of the Chief of Military History, 28 March 1950.
**Succeeded by Col. Thomas J. Sands, 3 March 1950.

. . . to Those Who Served

Foreword

Cross-Channel Attack is one of approximately a hundred volumes which the Department of the Army intends to publish regarding its part in World War II. This particular volume deals with the planning and the difficulties encountered incident to the mounting of the largest amphibious assault ever undertaken in military history. Much of the information it contains has not heretofore been a matter of public knowledge. For example, light is for the first time thrown upon the enemy's conflicting theories of defense against Allied air superiority and upon his paucity of first-class troops. This information is derived from the official records of the Wehrmacht and from signed statements of German participants. Many of the difficulties encountered in the planning, as well as in the execution stage of the operation, are here described to the public for the first time.

Where this history deals with the struggle ashore, it clearly illustrates the necessity for commanders to adjust their thinking to the means at hand, the terrain, and the influence of new weapons. It reiterates the indispensability of constant training in how to get order out of the confusion which is forever present upon the battlefield. It brings to mind in this connection the means used by a football team for meeting the problems of overcoming opposition on the playing field. The plays devised and the techniques used to attain its ends must be practiced again and again. Frequently it is the loss of effective direction of small units, incident to the battle's toll, which makes for failure rather than success.

Whether the reader approaches the book with the justified pride that he was a member or supporter of the winning team, or whether he reads to learn, is a matter for him to decide. The victor tends to prepare to win the next war with the same means and methods with which he won the last. He forgets the difficulty of reaching decisions, the planning problems, his faltering, his unpreparedness. The vanquished is wont to search far afield for new and improved methods, means, and equipment. The accomplishments of those who fought in this period were indeed great, as were the sacrifices. But from the national viewpoint it would seem desirable to read this volume with the self-critical eye of the vanquished as well as with the pride of the victor, an approach which the thoughtful reader will not find difficult.

ORLANDO WARD
Maj. Gen., U.S.A.
Chief of Military History

Washington, D.C.
1 October 1950

Introductory Note on the History of the European Theater of Operations

Chronologically this volume is first in the series narrating the events of World War II in the European Theater of Operations. It has been preceded in publication by *The Lorraine Campaign,* which covers the operations of the Third Army during the autumn of 1944 and which begins some two months after the close of the present volume. A co-operative history of the type represented in this series has distinct advantages but does not lend itself readily to the production and publication of volumes in proper chronological order. For this reason each volume will be designated only by title and will remain unnumbered.

Cross-Channel Attack has been planned and written as the introduction to the history of those campaigns in 1944 and 1945 which led to the destruction of the German armies in the west. It provides necessary background for the study of *all* the campaigns in the European Theater of Operations. The narrative of operations ends on 1 July 1944, with the Allies firmly established in Normandy. The concluding chapters show the successful fruition of plans and preparations reaching back as far as January 1942; but the seizure of the Norman beaches and the establishment of a lodgment area are only a beginning, a point of departure for the drive to the Elbe and the Baltic. Although *Cross-Channel Attack* includes discussion of certain problems of high command and logistics, a more complete treatment is accorded these subjects in two volumes now under preparation in this series: *The Supreme Command* and *Logistical Support of the Armies.*

The author of *Cross-Channel Attack,* Gordon A. Harrison, a former newspaper reporter and instructor at Harvard University, holds the Doctor of Philosophy degree from that institution. During the war he served as a historical officer with the Third Army, taking part in five campaigns. He joined the Historical Division, Department of the Army, in 1946.

HUGH M. COLE
Chief, European Section

Washington, D.C.
1 October 1950

Preface

This volume, introductory to a series on the European Theater of Operations, deals with the development of strategy and planning for the attack on northwest Europe in 1944 and with the first month of operations establishing Allied armies in France. The first seven chapters (about two-thirds) of the book are concerned with the prelude to the 6 June assault: the preparations and discussions of strategy on both the Allied and German sides from 1941 to 1944. The remaining three chapters describe the combat operations of the First U. S. Army in Normandy from 6 June to 1 July 1944. This apportionment of space was deliberately made with reference to the whole European Theater Series, and much of the material on plans, the state of German defense, preparatory operations, has strict relevance only when viewed from the larger perspective.

While attempting to set operations in northwest Europe in the framework of world-wide strategy, *Cross-Channel Attack* makes no pretense of telling the full story of that strategy. Other volumes under preparation by the Historical Division will focus on the Mediterranean and Pacific and discuss various aspects of the higher direction of the war.

It should be pointed out further that this is an American story of an Allied operation. It is based largely on Department of the Army records, and although these include a large number of British and Combined documents it has not been possible, nor was it intended, to develop in full the narrative of British participation. Every effort has been made to avoid a partisan viewpoint and to present fairly some of the critical problems of the Anglo-American alliance as they came into and were revealed by the cross-Channel project. Beyond that there is no attempt to achieve an "Allied" perspective or to weigh and balance American and British contributions. In the operational chapters British action has been summarized only when it occurred on the flank of First U. S. Army and materially affected American operations.

In the narrative of American operations in Chapters VIII–X, the basic unit treated is the division, although in recording the fragmented battles typical of fighting in the European theater it often becomes necessary to follow battalions and even companies and platoons on quasi-independent missions in order to describe fully what the division as a unit did. The actions are described in somewhat less detail than in other volumes of the series chiefly because the Department of the Army has already published monographs covering the period. The reader interested in greater detail will find it in [Charles H. Taylor] *Omaha Beachhead* (Washington, 1945) and [R. G. Ruppenthal] *Utah Beach to Cherbourg* (Washington, 1947). *Cross-Channel Attack* summarizes these two accounts with occasional corrections, additions, and reinterpretations, and with entirely new German material.

In a work based on thousands of cables, memoranda, plans, journal entries, etc., to have cited the source for every fact would have unduly burdened every page with redundant footnotes. Documentation is therefore selective, aimed first at citing authorities for all important or disputed facts and opinions, and second at providing those curious to know more with an adequate guide to the primary and secondary source material.

As is the uniform practice throughout this series, German units and headquarters are italicized. Exception is made for OKW and OKH which, though military headquarters, were also constitutional organs of the German state. German units are translated whenever exact English equivalents exist. The terms panzer, panzer grenadier, Luftwaffe, and Kampfgruppe, however, have been retained because they are of such common occurrence that they have been virtually assimilated at least into military English.

Cross-Channel Attack is in a real sense the product of co-operative enterprise. It depends heavily on information collected by army historians in the field during combat, on preliminary draft narratives by other historians after combat, on specific assistance given me during the writing and research, and perhaps most important of all on the privilege (which I have always enjoyed) of tapping the collective knowledge of colleagues working in related fields. When the first draft was completed I had to leave the Division temporarily and the whole burden of editing devolved for some time upon others. I am particularly grateful to Associate Editor Joseph R. Friedman and to Capt. Frank Mahin, Capt. James Scoggin, and Mr. Detmar Finke of the Foreign Studies Section for undertaking much of the onerous burden of checking facts and footnotes in my absence, and for performing an editing task that often amounted to collaboration.

It is a pleasure to acknowledge indebtedness to Col. S. L. A. Marshall for his indispensable series of interviews and manuscript studies of the airborne operations in Normandy and for his interviews with officers and men of the 1st and 29th Divisions. Other combat interviews to which I am indebted were conducted by Lt. Col. W. T. Gayle and Capt. R. G. Ruppenthal. Special thanks are due Captain Ruppenthal and Colonel Taylor for the excellent preliminary studies on UTAH and OMAHA beach mentioned above which I have used freely. Interviews conducted by Dr. Forrest C. Pogue with some forty British planners and commanders in the summer of 1946 immeasurably enriched the record available to me.

In exploring German sources, besides assistance by the Foreign Studies Section I received special help from Capt. Benjamin Schwartz. The bulk of the research in air force records on which the section on the Combined Bomber Offensive is based was very ably performed by Lt. Col. Charles A. Warner. The task of locating relevant documents and running down some of the more elusive facts was made easier and more pleasant by the willing efforts of many special research assistants and archivists who cannot all be named here. I appreciate the co-operation of members of the JCS Historical Section, the Air Forces Historical Section, and the Office of Naval History. I am specially grateful to Mr. Israel Wice and his assistants, to Mr. Royce L. Thompson, and to Miss Alice Miller.

The problems of dealing with an Allied operation largely from American records were greatly reduced by the generous help of the British Cabinet Historical Section under Brigadier H. B. Latham. I must particularly acknowledge the contributions of Lt. Col. H. A. Pollock and Lt. Col. A. E. Warhurst. Colonel Warhurst, author of the British Historical Section's preliminary narrative of operations in northwest Europe, has sent me copies of important documents missing from the files here and has supplied careful briefs of British action. Useful information was also supplied by the British Admiralty and the Air Ministry. Col. C. P. Stacey of the Canadian Historical Section gave me the benefit of his special knowledge. It should be pointed out, however, that the British and Canadian historians do not concur in many of the judgments in this book and that they are in no way responsible for the handling of the material, or for errors of fact or presentation.

For making available personal papers and other data I am indebted to the kindness of Gen. Dwight D. Eisenhower, Maj. Gen. Ray W. Barker, and Lt. Gen. Sir Frederick E. Morgan. Other commanders have helped clarify obscure points and have criticized portions of the manuscript. Footnotes acknowledge their contributions only in part. The warning must be repeated that their help in no way implies an endorsement of the use that has been made of it.

Mr. Wsevolod Aglaimoff in the course of planning and laying out the maps provided me with new fruitful perspectives out of his knowledge and experience as a military cartographer. Pictures were selected and prepared by Lt. Col. John Hatlem; aerial photographs were made by him specially for this volume through the co-operation of the 45th Reconnaissance Squadron, USAF. Miss Michael Burdett edited the footnotes and, with Mrs. Frances T. Fritz, copy-edited the entire manuscript. The tremendous job of preparing the index was carried out by Mr. David Jaffé. Miss Mildred Bucan typed the manuscript for the printer.

Cross-Channel Attack has been prepared under the general direction of Dr. Hugh M. Cole, Chief of the European Section, Historical Division. It has been a happy and rewarding experience to have had Dr. Cole's discerning counsel throughout the period of research and writing.

GORDON A. HARRISON

Washington, D.C.
1 October 1950

Contents

Charts

Maps

Illustrations

Illustrations are from the following sources:

U.S. Army Photos, pages: 7, 14, 20, 39, 50, 89, 118, 124, 132, 159, 163, 178, 216, 251, 256, 271, 273, 277, 285, 303, 310, 316, 343, 352, 385, 405, 424, 425, 427, 433, 437, 439

U.S. Air Force Photos, pages: 85, 195, 226, 229, 279, 285, 294, 306, 312, 331, 346, 354, 358, 362, 389, 391, 394, 399, 407, 409, 424, 427, 435

U.S. Navy Photos, pages: 161, 323

U.S. Coast Guard Photos, pages: 161, 299, 303, 314, 425

Captured German Photos, pages: 55, 134, 139, 150, 255

National Archives Photo, page: 199

CHAPTER I

The Roots of Strategy

The Common Ground

OVERLORD, the cross-Channel attack which hit the German-occupied coast of Normandy on 6 June 1944, was one of the last and by far the biggest of the series of amphibious operations by which the United States and the British Empire came to grips with the German–Italian–Japanese Axis in the course of World War II. But it was more than just another attack. It was the supreme effort of the Western Allies in Europe—the consummation of the grand design to defeat Germany by striking directly at the heart of Hitler's Reich. One of the last attacks, it was the fruition of some of the first strategic ideas.

The principles that eventually shaped OVERLORD were developed early but their application was discontinuous, interrupted by diffuse experimentation and improvisation. Neither ideas nor planning can be traced along a single line from a clear beginning to the ultimate action. OVERLORD was an Allied project. British and American planners worked together, but they also worked separately, particularly in the early years of the war. Sometimes their efforts paralleled each other; sometimes they were at cross-purposes. Within both the American and the British military establishments, furthermore, divergent opinions struggled for acceptance. The whole story of planning and preparing the cross-Channel attack is thus many stories which can be told only in terms of the planners and directors concerned, and the pragmatic organizations within which they worked.

At least a year and a half before the United States was drawn into the war, the groundwork for possible Anglo-American military collaboration against the Axis was being laid. The Navy Department took the lead in the summer of 1940 in establishing a permanent observer in London (Rear Adm. Robert L. Ghormley) whose job was specifically to discuss arrangements for naval co-operation in case the United States came into the war, and generally to provide a channel for the interchange of naval information between the two countries.[1] Army observers also traveled to London during 1940 on special missions, but the War Department did not set up a permanent liaison body until the spring of 1941. At that time Maj. Gen. James E. Chaney, a veteran of twenty-four years' experience in the Air Corps, was sent to London as a Special Army Observer directly responsible to Gen. George C. Marshall, the U. S. Army Chief of Staff. General Chaney's headquarters became known as SPOBS (Special Observers). Admiral Ghormley's group at the same time was reconstituted and he was designated Special Naval Observer, reporting directly

---

[1] Administrative History of U.S. Naval Forces in Europe, 1940–1946, MS, pp. 2ff. Hist Div files. See Bibliographical Note.

to Admiral Harold R. Stark, the U. S. Chief of Naval Operations.[2]

The establishment of Chaney's and Ghormley's groups stemmed from agreements with the British in early 1941 to exchange military missions in order to insure continuous co-ordination of ideas and techniques. The British, as a result of these agreements, set up in Washington the Joint Staff Mission, representing the British Chiefs of Staff. Heads of the Joint Staff Mission were co-ordinate representatives of each of the three service chiefs. Jointly the mission was responsible to the British Chiefs of Staff Committee as a whole. Originally the United States intended to establish a similar joint mission. But in the first place the United States had at that time no system of joint direction comparable to the British Chiefs of Staff. In the second place it was considered that a formally constituted military mission might lead to political commitments which, in view of U. S. neutrality, the government could not accept.[3]

The co-ordination provided by the interchange of information through U. S. observers and the British mission was supplemented during 1941 by two formal Anglo-American military conferences. The first was held in Washington between January and March; the second took place in August on shipboard in the Atlantic. At both conferences principles of combined strategy in Europe were discussed and tentative agreements reached on the policy that would govern combined conduct of the war when and if the

United States became Great Britain's ally. The agreement known as ABC–1, which was arrived at in the course of the first of these meetings, was especially important. Although its decisions were not binding on either nation and were not officially recognized by President Roosevelt, they were nevertheless accepted by the War and Navy Departments as a basis for planning in the event of U. S. participation in the war.[4]

The observer and military mission period came to an abrupt end in December 1941 after the Japanese attacked Pearl Harbor and Germany declared war on the United States. In January 1942 Anglo-American alliance became a fact and the British Chiefs of Staff came to Washington to reaffirm earlier informal agreements on combined strategy and to plan the combined conduct of the war. Their most important achievement was the establishment of permanent machinery for collaboration: the Combined Chiefs of Staff. *(Chart 1)* The Combined Chiefs of Staff were defined as consisting of the British Chiefs of Staff or their representatives in Washington (the Joint Staff Mission) and the United States opposite numbers.[5] Their duties as finally approved were to formulate and execute, under the direction of the heads of the United Nations, policies and plans concerning the strategic conduct of the war, the broad program of war requirements, the allocation of munitions, and the requirements for transportation.[6]

[2] *Ibid.;* [Henry G. Elliott], The Predecessor Commands: SPOBS and USAFBI (The Administrative and Logistical History of the ETO: Part I), MS, pp. 23–24. Hist Div files.

[3] Elliott, The Predecessor Commands, pp. 2, 25.

[4] Brief of ABC–1 Conversations. Pre-Inv file 308. See Bibliographical Note.

[5] U.S. ABC–4/CS–4, 14 Jan 42. OPD files, ARCADIA Conf Bk.

[6] CCS 9/1, War Collaboration Between United Nations. Approved at CCS 4th Mtg, 10 Feb 42. See Bibliographical Note for location and nature of CCS documents.

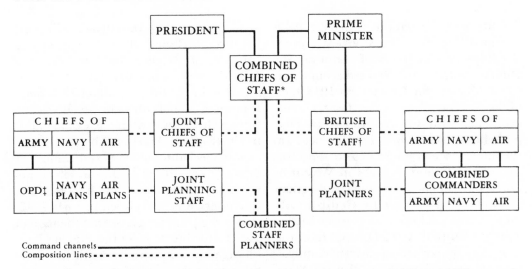

Command channels ―――――――
Composition lines ●●●●●●●●●●●●●●●●●●●

*Admiral Leahy (beginning in July 1942) represented Commander in Chief Roosevelt, and Field Marshal Dill represented Minister of Defence Churchill in the Combined Chiefs of Staff.

†The Joint Staff Mission met in Washington with the Joint Chiefs of Staff as representatives of the British Chiefs of Staff. In major conferences, such as Cairo, Tehran, Yalta, etc., the British Chiefs of Staff attended themselves.

‡The Operations Division was the agency most concerned with planning for European operations.

CHART 1.—SIMPLIFIED COMMAND AND PLANNING ORGANIZATION
FOR EUROPEAN OPERATIONS AS OF MAY 1942

The curious definition of the Combined Chiefs was compelled by the fact that there was no organization of United States Chiefs of Staff at that time equivalent to the British Chiefs of Staff Committee. It was primarily to provide "opposite numbers" to the British for membership in the combined organization that the U. S. Joint Chiefs of Staff came into being.[7] Initially they consisted of Gen. George C. Marshall, Chief of Staff of the Army, Lt. Gen. Henry H. Arnold, Commanding General of the Army Air Forces and Deputy Chief of Staff for Air, Admiral Harold R. Stark, Chief of Naval Operations, and Admiral Ernest J. King, Commander in Chief of the U. S. Fleet. In March 1942, the offices held by Stark and King were combined under King;[8] Stark was sent to London as Commander of U. S. Naval Forces in Europe. The three Joint Chiefs then corresponded to

[7] The only interservice directorate previously existing was the Joint Board founded 17 July 1903. The Joint Board, charged with co-ordinating all matters of joint interest to the services, consisted in 1942 of four Navy and four Army members: for the Army, the Chief of Staff, the Deputy Chief of Staff, the Deputy Chief of Staff for Air, and the Director of the War Plans Division; for the Navy, the Chief of Naval Operations, the Assistant Chief of Naval Operations, the Chief of the Bureau of Naval Aeronautics, and the Director of the War Plans Division of the Office

of Naval Operations. The Joint Board was primarily concerned with administrative matters and doctrine. It continued to exist after the establishment of the Joint Chiefs although its duties and importance dwindled. It was finally abolished by executive order in August 1947.

[8] Admiral King, Annapolis graduate of 1901, served during World War I as Assistant Chief of Staff to the Commander in Chief, U.S. Atlantic Fleet, winning the Navy Cross. In 1937 he moved into the group controlling broad naval operations and was, suc-

the British organization, which in 1942 included Gen. Sir Alan Brooke, Chief of the Imperial General Staff, Admiral Sir Dudley Pound, First Sea Lord, and Air Chief Marshal Sir Charles Portal, Chief of the Air Staff. The British Chiefs, however, met with the Americans only at periodic military-political conferences. In the interim they were represented on the permanent combined body in Washington by the Joint Staff Mission, the original members of which were Lt. Gen. Sir Colville Wemyss, Admiral Sir Charles Little, and Air Marshal A. T. Harris.[9] In addition to the three service members of the mission, Field Marshal Sir John Dill [10] sat as a member of the Combined Chiefs of

Staff representing the Prime Minister, Winston S. Churchill, in his capacity as Minister of Defence. In July 1942, the Joint Chiefs of Staff also acquired a fourth member in Admiral William D. Leahy, appointed Chief of Staff to President Roosevelt in his capacity as Commander in Chief of the Army and Navy.[11]

The mechanics of joint and combined direction of the Allied war effort developed very slowly although most of the machinery was established in early 1942. Just as the Joint Chiefs of Staff themselves were formed to parallel the existing British organization, so they established their principal subordinate agency, the Joint Planning Staff, along the lines developed

cessively, a member of the General Board of the Navy, Commander of the U.S. Fleet Patrol Force, and, with the rank of admiral, Commander in Chief of the Atlantic Fleet. He assumed command of the U.S. Fleet in December 1941. Admiral Stark, Annapolis graduate of 1903, had commanded a destroyer squadron in active service against submarines in the Mediterranean and the Atlantic in World War I, later serving on the staff of the Commander, U.S. Naval Forces Operating in European Waters. He was made Chief of the Bureau of Ordnance in 1934 and four years later became Commander, Cruisers, Battle Force. The following year, 1939, he was promoted to full admiral and assumed his post of Chief of Naval Operations.

[9] The Joint Staff Mission superseded the earlier British Military Mission in May 1941. Changes in personnel up to 1944 were: Chief of the British Army Staff—Lt. Gen. Sir Colville Wemyss (to March 1942), Maj. Gen. R. H. Dewing (March–June 1942), Lt. Gen. G. N. Macready; Chief of the British Admiralty Delegation—Admiral Sir Charles Little (to June 1942), Admiral Sir Andrew Cunningham (June–December 1942), Admiral Sir Percy Noble; Chief of the British Air Staff—Air Marshal A. T. Harris (to February 1942), Air Marshal D. C. S. Evill (February 1942–June 1943), Air Marshal Sir William Walsh.

[10] Field Marshal Dill, Sandhurst graduate and Boer War veteran, was Field Marshal Haig's Brigadier General, Operations, during the last Hundred Days before the 1918 Armistice. He served on the General Staff in India, was Director of Military Operations and Intelligence in the War Office, commanded two divisions in Palestine during the Arab rebellion, and

was Commander-in-Chief at Aldershot. As Chief of the Imperial General Staff from May 1940 through 1941, he was responsible for the reinforcement of the British armies in Egypt and the Middle East and for the decision to send British troops to Greece. Promoted to field marshal in December 1941, he was sent to Washington as Head of the British Joint Staff Mission and senior British member of the Combined Chiefs of Staff.

[11] Long after the Joint Chiefs of Staff had become an accepted functioning organization an attempt was made to give them a written charter. But it was discovered that definitions of authority at such high levels tended to confuse rather than clarify the positions of responsibility and trust established by intimate personal relationships. The attempted definition was rejected by President Roosevelt, and the corporate existence of the Joint Chiefs of Staff continued to stem from the Combined Chiefs of Staff charter.

Admiral Leahy, Annapolis graduate in the class of 1897, saw active war service against the Spanish Fleet in Santiago Harbor, in the Philippine Insurrection, and in the Boxer Uprising. During World War I, he served aboard ships of the line and also commanded a troop transport, winning the Navy Cross. He assumed command of the *New Mexico* in 1926 and in 1933 was made Chief of the Bureau of Navigation. Four years later (then an admiral), he became Chief of Naval Operations. In 1939, retired from the service, he was appointed governor of Puerto Rico. The following year he went to France as U.S. Ambassador. It was from this post that he was recalled to active duty by the President in 1942.

by the British. The U. S. Joint Planning Staff together with the British Joint Planners constituted the Combined Staff Planners, responsible to the Combined Chiefs of Staff.[12] In theory, plans and studies of U. S. policy and strategy were to come up through joint committees to be co-ordinated by the Joint Planners and then submitted for approval to the Joint Chiefs. If approved, they became the official U. S. view to be placed before the Combined Chiefs for acceptance as Allied policy. British studies would develop along parallel lines. In case of important discrepancies between American and British views, the problem might be referred by the Combined Chiefs to their planning staff for adjustment. The Combined Planners, being more of a co-ordinating than a working body, seldom initiated planning papers.

By 1943 the practice of joint and combined planning closely approximated the theory. But in early 1942 most actual planning on the U. S. side was done in the War and Navy Departments and co-ordination between the services was effected largely outside the formally established joint channels.[13] As far as the European war was concerned, the War Department and particularly the Operations Division took the initiative in planning and General Marshall assumed personal responsi-

bility for establishing and defending the U. S. view.

On the British side, the joint system had been worked out and was fully operative in 1942. The British Joint Planners directly responsible to the British Chiefs of Staff were throughout the war the chief planning body concerned with developing British strategy. Much of the operational planning, however, was done by various field commands. Especially important was the Combined Operations Headquarters, which was headed after September 1941 by Commodore Lord Louis Mountbatten.[14] At the time that Mountbatten became chief, Combined Operations was charged with responsibility for planning and executing raids against the Continent. It was also primarily concerned with all the technical problems of amphibious operations, and in particular with the development of landing craft.[15] In January 1942 Gen. Sir Bernard Paget, commander of the British Home Forces (the highest army field command in England), was brought into the planning picture by a directive from the Chiefs of Staff to study a cross-Channel attack plan written by the British Joint Planners.[16] Paget was asked to study this

---

[12] Combined Planners named in the original Combined Chiefs' charter were: for the U.S., Rear Adm. R. K. Turner (USN), Brig. Gen. Leonard T. Gerow (USA), Capt. R. E. Davison (USN), Col. E. L. Naiden (AC); for the British, Capt. C. E. Lambe (RN), Lt. Col. G. K. Bourne, Group Capt. S. C. Strafford (RAF).

[13] U.S. planning organization and techniques are considered at length in Ray S. Cline, Washington Command Post: The Operations Division, a volume now under preparation in this series.

[14] Mountbatten, who entered the Royal Navy in 1913, served at sea during World War I, for the last two years as a midshipman. After specializing in communications, he was assigned as Mediterranean Fleet Wireless Officer in 1931. Then followed assignments as commander of the *Daring*, the *Wishart*, and, in 1939, the *Kelly* and the 5th Destroyer Flotilla in Mediterranean operations. He came to Combined Operations Headquarters after commanding the *Illustrious*.

[15] Paper by Lt. Col. Paddy Corbett, The Evolution and Development of Amphibious Technique and Material, read before British Staff College, Camberly, England, May 45. Hist Div files.

[16] General Paget, winner of the Distinguished Service Order and Military Cross in World War I, entered the British Army in 1907. As commander of the

plan in consultation with the designate Naval and Air Force Commanders-in-Chief (Admiral Sir Bertram H. Ramsay and Air Marshal Sholto Douglas respectively). Beginning their association informally these three became in the course of the first six months of 1942 the nucleus of a formal planning body, the Combined Commanders. Later Mountbatten was officially added to their number and the Commanding General of U. S. Forces in the European Theater was informally included among them. The Combined Commanders held their first meeting in May 1942 and thereafter until early 1943 acted as the chief British planning agency concerned with the development of plans for a cross-Channel attack.[17]

To sum up, the informal military rapprochement between the United States and Great Britain which began in 1940 culminated in January 1942 with the formation of the Combined Chiefs of Staff. The Combined Chiefs were a co-ordinating agency at a very high level. The detailed work, not only of drawing up tactical plans but of outlining strategy, studying requirements, and testing principles against resources, was done very largely by separate U. S. and British bodies. At the strategy level, the most important in 1942 were the Joint Planning Staff and the Joint Planners for the Americans and the British respectively. On the

other hand, the agencies most directly concerned with drawing up plans for European operations in 1942 were, in the United States, the Operations Division of the War Department, and, in England, the Combined Commanders. Finally, over and above all these formally constituted planning and directing bodies stood President Franklin D. Roosevelt and Prime Minister Winston S. Churchill, the ultimately responsible persons for all military decisions, who exerted a direct and vital influence on planning that cut athwart all the formal channels of co-operation.

In the period before the United States entered the war, the planning of offensive operations against Germany was naturally desultory and inconclusive. In view of British weakness and aloneness on the edge of Hitler's Europe, and in view of America's jealously preserved isolation, the interesting thing is that planning took place at all. The notion of a British attack across the Channel could have had little reality and no urgency during the days when the German armies were in the flood tide of their initial victories on the Continent. Yet the British Joint Planners before the end of 1941 had drawn up an invasion plan. They called it ROUNDUP, a name suitably reflecting the concept of an operation in the final phase of the war against only token resistance. ROUNDUP was a plan for an operation with very small resources and bore little relation to the attack against Normandy in 1944. Nevertheless it was a beginning and some of its ideas persisted far into the OVERLORD planning period.

ROUNDUP was planned to exploit German deterioration. As a condition for the

---

18th Division in 1939 in operations in Norway, he successfully engineered its evacuation. He was promoted to lieutenant general and in 1940 was appointed Chief of General Staff, Home Forces, holding this position until he assumed command of the Home Forces in 1942.

[17] 21 A Gp, Note on the History of Planning for Operations in Northwest Europe, 30 Dec 43. Hist Div files.

PRESIDENT ROOSEVELT AND PRIME MINISTER CHURCHILL

invasion, it was assumed that the Germans had abandoned hope for victory, and were withdrawing their occupation forces to concentrate on the defense of the Reich. The purpose of ROUNDUP was to disrupt that orderly withdrawal. British forces would assault west and east of Le Havre on beaches from Deauville to Dieppe. The object would be initially to dominate an area between Calais and the Seine 75 to 100 miles deep. The invasion forces would then push north, take Antwerp and proceed into Germany across the Meuse River north of Liége. Total forces to be used were 6⅓ infantry divisions, 6 armored divisions, 6 army tank brigades, and supporting troops. Preliminary bombardment to soften the coast defenses would require three naval vessels, including one capital ship. The diffuse, small-scale landings and the tiny dimensions of the total force at once underlined the basic condition of enemy weakness set for the operations, and reflected the military poverty of the British at the time.[18]

The 1941 ROUNDUP was not taken very seriously and was never introduced officially into combined discussions. The immediate concern of both Americans and British was necessarily with basic strategic principles in the light of which long-range planning and production could be undertaken. The first Allied discussions of strategy took place when the war was still confined to Europe. It was clear, however, that Japan might at any time enter the conflict. In that event, if the United States was drawn into war with all three Axis members Allied military resources would be scattered and Allied strategy immensely complicated. A decision was urgently required as to where U. S. and British forces should first be concentrated. That decision was taken at the conference in early 1941 when the U. S. War and Navy Departments agreed with the British to defeat Germany first while remaining on the strategic defensive in the Pacific.[19] For Great Britain geography made the choice obligatory. American concurrence was dictated by reasons less obvious but scarcely less compelling. Germany was considered the dominant Axis member whose defeat would greatly weaken the war-making power of Japan. Only against Germany could the offensive power of both the United States and Great Britain be concentrated without uncovering the British Isles. Finally, the United States, desperately short of shipping, could not at first afford long lines of communication. "Time and space factors," wrote General Marshall in reviewing the early years of the war, "dictated our strategy to a considerable degree. To land and maintain American forces in Australia required more than twice the ship tonnage for similar American forces in Europe or North Africa." [20] The decision to take the offensive first against Germany was reaffirmed at the ARCADIA Conference in Washington on 31 December 1941 after the United States entered the war. It was reaffirmed without question despite the Japanese attack on Pearl Harbor.

---

[18] JP (41) 1028, 24 Dec 41. CCS files, CCS 381 (3-23–42) , par. I. This was the final version of the plan. An earlier version, JP (41) 823 (0) Draft, was dated 9 Oct 41; no copy has been located among Dept. of the Army records.

[19] Brief of ABC–1 Conv. See n. 4.

[20] George C. Marshall, *Biennial Report of the Chief of Staff of the United States Army, July 1, 1941, to June 30, 1943* (Washington, 1943) , p. 10.

In the very broadest sense, the ground-work for OVERLORD was thus laid. The early combined discussions tried further to explore ways and means of getting at Germany. But offensive plans necessarily remained vague so long as the needs for defense of the United Kingdom and, after Pearl Harbor, of American bases in the Pacific absorbed not only all resources on hand but the bulk of those immediately in prospect.

The conclusion was that direct offensive action against Germany was unlikely at least until 1943. At the ARCADIA Conference, the following agreement was reached:

In 1942, the methods of wearing down Germany's resistance will be . . . ever increasing air bombardment by British and American forces . . . assistance to Russia's offensive by all available means . . . [and operations] the main object [of which] will be gaining possession of the whole North African coast. . . . It does not seem likely that in 1942 any large scale land offensive against Germany, except on the Russian front, will be possible . . . [but] in 1943, the way may be clear for a return to the continent across the Mediterranean, from Turkey into the Balkans, or by landings in Western Europe. Such operations will be the prelude to the final assault on Germany itself.[21]

The program thus outlined was to a remarkable degree carried out. But it was not carried out without prolonged and searching re-examination of each step of the prelude. In the course of that re-examination the American and British Chiefs of Staff discovered an important difference of opinion in their approach to the problem of defeating Germany. The difference was adumbrated in an exchange of views in the fall of 1941 called forth by a Review of Strategy submitted by the British Chiefs of Staff for American consideration. In reply, American joint planners criticized the indirection of the British approach to offensive action. They noted "only minor attention" in the Review to possible land operations and expressed the opinion that although naval and air power "may prevent wars from being lost, and by weakening enemy strength, may greatly contribute to victory, . . . dependence cannot be placed on winning important wars by naval and air forces alone. It should be recognized as an almost invariable rule," they added, "that wars cannot be finally won without the use of land armies."[22]

That point, of course, had not escaped the British. The first British ROUNDUP plan was in itself a recognition of the need for ground action on the Continent and specifically admitted that "operations on the Continent will in some form be inevitable."[23] Further, in reply to American objections to their Review, the British Chiefs of Staff explained that the indirect offensive methods which they had listed, including blockade, bombing, and the encouragement of subversive activities in German-occupied countries, did not preclude an eventual large-scale landing on the Continent when the time was ripe.[24]

If there was, at this time, any real disagreement, it was over a question of emphasis. Neither operations, nor plans, nor

---

[21] U.S. ABC–4/CS–1, 31 Dec 41. ARCADIA Conf Bk.

[22] Joint Planning Committee Rpt, General Strategy —Review by the British Chiefs of Staff, 25 Sep 41, JB 325, ser 729. OPD files.

[23] ROUNDUP Plan cited n. 18.

[24] American Liaison (41) 8th Mtg, 21 Nov 41. Navy Dept files, Ghormley Papers.

even strategic principles were immediately at issue. The ARCADIA formula, cited above, outlined a program to which both British and American military leaders could subscribe without reservation, and it did not contradict anything in either the British Review or the American reply to it. The American protest was nevertheless significant for the future. It foreshadowed an American impatience to get on with direct offensive action as well as a belief, held quite generally in the U. S. War Department, that the war could most efficiently be won by husbanding resources for an all-out attack deliberately planned for a fixed future date. American impatience was opposed by a British note of caution; American faith in an offensive of fixed date was in contrast to British willingness to proceed one step at a time molding a course of action to the turns of military fortune. This opposition was by no means clear in 1941. It is sketched here in order to provide a vantage point for the understanding of Anglo-American strategy, and as a guide through a necessarily condensed and selective account of the debate on how to fight the war against Germany.

The complex bases for American and British strategic views will appear in the course of the narrative. At the risk of oversimplification, however, it may be useful here to generalize that the prime difference between those views derived from the fact that the British, close to the scene of the war, tended to focus on the difficulties of assault, and the tactical and logistical problems involved, while the Americans, some 3,000 miles away, found it easier to start with the large view of the strategic problem. British planners were deeply and continuously conscious that

to attack northwest Europe armies had to get across an ugly piece of water called the Channel, that this crossing took boats and special equipment, that when the troops landed they had to storm fortifications and fight a German Army that had all Europe by the throat. Americans were aware of these problems only at second hand and at a distance. They worked from maps. Each perspective, it should be noted, had a distinct contribution to make. If the British saw the tactical problems more clearly, the Americans were enabled to give freer rein to their imagination and to arrive at bolder offensive concepts.

These views need not necessarily have been opposed. They were opposed largely because the strategic problem as it developed in early combined discussion was not one of developing and carrying out the ideally best plan for defeating Germany. It was rather a problem of tailoring an ideal strategy to the changing political and military shape of a war in which the enemy at first had the initiative. The difference of opinion as to how the tailoring should be done was called forth primarily by the cry for immediate action.

That cry was taken up by many voices for a number of different reasons. In the first place, it was recognized that the sooner the Allies could wrest the initiative from the Axis the sooner they could stop dissipating resources to plug holes in the defense and start concentrating them for the defeat of the enemy. The combined Chiefs of Staff discussed at the ARCADIA Conference one plan for immediate action, called GYMNAST, which looked as though it might have a chance of success even when carried out by the relatively tiny forces then available to the United

States and Great Britain.[25] GYMNAST, a plan for the invasion of North Africa, was a highly speculative operation. For success it gambled on the nonresistance of the colonial French, and even if successful it was doubtful whether it would materially contribute to the offensive against Germany except in strategically tightening the ring around her. What it clearly would do, however, would be to put U. S. ground troops in action against the Germans. This consideration was particularly important to President Roosevelt, who thought that immediate action would stiffen American morale and have the reverse effect on the Germans.[26] Strongly championed by both the President and the Prime Minister, GYMNAST was accepted by the Combined Chiefs of Staff in January 1942. But the more pressing need to send immediate reinforcements to the Southwest Pacific to check Japanese expansion toward Australia forced postponement and at last in March drew from the Combined Planners a declaration that the project had become academic.[27]

In the meantime, both U. S. and British planners were independently investigating the possibility of being forced into action in 1942 in order to assist the Soviet Union. When Hitler attacked the USSR in June 1941, many observers felt that the Russians would fall before the German blitz as quickly as had most of the rest of

Europe. Then the Red Army tightened and held in front of Moscow and, when the snows came, struck back. Despite this success, however, neither American nor British military leaders were sanguine about the ability of the Russians to withstand a new German offensive in 1942. U. S. planners wrote: "Although Russia's strength was greatly underestimated by military authorities, including the Germans, a true test of Russia's capacity to resist the enemy will come this summer."[28] The outcome of that test, they believed, was the key to the European and possibly to the world situation. Defeat of the USSR would enable the Germans to dominate the whole of Europe, complete the blockade of England, and probably force England to capitulate. If so, then it followed that every possible effort should be made by the Western Powers to insure that Russia was not defeated.

At the end of February 1942, Brig. Gen. Dwight D. Eisenhower, Assistant Chief of Staff, War Plans Division, wrote: "The task of keeping Russia in the war involves . . . immediate and definite action. It is not sufficient to urge upon the Russians the indirect advantages that will accrue to them from Allied operations in distant parts of the world. . . . *Russia's problem is to sustain herself during the coming summer,* and she must not be permitted to reach such a precarious position that she will accept a negotiated peace, no matter how unfavorable to herself, in preference to continuation of the fight." The two ways of assisting Russia, General

[25] Full treatment of the GYMNAST–TORCH project will be found in George F. Howe, Operations in Northwest Africa, a volume now under preparation in this series.

[26] (Marshall) Notes of Meeting at the White House with the President and the British Prime Minister Presiding—5:00 P.M. (Dictated from rough notes), 23 Dec 41. C/S file 384 (Mtgs and Confs). See Bibliographical Note.

[27] CCS 11th Mtg, 10 Mar 42.

[28] JCS 23, Annex C, 14 Mar 42. This paper is actually a composite of directives and deployment studies dating back to 30 January 1942. See Bibliographical Note for location and nature of JCS documents.

Eisenhower noted, were Lend-Lease aid and early operations in the west to draw off from the Russian front large portions of the German Army and Air Force. He was dubious whether a sizable ground attack from England could be mounted soon, but at least, he thought, air operations could be initiated.[29]

The U. S. Joint Planning Staff, studying the whole question of U. S. troop deployment, went much further. They believed that a considerable land attack could be launched across the English Channel in 1942. Although it would have to be done at first largely by British forces, American participation would build up rapidly, and the prospect of such reinforcement should enable the British to mount the attack on a slimmer margin than would otherwise be possible. On this basis, the planners outlined what they thought would be a possible operation to take place in the summer of 1942 with a D Day between 15 July and 1 August. The operation was to open with a fifteen-day air attack, the strategic purpose of which would be to divert the German Air Force from the east. The immediate tactical objectives were to establish control of the air over the Channel and at least a hundred kilometers inland between Dunkerque and Abbeville, and to inflict the maximum damage on German military installations and lines of communication. During the air offensive, commandos were to raid the coasts of the Netherlands, Belgium, and Normandy. In phase two, beginning about D plus 30, major land forces were to cross the Channel with the mission of securing the high ground north

of the Seine and Oise Rivers, and of destroying enemy ground and air forces in the general area Calais–Arras–St. Quentin–Soissons–Paris–Deauville. The plan did not go into operational detail. The critical problem of landing craft received little attention beyond a listing of the barge requirements and a notation that both Americans and British would have to construct special craft.[30]

The British Joint Planners had come to the same conclusion as the U. S. War Department—that the approaching summer campaign of 1942 in Russia was likely to be critical and might require support by diversions in the west if Russia was to be kept in the war. On the other hand, the British were much more pessimistic about what could be done. The maximum feasible operation, they thought, would be a limited-objective attack—something like a large-scale raid—the main purpose of which would be to tempt the German Air Force into a battle of destruction with the Royal Air Force under conditions favorable to the latter.[31] For that concept, Prime Minister Churchill coined the code name SLEDGEHAMMER, and the Combined Commanders were directed to study and report on it. They found at once that the name was far more aggressive than the plan could be. They faced a tactical paradox. They were asked to strike where RAF fighters could engage the Luftwaffe on favorable terms. There was only one such area, since effective fighter cover from British bases extended at that time only over the beaches between Dunkerque and the Somme. This area, called

---

[29] Memo for CofS, 28 Feb 42. (Italics in the original.) OPD files, exec 4, env 35.

[30] JCS 23, App. II, JPS 2/6, 5 Mar 42.
[31] Capt M. McLaren, secy to Combined Commanders, Notes on the History of SLEDGEHAMMER, Sep 42. Hist Div files.

the Pas-de-Calais,[32] had the strongest German defenses of any portion of the French coast. It also had flat beaches unsuitable for British landing craft. The beaches furthermore had too few exits to pass the required number of vehicles inland to maintain the forces landed. Finally the ports in the area were too small to supply a force large enough to hold a bridgehead against the probable scale of German counterattack. In short, the one area where the RAF could supply fighter support and achieve the main purpose of defeating the Luftwaffe was precisely the one area which, from every other point of view, was unsuitable for assault.[33]

The problem seemed insoluble and the planners first concluded that no cross-Channel operation was possible in 1942 unless the Germans showed signs of collapse. This conclusion, however, was modified by a second report submitted by the Combined Commanders early in April. Assuming then that they might disregard requirements for the security of the British Isles and that "the maintenance problem"[34] could be "successfully overcome," they calculated that an invasion of the Pas-de-Calais could be carried out. But, they added, if the Germans countered in force, the beachhead probably could not be held and, if lost, it was doubtful whether the bulk of the men and equipment could be evacuated. The

British Chiefs of Staff did not wholly endorse this analysis, but they did tacitly accept the conclusion that establishment of a permanent bridgehead on the Continent would probably be impossible in 1942.[35]

General Marshall's Project

The first look at the cross-Channel project discovered only a host of difficulties that seemed all but insuperable. So long as attention was focused on an attack in 1942 all plans were pervaded with the sense that to do anything at all would be to act in desperation, to accept abnormal military risks for the sake of avoiding ultimate disaster. If the view in London was more pessimistic than in Washington, that was in large part because the major risks of action in 1942 would have to be borne by the British.[36] In addition the British, whose mobilization was already far advanced, were inclined to see operations through the glass of current resources which, in general, could be increased in one category only by reduction in another. The United States, on the other hand, even while struggling desperately to build up the stocks needed for defense in the Pacific, was still continuously aware of its huge potential resources. Although it was recognized that in 1942 American military power would only begin to make itself felt, plans even for that year reflected the Americans' basic optimism and recommended risks far greater than the British considered accepting.

---

[32] The Pas-de-Calais actually was the name of a department in the center of the coast considered for invasion. But the name was used by the planners, and will here be used, in the looser sense of the coast line washed by the Strait of Dover between Dunkerque and the Somme.

[33] Memo, Brig C. V. McNabb, SLEDGEHAMMER, 17 Jul 42. SHAEF G–3 files, Ref Lib Gp D. See Bibliographical Note.

[34] The British term "maintenance" is generally equivalent to U.S. "supply."

[35] McLaren, Notes on SLEDGEHAMMER, cited n. 31.

[36] This was freely admitted by General Marshall. Draft Memo, Marshall for Roosevelt, The Pacific Theater *versus* BOLERO, undtd (sent to the President 6 May). OPD file 381 gen sec. 2, case 62. See Bibliographical Note. Cf. below, p. 30.

GENERAL MARSHALL, *Chief of Staff, United States Army.*

It was in looking further ahead, however, that the American optimistic view made its chief contribution to strategy. Until mid-March, plans for 1942 had been considered without specific reference to long-range objectives. Except for the determination to attack in Europe, there *were* no specific long-range objectives. The general principles agreed to at ARCADIA did not form a concerted plan of action.

In March 1942, the Operations Division of the War Department (OPD) began work on an outline plan for a full-scale invasion of the European continent in 1943. It was to be projected as the basis for the deployment of forces and as a guide for strategy. The need for such a guide had become increasingly urgent as, despite the shelving of GYMNAST, President Roosevelt continued to press for immediate action.[37] On 25 March, the President called the Joint Chiefs of Staff and Secretary of War Henry L. Stimson to the White House to ask advice on future offensive operations. Specifically he wanted to know whether U. S. troops might profitably be used in Syria, Libya, and northwest Africa, as well as in northwest Europe. On 2 April, General Marshall gave the President the War Department's answer embodying OPD's outline plan for a cross-Channel attack in 1943.[38]

The War Department and General Marshall were convinced that the main U. S.–British ground offensive should be undertaken against northwest Europe. They rejected the Mediterranean areas suggested by Roosevelt because commitment of U. S. troops there would be strategically defensive. Although the conquest of North Africa would break Axis control of the Mediterranean and prevent an Axis move through West Africa, the victory would not in itself be decisive and could not be exploited for further decisive action against Germany.

The body of General Marshall's memorandum therefore, was concerned with exploring the concept of a cross-Channel invasion of France. The operation was conceived in three phases: a preparatory phase, the cross-Channel movement and seizure of bridgeheads between Le Havre and Boulogne, and, finally, consolidation and expansion of the bridgehead. Logistics set the earliest possible date for the beginning of phase two at 1 April 1943, except under emergency conditions.[39] The preparatory phase would begin at once with the organization, arming, and overseas movement of the necessary forces. During the summer of 1942 small task forces would raid along the entire accessible enemy coast line. General Marshall attached great value to these preparatory raiding operations which he defined as the "establishment of a pre-

---

[37] Cbl, Roosevelt to Churchill, 9 Mar 42. OPD file ABC 311.5 (1–30–42).

[38] The first memorandum was submitted by OPD on 27 March. The last draft bearing a date was prepared on 2 April. This was revised by General Eisenhower and the revision constituted the memorandum as finally presented to the British. This final version is undated and titled simply "Operations in Western Europe." Additional studies were made after 2 April, an analysis of U.S. troop build-up being dated as late as 6 April. For the final version and various drafts and appendixes see Pre-Invasion file 308. Copy of the original OPD memo is in AAF file 381, War Plans Sec. G. See Bibliographical Note. Discussion following is based on the memorandum plan and its appendixes.

[39] Actually it was noted that, if only U.S. shipping was available for U.S. troop and supply build-up, the invasion date would be delayed until late summer. By 1 April, it was estimated, U.S. shipping could transport only 40 percent of the forces required.

liminary active front." He thought they might serve to draw German troops from the east and so "be of some help to Russia." They might also be useful for deception either in persuading the Germans that no all-out offensive would be attempted or else in keeping them on tenterhooks for fear that any one of the raids might develop into a full-scale invasion. Thinking of national morale, a consideration always important to both the President and the Prime Minister, he noted that raiding together with air operations would be "of immediate satisfaction to the public." But, he added, "what is most important" is that the raids would "make experienced veterans of the air and ground units, and . . . offset the tendency toward deterioration in morale which threatens the latter due to prolonged inactivity."[40]

The main attack in the spring of 1943 was planned to employ 48 divisions supported by 5,800 combat aircraft. Landings would take place between Etretat north of Le Havre and Cap Gris Nez with the object of seizing the lower valley of the Somme and the high ground forming the watersheds of the Seine–Somme river system. Two main assaults were planned, on either side of the mouth of the Somme. The bridgeheads would be expanded to the southwest in order to seize Le Havre and the line of the Seine River. Although U. S. planners made use of some detailed data on terrain and estimates of the enemy, they did not attempt to examine tactical problems even to the extent that British planners had studied them in working on SLEDGEHAMMER. The main purpose of the Marshall Memorandum

was to pin down a strategic idea sufficiently so that production, training, and troop allocations and movement could be "coordinated to a single end." There was time for planning, but none for delaying the basic decision. For example, it was pointed out that under current production schedules only 10 percent of the tank landing craft required to carry U. S. troops in the assault would be available. Only a decision now could insure the required resources in time.

The Marshall Memorandum shifted emphasis from 1942 to 1943 while retaining for 1942 some activity which might satisfy political requirements. In the event that an operation should be required in 1942 to save the Russians or take advantage of sudden German deterioration, preparations were to be made to permit a cross-Channel assault on greatly reduced scale in the fall of the year. The maximum U. S. forces which could be on hand for such an assault were three and a half divisions, and the operation would be justified only by prospects of marked deterioration of the German army in the west.

In the second week in April General Marshall and Mr. Harry Hopkins, special emissary of President Roosevelt, went to London to seek a firm decision from the British Chiefs of Staff on the form, location, and timing of the British-American main effort. As it turned out, that decision was quickly reached with general agreement on the project outlined in the Marshall Memorandum.[41] Discussion then shifted to what could be done in 1942. General Marshall reported that by

---

[40] Memo, Operations in Western Europe, cited n. 38.

[41] British Chiefs of Staff, Comments on General Marshall's Memorandum, 13 Apr 42, COS (42) 97 (0). C/S file 381.

the end of August U. S. reinforcement of the Pacific, Iceland, and Northern Ireland garrisons should be complete and the United States could concentrate on pouring troops and supplies into England for offensive action. He thought two and a half infantry divisions, one armored division, and 900 U. S. aircraft could be in the United Kingdom by 15 September.[42]

General Brooke, Chief of the Imperial General Staff, said his planners counted on landing seven infantry and two armored divisions if forced to attack the Continent in 1942, but he frankly did not like the prospect. Such a small force could not hold against German counterattacks and its loss would seriously weaken England's defenses. Also, he was worried about India and the Middle East, where the Japanese and Germans might join forces and capture the oil fields in Iran and Iraq on which, he thought, "the whole of our effort in both theaters depended." [43]

Brooke and Air Marshal Portal, Chief of Air Staff, also raised objections to the September date.[44] Brooke believed that the operation would have to take place in August at the latest in order to capture a port before the third week in September, when bad weather was likely to prevail over the Channel. Portal thought that during the summer the German Air Force might win a complete victory over the Russians and so by autumn become a formidable enemy for the RAF. General Marshall agreed that an earlier target date would be advisable but felt he could not urge it since U. S. troops would not then be available. He clearly indicated that his main interest in a 1942 operation was to provide battle experience for the Americans in preparation for 1943. He was also concerned that, if something were attempted in 1942, it be an operation across the Channel in order to avoid dispersion of forces. He did not want the main project—operations on the Continent— reduced to the position of a "residuary legatee" for whom nothing was left.[45] Against this view, Brooke continued to stress the danger in the Middle East. He then reversed the American concept that SLEDGEHAMMER was a device to save the Russians. Operations in 1942, he said, depended on what success the Germans had against the Russians. "If they [the Germans] were successful," he believed, "we could clearly act less boldly. If, however, the Russians held the Germans or had an even greater measure of success, our object should be to detach air forces from the Russian front."[46] In short, he re-

---

[42] COS (42) 23d Mtg (0) , 9 Apr 42. OPD file ABC 381 BOLERO (3–16–42) sec. 5.

[43] *Ibid.* General Brooke, a graduate of the Royal Military Academy, Woolwich, had by 1941 acquired the reputation of being Britain's greatest expert on mechanization. For his service in France during World War I, he received the Distinguished Service Order with Bar, the Belgian Croix de Guerre, and six mentions in dispatches. In the early part of World War II, he commanded the British Second Army Corps, his defensive action making possible the evacuation of Dunkerque. He then organized and trained the British Home Forces in preparation for the expected Nazi invasion. He was made Chief of the Imperial General Staff in 1941, succeeding Field Marshal Dill.

[44] Portal, an observer and fighter pilot in World War I, entered the RAF College in 1922. In the 1930's he commanded the British forces in Aden and was Director of Organization, Air Ministry. Early in World War II, he served on the Air Council and was Air Officer Commanding-in-Chief of the Bomber Command. He became Chief of Air Staff in October 1940.

[45] COS (42) 118th Mtg, 14 Apr 42. OPD file ABC 381 BOLERO (3–16–42) sec. 5.

[46] War Cabinet Defence Com, DC (42) 10th Mtg, 14 Apr 42. C/S file 381. On quotation of indirect discourse, see n. 138.

jected the emergency operation and accepted only the operation of opportunity.[47] The opinion was in notable contrast to the U. S. Army view that a 1942 operation would be justified by the need for helping Russia in the war so that "an opportunity would be presented to us of defeating Germany next spring."[48] The point, however, was not argued, and the whole problem of a 1942 operation was returned to the planners for further study.

General Marshall's scheme for invasion in 1943, on the other hand, was received with enthusiasm, qualified only by a note of caution from British planners. The planners observed again the two deficiencies which had already crippled plans for a return to the Continent: the lack of landing craft (particularly craft capable of landing on the flat-gradient French beaches) and the lack of long-range fighter aircraft. They did not imply, however, that these deficiencies could not be made up during the coming year.[49]

For the rest, the British Chiefs of Staff and the Prime Minister found nothing in the plan to quarrel with. The U. S. commitment to deliver one million troops to the United Kingdom during the next year altered, in the opinion of Lord Mountbatten, "the whole picture of combined operations against the Continent. The plans, which we had been at present evolving, all fell short in one way or another for lack of essential resources. This would be all changed when the great flow of American forces began, and we should be enabled to plan that real return to the Continent, without which we could not hope to bring the war to a successful conclusion."[50]

The meeting at which Mountbatten so expressed himself was the concluding session of the conference with General Marshall. The tone of optimism was echoed by all those present and the whole meeting was informed with an extraordinary enthusiasm. Mr. Hopkins said that although American public opinion would have preferred an offensive against Japan, "the American nation was eager to join in the fight alongside the British." Mr. Anthony Eden, British Foreign Secretary, replied in kind. "The plan," he considered, "had much more than a purely military significance. It was, in fact, the great picture of two English-speaking countries setting out for the redemption of Europe." Forgotten for the moment was the opinion expressed a month before that the Allies in 1942 were on the verge of defeat.[51] Instead of anticipating the need for a "sacrifice" operation in order to save a chance to strike in 1943, the conferees looked forward to sharing in a victory not far off. Churchill closed the meeting by summing up the complete unanimity of opinion and adding a prediction that now "the two

---

[47] Churchill also made this reversal more explicitly a little later when he wrote: "The launching of SLEDGEHAMMER should be dependent not on a Russian failure but on Russian success and consequent proved German demoralization in the West." PM, Minute for Gen Ismay for CofS Com, 10 Jun 42, Annex to COS (42) 175th Mtg. Copy in Hist Div files.

[48] Remark by Col J. E. Hull, U.S. (P) 4th Mtg, 12 Apr 42. Pre-Inv file 287 (Combined Operations Conferences). A series of meetings was held between U.S. and British planners in the course of the April conferences in London.

[49] Memo, British Staff Planners, Main Considerations Affecting The Employment on the Continent in 1943 of the Anglo–American Forces envisaged in General Marshall's Paper, undtd. OPD file ABC 381 BOLERO (3–16–42) sec. 5.

[50] War Cabinet Mtg, 14 Apr 42, cited n. 46.

[51] JCS 23, cited n. 28.

nations would march ahead together in a noble brotherhood of arms."

The morrow brought soberer second thoughts, but the strategic decision, destined to last less than two months, at least laid some groundwork for the future. One immediate outcome was the establishment of machinery to concentrate U. S. troops in England. The build-up operation, called BOLERO,[52] was to provide a force of about one million men specifically equipped to carry out an air offensive in 1942, a major invasion of the Continent in 1943, and if agreed on, a continental operation in conjunction with the British in 1942. Special planning staffs, BOLERO Combined Committees, were set up in Washington and London to function under the direction of the Combined Planning Staff. The committees were not responsible for tactical planning but were to proceed on the assumption that the invasion would conform to the outlines drawn in General Marshall's memorandum.[53]

The establishment of BOLERO planning formalized and intensified the process of preparing United Kingdom bases for American troops, but the process had begun long before. As a result of the ABC–1 decisions of early 1941 the War Department had drawn up deployment plans to be put into effect if and when America came into the war. One of the provisions was the MAGNET plan to move U. S. troops into Iceland in order to relieve British garrisons there and to send troops to Northern Ireland to establish and defend air and naval bases for the use of U. S. forces. In January 1942 the first contingent of troops under the MAGNET plan was shipped to Northern Ireland, although, as a result of the emergency reinforcement of the Southwest Pacific area, the shipment had to be cut from a planned 17,300 to 4,000. Three more shipments arrived in Ireland before the end of May, bringing U. S. ground strength there to more than 32,000, including the 34th Division, the 1st Armored Division, and V Corps headquarters.[54]

At the same time the U. S. Air Force was beginning to set up house in the British Isles. On 26 January 1942, General Arnold submitted to General Marshall a plan to base 4,648 American planes in the United Kingdom, including 54 groups of heavy bombers, 10 groups of medium bombers, and 10 groups of pursuit planes.[55] The build-up was begun at once. Brig. Gen. Ira C. Eaker, with a portion of his staff, was ordered to England in January and by the end of Feb-

---

[52] There was considerable confusion in the early use of this code name, especially in the War Department where it was taken at first to indicate not only the build-up but the cross-Channel operation for which the build-up prepared. In the early days the confusion was symptomatic of a real conceptual identity between the operations. Decisions on the BOLERO build-up reflected attitudes toward the ROUNDUP attack. Cf. Robert E. Sherwood, *Roosevelt and Hopkins: An Intimate History* (New York, 1948), p. 569.

[53] In general the Washington Committee dealt with basic problems of policy; the London Committee, made up of representatives of various British supply ministries and representatives of the U.S. Army, handled the more technical details of the plan. See [Herbert French] Supply and Troop Buildup in the UK (The Administrative and Logistical History of the ETO: Part III), MS. Hist Div files.

[54] Elliott, The Predecessor Commands, pp. 15, 85–95. See n. 2.

[55] General Arnold, who had become Chief of the Air Corps in 1938, was directly responsible for the expansion of the American aircraft industry and the inception of the program for civilian training of flying cadets. In 1940 he was made Deputy Chief of Staff for Air and the following year was given the additional duty of Chief, Army Air Forces.

U.S. SOLDIERS IN IRELAND

ruary he had established the VIII Bomber Command. In June his command was subordinated to the newly arrived Eighth Air Force under Brig. Gen. Carl Spaatz.[56]

The air build-up schedule in the meantime was altered in a series of conferences in London in April between General Arnold and Air Chief Marshal Portal. The new basic plan, approved in June, drastically reduced the heavy bomber commitment: instead of 54 groups there would be 17. The force would include 10 groups of medium bombers and 6 of light, 12 groups of pursuit planes, and 8

[56] General Spaatz, a graduate of West Point in 1914 and of Aviation School in 1916, served with the First Aero Squadron of the Punitive Expedition into Mexico. During World War I, he flew in combat over St. Mihiel and Meuse–Argonne, receiving the DSC. In 1940 he was an official observer of the Battle of Britain and returned to the United States to take command, first of the Air Corps Materiel Division and, later, of the AAF Combat Command.

Before General Eaker undertook the assignment of establishing VIII Bomber Command, he had been

on special duty with the RAF in England in 1941, observing and flying new types of fighters and observing British fighter control methods.

groups of transports, a total of 3,262 aircraft.[57]

On 4 July American air crews in six bombers borrowed from the RAF participated in a daylight attack on German airfields in the Netherlands. It was not until 17 August, however, that the Eighth Air Force carried out its first bombing in its own aircraft. By that time the whole European strategy had been profoundly altered and the build-up of air and ground forces in the United Kingdom abruptly ceased to be a first-priority task.[58]

"Action in 1942—Not 1943"

The events between 15 April and the end of July 1942 produced, from the point of view of the U. S. War Department, a disturbing shift in Allied strategy. The April decision to concentrate on a build-up in the United Kingdom for a cross-Channel invasion in 1943 was supplanted in July by the agreement to ship U. S. and British forces into the Mediterranean to invade North Africa. The 1943 ROUNDUP, approved by acclamation in April as the first object of combined strategy in Europe, in July was laid aside in favor of extended preparatory and peripheral operations designed as prelude to a cross-Channel invasion of uncertain date. In General Marshall's view, this meant the dissolution of the strategy which had seemed so firmly established when he and Harry Hopkins left London in April.[59]

Of the many circumstances that combined to overturn the April agreements, one of the weightiest was the continued inability of planners to see any way out of the difficulties posed by SLEDGEHAMMER. A draft plan for the operation was submitted at the end of April to newly appointed British force commanders, Admiral Ramsay, Air Marshal Sir Trafford Leigh-Mallory, and Lt. Gen. Edmond Schreiber. Their report on 4 May was that with current resources of landing craft SLEDGEHAMMER was not a sound operation of war. The British Chiefs of Staff accepted the conclusion but directed that the plan be kept in readiness in case German collapse should make it feasible.[60]

In view of the new principle that SLEDGEHAMMER would take place only under conditions of marked German deterioration, planners now turned away from the uninviting prospect of a Pas-de-Calais assault. Air cover, they argued, would be less essential if the Germans were on the point of collapse and it therefore might pay to look farther afield for an assault area containing a major port. They selected the Cherbourg and Le Havre areas, preferring the latter because it contained more airfields.

But problems multiplied faster than solutions. It was discovered that it would take twenty-one days to land the six divisions with available shipping. When

---

[57] Elliott, The Predecessor Commands, pp. 130ff. See n. 2.

[58] See Wesley F. Craven and James L. Cate, eds., The Army Air Forces in World War II: I, Plans and Early Operations January 1939 to August 1942 (Chicago, 1948), pp. 654, 655ff.

[59] See, for instance, his letter to Dill, 17 Aug 42, stating his belief that the July decisions had altered

not only the strategy agreed upon in April but also the fundamental strategic agreements made at ARCADIA. C/S file TORCH I; cf. Cbl to Eisenhower, 6 Aug 42, draft in Memo, Handy for Classified MC. OPD file 381, ETO, sec. 2. Marshall wrote: "Torch operation is of necessity a substitution for Roundup and not a postponement of the same except for unexpected developments." See below, pp. 29–30.

[60] McLaren, Notes on SLEDGEHAMMER, cited n. 31.

Churchill was informed of this obstacle he replied, as one planner observed, in the manner of King Canute: he did not accept it.[61] Investigation should be made, he continued, into the use of floating piers and other devices to speed the landings. This observation, important for the future, had no immediate issue, for the Prime Minister had also put forward and secured War Cabinet approval of a principle that, in effect, threw out the whole SLEDGEHAMMER idea. The principle was that "there should be no substantial landing in France unless we intended to remain."[62] All planning to date had concluded that, whatever might be done in 1942, the establishment of a permanent bridgehead on the Continent was beyond British resources.

While planning for 1942 struggled vainly to solve the unbalanced equation between ends and means, simultaneous study of a 1943 cross-Channel assault was turning up its share of discouraging difficulties, and drawing conclusions that drastically modified the aggressiveness of the Marshall Memorandum. Planning for ROUNDUP was renewed for the first time on an organized combined basis even though arrangements remained informal. Col. Ray W. Barker, who had arrived in London about 1 April, was assigned shortly afterward to head the planning division of General Chaney's headquarters, which had been converted from SPOBS to United States Army Forces in the British Isles (USAFBI). Barker set up shop in Grosvenor Square. British planners under Brig. Colin McNabb

worked near by. Colonel Barker's group received copies of all the planning papers which had been developed up to that time by the British. Almost daily conferences were held between Americans and British and, about once a week, agreed-on papers were submitted to the Combined Commanders.[63]

By the middle of June 1942 the planners had developed a new appreciation and outline plan for ROUNDUP to be mounted in the spring of 1943. The plan was accepted by the Combined Commanders and submitted to the British Chiefs of Staff. It did not go into tactical details and was limited in scope to the establishment of bridgeheads including necessary airfields and port areas. The approach was cautious and the tactical idea quite different from that which produced OVERLORD. "If our invasion is to succeed," the planners wrote, "we must endeavor to disperse the enemy's mobile reserves on land and in the air. At the same time we must avoid such action as will allow the enemy to destroy isolated parts of our land forces in detail. It follows, therefore, that while we must endeavor to launch assaults on as wide a front as possible, the size of each assault and the rate of subsequent development must, if possible, be sufficient to meet the anticipated rate of enemy reinforcement in each area. . . ." How to dissipate the enemy's defense by a diffuse attack and at the same time be strong at each widely separated point was not fully explained.[64]

The plan to make three "almost" simultaneous assaults in the Pas-de-Calais and

---

[61] *Ibid.*

[62] COS (42), 51st Mtg, 8 Jun 42 (0). SHAEF SGS files; cf. McLaren, Notes on SLEDGEHAMMER. The War Cabinet approved the new principle on 11 Jun 1942.

[63] Interv with Gen Barker, WD, 4 Oct 46. See Bibliographical Note.

[64] Joint Memo, Combined Commanders for Br COS, 17 Jun 42. Pre–Inv file 281, Combined Commanders Papers.

on both sides of the Seine would leave a gap of some 150 miles between the northern and southern bridgeheads. In addition, subsidiary assaults were to be devised to lead to the early capture of Cherbourg and the Channel Islands. The planners did not go into this problem but merely noted that it was subject to further investigation. The first landings would require at least six divisions. "After the initial assaults the forces in each area are built up . . . as a preliminary to further offensive operations." No attempt was made at the time to foresee these. The Combined Commanders, in forwarding the plan, told the British Chiefs of Staff that they believed it was the only possible way of effecting a re-entry into France, but even that would not be feasible "unless the German morale was deteriorated by the spring of 1943 owing to another failure to defeat the Russians." [65]

Churchill was dissatisfied with the planners' caution. He retorted with a memorandum of his own sketching an operation with "qualities of magnitude, simultaneity and violence," and involving six landings by at least ten armored brigades in the first wave, and the debarkation of 400,000 men in the first week. If in fourteen days, he wrote, "700,000 men are ashore, if air supremacy has been gained, if the enemy is in considerable confusion, and if we held at least four workable ports, we shall have got our claws well into the job." [66] Churchill's object in sketching his impression of ROUNDUP in such terms was to give an idea of the "scale and spirit" which he felt

necessary if the undertaking was to have "good prospects of success." In reality, however, his concept required resources which seemed so far beyond reach that planners could not regard it seriously. They did not alter their view that ROUNDUP could go in only against a weakened enemy.

Furthermore, even Churchill's concept, for all its vigor, remained academic in the absence of broad, formative decisions. Planners, without allotted resources, without a target date, and without a command organization, worked in a schoolroom, trapped in circular arguments and unable to make real progress toward preparing a definite operation of war. Recommendations by the Joint Planning Staff that commanders be selected at once to carry out the operation and that steps be taken to secure the appointment of a Supreme Allied Commander produced no results. [67]

The truth was that the general approval of the ROUNDUP idea which General Marshall had won in April 1942 did not reflect any general conviction that the 1943 cross-Channel attack was really the best way of carrying out Allied strategy in Europe. Skepticism remained on both sides of the Atlantic. In Washington President Roosevelt was wavering, and the U. S. Navy was lukewarm. Roosevelt, early in May, wondered whether more troops should not be sent out to the Pacific to reinforce Australia. Admiral King thought they should, and wrote that the mounting of BOLERO should not be allowed to interfere with Pacific plans. He called holding the Japanese "our basic strategic plan in the Pacific Thea-

---

[65] Ibid.

[66] Memo, Churchill for Marshall, Operation ROUNDUP, 15 Jun 42. Hist Div files.

[67] McLaren, Notes on SLEDGEHAMMER.

ter."[68] It was perhaps only a turn of phrase but General Marshall felt it necessary to remind the President that sustaining Russia, not holding the Japanese, was the basic strategy. The proposals to reinforce Australia would mean cutting in half the number of divisions that could be shipped to England for a SLEDGEHAMMER operation. Operations in 1942 from England, he pointed out, already depended primarily on the British, who would be accepting risks far graver than any run by the Americans. The British had agreed to BOLERO on the understanding that it was the prime U. S. project. If it was not, BOLERO should be abandoned and the British notified.[69] President Roosevelt retreated. He told General Marshall that he had only asked if the Australian reinforcement could be done and he now agreed with him "and Admiral King" that it could not. He added: "I do not want 'BOLERO' slowed down."[70] On the same day, however, he expressed his impatience with continued inaction. The Atlantic theater, he believed, called for "very great speed in developing actual operations. I have been disturbed," he wrote, "by American and British naval objections to operations in the European Theater prior to 1943. I regard it as essential that active operations be conducted in 1942." He realized the difficulties, but ideal conditions could hardly be expected. Expedients must be improvised. "The necessities of the case call for action in 1942—not 1943."[71]

The President's impatience may have been reinforced by a visit of the Soviet Foreign Minister, Vyacheslav Molotov, to Washington at the end of May. Molotov came at the President's request primarily to discuss the Murmansk convoys of Lend-Lease war materials, but it was clear that he was still more vitally interested in the opening of a "second front." On his way he had stopped off at London to see Churchill, from whom he received only deliberately vague promises concerning the possibility of SLEDGEHAMMER.[72] In Washington he tried to pin the Americans down to a more definite commitment. What the Soviets wanted was an operation in 1942 on a large enough scale to force the Germans to withdraw forty divisions from the Russian front. Such an operation evidently could not be promised. The most that General Marshall would say was that a second front was in preparation, that the Western Allies were trying to create a situation in which a second front would be possible. The President, however, significantly extended Marshall's answer and sent word through Molotov to Stalin to expect a second front in 1942. Roosevelt did not say where or on what scale.[73] Precisely what weight this promise carried in subsequent discussion is difficult to assess. Probably the promise was of more significance as a symptom than as a contributing cause of Roosevelt's eagerness

---

[68] Memo, The Pacific Theater *versus* BOLERO, cited n. 36. Proposals to reinforce Australia would have increased ground forces by 25,000 troops, air forces by 100 planes. Another 215 planes were to be sent to the South Pacific.

[69] *Ibid.*

[70] Memo, Roosevelt for Marshall, 6 May 42, OPD file 381, gen sec. 2, case 62.

[71] Memo, Roosevelt for Secy of War, CofS, Gen Arnold, Secy of Navy, Adm King, and Hopkins, 6 May 42. C/S file 381.

[72] McLaren, Notes on SLEDGEHAMMER.

[73] Notes on White House Mtg, cited in Sherwood, *Roosevelt and Hopkins*, p. 563. The Molotov visit is treated at length by Sherwood, pp. 544–68.

for immediate action. In any case, other pressures built up after Molotov left Washington.

June 1942 marked the low ebb of British military fortunes. On the 13th, Generalfeldmarschall Erwin Rommel at Knightsbridge in Libya defeated British armored forces in the last of a series of battles which had started 27 May. The British army retreated across the Egyptian border to El 'Alamein. On Sunday, 21 June, British and Dominion troops, isolated in Tobruk by the withdrawal, were forced to surrender. The rest of the army dug in at El 'Alamein for the defense of Alexandria.

That month also marked the opening of the expected new German offensive on the Russian front. Expected or not, the event was disheartening. The prevailing opinion among military leaders in America and Britain was still that they would be lucky if Russia managed to stay in the war through 1942. In London the official estimates of the Russian situation included only two hypotheses: that Russia had been defeated by October 1942 (hypothesis "A"), or that Russia was still in the war in 1943 "but had suffered heavily in manpower and materiel...."[74]

The pressure was very great on Allied leaders to act at once wherever such action promised any fair chance of success. The pressure to act, moreover, coincided with an improved opportunity. Two decisive naval victories over the Japanese in May and June (Coral Sea and Midway) had relieved the immediate threat to Australia, and defensive requirements in the Pacific were thus no longer a sword of

Damocles hanging over plans for European operations.

Between the two North African disasters, on 18 June, the Prime Minister and the British Chiefs of Staff came to Washington to discuss the desirability of reorienting strategy. Churchill came because he had been greatly alarmed by reports from Admiral Mountbatten that the President was pressing for a 1942 operation.[75] It was clear to the War Department that Churchill's visit foreboded an eloquent attack on the April commitment to BOLERO. Secretary Stimson prepared for the President a strong defense of the BOLERO idea. He pointed out that all the reasons for adopting BOLERO were still valid and that no other operation could achieve the same end. No other operation, furthermore, should be allowed to interfere with it. It was of prime importance, he believed, to press unremittingly forward with BOLERO, not only because it was the best plan but because any deviation from it would be taken as "evidence of doubt and vacillation."[76]

At the same time General Marshall was again defending the idea before the Combined Chiefs. At an informal meeting with General Brooke and Field Marshal Dill the reasons for having made BOLERO the main effort were discussed and reaffirmed. Marshall's defense was at the moment completely successful and General Brooke agreed that BOLERO should be pushed and that the North African invasion should not be undertaken. The generals further accepted the principle

---

[74] JIC (92) 193 (Final), German Strength and Dispositions in 1943 under Certain Hypotheses, 21 May 42. SHAEF SGS files, Combined Commanders Papers.

[75] See CCS 27th Mtg, 19 Jun 42. Mountbatten had come to Washington earlier in the month, primarily to discuss the problems of landing craft.

[76] Ltr, 19 Jun 42, cited in Henry L. Stimson and McGeorge Bundy, *On Active Service in Peace and War* (New York, 1948), pp. 420–23.

that any operations in 1942 would adversely affect operations in 1943, and should therefore be contemplated only in case of necessity.[77]

On Sunday, 21 June 1942, at the White House this decision was significantly modified. Churchill vigorously attacked the BOLERO idea and urged GYMNAST, with the knowledge (Stimson believed) that "it was the President's great secret baby."[78] In the midst of the discussions at the White House came the dramatic news of the surrender of Tobruk. The news greatly strengthened Churchill's arguments for diverting the Allied effort from BOLERO to North Africa and correspondingly weakened General Marshall's efforts to save what he regarded as sound strategy from being upset by political considerations.[79] While arguing for BOLERO, however, General Marshall was deeply conscious of the gravity of the situation both in Egypt and in southern Russia, where German successes "threatened a complete collapse in the Middle East." [80] To meet that threat, Roosevelt and Marshall agreed to rush reinforcements of planes to the Middle East and tanks to the British armies in Egypt. Marshall hoped that these reinforcements would ease the pressure of the immediate emergency without disrupting basic

strategy.[81] The final upshot of the White House meeting was a compromise which left BOLERO the priority task but noted that it was "essential that the U. S. and Great Britain should be prepared to act offensively in 1942." The President and Prime Minister agreed that "operations in France or the Low Countries in 1942 would, if successful, yield greater political and strategic gains than operations in any other theater." Such operations would therefore be planned and prepared with all vigor, but if they proved unlikely to succeed, "we must be ready with an alternative." The best alternative was GYMNAST, which should be "explored carefully and conscientiously" and plans completed in detail as soon as possible.[82]

Although in form these conclusions reaffirmed the priority of BOLERO in Allied European strategy, against the background of the pessimistic reports of planners in England they actually yielded precedence to GYMNAST. This fact became increasingly clear as planners engaged in the last futile struggle with SLEDGEHAMMER. On 24 June General Eisenhower arrived in London to take command of all American forces in Europe, as Commanding General ETOUSA (European Theater of Operations, U. S. Army). He spent a week looking around and then wrote General Marshall that although a lot of planning had been done at low levels most of the basic decisions such as, for instance, the exact frontage of the assault had still not been made. He reported General Paget's complaint of the

---

[77] Memo, CCS for information, Minutes of an Informal Meeting . . . held in General Marshall's Office, June 19, 1942. OPD file ABC 381 (3–16–42) sec. 2.

[78] Stimson and Bundy, On Active Service, p. 425.

[79] Notes on War Council Mtg, 22 Jun 42. C/S file, Secy of War Confs, Vol. II. The War Council meeting at which General Marshall reported on the White House meeting was attended by the Secretary of War and Under and Assistant Secretaries as well as by Generals Arnold, McNair, Somervell, Knudsen, McNarney, Surles, and Eisenhower.

[80] Quoted in Sherwood, Roosevelt and Hopkins, p. 592.

[81] Notes on War Council Mtg, 29 Jun 42. C/S file, Secy of War Confs, Vol. II.

[82] CCS 83/1, Offensive Operations in 1942 and 1943, 24 Jan 42, Encloses memorandum by Maj. Gen. Sir Hastings Ismay reporting conclusions of a meeting held at the White House on 21 June.

lack of effective organization. Paget told him: "If we could only have the organization you have here, we could settle these matters in a morning. As it is we constantly go over the same ground and no real progress has been made."[83]

Lack of organization was a reflection of lack of conviction in high places that existing plans were practicable. A few days after his letter to Marshall, Eisenhower talked to the Prime Minister and found him "quite averse to attempting anything in Western Europe. . . . He believes it would be slaughter," Eisenhower noted, "because we are not strong enough." On the other hand, Churchill was perfectly confident about the northwest Africa operation—a confidence that Eisenhower at this time did not share.[84]

The Prime Minister's mind was, in fact, made up. On 6 July 1942 he presided over a meeting of the British Chiefs of Staff at which "it was unanimously agreed that operation 'SLEDGEHAMMER' offered no hope of success, and would merely ruin all prospects of 'ROUNDUP' in 1943."[85] The next step was to inform the Americans. This was done by two cables on 8 July, one to the Joint Staff Mission in Washington and the other a personal message from Churchill to Roosevelt.[86] Both reported the unfeasibility of SLEDGEHAMMER and recommended that the Americans proceed with planning for GYMNAST, while the British investigate the the possibility of attacking Norway (Operation JUPITER). Field Marshal Dill

had a preliminary talk with General Marshall. He found the latter's reaction so strong that he contemplated cabling a warning to his government that to press acceptance of GYMNAST at the expense of BOLERO would "drive U. S. A. into saying 'We are finished off with West and will go out in Pacific.' "[87] As Admiral King was out of town, official U. S. reaction was delayed. When King returned on 10 July, the Joint Chiefs met and General Marshall proposed just the step he had evidently discussed with Dill: turning from Europe to undertake an offensive in the Pacific. Admiral King approved, and remarked that the British, in his opinion, had never wholeheartedly supported BOLERO. Further, he believed, the Japanese were not going to sit tight much longer but were planning new attacks in the South and Southwest Pacific.[88] Marshall and King then sent a joint memorandum to the President stating their view that GYMNAST was indecisive, would prevent a SLEDGEHAMMER operation in 1942, and curtail or perhaps make impossible ROUNDUP in 1943. They concluded: "If the United States is to engage in any other operation than forceful, unswerving adherence to full BOLERO plans, we are definitely of the opinion that we should turn to the Pacific and strike decisively against Japan."[89]

The memorandum went to Hyde Park. The next day General Marshall heard rumors that he and King and Harry Hopkins would be sent to London but he still had no indication of the President's views. On 14 July the President telegraphed: "I

[83] Ltr, Eisenhower to Marshall, 30 Jun 42. OPD file 381, ETO, sec. I.

[84] Diary, Office of the Commander in Chief, 5 Jul 42. Cited hereafter as Diary of CinC. See Bibliographical Note.

[85] McLaren, Notes on SLEDGEHAMMER.

[86] See JCS 24th Mtg, 10 Jul 42.

[87] Draft Cbl in C/S file 381.

[88] JCS 24th Mtg, 10 Jul 42.

[89] Memo, King and Marshall for President, 10 Jul 42. C/S file BOLERO.

have definitely decided to send you, King and Harry to London immediately. . . . I want you to know that I do not approve the Pacific proposal."[90] In conversation with Marshall the next morning in Washington, Roosevelt called the proposal "something of a red herring" and was concerned lest it appear that "we had proposed what amounted to abandonment of the British."[91] General Marshall did not think so, but in any case the matter was dropped.

General Marshall's vehement defense of BOLERO stemmed in part from his feeling that the world situation was extremely critical. He was fearful, in particular, of a Russian collapse. The German summer offensive toward the Caucasus had broken through the Kharkov front and forced the Russians into a general withdrawal. "The present action in the Don Basin," General Marshall wrote on 13 July, "indicates Russia's possible inability to halt the massed power of Germany and her Allies. Considering the distribution of population in regard to density and race, the location of primary agricultural and industrial areas, and the railroad and road net of Russia, it is evident that unless this German offensive is soon halted Russian participation in the war will become negligible in magnitude, with the inevitable result of rendering all planning concerning ROUNDUP and all BOLERO movements (of ground troops at least) vain." The emergency for which SLEDGEHAMMER was planned was at hand, he believed, and failure to meet it would doom the chances of a cross-Channel attack in 1943. Inva-

sion of North Africa, in his view, would not achieve the necessary diversion to save the Russian armies from collapse. He cabled his views to General Eisenhower and asked Eisenhower to prepare a specific plan on how SLEDGEHAMMER might be carried out.[92]

It was with these convictions as to the desperate urgency of SLEDGEHAMMER that General Marshall on 16 July left for London. With King and Hopkins, he went as a personal representative of the President with large powers to settle strategy. The President's instructions required that SLEDGEHAMMER be strongly urged as the most important and perhaps imperative task for 1942. If it were found impossible, then Marshall should review the world situation with King and Hopkins and determine "upon another place for U. S. troops to fight in 1942."[93]

At the first London meeting, on 20 July, Churchill outlined his views and set the framework for subsequent staff discussions. The first question, he said, was the feasibility of SLEDGEHAMMER. Although the British had failed to devise a satisfactory plan, they would all listen sympathetically to any U. S. proposals. However, he went on to question the

---

[90] Tel, Roosevelt to Marshall, 14 Jul 42. C/S file BOLERO.

[91] Memo, Marshall for King, 15 Jul 42. C/S file WDCSA 381 War Plans Sec.

[92] Cbl, Marshall to Eisenhower, 13 Jul 42, C/S file BOLERO.

[93] Memo, Roosevelt for Hopkins, Marshall, and King, Instructions for London Conference,—July 1942, sgd orig in C/S file 381. This memorandum was drafted by the War Department, but Roosevelt made considerable changes in it, omitting the Pacific threat, and weakening the War Department's paragraph on commitment to ROUNDUP. The War Department draft on the latter point read that if SLEDGEHAMMER were given up, then the Allies should continue "our *planned* activities and *present* commitments in other areas. We should proceed with ROUNDUP preparations." In Roosevelt's revision, these two sentences were struck out. War Department draft included in Diary of CinC.

urgency of SLEDGEHAMMER. Might it not be argued that ROUNDUP depended only on what the Russians did, and not on what the Western Allies might do? He wondered whether the ROUNDUP concept need be confined to an attack on the western seaboard of France. He then discussed the value of invading North Africa and suggested that if the battle for Egypt went well it might be possible to attack even Sicily or Italy.[94] In a written review the next day the Prime Minister made his own conclusions clear, at least by implication. There were two main facts to be recognized, he believed: first, the immense power of the German military machine, which even without a defeat of Russia could still shift to the defensive in the east and move fifty or sixty divisions to France; second, the race in the west between attrition of Allied shipping and development of Allied air power. "It might be true to say," he wrote, "that the issue of the war depends on whether Hitler's U-boat attack on Allied tonnage or the increase and application of Allied air power, reach their full fruition first."[95] Emphasis on these two facts as the key to strategy meant postponing decisive land operations against Germany while carrying out a preliminary policy of attrition, chiefly through an increasing air offensive.

Although General Marshall was adamantly opposed to the concept, he found himself on weak ground in attempting to preserve the sanctity of the ROUNDUP idea while carrying out the President's mandate to take action somewhere in 1942. General Eisenhower was unable to defend SLEDGEHAMMER as an operation offering even a fair chance of tactical success. Eisenhower personally estimated that the chances of a successful landing were one in two and of being able to build up on the Continent to a force of six divisions about one in five. Still, he did point out that "if we are convinced that the Russian Army is now in a desperate situation . . ." the question of the tactical success or failure of SLEDGEHAMMER was of little moment, and "the only real test of SLEDGEHAMMER's practicability is whether or not it will appreciably increase the ability of the Russian Army to remain a dangerous threat to the Germans next spring." He admitted that the desperateness of the Russian situation was a matter of pure conjecture, in which there was "considerable difference of opinion." His conclusion, therefore, was that SLEDGEHAMMER should be kept alive until the first of September when a decision could be made on the basis of the Russian situation at that time.[96]

On the other hand, General Eisenhower strongly recommended against accepting GYMNAST as an alternative to SLEDGEHAMMER. "GYMNAST," he wrote, "is strategically unsound as an operation either to support ROUNDUP or to render prompt assistance to the Russians. Its execution now may be a logical alternative to 1943 ROUNDUP, but it is not a logical operation to insure execution of ROUNDUP. If undertaken now, *it should be done on the theory that the Russian Army is certain to be defeated* and that, consequently, we should take advantage of the relatively favorable situation now exist-

---

[94] Combined Staff Conf, 20 Jul 42. C/S file 319.1.
[95] Memo, 21 Jul 42, WP (42) 311. C/S file BOLERO.

[96] Memo (prepared by Gen Eisenhower with advice of Gens Clark and Lee and Col Barker), Conclusions as to the Practicability of SLEDGEHAMMER, 17 Jul 42. Diary of CinC.

ing to improve the defensive position that will be forced upon us in Europe and western Asia by a Russian defeat." [97]

Eisenhower's analysis anticipated in large measure the conclusions of the July conference. The British Chiefs of Staff were unalterably opposed to SLEDGE-HAMMER as an operation without reasonable chance of success. Since the SLEDGE-HAMMER force would necessarily be largely British and under British command, their opposition was decisive.[98]

Marshall reported to the President the failure of his first task. The President replied, asking for study of GYMNAST as the next most desirable operation, and concluding with a request for "speed in a decision." [99] Even with SLEDGEHAMMER ruled out, General Marshall was still reluctant to commit U. S. strategy irrevocably to the Mediterranean. He therefore arrived at a compromise with the British which began with agreement "that no avoidable reduction in preparation for ROUNDUP should be favorably considered so long as there remains any reasonable possibility of its successful execution before July 1943." That possibility depended on the Russians, and it was further agreed that "if the situation on the Russian front by September 15th indicates such a collapse or weakening of Russian resistance as to make ROUNDUP appear impracticable . . . , the decision should be taken to launch a combined operation against the North and North-

west Coast of Africa at the earliest possible date before December 1942." [100]

Not only did this agreement leave the door open for reconsideration but it made clear that the choice was between GYM-NAST and ROUNDUP and that a decision to go into North Africa should be made only after ROUNDUP was discovered impracticable. To General Marshall, as to General Eisenhower, the choice of GYMNAST meant acceptance of a probable Russian defeat, which in turn would prevent Allied invasion of Western Europe. General Eisenhower, reviewing the strategic situation on the eve of the conference's decision, admitted that GYMNAST seemed to be the only feasible and strategically valuable operation open to the Allies in 1942, but he added, "Since it is too much to hope that the Russians can continue fighting unaided, all through 1943, the final effect would be the abandonment of ROUND-UP." [101] The conclusion agreed to in conference with the British was only slightly less pessimistic. On American insistence, the agreement admitted that "a commitment to this operation [GYMNAST] renders ROUNDUP in all probability impracticable of successful execution in 1943 and therefore that we have definitely accepted a defensive, encircling line of action for the Continental European theater, except as to air operations and blockade. . . ." [102]

The door left open at the conference did not remain open long. On 25 July Harry Hopkins cabled Roosevelt urging an immediate decision in order to avoid

[97] *Ibid.* Italics in original. General Marshall agreed that SLEDGEHAMMER was not an operation he would choose if choice were possible. He believed, however, that choice was not possible, that "time was tragically against us." Memo for the President, 28 Jul 42. C/S file 319.1.

[98] Memo, Marshall for the President, cited n. 97.

[99] Cbl, 23 Jul 42. C/S file 381.

[100] CCS 94, Operations in 1942/3, 24 Jul 42. This paper states the decisions of the London Conference.

[101] Memo for Marshall, Survey of Strategic Situation, 23 Jul 42. Diary of CinC.

[102] CCS 94, cited n. 100.

"procrastinations and delays." [103] The President made up his mind at once. He called in Secretary Stimson and the Joint Chiefs of Staff [104] and, without discussion, read to them his decision to go ahead with GYMNAST. He saw no reason why the withdrawal of a few troops to the Mediterranean would prevent ROUNDUP in 1943. He desired action. To Hopkins, Marshall, and King, the President cabled, "Tell Prime Minister I am delighted that decision is made." [105]

The ambiguity of the "decision" which the President welcomed left the military leaders uncertain as to how definite the commitment to GYMNAST was. But it was perfectly clear that the North African project now had the inside track for planning and preparation. By agreement, ROUNDUP planning was to continue under the Combined Commanders and the ETOUSA plans section headed by General Barker. A separate U. S. staff would be sent to London to work on North Africa. Acceptance of the North African operation was sealed by baptism with a new code name: TORCH. [106] It was also determined that all currently planned operations (TORCH, SLEDGEHAMMER, and ROUNDUP) would be under a United States Supreme Commander. Pending the formal appointment of such a commander, General Marshall and Admiral King directed General Eisenhower to take immediate control of planning for TORCH. If and when TORCH was finally de-

cided on, the supreme commander of all operations in the theater would also command TORCH with a British deputy. [107] The nationality of the commander for ROUNDUP was not determined. It was laid down, however, that he would not have operational control of ground forces in the United Kingdom, that his function would be training and planning, and that troops would "only come under his operational command when the operation was mounted." [108]

After a week of uncertainty, [109] the President on the evening of 30 July informed the Joint Chiefs of Staff that he wanted to do TORCH but, before he cabled the Prime Minister of his decision, he would like an estimate of the earliest practicable date on which the operation could be launched. [110] The next day the British Joint Staff Mission was notified of the White House decision and cabled it to

---

[103] Cited in Sherwood, *Roosevelt and Hopkins*, p. 611.

[104] Admiral Leahy, General Arnold, and General McNarney.

[105] Cbl, 25 Jul 42. C/S file 381; Memo, Gen Deane for Admiral Willson, 25 Jul 42. C/S file WDCSA 381 War Plans Sec.

[106] Agreed at CCS 33d Mtg, 25 Jul 42.

[107] Later changed at British request in order to maintain appearance of an all-American operation and provide continuity of U.S. command in case the deputy had to take over. [Morton Yarman] TORCH and the European Theater of Operations (The Administrative and Logistical History of the ETO: Part IV), MS, p. 20. Hist Div files.

[108] General Marshall speaking at CCS 33d Mtg. This controverted an earlier (1 July) recommendation by the Combined Commanders that the ROUNDUP supreme commander also be charged with home defense of Great Britain. CC (42) 27, Notes on System of Command for Operation ROUNDUP. SHAEF SGS files, Combined Commanders Papers.

[109] At the CCS 34th meeting, 30 July, there was considerable vagueness expressed as to whether the TORCH decision had been made. Leahy and Dill "had the impression" that it had. Admiral King believed the President and Prime Minister had not yet decided to "abandon ROUNDUP in favor of TORCH."

[110] Memo, Gen W. B. Smith for JCS, Notes of a Conference Held at the White House at 8:30 P.M., July 30, 1942, 1 Aug 42. OPD files, exec 5, item 1, tab 14. General Smith reported: "The President stated very definitely that he, as Commander-in-Chief, had made the decision that TORCH would be undertaken at the earliest possible date."

the British Chiefs of Staff for relay to General Eisenhower. General Eisenhower was to assume the position of Supreme Commander pending final decision on a permanent appointment.[111]

In London, General Eisenhower took immediate steps to get the operation under way. As no new planning staff had arrived from the United States, it became necessary to employ American officers already in the United Kingdom. That meant denuding staffs which had been working on Continental planning. General Barker, selected as acting G–3 for TORCH, was one of the first to go. A TORCH planning committee was set up on a combined basis under Brig. Gen. Alfred W. Gruenther (U. S. A.), and the chief British planners who had developed ROUNDUP were also absorbed in the new adventure.[112]

ROUNDUP planning came virtually to a standstill.

The Period of Indecision
(July–December 1942)

President Roosevelt's decision to go ahead with TORCH [113] meant the indefinite postponement of ROUNDUP. That much was clear. It was not clear what effect the decision would have on grand strategy. The April agreements had provided for

a concentration on BOLERO in preparation for ROUNDUP in 1943. The July agreement rejected the principle of concentration and accepted instead a "defensive, encircling line of action." Regarding those two notions as contradictory, the U. S. Chiefs of Staff felt that strategy had been overturned. The British Chiefs of Staff, on the other hand, recalled the earlier ARCADIA principles which had emphasized preparatory operations (including attacks through the Mediterranean) in 1942 before the main attack across the Channel. The TORCH decision was clearly not at odds with those principles. Acceptance of "defensive, encircling action," they believed, meant only recognition of the need for a longer prelude to the final assault. They characterized the U. S. interpretation as heresy and were alarmed lest it take root.[114] But that it should take root was inevitable. For the U. S. Chiefs of Staff, under constant pressure to get on with the war against Japan, any delay and, more particularly, any uncertainty in the mounting of the decisive attack on northwest Europe inevitably unsettled the whole program for waging the war. Moreover, the connection between TORCH and an eventual ROUNDUP was at best indirect. If a North African invasion might be regarded, in the long run, as preparatory to a cross-Channel attack, the immediate relationship between TORCH and ROUNDUP would be competitive. Instead of building up forces in the United Kingdom, TORCH, if successful, would concentrate them in the Mediterranean. What then would be the next step?

---

[111] Cbl, JSM to Br COS, 31 Jul 42. OPD files, POD Super BOLERO, exec 1, tab 10; Memo, Marshall for WD Classified MC, Commander for TORCH, 6 Aug 42, OPD file 381, ETO, sec. 11, case 16.

[112] Yarman, TORCH, p. 18. See n. 107.

[113] The decision to do TORCH, as has been indicated, was primarily the President's, but Churchill had repeatedly taken the initiative in urging it. In April 1944 Churchill declared that he would "personally assume responsibility before God for the decision to do TORCH." See Ltr, Gen Wedemeyer to Gen Handy, 13 Apr 44. OPD files, OPD Misc, bk. 18.

[114] Cbl, Br COS to JSM, 13 Aug 42. Excerpts, supplied by British Cabinet Office Hist Sec, are in Hist Div files.

Lack of a long-range plan was particularly awkward for the United States in 1942 when mobilization was just getting started. The Army was in process of formation. Deployment had only just begun. Expanding productive capacity still had to be directed in accordance with priorities established to fit special military needs at least a year in advance. U. S. planners, studying the decisions of the London Conference, concluded that while they evidently abrogated the strategy implicit in the Marshall Memorandum of April they did not formulate any new strategy.

Through the summer and fall of 1942, the planners wrestled with the problem of calculating future needs in troops and materiel. In the weeks immediately preceding the July conference the Combined Planning Staff had drawn up two deployment papers, defining the basic combined strategy and translating it into terms of future commitments of troops and munitions in the various theaters of operations.[115] The first study assumed that the present strategic concept was: "To conduct the strategic offensive with maximum forces in the Atlantic-Western European Theater at the earliest practicable date, and to maintain the strategic defensive in other theaters, with appropriate forces." The second study, based on this assumption and on its implementation by the Marshall BOLERO plan, forecast that in April 1944 the offensive on the continent of Europe would be in progress. Neither study had been approved by the Combined Chiefs when the

TORCH decision forced reconsideration of the premises.[116] There began then a series of attempts to explain what had been decided at the London Conference. Neither the planners nor the chiefs could agree. What, in particular, was the extent of commitment of ROUNDUP? The British Chiefs of Staff, anxious to have the build-up of U. S. forces in the United Kingdom continue at the maximum rate, wanted to hold to the assumption that in the spring of 1944 operations would be either in progress or immediately in prospect on the Continent.[117] The Joint Chiefs could not see anything in the July decisions that would warrant such an assumption. The vague promise to consider crossing the Channel at some time when "marked deterioration in German military strength became apparent and the resources of the United Nations, available after meeting other commitments, so permit" [118] seemed to them an invitation to tie up troops and resources in the United Kingdom indefinitely with no assurance that they would be used in decisive action. The Joint Chiefs were in the meantime deeply conscious of the need to prosecute the war against Japan. They were in fact again wondering whether they should not reverse their basic strategy. The big issue to be decided, General Marshall argued in August, was whether the main U. S. effort should be in the Pacific or in the Europe–Middle East area.[119] The question which President Roosevelt a month earlier, before the London Conference, had called a "red herring" was now, at least, an issue of

---

[115] CCS 91, Strategic Policy and Deployment of United States and British Forces, 7 Jul 42; CCS 97, Strategic Hypothesis for Deployment of Forces in April 1944, 24 Jul 42.

[116] JCS 26th Mtg, 28 Jul 42.

[117] CCS 97/2, 8 Aug 42. See discussion in CPS (Combined Planning Staff) 28th Mtg, 7 Aug 42. OPD file ABC 370 (7–2–42).

[118] CCS 94.

[119] JCS 28th Mtg, 11 Aug 42.

all seriousness. Discussion of it centered largely upon the deployment of aircraft.

By the agreement of July the U. S. Chiefs of Staff withdrew fifteen groups of aircraft from allotment to BOLERO with the avowed intention of using them in the Pacific. The clause was written into the agreement, General Marshall later explained, only in order to remove the fifteen groups from the realm of combined discussion.[120] By assigning the groups formally to the Pacific, where by common consent strategy was primarily a U. S. responsibility, the Joint Chiefs reserved the right to dispose of them as they saw fit. When the whole question of future deployment was sent to the Joint Planning Staff, the fate of the fifteen groups uncovered a wide range of disagreement on basic strategy.[121] Naval planners wanted the planes shown deployed chiefly in the South and Southwest Pacific as of April 1943, thus assuming a considerable reorientation of strategy toward increased offensive effort against the Japanese. Specifically they recommended deploying aircraft according to the priority TORCH, Middle East, South Pacific, Southwest Pacific, United Kingdom. Army planners, still insisting on the primary importance of the whole European area, wanted equal priority for TORCH, the Middle East, and the United Kingdom. They pointed out that the Navy's deployment schedules would delay the arrival of planes in the United Kingdom by one to three months. General Arnold took up the cudgels to defend priority for the European theater. He pointed out that, of fifty-four groups of planes allotted to BOLERO-ROUNDUP by the Marshall Memorandum, only twenty-five remained for the air offensive against Germany. He believed that under the terms of the July agreements Germany was still to be considered the first objective of Allied strategy and that, therefore, no strengthening of the Southwest Pacific should be undertaken "until the modified BOLERO-TORCH plan has first been completely implemented."[122] That modified plan, he believed, far from entailing a reduction of air build-up in the United Kingdom put the chief burden of maintaining pressure against Germany on the air forces. The European theater, he believed, had become an air theater. He further argued that it was specious to separate TORCH and the Middle East from the United Kingdom, since the bomber offensive from England in fighting the German Air Force and weakening the German military potential contributed directly to the success of TORCH. The debate between General Arnold and Admiral King on this subject continued into the fall without arriving at any resolution.[123] Toward the end of October, planners reviewing the matter found that of the fifteen groups three had already been deployed: one to Hawaii, one to the Middle East, three squadrons to the South Pacific, and one squadron to Alaska. The remaining twelve groups the Joint Chiefs then decided should be held in strategic

---

[120] JCS 36th Mtg, 6 Oct 42.

[121] JPS 32d Mtg, 31 Aug 42. OPD file ABC 370 (7-2-42). See also notes on this meeting, 2 Sep 42. OPD file ABC 381 (9-25-41), sec. II.

[122] Memo, Arnold for Marshall, 29 Jul 42. OPD file ABC 381 (9-25-41), sec. III.

[123] See JCS 97 series which contains the gist of the running argument between General Arnold and Admiral King. For more detailed treatment of this subject see W. F. Craven and J. L. Cate, eds., *The Army Air Forces in World War II: II, Europe—Torch to Pointblank, August 1942 to December 1943* (Chicago, 1949), pp. 280-82.

reserve.[124] They were as far as ever from knowing what Anglo-American strategy was to be.

Although the Joint Chiefs did not agree on how far the BOLERO strategy had been or should be modified to step up the war in the Pacific, they were clearly pressing for some modification. Even before the TORCH decision, the concept of the "strategic defensive" in the Pacific had been defined to include "limited offensive operations." [125] That definition was not at once accepted by the Combined Chiefs, but in the middle of August they did agree to a strategic hypothesis [126] which for purposes of troop deployment assumed that by April 1944 there would be "an augmentation of forces in the Pacific by a readjustment of United States commitments in the European Theater . . . in order to further offensive operations against Japan." In context, however, this provision remained at least as vague as the earlier agreements. The same hypothesis also assumed that in 1944 preparations would continue for an invasion of the Continent as well as for deception purposes and in order to take advantage of a "favorable opportunity or emergency." Finally it was assumed also that North Africa in 1944 would be occupied by the Allies and "intensified operations" would be "conducted therefrom."

It was to this last assumption that the British Chiefs of Staff and the Prime Minister were giving their principal attention. In September Churchill outlined his conception of future strategy to the President. He was considering two possibilities after the assumed success of TORCH: attack into the "underbelly" by invasion of Sardinia, Sicily, or even Italy, and attack on Norway with the idea of giving more direct aid to Russia. ROUNDUP, he understood, was definitely off for 1943, but there still remained the possibility of an emergency cross-Channel operation and he believed that all the arguments advanced for SLEDGEHAMMER in 1942 would be even more valid in 1943–44.[127] The President was particularly interested in exploiting success in the Mediterranean. In November he proposed to Churchill that "you with your Chiefs of Staff in London and I with the Combined Staff here make a survey of the possibilities including forward movement directed against Sardinia, Sicily, Italy, Greece and other Balkan Areas, and including the possibility of obtaining Turkish support for an attack through the Black Sea against Germany's flank." [128] This was a welcome idea to the Prime Minister, who replied now that an attack against Sicily or Sardinia was an essential step following the cleaning up of North Africa.[129]

The idea, however, was anathema to the U. S. War Department. Maj. Gen. Thomas T. Handy, Assistant Chief of Staff, OPD, expressed adamant opposition to the British views, toward which Roosevelt seemed to be leaning. He believed that the Mediterranean operations were not logistically feasible, and that in any case they would not bring an Allied

---

[124] JCS 97/5, 26 Oct 42; JCS 39th Mtg, 27 Oct 42.

[125] CCS 91, cited n. 115. This paper, however, was never approved by the Combined Chiefs.

[126] CCS 97/3, Strategic Hypothesis as to Deployment of Forces in April 1944, 14 Aug 42. Approved at CCS 36th Mtg.

[127] Cbl, Eden to Halifax, quoting Cbl, Churchill to Roosevelt, 22 Sep 42. C/S file ETO.

[128] Quotation from Cbl, Roosevelt to Churchill, in Cbl, Churchill to Roosevelt, 18 Nov 42, incl in JCS 153, Plans and Operations in the Mediterranean, Middle East, and Near East.

[129] Cbl, Churchill to Roosevelt, cited n. 128.

force within striking range of Germany. He deplored the concept of an emergency cross-Channel operation. "Under no circumstance," he said, "can the U. S. agree to concentrate large forces in the U. K. there to be immobilized until the hypothetical break of German power as envisaged in the British concept." The only sound alternatives in his view were ROUNDUP as originally planned with a specific target date, or abandonment of the whole idea of defeating Germany first and turning to the offensive in the Pacific.[130]

In December 1942 Handy's views were echoed in a new strategic concept drawn up by a new committee, the Joint Strategic Survey Committee (JSSC) —a body of three senior officers whose sole job was to maintain a large perspective on the major problems of combined direction of the war and advise the Joint Chiefs on matters of policy.[131] The first task of the JSSC was to recommend to the Joint Chiefs a course of action for 1943. It was high time that such a course was settled. The North African invasion, launched on 8 November, met almost immediate success and raised with new urgency the question which the July decisions had left unanswered: What next?

The core of the strategy recommended by the JSSC was concentration on the build-up of a balanced force in the United Kingdom for a decisive cross-Channel attack before the end of 1943. In the meantime, an air offensive against Germany would be carried out from England, North Africa, and the Middle East. The

success of the North African operation would be exploited by air attacks on Germany and Italy "with the view to destroying Italian resources and morale and eliminating her from the war.[132] This much of the JSSC policy was accepted by the Joint Chiefs. However, the committee's recommendations for the Pacific, which amounted to continuation of the limited operations for defense and the minimum support of China, the Joint Chiefs drastically revised after a discussion in closed session. The revision greatly enlarged the concept of the strategic defensive against Japan. The Joint Chiefs declared that in the Pacific limited offensive operations would be carried out not only to secure Australia, New Zealand, Hawaii, Alaska, and the lines of communication but also "to maintain the initiative in the Solomon–Bismarck–East New Guinea area with a view to controlling that area and involving Japan in costly counter operations." In Burma an offensive should be undertaken to open supply routes to China.[133]

When these views were put before the Combined Chiefs, the British replied with their first fully developed statement of what may be called their peripheral strategy for the defeat of Germany.[134] Germany, they argued, needed a period of rest and recuperation; Russia was preventing that. The Allies therefore should do everything possible to assist Russia. Although Germany had to be reoccupied

---

[130] Memo, Handy for CofS, 8 Nov 42, American–British Strategy. C/S file 381.

[131] JCS 149/D, Charter of the Joint Strategic Survey Committee, 7 Nov 42.

[132] JCS 167, Basic Strategic Concept for 1943, 11 Dec 42.

[133] JCS 167/1, 20 Dec 42. The revision was done in the JCS 46th meeting. The revised paper, JCS 167/1, was submitted to the Combined Chiefs of Staff as CCS 135.

[134] CCS 135/2, American–British Strategy in 1943, 3 Jan 43.

eventually, the Allies were not yet ready to attack the Continental fortress. "To make a fruitless assault before the time is ripe would be disastrous to ourselves, of no assistance to Russia and devastating to the morale of occupied Europe." Even a maximum concentration on building up for a cross-Channel attack in 1943 would assemble only about twenty-five divisions in the United Kingdom by late summer, as compared to the original estimated requirement in the Marshall Memorandum of forty-eight divisions. In contrast to the unattractive prospect of a shoestring operation across the Channel, the British Chiefs of Staff sketched the rewards of pursuing operations in the Mediterranean. "If we force Italy out of the war and the Germans try to maintain their line in Russia at its present length, we estimate that they will be some 54 divisions and 2,200 aircraft short of what they need on all fronts. . . ." The operations they had immediately in mind were the invasion of either Sardinia or Sicily. But their plans for the Mediterranean did not stop there. Following Italian collapse the next step would be the Balkans, although it was not clear just what action would be possible in that area. In the meantime, while concentrating offensive action in the Mediterranean, the British Chiefs wanted the United States to build up an air force of 3,000 heavy and medium bombers in England and also continue to send ground divisions. They believed that, without prejudice to other operations, the build-up in the United Kingdom could reach twenty-one divisions by the fall of 1943—a force sufficient to effect a re-entry into the Continent under favorable conditions. As for the Pacific the British approved operations

to reopen the Burma Road, but they did not want any other expansion of the war against Japan. The reasons for tackling Germany first, they wrote, were still sound.

Although these views were in direct opposition to the strategic principles previously expressed by the U. S. War Department, the Joint Strategic Survey Committee found grounds for compromise. They believed that the ends sought by the British and the United States were the same: that is, to expel the Axis from North Africa, to eliminate Italy, and to do so by pressure rather than by occupation of the Italian peninsula. They thought the Combined Chiefs were further agreed that no large-scale operations should be undertaken against southern Europe with the ultimate view of invading Germany therefrom, and that, on the other hand, invasion of the Continent from the United Kingdom was essential to achieve decisive results. The chief disagreements seemed to be on the method of exerting pressure on Italy and on the timing of ROUNDUP. The U. S. Joint Chiefs wanted to force Italy's surrender by air bombardment from North African bases rather than by continued ground operations. The difference of opinion on ROUNDUP the JSSC thought might be due to misinterpretation. They criticized the British statement that concentration on the build-up for a cross-Channel attack in 1943 would interfere with the build-up of air forces for the bomber offensive. On the contrary, the JSSC believed: "The air offensive will of necessity hold precedence over the buildup for the land offensive, and continue to do so until the results of the air operations and the deterioration of the Axis situation in general can be better estimated in relation to prospective land operations." They concluded that this difference could probably be adjusted with the British without setting a definite date for ROUNDUP.[135]

This was the last formal word on U. S. strategy before the meeting of the Combined Chiefs of Staff with Roosevelt and Churchill at Casablanca in the second week of January, 1943. In its glossing over of deep differences of opinion and its ambiguous stand on the cross-Channel invasion, it reflected the lack at this time of a strong united conviction in the U. S. War and Navy Departments on what U. S. strategy should be. General Marshall admitted this when the President asked whether it was agreed that they should meet the British at Casablanca "united in advocating a cross-Channel operation." Marshall replied "that there was not a united front on that subject, particularly among the planners." Even among the Chiefs of Staff conviction was not strong. In Marshall's opinion, they regarded an operation across the Channel more favorably than one in the Mediterranean, "but the question was still an open one." [136]

The Casablanca Conference

When the Casablanca Conference opened on 12 January 1943 the Allies for the first time felt themselves able to choose the time and place for carrying the war to the enemy. Rommel had been decisively beaten in North Africa. Although the fighting in Tunisia continued, it was clearly only a matter of time before the

entire North African shore would be cleared. The Russians were already on the offensive after stopping the Germans in Stalingrad. Generaloberst Friedrich Paulus with more than 250,000 Germans was encircled and helpless before the city; the attempt to relieve him had failed. In the meantime the Russians had launched two other offensives to clear the Don Basin. In the Pacific, Japanese expansion had definitely been checked. The land and sea battles of Guadalcanal had both been won, although in January the island was still not entirely cleared. In the six months since the dark days of July Allied chances for victory had improved remarkably throughout the world.

In the generally brightening picture, however, there were still dark spots. Darkest was the German submarine menace in the Atlantic. Allied shipping losses had reached alarming proportions, and there was evidence that the German submarine fleet was steadily growing. The loss of shipping from all causes up to the end of 1942 exceeded new construction by about one million tons. During the year, 1,027 ships were sunk by enemy submarine attack.[137] This was a threat of the first magnitude. Without control of the seas the great U. S. war potential could not even reach the theaters of war; the Allies could not undertake the amphibious operations that were necessary throughout the world in order to get at the enemy. At the first meeting of the Combined Chiefs of Staff at Casablanca, Gen. Sir Alan Brooke put the matter bluntly. "The shortage of shipping," he believed, "was

---

[135] JCS 167/5, 10 Jan 43.

[136] Minutes of a Meeting at the White House on Thursday, 7 January 1943, at 1500. OPD files, POD exec 10, item 45.

[137] Samuel E. Morison, *The Battle of the Atlantic, September 1939–May 1943 (History of United States Naval Operations in World War II: I)* (Boston, 1947), p. 410. Over 1,770 ships were lost from all causes during the year.

CASABLANCA CONFERENCE. *Seated: President Roosevelt and Prime Minister Churchill. Standing, front row, left to right: General Arnold, Admiral King, General Marshall, Admiral Pound, Air Chief Marshal Portal, General Brooke, Field Marshal Dill, and Admiral Mountbatten.*

a stranglehold on all offensive operations and unless we could effectively combat the U-boat menace we might not be able to win the war."[138]

The other great weakness in the Allied position was a paucity of resources. Despite the large war potential of the United States, the troops, shipping, supplies, and material actually on hand at the beginning of 1943 were sufficient only for relatively small-scale offensive operations in one theater. The major strategic question before the Combined Chiefs of Staff at Casablanca was where and when these slender resources could be committed to make the maximum contribution to the defeat of Germany. The basic issue was similar to the problem faced in July: granting that the ultimate aim was to strike the decisive blow at Germany across the Channel, could such a blow be struck in 1943? Put another way the question was: if the prospects for a successful ROUNDUP in the summer were dubious, was it not better to concentrate on the Mediterranean where immediate operations offering a good chance of success were possible?

Churchill had no doubt that this was the correct strategy. In November he had written the President: "The paramount task before us is first, to conquer the African shores of the Mediterranean and set up there the navy and air installations which are necessary to open an effective passage through it for military traffic; and, secondly, using the bases on the African shore, to strike at the underbelly of the Axis in effective strength and in the shortest time." His opinion in January 1943 had not changed; he submitted then that "this surely remains our obvious immediate objective." [139]

It was not, however, obvious to General Marshall. He felt that there was a danger of fighting the war on a day-to-day opportunistic basis, of taking a series of un-co-ordinated steps promoted by immediate tactical considerations without considering the over-all strategy by which the Germans could be defeated most efficiently and in the shortest possible time. Granted that the victory in Africa opened the way for exploitation in the Mediterranean, the question still had to be asked how such exploitation would fit into "the main plot." Unless it could be proved to fit somewhere and constitute, moreover, the best means of advancing the plot at that time, it should not be undertaken no matter how tempting was the prospect of an easy military victory.

In answer to General Marshall's question, there was one obvious approach. What else could be done? General Brooke developed the argument from necessity. He pointed out that, on the Continent, Russia was the only Ally with large land forces in action. Comparing the Russian effort with the twenty-one divisions that the Western Allies could hope to land in France in 1943, he urged that "any effort of the other Allies must necessarily be so small as to be unimportant in the over-all

---

[138] CCS 55th Mtg, 14 Jan 43. Bound volumes containing the official U.S. minutes of the Casablanca (SYMBOL) Conference are in the OPD files. A single copy of the British official minutes is in the SHAEF SGS files. For all combined conferences the U.S. and British minutes are identical, but the latter include, in addition, the meetings of the British Chiefs of Staff at Casablanca. Since none of the minutes were stenographic, quotations here and throughout the text reproduce only secretarial summaries and paraphrases of the speakers' words.

[139] Note by Minister of Defence, 25 Nov 42, WP (42) 543, annex to 3d Br COS Casablanca Mtg. SHAEF SGS file 337/5, British Min of SYMBOL Conf.

picture." He contended that with limited resources the Allies could not expect to engage any considerable portion of the German land forces. The forty-four German divisions estimated to be in western Europe, he said, would "overwhelm us on the ground, and perhaps hem us in with wire or concrete to such an extent that any expansion of the bridgehead would be extremely difficult." [140] The argument on the relative futility of trying to influence the course of the land battle in Europe was lent considerable cogency by Molotov's prior request to General Marshall for the commitment in "the second front" of sufficient troops to draw off forty divisions from the Eastern Front.[141] This was ludicrously beyond the capacity of the Western Allies at that time.

Even if a landing on the Continent were feasible, it was likely to be much more costly than an assault in the Mediterranean. The British pointed out that the rail system of France would permit the simultaneous movement of at least seven German divisions from the east to reinforce the Atlantic Wall, whereas only one division at a time could be moved from north to south to meet an Allied attack in the Mediterranean. Use of the argument also revealed that direct assistance to Russia, the dominant consideration in July, was no longer a primary concern. It was further argued that such assistance could not be given. ROUNDUP preparations could not be completed before the middle of August; it was more likely that the operation could not be mounted before early autumn. In that case, it would not support the Russian summer campaign. Finally, it was un-

likely that the relatively small force which the Allies could put on the Continent would require the Germans to shift troops to defeat it. For the same reason it was doubtful whether even the German Luftwaffe could be brought to decisive battle. In sum, the argument was that ROUNDUP in 1943 would do no good and would invite disaster.

The Prime Minister continued to think of a SLEDGEHAMMER attack against the Continent in 1943, and in order to make it possible advised planning a Mediterranean operation to be accomplished cheaply and quickly after the windup of the North African campaign.[142] The chief arguments for continuing attacks in the Mediterranean, however, were the immediate strategic advantages to be gained from them. In the first place, since there were several plausible objectives in the Mediterranean, a skillful use of feints might well force the Germans to disperse a large number of troops to meet widespread threats to Sicily, Corsica, Sardinia, the Dodecanese Islands, and the coasts of Italy and Greece before any operation was actually launched. In the second place, if Italy could be knocked out of the war (and that in the British view was the major immediate objective of any action contemplated in the Mediterranean), the Germans would not only have to take over the defense of Italy but would also have to assume Italian commitments for defense of the Balkans. The Prime Minister was also drawn to the possibility of tempting Turkey into the war. He felt that by clearing the Mediterranean a valuable selling point would be gained for negotiations with Turkey. If Turkey could be brought in, the British planned to use the

---

[140] CCS 58th Mtg, 16 Jan 43.
[141] See above, p. 24.

[142] 1st Br COS Casablanca Mtg. See n. 138.

country as a base from which to attack the Românian oil fields and open the Black Sea route to Russia. They did not contemplate the use of Turkish troops in attacking outside of Turkey.

The British arguments in favor of the Mediterranean as the scene for 1943 attacks were, from a tactical standpoint, convincing enough, but they did not meet Marshall's objections that the Mediterranean could not be considered the main arena for meeting and fighting German military might. The Americans believed and consistently maintained that Germany's defeat "could only be effected by direct military action," [143] and that that action must be directed against the main body of the German Army in the west. The British thought Germany might be defeated primarily by destroying the enemy's will to resist through air attack and encirclement. They reasoned that "Germany's will to fight depended largely on her confidence in ultimate success." [144] Repeated victories by Russia and the Western Allies, even if on the perimeter of the German *Lebensraum,* would make Germany "realize that the prospects were hopeless." If despite that realization the Germans still refused to surrender, then direct attack from the west would be employed to deal the deciding blow.

The U. S. Chiefs of Staff did not discount the possibility of a sudden German collapse. On the whole, however, they held firm to the conviction that neither the air offensive nor victories in the Mediterranean could so significantly weaken the German's will to resist as to justify prolonged delay in mounting the final

attack. General Marshall stated the United States point of view in these terms: "It has been the conception of the United States Chiefs of Staff that Germany must be defeated by a powerful effort on the Continent, carrying out the 'BOLERO' and 'ROUNDUP' plans." Aid to Russia was important in order to absorb German strength, but "any method of accomplishing this other than on the Continent is a deviation from the basic plan." He then made it clear that if the Americans should agree to Mediterranean operations they would be accepting a temporary expedient compelled by immediate circumstances. They would not consider that they had thereby approved in principle any departure from their overall strategy. The question, Marshall submitted, was: "To what extent must the United Nations adhere to the general concept and to what extent do they undertake diversions for the purpose of assisting Russia, improving the tonnage situation, and maintaining momentum." That this distinction should not be missed, he asked pointedly whether the British Chiefs of Staff considered that an attack now against Sicily was a means to an end or an end in itself. Did they view it as "a part of an integrated plan to win the war or simply taking advantage of an opportunity"? [145]

However, having drawn this line between strategy and expediency, the U. S. Chiefs of Staff then agreed that circumstances made a Mediterranean operation expedient. After some discussion the Combined Chiefs decided that, as between the two possible invasions (Sardinia or Sicily), Sicily was the more profitable attack with the resources available.

---

[143] Admiral King speaking at CCS 58th Mtg.
[144] Air Marshal Portal at CCS 58th Mtg.

[145] CCS 58th Mtg.

The principal grounds on which the Americans conceded the argument were that they had large numbers of troops in North Africa which could not be readily employed outside the Mediterranean and that the Sicilian operation would "effect an economy of tonnage which is the major consideration." [146] Even in yielding, however, General Marshall said that "he was most anxious not to become committed to interminable operations in the Mediterranean. He wished Northern France to be the scene of the main effort against Germany—that had always been his conception." [147]

To this Air Chief Marshal Portal significantly replied that it was impossible to say where they should stop in the Mediterranean since the object was to knock out Italy altogether. The difference of opinion had not been resolved. It had only been temporarily abated for the sake of arriving at a vital decision to maintain the momentum of the war against Germany.

The question of how to proceed against Germany was posed at Casablanca in the context of the global war. While devoting all possible energy and resources to defeating Germany, it was clear that the Allies could not afford simply to turn their backs on Japan. It has already been pointed out that the U. S. Chiefs of Staff since July had veered toward a decision to increase substantially the effort in the Pacific. They spelled out their new point of view to the British for the first time at Casablanca. The United States desired to maintain pressure against the Japanese,

General Marshall told the British Chiefs of Staff, in order to forestall another "series of crises," which had wrecked offensive plans in the early part of 1942.[148] Maintaining pressure, of course, meant mounting attacks. Admiral King estimated that the attacks considered necessary would require roughly double the current U. S. forces in the Pacific. There was a danger, he pointed out, that without a great effort to assist Generalissimo Chiang Kai-shek China might pull out of the war. General Marshall added that helping China carry the fight against Japan "might have a most favorable effect on Stalin." [149] The U. S. Chiefs of Staff therefore especially recommended pushing operations in Burma.

The British frankly did not like this new attitude. In general they regarded the Pacific in much the same light as General Marshall regarded the Mediterranean—an invitation to diversions from the main effort. While admitting in principle the need for unremitting pressure against Japan, the British Chiefs of Staff feared it would mean weakening the offensive against Germany. General Brooke tried to force the issue by stating it as a problem of reviewing "the correctness of our basic strategic concept which calls for the defeat of Germany first." He believed that the Allies could not take on Germany and Japan at the same time. The Americans denied any intention of altering the basic strategy. On the contrary, "The whole concept of defeating Germany first," Marshall submitted, "had been jeopardized by the lack of resources in the Pacific." He recalled how the United States had nearly been forced to

---

[146] Marshall speaking at 2d ANFA Mtg, 18 Jan 43. The ANFA meetings were those presided over by the President and Prime Minister.

[147] CCS 60th Mtg, 18 Jan 43.

[148] 2d ANFA Mtg.

[149] CCS 56th Mtg, 14 Jan 43.

withdraw from TORCH because of the danger of reducing the slender resources in the Pacific. "A hand-to-mouth policy such as this was most uneconomical." It was essential to establish a sound position in the Pacific. That could not be done simply by defensive deployment. The Japanese themselves were busy consolidating and would certainly continue their attempts to advance if they were given a breathing spell. To forestall them the Allies must attack. Furthermore it would unduly prolong the war if the United States waited until after the defeat of Germany before securing positions from which the final offensive against Japan could be launched.[150]

The British at last yielded the point. They had already agreed to operations in Burma to open the road to China. They now approved plans to mount both overland and amphibious attacks against the Japanese in Burma during 1943. They further agreed to the seizure of Rabaul and reserved decision on a proposed attack against Truk.

Casablanca focused attention on 1943 and concluded with a statement that the operations envisaged in 1943 were designed to bring about the defeat of Germany in that year.[151] This was for the record—but there were reservations. The Americans in particular were not sanguine about the prospects of victory in 1943. General Arnold asked for a decision on what might be done in 1944 so that production schedules could be planned in advance. General Brooke replied that "we could definitely count on re-entering the Continent in 1944 on a large scale."[152]

The Combined Chiefs of Staff then proposed setting up a combined command and planning organization to plan for small-scale raids, a return to the Continent in 1943 under conditions of German collapse, a limited operation in 1943 to secure a bridgehead on the Continent for later exploitation, and last "an invasion in force in 1944." [153]

Even though a 1944 ROUNDUP lay far ahead in a somewhat clouded future, the conference undertook to give preliminary shape to its ultimate command organization. Roosevelt proposed a British supreme commander, but on Churchill's suggestion decision was postponed. At the moment the Prime Minister believed it was necessary only to select a commander to undertake the planning. This commander, he agreed, should be British, but he enunciated the principle that "the command of operations should, as a general rule, be held by an officer of the nation which furnishes the majority of the force." [154] At a later meeting the Combined Chiefs decided that it would be sufficient to select a British Chief of Staff, together with "an independent United States–British Staff." [155] In examining this proposal the President questioned whether "sufficient drive would be applied if only a Chief of Staff were appointed." [156] General Brooke thought that "a man with the right qualities . . . could do what was necessary in the early stages." [157] It was left at that—a curiously vague and inauspicious beginning for the

---

[150] CCS 60th Mtg, 18 Jan 43.
[151] CCS 155/1, Conduct of the War in 1943, 19 Jan 43.
[152] CCS 58th Mtg.

[153] CCS 169, Organization of Command, Control, Planning and Training for Cross-Channel Operations, 22 Jan 43.
[154] 2d ANFA Mtg.
[155] CCS 67th Mtg, 22 Jan 43.
[156] 3d ANFA Mtg, 23 Jan 43.
[157] *Ibid.*

staff that would write the OVERLORD plan and then become the nucleus of the supreme headquarters that carried it out.

If Casablanca did little to erase the vagueness surrounding the ultimate ground operations in northwest Europe, it at least arrived at more vigorous decisions on an air offensive from the United Kingdom. The Combined Chiefs directed the initiation at once of a combined U. S.–British bomber offensive aimed at "the progressive destruction and dislocation of the German military, industrial, and economic system and the undermining of the morale of the German people to a point where their capacity for armed resistance is fatally weakened." [158]

Most of the big decisions of the Casablanca conferences were made during the first week. General Brooke undertook to summarize these for the President and the Prime Minister:

Measures to be taken to combat the submarine menace are a first charge on the resources of the United Nations. . . . Our efforts in defeating Germany will be concerned first with efforts to force them to withdraw ground and air forces from the Russian front.[159] This will be accomplished by operations from North Africa by which Southern Europe, the Dodecanese Islands, Greece, Crete, Sardinia, and Sicily will all be threatened, thus forcing Germany to deploy her forces to meet each threat. The actual opera-

tion decided upon is the capture of Sicily. At the same time we shall go on with preparing forces and assembling landing craft in England for a thrust across the Channel in the event that the German strength in France decreases, either through withdrawal of her troops or because of an internal collapse. . . . The maximum combined air offensive will be conducted against Germany from the United Kingdom. By this and every other available means, attempts will be made to undermine Germany's morale. Every effort will be made, political and otherwise, to induce Turkey to enter the war in order that we may establish air bases there for operations against Roumania. . . .[160]

As an outline of a strategic concept for the guidance of planning, these decisions were not much clearer than the decisions of July 1942. Certainly the extent of commitment to an eventual cross-Channel operation was no more specific. But in providing for the establishment of a planning staff and in agreeing to push the BOLERO build-up despite continuing operations in the Mediterranean, Casablanca had, in fact, laid the groundwork for OVERLORD. During the next six months, planning and preparations in the United Kingdom would of themselves clear much of the academic mist from the face of the cross-Channel project and convert it from a map problem into a plan of action for which the necessary men and material were on hand or in prospect. And this would happen while the debate on strategy continued through a series of compromise decisions scarcely firmer than those with which the Casablanca Conference closed.

---

[158] CCS 166/1/D, The Bomber Offensive from the United Kingdom, 21 Jan 43. See below, Ch. VI.

[159] As noted above, it does not appear from the records that this was actually an important consideration. The strategic concept underlying Mediterranean operations was the much more general idea of attrition.

[160] 2d ANFA Mtg.

CHAPTER II

Outline Overlord

(January–July 1943)

Organization for Planning

Several months elapsed before the Casablanca decisions to go ahead with ROUNDUP plans and preparations began to bear fruit. In these months the European theater convalesced slowly from the TORCH bloodletting, reasserted its independence, and turned again to face northwest Europe across the English Channel.

Recovery was difficult, for, ever since the TORCH decision, the Mediterranean had enjoyed a ruthless priority on all resources of war. As already noted, TORCH had drawn top U. S. and British personnel into what was first a planning group and later became Allied Force Headquarters (AFHQ), which under Lt. Gen. Dwight D. Eisenhower carried out the North African invasion. At the same time General Eisenhower retained command of ETOUSA, the headquarters controlling U. S. forces in the United Kingdom. Despite the difficulties of this dual role the arrangement was preserved in order to insure that TORCH might draw at will on American resources in England. When Eisenhower moved to the Mediterranean, he appointed an executive deputy theater commander, Maj. Gen. Russell P. Hartle, to manage theater affairs in the United Kingdom. Hartle served in this capacity

from 2 November 1942 to the end of January 1943. Then, according to plan, with TORCH firmly established, AFHQ and ETOUSA were formally split. Early in February Lt. Gen. Frank M. Andrews was named commanding general of ETO-USA. New theater boundaries gave ETO-USA responsibility for operations in the whole of Europe except the Iberian Peninsula, Italy, and the Balkans.[1]

It was a large theater but, when General Andrews took over, it was occupied by only a handful of the U. S. Army. Before TORCH swept the larder, U. S. forces by the end of September 1942 had built up in the United Kingdom to about 188,-000 men, including one armored and three infantry divisions. In the course of the next five months, TORCH took three of the four divisions, and a total of over 150,000 troops. Although partially replenished by shipments from the United States, net U. S. strength in Britain had fallen to 107,801 by the end of February. This was the low point. The build-up thereafter began to recover slowly. However, the one division passed over by TORCH, the 29th, remained the only divi-

---

[1] See [Robert W. Coakley] Organization and Command in the ETO (The Administrative and Logistical History of the ETO: Part II), MS, Ch. III. Hist Div files.

sion in the United Kingdom until the fall of 1943.[2]

TORCH interfered even more drastically with the air corps build-up. The new Eighth Air Force was only beginning to accumulate its striking power when it was required to form the Twelfth Air Force to support TORCH. It surrendered to the Twelfth Air Force about half of its complement of aircraft (1,100 planes) and much of its key personnel including its commander, Maj. Gen. Carl Spaatz. General Eaker, who took command of what was left, complained that still worse than the loss of planes was the loss of priority on organizational equipment, spare parts, and replacements of aircraft and personnel.[3] The net result was that U. S. participation in the bomber offensive against Germany was set back eight or nine months and did not begin to become effective until the spring of 1943.[4]

Stock piles of supplies and equipment that had been accumulated in the United Kingdom to maintain a cross-Channel operation were also drawn into the Mediterranean, in some cases at a rate even faster than the movement of troops. Thus the level of supply of some items actually declined for the troops that remained in Britain. In addition monthly delivery of supplies to the United Kingdom which in September reached almost 240,000 long tons had dropped in February to 20,000 tons. BOLERO shipments began to pick up slowly in March but did not regain the September rate until July.

In the meantime planning for ROUNDUP continued under the aegis of the Combined Commanders. The new combined planning staff ordered at Casablanca was slow in taking shape. The difficulties, though relatively minor, seemed to require a large amount of discussion. Casablanca had been vague about both the mission and the form of the new staff. The specification that it would function under a chief of staff to an unnamed supreme commander implied that the planners could henceforth be regarded as the nucleus of the headquarters that would eventually control the operations. Beyond that, Casablanca recalled that a "special inter-allied staff" had already been working "for some months" on cross-Channel plans, and suggested that "this special planning staff should be adapted to the new conditions and strengthened by the addition of American personnel. They should work, under the direction of the Supreme Commander (or his deputy until he is appointed), in conjunction with the nucleus of his combined staff in London." [5]

But all this was not much more than a collection of working notes by the Combined Chiefs, reminding themselves in a general way of the nature of the problem they would have to solve later by means of a directive actually establishing the organization they recognized as needed. By

---

[2] [Morton Yarman] TORCH and the European Theater of Operations (The Administrative and Logistical History of the ETO: Part IV), MS, pp. 95ff. Hist Div files. Figures on troop strength are derived from Transportation Corps sources and indicate troops actually carried into and out of the United Kingdom. Slight discrepancies exist between them and the official troop assignment figures. A detailed account of troop build-up in the United Kingdom will be found in R. G. Ruppenthal, Logistical Support of the Armies, a volume under preparation in this series.

[3] Rpt, Eaker to Arnold, Oct 42, cited in Yarman, TORCH, p. 119.

[4] See below, Ch. VI.

[5] CCS 169, Organization of Command, Control, Planning and Training for Cross-Channel Operations, 22 Jan 43.

the end of February the British Chiefs of Staff had drafted such a directive, but it provided for a predominantly British organization, not very different from the Combined Commanders. Addressed to a British chief of staff for cross-Channel operations, it directed him to report to the British Chiefs of Staff and charged him temporarily with the command responsibilities of the supreme commander, pending the latter's appointment.[6]

This draft, as might have been expected, was unsatisfactory to the Americans, who amended it to make the chief of staff for cross-Channel operations responsible to the Combined Chiefs and limit his responsibility to planning. They added further that the Commanding General, ETOUSA, should be considered as the direct representative of the United States Chiefs of Staff and that he should be consulted on all plans with respect to the employment of United States forces.[7]

The American amendments were promptly accepted by the British and the new directive was approved by the Combined Chiefs on 5 March.[8] However, the question of when the new staff should be organized and what planning responsibility it should have was not thereby settled. The British Chiefs of Staff recommended delay. They understood that BOLERO build-up plans had been changed and that few American troops would actually be present in the United Kingdom during 1943.[9] They reasoned that the cur-

rent arrangements for planning by the Combined Commanders were therefore adequate and should be continued.[10] Under the circumstances they were reluctant to spare the necessary senior officers to form a special staff. Instead they suggested appointing a chief staff officer to the Combined Commanders, to be charged with "co-ordinating and driving forward the plans for cross-Channel operations this year and next year." This appointment was actually made, pending American approval of the other suggestions. General Brooke selected Lt. Gen. Frederick E. Morgan, and the Prime Minister and the Secretary of State for War at once approved the nomination.[11]

The U. S. Chiefs of Staff agreed to General Morgan's appointment but not to the reduced planning arrangements. The Combined Chiefs consequently turned again to consideration of the special combined staff. The directive of 5 March was reintroduced for fresh debate, and the month of April witnessed an interchange of proposals and counterproposals. Out

---

(43) 28th Mtg (0), 24 Feb 43. Marshall wrote that, because of an urgency in another theater, no shipping would be available for lifts to the United Kingdom in March and April and that the amount of shipping to be available in May could not be determined. Minutes also reproduce cable (COS (W) 492) from British Chiefs of Staff to Field Marshal Dill asking Dill to elucidate the urgency in another theater and call to the attention of the U.S. Chiefs of Staff the British belief that such diversion of shipping from BOLERO constituted an abrogation of Casablanca decisions. All COS documents, hereafter cited, are located in SHAEF SGS files, unless otherwise specified. See Bibliographical Note.

[10] COS (43) 58th Mtg, 6 Mar 43.
[11] COS (43) 63d Mtg, 12 Mar 43. For General Morgan's background and experience, see Lt. Gen. Sir Frederick E. Morgan, *Overture to Overlord* (New York, 1950), pp. 1–28.

---

[6] CCS 169/1, 25 Feb 43; cf. Cbl, Andrews to Marshall, 28 Feb 43. SHAEF SGS file 322.011/3.
[7] CCS 169/2, 2 Mar 43.
[8] CCS 74th Mtg. The directive was issued as CCS 169/3/D.
[9] COS (43) 105 (0) (Final), 8 Mar 43. Cf. Cbl, Marshall to Andrews, 22 Feb 43, cited in Min, COS

of this came a revision of planning tasks. The conviction had grown since Casablanca that no operations against the Continent, even of limted scale, would be possible in 1943. The order to plan such operations was therefore struck out and instead planners were directed to draw up a plan to keep the Germans guessing about Allied intentions during the year.[12]

Although this change in mission was the only basic alteration made during more than a month of discussion, one issue was raised that revealed an important difference in attitude between the U. S. and British Chiefs. This was the question of the target date for the 1944 cross-Channel invasion. Casablanca had specified only the year: "an invasion in force in 1944." The March 1943 directive read: "full-scale invasion in the spring of 1944." The British struck out "spring" in their first attempt at amending the directive. The Americans, in their reply, restored it. The final directive compromised: "A full scale assault against the Continent in 1944, as early as possible."[13]

The Combined Chiefs finally issued a directive on 23 April. By that time the new organization was already well under way. General Morgan had been told in March that, whatever the final arrangements, the chief responsibility for planning cross-Channel operations would be his. He was handed a file of planning papers and required to make recommendations on the form that he thought

the staff should take. On the understanding then that the supreme commander would be British, General Morgan recommended a British organization headed by a British chief of staff. He asked that the chief of staff be invested with "plenary powers, temporarily to impersonate the commander-to-be." This body should be the nucleus of an Allied headquarters, and General Morgan advised against the establishment of any British GHQ. He wanted, on the other hand, to have British, Canadian, and American army headquarters set up as soon as possible. Allied headquarters would deal directly with the armies until such time as the build-up of forces in the United Kingdom warranted the interpolation of army group headquarters. The Allied staff, General Morgan felt, should effect a "complete amalgamation of the British and American personnel, sub-branches being headed by American or British officers as found suitable." On the other hand it would be desirable to keep British and American administrative affairs separate. He recommended a thorough integration of the various services throughout the echelons of command as low as army. Finally he asked for a grant to his own organization of "the highest possible degree of autonomy, at least in the operational sphere."[14] In short, what General Morgan had in mind was a compact planning and co-ordinating staff which should enjoy the maximum freedom in carrying out its mission of preparing for cross-Channel operations and which would represent as completely as possible an integration of

---

[12] The debate can be followed in CCS 169 series and in CCS 80th and 81st Mtgs, 16 and 23 April 1943 respectively, with additional reference to the British Chiefs of Staff (COS) papers and meetings already cited. Cf. Interv, F. C. Pogue with Gen Morgan, 8 Feb 47. Hist Div files.

[13] CCS 169 series.

[14] All quotes from Memo, Morgan for Br COS, Cross-Channel Operations, 21 Mar 43, Annex to COS (43) 148 (0), 23 Mar 43.

GENERAL MORGAN, *chief OVERLORD planner.*

all services of both nations, combined to plan and ultimately to carry out the supreme effort of the Allies against Germany.

In general the staff established in April 1943 conformed to General Morgan's concept. It was christened COSSAC after the initial letters of Morgan's new title: Chief of Staff to the Supreme Allied Commander (designate), and its principal staff officers met officially for the first time on 17 April. General Morgan was not immediately given either the executive power he asked for or quite the untrammeled direction he requested over "all offensive enterprises of whatever kind initiated from the United Kingdom." [15] He was, however, granted sufficient power to tackle the task, and his attitude from the beginning was that of an executive rather than a planner. He told his staff at their first meeting that they should not consider themselves planners. "The term, 'Planning staff' has come to have a most sinister meaning—it implies the production of nothing but paper. What we must contrive to do somehow is to produce not only paper; but action." This would not be easy in view of COSSAC's lack of executive authority, but despite that General Morgan said: "My idea is that we shall regard ourselves in the first instance as primarily a co-ordinating body. . . . We differ from the ordinary planning staff in that we are . . . the embryo of the future Supreme Headquarters Staff." He wanted to model his staff on that of Marshal Foch at the end of World War I—"a really small body of selected officers who dealt with the major decisions on broad lines, the day-to-day work of the war being dele-gated completely to commanders of army groups." [16]

The original COSSAC staff was divided into five branches: Army, Navy, Air, Intelligence, and Administration and Logistics. Each branch, except Intelligence, was headed by two Principal Staff Officers, British and American. The Intelligence branch initially had only a single British head. The Principal Staff Officers, in turn, had separate staffs split vertically by nationality and horizontally into sections devoted to the preparation of the various plans for which COSSAC was responsible. Thus, for example, the Army branch headed by a British and an American Principal Staff Officer had two head planners (British and American) and under them British and American officers in three sections working respectively on plan OVERLORD, plan RANKIN (the plan for a return to the Continent under conditions of German collapse), and plan COCKADE (threat to hold the maximum number of German forces in the west in 1942). In addition there were three advisory sections. Naval and Air branches had more or less parallel divisions. The Intelligence and Administrative branches were subdivided by sea, air, and land; in the Administrative branch these subdivisions were doubled by nationality. The Principal Staff Officers were responsible for co-ordinating all joint problems before presenting them to COSSAC. Army, Navy, and Air branches prepared the outline appreciations and plans. The Intelligence branch was to supply the necessary information about

---

[15] Memo, Cross-Channel Operations, cited n. 14.

[16] COSSAC (43) 1st Mtg, 17 Apr 43. All COSSAC documents referred to are located in the collections of COSSAC papers and minutes of staff conferences in SHAEF SGS files. See Bibliographical Note.

the enemy and the Administrative branch analyzed the resources called for. The Administrative branch was also responsible for developing administrative and logistical plans within the operational framework.[17]

This organization, though fairly satisfactory at first, became cumbersome as COSSAC's duties and American representation increased, and as the staff took on more the complexion of a supreme headquarters. With the appointment toward the end of June of Air Marshal Sir Trafford Leigh-Mallory as Air Commander-in-Chief pro tem, the COSSAC United States and British air staffs were amalgamated into a single staff.[18] This process of fusing nationalities into a single combined organization had started informally earlier. The Intelligence branch had had a single head from the beginning. The Administrative branch was integrated very soon after its formation under Maj. Gen. N. C. D. Brownjohn (British). On 16 July, General Morgan decreed that a single Operations branch should be formed with sections grouped functionally but not separated by nationality. Complete integration of the combined headquarters, however, did not take place until the fall when Maj. Gen. Ray Barker, Deputy Chief of Staff, announced the abolition of any division along national lines in favor of a purely functional organization.[19]

It was impossible to keep COSSAC small. Even though the day-to-day work was in large part delegated to lower headquarters, the co-ordinating functions of COSSAC continued to expand up to the time when it came of age in January 1944 as the Supreme Allied Command. Not only did its planning duties increase to include, for instance, Civil Affairs and Publicity and Psychological Warfare, but it became imperative to assume the executive obligations implicit in COSSAC's responsibility for the cross-Channel operation. Thus in the fall of 1943 COSSAC took over the task of co-ordinating raiding and reconnaissance in northwest Europe in order to relate those activities to the ultimate invasion and to the 1943 diversion program.[20] A little later General Morgan assumed a similar responsibility for directing certain aspects of the partisan and underground movements on the Continent, so far as these were strategically related to the COSSAC plans.[21]

While organization of the COSSAC staff proceeded, the British took steps to form their Army, Navy, and Air high commands for the invasion. The whole frame of the British field command was firmly established in the spring and early summer, and each of the service headquarters, preceding similar U. S. organizations by several months, became the nucleus of the

---

[17] COSSAC (43) 12 (First Draft), Provisional Organization of COSSAC Staff, 25 May 43.

[18] See below. Leigh-Mallory had an anomalous appointment to make decisions on air matters without prejudice to the Air Commander-in-Chief when appointed. See COSSAC 12th Staff Mtg, 26 Jun 43.

[19] COSSAC (43) 29th Mtg, 8 Oct 43. Barker was presiding in the absence of Morgan, who was visiting Washington. See below, Ch. III.

[20] COS (43) 217th Mtg (0), 16 Sep 43; COS (43) 624 (0), 13 Oct 43.

[21] COSSAC's authority included operational control of all underground movements directed from London, the general direction of planning such movements, and the use and co-ordination of instructions on target priorities. See COSSAC (43) 58 (Final), Proposals for Control by COSSAC of SOE/ SO Activities in Northwest Europe, 20 Oct 43. ETOUSA concurred by indorsement on 11 Nov 43. SHAEF G-3 file Ops C, 322.7 II; cf. COS (43) 237th Mtg (0), 5 Oct 43.

eventual command over the combined invasion forces.[22]

By July the Second British Army, the First Canadian Army, and 21 Army Group all had functioning headquarters. The 21 Army Group, under command of General Sir Bernard Paget, took over from the Home Defence Command all planning, tiaining, and executive functions in regard to British expeditionary forces. General Morgan at once established close liaison with Paget's staff and depended on them thereafter for detailed information and advice on the employment of British ground forces. More than that, 21 Army Group became the principal advisers on ground tactics and all matters of army interest in the assault. This inevitably followed from the lack of any parallel U. S. organization. With V Corps still the highest U. S. tactical headquarters in the United Kingdom, the U. S. Army participated in COSSAC planning through theater headquarters, ETOUSA. In fact, since no table of organization was set up by the War Department for the U. S. half of the COSSAC staff, the American COSSAC planners functioned on detached service from the G–5 (plans) section of ETOUSA. Although both General Andrews and his successor, Lt. Gen. Jacob L. Devers,[23] took an active part in the planning, they could not supply an organization parallel to the British for detailed examination of army problems. This deficiency was not remedied until

October when First U. S. Army was established in England.

The British similarly outdistanced the Americans in creating naval and air commands for invasion. On 5 May the British Admiralty issued a directive to Admiral Sir Charles Little, Commander-in-Chief, Portsmouth, appointing him Naval Commander-in-Chief (designate) for the cross-Channel operations being planned by COSSAC.[24] The appointment was in addition to his normal duties as commander of all British naval forces operating out of the Portsmouth area. To handle his new assignment he was authorized a special planning staff to be known as Naval Staff (X).[25] His Chief of Naval Staff (X), Commodore J. Hughes-Hallett, who had commanded the naval force at Dieppe, became a member of the COSSAC staff in May.[26]

All U. S. naval forces operating from the United Kingdom were at that time under Admiral Stark, Commander-in-Chief Naval Forces in Europe. As in the case of the U. S. Army, tactical organization for the invasion was delayed until the fall when the Twelfth Fleet under Rear Adm. Alan G. Kirk was organized.[27] Stark's headquarters, therefore, was

---

[22] Information on establishment of British headquarters from Intervs, F. C. Pogue with Lt Col H. A. Pollock (13 Dec 46), Gen Morgan (8 Feb 47), Gen Barker (4 Oct 46), and Gen Paget (6 Feb 47). Hist Div files.

[23] General Andrews was killed in an airplane crash in Iceland on 3 May 1943. Devers was assigned to the European post after having served as Chief of the Armored Force at Fort Knox since 1941.

[24] Ltr, H. N. Morrison to Admiral Little. SHAEF SGS file 322.011/2.

[25] COS (43) 73d Mtg, 12 Apr 43.

[26] COSSAC Staff Conf, 1 May 43. SHAEF SGS file 337/14. At the beginning of World War II, Hughes-Hallett was serving as second in command of the *Norfolk.* In 1940 he became deputy director of Local Defence at the Admiralty and followed this tour of duty with appointment as chairman of the Admiralty's radar committee. He went to Combined Operations Headquarters in 1942. In August 1943 Commodore Hughes-Hallett was replaced on the COSSAC staff by Rear Adm. G. E. Creasy.

[27] There had never been any question that the British, who supplied the bulk of the naval forces, would have the Allied naval command.

charged with co-ordinating U. S. preparations for OVERLORD with ETOUSA and COSSAC, but had no specific tactical responsibility. Admiral Stark, in addition to supplying COSSAC with a U. S. naval staff, sent liaison officers to Admiral Little's headquarters and also to the Plymouth and Milford Haven Commands which were the bases from which the U. S. naval assault forces would sail.[28]

The beginnings of a Royal Air Force organization for support of ground operations on the European continent were made in March 1943. Air Marshal Portal then proposed the formation of a "Composite Group Headquarters" within the fighter command, both to test ideas for organization for Continental operations and to function as a command if a German collapse should require a return to the Continent before detailed preparations could be made. The composite group, established on 19 March, grew rapidly into a full-scale tactical air force.[29] The Tactical Air Force was formally recognized as existing from 1 June with Air Vice Marshal Sir John Henry d'Albiac in command.[30] Again the U. S. parallel organization came late on the scene with the reconstitution in England of the Ninth Air Force in October.[31]

Size and Shape of the Attack

When the COSSAC staff began work, it had a large amount of experience and data accumulated through two years of planning for ROUNDUP and through experimentation in minor cross-Channel operations. The most important practical experience came from the Dieppe raid in August 1942.[32] The raid carried out under joint British and Canadian command[33] and largely with Canadian troops —about one thousand British troops and fifty U. S. Rangers also took part—was originated in Mountbatten's Combined Operations headquarters in order to test amphibious tactics and techniques in a large-scale operation. The most ambitious attack on the French coast up to that time had been the raid on St. Nazaire in March 1942. But St. Nazaire was still only a hit-and-run commando foray. Dieppe was planned as a miniature invasion, involving the full use of combined arms and mass landings of infantry and armor with the object of seizing a beachhead. Except that there was no intention of holding the beachhead, Dieppe was drawn as closely as possible to the pattern of a full-scale amphibious attack. Specifically it was designed to test the newly developed LCT in landing tanks across the beaches and to find out whether it would be possible to take a port by direct frontal assault. It would also test naval organization in managing a considerable landing fleet (253 ships and craft), and air organization in gaining air supremacy over the landing area and providing support for the ground troops.

[28] Administrative History, U.S. Naval Forces in Europe, MS, pp. 237ff. Hist Div files.

[29] COS (43) 149 (0), 23 Mar 43; COS (43) 248 (0), 10 May 43. Also documents in British Air Ministry Collection, excerpted by U.S. Air Forces Historical Unit.

[30] D'Albiac was succeeded in January 1944 by Air Marshal Sir Arthur Coningham.

[31] For formation of U.S. commands for OVERLORD, see below, Ch. V.

[32] For full account of the Dieppe raid, see Col C. P. Stacey, *The Canadian Army, 1939–1945: An Official Historical Summary* (Ottawa, 1948), pp. 64–86.

[33] The Military Force Commander was Maj. Gen. J. H. Roberts, commander of the 2d Canadian Division. Naval and air force commanders were British, Commodore J. Hughes-Hallett and Air Marshal Sir Trafford Leigh-Mallory respectively.

BRITISH LANDING CRAFT ON BEACH AT DIEPPE

The raid was carried out on 19 August 1942 as planned. Tactically, it failed. Very heavy enemy opposition resulted in severe casualties and the planned withdrawal nine hours after the touchdown was carried out under difficulties reminiscent of Dunkerque. Besides nearly 1,000 dead, about 2,000 Canadians were left behind as prisoners. Of 6,100 men embarked on the expedition only 2,500 returned, including an estimated 1,000 men who never landed. Although the cost was severe, the Dieppe raid provided some valuable experience both for the tactics of amphibious operations and specifically for the planning for OVERLORD.[34] As concerned the latter, Dieppe seems in general to have impressed planners with the hardness of the enemy's fortified shell and the consequent need for concentrating the greatest possible weight in the initial assault in order to crack it.

Whether as a direct result of Dieppe or not, ROUNDUP planning in the winter of 1942–43 took a new turn. It had hitherto been assumed that attacks against the French coast should be widely dispersed in order to prevent the enemy from concentrating on the destruction of any one beachhead. In November 1942, General Barker and Maj. Gen. J. A. Sinclair, chief British planner, started on another tack. In examining the requirements for a suitable assault area for a major operation, they premised their study on the principle of concentration. Abandoning the ROUND-

[34] For the effect of the Dieppe raid on tactical doctrine, see below, Ch. V.

UP idea of many separate regimental and commando assaults, they assumed one main landing in an area capable of development into a lodgment for the whole Allied invasion force.[35]

They then analyzed the conditions essential for such an area. It first had to be within range of fighter planes based in the United Kingdom in order that air supremacy might counterbalance the unusual hazards of a major amphibious assault. At the time the study was made, fighter cover extended only over the coast between Cherbourg and Knocke (in the northwest corner of Belgium). Further to insure air supremacy, the area selected had to contain airfields or sites for airfields which could be made available to Allied fighters at an early date.[36]

The beach defenses had to be capable of reduction by naval fire, air bombardment, or airborne troops. It was desirable, obviously, that the beach defenses be as weak as possible, but the essential thing was that there should be a reasonable chance of neutralizing them. This requirement, in fact, ruled out only small beaches dominated by well-defended cliff positions and areas, such as the Netherlands, where the enemy could defend by large inundations which the Allies had no means of combatting.

The selected assault area must permit the Allied rate of build-up to compete with that of the enemy. From this, other conditions followed. The area had to contain one major port that could be captured quickly. It was also desirable that a group of ports be close at hand with sufficient combined capacity, when developed, to support the entire force in later phases of the operation. Since there was no hope of being able to put captured ports into workable condition until about three months after the landings, it was equally important that the selected assault area have beaches suitable for prolonged maintenance operations. They therefore had to be sheltered from the prevailing winds in order to insure continuous operations even in bad weather. More important, the beaches had to have sufficient capacity to receive and rapidly pass inland the required vehicles and supplies. The critical considerations here were not only the size and firmness of the beaches but also the existence of adequate vehicle exits and adequate road nets behind the beaches.

Having established the conditions essential to an assault area for a major invasion, Generals Sinclair and Barker then proceeded to examine various coastal sectors, matching each with the ideal. None fitted. Only one came close—the sector around Caen. The Netherlands was ruled out because it was out of the range of fighter cover, because its beaches were too exposed and, being backed by sand dunes, had inadequate exits for vehicular traffic. Finally the Germans could too easily defend them by flooding. A scarcity of beaches—and those small and exposed —disqualified Belgium unless enemy resistance was comparatively light and good weather could be counted on for at least

---

[35] Capt. M. McLaren, Secretary to the Combined Commanders, pointed out that the study reversed the ROUNDUP concept of maximum dispersion in order to prevent the enemy from concentrating on the destruction of any one bridgehead. Memo, Operation OVERLORD—Main Appreciation, 12 Dec 42. SHAEF G–3 file 370–43.

[36] This and the following four paragraphs are from CC (42) 108, Selection of Assault Areas in a Major Operation in Northwest Europe. A late draft (5 Feb 43) is in SHAEF SGS file, Combined Commanders Papers.

a week to allow capture of the group of ports from Dunkerque to Zeebrugge. Actually German defenses of the sector were very strong, and therefore the feasibility of invading it would depend on a substantial lowering of enemy morale. The Pas-de-Calais coast, which ROUNDUP planners had regarded as the most likely assault area, was rejected for a major operation because the beaches were exposed, strongly defended, and dominated by high ground on which the enemy had emplaced artillery. The larger beaches had few exits, and the ports in the area had insufficient capacity to maintain a large force. Inadequate beaches ruled out the Seine sector as well, except as an area for subsidiary assault. It was noted that in order to use the ports of Le Havre and Rouen both banks of the Seine would have to be cleared. On the other hand, simultaneous attacks on both sides of the Seine could not be mutually supporting and would therefore be subject to defeat in detail. The Seine sector could be attacked with a reasonable chance of success only *after* a main assault in the Caen area. Brittany failed to meet any of the major requirements except as to port capacity. It was above all too far from Germany and a lodgment there would result in long lines of communication in the advance east.

The process of elimination left only the Caen sectors and the Cotentin Peninsula. Caen was desirable from every standpoint except the lack of adequate ports. It was therefore suggested that Caen be made the area of main attack with a subsidiary attack on the east coast of the Cotentin to insure the early capture of Cherbourg. Even Cherbourg, however, could not supply a large invasion force, and it was

therefore deemed necessary to seize the Seine ports or the Breton group in addition. Decision on which group to secure would depend on the final objectives of the operation and the degree of enemy opposition expected. There were objections to both. To take the Seine ports would necessitate crossing the river. Dependence on the Brittany ports, as already noted, would mean long lines of communications. This risk, planners thought, would be acceptable only if it were considered "essential to build up a large force west of and protected by the River Seine."

This analysis revised during the early months of 1943 was at last approved by the Combined Commanders on 1 March and constituted the basic appreciation for subsequent cross-Channel planning. The immediate result was a new outline plan —the final effort of the Combined Commanders before they turned over the planning job to COSSAC. The new plan, SKYSCRAPER, provided simultaneous landings on the Caen and east Cotentin beaches with four divisions in the assault and six in the immediate follow-up. It required in addition eighteen Commandos [37] for special assault missions and four airborne divisions to interfere with the movement of enemy reserves. After the initial beachhead, including Cherbourg, had been established, planners assumed the next move would be to secure additional port capacity for the build-up. They advised advance toward the Seine ports, but thought the capture of Le Havre might well require a new landing northeast of the port in support of the

---

[37] A Commando was a specially trained and equipped British unit roughly equivalent in strength to a U.S. rifle battalion.

overland attack. Advance would then continue northeast to open the port of Antwerp and establish the armies between the Pas-de-Calais and the Ruhr.[38]

The avowed object of SKYSCRAPER was to provide a gauge of some of the major problems to be faced in the cross-Channel invasion. Chief of these was the large requirement for resources, especially in landing craft. Planners stated the case uncompromisingly. The requirement for ten divisions simultaneously loaded was an absolute minimum, they said. Even that would enable the Allies to take on only the present enemy force in the west, estimated to consist of an average of two coast defense divisions to each hundred miles of assault area. Furthermore the ten-division assault force would suffice only if enemy troop movements could be completely blocked.

SKYSCRAPER set its sights deliberately high. It was an attempt to break the deadlock which the tangle of interrelated contingencies had imposed on ROUNDUP planning. Planners were pressing now for a decision. "If we are to plan and prepare for the invasion of Western Europe against opposition," they wrote, "it must be on the understanding that the resources considered necessary are fully realized and that it is the intention to provide them." Therefore, they concluded, "To defer the decision is to decide not to be ready." But the sights seem to have been set too high. The British Chiefs of Staff argued that the vague notion of "determined opposition" could not be used as a criterion for the number of assault divisions needed.[39] They decided not to consider the general principles enunciated in the plan.[40]

Some of the SKYSCRAPER ideas carried over into the OVERLORD planning, since many of the Combined Commanders' planners were transferred to the COSSAC staff. On the other hand, rejection of the SKYSCRAPER approach by the British Chiefs of Staff emphasized a break in the planning. The idea of pressing for increased resources seemed to have been discouraged in advance. In any case a new beginning and a new approach were required. General Morgan made this point explicit when he told his staff to consider that much useful data had been collected but that no plan worthy of the name existed. They were to make the maximum use of previous planning studies in order to save time, but the problem, Morgan insisted, should be seen as something new—something to be tackled afresh as though no planning had gone before. He returned therefore to first principles and recreated the broad strategic frame.[41]

The over-all conception he presented was of a major land campaign culminating in the invasion and occupation of Germany with forces totaling possibly a hundred divisions. The opening picture was of Anglo-Canadian armies concentrated in the southwest, and the main

---

[38] Abstract from SKYSCRAPER Plan. Hist Div files.

[39] COS (43) 61st Mtg (0), 30 Mar 43.

[40] Formal grounds for tabling the paper were that COSSAC was about to begin planning for "definite operations" and that consideration of general principles would therefore be a waste of time. General Paget, commander of 21 Army Group, and one of the Combined Commanders, believed, however, that the British Chiefs of Staff were generally unfavorable to the plan because of the huge bill for resources. His interpretation is persuasive. See Gen Paget, Notes on the History of Planning for Operations in North-West Europe, 30 Dec 43. Hist Div files.

[41] COSSAC (43) 11, Plan for a Full Scale Invasion of the Continent in 1944, 25 May 43.

army waiting in the United States preparing to cross the Atlantic. The need for maximum fighter cover dictated that the assault should be made on the left flank, opposite the British forces. American forces might then be brought into the bridgehead and sent westward to take the ports through which the main American army from the United States could be disembarked. Since this plan would involve tangling administrative lines, it would perhaps be better "to contemplate the Anglo-Canadian bridgehead as the left flank guard of American assaults to be delivered further to the west." In any case the need for opening the Atlantic ports meant that the initial assaults were to be given a westerly rather than an easterly trend.[42]

The broad perspective led General Morgan to only one positive conclusion as to the choice of an assault area: it must be in France. Although both France and the Low Countries contained sufficient deepwater ports to receive the American armies, it was not reasonable to suppose that the ports of the Netherlands and Belgium could be opened up by assaulting forces. "To demand of the armies of the advanced guard that they should cover the use of the group of ports of the Low Countries is to demand that they should in effect themselves fight the battle of Germany."[43]

Landing Craft Requirements

Neither the precise area of the assault nor the question of whether one or many landings should be made was decided at this time. In large part, these decisions depended on the approximate scale of the operation. While General Morgan was conceiving the broad outlines of the operation, his staff worked to crystallize the concept in terms of landing craft and men. This problem brought them right back to basic difficulties faced by all the cross-Channel planners and solved by none of them. How could one calculate the size of the assault? What were the determining factors? The Combined Commanders had picked a figure of ten divisions, four in the assault and six preloaded to insure a continuous build-up during the time the craft used in the assault were returning or undergoing repairs for subsequent trips. All ten divisions were to land on the first four tides—that is, before the end of D plus 1.[44] But the only basis for this requirement was the Combined Commanders' feeling that "a return to the Continent against determined opposition" could not be successful with a smaller force. In rejecting the whole SKYSCRAPER idea, the British Chiefs of Staff pointed out that one could not estimate the number of divisions needed to overcome "determined opposition."[45]

In fact, however, no better estimate was possible. It was obviously absurd to forecast a year in advance the strength and nature of enemy opposition. The only possibility was to plan on the basis of German dispositions as they existed in the spring of 1943, assume a normal distribu-

---

[42] Note that this is the opposite of the SKYSCRAPER principle of pushing northeastward in order to maintain the pressure of the attack on Germany.

[43] COSSAC (43) 11, cited n. 41.

[44] SKYSCRAPER Plan; Memo, Gen Barker for Executive Planning Section (ETOUSA), Requirements of Landing Craft, 9 Mar 43. SHAEF SGS file 560 I.

[45] COS (43) 61st Mtg (0), 30 Mar 43. Note that the British Chiefs of Staff apparently reversed themselves on this point at the Washington Conference in May. See below, section following.

tion of reserves, suppose that German commanders would take the best possible steps for defense, and add hypothetical calculations from logistical tables on the capacity of the enemy to move in reinforcements from the east. The net calculation, however, could easily mean nothing, since the number of unknown factors was very large and there was ample time for the whole picture to change completely before the Allies were ready to attack.

The attempt to find how large an assault would be required for the job thus broke down on the impossibility of judging with any realism the size of the job. The alternative was to calculate how large an assault might be practicable with resources likely to be available and then try to see how an operation of such size might be assured a reasonable chance for success. In May Commodore Hughes-Hallett, chief British naval planner, made a guess pending lengthy examination. He thought landing craft might be procured for simultaneous assault by four divisions including 16,000 men in armored landing craft and 12,000 vehicles in LST's and similar ships. A fifth division might be preloaded to land within twenty-four hours.[46] But an estimate of the availability of craft was almost as shaky as an estimate of the need for them. Writing to General Handy in April, General Barker said: "Provision of landing craft . . . constitutes a continuing bottleneck which not only has to be met materially, but must also be overcome from the psychological and political aspects as well. In other words a shortage . . . can readily be made the excuse for failure

to do operations which otherwise might prove practical." He asked General Handy for a clear statement on U. S. production and assurance that the United States could provide the necessary craft for a cross-Channel attack.[47]

It was not easy to supply assurances on U. S. production of landing craft. In the first place the whole idea of using specially constructed craft in large numbers for amphibious operations was so new that no generally accepted doctrine had been developed. Thus in the spring of 1943 Admiral King was reported as saying: ". . . apparently now it is felt assaults cannot be made without specially designed craft." At the same time it was suggested that the landing craft bottleneck might be partly bypassed by larger use of "makeshift" craft such as barges and river "steamers."[48]

Except for small personnel boats the U. S. Navy had had no landing craft at all until 1937 when it experimented unsuccessfully with a tank lighter. The first successful vehicle landing craft was developed by Andrew J. Higgins, a New Orleans boatbuilder, but was not ordered by the Navy until September 1940 and not contracted for in large numbers until spring of 1942. During the first years of the war the majority of naval leaders re-

---

[46] Memo, 1944 Hypothesis, 15 May 43. SHAEF SGS file (1944 Operations).

[47] Memo, Landing Craft for Cross-Channel Operations, 20 Apr 43. SHAEF SGS file 560 I.

[48] JCS 71st Mtg, 30 Mar 43. The British planned to use barges and coasters in the invasion and had pointed out in April that they were busy converting barges for such use. They did state, however, that although miscellaneous vessels might be useful they ought not to be employed in the first assault. "There is no substitute for specialized landing craft in an assault against the most heavily defended coastline in the world, despite the fact that the morale of the German Army may have deteriorated sufficiently to justify an assault on the Continent." Note by Br JPS, CPS 63/1, 16 Apr 43.

sisted the development of landing craft as a foolhardy gamble with an untried weapon and a waste of resources badly needed for naval construction.[49]

The initiative in development of large landing craft was left to the British who, for obvious reasons, were much more seriously impressed with the need for such craft. British experimentation with specialized landing craft began after World War I as a result of the invention of the tank. Whereas experience had seemed to show that personnel could be landed on hostile shores by the regular vessels of the fleet, the tank clearly could be beached only from a special ramp boat. In 1920 the British produced a tank lighter which, with very few changes, became the LCM (1) (Landing Craft, Mechanized). Too small to carry the medium tanks used in World War II, the LCM (1) was nevertheless kept in extensive use for transporting other vehicles and supplies. In 1938 the British at last abandoned the theory that special craft were not needed to land troops. In that year they produced the prototype of the LCA (Landing Craft, Assault), a small wooden armored craft for ship-to-shore movement of assault infantry. The first large orders for LCA's were placed in September 1939, and subcontracted to small boat and yacht firms. Engines for both the LCM and LCA came from the United States.[50]

The LCM and LCA were designed for raiding operations. Production was undertaken only on a very small scale and mostly outside the established shipbuilding industry which was already working to capacity in attempting to meet vastly expanded requirements for merchant and naval war vessels. In June 1940 Prime Minister Churchill personally ordered the design and production of the first landing craft capable of carrying expeditionary forces. Worked out by the Combined Operations staff within the British Admiralty, this became the LCT (Landing Craft, Tank), designed to carry three 40-ton tanks and disembark them in three and a half feet of water on steep-gradient beaches such as those of Scandinavia. The first LCT was delivered in November 1940. Subsequent development of the LCT was comparatively rapid. In December 1941 orders were placed for the fourth model, LCT (4), the first landing craft designed specifically for the shallow-gradient beaches of the French coast. It was to be able to carry six medium tanks and to be capable of rapid mass production.[51]

While the LCT—the basic vehicle-carrying landing craft of World War II—was being perfected, the British also began experimenting with a much larger ocean-going ship capable of discharging vehicles directly across the beach. Three shallow-draft oilers used on Lake Maracaibo in Venezuela were procured and converted to prototypes of the LST (Landing Ship, Tank) by cutting off

---

[49] Lt. Hamilton S. Putnam and Lt. Craig A. Livingston, Commander-in-Chief Atlantic Fleet, Amphibious Training Command (United States Naval Administration in World War II), MS, Vol. I, Ch. VIII. Navy Dept files.

[50] This and subsequent information on British landing craft production was supplied by the British Admiralty.

[51] The production lag in the LCT (4) is worth note. When the boat was ordered the United States had just come into the war; planners in England had worked out only the first tentative plan for an eventual cross-Channel attack. When the first craft was delivered in September 1942, the 1942 season for amphibious operations in the Channel was already coming to a close.

the bows, installing bow ramps, and scooping out the insides to accommodate vehicles. Though designed with shallow draft, neither the converted Maracaibo nor the first model LST proved satisfactory. Improvements were gradually worked out through experimentation and study by both British and American designers. The final result was the LST (2), an ocean-going ship capable of grounding and discharging vehicles on the shallow-gradient beaches of France. The United States undertook the entire production of the LST (2) for both British and American use.

In the spring of 1942 the United States began a program for the mass-production of landing craft for the 1943 cross-Channel attack as envisaged in the Marshall Memorandum. The difficulties of expanding a comparatively small landing craft fleet into one for major amphibious operations were enormous. The Navy, which was to co-ordinate the program, and many of the shipyards that were to carry it out were almost wholly lacking in experience. The program was superimposed on already swollen naval construction schedules. Contracts therefore had to be let to small boatyards and manufacturing companies for whom the construction problems posed were unprecedented. The LCT's and LST's were built on inland waterways and it became necessary to find and train crews to sail them to Atlantic ports. The U. S. Coast Guard, which formed the Ferry Command in July, undertook this task with almost no technically competent personnel. Typical of the greenness prevailing to some extent throughout the landing craft program was the story of a young Ferry Command skipper who, piloting his craft down the

Niagara River at night, missed the turning into the Erie Canal and, despite warnings from the shore, sailed serenely toward the falls. By luck he ran aground a few hundred yards from the brink. He blandly reported afterward that he had seen the warning lights at the point where he missed the turning but had paid no attention because he could not figure out what they meant.[52]

Lack of experience delayed the program but did not seriously jeopardize it. A more serious difficulty, and one which persisted throughout the war, since it had no final answer, was the establishment of priorities. The material requirements for landing craft, chiefly steel and marine engines, had to compete with other high-priority building programs. The construction of a landing craft fleet in 1942 was completed only by the issuance of emergency directives and the creation of special expediting machinery. When the immediate emergency passed with the successful landings in North Africa, landing craft construction had to give way in the competition for materials to other war production which could claim greater urgency. The President's January list of "must" programs for 1943 omitted landing craft. Escort vessels and merchant shipping were a more immediate necessity. The need for escort vessels, in fact, was considered so urgent in the early months of 1943 that the machinery which had been set up to expedite production of landing craft was diverted to perform the same function for destroyer escorts. The 1942 landing craft program ended as scheduled in February with a record production of 106,146 light displacement

[52] Putnam and Livingston, Amphibious Training Command, cited n. 49.

tons. From then on it declined and in May was stabilized at about 60,000 tons monthly. This figure was carried forward for deliveries during the first half of 1944.[53]

In March 1943 the question of increasing the production of landing craft, particularly for a cross-Channel invasion, came before the Joint Chiefs of Staff. The British at that time asked the United States to examine the possibility of increasing production, because a shortage of LCT's and LST's was likely to make a cross-Channel invasion in 1944 difficult. They added that Britain could not do anything about it since British production was already proceeding at the maximum rate. The British request was met with some suspicion.[54] The Joint Chiefs were inclined to question whether the British were making full use of their own resources. Admiral King stated flatly that any substantial increase in the rate of production of landing craft would cause serious delays and conflicts with other programs.[55] The Navy recalled with alarm the dislocation in naval construction caused by the 1942 landing craft program. After noting that the present schedules for delivery of craft during 1943 and early 1944 would "in no way near approximate previous deliveries except in the case of

LST's," a Navy spokesman strongly recommended that no change be made in current production schedules. "It should be remembered that in order to get the present LST's on time we have to cut across every single combatant ship program and give them over-riding priority in every navy yard and in every major civilian ship-building company. We have not and will not for the next 6 months recover from all the derangements suffered from the last over-riding Amphibious Boat Program. In my opinion anything approaching a repetition of the previous program would be disastrous from a standpoint of all other Naval construction. . . ."[56]

Allotment of Resources, May 1943

From the point of view of the COSSAC planners in London, the failure to take timely steps to increase landing craft production looked at best like shortsightedness and at worst like a deliberate attempt to sabotage the cross-Channel invasion. Washington, however, had a larger, more difficult perspective. The Joint Chiefs were concerned not only with a European invasion but with establishing the best possible balance of forces to carry on the global war. In the spring of 1943 they were still operating under the Casablanca statement of strategy which required that defeat of the German submarine should be a first charge on the resources of the United Nations. The German submarine had not yet been defeated; on the contrary

---

[53] George E. Mowry, *Landing Craft and the WPB (Historical Reports on War Administration: WPB Special Study No. 11)*, rev. ed. (Washington, 1946), pp. 7, 19–21, 25.

[54] One of the principal American planners noted that lack of landing craft might be *one* reason for the difficulty of launching an invasion in 1944, but, on the other hand, "we have never had tangible indication that the British intend to launch [a] cross-Channel operation." Penciled note on Gen Wedemeyer's copy (Copy 4) of CPS 63, Production of Landing Craft, 19 Mar 43, incl to JCS 248, 26 Mar 43. P&O Implementing Section files.

[55] JCS 71st Mtg, 30 Mar 43.

[56] Memo, W. S. Farber for Admiral Horne, Rates of Production for Landing Craft, App. A to Min, JCS 71st Mtg. Rear Adm. Farber was head of the Fleet Maintenance Division (December 1940–October 1943). Vice Adm. Horne was Vice Chief of Naval Operations for Materiel.

the United Nations in March had lost a near record tonnage of shipping.[57] Any decision to curtail the production of escort vessels would not therefore have seemed justified. Requests to increase landing craft production were at this time extremely vague. No one could say how many more LCT's or LST's would be required. No one could state categorically that the current production schedules would not yield sufficient craft for proposed operations. It has already been pointed out that the planners' estimates for a cross-Channel invasion had varied from a five- to a ten-division lift. By May the only conclusion reached was General Morgan's warning that although requirements of landing craft could not yet be forecast they would be "large enough . . . to present a very serious problem, which has no precedent." [58]

It was with this basic uncertainty as to their needs that the British planners arrived in Washington in May 1943 to settle, among other things, the allocation of resources for 1944 operations in the European theater. The availability of resources was a planning problem and scarcely a whisper of it reached the high council chambers where the President and Prime Minister, with the advice of the Combined Chiefs, sought to mark out world-wide strategy. Yet the whole discussion was colored by the higher level debates on strategy and, in turn, decisions on landing craft made at planning level

were to become pivots of higher strategy. For the future of cross-Channel operations in particular, the work of the planners in Washington in May was vastly more significant than the pronouncements of the President and Prime Minister. The repercussions of landing craft decisions were to be felt all during the following year until Churchill at last complained with some bitterness that "the destinies of two great empires . . . seemed to be tied up in some god-dammed things called LST's whose engines themselves had to be tickled on by . . . LST engine experts of which there was a great shortage." [59]

At the Washington Conference the first British statement of requirements for a 1944 cross-Channel invasion included 8,500 landing ships and craft to provide a lift for ten divisions simultaneously loaded for the assault. American planners, comparing this figure with estimated production rates, came up with the conclusion that the demand was impossible of fulfillment. It was, in fact, so far out of line with reality that the U. S. Chiefs of Staff at once suspected the good faith of the British in proposing it. They wondered whether the impossible bill for shipping had not been presented to provide the British with an excuse for not doing the operation.[60] They ignored the fact that the estimate of ten divisions for the assault had been arrived at by *combined* planners in London and had been specifically agreed to by ETOUSA.[61] In

[57] History of the Commander-in-Chief Atlantic Fleet (United States Naval Administration in World War II) , MS, p. 463. Navy Dept files; cf. Samuel E. Morison, *The Battle of the Atlantic (History of United States Naval Operations in World War II: I)* (Boston, 1947) , pp. 315, 326, 344, 403.

[58] Memo, Morgan for Br COS, Landing Craft Requirements for Cross-Channel Operations, 24 May 43, COSSAC (43) 5.

[59] Quoted in Memo, ASW (J. J. McCloy) for Marshall, 26 Apr 44. OPD files, misc bk. 18.

[60] JCS Mtgs, 14–19 May 43.

[61] ETOUSA approval noted in Memo, Barker for Executive Planning Section (ETOUSA) , Requirements for Landing Craft, 9 Mar 43. SHAEF SGS file 560 I.

the context of British arguments at the Washington Conference for further operations in the Mediterranean and of their openly expressed doubts as to the feasibility of a cross-Channel invasion unless German strength in the west could be drastically reduced, the suspicion appeared logical. Admiral King, in particular, was convinced that the British had no intention of invading the Continent in the spring of 1944. He thought they would wreck the prospects of ROUNDUP "on the matter of the number of landing craft." General Marshall, taking a more temperate and optimistic view, agreed that ROUNDUP in its conception as a ten-division assault must be recognized as "a logistic impossibility" in the spring of 1944.[62]

It was clear, then, that to argue against the British concept of continuing attacks in the Mediterranean which the Joint Chiefs consistently maintained were incapable of decisive results it was necessary to reduce the size of the contemplated cross-Channel invasion to something within the range of logistic possibility. The Joint Chiefs discussed such an operation as a "glorified SLEDGEHAMMER" and conceived it as employing some twenty divisions, which meant scaling down the number of actual assault divisions to a logistically reasonable force. Thus, their doubts as to the seriousness of British commitment to a Continental invasion in 1944, whether justified or not, helped shape their position that planning should be for an operation possible with the resources which would certainly be on hand in the spring of 1944. In other words the search for a tenable ground to argue against Medi-

terranean strategy predisposed the U. S. Chiefs of Staff to an acceptance of 1943 production rates as a limiting factor on the scale of Continental operations in 1944. It became politic to avoid discussing the possibility of increasing landing craft production. The issue had to be rescued from the quicksands of hypothesis.

It was. British planners arguing for a ten-division assault felt themselves on unsure ground. Rear Adm. C. M. Cooke of the U. S. Joint Planning Staff commented that each of the British planning papers seemed to contain a different assessment of landing craft requirements, and that their original figure of 8,500 had been "talked down" to 4,000.[63] As the British Chiefs of Staff had previously admitted, there were no grounds for defending the arbitrary estimate of ten divisions in the assault except a feeling that overwhelming strength would be needed. Since this was obviously relative and no one could foretell what it would be relative to, the argument could not carry much weight.

The Joint Chiefs of Staff instructed their planners to re-examine American and British capabilities for supplying troops and landing craft. The planners reported that, assuming two operations in the Mediterranean after the conquest of Sicily, landing craft could be made available in the United Kingdom by the spring of 1944 sufficient to lift five divisions simultaneously, three for the assault and two for the immediate follow-up. They believed a "second follow-up force of two divisions can be floated by landing craft used in the assault on their first turnaround augmented as practicable by miscellaneous craft which can be pro-

---

[62] JCS 85th Mtg, 19 May 43.

[63] Ibid.

vided in the United Kingdom."[64] Detailed figures actually revealed a deficit of lift for 500 vehicles, but this was considered small enough to be acceptable for planning purposes. Troops available in the United Kingdom at the target date were estimated to total from twenty-six to thirty divisions depending on whether cannibalization of four British divisions proved necessary in order to find line of communications troops.

These planning figures were accepted without significant debate and it was agreed that General Morgan would be ordered to confine his plan to the detailed allotment of 4,504 landing ships and craft which planners figured would be available.[65] In addition to the five divisions seaborne in the assault, Morgan would plan to use two airborne divisions for which he was allotted an admittedly inadequate number of transport aircraft.[66]

The whole calculation was necessarily based on a number of highly debatable assumptions, which had not been agreed on by the various planning groups and which had not been tested by a large-scale amphibious operation against a defended coast. By May the COSSAC naval staff had adopted a "Standard Method for Forecasting Landing Craft Requirements." But this was not used at the Washington Conference. The Washington estimates were based on quite different assumptions. For instance, while COSSAC allotted 3,000 vehicles to each assault division to be carried in major landing ships or craft, Washington planners figured 4,380.[67]

The Washington estimates of the average capacity of the various types of craft also differed significantly from COSSAC's reckoning.[68] These discrepancies are understandable when the nature of the problem of estimating ship capacities is considered. In the first place a "vehicle" is a flexible term covering everything from a $\frac{1}{4}$-ton trailer to a tank retriever. In actual loading for the operation, for instance, VII Corps LCT's carried from three to twenty-eight vehicles, depending on the type. In striking an average for an assault force, much depended on the exact composition of the force. Furthermore the average was not likely to obtain when applied to smaller units of the assault which, for tactical reasons, might have to be loaded without regard to economy of space. Thus, the higher the average capacity for planning purposes, the more inflexible the tactical employment of the force. Until the tactical plan was known, planning estimates would naturally vary according to the planner's knowledge of, or feeling about, the difficulty of the actual operation contemplated. Throughout the planning period it was generally true that the Americans tended to be more optimistic than the

---

[64] CPS 71, Report by Sub-Committee on Availability of Landing Craft for ROUNDHAMMER, 20 May 43. ROUNDHAMMER was the code name used at the Washington Conference for the cross-Channel attack. Conceived as an operation midway in size between the old SLEDGEHAMMER and ROUNDUP, it borrowed part of each code name.

[65] Of these, 3,257 would be supplied by the British; 1,247 by the United States.

[66] This was to represent no real problem, however. See below, Ch. V.

[67] Washington estimated only 2,760 vehicles for the follow-up divisions, thus striking an average for the five divisions of 3,730. What are called in the text "Washington estimates" are all those of the subcommittee referred to in note 64.

[68] Washington figures: LCT (3) and (4)—15 vehicles; LCT (5) and (6)—12 vehicles; LST—50 vehicles. COSSAC figures: LCT (all types)—10 vehicles; LST—60 vehicles.

British about the difficulties of the assault and hence more willing to push planning figures upward toward the theoretical maximum. The most optimistic Americans were those on this side of the water.

One of the greatest weaknesses of the Washington calculations which fixed COSSAC's resources was that they did not take into account possible loss or damage to craft in the assault or the time required for ships to turn around and come back for the build-up forces. As one of the chief COSSAC planners pointed out, the provision of sufficient landing craft for the assault and first twenty-four hours did not necessarily insure an adequate build-up.[69] The build-up would depend in large part on what ships came back from the assault. How long would it take them to return, how many would be lost, how many damaged, how fast could the damaged craft be repaired? It would have been impossible for the Washington planners to have arrived at any firm estimates along these lines because the choice of an assault area had not then been settled and consequently the nature of enemy opposition could not even be guessed at nor the length of the sea voyage determined.[70]

Another important factor largely omitted from reckoning at Washington was the need for close-support craft. The principal types mounted guns, rockets, or mortars on LCT hulls or similar bottoms. They therefore had to be figured into the total production requirements for landing craft, even though they provided no assault lift. The failure to allot them in anything like adequate numbers, in fact, forced COSSAC to convert some LCT's and thus increased the shortage of landing craft.[71]

The net effect of the Washington Conference decisions was narrowly to restrict not only the size of the cross-Channel assault but the degree of flexibility with which tactical dispositions could be planned. As planning progressed it would become increasingly apparent that the allocations agreed to by the Combined Chiefs of Staff in May 1943 were wholly inadequate for the job. But for the moment the figures were accepted without serious demur from any quarter.

It has already been suggested that this ready agreement to mount the cross-Channel invasion on a shoestring sprang at least in part from the context of the Washington Conference. American concern with getting a firm decision on a definite operation with a definite target date led to a willingness to accept an operation scaled to resources evidently within the capacities of the Allies. The British were not likely to take serious issue. They attached little importance to long-range commitments and con-

---

[69] Memo, Brig Gen K. McLean (Br Army Ops Branch), Landing Craft Requirements (Comment on Memo by Naval Chief of Staff, 15 May), 26 May 43. SHAEF SGS file 560 I.

[70] It is interesting, in this connection, that both Washington and COSSAC planners in May were contemplating shore-to-shore sailings of the small assault craft (LCA's and LCVP's). This could have been feasible only if the force sailed from Dover to assault the Pas-de-Calais coast. The longer voyage to the Caen area could not have been made in rough Channel weather by LCA-type boats. Commodore Hughes-Hallett planned to sail a portion of the LCA's from Dover and carry the rest on LSI (S) 's. Washington planners did not contemplate carrying any of the smaller craft aboard larger ships. See

---

Memo, Hughes-Hallett for CCO, Cross-Channel Operations: 1944 Hypothesis (Requirements for LCI (S)), 22 May 43. SHAEF SGS file 560 I; cf. CPS 71, App. B, 20 May 43.

[71] See below, Ch. III.

sistently deprecated discussions of strategic principles. They were always more interested in the operation which came next on the war agenda.[72]

For the British in May 1943, the next logical operation was a follow-up in the Mediterranean of the invasion of Sicily, which was scheduled for July. The main project for 1943, they said, was the elimination of Italy. "The collapse of Italy," said the Prime Minister, "would cause a chill of loneliness over the German people, and might be the beginning of their doom." [73] The British Chiefs of Staff contended that Mediterranean operations were not only the most important immediate objective but that they were also essential in order to create conditions which would permit the mounting of ROUNDUP in the spring of 1944.[74] In General Brooke's opinion, without further Mediterranean operations, ROUNDUP would not be possible before 1945 or 1946. In a detailed estimate of the probable situation in northwest Europe in 1944, the British planners concluded that the Allies could not hope to compete successfully with enemy build-up either on the ground or in the air unless the enemy's ability to reinforce his coastal defenses was weakened by forced withdrawals to take over the defense of Italy and Italian commitments in the Balkans. They pointed out that there were definite limitations to the weight which the

Allies could throw against the Continent —limitations chiefly due to landing craft but also inherent in the nature of amphibious operations. To ignore these would be to risk entering a build-up race in which the Allies could probably never hope to achieve the necessary margin of superiority. Furthermore, failure to maintain the momentum of attack in the Mediterranean would cast away an unrivaled opportunity to inflict mortal injury on Germany and would give her a chance to prepare to parry the final blow. "The final blow," they admitted, "can only be struck across the Channel; it cannot be delivered from the Mediterranean." [75] But it was essential to do everything possible to exhaust and weaken Germany before the blow was struck.

With the conclusion the U. S. Chiefs of Staff agreed. It was the method they challenged. They did not believe that such "minor" operations in the Mediterranean as were within the capabilities of the United Nations would draw German forces from Russia even if they resulted in the collapse of Italy. They believed that the main effort against Germany in 1943 would have to be made by the Soviet Union and that the United States and Great Britain were incapable of effective intervention. On the other hand, the Soviets would probably still need help in 1944. The Western Allies could put themselves in a position to render really effective aid then provided that they did not dissipate their resources on side shows in 1943.[76] Tentatively the Americans suggested that a

---

[72] See, for instance, CCS, 288/2, 29 Jul 43, in which the British Chiefs of Staff, proposing an agenda for the Quebec Conference, wanted to "dispense with lengthy discussions on over-all strategic concepts or global strategy" and talk about specific operations.

[73] 1st White House Mtg, 12 May 43. OPD files, Min of TRIDENT Conf.

[74] CCS 87th Mtg, 18 May 43; CCS 234, Defeat of the Axis Powers in Europe (Elimination of Italy First), 17 May 43.

[75] CCS 234.

[76] CCS 235, Defeat of Axis Powers in Europe, 18 May 43.

limited bridgehead operation against the Continent might be attempted during 1943. But they did not press the point against British objections that the bridgehead would lock up the Allied divisions employed, cause the Germans to concentrate in France, and so make later invasion more difficult. The President expressed the gist of the American point of view at the first plenary session. He disliked the idea of possibly playing into German hands by committing large United Nations armies in Italy where they were in danger of suffering attrition. On the other hand he agreed with the Prime Minister that American and British forces should not be idle between the conclusion of the Sicilian campaign and the spring of 1944.[77]

In the final decision of the conference the latter consideration prevailed. The debate was resolved more easily than similar debates at later conferences, because it did not involve an immediate choice between alternative courses of action. The Americans opposed Mediterranean operations not in themselves but only as they might delay attack on northwest Europe. The British opposed not the cross-Channel attack but only the exclusive devotion of resources to it which would rule out action in the Mediterranean. The British feared an immediate opportunity would be thrown away through narrow concentration on the main goal. The Americans feared that by taking the immediate opportunity the chance to pursue the main goal might be lost or seriously delayed.

The conference was able to straddle the disagreement. The Joint Chiefs of Staff secured a firm commitment on the

size and target date for the cross-Channel operation. The decisions of the conference as they affected the plan which COSSAC would soon christen OVERLORD provided that "forces and equipment" should be established in the United Kingdom "with the object of mounting an operation with target date 1 May 1944 to secure a lodgment on the Continent from which further offensive operations can be carried out."[78] The Combined Chiefs agreed to allot five infantry divisions for the assault, two infantry divisions for the initial build-up,[79] two airborne divisions, and an additional twenty divisions to be available in England for movement into the lodgment area.

The decision on the target date was made without much debate. The Joint Chiefs of Staff first proposed 1 April as the earliest date when suitable weather could be expected and as the date that coincided with the conclusion of the planned bomber offensive designed to prepare the attack chiefly by knocking out German air power.[80] General Brooke proposed a postponement of one month to avoid the spring thaw in Russia and so permit the Soviet Union to launch a

---

[77] 1st White House Mtg, TRIDENT Conf.

[78] Draft Supplementary Directive to COSSAC, Amphibious Operations from the UK, incl B to CCS 250/1, 25 May 43.

[79] There is some confusion on the term "follow-up." The Washington agreement reads five divisions in the assault and two in the follow-up. By later usage, however, this is a misnomer. The follow-up as generally used in the planning period and as consistently used in this book means divisions not taking part in the initial assault but preloaded in craft and shipping to come in immediately behind the assault units. Build-up units are those landed on subsequent trips by craft already employed in the assault and follow-up waves—or more generally any units which are not actually on board ship at the time the assault is mounted.

[80] See below, Ch. VI.

co-ordinated offensive. This was agreed. Admiral King even indicated that a still later date might be acceptable and he commented that target dates were seldom met anyway. The Joint Chiefs were mainly concerned that some date be fixed to pin down the commitment to the operation and insure a certain urgency in the planning and preparation.

The Joint Chiefs yielded to British arguments so far as to sanction further operations in the Mediterranean but only with provisos that strictly limited Mediterranean commitments. Each specific operation in the Mediterranean to follow HUSKY (the invasion of Sicily) was to be subject to approval by the Combined Chiefs of Staff. General Eisenhower, Commander in Chief in North Africa, could use for his operations only the forces already allotted to his theater. It was further agreed that four U. S. and three British combat-experienced divisions in the Mediterranean would be held in readiness from 1 November onward for transfer to England to take part in the cross-Channel operation.[81] This was a particularly important decision in hardening the resolution to turn in 1944 from the Mediterranean to northwest Europe.

The COSSAC Plans

The decisions of the Washington Conference were made known to COSSAC late in May. In the meantime the COSSAC staff had begun developing plans for the three operations for which it was responsible. These included, in addition to the cross-Channel attack itself, actions to make the Germans believe the Allies would invade Europe during 1943, and operations to take place in case of German collapse.

Cockade

The main objective of the diversionary scheme for 1943, planned under the code name COCKADE, was to pin German forces in the west by encouraging German expectations of an Allied invasion during that year. In addition, by including an actual amphibious feint, General Morgan hoped to provoke an air battle that would contribute to the destruction of the German Air Force.

This over-all plan included three separate operations, each threatening a different portion of the enemy-held coast. The U. S. Army's allotted portion of the plan was Operation WADHAM, embodying a threat to the Brest Peninsula and designed to persuade the Germans into overestimating the strength of U. S. forces in the United Kingdom.[82] The threat was carried out by forces under V Corps. At the same time British forces in Scotland simulated preparations for attack against Norway (Operation TINDALL). But the heart of COCKADE was Operation STARKEY [83] directed against the Pas-de-Calais and designed to include, as an amphibious feint, a landing exercise, HARLEQUIN. Plagued, as usual, by the shortage of landing craft, COSSAC was obliged in the end to halt HARLEQUIN short of embarkation, but the rest of the STARKEY plan was carried through, cul-

---

[81] CCS 242/6, Final Report to the President and Prime Minister, 25 May 43.

[82] For additional details on WADHAM see *V Corps History* (Paris, 1945), p. 20.

[83] COSSAC (43) 4 (Final), Operation 'Starkey,' 26 Jun 43.

minating in minesweeping operations in the Channel at the beginning of September.

It is peculiarly difficult to assess the effects of operations like COCKADE. Neither in the routine Allied intelligence reports nor in surviving German records is there evidence of specific and overt German reaction. No new troop dispositions were ordered in expectation of immediate invasion of France. On the other hand, the German defenders in the west were in some stage of alert during most of 1943 and it is plausible to suppose that knowledge of Allied activities contributed at least in some measure to their tenseness. General Morgan, though uncertain as to enemy reaction, believed that certain naval activity in the Channel and the flooding of the lowlands behind Caen and the Cotentin beaches might be "reasonably ascribed" to the feints.[84] Whatever the full effect may have been on the enemy, COCKADE had one clear value for the Allies in providing experience for planning the successful diversionary activities of 1944.

Outline Overlord

The duties of COSSAC in supervising the execution of COCKADE continued, as noted, through the summer of 1943, but the staff's chief planning energies were turned at the beginning of June to the preparation of OVERLORD. Six weeks later they had written the outline plan. Before examining the details of that plan, it is important to observe its general character.

Outline OVERLORD, in the strict sense,

was not an operational plan at all.[85] It was not a blueprint for maneuver. No field order could have been issued on the basis of it, and no troop dispositions made. It was a plan for planning, not a plan for action. Its tone was discursive, not precise and peremptory. It reflected the fact that it was drawn by a staff in the absence of the commander, and it made a patent effort to refrain from tying the commander's hand, especially in examining the later phases of the operation. It was designed to answer the question implicit in the May decisions of the Combined Chiefs of Staff. Given certain resources, was an operation against the Continent possible in the spring of 1944? COSSAC arrived at an answer in Outline OVERLORD, first by narrowing down the problem through rejecting courses of action that seemed impossible with the given means, and then by outlining certain conclusions as to the size and shape and limiting conditions of a feasible operation. Within that outline, details were only tentatively sketched in.

Previous planning had already observed that geography placed rigid limits on the operation. Earlier planners concluded that only two geographically feasible assault areas existed—the Caen region and the Pas-de-Calais. Although

---

[84] COS (43), 207th Mtg, 4 Sep 43; cf. Morgan, *Overture to Overlord*, pp. 100–103.

[85] COS (43) 416 (0), Operation OVERLORD, Report and Appreciation, 30 Jul 43, cited hereafter as Outline OVERLORD. Department of the Army files contain several copies of the plan. The one used is in SHAEF SGS file 381 Ia.

The OVERLORD Plan consists of a Digest, three main parts: (I, Selection of a Lodgement Area; II, Appreciation and Outline Plan for the Opening Phase up to the Capture of Cherbourg; III, The Development of Operations after the Capture of Cherbourg), and twenty-four appendixes (with maps) which include discussions of alternative courses of action and studies of special problems. Digest of the plan is reprinted below as Appendix A.

the most recent appreciation made at the end of 1942 had rejected the Pas-de-Calais, General Morgan revived the idea. The Pas-de-Calais had certain obvious attractions, inherent chiefly in its proximity to England. Morgan, though recognizing its disadvantages, was reluctant to dismiss it out of hand. He therefore ordered that the British Army operations branch of COSSAC prepare an estimate and outline plan for an assault on the Pas-de-Calais while the American branch worked on an operation against Caen.

This order was given early in June 1943 and about two weeks later the British planners had delivered their answer. They agreed with the earlier planning conclusion. An attack on the Pas-de-Calais, they said, must be considered strategically unsound.[86] The British appreciation, embodied later in an appendix to the OVERLORD plan, reinforced the reasoning of earlier planners. The COSSAC staff found only four beaches in the Pas-de-Calais suitable for assault. These could receive a theoretical maximum of two assault divisions on D Day provided no delay were imposed by landing obstacles or enemy resistance. Since there were no ports in the region and the beaches were unsheltered, blocked, and heavily defended, it seemed obvious that the Allies' rate of build-up could not hope to compete with the enemy's. The expansion of the beachhead, moreover, to include major ports for the subsequent maintenance of the invasion force would require long flank marches east to Antwerp or southwest to the Seine ports, both across the whole front of the German army. They

summed up: "Not only does the strength of the defences demand a weight of assault which the restricted capacity of the beaches cannot admit, but the restrictions imposed by the beaches do not allow a rapid build-up. Further, even if assault were practicable, the geography of the area does not permit of the capture of sufficient ports to maintain the force, and the terrain does not allow of the defence and exploitation of the bridgehead by the occupation of successive natural obstacles."[87]

Before the end of the month planners had ruled out assaults at Le Havre and on the Cotentin Peninsula.[88] But with rejection of the Pas-de-Calais, the decision had actually been made that the main attack would take place in the vicinity of Caen. *(Map I)** Assault landings would be confined to three beaches (Lion-sur-Mer–Courseulles, Courseulles–Arromanches-les Bains, and Colleville-sur-Mer–Vierville-sur-Mer).[89] This, General Morgan decided, was the maximum area that could be successfully attacked with the limited forces at his disposal. He rejected the earlier idea of a simultaneous landing on the eastern beaches of the Cotentin, although he recognized its value, and told the British Chiefs of Staff that he would like such a landing if he could have craft for an extra assault division.[90]

* Maps numbered in Roman are placed in inverse order inside the back cover.

[87] Outline OVERLORD, App. C.

[88] COSSAC (43) 13th Mtg, 2 Jul 43.

[89] These beaches in the event were the center of the OVERLORD assault after the operation was expanded from three to five assaulting divisions. The first two beaches were British in both the COSSAC and the later plan. The last-named (Colleville–Vierville) was the beach later called OMAHA.

[90] JP (43) 260 (Final), Commentary on Operation OVERLORD, 3 Aug 43. SHAEF SGS file 381 Ia.

[86] COSSAC (43) 11th Mtg, 19 Jun 43.

As it was, the plan was to land two British divisions over the two eastern beaches in the Caen sector, one U.S. division over the western beach, and two-thirds of one British airborne division in the vicinity of Caen.[91] In addition, various subsidiary assaults would be necessary by commandos and parachutists to neutralize key enemy costal batteries, secure crossings over the River Aure, and form a defensive flank on the Vire. Details of these missions were left for later planning.

D Day was, of course, not selected, but some of the weather and tidal conditions governing its selection were discussed. Since the target date (Y Day) was 1 May, D Day would fall some time during the month. There were likely to be twenty-three days in May on which the prevailing wind force would permit the beaching of landing craft. Quiet spells of four days or more could be expected twice during the month.[92] But forecasting them was another matter. The odds were ten to three that a three-day spell of good weather could be predicted twenty-four hours in advance. The incidence of suitable weather for the airborne operation was still under investigation when the plan was issued, and it was simply noted that this would probably impose still narrower limitations on the choice of D Day.

The question of whether the assault should take place in daylight or darkness was not definitely decided though it was pointed out that the Navy required daylight in order to control the operations of a large fleet and in order to direct effective fire support. This requirement, the planners added, was likely to be decisive, even though, from the Army's standpoint, an approach to the shore by night would be desirable to help preserve surprise up to the last moment.

It was noted that the initial landing should take place about three hours before high water in order that a good-sized force might be landed on the first tide. Calculations to tie in weather, tide, and hours of daylight would be made only in later planning, when the optimum conditions for H Hour were finally settled.

The choice of the Caen area meant a decision to delay the capture of ports needed for the maintenance of a large invasion force. Cherbourg, even if captured early, would not be adequate to support the twenty-nine divisions which were to be put into the lodgment area. Throughout the initial phases of the operation a large proportion of supplies would have to be landed across the invasion beaches. General Morgan accepted the risk of prolonged beach maintenance because he counted on the completion of at least two artificial ports which were then being developed.

The bold and revolutionary idea of prefabricating ports in England and towing them across the Channel had been talked about in 1942, but experimentation did not begin in earnest until the summer of 1943. The essential ingredients of the artificial ports (which, in the prevailing fashion of code names, were called MULBERRIES) were the breakwaters to supply sheltered water in which small craft could ferry supplies to the beaches, and a floating pier (connected by treadway to the beach) at which

---

[91] Presumably at the same time as the seaborne landings, although the plan does not make this clear.

[92] A quiet spell was defined as a period in which the maximum wind force was nine knots.

larger vessels could unload directly into trucks. The solution at last developed for the breakwater was to combine sunken ships with the so-called phoenixes—hollow, floating concrete caissons about six stories high. The phoenixes were to be towed across the Channel and then sunk, by opening sea cocks, and anchored in position. The pier was developed as a floating platform devised so that with the rise and fall of the tide it could slide up and down on four posts which rested securely on the bottom of the sea.[93]

When General Morgan made his plan, depending on these devices, the MULBERRIES were still on the drawing boards. In fact, engineers were still experimenting with various breakwater devices and the vast concrete phoenixes had not even been ordered. This circumstance again underlined the tentativeness of COSSAC's approach. It was still necessary to assume resources that were not at hand and conditions that could hardly be foreseen.

For this reason, such things as the detailed composition of the assault forces were left for later planning. It was noted only that an unusually high proportion of armor and antiaircraft would probably be required in the first waves. COSSAC's view was that the Allies could count on surprise to get them safely ashore and through the first crust of the enemy's defenses. The critical phase of the operation would be the first battles with the enemy's reserves. Because enemy counterattacks could be expected from D Day on, the Allies needed to have the maximum of armor at their disposal as early as possible. "The normal German system," COSSAC observed, "is to concentrate reserves well forward behind threatened sectors, in order to get the maximum forces into action on D Day. . . . The crux of the operation will be our ability to land forces quickly enough, first, to hold the initial German counterattacks, and then to defeat and drive off the large German reserves which will be brought in against our bridgehead."[94]

The basic problem was to establish and maintain a reasonable margin of superiority over the enemy. In this, General Morgan was handicapped from the outset by limitation of resources. The Combined Chiefs of Staff had instructed him to use three divisions in the assault and two in the immediate follow-up and had allocated a specific number of landing craft and ships for the simultaneous loading of these five divisions. When the COSSAC staff tried to match men and vehicles with allocated shipping and form five naval task forces each to carry one division, they found that a large percentage of the two follow-up divisions could not be tactically loaded and that they had more than 1,200 minor landing craft left over which were not seaworthy enough when loaded to make the long cross-Channel trip to Caen under their own power.[95]

The fact that overheads such as antiaircraft and special engineer units would have to be landed on D Day and D plus 1, and that a high proportion of tanks

---

[93] [Clifford Jones] NEPTUNE: Training, Mounting, the Artificial Ports (The Administrative and Logistical History of the ETO: Part VI), MS, II, 112 ff. Hist Div files.

[94] COSSAC (43) 29, Strategical Background, Cross-Channel Operation, 1944, 25 Jun 43.

[95] The leftover craft included 195 LCM (1)'s, 376 LCM (3)'s, and 660 LCVP's. Outline OVERLORD, App. Z.

would have to be carried in the assault, put an additional strain on shipping resources. The net effect was to compel reduction of the immediate reinforcements for the assault and delay their landing. On D Day only four follow-up reinforced regiments would be landed instead of two divisions as specified in the Combined Chiefs of Staff directive.[96]

On D plus 1 only one and a third divisions could be landed instead of the two estimated by Washington planners. Furthermore, COSSAC warned that 75 percent of the vehicles in the D-plus-1 build-up divisions would have to be loaded in ordinary shipping. Not only were there risks and difficulties in using large ships so early in the operation, but the units carried in them could not be unloaded in tactical order. It would take twenty-four hours after they got ashore before they could be organized and equipped for action. "It should be clearly noted," the plan warned, "that landing units in this manner means that the forces ashore on D Day are not reinforced until D plus 2 with formations operationally available, except to the extent of about a brigade group [regimental combat team]." [97]

COSSAC was directed to employ two airborne divisions in the assault, but the allotment of 632 transport aircraft was far short of what was needed. This was not lift enough even for the two missions deemed essential: the capture and neutralization of the coastal batteries at Grand-camp-les Bains and Ouistreham-Riva-

Bella and the capture of Caen. The capture of Caen alone was estimated to require a full airborne division. COSSAC's decision was nevertheless to employ airborne troops on both missions, with the main air landings in the vicinity of Caen. The planners felt that Caen, an important bottleneck in communications from the hinterland to the beaches, had to be seized "to avoid defeat in the early stages." [98]

General Morgan was always conscious that the Allies, with such limited resources in the early stages, could hope at best for only a slender margin of superiority. It was thus essential to do everything possible to reduce the enemy's capacity to resist. Steps were to be taken immediately (as of July 1943) to soften German resistance by all available means: direct sea and air action, psychological, political, and economic pressures, and sabotage and deception. This softening was to constitute the preliminary phase of the operation and was to be systematized to produce conditions considered essential to the success of OVERLORD. During this phase the main effort of the Allied forces would be to reduce German fighter strength in western Europe, by bombing fighter production plants and airfields and by bringing the German fighter force to battle under conditions favorable to the Allies. At the same time, "but without detriment to the main aim," the Allied air offensive would continue the progressive destruction and dislocation of the German military and economic system and the undermining of the morale of the German people. It was expected that in these ways the Allies could

---

[96] Although the plan stated that the limiting factor was the capacity of defended beach exits to pass vehicles inland, General Morgan later complained that the weakness of the planned follow-up was due to shortage of suitable landing craft. COSSAC (43) 57 (Final), 30 Sep 43. SHAEF SGS file 560 I.

[97] Outline OVERLORD, Part II, par. 85.

[98] *Ibid.*, Part II, par. 96.

insure themselves of absolute air supremacy by D Day. That was set as a condition for the operation "since only
through air power can we offset the many
and great disabilities inherent in the
situation confronting the attacking surface forces." [99]

In the preparatory phase, beginning an
undetermined time before D Day, the air
offensive would be intensified and begin
to hit hard at the enemy's airfields and
those portions of his transportation system within fighter range of the Caen area.
Immediately before the assault, air attack
would focus on rail and road nets directly
feeding into the battle area. Not until the
assault phase itself—a matter of hours before the landings—would aircraft attack
the enemy's beach defenses.

Important as it was thought to be to
make the fullest utilization of Allied air
power, it was considered still more important to conceal as long as possible the
actual assault area. COSSAC planners believed that it would be possible to preserve a high degree of tactical surprise,
for, the staff pointed out, "It was evident
from the weakness of the local defenses
that the Germans did not consider it likely
that we could make an assault in force in
the Caen sector." [100] All preparations
therefore should studiously avoid calling
attention to the assault area.

Further to contribute to surprise as well
as to reduce enemy strength in the invasion area, two major diversions were to
be staged. One would be carried out from
the United Kingdom: a feint aimed at
the Pas-de-Calais coast to begin about D
minus 14 and continue during the first
two weeks of the invasion. It was to follow

the general lines of the 1943 operation
pointed at the same area and would include an actual expedition using some of
the small craft which were unsuitable for
the main assault. A second diversion
would be mounted from the Mediterranean against the south coast of France
to give the impression of an imminent
major landing there. This was to start
with a threat before the Normandy
landings, but preparations would be
made for an actual landing if German
forces were withdrawn from southern
France to meet the OVERLORD attack. Both
of these diversions became tremendously
important in later planning and in the
invasion itself, but in the outline plan
COSSAC did little more than suggest the
idea.[101]

Everything possible should be done before the invasion to reduce the enemy's
capacity to resist on the ground and in the
air. But this was a highly theoretical
specification. How much capacity to resist could safely be left to the enemy? At
what point could preparations be said to
be complete and the necessary conditions
for the invasion set up? The answer could
not be securely pinned to reality, since it
was patently impossible to estimate enemy
capabilities so far in advance. The best
answer was hypothetical. Rejecting the attempt to assess the actual enemy, General
Morgan calculated the maximum enemy
which in his opinion the Allies could take
on.

Static troops defending the coast line
were not taken into consideration; it

---

[99] COSSAC (43) 29, cited n. 94.

[100] COSSAC (43), 13th Mtg, 2 Jul 43.

[101] The diversion against southern France was later
planned as an actual operation under the code name
ANVIL; the feint against the Pas-de-Calais remained
a threat, planned and carried out as Operation FORTI-
TUDE.

was assumed that they would be defeated by the landing itself. Having got ashore, the invasion forces would be able, it was thought, to withstand counterattack by two German divisions. A third German offensive division could be in the area on the assumption that it would have to be held in reserve for the defense of the Cotentin. By D plus 2 the bridgehead could probably hold against attack by two additional enemy divisions. By D plus 8 the enemy should not have more than a total of nine offensive divisions in the area if the Allies were to have a reasonable chance of gaining their objectives. The Germans by that date would have had time to move all available divisions in France and the Low Countries into the bridgehead area, except those pinned down by diversionary threats to other areas. It was believed that threats could keep a maximum of three enemy reserve divisions away from the bridgehead. In other words, the total German offensive striking force in France and the Low Countries on the invasion date should not exceed twelve divisions if the invasion was to succeed.

These calculations evoked considerable criticism. General Barker, Morgan's deputy, protested the inclusion of any conditional clauses in the plan because he felt that they would make the plan harder to sell in Washington. The U. S. Joint Chiefs of Staff, he knew, believed that the British were cool toward the idea of a Continental invasion, and he foresaw that specifications as to the maximum enemy forces that could be defeated in France would only reinforce their belief.[102] The Joint Chiefs, in fact, reacted

as General Barker predicted. Barker had to explain that the clause did not mean that the operation would have to be canceled if more than twelve enemy divisions could be brought to oppose it. COSSAC meant only that a maximum of twelve divisions could be defeated by the Allied ground forces; if there were any more, they would have to be reduced by air power or other means.[103] This interpretation was accepted, and the conditions stood. Later on, however, at the conference with the Russians, they were again queried when Stalin simply asked: "And what if there are thirteen divisions?"[104]

It was not so much a question as a needle jab to elicit further assurance of the Allies' firm intention to mount the operation. As far as General Morgan was concerned, it was not his business to settle Allied intentions, but it was his job to determine whether OVERLORD was feasible. Since his own resources were limited by directive and since no such limitation was imposed on the enemy, he could not very well return an unqualified verdict. As to the artificial rigidity of the conditions, the plan itself provided a qualification. "It will be realized that the conditions under which the operation might be successful do not depend solely on the numerical strength of the reserves available to the Germans. The scale of German resistance will depend on such things as the state of the French railways and the strength, quality, and morale of the enemy's front line units."[105]

---

[102] Interv with Gen Barker, 4 Oct 46. Hist Div files.

[103] JCS 442/1, Operation OVERLORD, 6 Aug 43; cf. Marshall's statement to the same effect at CCS 108th Mtg, 15 Aug 43.

[104] 1st Plenary Mtg at Tehran, 29 Nov 43. OPD files, U.S. Min of EUREKA Conf.

[105] Outline OVERLORD, Part II, par. 118.

The first objective of the main assault was to secure a bridgehead including Grandcamp, Bayeux, and Caen by the end of D Day. Initial follow-up forces consisting of two regiments in each sector (British and American) would land on D Day and assist assault forces in consolidating this bridgehead. Subsequent expansion of the bridgehead would take the form of thrusts south and southwest from the Caen–Bayeux area to defeat the enemy west of the Orne River, outflank his forces between the Orne and the Dives Rivers, and finally secure sufficient depth to make the turning movement to attack up the Cotentin toward Cherbourg. These operations would cover the first eight days of the invasion; by that time twelve divisions would be ashore. During the next six days, expansion southwestward would continue while a force entered the Cotentin with the mission of capturing Cherbourg by D plus 14. An armored force at the same time would strike southeast toward Alençon to cover the opening of airfields southeast of Caen. Eighteen divisions would be ashore on D plus 14 and the planners estimated that at that time "the German forces should have been decisively beaten." [106]

After the capture of Cherbourg and the defeat of German forces west of the Orne River, COSSAC planners believed the enemy would fall back with part of his forces on Brittany for the defense of the ports there and withdraw the rest east of the Seine for the defense of Paris. It would

then be up to the Supreme Commander to decide whether the Allies' next move would be to capture the ports on the Seine or those in Brittany. Although his decision would depend on estimates of his own and enemy capabilities at the time, COSSAC presumed that unless the Germans were on the point of collapse the Allies would be compelled to go after the Brittany ports in order to build up a large striking army with which to force the line of the Seine. To cover the entry into Brittany it would be necessary to drive the retreating Germans eastward in order to secure the line of the Eure River from Dreux to Rouen and thence the line of the Seine to the sea. This task would be carried out by British and Canadian armies while the American army was attacking Brittany. In these moves, the planners warned, five guiding considerations should be kept in mind: the vital necessity not to outrun heavily strained communications, the importance of early capture of a group of enemy airfields in the Dreux–Evreux region and of ground for the development of airfields in the le Mans–Châteaudun area, the value of the Seine below Rouen as a complete obstacle, the importance of Dreux, Chartres, and Orléans as centers of communication, and the value of the Coteaux du Perche as a bastion west of Dreux and Chartres.

In this latter phase, culminating on about D plus 50 in the occupation of the lodgment area proper bounded by the Loire and Seine Rivers, COSSAC put great stress on the development of airfields. By D plus 24, for instance, it was anticipated that twenty-seven Continental airfields should be in operation, on which sixty-two squadrons could be based. The securing of the lodgment area, planners

---

[106] *Ibid.*, Part III, par. 44; cf. Commentary on Operation OVERLORD (cited note 90), in which the planners point out that the advance calculated up to D plus 14 was sixty miles as compared with the advance of the right flank of Eighth Army in Sicily of only thirty miles in three weeks against much less serious opposition.

figured, would be followed by a long period of reorganization and consolidation. The next phase, the primary objective of which would be the capture of Paris and the Seine ports, was conceived as a major operation which the Germans would resist heavily. Its completion would be followed by another pause of some three months while the enemy was cleared out of the whole of France south of the Loire and Dijon and the surrender of the Channel Islands was forced.

The maneuver thus envisaged an evenly spaced series of battles, evenly opposed. The planners blueprinted an operation in which the invading armies struck hard for an initial foothold, built up and pushed forward on all fronts to gain maneuver room, paused, gathering strength for the next push, and so proceeded by bounds, cracking the enemy lines with separate, massed, and carefully prepared attacks for each new objective. The plan did not foresee the battle of attrition in Normandy nor the breakout that followed, nor the long-sustained armored drives in pursuit of a broken enemy.

Crushing defeat of the enemy, sending him in headlong and disorganized retreat, was a fortune of war which could be hoped for but not planned. Besides, by the terms of his directive, General Morgan was to plan not the annihilation of the German armies but the establishment of a lodgment area from which further offensive operations could be carried out. His attention was thus naturally focused on seizing and consolidating ground, capturing ports and airfields, and building up an army which could hold its gains and prepare to strike for further conquest.

Rankin

Outline OVERLORD was finished and submitted to the British Chiefs of Staff for review before COSSAC got around to the third task: planning for occupation of the Continent in case of German collapse. RANKIN, as the collapse operation was named, proved an exceptionally difficult concept to grasp and translate into a plan of action. In the first place it was not at all clear what collapse meant. SLEDGEHAMMER and ROUNDUP had both been made contingent on a kind of collapse and planners then attempted to define the concept. They came up with a rather vague notion of marked "deterioration of German morale," which seems not to have contemplated any failure of the Nazi government or any withdrawal of forces from the west. Rather it denoted a general weakening of the will to resist (as a result, of course, of a weakening of the means)—a nebulous idea at best. But nothing more specific was then needed. SLEDGEHAMMER and ROUNDUP both were planned by the British as operations involving the maximum available Allied forces as if to meet determined enemy opposition. Plans were then shelved pending some future intelligence estimate which might indicate an enemy situation sufficiently weak to give the attacks a reasonable chance of success.

OVERLORD, in contrast, was designed from the beginning as an operation with a specific target date, to go in against full enemy opposition. Such conditions as were laid down concerning maximum enemy resistance were conditions to be brought about by the Allies during the period of preparation. They were tactical rather than strategic conditions—that is, they affected only the limitation of the number of German troops that could be committed against the lodgment area; they did not include any general undermining of Germany's military or political potential. The possibility of such general deterioration, however, remained and, since OVERLORD was being prepared entirely without regard for it, it became necessary to make separate plans to take advantage of collapse when and if it occurred.

General Morgan was instructed by the Combined Chiefs that his organization should provide for "the need to re-enter the Continent with all available forces at the shortest possible notice in the event of a sudden and unexpected collapse of German resistance. The aim would be to seize critical political and military centers in Germany in the shortest possible time." [107] Soon after the COSSAC staff was established General Morgan asked the British Chiefs of Staff for a clarification of this directive, because, he said, his main object was given him as "the defeat of the German fighting forces in North-West Europe," whereas the directive to prepare for German collapse presupposed that the enemy had been defeated. He wanted specifically a restatement of his major object, a closer definition of the phrase "German disintegration," and more detail on the "critical political and military objectives." [108]

The reply of the British Chiefs of Staff was not delivered until 21 June. In the meantime General Morgan changed his mind about the need for definition. In a directive to his staff on 22 May, he said:

"Little is to be gained by seeking to define the phrase 'German disintegration'. Quot homines tot sententiae." Instead he suggested a flexible plan capable of variation between the extremes of an invasion of the Continent to break through a screen of resistance, and a landing against no opposition at all. The first plan prepared should suppose no resistance, since the state of Allied resources would not immediately permit undertaking an opposed landing. He recognized the difficulty of getting hold of a planning hypothesis. Since the time of the return could not be predicted, no precise estimate was possible of conditions on either side of the Channel. But, he pointed out, "Nebulous though the setting may be, there can be nothing nebulous in the event, which must be characterized by the utmost speed and precision of movement." The problem was basically similar to mobilization in peacetime. The solution consisted, first, in providing machinery to anticipate the event as far ahead as possible and, second, in phasing preparations so that they will "gain or lose momentum as the critical moment is judged to be approaching or receding." [109]

The solution at last selected was to break up the concept of enemy collapse into three definite degrees of collapse and provide three corresponding courses of action for the Allies. The three conditions were case A, which supposed a substantial weakening of organized resistance in France and the Low Countries, case B, which assumed German withdrawal from the occupied countries, and case C, unconditional surrender and cessation of

---

[107] CCS 169/8/D, 23 Apr 43.
[108] COSSAC (43) 2, 29 Apr 43.

[109] COSSAC (43) 9, Plan for Return to the Continent in Face of German Disintegration, 22 May 43.

organized resistance in northwest Europe.[110]

If the deterioration of German military power in the west was not accompanied by surrender or withdrawal, Allied action would depend on the relative strength of German and Anglo-American forces at any given date. Before January 1944, it was thought that no assault against organized resistance, however weakened, would be possible. In January and February a substantial weakening of the German forces might make possible a limited bridgehead operation. Since this date would find preparations for OVERLORD far advanced, the only feasible operation would be one that made use of these preparations. The RANKIN plan thus indicated a modification of OVERLORD to secure the Cotentin Peninsula if it became desirable to set the date forward to January or February. After 1 March a drastic reduction in German strength would permit a modified OVERLORD assault with substantially OVERLORD's objectives.

Case A thus involved no special planning difficulty. The problem of following up a German withdrawal from France was more complicated. If such withdrawal was made, it would be done presumably with the idea of strengthening the German position. It could therefore be expected that the maximum obstacles would be put in the way of Allied occupation. If withdrawal was begun in the winter, Allied landing would have to wait for the evacuation of a major port, since beach maintenance in winter weather was impossible on the Channel coasts. The Germans seeking to establish a defensive position at the West Wall (the Siegfried Line)

—the only position that would permit the necessary economy of troops—would start pulling out from the south and southwest. The first port to be vacated would be Bordeaux. But this was too far from where the Allies could be deployed against the Germans to be useful as a port of entry. The landing of substantial military forces could be begun only when Cherbourg was freed. The problem was to get as far east as possible in order to get as near as possible to the final German defense line and insure fighter protection from United Kingdom bases. At the same time landings could not be made so far east that they would be under attack by German mobile forces operating in advance of their main line of defense. Le Havre and Rouen were ruled out as initial ports of entry because the Germans were expected to make a preliminary stand at the Seine to protect and organize the retreat. Landing at Cherbourg, forces would be built up in the Cotentin. But this was likely to be a slow process in view of anticipated demolition of the port. "There can . . . be no thought of forcing the SEINE at an early stage, nor indeed can any major effort be contemplated at any time to speed the enemy's withdrawal other than by air action." It was pointed out further that a grave disadvantage of landing as far west as Cherbourg was "the immense bridging liabilities which the enemy's legacy of large scale demolitions" was likely to cause. The store of Allied bridging equipment in the United Kingdom was not likely to prove adequate for such an undertaking before 1 January 1944.[111]

Advance beyond the initial bridgehead would depend on the rate of enemy with-

---

[110] COSSAC (43) 40 (Final), Plan RANKIN, 13 Aug 43.

[111] Ibid.

drawal. It could be retarded by delay in the build-up but could not be accelerated. When the enemy reached his final defensive position, "There must of necessity be a considerable pause while we build up sufficient forces for an advance Eastwards." [112]

The plan throughout was conservative in estimating the time needed to build up strength before joining the final battle. The conclusion was that German collapse as envisaged under cases A and B might permit the Allies to return to the Continent before May 1944 but that such collapse would not materially advance the time for decisive action. In short, the RANKIN A and B plans offered little military advantages and the grounds for considering them were chiefly that politically it might be necessary to press into the occupied countries as soon as the Nazi grip on them relaxed.

As preparations for OVERLORD pro-

ceeded, the only RANKIN operation seriously considered was that under case C— total collapse accompanied by unconditional surrender. The plan here involved no purely military considerations, being a scheme for rapid occupation. [113]

Although no RANKIN plan was ever put into effect, detailed consideration has been given to the planning because it reveals that the Allied timetable for the war in western Europe was actually much more dependent on Allied preparations than on the state of the enemy.

The RANKIN project was kept before the planners and periodically re-examined, but its importance as a plan steadily dwindled as the OVERLORD target date approached and the proliferation of OVERLORD plans and preparations focused attention more and more on the big invasion.

---

[112] *Ibid.*

[113] The relation of RANKIN C to later occupation plans (ECLIPSE) will be dealt with by F. C. Pogue in The Supreme Command, a volume now under preparation in this series.

CHAPTER III

Overlord in the Balance
(August–December 1943)

Strategy Reviewed:
The Quebec Conference

When the Combined Chiefs of Staff parted at Washington in May 1943, they left with the sense that many of their decisions had been necessarily tentative and would have to be re-examined in the light of what happened in the next few months in Russia and in the Mediterranean.[1] Near the end of July the Joint Strategic Survey Committee reviewed the principal developments for the guidance of the Joint Chiefs and found especially noteworthy the "substantial improvement in the submarine situation and prospects, satisfactory progress of the bombing offensive, unforeseen degree of success attained with HUSKY [the invasion of Sicily], indications of the impending collapse of Italy, decision to carry the war to the mainland of Italy . . . and apparent loss of the initiative by the Germans on the Eastern Front."[2] This was actually a cautious statement of successes which in two and a half months had definitely tipped the balance of military power in favor of the Allies throughout the world.

At the Casablanca Conference, it will be remembered, the Allies had decided that the first charge on their resources should be the defeat of the German sub-

marine. By the summer of 1943 that defeat had all but been accomplished. Sinkings of Allied ships would continue, but on a diminishing scale, while the destruction of enemy U-boats accelerated. The turning point in the war on U-boats came dramatically in the spring of 1943.

The Allied counteroffensive began in a small way in the early months of 1943. Although sinkings continued heavy, reaching a peak in March of 141 ships lost, the Germans were also beginning to lose more heavily, and, though the Allies were then unaware of it, the German Admiralty was worried.[3] Early in February 1943 Grossadmiral Karl Doenitz expressed alarm at the fact that the Allies now seemed to have exact knowledge of the disposition and in some cases of the number of German U-boats in operational areas. At the end of the month he reported to Hitler that nothing had been sunk that month because nothing had been sighted.[4] He attributed the failure to bad weather and lack of reconnaissance. But it was not bad weather that destroyed

---

[1] CCS 95th Mtg, 24 May 43.

[2] JCS 422/1, QUADRANT, 25 Jul 43.

[3] See Naval Int Div (Br), History of U-Boat Policy, 1939–1945, 26 Feb 43. Navy Dept files. This consists of translations of extracts from documents in the files of the U-Boat Division of the German Admiralty.

[4] *Ibid.* Actually the Allies in February lost 83 ships totaling 420,238 tons. See Commander-in-Chief Atlantic Fleet (U.S. Naval Administration in World War II), MS, p. 463. Navy Dept files.

nineteen U-boats in February and fifteen in March.

For the Germans much worse was to come. In March on the suggestion of the Canadian Chief of Naval Staff, American, British, and Canadian naval commands held a conference in Washington to reorganize the Atlantic convoy system. Up to that time Atlantic convoys had been operated on a combined basis with ships of all three nations participating. Friction and inefficiency resulted. It was decided therefore to turn over naval responsibility for the North Atlantic entirely to the British and Canadians. The United States Atlantic Fleet would escort convoys between the eastern seaboard and North Africa, as well as certain special fuel convoys. The change, effective at the end of April, contributed to the conspicuous success of the Allied antisubmarine offensive beginning in May. A still greater contribution, however, was made by the long-range aircraft which the conference recommended be allocated to coastal areas for antisubmarine work. The Combined Chiefs of Staff assigned nearly all the aircraft requested (about half from British and half from American sources) and specified that all planes would be equipped with radar and operated by crews specially trained in antisubmarine warfare. Steps were being taken also to supplement land-based air patrols with carrier aircraft. During the winter four baby flattops were in process of conversion for Atlantic convoy use. The first was delivered in March. In June, three were operating in the South Atlantic.[5]

With a better-organized convoy system, new aircraft, and new detection methods, the Allies struck hard at the enemy's

underwater fleet in May. That month German U-boat losses soared to 30 percent of all boats at sea. Admiral Doenitz told Hitler: "These losses are too high. We must conserve our strength, otherwise we will play into the hands of the enemy." But as to the cause of the disaster Doenitz could only speculate. He knew that British aircraft were using a new microwave radar and suspected that the same device was employed on Allied surface vessels. He knew that, whatever the new device was, it apparently enabled planes and destroyers to hunt out German submarines in the dark and in the fog and destroy them. He knew also that the submarines had no radar detection set that could warn them of the impending attack. In fact, he said, "We don't even know on what wave length the enemy locates us. Neither do we know whether high frequency or other location devices are being employed. Everything possible is being done to find out what it is." Hitler added a dark intuitive note. Perhaps, he suggested, the new device involved principles with which the Germans were not familiar. "The crisis must be overcome by all possible means."[6]

But it was not overcome. It deepened and spread. In June, German submarines chalked up only nineteen Allied sinkings; in August, only three; and in September almost all U-boats had been withdrawn from the Atlantic, with the result that the U.S. Navy could virtually abolish the convoy system in coastal waters.[7]

---

[5] Commander-in-Chief Atlantic Fleet, pp. 481ff.

[6] Berghof Conference, 31 May 43, Office of Naval Intelligence, *Fuehrer Conferences, 1943. Fuehrer Conferences* is a selection of translated documents from German naval archives.

[7] Independent sailings were authorized for all ships except those carrying aviation fuel and those slower than eleven knots. See Commander-in-Chief Atlantic Fleet, p. 581.

GERMAN SUBMARINE UNDER AERIAL ATTACK

The reckoning at the end of 1943 was that three million gross tons of Allied and neutral shipping had been sunk as compared with more than eight million the year before.[8] But enemy success was much less than even these figures show, for during the year Allied shipyards had put fourteen million tons of new shipping on the seas as against only seven million in 1942. In other words the net loss in 1942 of about a million tons became in 1943 a net gain of almost eleven million. At the same time estimated sinkings of U-boats increased from 85 in 1942 to 237 in 1943.

The spring of 1943 marked a sudden intensification of the air war against Germany almost as dramatic as the antisubmarine campaign. After the reduction of U.S. Air Forces in the United Kingdom in the fall of 1942 to furnish air support for the North African campaign, American air power in Great Britain remained virtually static until the spring. From December 1942 through April 1943, the Eighth Air Force based in the United Kingdom had just six groups of heavy bombers operational each month. During May, the number of groups doubled; in June, thirteen groups were operational, in July, fifteen, and in August, sixteen and three-quarters.[9]

The build-up was reflected gradually in intensified operations. March and May each saw nine operations carried out, but in March they involved 956 sorties and the dropping of 1,662 tons of bombs. In May 1,640 sorties were flown and 2,851 tons of bombs dropped.[10] In short, the average mission in March involved about 106 planes; in May it involved 180. This was still a long way from the June 1944 peak when the average operation was undertaken by 1,000 heavy bombers. Nevertheless the sudden spurt forward in the spring of 1943 was a step decisively in the direction of bringing crushing air power to bear on the enemy's war machine.

A similar increase in effort by the British Bomber Command at the same time was noted by the Chief of Air Staff, Sir Charles Portal. The bomb tonnage dropped on enemy territory during the second quarter of 1943, he reported, more than doubled the tonnage in the first quarter. Even after making allowances for weather, this achievement, together with the accelerated build-up of the Eighth Air Force, represented a notable net increase in the pressure of the combined air offensive. It was too early to see certain or decisive results, but the promise of things to come was clear. Air Marshal Portal remarked that already Germany was being forced into a defensive air strategy.[11]

What the Joint Strategic Survey Committee referred to as an "unforeseen degree of success attained with HUSKY" was the relatively quick victory in Sicily accompanied by signs of complete Italian demoralization. The forces of Field Marshal Harold R. Alexander (General Patton's U.S. Seventh Army and General Montgomery's British Eighth Army) in-

---

[8] Commander-in-Chief Atlantic Fleet, p. 462.

[9] Figures are from *Statistical Summary of Eighth Airforce Operations, European Theater, 14 Aug 1942–8 May 1945*, Hq Eighth Air Force, 10 Jun 45.

[10] Bad weather in April reduced operations so drastically that a comparison of April sorties and bomb tonnage with May figures would be misleading. For a detailed account of operations see Craven and Cate, *The Army Air Forces*, II, Ch. 10.

[11] CCS 109th Mtg, 16 Aug 43.

vaded Sicily on 10 July 1943; thirty-nine days later (on 17 August) organized resistance had ended. The overrunning of the island had the immediate effect of convincing the Italians that their cause was hopeless. On 25 July Mussolini was forced out. On 8 September the Italian government formed by Marshal Pietro Badoglio capitulated. The imminence of Italian collapse had been apparent to both the Allies and the Germans some weeks in advance, and both sides were hurriedly preparing for the next move.

The Germans, believing that there might still be some fight left in the Italians although their leadership had altogether broken down, in May had made plans for moving *Army Group B,* under Generalfeldmarschall Erwin Rommel, into Italy. The move was accomplished during July and August while a pretense of co-operation with the Badoglio government was maintained.[12]

The prospect of an early Italian collapse convinced the U.S. Chiefs of Staff that the time had come for bold action. At the Washington Conference in May and for some weeks subsequently the principal Mediterranean post-HUSKY operations envisaged were the seizure of Sardinia and limited-objective attacks on the toe or heel of the mainland. Both the Combined Chiefs of Staff and General Eisenhower favored the mainland operations as more likely to produce decisive results, but feasibility depended on the progress of

HUSKY.[13] Planning therefore proceeded concurrently for all contingencies, and decision was deferred. General Marshall thought the choice might be made toward the end of July. It was actually about the middle of the month that the Combined Chiefs proposed scrapping all their earlier conservative plans in favor of a direct assault on Naples with a view to full-scale exploitation up the peninsula.[14]

Before this decision was made, General Eisenhower had asked that he be given additional troops to follow up the victory of Sicily. Specifically he asked for the diversion to the Mediterranean of one convoy scheduled for the United Kingdom. The Combined Chiefs of Staff approved his request though it meant a net loss to the United Kingdom build-up for OVERLORD of 66,000 troops.[15]

British planners then proposed that General Eisenhower's striking power be still further increased.[16] But as their proposal would have reduced the OVERLORD build-up by another 50,000 troops and might have caused postponement of either OVERLORD or operations in the Pacific, the U.S. Chiefs of Staff demurred. They pointed out that, no matter how important an action in the Mediterranean might be, it could not substitute for action required in the Pacific or northwest Europe. In advocating the assault on Naples, they said, they had intended a bold plan which involved risks, justified,

[12] General der Kavallerie Siegfried Westphal, Der Feldzug in Italien, MS, Ch. IV. Hist Div files. The story of Italian collapse and surrender is treated in full by H. M. Smyth in The Sicilian Campaign and the Surrender of Italy, a volume now under preparation in this series.

[13] Meetings at Algiers between Churchill, Marshall, Eisenhower, and others, 29 and 31 May 43. Min of TRIDENT Conf.

[14] CCS 102d Mtg, 16 Jul 43. The debate during July on what to do in the Mediterranean may be followed in the CCS 268 series and in CCS 103d Mtg, 23 Jul 43, and CCS Spec Mtg, 26 Jul 43.

[15] Rpt, Combined Planning Staff, 15 Jul 43, CCS 268/2; Msg to Eisenhower, 21 Jul 43, CCS 268/5.

[16] CCS 268/2.

in their opinion, by the Italian collapse. They criticized the British proposal as overinsuring the operation at the cost of prejudicing agreed strategy elsewhere. They could not approve the Naples assault so conceived.[17] On this point the Joint Chiefs of Staff stood fast and on 26 July the British yielded.[18] The order went out to General Eisenhower to plan an attack on Naples with only those resources already allotted to his theater. These, of course, now included 66,000 more men that had been earmarked for the Mediterranean by the Washington Conference.

Pressure on Germany from the west and south by the spring of 1943 was at least sufficient to blunt Germany's offensive capabilities in these directions. But from Germany's standpoint much worse was happening in the east. In the two preceding summers the Germans had set their armies rolling across huge expanses of Russian territory, though the decisive victory on both occasions remained just beyond their grasp. In July 1943 they tried again. They massed armor south of the Russian salient at Kursk. The armor broke through only to be destroyed in great tank battles in the rear of the Russian main lines. The Russians waited only a week for this situation to develop before they launched their first major summer offensive with three armies attacking about fifty German divisions in the vicinity of Orël. On 5 August the city fell. More important, the Russians had finally and permanently seized the initiative and had begun the dogged battle of attrition in which the prize was not territory but

destruction of the German armies. The seesaw campaign in which the Germans advanced in the summer and retreated in the winter was over. Henceforth the main German armies in the east would walk in only one direction—back toward the homeland.

The war was, of course, not won in August 1943, and it could not have seemed so. But at least the brightening of Allied prospects was unmistakable. The optimistic might see victory dead ahead; the most pessimistic could feel maneuver room between their backs and the wall. It is certain that when the Combined Chiefs of Staff met at Quebec for another of the great plenary conferences they faced the future with a new sure knowledge of their power. This knowledge in turn sharpened the urgency to crystallize strategy. It was more clearly than ever up to the Allies to determine when and where the ultimate decision of arms would be sought.

The Quebec Conference, which opened on 12 August, had, unlike the earlier meetings at Casablanca and Washington, no decisions to make on immediate operations in Europe. The next step in the Mediterranean, the invasion of Italy in the Naples areas, had already been decided. This fact cleared the decks for a full-dress debate on European strategy. Fundamental disagreement between the U.S. Chiefs of Staff and the British on how to defeat Germany had been adumbrated in September 1941, and thereafter had underlain all their discussions on strategy. But during the first half of 1943 the opposition of strategic principle had been blurred because the immediate and pressing issue had always been to decide

---

[17] CCS 103d Mtg, 23 Jul 43.
[18] CCS Spec Mtg, 26 Jul 43.

QUEBEC CONFERENCE. *Seated, left to right: Prime Minister Mackenzie King of Canada, President Roosevelt, and Prime Minister Churchill. Standing: General Arnold, Air Chief Marshal Portal, General Brooke, Admiral King, Field Marshal Dill, General Marshall, Admiral Pound, and Admiral Leahy.*

whether or not to carry out a specific operation in the Mediterranean. Once the Allies were committed in North Africa, to reject exploitation in the Mediterranean meant to choose idleness for a considerable Allied force and to surrender the clear military advantage of maintaining momentum against the enemy. But attacks in the Mediterranean had always been conceived as having limited, not decisive, objectives. The ultimate aim, the British had argued, was to knock Italy out of the war. With the invasion of the Italian mainland, the course of action begun by TORCH would therefore reach its goal. After the defeat of Italy, continued attacks into the Axis underbelly would require new tactical and strategic justification. With the close of the 1943 summer offensive, furthermore, the old argument in favor of Mediterranean ventures as interim operations designed to maintain pressure on the enemy while preparations for OVERLORD were completed would no longer apply. On the contrary, for the first time since TORCH, Mediterranean operations and the cross-Channel attack became clear-cut alternatives competing for consideration as the Allied main effort.

From every standpoint the Quebec Conference seemed to present both the urgent need and an ideal opportunity to seek a firm resolution on future strategy in Europe. Aware of this, the Joint Chiefs of Staff made particularly careful preparations to present their views. They analyzed at length the procedure of previous conferences, the debating techniques of the British, and even the precise number of planners required to cope on equal terms with British staffs. Quite frankly they went to Quebec determined to make their ideas prevail by all the means at their disposal.[19]

This was to be, it must again be emphasized, a friendly debate between Allies seeking the same end. Nevertheless it was serious, for each Ally brought to it deep and honest convictions. It therefore became a matter of grave importance for each to find the strongest possible grounds on which to rest his case. The American ground in earlier conferences had been relatively weak. In the first place the British Chiefs of Staff had more readily available and more complete information on

the European war because they were closer to the scene, because they had presided over planning for European operations almost two years before the Americans became involved, because they were served by a well-developed intelligence system for which the newly arrived Americans had no equivalent, and finally because their own planning staffs were generally more numerous and more experienced.[20] These inequalities evened out only gradually as the U.S. Army grew and organized itself in the European and Mediterranean theaters.

In the second place, the British Chiefs of Staff were a much more tightly knit organization than the U.S. Joint Chiefs. This also was due to a longer familiarity with the problems of the European war, which had permitted them to iron out through long association and discussion both individual and service differences. It was more directly due, however, to the influence of the Prime Minister and the War Cabinet, who provided a large amount of daily guidance in strategic and political matters.[21] Through Lt. Gen. Sir Hastings Ismay, Military Chief of Staff to the Minister of Defence, who attended most Chiefs of Staff meetings, the military and political leaders were kept in close contact with each other and welded into a relatively homogeneous directorate

---

[19] Both the Joint Strategic Survey Committee and the Joint War Plans Committee made thorough examinations of British techniques of argument and ways of meeting them. See JPS 189, Preparations for the Next U.S.–British Staff Conference, 25 May 43; JCS 422/1, QUADRANT, 25 Jul 43; Memos and staff studies in OPD file ABC 337 (25 May 43) *passim.*

[20] The British brought a staff of 93 to the Washington Conference in May, and in addition made considerable use of the Joint Staff Mission and diplomatic personnel already in this country. The Americans by contrast took only 56 officers to Quebec. See JPS 189 and various commentaries thereon in OPD file ABC 337 (25 May 43).

[21] Cf. Winston S. Churchill, *The Grand Alliance* (New York, 1950), p. 28; Eisenhower, *Crusade in Europe,* p. 61.

of the total British war effort.[22] The unity of British political and military policy was further insured by the British system of cabinet responsibility. Churchill, as Minister of Defence, together with his War Cabinet, was directly answerable to the House of Commons for military decisions. It behooved him then to keep in close touch with his military chiefs and to make certain that he fully understood and approved their decisions, even as to detail, in order that he could defend them later, if necessary. Churchill was personally inclined, furthermore, to occupy himself even more intimately with military affairs than his position required. As a long-time student of tactics he could contribute substantially at the planning level to the conduct of the war. He attended and took active part in many of the regular Chiefs of Staff Committee meetings. He intervened constantly in the planning of operations, not only to enunciate principles but to suggest tactical detail. As already noted, he played a leading role in the development of landing craft and the artificial ports. He concerned himself in the details of artillery and armored tactics.[23]

In all these matters he had a lively personal interest. He sent along to the Army a stream of memoranda containing all manner of suggestions, some practical, some not. But all had in common a bold enthusiastic approach designed either to shock the planners out of what Churchill always feared was a narrow professional

view of the war or to cheer up his subordinates when the outlook was black.[24] After Dunkerque, when dispatches of disaster were piling up in the War Office and men were returning from the Continent stripped of their weapons and often of their clothes, when there seemed to be no hope of giving them even rifles with which to defend their country, the Prime Minister wrote: "We are stronger than ever before. Look how many extra men we have here now. Form Leopard Brigades to tear and claw the enemy." [25]

Churchill's close personal leadership never amounted to dictatorship. Although he generally called the British tune in discussions with the Americans, it would be a mistake to assume an identity between his views and those of the British Chiefs of Staff. Similarly it should be noted that what appeared as "British" views at the conferences were not necessarily endorsed by all British military men. "British" doubts concerning the feasibility of OVERLORD, for instance, were never shared by General Morgan and his staff.

Despite these differences of opinion, it remains true that there was a British point of view on strategy which Churchill and the British Chiefs of Staff consistently maintained. That view favored opportunistic, peripheral operations aimed initially at the reduction of German

---

[22] Ismay held this position under Churchill all during the war. Before Churchill became Prime Minister, Ismay was secretary of the Chiefs of Staff Committee. Interv, F. C. Pogue with Gen Ismay, 17 Dec 46. Hist Div files.

[23] See Note by the Minister of Defence, 7 Oct 41, cited in Churchill, The Grand Alliance, pp. 498–500.

[24] This was the interpretation of both General Barker and General Morgan on the basis of their experience on the COSSAC staff. See Intervs, F. C. Pogue with Barker, 4 Oct 46, and Pogue with Morgan, 8 Feb 47. Hist Div files. It is worth noting in this connection Churchill's impatience with the stodgy military professional which runs through his account of World War I as a kind of leitmotif. See esp. Winston S. Churchill, The World Crisis: 1915 (New York, 1923), pp. 540–46.

[25] Interv with Gen Ismay, cited n. 22.

power by indirect attack (by air over western Europe and by sea, air, and land in the Mediterranean), with the ultimate object of so weakening German defenses in France that a cross-Channel attack might be launched in the final phases of the war against an enemy whose will to resist was gravely shaken.[26] It was never clear precisely what degree of deterioration this involved and no doubt opinions would have differed widely. What was central, however, to British strategy and consistently maintained by its advocates was that the date for the final assault across the Channel had to be contingent and indeterminate.

On the American side there was rather less unanimity in the direction of the war. In the first place, traditional American isolationism had made this country wary of political involvement in Europe. The Joint Chiefs of Staff tended therefore to develop a purely military perspective that considered political implications chiefly with an eye to avoiding them. This perspective accurately reflected the popular obsession with winning the war as quickly and as cheaply as possible—an obsession which allowed little room for consideration of America's postwar position.[27] One

effect was to make the Joint Chiefs of Staff relatively independent of the President and State Department in formulating strategy. The President, unlike Churchill, seldom intervened in detailed military planning. He tended to make only the large decisions as between fully developed alternative courses of action. He was occupied almost exclusively with large perspectives and the political problems involved in the liberation of occupied countries, the employment of United Nations [28] forces, and dealings with foreign governments affected by proposed military operations. The President generally appeared at the Allied conferences as a defender of the strategy worked out by the Joint Chiefs of Staff.[29] Though apparently reasonably convinced of its soundness, he was still in the position of a man who having accepted persuasion from one quarter was psychologically prepared to listen to advice from another. The President, in short, because of his position, his experience and personality, and American opinion, did not create a unified American front comparable to the British front molded and inspired by the Prime Minister.[30]

In part, the lack of complete unity in American views can be traced to the di-

---

[26] On the question of possible British political interests in the Mediterranean see below, p. 96, and cf. Eisenhower, *Crusade in Europe*, pp. 194, 284; Stimson and Bundy, *On Active Service*, p. 447.

[27] The President was always conscious of this popular feeling. See, for example, Mtg, Roosevelt, Hopkins, and JCS on board ship, 19 Nov 43. Dep C/S file 110.00 A 48–41 dr 155. The President said "that we should not get roped into accepting any European sphere of influence. We do not want to be compelled, for instance, to maintain United States troops in Yugoslavia." See also Memo, Col Gailey (OPD) for Gen Handy, Information from the White House, 30 Jun, quoting portions of Cbl, Roosevelt to Churchill, 29 Jun 44, in reference to the British proposal to divert ANVIL resources to the Adriatic. Roosevelt

wrote: "I would never survive even a minor set-back in Normandy if it were known that substantial troops were diverted to the Balkans." OPD files, exec 10, item 71 (Information from the White House).

[28] The term "United Nations" to designate the Allies was apparently first used by Roosevelt at the end of 1941. See Sherwood, *Roosevelt and Hopkins*, p. 458; cf. *Ibid.*, pp. 548–49.

[29] An exception, of course, was the President's initiative in pushing the North African operation. See above, Ch. I.

[30] Cf. on this point Stimson and Bundy, *On Active Service*, pp. 428, 439, and Ch. XVII *passim;* Sherwood, *Roosevelt and Hopkins*, p. 446.

vergent interests of the services. Before the establishment of the Joint Chiefs of Staff in 1942, the U.S. Army and Navy had had little experience in the sort of close co-operation now demanded of them. Agreement on joint strategy did not prove too difficult, but day-to-day implementation continually revealed disparities between the Army and Navy points of view. It was not only that the services had different habits of thought and organizational jealousies; they were split by the geography of the war. The Army's primary interest was in Europe where the bulk of its forces would be used. The Navy had a similar primary interest in the Pacific. The naval members of the Joint Chiefs of Staff, Admirals Leahy and King, were not opposed to OVERLORD, nor to the basic strategy of defeating Germany first. They simply lacked the U.S. Army's single-minded enthusiasm for European projects. On the one hand, while there remained any doubt as to whether OVERLORD would be mounted, they questioned the wisdom of hoarding resources in the United Kingdom and so delaying the day when the all-out offensive in the Pacific could be started.[31] On the other hand, they were more open than the Army to persuasion that OVERLORD might be unnecessary.

In July 1943 naval representatives on the Joint War Plans Committee and the Joint Planners actually proposed shifting U.S. strategy away from the OVERLORD idea.[32] They argued that world conditions which had made the cross-Channel project the best means of seeking a decision with Germany had so changed as to "cast grave doubt over the ROUNDUP concept." The decisive defeat of the German armies, they believed, would, if necessary, be accomplished by Russia. They accepted the original British idea of a cross-Channel operation in the final stages of the war, and concluded that, "without prejudice to Pacific and Burma operations, the continuing success and great momentum of our Mediterranean operations must carry on, at least until after Italy is knocked out of the war." The decision by the Combined Chiefs of Staff in May, to withdraw seven divisions from the Mediterranean for use in OVERLORD, appeared to them unsound, since it would remove pressure from Germany, preventing a maximum effort in Italy and a possible opportunistic exploitation of Italian collapse through invasion of southern France. "If Germany chooses to fight in Italy," they wrote, "that is the place to fight her. There is, indeed, no doubt but that the combination of this constant wastage of Axis air power [through the combined bomber offensive] plus the elimination of Italy represents the maximum possible 1943 Anglo-American contribution towards the defeat of the European Axis."

The proposals, in short, completely reversed the American strategic principles consistently defended up to that time by the Joint Chiefs of Staff. The paper, representing "a new trend in U.S. thinking," went informally to Generally Marshall.[33] It was considered so seriously that

---

[31] For instance, see JCS 83d and 84th Mtgs, 17, 18 May 43; see also above, Ch. I.

[32] JPS 231, Adequacy of the TRIDENT Strategy, 26 Jul 43. Colonel Bessell, Army member of the JWPC, concurred in the memorandum but his concurrence did not represent War Department opinion. See JCS 444/1.

[33] Copy of JPS 231 (with attached buck slip) in C/S file 381 II.

when General Barker, deputy COSSAC, arrived in Washington with the OVERLORD plan he observed a "weakening" of the American attitude toward OVERLORD. He reported to General Morgan that the weakening was induced, "as previously," by U.S. naval authorities. He thought he had come just in time to strengthen the War Department's hand.[34] Actually the War Department planners had not weakened. They had already begun a thoroughgoing attack on the naval position and had presented a separate analysis of strategy for consideration by the Joint Chiefs of Staff. This returned to the traditional U.S. view on OVERLORD and reaffirmed the May decisions of the Combined Chiefs of Staff, especially in regard to the withdrawal of the seven battle-trained divisions from the Mediterranean. Admiral King did not defend the naval planners' report in the Joint Chiefs' next meeting on 7 August, and the traditional War Department view was accepted again as U.S. strategy.[35]

The flurry of planners' memoranda at the end of July 1943 was the Navy's only open challenge of General Marshall's European strategy. Admiral King himself was apparently content that, in discus-

sions with the British, U.S. views on European operations should be the War Department's view for which General Marshall was the spokesman.[36] As European matters were the principal and by far the most controversial concern of the Combined Chiefs of Staff, General Marshall assumed the chief responsibility for defending U.S. strategy in debate with the British. To this responsibility Marshall brought both conviction and diplomatic skill. He was firm in his belief that the strategy evolved by the War Department was the correct strategy, yet he was always willing to attend the possible merits of rival suggestions. He fought hard for ROUNDUP in July 1942 and lost primarily to the President's insistence on immediate action. Thereafter Marshall rode two horses, struggling to keep tight rein on Mediterranean commitments in order that BOLERO could proceed apace. He managed this feat by a series of compromises. But, at Quebec, as has been suggested, the roads diverged. It seemed essential to choose between them. For

---

[34] Morgan's notes on telephone conversation with Barker, 5 Aug 43. SHAEF SGS file 381 Ia.

[35] The original JWPC paper (JPS 231), which set forth the naval point of view, was never presented to the Joint Chiefs of Staff, but it formed the basis for JCS 444, which did reach them. The latter paper is a slightly toned down version of JPS 231 based on the same strategic principles. The formula at the 7 August meeting was to call for a "reconciling" of the reports of the Navy planners, JCS 444, and the Army planners' rejoinder, JCS 444/1. In fact what happened was that the Army views were accepted *in toto* and formed the basis for the U. S. Chiefs of Staff memorandum submitted to the British at Quebec as CCS 303. See OPD file ABC 381 Europe (5 Aug 43) and ABC 337 (25 May 43).

[36] On the other hand, General Marshall was scrupulous in letting Admiral King speak first on Pacific matters.

A graduate of the Virginia Military Institute in 1901, Marshall was commissioned in the infantry. During World War I he was assigned to general staff duty and went overseas with the 1st Division, with which he served at Lunéville, St. Mihiel, Picardy, and Cantigny. He worked on the plans for the St. Mihiel offensive and then became Chief of Operations of First Army in the midst of the Meuse–Argonne offensive. In May 1919 Marshall was appointed aide to General John J. Pershing and held that assignment for the next five years. In 1936 and again in 1937 he commanded Red Forces in army maneuvers. The following year he came to the War Department first as Assistant Chief of Staff, War Plans Division, and then as Deputy Chief of Staff. After a two months' tour as chief of a military mission to Brazil in 1939, he was appointed Chief of Staff of the Army.

the first time since July 1942 Marshall accepted the need for a showdown with the British and undertook to lead the fight. To his colleagues he said: "We must go into this argument in the spirit of winning. If, after fighting it out on that basis, the President and Prime Minister [decide] that the Mediterranean strategy should be adopted . . . the decision [should] be made firm in order that definite plans could be made with reasonable expectation of their being carried out." [37]

Deeply as General Marshall opposed the Mediterranean strategy, he still preferred to settle on that rather than face a series of emergency operations and a generally hand-to-mouth strategy. This opposition between a settled plan and a dependence on opportunity was probably the most serious difference between the American and British points of view—a rift wider and more difficult to reconcile than any differences over where and when the campaigns in Europe were to be fought.

The British said in effect, "How can we tell what we should do six months or a year hence until we know how we come out of next month's action?" The Americans retorted, "How do we know whether next month's action is wise unless we know where we want to be a year from now?" The positions were difficult to reconcile because ultimately both stemmed from the respective resources and experiences of the two nations. For a year and a half Great Britain stood alone on the edge of a hostile Europe fearful a good part of the time of being herself invaded by the Nazi conquerors. She stood

counting up her resources and matching them against her responsibilities for the defense of her own shores and her life lines throughout the world. The deficit in means must have seemed appalling.

From 1940 on it was obvious to British strategists that, if the war was to be won, eventually British armies would have to return to the Continent. But all their plans for such an eventuality had to recognize that a maximum effort might hurl about twenty divisions against the Atlantic Wall. Planners in 1941 and 1942 were bound to face strategy as primarily a problem of what could be done with such a relatively small army. Their invariable conclusion was that nothing could be done except under conditions of German collapse or a very great weakening in German morale. It should not be forgotten that the ground war in Europe at this time was being fought by massed German and Russian armies of hundreds of divisions. How could the scales of this conflict be tipped by the addition of twenty divisions? On the other hand if those twenty divisions (the core of an expeditionary force of about one million men) were committed in an unsuccessful enterprise, it was probable that they could never be reconstituted. England's striking power on land would thus be fruitlessly dissipated. It is not strange then that the strategists looked to the fringes of the Continent, outside the area where the bulk of the German Army was engaged. Their best hope for eventual success seemed to be to nibble the Nazi monster down to size. When this might happen no one could foretell. It depended partly on Russian success, partly on their own success. If they could get away with the first nibble they might try

---

[37] JCS 104th Mtg, 15 Aug 43.

a larger bite. Militarily they did not want rigid plans and long-range target dates. They did not want what General Brooke later called "a lawyer's agreement" to tie their hands.[38] They wanted maximum freedom to exploit whatever situation arose and promised the best chance of furthering their initial object of wearing down the German military power in preparation for the final blow. The Mediterranean, because of the weakness of Italy and because of the unusual number and variety of legitimate military objectives, was an ideal area in which to work out their policy. Moreover, since the eighteenth century the Mediterranean had been an area of British political interest. Military aims and traditional political concern thus both focused on the European underbelly.[39]

America came into the war with historic consciousness of her great, unbeaten power. Although she was dangerously unprepared, her psychology from the beginning was offensive. Americans were confident they could build huge armies, navies, and air forces. For example the War Department "Victory Program,"

prepared in September 1941 in answer to the President's request for an estimate of the Army's needs for waging war, contemplated an army of 215 divisions.[40] The thought was then that the USSR might succumb and that America had to be ready to take on the German Army alone, except for the relatively small contributions of Great Britain. After Pearl Harbor the War Department published a Troop Basis calling for an army of more than ten million men.[41] As the war progressed Soviet success made a huge U.S. field army unnecessary. But the very fact that Americans at the beginning contemplated taking on the German Army by themselves and felt it possible is a clue to their psychology. As U.S. war power accumulated, Americans became impatient to bring on the decisive trial of strength. It was evident that such a trial could never be made in the Mediterranean. Moreover, the attempt to nibble away at the German power, the Joint Chiefs of Staff believed, would only result in attrition of their own strength. However great the reservoir of American military power, its application was limited by the logistical difficulties of long sea communications and the chronic shortage of shipping. Every division sent into the Mediterranean was a division lost for the main battle. It could not be moved to another theater without expending the same amount of shipping as

[38] SCAEF 12th Mtg, 27 Mar 44. SHAEF SGS file 381 I. Brooke was at the time refusing to make commitments on the invasion of southern France as a diversion for OVERLORD (see Ch. V). He said that "it was not militarily sound to run a war on a lawyer's agreement by making commitments ahead of time, thereby losing the necessary and desired flexibility to meet the ever changing conditions and circumstances."

[39] See n. 26. It is impossible to assess what force political consideration may have had at any juncture in the debate, for neither the Prime Minister nor the British Chiefs ever put a political argument on the contemporary record. Even at this time (1950) Mr. Churchill apparently still does not defend the Mediterranean strategy on political grounds. See Churchill, *The Grand Alliance*, pp. 660–61.

[40] Joint Board Estimate of United States Over-all Production Requirements, 11 Sep 41, JB 355, ser 707. OPD files.

[41] Both of these estimates were primarily for purposes of planning war production and not mobilization, but they are nonetheless symptomatic of the Army's expansive thinking. Cf. other estimates in early 1942 cited in K. R. Greenfield, R. R. Palmer, and B. I. Wylie, *The Organization of Ground Combat Troops* (Washington, 1947), p. 198.

would be required to send a fresh division overseas from the United States.[42] Its very presence in the Mediterranean sucked in shipping to sustain it and more divisions to reinforce it. The Mediterranean, General Marshall thought, was a vacuum into which American's great military might could be drawn off until there was nothing left with which to deal the decisive blow on the Continent.[43]

And what if, after committing the country's resources to the Mediterranean, they should be boxed up there, and destroyed? The Americans could not forget that the Mediterranean was practically a closed lake to which Spain held the western key. What if the Allied armies, after fighting hard for minor victories, should be cut off from the sources of supply? The possibility did not seem unlikely. Franco was a Fascist who had certain reasons to be grateful to Hitler and might be persuaded at least to turn the other way while German armies marched through to Gibraltar. This fear of being locked up in the Mediterranean was never shared by the British, who had long been accustomed to faith in Gibraltar and diplomatic bulwarks in the Iberian Peninsula. But it remained a strong factor in American hostility to Mediterranean commitments until well into 1943, when it was finally concluded that the Germans no longer had enough spare divisions to seize the Iberian Peninsula.[44]

The differences of strategic concept were fully recognized by both the U.S. and British Chiefs of Staff. At Quebec they were squarely faced in a debate brought on by the Joint Chiefs' submission of a paper outlining strategy for the defeat of the Axis in Europe.[45] Their paper called for no action. It was a simple statement of principle, giving "over-riding priority" to OVERLORD over all other European operations. At first reading General Brooke found it for the most part unexceptionable. He agreed that OVERLORD "should constitute the major offensive for 1944 and that Italian operations should be planned with this conception as a background." [46] That agreement, however, was not so positive as it sounded. The British view was that the Italian operations were *essential* steps on the road that led to OVERLORD. Being essential rather than diversionary, they acquired in British eyes at least an equal importance with the operation for which they prepared. The British objected therefore to assigning "over-riding priority" to the cross-Channel attack. The Joint Chiefs believed that, without such priority, Mediterranean operations would compete successfully for Allied resources and so perhaps make OVERLORD impossible when the time came to mount it. For three days the debate precipitated by that phrase "over-riding priority" raged, often behind closed doors with no secretaries present.

It was no mere verbal dispute. It tackled head on the issue of whether or

---

[42] JCS 293, Limited Operations in the Mediterranean in 1943–44, 7 May 43.

[43] CCS 83d Mtg, 13 May 43.

[44] The fear of a German move through Spain was frequently expressed. See, for instance, JCS 52d and 57th Mtgs, Jan 43; CCS 151/2, 17 Feb 43 and JCS Spec Mtg, 26 Jul 43. Appreciation that such a move was no longer possible was contained in JCS 438/1, JIC Rpt, Estimate of the Enemy Situation, 1943–1944, European–Mediterranean Area, 7 May 43.

[45] See discussions of the Quebec Conference agenda, CCS 288 series.

[46] CCS 108th Mtg, 15 Aug 43.

not the Allies should base their strategy on a single-minded concentration on a cross-Channel attack in 1944. That there should be no doubt of the seriousness of the issue, General Marshall stated the American view in strong terms. If the Allies relied on opportunism, he said, they would be "opening a new concept which . . . weakened . . . [the] chances of an early victory and rendered necessary a reexamination of . . . [the] basic strategy with a possible readjustment towards the Pacific." [47] The threat had been used before, and was probably not taken very seriously. But there was no mistaking the new firmness in the American stand. "The United States Chiefs of Staff believe that the acceptance of this decision [to grant over-riding priority to OVERLORD] must be without conditions and without mental reservation. They accept the fact that a grave emergency will always call for appropriate action to meet it. However, long range decision for the conduct of the war must not be dominated by possible eventualities." [48] The debate continued.

On 17 August 1943, the Combined Chiefs at last agreed to a statement of policy which on the face of it was acceptance of the American principle, but the wording was pregnant with mental reservations. Instead of giving OVERLORD "over-riding priority," they proclaimed: "As between operation OVERLORD and operations in the Mediterranean, where there is a shortage of resources, available resources will be distributed with the main object of insuring the success of OVERLORD. Operations in the Mediter-

ranean Theater will be carried out with the forces allotted at TRIDENT except as these may be varied by decision of the Combined Chiefs of Staff." [49] Possible eventualities still were riding high.

American attempts to crystallize strategy were, of course, at bottom merely efforts to force the British Chiefs of Staff into a hard and fast commitment on OVERLORD. How far they succeeded at Quebec is difficult to appraise. General Brooke, when directly challenged as to his faith in OVERLORD, replied that he thought OVERLORD would succeed provided that the conditions of restricted enemy opposition as laid down in the plans were met. The Prime Minister in the course of both plenary sessions underlined these conditions. If they were still unfulfilled when the target date became imminent, then he asked that the Combined Chiefs review the operation. So that they would have a second string to their bow, he suggested that planning be directed now for an alternative operation against Norway. In conversation with Marshall, on the other hand, Churchill said that he "had changed his mind regarding OVERLORD and that we should use every opportunity to further that operation." [50] He also told General Ismay after the conference that "the thing looked good." [51] He would not, however, commit himself on the issue of the relative priorities of OVERLORD and the Mediterranean. In general it may be said that the British Chiefs and the Prime Minister at Quebec endorsed the principle of a cross-Channel invasion in 1944 but still

---

[47] *Ibid.*

[48] CCS 303/1, Strategic Concept for the Defeat of the Axis in Europe, 16 Aug 43.

[49] CCS 303/3, 17 Aug 43. TRIDENT was the code name for the Washington Conference of May 1943.

[50] JCS 106th Mtg, 16 Aug 43.

[51] Interv with Gen Ismay cited n. 22.

entertained considerable reservations as to its feasibility at that date. It would take another stormy meeting in the winter to settle these for good.

In the meantime, the reservations were less important than the decisions. In effect the Combined Chiefs at Quebec abided by their agreements of the Washington Conference. They resisted suggestions that the seven battle-trained divisions ought not to be moved out of the Mediterranean. They approved General Morgan's OVERLORD plan and ordered him to continue plans and preparations. They further suggested that the plan should be enlarged. The Prime Minister asked for an increase of the assaulting forces by at least 25 percent. He also desired a landing on the east coast of the Cotentin. General Marshall agreed. Although these recommendations were not embodied in a directive, they constituted an authorization to Morgan to overstep the limitations imposed on his planning by the Washington agreements.[52]

The OVERLORD planners had also asked for a diversion against southern France to prevent the Germans from moving troops from the south to meet the main Allied assault in Normandy. The Quebec conferees accepted with very little discussion the desirability of such a diversion and ordered General Eisenhower, then commanding general of the North African theater, to draw up plans for an actual operation. It was to be timed to coincide with OVERLORD and have as its objective the establishment of a lodgment in the Toulon–Marseille area with subsequent exploitation northward. The British expressed some tentative doubts about the plan. General Brooke believed that the invasion should be attempted only if the Germans had been "forced to withdraw a number of their divisions from that area,"[53] and the Prime Minister wondered whether air nourishment of the French guerilla forces in the region might not constitute an acceptable alternative. In the absence of a specific plan and before the Italian venture had been undertaken, the whole project was evidently highly speculative and the most that could be decided was to explore the possibilities.

Even the possibilities were admittedly very limited. General Eisenhower was directed to plan on the basis of resources already allotted to his theater, and it was estimated that this would allow him an amphibious lift for only 27,000 troops and 1,500 vehicles—a lift, in other words, for about one division. It was further noted that "the ships and craft shown do not provide a balanced assault lift. . . ." However inadequate these resources might be, the Quebec planners ruled that nothing more would be available. "Augmentation is not considered practicable without drawing from OVERLORD."[54]

Despite this ruling, planning would reveal in the months ahead that augmentation was essential, and in consequence the southern France invasion, though conceived by the Americans as an integral part of OVERLORD, would actually become another competitor for scarce re-

---

[52] Capt Mansergh (COSSAC Naval Staff), Rpt on QUADRANT at COSSAC (43) 23d Mtg, 30 Aug 43.

[53] 1st Plenary (Citadel) Mtg, 19 Aug 43. OPD files, Min of QUADRANT Conf.

[54] CCS 328/1 Directive to General Eisenhower, 27 Aug 43, Annex V. The origins and development of the southern France operation will be discussed in detail by Maj. J. D. T. Hamilton in Southern France and Alsace, a volume under preparation in this series.

sources. On the other hand, by providing a means to employ forces already located in the Mediterranean in direct support of the attack against northwest Europe, it would prove a useful talking point against British advocacy of Balkan adventures or an increased effort in Italy.

For the fate of OVERLORD, the casual suggestion to increase its size was probably the most significant product of the Quebec Conference. It set in motion plans and preparations that acquired their own momentum, which with the mere passage of time became increasingly difficult to reverse. This fact underlines an important characteristic of all the debates among the Combined Chiefs of Staff. The debates always prefaced action. Action was required by circumstances regardless of whether minds met or not. There was never any question of allowing differences to split the Anglo-American alliance. However great was the disparity in strategic thinking, the community of basic interests ran deeper. The need for common action was more vital than any principle under debate. Thus, although neither Americans nor British perceptibly yielded their separate points of view, practical decisions were made as if such yielding had taken place. The deadlock of ideas was broken by the practical politics of compromise, enforced by the necessity of continuously acting against the enemy.

Compromise, furthermore, was made possible, as well as necessary, by the equality of the Allies. The realization that neither America nor Great Britain could act alone was implicit in every discussion and every decision. England's base and America's resources were alike indispensable for a decisive trial of strength with Germany. Each nation separately would have been doomed to a long and possibly futile struggle.

Quebec was as inconclusive as the previous meetings had been in attempting an unalterable definition of European strategy. But operation OVERLORD came through the debates unscathed by any serious criticism. OVERLORD was the weapon. Once forged, it would argue for its own use more eloquently than all the words in council.

Landing Craft Again

General Morgan did not wait for the decisions at Quebec to begin a re-examination of his completed plan with the view to strengthening it. One of his first steps after the plan had been delivered to the British Chiefs of Staff was to ask his naval staff to estimate, first, the number of additional landing craft that would be required to load the vehicles of the two follow-up divisions tactically so that they could be used on D plus 1, and, second, the number of craft needed to lift another assault division. The figures supplied him on 27 July 1943 almost immediately became irrelevant.[55] Instead of being able to contemplate a larger assault, Morgan saw his already inadequate supply of landing craft dwindling away.

Of the 653 LCT's which the Washington Conference allotted to OVERLORD and which General Morgan from the outset complained constituted a bare and dangerous minimum for the task, 44 had

---

[55] Memo, Capt Mansergh for COSSAC, Appreciation of the Effect of the Provision of Extra Landing Craft and Shipping for Operation OVERLORD, 27 Jul 43. SHAEF SGS file (1944 Operations).

been taken by the British Navy for net protection duties at Scapa Flow. It was possible, though not certain, that some might be released in time to take part in OVERLORD. Still more serious, a large number of LCT's had to be converted into close-support craft for the assault because the Combined Chiefs had made almost no provision for such craft. Although the burden of neutralizing the enemy coastal and beach defenses would be undertaken by the air forces and naval vessels, the heavy preparatory fires would have to be lifted some minutes before the assault craft actually touched down. It was never imagined that preparatory fire could destroy any significant proportion of the enemy defenses. The most it could do would be to prevent the enemy from manning his guns effectively while the bombardment was in progress. It was therefore essential for the assaulting force to keep up neutralizing fire until the last possible moment. That meant small craft, armored and equipped with guns and rockets, which could maneuver close to the shore and fire as the assault waves rolled in. To perform this vital task, the Washington Conference allotted OVERLORD just thirteen LCG's (Landing Craft, Gun). Early in August 1943, COSSAC was informed that only seven of these craft could be delivered in time; the rest would be a month late. General Morgan took the opportunity to raise the whole question of the inadequacy of the planned close support. As a result, the British Chiefs of Staff invited him on 12 August to prepare a detailed report on the shortage of landing craft "and other naval equipment" for OVERLORD.[56]

General Morgan rolled up his sleeves and accepted the invitation with zest. He told 21 Army Group, which was particularly concerned over the shortage of support craft, that he would take full advantage of the opportunity offered him to expound the subject of landing craft shortages. "I am aiming," he said, "to give the Chiefs a proper earful." [57]

Facts for the earful were supplied by his naval staff, which calculated shortages based solely on current allocations and the three-division assault plan. Altogether about one-quarter of the 648 LCT's planned for the assault lift were, for various reasons, no longer available. In addition to the 44 already noted which were being used at Scapa Flow, 36 were to be converted to LCT(R)'s (rocket-carrying craft), 48 would be armored to carry direct-support high-explosive weapons, and 36 would probably be needed for close support of the U.S. assault division. The latter estimate, in reality, was very low. General Devers, ETOUSA commanding general, subsequently calculated that the American assault division would require 56 support craft of the types that used LCT hulls or the equivalent. The net deficit Navy planners set at 164 LCT's as well as 7 LCI(L)'s that had been converted into headquarters ships.[58]

How was this deficit to be made up? The U.S. Chiefs of Staff held out little hope that the craft might come from

[56] COS (43) 186th Mtg (0), 12 Aug 43.

[57] Ltr, Morgan (COSSAC) to Maj Gen W. D. Morgan (CofS 21 Army Group), 18 Aug 43. SHAEF SGS file 560 I.

[58] COSSAC (43) 50, Landing Craft for OVERLORD, 10 Sep 43; Memo, Devers for COSSAC, Support Craft Required per U.S. Assault Division, 15 Oct 43. SHAEF SGS file 560 I.

American sources. The United States, they decided, could not assign additional LCT's to the United Kingdom to replace those diverted from OVERLORD to Scapa Flow defense duties.[59] The Joint Chiefs declared that the United States had never built any gun-support craft and did not intend to.[60] On 10 August Admiral King wrote to Admiral Stark: "Production in the U.S. and requirements of other theaters will permit no advancement of present schedule of BOLERO landing craft to come from the United States mainland. The above matters are being studied at the present time and you will be informed when decisions are reached."[61] The decision was reached a few days later to explore the possibility of increasing production, and Admiral King then said he felt sure some increase could be achieved. But there was considerable doubt whether any increases, even if effected, could be felt in time for OVERLORD. The program of U.S. landing craft production remained for several weeks clouded with uncertainty.

British production offered no better hope. The shipbuilding industry in the United Kingdom was near the saturation point, especially as regards the employment of available skilled labor. The manufacture of landing craft had already been expanded to the point where it was consuming a quarter of all the steel worked into new hulls. To increase it further would have involved a host of technical difficulties which seemed un-

economical to British authorities.[62] Not until later in the fall did the need for more craft appear so urgent that the Prime Minister intervened to cancel certain ship construction in order to make way for an increase of about sixty landing craft for OVERLORD. At the moment, General Morgan's request for a revision of the whole shipbuilding program was turned down by the British Chiefs of Staff.[63]

The problem of how to make good the deficit in landing craft for a three-division assault had received only a preliminary examination when word came from Quebec that the Prime Minister wanted the assault increased to four divisions.[64] The British Chiefs of Staff asked General Morgan to report on that possibility. By the end of September, COSSAC completed a thorough re-examination. So much debate and hypothesis had by that time clouded the issue that General Morgan undertook to start afresh, recalculate his requirements, and restate his tactical thinking.

"My original Directive" he began, "placed at my disposal a quantity of landing craft which bore little or no relation, as to numbers and types, to the actual requirements of the proposed operation." Now, he continued, it was proposed to strengthen the operation, which he fully conceded needed strengthening. But did this mean adding a fourth division to the assault? General Morgan thought not. He pointed out the dangerous weaknesses of the plan as it stood, weaknesses which were thrust on it by the

---

[59] COS (43) 175th Mtg (0), 29 Jul 43.
[60] Memo, Adm Creasy for COSSAC, Provision of Support Craft—Progress Report, 2 Sep 43. SHAEF SGS file 560 I.
[61] Ltr, King to ComNavEu, 10 Aug 43. SHAEF SGS file 560 I.

[62] Information supplied by the British Admiralty.
[63] COS (43) 566 (0), Availability of Landing Craft (Tanks) for OVERLORD, 22 Sep 43.
[64] Cbl cited at COS (43) 209th Mtg (0), 7 Sep 43.

inadequacy of the landing craft allotted. "Detailed analysis of the present plan shows that while the three assault divisions are only barely adequately mounted in craft of suitable types, the immediate follow-up formations are most inadequately mounted, and there is a dangerous gap on D-plus-1 day." A large proportion of the follow-up forces being mounted in ordinary shipping could not be tactically loaded and thus would not be operationally available on the far shore until twelve hours after landing. In short most of them were "follow-up" in name only; they would not be in position immediately to reinforce the assault troops. General Morgan therefore recommended that, before any consideration be given to increasing the number of assaulting divisions, all additional landing craft that could be raked up should be put in to strengthen the follow-up and provide a floating reserve. "We already have far too high a proportion of our goods in the shop window," he said. "To consider any increase in this proportion without adequate stocking of the back premises would in my opinion be basically unsound." [65]

Morgan's new calculations of craft needed to permit the landing of two full divisions in the follow-up for use on D plus 1 showed a deficit of 251 LCT's for a three-division assault and 389 for a four-division assault. In addition, for a four-division assault there would be a shortage of more than 150 support craft using LCT or equivalent hulls.

Quite apart from this very large landing craft requirement, the four-division assault struck General Morgan as unwise because it would necessitate broadening the assault front. Extension to the east he believed would bring the assaulting troops within range of the Le Havre coastal guns, which were among the most formidable in the Atlantic Wall. Extension on the right flank of the assault would involve landing on the beaches northwest of the Carentan estuary. Reversing his previous stand that this would be desirable, General Morgan now noted that the Germans had already begun flooding the hinterland of the Cotentin and that therefore the contemplated assault in that area was unsound.

The British Chiefs of Staff were not impressed with this argument and continue to advocate a four-division assault, the fourth division to be American and to be employed against the east Cotentin. No suggestions were made as to how the evident difficulties might be overcome. [66]

However the strengthening of OVERLORD was to be accomplished, there was general agreement that strengthening was needed, and that this would require large new increments of landing craft. In the urgent need to find these craft, the question of their tactical employment for the moment took a back seat.

In September Donald Nelson, chairman of the U.S. War Production Board, went to London and talked to General Morgan and his staff about landing craft requirements. As a result of his conversations he cabled Charles E. Wilson his conviction that LST's and LCT's were the "most important single instrument of war from the point of view of the Euro-

---

[65] COS (43) 596 (0) , 30 Sep 43.

[66] COS (43) 236th Mtg, 4 Oct 43.

pean Theater," and that the requirements for them had been "grossly understated." [67]

Planning adequate supplies of landing craft, however, was still complicated by the competition of other parts of the war production program for critical war materials, particularly steel plate and marine engines. Equally important was the competition between landing craft and other shipping for priority in the nation's crowded shipyards. The Navy's 1944 shipbuilding program called for a 50 percent increase of tonnage over the previous year, while the Maritime Commission's schedules for merchant shipbuilding remained about the same as before. To superimpose on this large shipbuilding commitment an increase in landing craft production schedules required a careful scrutiny of strategic needs for various types of shipping. Furthermore, if changes were to be made in apportioning materials and facilities, they had to be made long in advance of anticipated needs since readjustments in the program required time—time to cancel contracts for one type of vessel and let contracts for another, time to complete construction already under way on one type and initiate construction of another. A large part of the Navy's 1944 shipbuilding program consisted of small vessels and destroyer escorts which used mostly the same tools, materials, and yards as landing craft.[68]

Time was already short when the question of increasing landing craft production was officially raised at Quebec and Admiral King told the Combined Chiefs of Staff that he was examining the possibility of building more landing craft by halting the construction of 110-foot subchasers. This, he thought, might result in an increase of 25 percent, but the estimate was not yet firm.[69] On 20 August 1943, planners, after tentative studies, reported that any acceleration in landing craft production would probably not be felt before 1 April 1944.[70]

On 13 September the Chief of Naval Operations submitted a new schedule calling for a 35 percent increase in landing craft production, saying that it "was designed to meet the requirements of the operations agreed upon in QUADRANT." The Joint Staff Planners commenting thereon agreed, with qualifications.[71] "Landing craft destined for OVERLORD," they pointed out, "will arrive in time for the operation [that is, craft already allotted] though the complete allotment of some types from the United States will not arrive as early as desired by COSSAC. The most critical situation will exist in LCT (5 and 6)'s. The only solution (if the late arrival cannot be accepted) seems to be additional withdrawals from the MEDITERRANEAN. There is no increased U.S. production in this type of craft. . . . The QUADRANT decision relative to OVERLORD will therefore not be affected

[67] Cbl, Nelson to Wilson, 27 Sep 43, cited in George E. Mowry, *Landing Craft and the WPB (Historical Reports on War Administration: WPB Special Study No. 11)*, rev. ed. (Washington, 1946), p. 29. Wilson was chairman of the Production Executive Committee, War Production Board.

[68] Mowry, *Landing Craft and the WPB*, pp. 33–34, 51–52.

[39] CCS 111th Mtg, 18 Aug 43.

[70] CCS 314/3, Allocation of Landing Craft (Operation OVERLORD—Vehicle Lift), 20 Aug 43.

[71] JCS 462/3, Landing Ships and Craft—Means to Increase U.S. Production, 1 Oct 43, with incl, Ltr, Vice Chief of Naval Operations to Chiefs of Bureaus, 13 Sep 43.

by the increased production of landing craft."

At the end of October 1943 logistical planners had prepared another study which indicated that landing craft production could be further increased, but no decision was made and the 1 November production schedules virtually repeated the 1 October schedule. In the meantime General Morgan, visiting Washington, was led to believe that "if sufficiently powerful pressure was applied at the right spot, U.S. landing craft production . . . [could] in fact be increased. . . ." Although he observed that it was "extremely difficult to find out just exactly whence to have this pressure applied . . . ," he still hoped to be able to "bring matters to a head."[72] In that hope he was evidently disappointed. As time passed and action was postponed the prospects of producing more craft in time for OVERLORD faded.

Thenceforward procurement of landing craft for OVERLORD proceeded on the basis of making the most of existing supply. The principal methods of stretching the supply were reallocation from the Mediterranean theater, a comb-out of training facilities in the United States and United Kingdom, increase in serviceability rates, and increased loading. All these expedients were fully explored in the months following General Eisenhower's assumption of the Supreme Command in January 1944, but up to the last minute the situation remained tight and threatened to compromise the tactical dispositions for the assault.

Questions of Command

For OVERLORD planners the months following Quebec were filled with frustrations. The order to re-examine the strength of the assault brought them up against the apparently unanswerable question of landing craft availability. Still more baffling was the seemingly simple directive to carry on with plans and preparations. What did it mean? General Morgan's original job—the only job for which he had a clear-cut directive —was finished. He had been told to study the possibilities of mounting a cross-Channel invasion of a certain size at a certain date and say by means of an outline plan whether such an operation was feasible. The verdict had been returned. To continue planning could mean only to plan tactically, to fill in the detail of how the operation as outlined could be carried out. But this was no job for a small planning group designed as the nucleus for the Supreme Headquarters. It could be done only by the tactical headquarters which would have direct control of the operation: army group, army, and corps. The Quebec order, therefore, was actually an order to COSSAC to farm out and co-ordinate tactical planning. Such a task obviously required executive authority. General Morgan was legally only the chief of a planning group, without command functions. He was, as he pointed out, a relatively junior officer.[73] It was out of the question to give him the substance of command, but he was at length given the shadow. The

---

[72] Ltr, Morgan to Barker, 28 Oct 43. Barker Papers. See Bibliographical Note.

[73] Ltr, Morgan to Hollis (Secy of War Cabinet), 2 Sep 43. SHAEF SGS file 322.011/2.

Combined Chiefs of Staff in September made him temporarily responsible for "taking the necessary executive action to implement" the COSSAC plans, pending the appointment of a supreme commander.[74] That this was a stopgap expedient scarcely adequate for the situation was apparent to everyone and to no one more painfully than to General Morgan himself. He wrote to General Devers: "While I hate the sight of this whole business I am completely at a loss to suggest anything better, short, of course, of appointing the great man himself which appears to be utterly impossible."[75]

The quasi command thus conferred on General Morgan had grave limitations. Although, with the backing of the Combined Chiefs, he could now take "executive action" he could not, on his own, make command decisions. One command decision, in particular, was immediately required if preparations for OVERLORD were to go forward: what was to be the organization of command of the ground forces in the assault and in the successive phases thereafter?

The basic principles of combined command had been outlined in 1942 and agreed to by the Combined Chiefs of Staff in the fall of that year.[76] They stemmed from the principle approved at the ARCADIA Conference that one Allied commander should have supreme command in each theater of operations.[77] But agreement on principle still left a wide area for debate on the detailed organization of the command for specific operations. The COSSAC plan for OVERLORD contemplated the carrying out of a single tactical mission by a task force of army size and mixed nationality. There was no question of the need for a single unified command over all ground forces in the assault phase. The closest co-ordination was essential, both because the immediate objective was the establishment of a single bridgehead and because the enemy could be expected to probe out the boundary between U.S. and British forces and, reasoning that it represented a point of special weakness, attempt to drive a wedge into it. There was, on the other hand, no question of the necessity for having both American and British troops take part in the assault.[78] Military and political considerations both required it. The administrative and logistical organizations of the U.S. and British armies were so different that to attempt to pass one army through the beachhead established and organized by the other would have involved critical difficulties. Even if these difficulties could have been accepted, it was still unthinkable that the first blow of the supreme offensive of the

[74] Annex I to COS (43) 206th Mtg (0), 3 Sep 43.
[75] Ltr, Morgan to Devers, 2 Sep 43. SHAEF SGS file 322.011/2.
[76] CCS 75/3, System of Command for Combined United States–British Operations, 21 Oct 42.
[77] The Chiefs of Staff Conference, ABC–4, JSSC 2. 25 Dec 41. ARCADIA Conf Bk. (Marshall's words at this meeting are quoted in Sherwood, *Roosevelt and Hopkins*, pp. 455–57.) The principle of unity of command was embodied first in the Directive to the Supreme Commander in the ABDA Area, ABC–4/5, 10 Jan 42. ARCADIA Conf Bk. The directive assigned command over "all armed forces, afloat, ashore, and in the air," that belonged to the four participating powers (Australia, the Netherlands, United Kingdom, and United States).
[78] In July General Barker had written: "It can be accepted as an absolute certainty that the PM would not, for one moment, allow the assault to be made wholly by American troops. The same is true with relation to the U.S. Government. We must be practical about this and face facts." Memo, Barker for Morgan, 4 Jul 43. Barker Papers.

Western Allies should be struck by the armies of only one of them.

The situation envisaged by OVERLORD was actually not very different from that existing in the attack on Salerno where a British corps was subordinated to an American army controlling the assault. Apparently, however, it seemed different, for the Salerno experience with mixed tactical command was conspicuously absent from the discussion of the OVERLORD problem.[79]

In the OVERLORD plan, COSSAC recommended that one U.S. division be employed on the right of the assault, two British divisions on the left, and that all three be initially under a British army commander.[80] As soon as an American army was established on the Continent, Allied field command would pass to a British army group, which would continue to exercise operational control until the capture of the Brittany peninsula or the establishment of a U.S. army group in France, whichever occurred first. Morgan's reason for recommending initially a British chain of command was his feeling that it would be easier for British commanders to organize and coordinate an assault from a British base. It is clear, further, that General Morgan wrote the OVERLORD plan under the impression that the supreme commander would also be British.[81]

Planning recommendations are one thing; decision another. It was true that the OVERLORD plan had been approved without change by the Combined Chiefs; but, when General Morgan pressed for a ruling on whether this over-all approval could be taken to apply to the recommendations on command, he was told that the Combined Chiefs had not been aware of any "special implications" of approving the command system, and that in any case details of the plan were subject to change by the supreme commander when appointed.[82] General Morgan replied that a firm decision was required at once if the operation was to take place on schedule, and he asked the Combined Chiefs to make that decision.[83]

The British Chiefs of Staff then decided to accept General Morgan's proposals in the OVERLORD plan as representing their own point of view, and asked for American comment.[84] The Americans at once began formulating counterproposals. They had not agreed on any formal reply to the British, however, when the whole question was deflected by the introduction of a new and more pressing problem: the need for immediate establishment of an over-all tactical air command.

A tentative organization of the British tactical air forces for support of the invasion had already been set up under Air Marshal Sir Trafford Leigh-Mallory, who had been authorized to make planning decisions on the use of the combined U.S. and British tactical air forces without prejudice to the later appointment of

---

[79] See, however, below (pp. 110–11) for citation of the Salerno experience in a different connection.

[80] COS (43) 416 (0), Operation OVERLORD, Report and Appreciation, 30 Jul 43, Part I, par. 40. SHAEF SGS file 381 Ia.

[81] At the first meeting of the COSSAC staff, 17 April 1943, Morgan announced that Casablanca had decided the invasion was to be commanded by a British supreme commander with an American deputy.

[82] COS (43) 206th Mtg (0), 3 Sep 43.

[83] COS (43) 525 (0), Operation "OVERLORD"—Command and Control, 11 Sep 43.

[84] COS (43) 217th Mtg (0), 16 Sep 43.

another air commander-in-chief.[85] At Quebec in August 1943, the Combined Chiefs agreed to name Leigh-Mallory Commander-in-Chief, AEAF (Allied Expeditionary Air Force), but delayed writing a directive.[86] This action, in effect, formalized his authority to make combined planning decisions on air matters for OVERLORD, but he remained without a combined command. About the middle of September Maj. Gen. Lewis H. Brereton arrived in England from the Middle East with orders to organize a U.S. tactical air force in the United Kingdom. This became the Ninth Air Force, formed initially with the headquarters of the Ninth Air Force from the Middle East and planes from the Eighth Air Support Command taken over from General Eaker's command.

In October the British Chiefs of Staff pressed for the immediate integration of U.S. and British tactical air forces under Leigh-Mallory's command, and submitted to the U.S. Chiefs on the 12th a draft directive outlining AEAF powers and responsibilities.[87] Their earlier request, meanwhile, for U.S. views on Morgan's command and control recommendations was still unanswered. On 19 October the Joint Chiefs commented on both British papers in the same vein. To the proposed directive to the Commander-in-Chief, AEAF, they replied, "It is the view of the United States Chiefs of Staff that the issuance by the Chiefs of Staff of directives to subordinates of the Supreme Allied Commander is unsound." This

principle applied equally, the Joint Chiefs believed, to the proposed successive command of ground forces in the assault. To specify the organization of command under the supreme commander would be to encroach on his prerogative.[88]

These two negative replies funneled the discussions on OVERLORD command into a single debate over the authority of the supreme commander, as the Combined Chiefs began the delicate job of writing a directive for him. When they undertook the task, the identity of the supreme commander was still unsettled, but it was known at least that he would be an American and there was a strong presumption that the choice would be General Marshall.[89] It was therefore a good bet that decisions left to the discretion of the supreme commander would in fact reflect American views on command.

In contrast to the British, the U.S. Army always insisted on permitting a field commander the maximum freedom and discretionary power in the exercise of his command. The Americans believed that it was sufficient for the Combined Chiefs to assign the supreme commander a mission and leave to his discretion all the details of how that mission should be carried out. They viewed with alarm the British tendency to extend the control from the highest level down through the echelons of command, narrowly specifying the functions of subordinate commanders. When Eisen-

---

[85] COS (43) 138th Mtg (0), 26 Jun 43. See above, Ch. II.

[86] CCS 113th Mtg, 20 Aug 43.

[87] CCS 304/2, Directive to the Supreme Allied Commander for Operation "Overlord," 12 Oct 43.

[88] CCS 304/3 and 304/4, 19 Oct 43. All the papers in the 304 series bear the title as given in note 87 except 304/1 and 304/4. The subject of these latter two is "Command and Control for Operation 'Overlord'."

[89] See below, pp. 112–14.

hower heard, after his appointment to the supreme command of OVERLORD, that the British Chiefs of Staff proposed to dictate the detailed composition of the tactical air forces under him, he complained not only against the specific proposal but against what he called the British tendency to freeze organization so that commanders could not use trusted subordinates in their proper spheres.[90] The British position seems to have been precisely that they were hesitant to trust their subordinates. The Prime Minister wrote: "In practice it is found not sufficient for a Government to give a General a directive to beat the enemy and wait to see what happens. . . . The General may well be below the level of his task. . . . A definite measure of guidance and control is required from the Staffs and from high Government authorities. It would not be in accordance with the British view that any such element should be ruled out." [91]

It was against this background of differing conceptions of the basic principles of command that the specific debates on OVERLORD command took place between the Americans and the British. The principal objections which the Americans advanced to COSSAC's proposals on successive command in the invasion were, first, that they would have subordinated American units of division size and smaller to direct British command in violation of the Casablanca declaration, and, second, that they seemed to exclude the supreme commander from operational control of the assault and early build-up phases.

General Devers, in the first formal commentary on the COSSAC proposals, argued that both objections could be met by having the assault divisions controlled by U.S. and British corps commanders whose efforts in turn would be co-ordinated under direct command of the supreme commander through an advance headquarters. COSSAC replied that the Devers plan was probably unworkable. Supreme Headquarters would not be set up for tactical command. It would not be organized to control the detail that normally flowed through a field army. Furthermore it would be impossible for the supreme commander to be physically located so that he could exercise field command of the assaulting forces and at the same time carry out his basic mission of co-ordinating the whole operation through relations with ETOUSA, the air and naval commands, and U.S. and British army group headquarters and service ministries, all either located in London or having established liaison and communication with the capital.[92]

Despite this criticism, the War Department continued to advocate some measure of direct control by the supreme commander in the assault. The Devers plan, however, was modified to restore an army commander to take direct command. The War Department believed that the assault army should be American, not British, and this view was apparently accepted as a basis for discussion although it was not at once embodied in a written agreement. War Department thinking, reflected in a series of draft

---

[90] Cbl, Eisenhower to Marshall, W8967, 31 Dec 43. WD Cable log.

[91] Minute, 24 Oct 43, Annex II to Min, COS (43) 209th Mtg (0), 25 Oct 43.

[92] Ltr, Devers to Morgan (unsgd), 4 Sep 43; Memo, Comments on General Devers' Letter on Plan for Command and Control of Operation "OVERLORD." SHAEF SGS file 322.011/2.

memoranda and reports during September and October,[93] envisaged a command setup somewhat as follows: the assault would be initially under the Commanding General, First U.S. Army, whose forces would consist of airborne troops, a British corps, U.S. corps, and Canadian corps, each to contribute one division to the assault. "During the period from a date prior to the assault to be designated by SAC [94] until CG, First U.S. Army relinquishes the overall command of forces on the continent to British 21st Army Group, control of operations will be exercised directly by SAC to First Army." [95] After the first three corps had built up on the Continent, a British army headquarters would be established. At the same time the Continental field command would pass to 21 Army Group. The supreme commander's control of the operation would then be exercised through army group to U.S. and British armies. On the arrival of the second U.S. army, First U.S. Army Group would assume direct command of all American forces under the supreme Allied commander.

There was no argument about the arrangements thus outlined for the build-up phase. General Morgan, however, was still unable to accept the concept of the supreme commander's direct intervention in the assault. He was, in fact, unable to understand just what was meant. After considerable discussion of the matter in Washington during his visit in October, he wrote:

There persists here the thought that S.A.C. should have some direct connection with the army of assault. Now, what this direct connection is to consist of I cannot for the moment say. I am completely bogged down for the moment in the differences between our two languages. It seems that the word "command" has two different meanings in our two services. All I can get out of General Marshall is that he has a sensation that he should in some way control the assaulting army, although I am quite sure that his conception falls far short of what we understand by the term "command". As far as I can make out, it also falls far short of the American conception of command. But how to define it I must confess completely puzzles me. . . .[96]

General Barker, acting head of COS-SAC in Morgan's absence, took up the problem with his staff in London and replied at length. He did not feel that General Marshall need be apprehensive about the degree of control he could exercise over the assaulting army. But the control should be that appropriate to a supreme commander, not the control normally exercised by a tactical headquarters. General Barker wrote:

I think it goes without saying that the assault must be directly commanded by an Army Commander. Furthermore, the fact that an Army Group Commander must perforce take over direct command of the operation at a fairly early stage, say D plus 5 or 6 or thereabouts, makes it essential that said Army Group Commander should be closely associated with the planning and execution of the assault, otherwise there is likely to be a break in continuity of command, or at least some friction in the change-over as well as in the planning for the buildup. After all, the SAC can and would intervene at any time the situation seems to warrant it. The Salerno operation is a good example of the di-

---

[93] OPD file ABC 381 (22–1–43) sec. 1.

[94] The Supreme Allied Commander.

[95] Draft Memo, Col Roberts (JWPC) for General Handy for CofS, 18 Oct 43. OPD file ABC 384 Europe (5 Aug 43) sec. la.

---

[96] Ltr, Morgan to Barker, 28 Oct 43. Barker Papers.

rect intervention of a Commander-in-Chief when the operation gets sticky. He would, of course, have a senior staff officer from his staff on liaison with the Army Commander.

You will recall that Alexander and Eisenhower both intervened in Clark's battle at Salerno, and as the result, Eisenhower ordered the whole weight of the Air and Naval forces to concentrate on the battlefield. In the assault stage of OVERLORD, it is these two weapons, the Air and the Navy, that SAC would employ to influence the course of the battle. Our headquarters will have direct telephonic, telegraphic and radio contact with Army, Army Group and the Air and Naval Headquarters, as well as with our liaison officers at these headquarters. In consequence, the SAC will be in the closest touch with the battle and can intervene quickly should the necessity arise.[97]

General Morgan agreed and wrote that he would "make arrangements for [General Marshall as SAC] to be able to participate directly in Bradley's battle when it takes place. What though the planning must have been through the other system, that is, through the 21 Army Group, I am myself satisfied that this is the practical solution having in view the fact that the Commander himself will not be present throughout the whole proceedings." [98]

American concern with expanding the authority of SAC took another direction. In the same memorandum in which the Joint Chiefs criticized the COSSAC proposed chain of command, they recommended defining the supreme commander's sphere of command to include the whole of Germany for purposes of conducting air operations.[99] The British at once demurred, saying that the pro-

posal amounted to giving the supreme commander all responsibility for strategic bombing. This responsibility, they felt, should remain with the Combined Chiefs of Staff. General Marshall observed that "operation POINTBLANK [the strategic air offensive] is intended as a preparation for OVERLORD and may now be extended to operations from Italy. Thus it is a part of OVERLORD." [100]

Although there was no argument over SAC's right to control the strategic bomber forces once the invasion had begun, the British strenuously objected to turning over command before that date. The furthest they would go at the moment was to specify in the draft directive to the Commander-in-Chief, AEAF, that the strategic air forces would be "detailed from time to time by the Combined Chiefs of Staff to operate with all or part of their effort to meet the requirements of the Supreme Commander." [101] They believed that SAC control of the Eighth Air Force and RAF Bomber Command was unsound. Air operations were specialized; air channels had been organized through four years of war; air operations affected all enemy fronts; and, finally, the air offensive already in progress was designed to establish conditions for OVERLORD. This system could not be improved on by putting SAC in command.[102] The Joint Chiefs could not accept the argument. What-

---

[97] Ltr, Barker to Morgan, 3 Nov 43. Barker Papers.
[98] Ltr, Morgan to Barker, 8 Nov 43. Barker Papers.
[99] CCS 304/4, 19 Oct 43.

[100] CCS 124th Mtg, 22 Oct 43.
[101] CCS 304/7, 4 Nov 43. This is a "split" paper. The first five paragraphs of the draft directive inclosed were agreed on by U.S. and British planners. The final paragraphs, dealing with the control of the strategic air forces, were reported in two versions representing opposing U.S. and British views.
[102] Cbl, Br COS to JSM, 10 Nov 43. SHAEF SGS file 322.011/2.

ever the technical objections might be, they held it was unthinkable that the supreme commander of any operation should not have absolute command of all forces needed by him to carry out that operation. "A committee," said General Marshall, "cannot fight a battle." [103]

The upshot of the debate was a temporary deadlock. It was decided then to put the question aside until it became critical. At the moment it was more important to issue a directive to the Commander-in-Chief, Allied Expeditionary Air Force, authorizing him to organize the U.S. and British tactical air forces into a single command under SAC. The essential outlines of this command were agreed to by the Combined Chiefs of Staff, and, despite U.S. objections to issuing directives to subordinate commanders, they were embodied in a directive to Air Marshal Leigh-Mallory early in November.[104] The AEAF headquarters was established as of 15 November, to take immediate control of the RAF Tactical Air Force and the Air Defence of Great Britain. The date at which the Ninth Air Force would pass to AEAF command was tentatively set for 15 December.[105]

Designed first as an appendix to the directive to the supreme commander, the AEAF directive was issued separately as it became apparent that full agreement

on the definition of SAC's authority could not immediately be reached. Consideration of the latter problem, in fact, was deferred to January.[106] In the meantime at the Cairo Conference in December the supreme commander was at last appointed. General Eisenhower, then commander in chief in the Mediterranean, was notified of his appointment about the middle of December and arrived in England to take command the middle of January. It was another month before the formal directive from the Combined Chiefs was issued to him. But the debate over the directive after his appointment was mainly verbal. The few substantial issues at stake were settled by being dropped. In effect the whole directive was trimmed down to what both sides could agree to and the settlement of such questions as the control of strategic air was left for later discussion in which the supreme commander's determination of his own requirements would be the decisive factor.[107]

The appointment of General Eisenhower ended almost a year of uncertainty which kept many of the preparations for invasion in long suspense. When the question of selecting a commander for cross-Channel operations was broached at the Casablanca Conference, it was shelved on the grounds that it was unnecessary to appoint a commander so early in the proceeding. Informally it was agreed that the commander, when appointed, would be British. Casablanca's perspective, it will be remembered, was confined principally to 1943.

---

[103] CCS 126th Mtg, 5 Nov 43.

[104] The directive was issued through COSSAC, saving the letter of SAC's right to appoint his subordinates.

[105] COS (43) 717 (0), Formation of an Allied Expeditionary Air Force, 17 Nov 43. Air Defence of Great Britain replaced Royal Air Force Fighter Command. "Despatch by Air Chief Marshal Sir Trafford Leigh-Mallory" (submitted to the Supreme Allied Commander in November 1944), *Fourth Supplement to The London Gazette No. 37838*, 31 December 1946, pp. 37–38.

[106] After the paper referred to in note 101 (dtd 4 Nov 43), the next CCS memorandum on command (CCS 304/8) was dated 6 January 1944.

[107] For full text of this directive see below, App. B.

If a cross-Channel invasion had been attempted that year, the British would inevitably have made by far the greater initial contributions of resources. It was on that basis, and in consideration of the fact that General Eisenhower was commanding in the Mediterranean, that the agreement was made. COSSAC was given to understand immediately after Casablanca that the matter was settled. The Prime Minister informed General Sir Alan Brooke that he would be appointed supreme commander as soon as it seemed advisable to make a formal appointment.[108]

These arrangements were much less settled than they seemed. Churchill, while agreeing to the choice of a British commander, formally enunciated the principle that the nation contributing the majority of the forces to any combined enterprise should command it. When it became apparent that no cross-Channel operations would be launched during 1943 and that for the 1944 operation the United States would furnish the bulk of the troops and matériel, the Casablanca decision on the high command was changed. As early as July 1942 the Prime Minister had suggested to President Roosevelt the appointment of General Marshall to command cross-Channel operations.[109] Churchill apparently repeated the recommendations at Quebec a year later.[110] Although no agreement was reached, rumors of Marshall's appointment leaked to the press, and received increasing credence even from those officially concerned with

OVERLORD.[111] When President Roosevelt was asked by General Morgan in October for confirmation that General Marshall would be given the command, the President replied only that he was still not sure.[112]

Behind the President's reluctance to appoint General Marshall to the OVERLORD command was the feeling that no one could satisfactorily replace him as Chief of Staff of the Army and member of the Combined Chiefs of Staff.[113] In particular it was felt that General Marshall had established a working relationship with Congress which would be jeopardized by bringing in a new man whom Congress did not know. There was also a very general sense in the American camp that a field command in one theater was not a big enough job for the man who for four years had occupied the top position in the U.S. Army and had taken a leading part in formulating strategy throughout the world. Partly in an effort to create a job suitable for their Chief of Staff, the Americans at the Cairo Conference suggested combining the European and Mediterranean theaters under a single commander who would have the direction of all operations in Europe.[114] The suggestion

---

[108] Interv with Gen Ismay, cited n. 22; cf. Stimson and Bundy, On Active Service, p. 439.

[109] Sherwood, Roosevelt and Hopkins, p. 615.

[110] Stimson and Bundy, On Active Service, p. 439.

[111] Ltr, Col Edwards (OPD) to Gen Edwards (CofS ETOUSA), 5 Sep 43. Pre-Inv files, Devers Correspondence. Colonel Edwards wrote: "The newspapers have just announced and rather firmly, that SAC is to be Gen. Marshall and suggest that Gen. Eisenhower may be C/S [Chief of Staff of the Army]. This should clear the atmosphere."

[112] Interv with Gen Ismay, cited n. 22.

[113] See the account in Katherine T. Marshall, Together: Annals of an Army Wife (Atlanta, 1946), pp. 69ff.

[114] CCS 408, Command of British and U.S. Forces Operating Against Germany, 25 Nov 43; CCS 126th Mtg, 5 Nov 43. During a meeting with the Joint Chiefs of Staff on shipboard on the way to Cairo, President Roosevelt said that it was his idea "that

stemmed also from American conviction that a single command over related operations was more efficient than co-operation between co-ordinate commanders. It was turned down by the British on the grounds that a single field command over such disparate operations was unfeasible and that the proposal therefore would only mean the creation of an unnecessary intermediary between the Combined Chiefs of Staff and the theater commanders.[115]

Shortly after the British had refused to entertain the idea of amalgamating the Mediterranean and European commands, President Roosevelt decided that General Marshall should remain at his post as Chief of Staff, and that General Eisenhower, the next logical choice, should take command of OVERLORD.

While principles were being discussed on the highest levels, the organization in the theater of various headquarters that would assume control of the operation proceeded. In the early summer the British had constructed the skeleton of their tactical command for OVERLORD, complete with the creation of headquarters of the Second British Army, the First Canadian Army, and 21 Army Group. At that time the highest U.S. ground force command in the United Kingdom was still V Corps. In May, General Devers strongly urged the War Department to establish a U.S. army headquarters.[116] It was required to parallel British organization, to "initiate

actual planning for the 1944 operation," and finally as part of the scheme to make the Germans believe that an attack across the Channel would be made in 1943. Two months later General Devers further recommended that a skeleton headquarters for a U.S. army group also be sent to England.[117]

Despite this urging, which was reinforced by General Morgan, the War Department did not become convinced of the necessity for an immediate appointment of an army commander until the end of August 1943, and insisted then on still further delay in naming an army group commander.[118] The choice of an army commander was unanimous: he was to be Lt. Gen. Omar N. Bradley, American commander in the battle of Tunisia.[119] His release from the command of II Corps then in Sicily was arranged during the last week in August, and effected on 7 September. After conferences in Washington, Bradley arrived in the United Kingdom in October. On the 20th of that month the headquarters of the First U. S. Army was at last opened. The headquarters had been activated in the United States during September with cadre from the Eastern Defense Command.[120]

Army group headquarters was to be allowed to develop gradually out of the theater as the need for it grew. At the time that General Marshall arranged for the appointment of General Bradley as army

---

Marshall should be commander-in-chief against Germany commanding all British, U.S., French and Italian troops." JCS Mtg, 15 Nov 43. Dep C/S file 110.00 A 48.41 dr 155.

[115] CCS 408/1, 26 Nov 43.

[116] Ltrs, Devers to Marshall, 18 and 19 May 43. Pre-Inv files, Devers Correspondence.

[117] Ltr, Devers to Marshall, 6 Jul 43. Pre-Inv files, Devers Correspondence.

[118] Ltr, Barker to Devers, 30 Aug 43. Pre-Inv files, Devers Correspondence.

[119] For Eisenhower's appraisal of Bradley's qualifications, see Eisenhower, *Crusade in Europe*, p. 215.

[120] See Cbls, Marshall to Eisenhower, No. 5968, 25 Aug 43; No. 6595, 1 Sep 43; No. 6904, 4 Sep 43. WD Cable log.

commander he was still not ready to name a commander for army group. General Devers then proposed that a single superior U.S. headquarters, a U.S. GHQ, be established to direct both operations and administration, following the precedent of World War I.[121] Devers' proposed GHQ was to consist of a field headquarters and a rear echelon to handle theater functions. It was to be formed gradually by doubling the staff sections of ETOUSA to constitute forward and rear components. Once the field headquarters moved to the Continent, the theater functions might be redefined to permit, presumably, a greater independence of operational and administrative commands.

The Devers proposal did not suit General Marshall, who believed that a maximum separation of operational and administrative functions was desirable.[122] On 18 September the War Department agreed in principle to the establishment of a U. S. army group headquarters, and planning for it was delegated to General Bradley in addition to his duties as army commander.[123] So strongly did General Marshall feel that the new headquarters should not be burdened with theater responsibilities that he recommended to General Devers a physical separation of army group from ETOUSA. "I desire that the organization of the Army Group Headquarters be initially controlled directly by Bradley under your supervision and that it not be merely an offshoot, or

appurtenance to ETO Headquarters."[124]

First U. S. Army Group (FUSAG) was activated on 16 October. Its first assigned task was operational planning under the direction of ETOUSA. The operational missions of both FUSAG and First Army were to be assigned later by COSSAC. By this time, however, it had already been decided that First U. S. Army would command at least all American troops in the assault and that 21 Army Group, chiefly because it was early on the scene and had participated in COSSAC planning, would have over-all ground command in the assault and early build-up phases. In effect, those decisions meant that the role of FUSAG would be to take over command of U. S. troops when two American armies had become operational on the Continent, that is to say, after the establishment of the initial lodgment area.

It does not appear that the decision giving initial ground command to 21 Army Group was ever formally confirmed by the Combined Chiefs of Staff. When General Morgan returned to London in November after more than a month's stay in Washington, he carried back the instructions and full confidence of General Marshall. "He knows exactly what I want," General Marshall told General Devers in asking the latter for full co-operation with COSSAC.[125] It was presumably in the light of General Marshall's instructions that General Morgan, shortly after his return, began to draft a directive to the Commander-in-Chief, 21 Army Group, which finally fixed the chain of command for OVERLORD.

---

[121] Cbl, Devers to Marshall, W4421, 13 Sep 43. WD Cable log.

[122] Marshall's views on command in Europe are stated in Cbl, Marshall to Devers, R3267, 18 Sep 43; Dir to Devers, 24 Sep 43. OPD Misc Exec office file.

[123] Cbl, AGWAR to ETOUSA, 18 Sep 43. Pre-Inv files, Devers Correspondence.

[124] Ltr, Marshall to Devers 24 Sep 43. OPD file ABC 381 (22–1–43) sec. 1.

[125] Cbl, Marshall to Devers, R5583, 11 Nov 43. WD Cable log.

That directive, issued on 29 November, significantly under the letterhead of "Supreme Allied Headquarters," told the 21 Army Group commander that he would be "jointly responsible with the Allied Naval Commander-in-Chief and the Air Commander-in-Chief, Allied Expeditionary Air Force, for the planning of the operation, and, when so ordered, for its execution until such time as the Supreme Allied Commander allocates an area of responsibility to the Commanding General, First Army Group." He was also told that operations in the assault phase would be carried out by U. S. and British corps under "the unified command of the Commanding General, First (US) Army," and that "the Commanding General, First (US) Army . . . [would] remain in immediate control of land operations until such time as the forces landed warrant, in your opinion, the introduction of a second army headquarters . . . to take over a portion of the front." [126]

It will be noted that this directive made the commander of 21 Army Group an over-all ground commander in the initial phases co-ordinate in authority to the air and naval commanders in chief, but it specifically limited his tenure to the first part of the operation. In the earliest attempts at devising a formula for unified combined command, logic and—it might be added—the natural rivalry among the services for coequal dignity had seemed to demand separate commanders in chief under the supreme commander for all three services, Air Force, Navy, and Army. The Casablanca declaration on command had provided for three "assistant" supreme commanders for each of the services. Mediterranean operations had in effect practiced the doctrine of three coequal commanders, although the operations themselves were small enough so that the "ground commander" was never more than the equivalent of an army group commander. The issue of a ground commander for OVERLORD was raised in intramural discussions in the Operations Division of the War Department in September and came before the Joint Chiefs, but was shelved there. The concept of a ground commander seemed objectionable on practical grounds. Since the supreme commander would be American, it was considered in September that the ground commander, if there was one, would also have to be American. But, as one officer in OPD pointed out, the "ruling factor" determining in practice the nationality of the ground commander would be the availability of a suitable individual to fill the position. He observed further that no U. S. commander had the battle experience and reputation to challenge the qualifications of the British generals, Montgomery and Alexander, for the job. The conclusion was obvious: it would be impolitic of the Americans to suggest the creation of the job.[127]

The command organization for OVERLORD, which was at last agreed on in the closing months of the year, was retained in principle after the assault was broadened from a three- to a five-division front. The successive command already established was then phased forward. Two armies (U. S. and British) were then to make the assault under the direct command of 21 Army Group. General Montgomery, commander of the army group,

[126] Ltr, COSSAC to CinC 21 A Gp, Operation 'OVERLORD,' 29 Nov 43, COSSAC (43) 76.

[127] Ltr, Col Edwards (OPD) to Gen Edwards, 7 Sep 43. Pre-Inv files, Devers Correspondence.

GENERAL MONTGOMERY, *ground commander of the Allied assault on the Normandy beaches.*

was given a *de facto* ground command for the assault phase—the same kind of unified command that under the COSSAC plan would have been exercised by First Army.[128]

The Cairo–Tehran Conferences

In late October 1943, the Combined Chiefs of Staff began looking forward to their next staff conference and the issues which they expected to be raised there. Most of the indications were that the Quebec compromises would be reopened and the debate would go on as before.

In proposing an agenda for the conference, the British Chiefs of Staff emphasized their opinion that the most important point for discussion would be a "general review of our future strategy in the light of the events which have taken place since QUADRANT." [129] That this meant a further British attempt to shift additional Allied weight to the Mediterranean had already become clear through an exchange of views on the disappointingly slow progress in Italy.

On 24 October, General Eisenhower sent a long cable to the Combined Chiefs of Staff outlining the situation in Italy.[130] It was, he said, much changed since the Salerno landings, and the change was seriously and dangerously to the disadvantage of the Allies. At the moment the Allies had eleven divisions in the peninsula. They were opposed by nine German divisions, which, it was estimated, could be reinforced by fifteen more that were located to the north. At the current rate of build-up the Allies would have only sixteen to seventeen divisions by the end of January. There was thus a real possibility that the Allies might lose the critical build-up race and be not only stopped but defeated. What General Eisenhower feared most of all, however, was that, although he might be able to batter his way up the peninsula to Rome, his armies would arrive on their objective too weak to hold it. He could not stand south of Rome because it was important to take the capital as a symbol of victory in Italy, to capture the airfields north of it, and above all to retain the the initiative at least until after OVERLORD. Otherwise, the Germans would be free to withdraw divisions from Italy to oppose the Normandy landings and the main purpose of the Mediterranean campaign would be compromised. General Eisenhower concluded that he must keep pushing north; to do so without fatally exhausting his armies he needed landing craft to take advantage "of the enemy's inherent weakness," the exposure of his flanks to amphibious envelopment.

After receiving Eisenhower's report, the British Chiefs of Staff urgently cabled Washington asking that General Eisenhower be backed to the full. Specifically they wanted delay in the agreed schedules for transferring landing craft from the Mediterranean to OVERLORD. They wanted this "even if the 'OVERLORD' programme is delayed." [131] For the moment the Joint

---

[128] Montgomery, however, never received the formal designation of ground commander, and there actually remained some confusion, at least on his part, as to the duration of his command over ground forces on the Continent. The ground commander problem will be fully discussed by F. C. Pogue in The Supreme Command, a volume under preparation in this series.

[129] CCS 125th Mtg, 29 Oct 43.

[130] Cbl, Eisenhower to CCS, NAF 486, 24 Oct 43. WD Cable log.

[131] CCS 379, Operations in the Mediterranean, 26 Oct 43.

Chiefs simply replied that the British exaggerated the seriousness of the Italian situation and reminded them of their agreement to consider that OVERLORD and not the Italian battle was the "primary ground and air effort against Germany." [132] But it was clear that strategy was on the block again. Again a relatively minor practical decision, this time involving the convoy schedules for moving landing craft, raised the large issue of how the war in Europe was to be fought.

The landing craft problem was temporarily settled by an agreement that General Eisenhower might retain, until 15 December, sixty LST's scheduled for transfer to the United Kingdom a month earlier.[133] But no one doubted that the stopgap settlement was as unreliable as a cork in a volcano. In fact, the cable to General Eisenhower conveying the Combined Chiefs' decision [134] had no sooner been drafted than the British representatives began to argue that General Eisenhower had evidently not asked for enough resources, that he should be provided with at least a two-divisional amphibious lift even though he had requested only one.[135]

There were other straws in the wind that pointed to the resumption of the debate on European strategy. Immediately after the surrender of Italy in September 1943, the British had attempted to pluck off the Dodecanese Islands at the entrance to the Aegean Sea. They thought that the islands would fall readily into the vacuum of the general Italian collapse. German reaction, however, was unexpectedly swift and determined, and Italian assistance to the British, on the other hand, was of even less value than anticipated. As a result, within a few weeks the British had been ejected from their bridgeheads with a loss later estimated by the Prime Minister at 5,000 first-class troops.[136] Before this happened, in late September, the commanding generals of the Middle East and Mediterranean theaters had fully examined the possibilities of reinforcing the Aegean attack and saving the forces already committed there. They concluded that the only operation which could reestablish the Allied position was the capture of Rhodes. In view of heavy German air activity and the enemy disposition to resist strongly in the area, this operation was envisaged as requiring a very considerable contribution of resources from the Mediterranean which could be taken only from the Italian campaign. General Eisenhower, further, saw in an Aegean offensive a constant and probably mounting drain on Mediterranean resources which would seriously affect his capacity to prosecute the war in Italy. The other commanders concerned agreed and it was decided to postpone the proposed invasion of Rhodes. At the moment the Combined Chiefs did no more than take note of these decisions.[137] Since the operation was "postponed," however, and not canceled, it could be expected to come up again, particularly since the Prime Minis-

---

[132] CCS 379/1, 29 Oct 43.

[133] CCS 379/5, 4 Nov 43. At the Cairo Conference, the date for transfer of the craft was extended to 15 January 1944. CCS 132d Mtg, 30 Nov 43; Cbl, CCS to Eisenhower, FAN 281, 1 Dec 43. WD Cable log.

[134] Cbl, CCS to Eisenhower, FAN 271, 5 Nov 43. WD Cable log.

[135] CCS 126th Mtg, 5 Nov 43.

[136] 2d Plenary Mtg at Cairo, 24 Nov 43. OPD files, Min of SEXTANT Conf.

[137] See CCS series 365, Future Operations in the Eastern Mediterranean.

ter had always taken a special interest in the eastern Mediterranean.

One of the arguments for pushing operations in the eastern Mediterranean was that success in that area might persuade Turkey to enter the war on the side of the Allies. The project of using diplomatic pressure on Turkey to bring her into the war had been approved in principle by the Combined Chiefs at Casablanca.[138] Since that time various diplomatic overtures had been made through the British. Although Turkey remained coy in the face of both implied threats and open blandishments—threats that without active participation in the struggle against the Axis Turkey's position might be weak at the peace table, and direct offers of military assistance if she did come in— it still seemed possible at the end of 1943 that an alliance with Turkey might be achieved. The project was given impetus by reports that the Soviet Union was especially interested in getting direct and immediate support from the Mediterranean area so as to draw off more German strength from the main Eastern Front.[139]

There were thus three post-Quebec developments that would tend to supply fresh fuel for the British argument for heavier Mediterranean commitments. To these a fourth consideration, indirect and intangible, but nevertheless important, may be added. Red Army successes in the 1943 summer offensive had been impressive. The German armies were backed up to the line of the Dnepr. The Russians did not pause. Bridgeheads were thrown across the river. The Germans fought to

avoid annihilation on various parts of the front and in the process fell back as much as a hundred miles in the south. By November the main German armies were split by the Pripet Marshes; Kiev had fallen; the forces in the Ukraine were threatened with encirclement; the Crimea was cut off. Although the German armies gave no sign of collapse, they were fighting to escape destruction and steadily retreating. It seemed impossible that they could any longer hope for victory. In the meantime the tempo of the Allied air offensive from Great Britain had stepped up. There were increasing reports of fading morale among enemy prisoners, partly induced, it was thought, by letters from home describing the devastation rained by Allied planes on German cities. In London hopes were raised that enemy disintegration was near, that the closing months of 1918 were about to be reenacted. There was some feeling that plan RANKIN (the plan for return to the Continent in case of enemy collapse) was more likely to be executed than OVERLORD.[140] If collapse were, in truth, so near, then the strategy of throwing everything into the immediate battle in the Mediterranean and so avoiding, perhaps, the necessity of ever having to strike the big costly cross-Channel blow took on a new plausibility.

In the continuing policy discussions during the weeks before the Cairo Conference the Joint Chiefs of Staff found only one new consideration important enough to warrant a possible re-examination of their positive commitment to the OVERLORD concept: that was the sugges-

---

[138] See above, Ch. I.

[139] Cbl, Deane to JCS, No. 51, 9 Nov 43. WD Cable log.

[140] Ltr, Barker to Morgan, 20 Oct 43. Barker Papers; JCS 533/7, Recommended Line of Action at Next U.S.–British Staff Conference, 18 Nov 43.

tion of a Soviet preference for immediate support via the Mediterranean over the stronger but delayed attack on northwest Europe.[141] If the Russians were actually to urge accelerated operations in the Mediterranean, it would be a complete reversal of their previous stand that they wanted a second front, that they wanted it in northwest Europe, and that they did not consider Allied attacks in the Mediterranean as a substitute. Yet in November it seemed quite possible that the Soviet Union might make just this reversal. The circumstances are worth examining in some detail.

In October, U.S. and British military and diplomatic representatives met with the Russians in Moscow to discuss various problems of military collaboration.[142] Marshal K. E. Voroshilov put before the conferees three Soviet proposals for hastening the successful conclusion of the war: (1) preparations by the United States and Great Britain during 1943 to insure an invasion of northern France; (2) inducements to Turkey to enter the war on the side of the United Nations; (3) inducements to Sweden to permit the use of air bases for the war against Germany. In answer to the first proposal Maj. Gen. John Russell Deane and General Ismay outlined the conclusions of the Quebec Conference and reassured the Soviets that the decision to mount OVERLORD was firm. General Deane found it

worth remarking that these assurances were accepted by the Russians and that the Russians did not press to have the target date on OVERLORD put forward. Still more remarkable to General Deane was their calm acceptance of statements that OVERLORD might have to be delayed. Reporting on this to the Joint Chiefs of Staff, General Deane said that it opened up the possibility that the USSR's attitude on a second front in the west had been altered by recent successes of the Red Army, that the Russians were now laying greater stress on immediate assistance. General Deane's impression was strengthened when Molotov complained that Allied pressure in Italy had been insufficient to prevent the Germans from moving divisions to the Eastern Front. Soviet leaders could not understand why two nations of the combined resources of the United States and Great Britain could not tie up more than a handful of enemy forces.[143]

General Deane was convinced by all these signs that the Russians were working around to a demand that American and British armies intensify the campaign in Italy or perhaps launch an invasion of the Balkans. He cabled the Joint Chiefs of Staff on 9 November to be prepared for such a demand at the Tehran Conference. He told them that it was quite likely that Russian enthusiasm for a cross-Channel attack had cooled. He believed the Red Army was now confident

---

[141] Min of Mtg, Roosevelt, Hopkins, and JCS, 19 Nov 43, cited n. 27. Cf. below, n. 144.

[142] The principal U.S. representatives were Secretary of State Cordell Hull, Ambassador W. Averell Harriman, and Maj. Gen. John R. Deane. Deane, following the conference, was to establish a U.S. military mission to the Soviet Union. The British were represented by Foreign Secretary Anthony Eden and Gen. Sir Hastings Ismay.

[143] General Deane reported in detail to the Joint Chiefs of Staff in a series of cables in October and November 1943. See esp., Cbls No. 2, 19 Oct; No. 4, 21 Oct; No. 28, 29 Oct; No. 34, 31 Oct; No. 47, 6 Nov; No. 51, 9 Nov. WD Cable log. The story of the conference is briefly but accurately told in Deane's book: John R. Deane, *The Strange Alliance* (New York, 1947), pp. 16ff., 35.

of its ability to move into Berlin without benefit of the squeeze from the west.

The prospects of mounting OVERLORD as planned could not have seemed very bright to the Joint Chiefs of Staff as they traveled to Cairo for the first conversations with the British before the meeting with the Russians.[144] Shortly after their arrival the Joint Chiefs asked Ambassador John G. Winant for his impressions of British thinking so that they might be prepared for the inevitable debate.[145] Mr. Winant began by saying that "he thought the British had no idea of abandoning . . . [OVERLORD] but that they did oppose a fixed date for it." The British, he said, were anxious to mount the operation at the right "psychological moment" and they didn't think that moment could be predicted so far ahead of time. British defeat in the Dodecanese had much upset the Prime Minister and had confirmed him in the opinion that the Germans were still superior to both Great Britain and the United States on land. British military men, Ambassador Winant added, felt that the Prime Minister's views on the Dodecanese defeat were "considerably out of perspective," but they agreed in fearing the German capacity to build up rapidly on the ground to oppose the OVERLORD landings, despite Allied superiority in the air. In short, he believed, the British still doubted that the Allies could attack successfully at a fixed date which was dependent only on the state of Allied preparations; they still wanted to wait for a moment of German weakness.[146]

Winant's interpretation of British views was confirmed in the course of the conference. Early in the proceedings the Prime Minister emphasized the British commitment to OVERLORD but begged for some "elasticity" in order to expedite Mediterranean operations.[147] The necessary elasticity he thought could be achieved by delaying OVERLORD about five or six weeks. Landing craft destined for transfer from the Mediterranean to the United Kingdom could be held in the Mediterranean long enough to carry out amphibious assaults behind the German lines in Italy and undertake the invasion of Rhodes.

The Prime Minister's views were further elaborated and formally presented by the British Chiefs of Staff the following day.[148] They proposed the following actions: push the offensive in Italy until the Pisa–Rimini line was reached, nourish guerrilla movements in Yugoslavia, Greece, and Albania, induce Turkey to enter the war, open the Dardanelles supply route to the Soviet Union, and promote chaos in the Balkans. They added that, if these actions meant delaying OVERLORD, then that delay should be accepted.

These proposals, counter to U.S. strategy built around the absolute priority of OVERLORD, should have called forth a debate at least as vigorous as that at Quebec. Actually, the Joint Chiefs of Staff promptly accepted the British program as

---

[144] See Mtg, Roosevelt, Hopkins, and JCS, 19 Nov 43, cited n. 27. At that meeting Marshall expressed the opinion that the British might like to "ditch" OVERLORD now in order to go into the Balkans. Roosevelt thought the Russians might press for an attack up the Adriatic to the Danube to tie up with Russian forces entering România.

[145] JCS 127th Mtg, 22 Nov 43.

[146] Ibid.

[147] 2d Plenary Mtg, 24 Nov 43.

[148] CCS 409, "Overlord" and the Mediterranean, 25 Nov 43.

a basis for discussion at the Tehran Conference and afterward. The Joint Chiefs' acquiescence did not mean that they had relaxed their conviction of the transcending importance of OVERLORD. In accepting British proposals *as a basis for discussion* with the Russians, they were underlining the fact that final decision had to take into account Soviet views. They did not thereby agree to argue for the British stand; they intended only to present it in order to elicit Soviet reaction.[149]

There the matter rested when the preliminary Cairo conferences broke up and the Combined Chiefs of Staff traveled to Tehran for the central and critical meeting with the Russians. The keynote of the Tehran meetings was set by the first plenary session on 28 November 1943 between President Roosevelt, Prime Minister Churchill, and Marshal Stalin.[150] Because the main object of the Tehran Conference was to get the Soviet views on strategy as a basis for co-ordinating United Nations' policy, it was Marshal Stalin who at that first meeting called the tune. He wasted no time making clear the Russian view. After listening to some preliminary oratory by the President and Prime Minister, he cut short his own introductory remarks with a blunt "Now let us get down to business." Within a few minutes he announced all the major elements of USSR strategy as it affected the Western

Powers. He declared first that, as soon as Germany had been defeated, the Soviet Union would join with the United States and Great Britain in the offensive against Japan. Announced casually as though it were a point well understood, this was actually his first official assurance of Russian intentions in the Pacific, and it had, as will be seen, profound effect on Anglo-American strategy. Stalin then took up the Italian front. Allied victories there, he thought, had been important, but "they are of no further great importance as regards the defeat of Germany." The USSR, he continued, believed that the most suitable point of attack against Germany was northwest France. Thus in a few sentences he scouted General Deane's prognostications of a change in the Soviet attitude. The Americans were pleased, if somewhat surprised.

The Prime Minister wanted to know whether operations in the eastern Mediterranean to take some weight immediately off the USSR would not be acceptable even though they might mean a delay of a month or two in mounting OVERLORD. Stalin replied that he did not consider it worth while to scatter British and U.S. forces. On the other hand he was very much interested in the suggestion made by both the President and Mr. Churchill that an invasion of southern France was being considered as a diversion for OVERLORD. He did not look on it exactly as a diversion. Simultaneous attacks from the northwest and south appealed to him as a single pincer attack the pattern of which was familiar from many Red Army victories.

Stalin's interest in an assault on southern France caught the U.S. and British

---

[149] CCS 131st Mtg, 26 Nov 43.

[150] This and the following narrative of the Tehran (EUREKA) Conference are from the official U.S. minutes of the meeting, bound with the minutes of the Cairo (SEXTANT) Conference. OPD files. The records kept by the U.S. and British secretaries of the plenary political-military meetings at Tehran were not afterward co-ordinated. For purposes of the discussion here, however, the discrepancies are unimportant and the U.S. minutes have been used throughout.

TEHRAN CONFERENCE. *Left to right: Marshal Stalin, President Roosevelt, and Prime Minister Churchill.*

delegations unprepared.[151] The President and Prime Minister told Stalin that no detailed examination of the project had yet been made, but that their staffs would study it. It was a curious approach, possibly calculated to avoid making any firm commitment. But it ignored a large amount of quite detailed planning work already done for the operation. It ignored General Eisenhower's recommendations made to the Combined Chiefs of Staff on 29 October, opposing the operation in view of inadequate resources.[152] Most important of all it ignored the fact that the bulk of the planning staffs had been left in Cairo. The only material on hand at Tehran to "start" the study was a copy of the 9 August outline plan which was very much out of date.[153] It was on the basis of this old plan that the skeleton planning staff at Tehran drew up a draft memorandum for the President's consideration. Following the August plan, the memorandum recommended a two-division assault with a build-up to ten divisions. There was, however, no reliable information as to the resources likely to be available. On the critical matter of landing craft supplies, the memorandum was necessarily vague; its general conclusion was that there probably would be enough craft "to move two assault divisions by short haul from Corsica and Sardinia to

Southern France under favorable weather conditions. . . ."[154]

On the basis of this study and under considerable urging by Marshal Stalin, the Americans and British before leaving Tehran committed themselves to mounting OVERLORD with a supporting operation against the south of France during May 1944. It was clear that Marshal Stalin considered the two operations as a single, inseparable military undertaking.

This was the Soviet view of what Anglo-American armies should do to hasten the end of the war in Europe. The view was hammered in during the conference, as in every meeting the Soviet representatives, abetted by the Americans, sought to pin down the most unequivocal possible agreement on OVERLORD.[155] All other operations in the Mediterranean Stalin waved aside as diversion. "He had no interest in any . . . [Mediterranean] operations other than those into Southern France."[156] He admitted the desirability of getting Turkey into the war, but doubted that it could be done. In any case he felt that Turkey's participation was a comparatively unimportant matter. The important point was that he did not wish the Western Allies to contemplate any diversion whatsoever from OVERLORD. OVERLORD was the main question, not Turkey or Rhodes or the Balkans. To make sure that there would be no wavering in the preparations for OVERLORD, Marshal Stalin

---

[151] This can readily be deduced from the records and was specifically stated by Colonel (now Brig. Gen.) Bessel in conversation with the author, 5 March 1947. It is further confirmed by statements of General Ismay to Dr. F. C. Pogue, in the interview cited above, note 22.

[152] Cbl, Eisenhower to CCS, NAF 492, 29 Oct 43. WD Cable log.

[153] JPS 249, Plan for Invasion of Southern France, 9 Aug 43.

[154] Unnumbered Memo, Operation Against Southern France, 29 Nov 43. OPD file ABC 384 Europe (5 Aug 43) sec. 9a.

[155] It is clear that the Soviet views had force in the conference because they were also American views. For a plausible analysis of President Roosevelt's role at Tehran see Sherwood, *Roosevelt and Hopkins*, pp. 789ff.

[156] Plenary Mtg, 29 Nov 43. Statement not reported in British minutes.

urged that a supreme commander be appointed at once. He felt that the operation could not progress until someone had clear and single responsibility for it. Both Stalin and Churchill emphasized that the choice was the President's to make; all agreed that the appointment should be settled within the next fortnight.

The air was cleared when the Americans and British gathered again at Cairo. The question of postponing OVERLORD in favor of Mediterranean diversions was scotched at last. The one big problem that remained alive and would grow from now on more robust and obstreperous was how to carry out the commitment to invade southern France (Operation ANVIL) at the same time as OVERLORD. In agreeing to ANVIL, the Prime Minister had stipulated that the strength of the assault be not less than the two divisions which the Tehran staff had indicated were feasible. But back in Cairo the Combined Planners looked over the landing craft figures and reported that there was actually enough lift for only one division in the assault and two-thirds of a division in the immediate follow-up. Estimating that a two-division assault would require a simultaneous lift for 45,500 men and 7,740 vehicles, planners calculated a probable shortage of lift for 6,500 men and 3,200 vehicles. That deficit might be made good, they reasoned, by diverting from the Pacific one month's allocation of landing craft—or a total of 26 LST's and 26 LCT's—and then taking 5 LCT's from OVERLORD. With reference to the latter recommendation, the planners noted that OVERLORD was already getting 24 more LCT's than had been counted on at the Quebec Conference and that therefore the diversion of these five craft was "not

materially at the expense of that operation." The diversion of a month's supply of craft from the Pacific would probably force the postponement of an operation planned against Truk, and they suggested that, if that operation could not be delayed, then it would be necessary to make up the deficit for it by transferring craft from the South Pacific.[157]

Here was the sign of things to come. The "numbers racket" of shuffling allocations of landing craft around the globe, a half dozen here, a half dozen there, had begun and it would not end until late in 1944.

One possible source for more landing craft was the cancellation of a proposed amphibious assault (BUCCANEER) against the Andaman Islands, in connection with operations to open the Burma Road. The British, who had always felt that offensive action against Japan could wait until after the defeat of Germany, now took the initiative in urging cancellation. "It appeared," said Air Marshal Portal, "that in order to carry out a successful operation in the South of France, other operations would have to suffer." [158] Specifically, he thought, the operation that should suffer was BUCCANEER. The Joint Chiefs of Staff were opposed at first, but after consultation with the President they finally agreed to accept a smaller amphibious assault requiring not more than half the lift. The surplus craft could thus be diverted to Europe.[159]

---

[157] CCS 424, Amphibious Operations Against the South of France, 5 Dec 43.

[158] CCS 133d Mtg, 3 Dec 43.

[159] This decision and its impact on strategy in Burma as well as on U.S.–China relations will be discussed in full by C. F. Romanus and R. Sunderland in Command Problems, 1940–1944, a volume under preparation in this series.

In the course of the discussion Admiral King expressed alarm over the tendency to regard the Pacific area as a pool of resources for the European theater.[160] But in view of the priority of OVERLORD and ANVIL as the paramount operations of 1944, and the chronic shortage of landing craft, it was in fact inevitable to regard any non-European theater of operations as potentially a stock pile to be raided in order to fatten the ETO. The point was perhaps best made by a cable which General Marshall sent in December to all theater commanders and defense commands. "The landing craft situation is critical," General Marshall wired, "and will continue to be so for some time to come. Any possible increase in production is far behind the increasing demand for landing craft. You are directed to make every landing ship and craft available for and apply them to the maximum battle effort." [161] The word went around the world: to Cairo, Algiers, Tehran, Chungking, Southwest Pacific Area, Fort Shafter (Hawaii), Nouméa (New Caledonia), Quarry Heights (Canal Zone), Anchorage, and Adak Island (Alaska). Every craft saved was precious; wherever it was on the globe its fate was tied up with the fate of OVERLORD.

The net effect of the reallocation of craft at the Cairo Conference was to give OVERLORD an additional 26 LST's, 24 LCI(L)'s, and 64 LCT's above the allocations set at Quebec; and to give ANVIL an additional 41 LST's, 31 LCI (L)'s, 3 XAP's, and 6 LSI(L)'s.[162] These were significant additions but their impressiveness would pale before the increasing demands of the big invasion, as continued planning brought out the military realities of the task to be done.

---

[160] CCS 135th Mtg, 5 Dec 43; JCS 132d Mtg, 28 Nov 43.

[161] Cbl, R6820, 11 Dec 43. WD Cable log.

[162] CCS 428 (rev) , Relation of Available Resources to Agreed Operations, 15 Dec 43.

CHAPTER IV

The German Army In France 1940—1943

Organization of the West

German leaders in the fall of 1943 read their newspapers and pored over intelligence reports with special interest. Crisis in the east had been reached and passed; there would be no more massed German offensives, no decisive victories. Crisis in the west was approaching. In October, news of the military conference in Moscow convinced Hitler and his staff that the opening of the second front was imminent. The conclusion was modified later as press releases from the Tehran Conference were taken to indicate a postponement of the invasion for perhaps two or three months. The best guess then was that the Allies might attack any time after February 1944, but probably in the spring. Whatever the exact time schedule, most German leaders had little doubt that invasion was close at hand.[1]

While the Moscow Conference was going on, Generalfeldmarschall Gerd von Rundstedt, Commander in Chief in the West, was putting the final touches on a long, frank, pessimistic report on the state of his defenses. The burden of the report was that his army was not in any way prepared to resist the expected Allied attack. In three years of occupation little had actually been accomplished to make Fortress Europe a military reality.[2]

With the conquest of France in June 1940, Hitler believed that he had won the war.[3] He had no plans ready for the next step. He could not understand why any more victories should be necessary to convince Great Britain that it was hopeless to prolong the struggle. But Britain's stubbornness, though inexplicable, was clearly a fact. Hitler noted in July that the British Government was apparently

---

[1] *Oberkommando der Wehrmacht* (see n. 19) / *Wehrmachtfuehrungsstab, Kriegstagebuch* (referred to hereafter as *OKW/WFSt, KTB) 1.IX.–31.XII.43,* 11 Dec 43; cf. MS # B–283 by Blumentritt, *OB WEST* (see n. 2) Chief of Staff, who after the war wrote that following the declarations from Moscow and Tehran the German commanders knew that Germany was to be beaten; before that time they still hoped for an agreement with the Western Powers. See, however, later estimates of Allied intentions in Ch. VII, below.

[2] *Beurteilung der Lage Ob. West am 25.X.43,* 28 Oct 43 (cited hereafter as Rundstedt Report, 25 Oct 43), *Oberbefehlshaber West* (referred to hereafter as *OB WEST) Ia Nr. 550/43. Oberkommando des Heeres* (see n. 19), *Generalstab des Heeres/Operationsabteilung* (referred to hereafter as *OKH/Op.-Abt.),* 28 Oct 43. The German term *"Oberbefehlshaber West,"* which may mean either the Commander in Chief West or his headquarters, has been rendered as *"OB WEST"* when it refers to the headquarters and as "Commander in Chief West" when it refers to the person.

[3] See The Private War Journal of Generaloberst Franz Halder, 22 Jul 40 (trans), MS. Hist Div files. Cited hereafter as Halder Diary. Halder was Chief of the General Staff of the German Army from 1938 to September 1942.

set on fighting to the finish,[4] and he therefore began serious consideration of plans to deliver the *coup de grâce*.[5] The obvious and most convincing method was invasion.

The projected invasion was given the code name *SEELOEWE* (SEA LION) and Army and Navy planners set to work in a race against time to solve the manifold and unfamiliar problems of a large-scale amphibious operation. The first big problem was that there were no landing craft, and very little shipping of any description. By gathering up all the barges from inland waterways at the cost of paralyzing large sections of industry, the Germans could reckon on barely enough shipping space to put an effective force ashore in England.[6] But towed barges at the mercy of the slightest wind-roughened seas were hardly ideal. The perils of improvisation, furthermore, would be heightened by the lack of naval protection. The only way to guard the convoys seemed to be to mass all submarines and light surface vessels on the North Sea flank and at the same time mount a diversionary expedition on the Atlantic side to draw the British Fleet away from the main crossing. The Navy was decidedly cool toward the project. Grossadmiral Erich Raeder, the Navy Commander in Chief, as early as July had uncovered so many risks that he strongly recommended against the operation except as a last resort.[7]

Hitler agreed. Quite apart from the dangers of *SEELOEWE,* Hitler did not like the political implications of conquering England by invasion. He saw that the defeat of England would be followed by disintegration of the British Empire. The beneficiaries of such a collapse, he thought, would be Japan and the United States, not Germany.[8] He wanted not the destruction but the surrender of Great Britain. To force surrender, he believed it was necessary to deprive the British finally and completely of all hope in ultimate victory. They therefore must be confronted with a solid political front on the Continent embracing Spain, Italy, and a vanquished Russia.[9] Defeat of Russia was particularly important. Hitler thought that England drew hope chiefly from the continued independence of the Soviet Union and the United States. By knocking out Russia, the Germans would remove one source of hope and considerably dim the other; Russia's defeat would leave Japan strong in the Pacific and would probably prevent the United States from becoming an effective ally of Great Britain in Europe. "With Russia smashed," Hitler argued, "Britain's last hope would be shattered." On 31 July 1940 Hitler decided that Russia's destruction "must therefore be made a part of this struggle [against England]."[10] He set the spring of 1941 as the target date and ordered preparations made for a lightning blow to knock out Russia in not more than five months.[11]

The decision to attack Russia resulted immediately in a reorganization and ex-

---

[4] Halder Diary, 13 Jul 40.

[5] Conf, 20 Jun 40, ONI, *Fuehrer Conferences, 1940,* Vol. I.

[6] Annex 2, Conf, 25 Jul 40, *Ibid.,* Vol. II. It was planned to land 90,000 men in the first six days.

[7] Confs, 11 Jul 40 and 13 Aug 40, *Ibid.,* Vols. I and II, respectively. Cf. Halder Diary, 31 Jul 40.

[8] Halder Diary, 26 Jul 40.

[9] *Ibid.,* 31 Jul 40. Planning proceeded fitfully for an alliance with Spain and the seizure of Gibraltar.

[10] Halder Diary, 31 Jul 40.

[11] *Ibid.,* 17 Aug 40.

pansion of the Army. The goal set was
to build up from 143 to 180 divisions.[12]
As all three of the army groups that defeated France, *A, B,* and *C,* were to be
shifted to the Eastern Front by the spring
of 1941, it became necessary to create
a new headquarters to take over the occupation of France. This was *Army
Group D,* formed during September and
October under command of Generalfeldmarschall Erwin von Witzleben. In order
to relieve the Army High Command at
once for exclusive attention to the east, a
theater commander, *Oberbefehlshaber
West* (Commander in Chief West) was
designated about the same time to take
charge of all offensive or defensive operations that might be mounted in the west.
Field Marshal Rundstedt, still in command of *Army Group A* (the force earmarked for *SEELOEWE*), was concurrently appointed Commander in Chief
West with full command over *Army
Group A* and tactical command over
Army Group D and *Armed Forces Commander Netherlands (Wehrmachtbefehlshaber Niederlande).*[13]

While these command changes were
being effected, the German commanders
were rapidly becoming convinced that
SEELOEWE was not a sound operation
of war. The Navy had set the period
20–26 September as the earliest date on

which it could be ready.[14] But readiness
even on this date hinged on the ability
of Reichsmarschall Hermann Goering's
Luftwaffe to knock out the British Royal
Air Force. In the Battle of Britain Goering tried and failed as British fighter
pilots demonstrated skill and courage
that took heavy toll of the attackers.
There followed a succession of postpone-
ments, which gained nothing; the Royal
Air Force remained unconquered and
the weather, the final insuperable obstacle, only became more stormy and un-
predictable as the season advanced. With
an improvised landing fleet, composed
largely of river barges only a third of
which were self-propelled, the Germans
needed a relatively long period of almost
flat calm.[15] Such periods were rare in October and could not be forecast. By the
middle of October *SEELOEWE* had been
definitely called off. Preparations were to
be continued for a landing in the spring
but chiefly as a deception measure to keep
up the pressure on the British.[16]

Rundstedt thus remained in France
with his *Army Group A* during the
winter of 1940–41.[17] In April 1941 he
was moved out, and command in the
west passed to von Witzleben, commander of *Army Group D.* Witzleben
was left with three armies, the *Seventh*
and *Fifteenth* occupying the long coast
line from the Spanish border to Antwerp,
and the *First* disposed in the interior
with headquarters near Paris.

The threat of invasion or even of damaging raids by the English against the

---

[12] Memo, *Heeresaufbau auf 180 Divisionen,* 10 Sep
40, *OKW/Wehrmachtfuehrungsamt, Abteilung
Landesverteidigung, Gruppe II, Nr. 1650/40.* Translation found in German Manpower, MS. Hist Div
files. This is a study by German Military Documents
Section, WD G–2, prepared in 1946 from original
German records.

[13] Order, *Oberbefehlshaber West,* 26 Oct 40, *Oberbefehlshaber des Heeres* (referred to hereafter as
Ob.d.H.). *OKH/Op.Abt., Befehlsbefugnisse 30.V.40–
2.II.42.*

[14] Halder Diary, 30 Jul 40.

[15] *Ibid.,* 26 Jul 40.

[16] Order, *Aufgaben und Gliederung im Westen ab
Oktober 1940,* 17 Oct 40. *Heeresgruppe A, KTB 25.-
VI.–17.X.40, Anlagen, Teil III.*

[17] *Heeresgruppe A, KTB West, 1.I.–13.IV.41.*

Continent in 1941 was so slight as to be negligible. Nevertheless, Witzleben began taking certain steps to put his defense in order. In June, the former Inspector of Western Fortresses was appointed Inspector of Land Fortresses in the West and attached for tactical purposes to *OB WEST*. His headquarters was moved from Metz to Paris near that of Witzleben, and his first task was the inspection of the defenses of the Channel Islands.

The military reason for defending the Channel Islands was chiefly to protect coastal traffic. Hitler, however, attached to the islands a far greater political importance. He believed the British would be forced to retake them for the sake of prestige.[18] Conversely they were precious to him as the only British territory directly under his domination. In midsummer 1941 the *319th Division,* reinforced with machine gun, artillery, antitank, and antiaircraft units to the strength of about 40,000 men, was ordered to the islands. This garrison comprising some of the best troops and best equipment in the west was to remain on Channel guard duty, inactive and useless for the rest of the war.

Up to the end of 1941 the only German-built fortifications on the French mainland were seven heavy coastal batteries between Boulogne and Calais emplaced for the shelling of England during preparations for *SEELOEWE,* a few other naval coastal batteries, and some U-boat pens. The coastal battery emplacements were built for the Navy by Organization Todt, the construction organization formed in 1938 to build the West Wall. After *SEELOEWE* was called off, Hitler directed Organization Todt to construct bombproof U-boat pens along the Atlantic coast, especially at Brest, Lorient, and St. Nazaire. That project, to protect what Hitler came more and more to regard as his principal offensive weapon against the Western Powers, absorbed most of the labor and materials available for fortification of the west. When Witzleben in September 1941 proposed that the Army begin work on permanent defenses, the Army High Command (OKH)[19] had no construction battalions to give him and he had to make informal arrangements with the Navy to borrow such of their workers as were idle. Despite the difficulties, Witzleben at the end of 1941 ordered the armies, corps, and divisions under him to reconnoiter defense sites along the coast and begin construction.[20]

This was the first step toward fortifying the west against eventual Allied invasion, but without the necessary allotment of labor and materials it could not accomplish much. The actual building

[18] Interpretation of Warlimont (see n. 52) in *Geschichte des Oberbefehlshaber West,* edited by Generalleutnant Bodo Zimmermann (Ia (G–3) of *OB WEST*). This is a million-word manuscript prepared in part by Zimmermann, in part by generals and general staff officers associated with *OB WEST,* OKW, OKL (Oberkommando der Luftwaffe), OKH, OKM (Oberkommando der Kriegsmarine), and various subordinate commands. It was written under the auspices of the Historical Division of the U. S. War Department between 1946 and 1948. Cited hereafter as MS # T–121 (Zimmermann *et al.*).

[19] Oberkommando des Heeres. Until December 1941 this was the headquarters and staff for Generalfeldmarschall Walther von Brauchitsch, Commander in Chief of the Army. At that time Hitler took direct command of the Army and OKH was directly subordinated to him. In addition it was nominally subordinate for certain purposes to the Oberkommando der Wehrmacht (OKW, Armed Forces High Command).

[20] MS # T–121 (Zimmermann *et al.*).

FIELD MARSHAL VON RUNDSTEDT AND GENERAL JODL. *Von Rund-stedt (left) was Commander in Chief West; General Jodl was chief of Armed Forces Operational Staff.*

of the Atlantic Wall cannot be said to have begun before the spring of 1942. By then the first Russian winter counter-offensive, coupled with American entry into the war, had forced Hitler to reckon more seriously with prolongation of hostilities and the consequent possibility of major action in the west.

Early in March 1942 Field Marshal Rundstedt was appointed Commander in Chief West to replace Witzleben.[21]

Rundstedt was one of the senior officers and leading military personalities in Germany. He had been in charge of early planning for the Polish campaign of 1939 and had commanded an army group in that campaign. In 1940 in France he again commanded an army group. After the victory over France, he was placed in charge of planning and preparations for the invasion of England. On the abandonment of that project, Rundstedt participated in the first offensive against Russia as commander of *Army Group South* until the end of 1941, when he was relieved because of ill health. In March 1942 he reported to Hitler that his health was restored and a

---

[21] Officer's Personnel Files, Field Marshal von Rundstedt. *OKH/Heeres-Personalamt, Personalakten.* Witzleben was put in the OKH Fuehrer Reserve, that is, in a pool of officers unassigned but on active duty and available for service. Rundstedt's appointment as Commander in Chief West was "acting" as of 8 March and was made permanent on 1 May 1942.

week later received the command in the west.

Two weeks after Rundstedt's appointment, Hitler issued his basic order for the defense of the west.[22] Sole responsibility for the defense of all German-occupied territory in the west including the Netherlands was given to the Commander in Chief West, and he, along with the commander in Denmark, was placed directly under the Armed Forces High Command (OKW). This extended a process begun earlier of splitting the theaters of operation between OKW and OKH, as though they were coequal commands. By the beginning of 1943 OKW had become directly responsible for all western theaters (France and the Low Countries, North Africa and Italy, the Balkans, and Scandinavia) while OKH devoted exclusive attention to the east. The division recognized, in the first place, that OKH had its hands full with the increasing difficulties of the war in Russia. It also, in part, reflected the fact that the defense of the west particularly called for co-ordination between the three services.[23]

Co-ordination was effected, however, in name only. OKW, headed by General-feldmarschall Wilhelm Keitel, was no true joint staff. Naval and air force members were relatively junior officers.[24]

Reichsmarschall Hermann Goering and Admiral Raeder, furthermore, remained outside and above it in personal relationship with Hitler. Goering as Reichsmarschall outranked Keitel who, as chief of all the armed services, should have been his superior. In addition, Goering held a top Cabinet post as Minister of Aviation which further set him out of reach of OKW. Finally, the Army, wedded to the notion of Germany as a Continental power, had long opposed unification of the services on the basis of equal representation and authority.[25] The effect of the Army view together with the independence of Goering and Raeder was to reduce OKW to the position of a second Army staff. As long as it had no direct responsibility for any one theater of operations OKW retained a certain perspective and capacity to co-ordinate the German war effort, even though the bulk of its co-ordination had to pass through Hitler himself. With the splitting of the western and eastern theaters, OKW, for all practical purposes, lost

---

[22] Translation of Fuehrer Directive No. 40 is reproduced below as Appendix C.

[23] *OKW/WFSt, KTB 1.I.–31.III.43*, 2–3 Jan 43; Recapitulation of Fuehrer Directives establishing OKW Theaters, 28 May 42, *OKW/WFSt, Quartiermeister im WFSt. Wehrmachtbefehlshaber Suedost (A.O.K. 12) Taetigkeitsbericht* and *Anlagen, VI.42.* See also The German High Command, a study by German Military Documents Section, WD G–2, 1946, MS. Hist Div files.

[24] See the Navy's complaint to Hitler on 13 April 1942 that there was no high-ranking naval officer on the Armed Forces High Command (OKW) and that

strategy was suffering thereby. Annex 8, Conf, 13 Apr 42, ONI, *Fuehrer Conferences, 1942.* What the Navy asked for (and apparently got) was not representation on OKW but a flag officer to provide liaison at the Fuehrer Headquarters. This underlined the fact that such co-ordination between the services as existed operated on a personal basis through Hitler and not through any formal joint organization. Part of the Navy's protest was directed at the very efficient liaison which Goering had established at the Fuehrer Headquarters for the Luftwaffe, although the Luftwaffe was actually no better represented on OKW than the Navy.

[25] Memo, *Standpunkt Heer und OKW, betreffend Denkschrift des Oberbefehlshaber des Heeres ueber Organisation der Wehrmachtfuehrung (7.III.38)*, 22 Mar 38. OKW file 1866; cf. MS # C–045 (Natzmer et al.) , a postwar study of the historical evolution of OKH, which clearly describes the German Army's opposition to any unification of the services as co-equal participants.

GERMAN HIGH COMMAND. *Left to right: Admiral Raeder, Navy; Field Marshal Keitel, chief of OKW; Hitler; and Reich Marshal Goering, Air Force.*

even that limited power to co-ordinate. Henceforth the only unity of command in Germany rested in the person of Hitler, who no longer had adequate machinery through which to exercise it.[26]

In the various theaters of operations after 1940 no effective machinery was ever established to exercise unified command.[27] In the west, during an actual enemy invasion, the army commanders in the battle areas were to have tactical control over the air force and naval units in their sectors. But the failure to give *OB WEST* a supreme command meant that co-ordination of the defense rested largely on such informal co-operation and liaison as the local commanders might choose to establish. The divided command would gravely handicap German preparedness. In the meantime, the chief positive result of the new top-level command organization was to free the OKW operational staff (the *Wehrmachtfuehrungsstab, WFSt,* under General der Artillerie Alfred Jodl) from responsibility for the war in Russia and so permit it to concentrate on the operational needs of the west, Italy, the Balkans, and Norway and Denmark.

Hitler's basic order sketched out the tactical doctrine that henceforth governed all planning for the defense of France. He decreed that the coast defenses should be so organized and troops so deployed that any invasion attempted could be smashed before the landing or immediately thereafter. The main defensive preparations were to be made in the places most suitable for large enemy landings. Beaches where only small surprise landings were possible were to be defended by strong points tied in, if possible, with the coastal batteries. The rest of the coast would be patrolled. All positions were to be designed for defense to the last man of the garrison. All should be equipped with weapons and supplies so that even if overrun by the enemy they would not be forced to surrender for lack of means to continue the fight.[28]

Five days after the issuance of this order, Hitler was profoundly shocked by the successful British raid on St. Nazaire. The spectacle of British ships, including a destroyer, sailing with impunity up the mouth of the Loire reputedly made him furious and focused his attention on the inadequacies of the French coastal defenses. The only immediate outcome, however, was the relief of Generalleutnant Karl Hilpert, *OB WEST* Chief of Staff. Hilpert was replaced by Generalmajor Kurt Zeitzler, who was close to Hitler, and who afterward became Chief of the General Staff of OKH.[29]

Later more sober study of the St. Nazaire experience showed even to Hitler that the responsible commanders in France did not have the resources to deal

---

[26] The organizational structure and evolution of OKW and OKH have been described in great detail by committees of German officers working under the auspices of the Historical Division between 1946 and 1948. See MSS # T–101, The German Armed Forces High Command (Winter *et al.*) and # T–111, The German Army High Command (Halder *et al.*).

[27] The only instance of a joint staff was *Gruppe XXI,* formed in early 1940 by upgrading the *XXI Corps.* Under the command of General der Infanterie Nikolaus von Falkenhorst, it was charged with the preparation and conduct of the Scandinavian campaign in 1940. *Gruppe XXI, KTB 20.II.–8.IV.40.*

[28] Fuehrer Directive No. 40. See below, Appendix C.

[29] Officer's Personnel Files, Generaloberst Kurt Zeitzler. *OKH/Heeres-Personalamt, Personalakten.* Still later Zeitzler was implicated in the 20 July 1944 conspiracy against Hitler and dismissed.

with determined enemy forays. While Allied strength was increasing, German strength had been gradually weakened to nourish the operations against Russia. Admiral Raeder told Hitler bluntly: "We have no means of repulsing an enemy attempt." Even better defenses at St. Nazaire, in the opinion of Raeder, would not have stopped a determined Allied attack; the only thing that could have helped would have been strong naval forces and adequate air reconnaissance. Then he ventured a prophecy: "In view of the shortages everywhere and the necessity of using numerous makeshift defense measures, experience will show that there will constantly be new shortcomings in our defenses and new demands made upon them." [30] Despite this accurate forecast of things to come, Hitler was not then, and never would be, convinced that defense could not be made invulnerable if enough concrete and resolution could be poured into it. His retort to the St. Nazaire raid was to direct that submarine bases be so well protected that successful raids on them thenceforth would be impossible.

In August 1942 he expanded his notions of a concrete coastal wall. In a conference with Field Marshal Keitel and other high-ranking Army officers he proposed that fortress construction in France should proceed with "fanatic energy [*Fanatismus*]" during the coming winter. The object must be to build many small strong points to house from thirty to seventy men each, armed with machine guns and "a few other weapons," chiefly anti-tank guns. A continuous belt of interlocking fire must be created emanating from concrete structures designed to be proof against Allied bombing and naval shell-fire.[31] Behind this emphasis on fixed defenses lay the realization of a grave shortage of troops. Already in the summer of 1942 Hitler estimated that ten to twelve more divisions were needed to establish a solid defense along the *OB WEST* coast line, but reserves to make up this deficit were not available.

As the summer came to an end, prospects of victory in Russia were again clouded by the north winds. In the meantime the large-scale raid by Canadian troops at Dieppe in the latter part of August, though considered an absolute failure by the Germans, nevertheless forcibly called attention to the increasing threat of full-scale invasion by the Western Powers. On 29 September, Hitler called in Goering, Reich Minister Albert Speer (Chief of Organization Todt), Rundstedt, Generalleutnant Guenther Blumentritt (who had relieved Zeitzler as Chief of Staff *OB WEST* only a few days before), General der Pioniere Alfred Jacob (Chief Engineer of OKH), Generalleutnant Rudolf Schmetzer (Inspector of Land Fortresses for *OB WEST*), and certain other staff officers for a three-hour conference in the small Cabinet sitting room of the Reich Chancellery.[32] The Fuehrer began by expressing his confidence that Russia would be defeated in 1943 by a German push in the spring toward Mesopotamia in the south. He then

---

[30] Conf, 13 Apr 42, ONI, *Fuehrer Conferences, 1942.*

[31] Memo, *Aktennotiz ueber Fuehrerbesprechung am 2.VIII.42 im Fuehrerhauptquartier,* 3 Aug 42, *General der Pioniere und Festungen b.Ob.d.H. OKH/Op. Abt., Kuestenschutz Kanalkueste 20.VI.42– 18.V.44.*

[32] *Fuehrerrede zum Ausbau des Atlantik–Walles am 29.IX.42,* 3 Oct 42. OKH/Op. Abt., *Kuestenschutz Kanalkueste 20.VI.42–18.V.44.*

admitted grave concern over the possibility of the creation of a second front in the west. There was no question of capitulation, he said, "but I must freely admit . . . that a major landing of the enemy in the west would bring us to a generally critical position." The gravest present threat was to Norway, he believed, but ultimately it was France that would be invaded because such an operation would require the least amount of shipping tonnage.

Hitler then went on to analyze the Dieppe experience. Even though the British field order for the raid, clearly specifying a withdrawal of forces after nine hours, was captured and studied by the Germans, apparently the German generals involved reported and Hitler believed that Dieppe was actually a major landing attempt that failed. On that premise he compared the introduction of large-scale amphibious operations at Dieppe to the introduction of the tank at Cambrai in World War I. In both cases, he pointed out, the British had failed through having planned only the meeting engagement, leaving the follow-up to the initiative of the field commanders who were too timid to exploit their advantage. After Cambrai both British and Germans drew the false lesson that the tank was technically a failure and so "they poured out the baby with the bath." He warned now against a false deduction on the German side that amphibious operations against the coast of France were proved impossible by Dieppe. This time, he said, the British cannot arrive at a similar conclusion, simply because they have no alternative but to try again.

The Germans must prepare the strongest possible defenses. The defenses must be prepared, furthermore, on the assumption that the Allies would enjoy air and naval supremacy. The crushing weight of Allied bombs and shells, he believed, could be withstood only by concrete. Not only that, but massive concrete works, he believed, had a psychological as well as a physical strength. Hitler pointed out that the very existence of the West Wall had deterred Daladier in 1938 from threatening military action during the Czechoslovakia crisis. The West Wall repeated along the coast would have the same deterrent effect on the Western Allies. Hitler asked for 15,000 concrete strong points for the new "Atlantic Wall" to be defended by 300,000 men. The goal was an impervious, permanent defense ring. Since the amount of time available to build it was uncertain, construction was to follow a strict priority. In Hitler's view, the most important job was to protect the U-boat bases. He listed for defense thereafter: harbors for coastal traffic, harbors suitable for enemy landings (a reflection of the Dieppe experience), the Channel Islands, and finally landing places on the open coast. Beaches deemed most likely to be used in a major invasion attempt were to be fortified first. But, as Hitler pointed out, since the Navy could not guarantee that any portion of the coast was safe, the whole would have to be walled up eventually.

It was an ambitious program. Hitler ordered that it be completed by 1 May 1943; Organization Todt thought it would be lucky to get 40 percent finished by that time. At such a rate the defense of the coast proper, having the lowest priority, became a very long-range program which would probably not be completed before the Allies struck. In any case it was fantastic to suppose that even a first-class military power could be strong everywhere along the entire coast line from the Mediterranean to Norway. It followed that defense preparations would be concentrated in accordance with estimates of Allied intentions. But German intelligence services notably failed to supply reliable information about the Western Allies. The sparseness of accurate intelligence, the plethora of rumors, and the natural jitteriness of being on the strategic defensive led to constantly revised guesses that at one time or another pointed out grave threats to virtually every section of the coast. Division commanders, corps commanders, army commanders freely contributed predictions that their own sectors had been selected for the enemy landings. They were moved sometimes by logic, more often by desire to compete for the limited supplies of troops and materiel. They seldom had any sure knowledge of what was being brewed across the Channel. Hitler's intuition was no less erratic: at various times he picked the Gironde, Brittany, the Cotentin, the Pas-de-Calais, and Norway. In late 1943 a captured British agent indicated that the Allies intended to strike in the Netherlands.[33] He was not believed, and the Netherlands actually remained about the only sector in the west exempt from special attention as a threatened area.

Although the Germans could never be sure that any sector of the coast was safe, the necessity for concentrating their own forces led them to categorize roughly the degrees of danger. It was common consensus from the beginning that the sector of the *Fifteenth Army* from the Seine to the Schelde was most gravely if not uniquely threatened. This estimate, however, was based on reasoning, not on intelligence. It was thought the Allies would strike here because it was close to Germany and the Ruhr, and because the short Channel crossing would simplify the problems of air support and sea reinforcement. Strategically Allied success in this sector would cut off the whole of the German forces to the south.

The conclusion that the *Kanalkueste*[34] was the most likely place for a major landing, arrived at in the early days of planning the Atlantic Wall, was never seriously shaken by any later information. Even when other sectors appeared threatened, the threats were deemed diversionary. Rationalization had a persuasiveness that the meager reports of fact never had. Furthermore, once the concrete was poured, the original estimate became peculiarly difficult to alter. During 1942, for instance, four times as much concrete was allotted the left corps of *Fifteenth Army* as to the *LXXXIV Corps* in Normandy and Brittany.[35] By May 1943 the concentration of troops along the *Fifteenth Army* coast was almost three times as heavy as in *Seventh Army*—the army that would oppose the invasion.[36]

In the summer of that year a new importance was given to the Pas-de-Calais area. It was here that Hitler planned to install his *Vergeltungs* (vengeance) weapons, the long-range rockets and pilotless

[33] *OKW/WFSt, KTB 1.IX.–31.XII.43*, 31 Oct 43.

[34] Term generally coinciding with the sector of *Fifteenth Army*. It includes the Pas-de-Calais area and the Somme–Seine coast.

[35] MS # B–234 (Generalleutnant Max Pemsel, CofS *Seventh Army*).

[36] *Schematische Kriegsgliederung*, 1 May 43. *OKH/Op.Abt.*; see also Rundstedt Report, 25 Oct 43.

ENEMY COAST ARTILLERY *in the Pas-de-Calais area. Heavy concrete casemate under construction (above), and (below) laborers at work on casemate.*

aircraft from which he expected a complete reversal of the course of the war. He believed that the V-weapons would prove so dangerous to England that the Allies, whatever their previous plans might have been, would be forced to attack directly to overrun the launching sites. This estimate, of course, entailed the further conclusion that the bulk of the German defenses should be emplaced to defend the rocket sites. In June 1943 Hitler assigned construction priority to those portions of the Atlantic Wall defending rocket-launching areas.[37]

Although by far the strongest fortified portion of the French coast, even the *Kanalkueste* never became anything like the impregnable fortress that German propaganda advertised. Hitler, having ordered the creation of a wall of concrete and fire which could stop any invasion at the water's edge, apparently believed that such a wall would be built and paid little further attention to it. He never saw any portion of the western fortifications. After leaving Paris in triumph in the summer of 1940 he did not set foot on French soil again until a week after the Allied invasion in June 1944.[38] Absorbed with the struggle against Russia, he scarcely heeded the stream of memoranda in which the Commander in Chief West pointed out

and reiterated the entire inadequacy of German preparations for the defense of France.

In the spring of 1943 Rundstedt went to Berchtesgaden to present his case in person. But Hitler was still not interested in bad news from the west. He was looking forward to great victories in the east. He talked of how two thousand German tanks would annihilate at least ninety Russian divisions in the new spring offensive. Rundstedt, after abrupt dismissal, returned to France and embarked on a comprehensive survey of the state of his defenses. It was this survey which resulted in the detailed report of 25 October. This he forwarded to OKW with a special request that it be brought to the personal attention of Hitler.[39]

Impact of the Russian and Mediterranean Fronts

Rundstedt said little about the Atlantic Wall. He mentioned delays in naval construction due to a faulty priority system which had only just been straightened out. But for the most part he was less interested in the state of the permanent defenses than in the combat value of his troops. The wall, he said, was valuable for fighting as well as for propaganda, "but it must not be believed that this wall cannot be overcome." Strongly defended fortifications might be a more or less efficient means of weakening the attacking enemy by splitting his forces, but victory in the west could be achieved only by rapidly mounted, strong counterattacks.[40]

In the light of this basic requirement, Rundstedt pointed out how thin his line

---

[37] *OKW/WFSt, KTB 1.VII—31.VIII.43*, 14 Jul 43, referring to conference of 28 June. The term, "V–1," recommended by Reich Minister Josef Paul Goebbels and approved by Hitler, was adopted as "an instrument of propaganda" by directive of OKW: "The V used in this designation is . . . to counteract the enemy's usage of this letter (Victory), and the numeral 1 is to point toward other possible means of stepping up this type of warfare by remote control against England." *Seekriegsleitung/1.Abt., KTB 1.–30.VI.44*, 25 Jun 44.

[38] MS # T–121 (Zimmermann *et al.*). See below, Ch. X.

[39] MS # T–121.

[40] Rundstedt Report, 25 Oct 43.

of defense really was. The average coastal sector of a single division ranged from 50 miles in the *Fifteenth Army* sector to 120 miles in the *Seventh Army* sector and 217 miles along the Atlantic coast.[41] The coastal divisions, moreover, were almost all understrength—a good many had only two regiments. Their armament, particularly in antitank weapons and artillery, was often inadequate for a maximum defense of their positions. Most serious of all, in Rundstedt's eyes, was their almost total lack of transport.

All these deficiencies were the direct result of the drain on the German war economy to maintain the Russian and Mediterranean fronts. The opening of the Russian front in 1941 had turned the west into a kind of replacement center. Toward the end of that year the Commander in Chief West was already complaining that his troops were being siphoned off at a dangerous rate.[42] The complaint was futile; the process, in fact, had only just begun. From 1942 "the hard-pressed Eastern Front always short of forces looked with envy at the apparently sleeping army in the west, and at every crisis the higher commanders in the east . . . demanded that the reservoir be tapped. In the need of the moment these troops were usually conceded."[43]

In 1942 the process of east–west troop

exchanges was regularized. In May the Commander in Chief West issued an order concerning the reconstitution of divisions shifted from the Russian front to France emphasizing speed in re-equipping these divisions and the importance of maintaining the special toughness (*Ost-Haerte*) of the troops. In the same order Rundstedt warned against allowing the troops who had returned from the east to patronize those troops permanently stationed in the west. The latter, he pointed out, had done their duty and it was not their fault that they could not be used for fighting in the east.[44] In short, it was made a matter of policy that the west should be permanently garrisoned only by troops who because of various disabilities could not be used in the hard fighting in Russia. OKH, in October, proposed a regular monthly exchange of two divisions between *Army Group Center* and *OB WEST* and one division between *Army Group North* and the Norway garrison. OKH listed ten infantry divisions under *OB WEST* command which were immediately suitable for exchange with the east. At the same time it was proposed not to transfer any mobile divisions (armored and motorized) until spring to avoid using them up in winter fighting in Russia. But that was like trying to hold on to a parasol in a hurricane. A month later, Hitler ordered the immediate transfer of the *6th Panzer Division* from the west to the sector of Stalino–Volchansk. In the first eleven months after October 1942 the east–west exchange system took

---

[41] Note that this compared to an average sector on the Russian front of 32.5 miles to a corps. *OKH, Generalstab des Heeres* (cited hereafter as *OKH, Gen.St.d.H.*) /*Organisationsabteilung, KTB Anlagen,* 1943.

[42] Ltr, *OB WEST to OKH/Op.Abt.,* 19 Dec 41, *OKH/OP.Abt., Gliederung West, Bd. IV, 9.VIII.41–4.I.42.*

[43] MS # B–672 (Generalmajor Horst Freiherr Treusch v. Buttlar-Brandenfels (OKW)). This is a commentary on Zimmermann's preliminary narrative of *OB WEST* (MS # B–308).

[44] *Grundlegender Befehl des Oberbefehlshabers West Nr. 3, Aufgaben der Ost–Divisionen,* 10 May 42. *OKW/WFSt, 1. Generalstabsoffizier Heer* (referred to hereafter as *OKW/WFSt, Op. (H)), Grundlegende Befehle West 22.X.42–7.V.44.*

twenty-two infantry and six armored or motorized divisions out of the west. This was in addition to a constant weeding out of the best personnel and equipment from divisions considered unsuitable as a whole for east duty.[45]

Thus in 1943, a year of increasing threats of attack from the west, the German armies in France had not even held their own. General Blumentritt, the *OB WEST* chief of staff, in September summarized the deterioration for the high command. A year ago, he pointed out, the Atlantic Wall had been garrisoned with twenty-two infantry divisions most of which had three regiments. In reserve were six infantry and seven fully mobile, first-class armored or motorized divisions. Now, he continued, in a much more dangerous situation, the garrison infantry divisions had increased to twenty-seven, but this increase was largely nullified by the reduction of most of the divisions to two regiments. In reserve were six armored or motorized divisions and seven infantry divisions, of which three were new organizations. In other words, though the holding strength remained about constant in numbers the quality had certainly declined; the striking power had decreased slightly in numbers and very substantially in mobility.[46]

There was no appeasing the hunger of the Eastern Front. The continual protests of the Commander in Chief West and even Hitler's own resolution toward the end of 1943 to halt the weakening of the west were alike swept aside by the demands for more and more men to halt the tide of Russian victories. The German Army went into Russia in June 1941 with 3,300,000 men.[47] By the spring of 1943, despite every effort to get replacements, the eastern army had been reduced by 600,000. Built back up to three million for the summer offensive, it suffered another net reduction of a half million by September.[48] In 1943 alone, the Germans estimated that they had a total of 2,086,-000 casualties in the east, of which 677,-000 were permanent losses (that is, the killed and missing, unfit, and one-third of all wounded).[49] The net losses continued to mount so that in the year from July 1943 through June 1944 the gap between

---

[45] Various papers in *Austausch Ost–West, 1.IX.42–28.II.44, OKH/Op.Abt.* A total of 28 infantry divisions, 4 armored divisions, 2 motorized divisions, and 4 smaller units were alerted for service in the east after 1 October 1942.

[46] *OKW/WFSt, KTB 1.IX.–31.XII.43.* For figures as of 1 Sep 42, cf. Memo, *West–Divisionen, die ab 1.10.42 zur Verlegung in den Osten geeignet sind,* 1 Sep 42. *OKH/Op.Abt., Austausch Ost–West 1.IX.–42–28.II.44.* The panzer and panzer grenadier divisions contained substantially more men than the two-regiment infantry divisions. See below, Ch. VII.

[47] This is approximately the same strength as the maximum build-up of the U.S. Army on the Continent in 1945.

[48] *OKH, Gen.St.d.H./Organisationsabteilung* (referred to hereafter as *OKH/Org. Abt.*), *KTB Anlagen,* 1943.

[49] Memo, *Berechnungsunterlagen fuer Schaubild "Zugaenge und Abgaenge des Ostheeres vom November 42 bis Oktober 43" (Stand 5.XII.43),* 14 Dec 43. *OKH/Org.Abt., KTB Anlagen 1.XII.–10.XII.43.* German losses (killed, missing, and wounded) from June 1941 to December 1943 totaled 3,726,000, of which 3,513,000 were lost on the Eastern Front. Rpt, *Personelle blutige Verluste vom 22.Juni 1941 bis 31.Dezember 1943,* 4 Jan 44. *OKH/Generalquartiermeister, der Heeresarzt, OKH/Org.Abt., Arzt Meldungen, Monatsmeldungen ab 1.VII.43.* The proportions of wounded to total casualties and of seriously wounded to those returnable to duty were almost identical in the U.S. Army. See [John E. Henderson] The Procurement and Use of Manpower in the European Theater (The Administrative and Logistical History of the ETO: Part IX), MS, pp. 84–85. Hist Div files.

losses and replacements amounted to 535,000.[50]

Even these figures do not truly reflect the exhaustion of the German Army. Of 151 German Army divisions listed in the OKH order of battle for the Russian front in December 1943, ten panzer and fifty infantry divisions were "fought out" (*abgekaempft*) or, in other words, of negligible combat value. Eleven of the named infantry "divisions" were actually only Kampfgruppen. At the same time there were twelve full divisions in Italy, while *OB WEST* had forty-six divisions plus two regiments that were operational and another seven divisions in process of formation. These figures strikingly reveal the strain exerted by the Russian war: *the number of divisions in the east which needed replacement and reconstitution was greater than the total number of divisions in the two western theaters.*[51]

The war in Russia was always the principal vacuum into which German resources were sucked and destroyed, but Allied attacks on North Africa in November 1942 and subsequent Allied Mediterranean operations superimposed an additional strain which contributed substantially to the weakening of the west. General der Artillerie Walter Warlimont of OKW [52] concluded after the war that the invasion of North Africa, which came as a complete surprise to Hitler, was actually "decisive for the whole conduct of the war"

for it established a "springboard for a thrust into the groin of Fortress Europe, the naturally weak and practically unprepared south flank." [53] One immediate result of Allied landings in North Africa on 8 November 1942 was to force German occupation of the whole of France and add some four hundred miles of Mediterranean coast line to *OB WEST's* responsibilities.

Plans for the occupation of Vichy France were completed in July 1942. Troops were alerted on 7 November, the day before the Allied landings in North Africa. Ten divisions under two armies (the *First* and *Army Felber*) moved across the Demarcation Line on 11 November and, without opposition from the French, occupied the Spanish border and the Mediterranean coast as far as Toulon. The area from there east and as far north as a line between Lyon and the Swiss border was taken over at the same time by the Italian *Fourth Army*, which moved in with six divisions and three corps headquarters. In December the units under the German *First Army* withdrew and *First Army* responsibility was thereafter limited to the Atlantic coast line as far north as the Loire River. The Mediterranean became the responsibility of *Army Felber*.[54]

These arrangements lasted about six months. In June 1943 Rundstedt notified General der Infanterie Hans-Gustav Felber that Italian collapse seemed possible and he was therefore to prepare to relieve

---

[50] Chart, *Gesamt Zu- u. Abgaenge des Feldheeres in der Zeit vom 1.VII.43–30.VI.44,* 3 Jul 44. *OKH/-Org.Abt., KTB Anlagen,* 1944.

[51] *OKH/Org.Abt., KTB Anlagen, 1.XII.–10.XII.43; OKW/WFSt, KTB 1.IX–3.XII.43,* 3 Nov 43. To this Russian pressure U. S. lend-lease contributed enormously. See Pogue, The Supreme Command.

[52] Warlimont was deputy chief of the Armed Forces Operations Staff (WFSt).

[53] MS # T–121 (Zimmermann *et al.*) .

[54] *Armeeoberkommando 7* (referred to hereafter as *Seventh Army*) , *KTB IX.–XII.42* and *Anlagen; Armeeoberkommando 1* (referred to hereafter as *First Army*) , *KTB 10.VII.–31.XII.42* and *Anlagen; Hoeheres Kommando XXXXV (Armee Felber), Korpsbefehle, Ia 22.III.40–29.IX.42.*

the *Fourth Army*. His local commanders were to try to get the Italians to continue fighting on the side of the Germans, but those who could not be persuaded were to be disarmed. Labor troops were to be formed of those willing to work, and the rest were to be regarded as prisoners of war.

During the campaign in Sicily and through the fall of Mussolini the *Fourth Army* held on in France. But on 10 August the Italian supreme command proposed withdrawal of the army to defend Italy against the expected Allied invasion of the mainland.[55] Two days later Felber was relieved by General der Infanterie Georg von Sodenstern. During the next few weeks the command in the south was renamed the *Nineteenth Army* and preparations were completed to relieve the Italians. The relief, which absorbed four German divisions, was carried out early in September. Except for a brief fight at the Mount Cenis tunnel by units of the Italian *5th Alpini Division* the relief was peaceful. But in the course of it about 40,-000 Italian troops were made prisoner and sent into the interior of France as labor troops. No more than a handful volunteered to fight beside the Germans.[56]

Southern France was only one of the vacuums created by Italian collapse. As soon as collapse seemed imminent the Germans made plans to shift troops into the Italian peninsula and into the Balkans. The total number required was not large, but the added strain was severe. The planned 1943 summer offensive in Russia (Operation *ZITADELLE*), becoming an exhausting defensive action, drew off so many troops that OKW in July could find only twelve divisions available for occupying Italy.[57] All of these were already either in northern Italy or under *OB WEST* command. Impoverished by contributions to the Russian war, *OB WEST* was now to be beggared to nourish the Mediterranean. Before 1 September, Rundstedt had given up eight infantry and nine panzer divisions to Africa and Italy and one infantry and one panzer division to the Balkans. These comprised, moreover, some of the best-quality troops remaining in the west after earlier withdrawals for Russia.[58]

Besides forcing direct contributions of troops, Allied attacks in Italy weakened the whole defense system of the west by creating invasion threats to southern France. Although Rundstedt never reckoned with a major landing on his Mediterranean coast, he did count as probable a diversionary attack tied in with a large-scale invasion in the northwest. In his October report he pointed out that the Rhône Valley was a natural invasion route to the north and that the ports of Toulon and Marseille would undoubtedly be tempting to the Allies. General Sodenstern in August 1943 noted the clear strategic connection between thrusts from the north and south and recalled that the

---

[55] A more likely reason was to get troops for the defense of Italy against the Germans and particularly to defend Rome. See Mario Roatta, *Otto Milioni di Baionette* (Milan, 1943), p. 287.

[56] *OKW/WFSt, KTB 1.VII.–31.VIII.43*, 23–28 Aug 43; *First Army, KTB 1.VII.–30.IX.43* and *Anlagen*; *Armeeoberkommando 19* (referred to hereafter as *Nineteenth Army*), *KTB 20.VI.–31.XII.43* and *Anlagen*.

[57] *OKW/WFSt, KTB 1.VII.–31.VIII.43*, 14 Jul 43.

[58] *OKW/WFSt, KTB 1.IX.–31.XII.43*, 11 Sep 43. Total withdrawals for Russia and the Mediterranean up to 1 September 1943 were thus 31 infantry and 16 mobile divisions. The figures given by Rundstedt in his report as of 1 October 1943 were 36 infantry and 17 mobile divisions.

Rhône Valley had been a historic route to the upper Rhine for invading armies since the wars of Caesar.[59]

The "three-front" war all but exhausted the normal German manpower reservoirs. The Germans then turned to extraordinary sources to fill up the decimated ranks of the west army. The principal last-ditch sources were foreign personnel (chiefly Russian), young recruits of the classes of 1925 and 1926, convalescents often with physical disabilities, organizational overhead, and troops in occupied areas comparatively safe from invasion threats, like Norway and Denmark. Divisions that remained in the west but had their rosters combed out for replacements for eastern service were replenished with men rated less fit for combat. Divisions transferred to the east were replaced with new formations, sometimes with good personnel, more often with a mixture of fit and unfit, experienced and green, German and foreign.

In June 1941 the German Army was entirely German and prided itself on its "racial purity." With the opening of the Russian campaign, German propaganda began to internationalize German war aims as a crusade against Bolshevism. At the same time the requirements for men to administer and defend vast occupied territories while well over two million men fought in the Russian battlefields made imperative the opening of almost any conceivable additional source of manpower. "Racial Germans" (*Volksdeutsche*), especially from Poland, were given conditional German citizenship and under this fiction made subject to the draft. As time went on the fiction was ex-

tended often to persons who could not even speak German. Recruiting was begun also in the occupied territories of Russia and units formed of the so-called *Freiwilligen* (volunteers). As the pressure for more and more men developed, the *Freiwilligen*, too, lost more and more of their volunteer character. In the late fall of 1941 Hitler authorized the employment of Russian prisoners in the German Army, formalizing a procedure already applied by field commanders. The majority of the *Hilfswillige* (auxiliaries) were employed as labor troops in war areas. Through increasing admixture with these three categories, *Volksdeutsche*, *Freiwillige*, and *Hilfswillige*, the "racial purity" of the German Army became more and more dilute.[60] In 1944 the Army included as "volunteers" from occupied and allied territories: French, Italians, Croatians, Hungarians, Românians, Poles, Finns, Estonians, Letts, Lithuanians, North Africans, Negroes, Asiatics, Russians, Ukrainians, Ruthenians, Kazaks, North-Caucasians, Georgians, Azerbaijani, Armenians, Turkomans, Volga-Tatars, Volga-Finns, Kalmucks, Crimean Tatars, and even Indians.

The *Volksdeutschen*, drawn chiefly from territories which Germany intended to integrate with the Reich, were originally classified in four categories according to the degree of their overt sympathy with the Nazi party. The majority were placed in the third category (*Volksliste drei*) comprising racial Germans who despite previous integration in the Polish national culture were deemed amenable to Germanization.[61] *Volksliste drei* persons were

---

[59] Notes written in August 1943, appended to MS # B–276 (Sodenstern).

[60] German Manpower. MS cited n. 12.

[61] Category I included the active Nazis; II, the passive Nazis who had, however, preserved their

given a ten-year probationary citizenship and drafted if of military age. Although integrated for the most part in the Army they were forbidden to rise above the rank of private first class.[62]

Rundstedt, in October 1943, commented on the lower morale of the *Volksdeutschen,* due, he thought, not to ill will on their part but to the fact that their families were not being treated like the families of front-line German soldiers. But the reliability of the *Volksdeutschen* concerned him much less than that of the volunteer Russian combat battalions which his command had been forced to accept in the latter part of the year.[63] The original idea back of the formation of the *Ost* (east) battalions was to employ anti-Red Russian peoples (generally prisoners of war) in the crusade against the Soviet Union. When the third great German summer offensive soured in 1943 and the German armies began a retrograde movement that had all the earmarks of final retreat, the anti-Bolshevik recruits became increasingly unreliable and it was decided to transfer them to the west in exchange for German troops. In September OKW ordered the exchange on the basis of two *Ost* battalions for one German battalion.[64] At that time OKH reported that 15,800 *Osttruppen* were trained and that 25,000 more would be trained in November and December. During September and October, about forty-five Cossack, Georgian, North-Caucausian, Turkoman,

Armenian, Volga-Tatar, Azerbaijanian, Volga-Finn, and miscellaneous *Ost* battalions were brought into the *OB WEST* sector.[65] The original ratio of one German for two *Ost* battalions was considerably modified to the advantage of the Russian theater. Plans at the end of October were to exchange thirty-two more *Ost* battalions for twenty-six German battalions of which *OB WEST* would furnish twenty and Norway and Denmark the remaining six. By May 1944 *Seventh Army* alone had twenty-three *Ost* battalions of infantry.[66] This represented about one-sixth of the total number of rifle battalions in the Army. In the *LXXXIV Corps* sector in Normandy and Brittany, out of forty-two rifle battalions, eight were composed of *Osttruppen.*

Besides recruiting prisoners of war, the Germans added to their military manpower by relaxing physical standards. At the end of 1943 the physical fitness categories were cut down from four to three. The limited service classification was abolished and men were to be graded as fit for service at the front, fit for service in Germany, or totally unfit. Those with relatively minor ear, stomach, and lung ailments were to be sent to the front. Convalescence time was ordered cut down.[67] No accurate picture of the physical state of the German Army in the west is possible. Physical standards were unquestionably much lower than in Allied armies. But although the majority of troops in the west were considered unfit for combat in

Germanic spirit; and IV, those hostile to integration into the German state. See *Der Prozess gegen die Hauptkriegsverbrecher vor dem Internationalen Militaergerichtshof* (Nuremberg, 1947), III, 653.

[62] WD TM–E # 30–451, Military Intelligence Division, The German Replacement Army *(Ersatzheer).*

[63] Rundstedt Report, 25 Oct 43.

[64] *OKW/WFSt, KTB 1.IX.–31.XII.43,* 25 Sep 43.

[65] *OKH/Op.Abt., Kraefte Westen, Allgemein, Band III, 24.VII.42–1.XI.43.*

[66] *Kriegsgliederung,* 18 May 44. *Seventh Army, KTB Anlagen 1.I.–30.VI.44.*

[67] *OKW/WFSt, KTB 1.IX.–31.XII.43,* 5 Dec 43.

Russia, the cause of unfitness was often inadequate training, lack of transport, and lack of equipment rather than the physical condition of the men.

In the whole German Army the average age in 1944 was 31.5 years, four and a half years older than the average age of the German Western Front Army in 1917 and more than six years older than the U. S. Army in 1943. Of an Army of 4,270,000 in December 1943 more than a million and a half were over 34 years old.[68] In the west the older-age classes as well as a large proportion of the relatively unfit were assigned to the static coastal divisions. Even so, repeated raids were made on the static divisions to sort out their best men for east duty. Eventually these divisions acquired a substantial number of the overage, the very young (classes of 1925 and 1926), men with third-degree frostbite, *Volksdeutsche* (which were used up to 8 percent of division strength), and *Osttruppen*. The average age of the *709th Division* which held the east coast of the Cotentin was thirty-six.[69] The fact that one whole division was almost entirely composed of men suffering from stomach ailments is dramatic, if somewhat misleading, evidence of the lengths to which German leaders went to fill up the ranks of the Army. It is misleading because, in contrast to the static coastal divisions, the offensive divisions (infantry, parachute, armored, and SS) contained excellent personnel. Though relatively new organizations, most seem to have been adequately trained and equipped by the time of the invasion.[70]

Many of the deficiencies of the German Army in the west at the end of 1943 were substantially made up in the first six months of 1944; others were chronic and could at best only be patched over with makeshift measures. The most serious of the latter was the lack of manpower and especially of first-class combat soldiers. It should be remembered, however, that this constituted primarily a strategic weakness. While it affected the strength of the Atlantic Wall defenses both in reducing the numbers and quality of the coastal garrisons, its real importance was not for the battle of the beaches but for the campaign to follow. In naturally strong coastal defenses even a relative handful of second-class troops could give good account of themselves. The drain of the three-front war meant above all that there were no strategic reserves. Losses could not be made up. The divisions in the west could not hope for replacement when they were fought out. The defensive crust could be thickened and spiked and made very formidable indeed, but only at the expense of putting everything forward. The

---

[68] *OKH/Org.Abt., KTB Anlagen,* 1943.

[69] Oberstleutnant Hoffmann, *Bericht Kampfgruppe von Schlieben 6.–22.VI.44,* cited hereafter as Hoffmann Report. *Seventh Army, KTB Anlagen 1.I.–30.VI.44.* Hoffmann was the commander of the *3d Battalion, 919th Regiment,* of the *709th Division.* After von Schlieben's forces had been bottled up in Cherbourg in June 1944, Hoffmann escaped by E-boat with orders to report to the *Seventh Army.* See below, Ch. X.

[70] MS # C–024 (Kraemer). This manuscript by Generalmajor der Waffen-SS Fritz Kraemer, *I SS Panzer Corps* chief of staff, represents a minority judgment among the views of the German generals reporting after the war on their difficulties. It is accepted here because as an admission contrary to interest it seems to carry more weight than the generally unspecific assertions of other commanders. The gist of the opposing view was that the troops were not so thoroughly trained as they might have been. But this is a relative judgment and it is seldom clear what standards the commanders had in mind. For a discussion of certain deficiencies in training and equipment, see below, Ch. VII.

enemy was hollow and he would be shown so in the later phases of OVERLORD.

Rebuilding the Western Defenses

Rundstedt's report of 25 October on the weakness of the western defenses was read by Hitler; his reply was the issuance on 3 November of Fuehrer Directive No. 51, the second basic order dealing with the west.[71] The order was, in fact, elicited not only by Rundstedt's bill of particulars but by the military reverses that the German armies suffered in the east and south in the course of the year and the growing conviction that the Allies would soon seek a decision in the west. The bitter and costly fighting of the last two and half years against Bolshevism, Hitler wrote, had strained to the utmost German military capacities. That strain had to be borne, but now while the danger in the east remained it was outweighed by the threat from the west where enemy success would strike immediately at the heart of the German war economy. Therefore, there should be no more weakening of the west in favor of other theaters. Threatened portions of the coast line were to be strengthened by the maximum emplacement of coastal artillery, fixed antitank weapons, dug-in tanks, mines, and so on. At the same time, as security against the possibility of any enemy eruption through the coastal crust, the maximum mobile reserves should be created for rapid counterattack.

The Army would submit a plan to equip every panzer and panzer grenadier division with ninety-three Mark IV tanks or assault guns and with strong antitank

defenses by the end of December 1943. Reserve panzer divisions should be fully equipped;[72] antitank guns and machine guns were to be delivered in quantity to *OB WEST* units. It was forbidden to transfer armored units out of the west without Hitler's specific approval. *OB WEST* would conduct exercises to plan the shift of partly mobile units from portions of the coast not threatened by attack. The Luftwaffe and Navy were ordered to strengthen their defenses. Hitler concluded with an exhortation to maximum effort in preparing for the expected "decisive struggle in the west."

The order against weakening the west could not, or at least would not, be strictly carried out. On 23 November *OB WEST* was directed to speed up the reorganization of the *60th Panzer Grenadier Division* for immediate transfer to the east. On 3 December, 10,000 men of the class of 1925 were ordered pruned from divisions in the west to be replaced with men who had been previously deferred for occupational reasons. At about the same time the number of heavy weapons allotted to the west was reduced in favor of the east. During 1944 the troop transfers would continue.[73]

These continued transfers, however, were in the course of the first half of 1944 more than made up. The failure to adhere to the letter of Directive 51 revealed the continuing pressure of the war in the east, but more striking was the vigor and success with which the rebuilding of the west was undertaken despite that pressure. November 1943 thus marked an im-

---

[71] Translation reproduced below as Appendix D.

[72] See below, Ch. VII, for discussion of various types of German divisions.

[73] *OKW/WFSt, KTB 1.IX.–31.XII.43*, 23 Nov, 3 and 11 Dec 43.

portant new beginning in German defense preparations in the west. The new beginning was signalized in the same month by the introduction of Generalfeldmarschall Erwin Rommel, the famed desert tactician, into the western scene.

The circumstances of Rommel's selection are somewhat confused. Since the summer of 1943 Rommel had been in northern Italy at the head of *Army Group B*—the force that moved in when it became clear that the Mussolini partnership was on the point of collapse. Meanwhile, operations in Sicily and against the Allied landings in the south were directed by Generalfeldmarschall Albert Kesselring (*OB SUED*). At Hitler's wish, plans had been worked out and orders issued as early as August 1943 for the eventual assumption of command by Rommel over all German forces in Italy. The intention of making Rommel the theater commander in Italy was adhered to until the latter part of October, when, for reasons unknown, Hitler changed his mind and on the 25th appointed Kesselring instead.[74] This choice in effect left Rommel and his staff surplus at a time when Hitler and OKW were seeking new means to strengthen the west against Allied invasion threats. Hitler himself had long been convinced of the desirability of having a high command in reserve and he seized this opportunity.[75] Three days after Kesselring's appointment OKW had entered

formal proposals for the constitution of a reserve army group headquarters under Rommel earmarked for commitment wherever the main Allied invasion should come. The new headquarters was formed from the staff of *Army Group B* less various special staff officers and about half of the enlisted personnel. The reduced headquarters thus formed was redesignated *Army Group for Special Employment,* subordinated directly to OKW and transferred temporarily to Munich pending the commencement of its new duties.[76]

These were outlined in orders of 6 November. In preparation for his ultimate combat task Rommel was ordered to make tours of inspection of the coastal defenses of the west. He was to inspect first the defenses of Denmark and then those of Artois (roughly the *Kanalkueste*); thereafter he would on order examine the defense preparations in the Cotentin, the Netherlands, and Brittany. In each case he was directed to prepare operational studies for the employment of forces in defense and counterattack. He would examine the mobility, concentration, and combat readiness of all troops, but especially of the reserves. He would determine what units might be drawn from unthreatened portions of the coast, from reserve or school troops, and from home units to build a counterattacking force. He would make recommendations on the employment of armor in the operational zones.[77]

---

[74] With the new title of *OB SUEDWEST* and Commander, *Army Group C.* Details of the changes in German command in Italy will be found in H. M. Smyth, The Sicilian Campaign and the Surrender of Italy, a volume now under preparation in this series.

[75] MS # C–069a (Blumentritt); MS # C–069c (Buttlar-Brandenfels); and MS # C–069d (Zimmermann).

[76] *OKW/WFSt, KTB 1.IX.–31.XII.43,* 17 Oct 43 *et seq.* Rommel actually turned over comand in Italy on 21 November. See *Karteiblatt, Heeresgruppe B. OKH/Org. Abt.*

[77] Rad, Hitler to *OKH, Gen.St.d.H.,* 6 Nov 43. *OKH/Org.Abt., Bd. Chefsache 7.V.43–4.II.44;* cf. *OKW/WFSt, KTB 1.IX.–31.XII.43,* 28 Oct and 6 Nov 43.

FIELD MARSHAL ROMMEL *(left) inspecting coastal defenses.*

Hitler seems to have had a number of reasons for assigning this mission to the Rommel staff. He saw it as a means of securing effective personal control of the all-important battle with the main forces of the Western Allies, and probably was responsible for the suggestion that the Rommel staff be committed directly under OKW, bypassing the theater command.[78] Although OKW successfully argued that the proposal was not feasible in view of the smallness of Rommel's staff and the rank and importance of the theater commanders involved, the later his-

tory of the Rommel command in France suggests that the idea was only scotched, not killed. When Rundstedt was informed of the new command, OKW was careful to point out that it was not intended in any way as an abridgment of Rundstedt's authority. On the other hand, it was a recognition of the increasing burden of operational, training, and administrative responsibilities that were heaped on *OB WEST* in its multiple role as a defense command, an occupying force, a training command, and the base for the V-weapon war on England. The particular selection of Rommel undoubtedly had an additional morale motive. For the long-neg-

---

[78] *OKW/WFSt, KTB 1.IX.–31.XII.43,* 28 Oct 43.

lected west garrison troops the appointment of a commander with Rommel's reputation in combat was a stimulant and a dramatization of the new importance assigned to the west. Finally, the reserve command, considered in context with Directive 51, expressed a shift in Hitler's tactical thinking away from exclusive dependence on an impregnable wall defense toward the traditional German reliance on mobile operations.[79] Just how far Hitler intended to depart from his earlier insistence on a pure fortress defense, in which each inch of occupied ground was to be held to the last man and the last bullet, is not clear. It is clear and of considerable importance that this directive tended in that direction and that it was so interpreted by Rundstedt. Rundstedt was thereby encouraged to re-examine ways and means of shaking his army loose from the concrete of the Atlantic Wall, and the question of how the battle for France was to be fought was posed again with a new urgency.

German defense preparations in the west and the German conduct of operations in France can be understood only against the background of disagreement over tactics among the various commanders involved. In terms of abstract doctrine the disagreement was basic and clear-cut: it opposed the notion of linear defense to defense in depth, static warfare to mobile operations, the holding of ground to battles of annihilation, the primary dependence on concrete fortifications to the primary dependence on armored striking power. In practice, however, disagreements were blurred without being reconciled by the fact that few commanders believed in simple dependence on either alternative and that, since doctrine was at the mercy of limited means, it tended to shift in response to the expected availability of resources. It is extremely difficult therefore to line up the commanders on either side of the argument. But, although the line was neither clear nor fixed, it was nonetheless real and significant. Since Hitler and Rundstedt at the top of the hierarchy never arrived at clear-cut decisions themselves as to the basic tactics, shifting and relatively minor differences of emphasis in the lower command resulted in confusion and unworkable compromises particularly in the disposition and training of troops. The discussion of the varying points of view that follows can do no more than suggest the bases of that confusion without attempting to describe in full the stand of any one commander.

The problem of the defense of the west was immensely complex and perhaps insoluble. Hitler, at least after the possibility of defeating Russia had faded in 1943, looked forward to the forthcoming struggle in the west as his last chance to gain a decisive victory. On the other hand, his obsession with political prestige and his consequent reluctance to surrender ground voluntarily in order to gain strategic or tactical advantage committed him to a policy of rigid terrain defense not only in France but throughout the occupied territories. This basic conflict over the purpose of defense, whether it was to hold ground *in perpetuum* or gain military advantage for victory at arms was never decided. Plans were made, for instance, to evacuate Norway and Denmark in case of an invasion of France. OKW recommended in late 1943 that the troops

---

[79] MS # B–672 (Buttlar-Brandenfels).

in Italy be withdrawn to the north to save divisions for the main battles to be fought in Russia and France.[80] Hitler himself, as already noted, talked in his Directive 51 of the ruthless evacuation of coastal areas not under threat of attack to feed the main battle area when the time came. But when the time did come the evacuation was not carried out, probably both because Hitler no longer believed it possible and because he could not reconcile himself to the surrender of any portion of his conquests. The policy of rigid defense, meant, in the first instance, an impossible policy of defense for its own sake.

A certain rigidity of defense in the west, however, was required by purely military considerations. It was essential to hold the Allies at arm's length from the critical industrial areas of Germany, and it was highly desirable to take advantage of the strong position afforded by the sea barrier. These military arguments in favor of a stand at the coast line, however, were subject to interpretation, and the rigidity they seemed to dictate was only relative. The decision to build an Atlantic Wall was the initial admission that the elastic defense principles applied so successfully by the Russians in their vast territories could not be adopted in the west and that basically the German armies in the west must stand on a line. There was never any debate over the need for making this line as strong as possible through the construction of a system of permanent and field fortifications. The debate concerned only how the line was to be held: what de-

pendence was to be placed on stopping the enemy at the line itself, and where reserves should be located and how employed.

Hitler believed in 1942 and probably again in 1944 [81] that the line could be made so strong that the enemy landing attempt could be smashed at the water's edge within the first twenty-four hours. Rundstedt concurred that this was the ideal. He pointed out that the experiences of Dieppe and Sicily both confirmed that the enemy's weakest moment was at the time of landing. While still afloat he would be without cover and have reduced fire power.[82] Later reports on the Salerno landings led to the same conclusion through the observation that any other defensive course was foredoomed to failure. Generalmajor Viktor Marnitz reported that at Salerno the German reserves, although located near the coast (from three to five kilometers inland), had been unable to counterattack across the open terrain under heavy Allied naval artillery fire.[83] Allied air attacks contributed to the difficulties of forming counterattacks. Strong points along the coast had held out well but for the most part the Allies had avoided them, landing between them and infiltrating inland to seize transportation junctions. Allied troops had not been

---

[80] *OKW/WFSt, KTB 1.IX.–31.XII.43*, 4 Oct 43. This reversed the opinion of a month earlier that, even if the line in Italy were shortened, the troops thereby relieved would have to be used in the Balkans. *Ibid.*, 8 Sep 43.

[81] He did not long hold to the principles of counterattack outlined in Directive 51. See MS # B–672 (Buttlar-Brandenfels) and below, Ch. VII.

[82] *Grundlegende Bemerkungen des Oberbefehlshabers West Nr. 27, Auswertung weiterer Erfahrungen*, 24 Jul 43, and *Nr. 28 Erfahrungen und Folgerungen aus den Landungskaempfen von Salerno*, 25 Dec 43. *OKW/WFSt, Op. (H), Westen, Grundlegende Bemerkungen 4.V.42–27.XII.43*.

[83] Rpt, *Auszug aus Bericht Generalmajor v. Marnitz*, appended to *Grundlegende Bemerkungen des Oberbefehlshabers West Nr. 28*, cited n. 82. Marnitz was director of fortress engineer courses at Engineer School I.

held up by any kind of natural obstacles; on the contrary they had seemed able to take advantage of all kinds of unfavorable terrain. General Marnitz's recommendations were to smash the Allied attack before landing by holding the reserves close up and withholding coastal artillery fire to the last moment. If some troops got ashore they would be forced to spread out by stubborn resistance in a number of small resistance nests. Any of the enemy forces that pierced the coastal defenses should be counterattacked by local reserves after they were beyond the range of naval guns.

Rundstedt in forwarding this report concurred in its contents, but in a later communication he made one significant addition. Smash the enemy in his boats, if possible. If he lands, counterattack immediately with local reserves. *But if, despite everything,* he still succeeds in getting through the first line of defense, then hold him by fire from positions echeloned in depth long enough to permit counterattack by *corps and army reserves*. Counterattack by purely local reserves could be considered part of the concept of static defense. Riposte by corps and army reserves introduced the concept of flexible, mobile war, particularly when limited means made it impossible to achieve both an optimum strength on the first line and an adequate pool of reserves.

General der Panzertruppen Leo Freiherr Geyr von Schweppenburg, the armored expert in the west, wanted to push the mobile tactics thus adumbrated to the point of falling back entirely from the coast with all mobile units, leaving only the static defenses to stave off the enemy as long as possible and inflict maximum losses. He wanted to seek a decision in the interior with a massed armored counterattack. The Luftwaffe, he felt, should not be committed in the battle for the beaches but saved to cover the counterattack.[84] Sodenstern agreed, with an interesting variation which he described in reflections jotted down in the summer of 1943.[85] The relative weakness of German forces, he felt, required that they defend the coast only long enough to determine the center of gravity of the enemy attack. Strategic reserves should be assembled on both sides of the Seine northwest of Paris and on the upper Loire. The area between the Seine and Loire would be the battlefield. Since Allied air superiority would make extensive German troop movements impossible, the Allies should be compelled to maneuver into the area chosen for the battle by means of switch lines contrived to canalize the Allied attack.

The notion of gambling everything on fully mobile defense with massed counterattacks mounted inland was never seriously entertained. Rundstedt seems generally to have conceived of the main battle as taking place in the coastal area. He vacillated chiefly in the reliance which he wanted to put on mobile counterattack within that area. To make such an attack possible, German forces, of course, had to be able to maneuver freely. Salerno and Sicily had shown that armor could not fight successfully within the range of naval artillery. Rundstedt pointed out to OKW that armor therefore could not influence the battle unless German aircraft, especially torpedo planes, could interfere with

---

[84] MS # B–466 (Geyr von Schweppenburg). Cf. below, Ch. X.

[85] MS # B–276 (Sodenstern).

the firing of Allied warships.[86] In addition, German mobility obviously depended on the quality and quantity of equipment and personnel. In his October report, Rundstedt admitted that the German divisions in the west had neither the men nor the machines to fight in open terrain against an enemy so materially strong as the Allies were sure to be. The conclusion was thus forced that the only hope of redressing Allied superiority lay in taking the maximum advantage of the water barrier. That was how the situation looked in October. After the Hitler directive in the next month, Rundstedt modified his view. If the promise to strengthen the west meant the provision of new troops and more mobile divisions, it might be possible to return to the idea of mass counterattack. He therefore proposed the formation, partly on paper, partly on the ground, of a central reserve. Specifically he suggested earmarking six infantry divisions to be withdrawn after the Allied landings from coastal zones not threatened by attack. Made mobile by vehicles contributed by each of the armies, these divisions would be organized under two corps controlled by an army headquarters. Existing panzer and panzer grenadier reserves would be commanded by a reserve panzer corps and the entire force put under the special army group headquarters that was being formed under Rommel.[87]

There is no question that the Rundstedt plan considerably extended the ideas underlying Directive 51. OKW at once objected to the proposal to withdraw entire divisions from the unthreatened portions of the coast and suggested instead that only regimental Kampfgruppen be pulled out in order not to denude any section of its defenses.[88] More basic objections were raised by Generaloberst Hans von Salmuth, who as commander of the *Fifteenth Army* defending the coast which the Germans thought most likely to be the scene of the major Allied invasion attempt occupied a key position in the command hierarchy. Salmuth criticized Rundstedt's suggestion as contravening all the hitherto accepted principles of defense in the west. It assumed, he said, that the Allies would break through the cordon defense and would succeed in establishing a bridgehead. If that happened, he believed the Allies pouring ashore unhindered would soon establish a superiority of force that would be tantamount to victory. The central reserves would take too long to assemble; it would be delayed and partially destroyed by Allied air attack. It was probable therefore that it could never be committed in mass and that late and piecemeal commitment would be ineffective. All reserves, Salmuth believed, should be held as close as possible to the coast and should be under army control.[89] The main objection to Salmuth's argument, as Rundstedt pointed

---

[86] Ltr, *OB WEST (Ia Nr. 696/43)* to *OKW/WFSt,* 26 Nov 43. *Seventh Army, KTB Anlagen, Chefsachen 2.III.43–1.VIII.44.*

[87] Rad, *OB WEST* to *OKW/WFSt,* 14 Nov. 43. *Seventh Army, KTB Anlagen, Chefsachen 2.III.43–1.VIII.44.* At the time Rundstedt made this proposal he was not sure of getting the reserve army group headquarters. If he did not, he expected to employ simply an army command. See Order, *OB WEST* to

army commanders, *Vorbereitung fuer den Kàmpf,* 18 Nov 43. *OKH/Org.Abt., Bd. Chefsachen 7.V.43–4.II.44.* In place of the reserve panzer corps a special armored staff was later created. See below, Ch. VII.

[88] *OKW/WFSt, KTB 1.IX.–31.XII.43,* 15 Nov 43.

[89] Ltr, Salmuth to *OB WEST* with personal covering letter to Rundstedt, 25 Dec 43. *Fifteenth Army, KTB Anlagen, Chefsachen 26.X.–27.XII.43.*

out in reply, was that it relied too much on a correct guess as to where the Allies would strike. For Salmuth this was not a very grave objection since he was convinced that the Allies would make their main attack in his sector. Rundstedt agreed that the likelihood existed, but pointed out that it was by no means a certainty.[90]

To Salmuth's argument that the central reserves could not be assembled and committed fast enough to be of use in a decisive mass counterattack, Rundstedt made no reply. His continued advocacy of such a reserve implied a belief that if victory was to be won the difficulties had to be overcome, though precisely how was never quite clear. Rundstedt's conviction, shared by most of the commanders in the west, was that no matter how strong the Atlantic Wall was made it could be broken. The only relevant questions were what dependence to put on the wall and how to divide the available forces between local and central reserves. The *Nineteenth Army* commander, Sodenstern, argued that the impossibility of establishing an unbreakable cordon defense vitiated the whole concept of the Atlantic Wall since a break-through anywhere would make all the fortifications useless.[91] Rundstedt maintained that a rigid defense in a series of strong points held to the last could so splinter and weaken the enemy that his penetrations could easily be cleaned up and the whole invasion attempt thus be defeated before the enemy's superior material force could be concentrated and gain momentum. As far as the troops defending the coastal strong points

were concerned, there should be no withdrawal. Each strong point should be fought separately. But this kind of resistance would only soften up the enemy for the decisive counterattacks. To be decisive they must be mounted in force. "No dispersion," said Rundstedt, "no piecemeal commitment and no thin water soup!" Divisions should be committed intact to hit the flanks of the enemy penetrations.[92]

General der Artillerie Erich Marcks, commander of *LXXXIV Corps* in Normandy, was persuaded by the weakness of his forces to embrace the same tactics. He told an inspecting officer from OKW in January 1944 that even a doubling of his present troop strength would make possible only a thin screen at the coast which could still be torn at any point by the enemy. Instead of a wall defense, he therefore proposed the construction of numerous small field fortifications with some depth whose mission was not to stop the enemy but to split the attacking forces and gain time for the bringing up of German reserves. He felt that a corps reserve of armor and mobile infantry could be built up behind the coast but near enough to be committed within twenty-four hours.[93]

OKW generally remained skeptical whether, in view of Allied superiority in the air and the limited mobility of German units, large-scale counterattacks could be mounted. But, on the whole, Jodl and his staff concurred that depth of defense was desirable. In response to re-

---

[90] Ltr, Rundstedt to Salmuth, 27 Dec 43. *Fifteenth Army, KTB Anlagen, Chefsachen 26.X.–27.XII.43.*

[91] MS # B–276 (Sodenstern).

[92] *Grundlegender Befehl des Oberbefehlshabers West Nr. 20, Grundsaetze fuer die Fuehrung der Kuestenverteidigung, 18 Dec 42. OKW/WFSt, Op. (H), Westen, Grundlegende Befehle 22.X.42–7.V.44.*

[93] MS # B–672 (Buttlar-Brandenfels).

peated pleas by Rundstedt in the summer of 1943 OKW authorized the construction, if practicable, of a secondary position still within the coastal zone.[94] In June 1943 the Commander in Chief West ordered local commanders to reconnoiter rear areas for suitable locations for heavy weapons in accordance with their own estimate of the situation and enemy intentions. He also suggested that prepared positions for antitank guns and machine guns would be of considerable importance in delaying the enemy troops that might break through the first line of defense. At the moment there was little possibility of actually starting construction.[95] Nothing was started until the end of October, when Rundstedt ordered further reconnaissance by corps and armies and the beginning of field construction. The secondary position was to be built with maximum flexibility to include prepared switch lines and to take in already established airfields, ammunition dumps, and shelters for reserves and staffs. Antiaircraft guns would be emplaced for ground firing and all-around defense. Some 31,-000 French laborers were initially used on the job.

At the end of 1943 the discussion of defense tactics had produced no unequivocal decision. Rundstedt's own orders with their dual emphasis on holding coastal positions to the last and at the same time building mobile reserves, while in one sense perfectly consistent, were nevertheless subject to interpretation as supporting either primarily static or primarily mobile defense.[96] Since the practical problem was the allocation of limited time and resources, insufficient for the full development of both fortifications and troop build-up and training, Rundstedt's pronouncements actually straddled the issue. In the closing months of the year the doctrine of decision by counterattack in force, though qualified and not unchallenged, seemed to have achieved general acceptance in *OB WEST* and the apparent endorsement of OKW and Hitler. The outline of the battle as sketched by the chief of staff of *OB WEST*, General Blumentritt, envisaged the fighting in four main stages: first, the fire fight while the Allies were still on the water; second, the struggle on the beaches; third, the battles in the coastal zone between German local reserves and Allied units that had penetrated the main line of resistance; and, finally, the decisive beachhead battle in which *OB WEST* would commit large motorized units to throw the Allies back into the sea.[97]

In accord with this outline, Rundstedt ordered a winter construction program to step up work on the fortifications with special attention to casemating coastal artillery and antitank guns; at the same time, as already noted, he began planning for the formation of the central reserve. But the latter plans would go awry chiefly

---

[94] Ltrs, *OB WEST* to *OKW/WFSt*, 2 Apr 43 and 27 Jun 43. *OKH/Op.Abt., Kuestenschutz Kanalkueste 20.VI.42–18.V.44; OKW/WFSt, KTB 1.VII.–31.VIII.43*, 11 Jul 43.

[95] *Grundlegende Bemerkungen des Oberbefehlshabers West Nr. 26*, 6 Jun 43. *OKW/WFSt, Op. (H), Westen, Grundlegende Bemerkungen 4.V.42–27.XII.43.*

[96] Rundstedt could thus find himself in nearly perfect agreement with both Salmuth and Geyr, whose respective tactical concepts were wholly opposed. See MS # B–466 (Geyr von Schweppenburg); cf. MS # B–720 (Generalleutnant Dr. Hans Speidel, CofS, *Army Group B*).

[97] Ltr, CofS, *OB WEST*, to subordinate armies, 10 Jan 44. *Seventh Army, KTB Anlagen, Chefsachen 2.III.43–1.VIII.44.*

because the man slated to command the reserves and conduct the battle against the invaders was to be Field Marshal Rommel. There was scarcely a general in the German Army less in sympathy with the grandiose scheme of massed counter-attacks under the bomb sights of virtually unopposed Allied air fleets. Thus at the moment when the concept of mobile defense in the west seemed to enjoy highest favor, it was in reality on the point of most complete repudiation by a commander convinced that it was a dangerous fantasy.[98]

---

[98] See below, Ch. VII.

CHAPTER V

Overlord Revised

U.S. Organization and Training for the Assault, January 1944

General Eisenhower arrived in London on 14 January 1944 to take up his new duties as Supreme Commander, Allied Expeditionary Force. With his arrival, the whole character and tempo of planning and preparing for OVERLORD changed. Gone was the basic uncertainty—the sense of planning for a more or less probable contingency in a more or less indefinite future. OVERLORD was now a definite commitment. A commander at last was charged with responsibility for its success and authority to make his arrangements to insure that success. The twenty weeks that remained before the troops were loaded in ships for the fateful thrust across the Channel were weeks of decision when the plans, studies, suggestions, and acquired experience of the past three years were transformed into the working blueprints of action.

It was a task of complexity and disturbing size which at times made commanders despair that it could be accomplished in time. But for the most part the groundwork had been solidly laid. By January there could be no concern over the availability of troops to do the job. Already about half of the required U.S. combat divisions were in the United Kingdom and the arrival in time of the remainder was assured. The flow of combat divisions, which had been delayed to permit an intensive build-up of the air forces and serv-

ice troops, began in the fall of 1943 and continued from then until D Day at the average rate of about two divisions a month.[1]

U.S. corps and army headquarters for the control of the initial phases of the invasion were already established in the United Kingdom and the chain of command was settled. On 23 October 1943, First U.S. Army under Lt. Gen. Omar N. Bradley took over operational command of American ground forces in the United Kingdom.[2] At the same time VII Corps, which arrived during the month, was assigned to First Army. Over-all ground command for the assault phase had been given to 21 Army Group. Early in January General Paget was replaced as commanding general by Gen. Sir Bernard L. Montgomery.[3] General Montgomery ar-

---

[1] As of 1 January there were 749,298 U.S. troops in the United Kingdom including most of eleven divisions. The divisions, in order of arrival, were: 29th, 5th, 101st Airborne, 3d Armored, 28th, 2d, 1st, 2d Armored, 9th, 82d Airborne, and 8th. The 1st, 2d Armored, 9th, and 82d Airborne Divisions had been in combat in the Mediterranean.

[2] [Robert W. Coakley] Organization and Command in the ETO (The Administrative and Logistical History of the ETO: Part II), MS, I, 276–77. Hist Div files.

[3] General Montgomery came to this post with a brilliant record that dated back to World War I, in which he had been awarded the DSO and been mentioned six times in dispatches. At the beginning of World War II he commanded the 3d Division in France and, after escaping from Dunkerque, took over the 5 Corps. In 1942 and 1943 as commanding general of the British Eighth Army in Africa, Egypt, Sicily, and Italy, he achieved renown as the man who mastered Rommel.

GENERAL EISENHOWER, *Supreme Allied Commander.*

rived in England on 2 January 1944. He had stopped off at Algiers to receive General Eisenhower's instructions and then at Marrakesh to see the Prime Minister, who was convalescing there from an attack of influenza. His chief of staff, Maj. Gen. Sir Francis de Guingand, went ahead and on his arrival at once tackled the problem of reorganizing the army group staff and replacing most of its key personnel with officers from the British Eighth Army. In addition he undertook to establish parallel U.S. staffs to convert the British army group into a temporary combined headquarters which would function as such as long as U.S. troops were under its command.[4]

U. S. naval organization had also become pretty well set by the first of the year, after passing through many complicated command patterns from the time the first U.S. naval officers arrived in England as observers in 1940.[5] The end product—the command for combat—reflected some of these past complications. In January Admiral Harold R. Stark was still the senior U.S. naval commander in Europe, with the title of Commander of Naval Forces in Europe (ComNavEu). Until the fall of 1943 he exercised administrative command over various task forces sent by the Commander in Chief of the U.S. Fleet to operate in European waters. In addition, he commanded certain naval administrative units in the United Kingdom. On 9 September 1943 Admiral King ordered consolidation of all U.S. naval forces in Europe under a new command, the Twelfth Fleet, to be headed by Admiral

Stark. But, although this simplified the appearance of the command, the fact remained complicated. At the same time, Admiral King directed that a task force be formed to control operations and training for the cross-Channel assault. This became Task Force 122 under command of Rear Adm. Alan G. Kirk.[6] Operational and administrative command thus remained divided. Two other important subordinate commands were formed under Twelfth Fleet: the Eleventh Amphibious Force under Rear Adm. John L. Hall, and Landing Craft and Bases, Europe, which was created in the summer of 1943 to receive and control the buildup of landing craft for the invasion. The commander was Rear Adm. John Wilkes.[7]

Admiral Stark, as ComNavEu, was responsible for co-ordinating with ETO-USA and COSSAC all U.S. naval preparations for the invasion; as commander of Twelfth Fleet he was the administrative chief responsible for providing the task forces under him with facilities for training and operations. Admiral Kirk's Task Force 122 controlled the training, preparation, and operations of all U.S. naval forces. Under him, Admiral Hall's Eleventh Amphibious Force commanded U.S. amphibious forces afloat. Command of bases and responsibility for support and maintenance of forces afloat rested with Admiral Wilkes.

The Allied naval command had been established for planning purposes on 5 May 1943. On 25 October Admiral Little was replaced as Commander-in-Chief Al-

---

[4] Interv with de Guingand, 1947. Hist Div files.

[5] Material on naval organization is found in Administrative History of U.S. Naval Forces in Europe, 1940–1946, MS, pp. 237–47. Hist Div files.

[6] Admiral Kirk had been commander of Amphibious Force, Atlantic Fleet.

[7] Hall was former commander of the Eighth Amphibious Force in the Mediterranean. Wilkes from December 1942 to August 1943 had commanded the U.S. cruiser Birmingham.

INVASION TRAINING IN ENGLAND. *Amphibious exercise off beach (above), and troops coming ashore from a beached LCI (L) (below).*

lied Naval Expeditionary Force (ANCXF) by Admiral Sir Bertram H. Ramsay.[8] It was not until 1 April, however, that Admiral Ramsay assumed operational control of U.S. naval forces and even then his command remained formal until the eve of the invasion.[9] The principal duty of ANCXF in January was still the preparation of an Allied naval plan.

Air force organization was settled in January except for the control of strategic air. Air Marshal Leigh-Mallory's AEAF headquarters, in addition to directing preliminary operations against the enemy, was working on an over-all air plan for the assault.

The training of troops for the assault was never a primary responsibility of the theater. It was assumed that divisions would arrive in the United Kingdom fully schooled in their tasks. The cross-Channel attack, however, posed many special technical problems for which solutions could not be worked out at a distance. The British had been experimenting with assault tactics and equipment since 1940 through the Combined Operations Headquarters. After April 1942 American officers shared in this work and an attempt was made to work out a combined amphibious doctrine specially adapted to the conditions of the Channel assault.[10] As doctrine and planning developed and the American Army grew in the United Kingdom, it became imperative to set up an American training center that would both test the new tactical ideas and techniques and apply them in the training of troops. Negotiations to establish such a center had begun in late 1942, but the problems in the way were considerable. During the first six months of 1943 there were few trainees and fewer facilities, as the bulk of U.S. ground troops and landing craft continued to be absorbed by the Mediterranean theater. Moreover, it took time to locate suitable training grounds in the crowded island of England and to iron out the legal difficulties of taking over hundreds of pieces of private property, including farmlands and villages. (The area finally selected, in fact, was so small that firing exercises were narrowly limited.) In April 1943 the Assault Training Center was activated with Lt. Col. Paul W. Thompson in command. But it was September before it opened its first training courses at Woolacombe.[11]

Nearly all the U.S. troops earmarked for the OVERLORD assault underwent some training at Colonel Thompson's center, although the amount and intensity varied. The 29th and 4th Divisions sent all their regiments through the course. One regiment of the 29th, the 116th Infantry, returned for a refresher course. Out of the 1st Division only the 16th Infantry took the training. But the 1st Division arrived

---

[8] Ltr, H. N. Morrison to Admiral Ramsay, 4 Nov 43. SHAEF SGS file 322 (ANCXF). Admiral Ramsay had retired in 1938 after forty-two years in the Royal Navy, the last three of which he had served as Chief of Staff, Home Fleet. At the outbreak of World War II in 1939 he was recalled to active duty as Flag Officer Commanding, Dover. While serving in this post he organized the naval forces for the withdrawal from Dunkerque. Later he helped plan the TORCH operation, commanded a task force in the Sicilian invasion, and became British naval commander in the Mediterranean.

[9] Ltr, Smith to CinC 21 A Gp, FUSAG, and AEAF, 6 Apr 43. SHAEF SGS file 322 (ANCXF). The naval command set up was analogous to that of the Allied Expeditionary Air Force. See above, Ch. III.

[10] Rpt, History of American Section, Combined Operations Headquarters, 23 Sep 43. Pre-Inv file 289.

[11] [Clifford Jones] NEPTUNE: Training, Mounting, the Artificial Ports (The Administrative and Logistical History of the ETO: Part VI), MS, I, 165, 168ff. Hist Div files.

ASSAULT TRAINING. *Hitting the beach (above), and training with live am-munition (below).*

in England fully battle-tested through participation in both the North African and Sicilian assaults. The 82d Airborne Division, similarly experienced in combat in Sicily and Italy, did not attend the center. The 101st Airborne Division, however, despite intensive training in the United States did send two groups (two thousand men in all) for special short courses in the technique of assaulting fortified positions.[12]

Besides carrying out its primary mission of preparing troops for the assaults, the Assault Training Center made a vital contribution to amphibious doctrine. Through experimentation with new equipment, combined exercises, close liaison with the British, and conferences on tactics, Colonel Thompson's staff learned as well as taught, and their new wisdom not only improved tactical methods but in many important ways modified tactical concepts.[13] In January 1944, when Eisenhower took command, the specialized program of the Assault Training Center was in full swing; one division was already graduated, another was in training. Tactical methods, though still not firm in all respects, had at least been extensively reviewed and tested.

All the major problems attendant on the assembling, grouping, and training of invasion forces had thus been settled. It required only time and a few minor rearrangements to ready the troops for the attack. The status of planning, however, was much less satisfactory. Despite nearly three years of study and ten months of more or less intensive and specific planning for OVERLORD, many of the basic

problems still remained to be settled—the strength of the assault, for instance, and whether it should take place by day or by night.

It was recognized at least as early as Casablanca that the only plan worth working on was one drawn by the people who would ultimately execute it. Hence the decision to constitute COSSAC as an embryo of a supreme headquarters. Various attempts were then made to confer on General Morgan a kind of substitute commander's authority. But the device did not work. After the publication of the OVERLORD outline plan in July 1943, COSSAC found it impossible to make any further substantial contribution to OVERLORD tactical planning for reasons that have been described. General Eisenhower, General Montgomery, and their staffs, as well as the Allied naval and air commanders, found in January that as far as plans were concerned they had to go back and pick up where COSSAC left off in July. They had, however, an accumulated mass of special studies which greatly facilitated the problems of revising the master plan and preparing detailed unit field orders.

The Anvil—Overlord Debate

It was clear to planners after the Quebec Conference that the OVERLORD plan, as written by COSSAC in July 1943, would have to be revised to strengthen the assault. Although COSSAC examined some of the implications both of adding to the weight of the attack and of broadening the front, the planners came to no conclusion. General Morgan could not have rewritten the plan in any case, since he still functioned under the May directive of the Combined Chiefs of Staff which

---

[12] *Ibid.*, I, 193–96.

[13] For discussion, see below, The NEPTUNE Plans: Organization and Tactics of the Assault Forces.

limited his resources in men and shipping. He could not secure additional resources primarily because he could not exercise the necessary command authority.

When COSSAC received the Supreme Commander and emerged from its planning staff chrysalis to become the Supreme Allied Headquarters, its formal written plan for the invasion was still the July outline plan. But informally the staff had long been thinking in terms of a larger assault. If landing craft were available, planners hoped to be able to attack with four divisions and have one more division in floating reserve. Still this was only a hope—not a plan. The process of producing a new plan to realize the hope for a strong assault began with the arrival in London of General Montgomery and General Eisenhower's chief of staff, Maj. Gen. Walter Bedell Smith.[14]

On 3 January 1944 Generals Montgomery and Smith were formally briefed on the COSSAC OVERLORD plan by Brig. Kenneth McLean, the chief COSSAC Army planner. After the presentation, General Montgomery criticized the narrow front of the assault and spoke of carrying out simultaneous assaults in Brittany, around Dieppe, and on the west coast of the Cotentin. He also criticized planning figures on the capacity of available landing craft. The meeting broke up without decision. In the days following General Montgomery's first sweeping protest against the narrow restrictions placed on the original plan, discussion settled down to suggestions that the planned invasion front be extended from twenty-five miles to about forty miles and that five divisions be used in the assault.[15] The extended front was to run from les Dunes de Varreville on the east coast of the Cotentin to Cabourg (east of the Orne River). Two armies should be employed: the First U.S. Army on the right and the Second British Army on the left with an inter-army boundary approximately at Bayeux.[16]

General Montgomery insisted that it was essential in order to avoid confusion of administration and supply that armies and corps go in on their own fronts and not through bridgeheads established by other units.[17] Other reasons for broadening the front were that it would be harder for the enemy to define and locate the limits of the attack and conversely easier

---

[14] General Smith at the outbreak of war was serving as Secretary, General Staff of the War Department. In February 1942 he became secretary to the U.S. Joint Chiefs of Staff as well as American secretary of the Combined Chiefs of Staff. Appointed as General Eisenhower's chief of staff in September 1942, he served in this position in Allied Force Headquarters until the end of 1943. At that time he became SHAEF chief of staff, replacing General Morgan who became deputy chief of staff. General Eisenhower had been ordered to the United States for consultations and had sent Smith to London.

[15] Interv, F. C. Pogue with Maj Gen Kenneth R. McLean, 11-13 Mar 47. McLean said flatly that Montgomery's decision was to use a five-division front. Compare, however, notes by Lt. Col. H. Mainward (military assistant to Montgomery) on a meeting of Army commanders, 7 January 1944, where the decision reported was to try for an eight-brigade assault for four divisions each on a two-brigade front. Naval representatives said that, although eight brigades were the maximum that could be landed, they could be drawn from five divisions rather than four, if the Army preferred. Documents in Hist Div files.

[16] Mainward, notes cited n. 15. Bayeux was to be inclusive to the U.S. Army.

[17] This had been pointed out much earlier as one of the important lessons from TORCH. The Eastern Assault Force G-4 wrote: "It was fundamental to avoid intermingling of British and American Supply systems." See Lessons from Operation TORCH, 16 Dec 42. Pre-Inv file 465.

for the Allies to break out of the initial bridgehead. A wider frontage would give the Allies a larger number of vehicle exits from the beachhead and so facilitate the penetration inland and subsequent build-up. Finally a landing west of the Vire estuary would facilitate the early capture of Cherbourg, on which General Montgomery placed even greater stress than COSSAC, principally because he was suspicious of the value of the untried artificial ports.[18]

Details of tactical dispositions and objectives were not examined at this point. Even the question of whether to assault the beaches of the east Cotentin was apparently unsettled. What General Montgomery did achieve—and what was most important at that time to achieve—was to press, as a commander, for a decision that the assault be strengthened. He said in effect, "Give me five divisions or get someone else to command."[19] Of the COSSAC principal staff officers none agreed entirely with Montgomery's proposals. General Morgan, General McLean, and General Barker had always wanted the greater weight in the assault, but still questioned the soundness of expanding the front. Maj. Gen. Charles A. West, G–3, opposed any expansion, because he believed it would only spread thin the available forces.[20] The naval and air staffs had evi-

dent technical objections since the effectiveness of their support and preparation was directly proportionate to the concentration of the ground attack. Most of the COSSAC staff, whether or not they agreed with General Montgomery, felt immense relief that the matter was at last being brought to a head.[21] Planning was on solid ground again and now could move forward. Planners were ordered to go ahead with the revised plan to employ one airborne and five seaborne divisions in the assault on the assumption that the necessary additional resources in shipping and air transport would be forthcoming.

Montgomery and Smith then tackled the problem of getting the required landing craft. The most obvious source was the Mediterranean theater. But withdrawal from the Mediterranean would necessitate the cancellation of the ANVIL assault on southern France. One of General Eisenhower's last jobs as Commander in Chief of the Mediterranean theater had been the drafting of a plan for a two- or three-division ANVIL to coincide with OVERLORD and so constitute a concentric offensive against the enemy forces in France.[22] That plan, it will be remembered, was developed during December in compliance with the directive of the Combined Chiefs of Staff issued at Cairo after the meeting with the Russians.

On 5 January General Smith cabled General Eisenhower in Washington to report Montgomery's argument for a

---

[18] Notes for the Commander-in-Chief's Meeting with the Supreme Commander on Friday 21st January 1944. Copy furnished by British Cabinet Office Hist Sec. Hist Div files.

[19] Gen McLean's interpretation. See Interv cited n. 15. Eisenhower has said that in December 1943, he instructed both General Montgomery and General Smith to "seek for an intensification of effort to increase troop lift in Overlord. . . ." Cbl, Eisenhower to Marshall, 8 Feb 44. SHAEF SGS file 381 I (Overlord–Anvil).

[20] Interv with McLean; Interv, F. C. Pogue with Gen West, 19 Feb 47. Hist Div files.

[21] Interv with McLean.

[22] Eisenhower preferred a three-division assault, but made alternative plans to employ only two divisions in case the additional resources were not available. The three-division plan, actually not feasible, was dropped from reckoning in the later debate.

stronger and broader OVERLORD assault.[23] "Additional lift," he said, "can only be obtained at the expense of ANVIL. . . . Montgomery is insistent on the immediate recommendation to abandon ANVIL except as a threat previously agreed upon by the COSSAC and AFHQ staffs before the reinforcement in landing craft was decided upon at the Cairo Conference." Smith added that, although he had refused to make such a recommendation without General Eisenhower's "personal approval," he nevertheless agreed with it. He felt that ANVIL as a one-division threat would be just as effective as the contemplated three-division assault. In this General Morgan and the bulk of the planners in England concurred.[24] Morgan, like most of the planners, believed the ANVIL assault, as planned, was so remote from the OVERLORD area and from any military objectives vital to the Germans that the enemy would not find it worth while to divert more than two or three divisions from the main battle in the north in order to cope with it. The same diversion, he thought, could be achieved by a threat requiring amphibious lift for only one division. Eisenhower agreed that "OVERLORD must be more broadly based" but he did not think ANVIL as a threat would be as effective as the operation itself.[25]

Pending the outcome of the debate thus initiated, planners proceeded with an examination of the additional resources needed for the "Montgomery plan" and the implications of finding them.[26] To get the landing craft they estimated it would be necessary to return half of the two-division ANVIL lift to the United Kingdom. In addition the OVERLORD target date would have to be postponed from 1 May to 1 June in order to secure an additional month's production, and the number of vehicles per assault division would need to be cut to 2,500.[27] The broadened assault front would also increase the fighter plane commitment by eight squadrons. To lift a complete airborne division instead of the two-thirds originally planned would necessitate finding 200 more transport aircraft.[28]

The bill for the principal types of landing craft—as always the critical commodity—included an additional 72 LCI (L)'s, 47 LST's, and 144 LCT's.[29] The bill was submitted to the Combined Chiefs of Staff by General Eisenhower a week after he arrived in London. He was anxious that it be met, if possible, without interfering with ANVIL and indicated his willingness to postpone OVERLORD until after 1 June even though that meant the loss

[23] Cbl, Smith to Eisenhower, 5 Jan 44. Eisenhower Personal Files. See Bibliographical Note. Montgomery added his personal appeal when he cabled on 10 January, "Will you hurl yourself into the contest and what we want, get for us." SHAEF SGS file 560 II.

[24] COSSAC (44) 5, Operation 'ANVIL,' 6 Jan 44. SHAEF SGS file 370.2/2 I.

[25] Cbl, Eisenhower to Smith, 6 Jan 44. Eisenhower Personal Files.

[26] The "Montgomery plan" was a convenient appellation used by General Morgan and others at the time. See Ltr, Morgan to COSSAC G-4, 13 Jan 44. SHAEF SGS file 800.1 I. It should not be taken to indicate, however, that the idea of an expanded assault was uniquely Montgomery's.

[27] Former calculations had varied, but all exceeded 3,000. See above, Ch. II.

[28] COSSAC (44) 9, Reply to Joint Planning Staff Questionnaire (COS (44) 11 (O)) On Implications of Proposed Modification of Operation 'Anvil,' 8 Jan 44. SHAEF SGS file 370.2/2 I.

[29] The other requirements: 1 LSH (headquarters ship), 6 LSI (L)'s or APA's, all carrying a full complement of LCA's or LCVP's (British and U.S. ship-to-shore ferrying craft respectively), and 64 motor vehicle cargo ships. These requirements could all be met with relative ease and therefore do not figure in the struggle for adequate assault lift.

of a month of good campaigning weather. The postponement was seconded by the British Chiefs of Staff, and agreed to by the U. S. Joint Chiefs of Staff on 31 January. Besides insuring extra landing craft, the later date would increase the chances of favorable weather on the Russian front and thus make it possible for more closely co-ordinated action between the Allies.[30]

The ANVIL question was not to be resolved so easily. On the contrary the issue sharpened and the differences of opinion intensified. In early January 1944 when the British Chiefs of Staff first debated the cancellation of ANVIL, both Air Marshal Portal, Chief of Air Staff, and Admiral Sir Andrew B. Cunningham, First Sea Lord, recommended the mounting of a two-division ANVIL as a useful diversion to OVERLORD.[31] On 4 February, the Prime Minister bluntly stated that ANVIL and OVERLORD were not strategically interwoven because of the great distance (500 miles) of rugged country between them and the defensive power of modern weapons. He therefore doubted the value of a diversionary landing in southern France, regardless of the available resources. The Chiefs of Staff had then come to share his doubts.[32] Less than two weeks later a War

Department representative in London could say, in reference to the ANVIL–OVERLORD debate, that he had met the "customary attitude on the part of British planners." He found them maintaining that OVERLORD was the only operation "that will pay us dividends," and that "ANVIL might be an operation in the Marshalls" for all the connection it had with OVERLORD.[33]

As the British thus developed increasing hostility to the southern France invasion, the U.S. Chiefs of Staff reaffirmed an uncompromising stand that ANVIL was required "to make effective use" of the French and U.S. divisions in the Mediterranean and to draw German divisions away from northern France.[34] The most a threat could do, they thought, would be to contain the enemy divisions already deployed in the ANVIL area. Furthermore, they recalled that they were committed to the southern France assault by agreement with Marshal Stalin at Tehran. In brief, the U.S. point of view (shared by General Eisenhower) was that ANVIL and OVERLORD were parts of a single operation, and that it was unsound to cancel one part for the ostensible purpose of strengthening the other.

"Judging from the discussion and differences of opinion at the present time," General Marshall wrote to Eisenhower in February, "the British and American Chiefs of Staff seemed to have completely reversed themselves and we have become Mediterraneanites and they heavily pro-

---

[30] Various cables in SHAEF SGS file 381 I (Overlord–Anvil).

[31] COS (44) 5th Mtg (O), 7 Jan 44. SHAEF SGS file 370.2/2 I. Admiral Cunningham, who replaced Admiral Pound as First Sea Lord in October 1943, had entered the Royal Navy in 1898 and participated in World War I. As Commander-in-Chief, Mediterranean, between 1939 and 1942, he directed operations against the Italian Fleet at Taranto and Matapan and evacuated the British Army from Greece. After heading the Admiralty delegation in Washington in 1942, Cunningham was made Naval Commander-in-Chief, Expeditionary Force, North Africa.

[32] COS (44) 35th Mtg (O), 4 Feb 44 with Annex, Minute to the Prime Minister from Gen Ismay.

SHAEF SGS file 370.2/2 I; cf. CCS 465/4, Firm Recommendations with Regard to Operations "Anvil" and "Overlord," 4 Feb 44.

[33] Cbl, Hull (OPD) to Handy, 15 Feb 44. SHAEF SGS file 560 II.

[34] CCS 465/3, 31 Jan 44.

OVERLORD." [35] As Marshall was well aware, no reversal in opinion had in fact occurred. What *had* happened was that Allied plans for the battle in Italy had once again bogged down before unexpectedly heavy enemy opposition. The British, in asking the cancellation of ANVIL, were thinking at least as much of the need for additional resources with which to prosecute the Italian campaign as they were of diverting landing craft to strengthen OVERLORD. On 22 January, U.S. VI Corps units had landed at Anzio. The landing behind the enemy lines facing the Fifth Army was designed to force the Germans to pull out and leave the road to Rome open. Instead of pulling out, the Germans held the Fifth Army attack at the Gustav Line and counterattacked the beachhead. The beachhead was successfully defended but it soon became apparent that no quick link-up with the main armies was going to be possible.[36] The British had concluded early in February that the Germans meant to fight it out in central Italy and they saw this development as altering the Allied strategic decisions made at Tehran. They thought General Alexander, commander of 15 Army Group, controlling the ground forces in Italy, would need at least some of the troops earmarked for ANVIL and that the amphibious lift for one division should be reserved for his use for possible new operations similar to the Anzio "end run." The British Chiefs of Staff declared: "Germany . . . is now apparently playing our game [of tying up German forces in the Mediterranean]

and we must do all we can to pin down her forces and commit them still further. . . . We have no choice but to prosecute the Italian Campaign with vigor. . . ." [37]

The U.S. Joint Chiefs had no quarrel with the determination to prosecute the Italian campaign. Again the issue was to what extent strategic decisions and planning should be suspended to await battle developments. General Marshall's view was that planning and preparations should proceed for ANVIL but that, if by April the Allies had still not been able to establish themselves north of Rome, then ANVIL should be abandoned. If, on the other hand, ANVIL were called off at once, then there would be no possibility of mounting it in the spring.[38]

Early in February it became apparent to the Combined Chiefs of Staff that their differences could not be resolved by exchange of cables. The U.S. Chiefs of Staff therefore delegated their authority to General Eisenhower to carry on discussions with the British and sent to London Maj. Gen. John E. Hull and Rear Adm. Charles M. Cooke, Jr., with planners from the War Department to act as advisers. Eisenhower found himself actually on a middle ground between the War Department and British staff views. He agreed with the War Department's estimate of the importance of the southern France diversion, but he was closer to the planning difficulties of OVERLORD and therefore more dubious as to the feasibility of ANVIL.[39]

---

[35] Cbl, Marshall to Eisenhower, 7 Feb 44. SHAEF SGS file 381 I (Overlord–Anvil).

[36] The attack toward Cisterna on 28–29 January failed. Thereafter the Allied forces at Anzio remained on the defensive until May.

[37] CCS 465/4; Minute, Ismay for the Prime Minister, cited n. 32.

[38] Cbl, Hull to Handy, cited n. 33; CCS 465/10, 21 Feb 44.

[39] See, for instance, Cbl, Eisenhower to Marshall, 6 Feb 44. SHAEF SGS file 381 I (Overlord–Anvil).

During February the SHAEF staff struggled to devise an acceptable compromise. The possibility of compromise hinged, in the first instance, on finding enough landing craft for a five-division OVERLORD assault. Lift for four seaborne divisions and one airborne was promised by the War Department. The problem was to get additional lift not only for the fifth assault division but also for four armored brigades (or the equivalent), five regiments of self-propelled field artillery, shore groups, air force units, naval personnel, and two-thirds of a follow-up division which planners figured had to be carried in landing craft, tactically loaded, for immediate employment on landing. The rest of the follow-up (one and one-third divisions) would be carried in shipping and would therefore not be operationally available until D plus 2. Assault forces requiring simultaneous loading consisted of a total of 174,320 men and 20,018 vehicles. These figures included a large number of nondivisional troops equivalent in personnel and vehicular strength to between two and three divisions.[40]

As the result of conferences at Norfolk House (SHEAF headquarters) during the week of 13 February, a compromise shipping plan was worked out. SHAEF first proposed to reduce the current planning allocation by one LSI(H), 48 LST's, and 51 LCI(L)'s with a resulting loss of lift for 21,560 men and 2,520 vehicles. This loss would then be made up by overloading transports (APA's), carrying vehicles in the APA's, using AKA's (cargo ships) in the initial lift, and finding (presumably from new production) an additional 27 LCT's. This plan was subsequently revised to exchange the 6 AKA's with the Mediterranean theater for 20 LST's and 21 LCI (L)'s, on the grounds that the large cargo vessels could more easily be used in the calmer southern waters. The exchange would still leave an estimated two-division lift for ANVIL although it was doubtful whether Gen. Sir Henry Maitland Wilson (Commander-in-Chief Mediterranean) would accept the loss of tactical flexibility which use of the AKA's involved.[41] The SHAEF compromise still left a shortage of about fifteen LST's. General Eisenhower requested allocation of at least seven more LST's from U.S. production. The remainder of the deficit would have to be made up by increased loading of LST's on the third tide (morning of D plus 1) and increased seviceability.

The serviceability rate of landing craft —or, in other words, the percentage of craft on hand which at any given date would be operationally available—was always a planning figure to conjure with. So narrow were the planning margins that a difference of 5 percent in the estimates of serviceability might mean the difference between adequate and inadequate lift for the assault. The serviceability rate was contingent chiefly on repair facilities and the stock of spare parts—both of which were critically limited in the United Kingdom.[42] COSSAC in Outline OVER-

[40] Various cables between SHAEF and WD 5–9 Feb 44. SHAEF SGS file 560 II. A divisional slice for the assault at this time was figured at 24,000 men and 2,500 vehicles (of which 1,450 were organic). See CCS 465/7, 8 Feb 44.

[41] Memo by First Sea Lord, Landing Ships and Craft for "Overlord," incl to Ltr, Hollis to COSSAC, 21 Feb 44. SHAEF G–3 file GCT 451–94–1 Ops A.

[42] See, for instance, Cbl, McCloy to Forrestal, 20 Apr 44. SHAEF SGS file 560 II.

LORD had planned on an average serviceability rate of 85 percent for all craft and
90 percent for ships.[43] These figures were
substantially approved at the Quebec
Conference. On advice of U.S. naval planners, however, the rate for U.S. craft was
raised in January to 95 percent for LST's
and 90 percent for LCT's. The British insisted on retention of the lower COSSAC
figures. SHAEF accepted both estimates
and distinguished in planning between
U.S. and British craft, allowing the serviceability rate set by each country.[44]

The SHAEF shipping compromise was
severely criticized by planners of 21 Army
Group, mainly on the grounds that
SHAEF considered the problem of providing lift only from a logistical and not
from a tactical point of view. For example,
they pointed out that SHAEF had not
shown separately the Commando-Ranger
lift for special assault missions against fortified positions. This separation was important, the army group planners argued,
because there could be no question of
loading to full capacity the LSI's carrying
Commandos, and of course the excess capacity could not be used for lift of other
assault troops. The SHAEF proposals, by
pushing the loading of shipping toward
the full theoretical capacity of the vessels,
sacrificed flexibility, particularly in that
they prevented the preloading in craft of
adequate reserves. Army group thought it

extremely important that reserve units for
the assault waves be tactically loaded in
craft so that their employment would not
be affected by losses or time delays of the
LCA (ship-to-shore) craft used in the
initial assault. By increasing the personnel lift on the first tide of the assault
without any corresponding vehicle increase, the SHAEF proposal either would
land men who could not proceed with
their task until their vehicles arrived, thus
causing congestion on the beaches, or
would compel half-loaded personnel ships
to wait offshore, thus exposing both ships
and men to unjustifiable risks.[45]

The validity of these objections was
fully conceded by General Eisenhower,
but he considered the sacrifices and risks
worth accepting in order to permit the
simultaneous diversionary attack on
southern France. Although at first
strongly opposed, General Montgomery
at last agreed and the proposals were submitted to the British Chiefs of Staff.[46] The
Chiefs of Staff disapproved the compromise on the grounds, first, that it skimped
both ANVIL and OVERLORD and, second,
that the slow progress of the Italian campaign made the possibility of providing
the necessary build-up forces for ANVIL "so
remote as to be negligible." [47] Employment, as planned, of ten divisions in
southern France, General Brooke pointed
out, would leave only twenty divisions to

---

[43] Ltr, Gen Brownjohn to Morgan, 29 Jul 43.
SHAEF SGS file 800.1 I.

[44] Special Meeting Held in Room 126, Norfolk
House, 17 Feb 44. SHAEF SGS file 381 I (Overlord–
Anvil). Both figures actually proved pessimistic. The
assault forces used 4,266 landing ships and craft,
which represented 99.3 percent of all U.S. vessels on
hand and 97.6 percent of all English vessels. See
*Report by Allied Naval Commander-in-Chief Ex-
peditionary Force on Operation* NEPTUNE (London,
1944), I, 8, 128.

[45] Memorandum on Implications of the SHAEF
Proposal to Reduce the Allocation of Landing Ships
and Landing Craft, 17 Feb 44. SHAEF SGS file 381 I
(Overlord–Anvil).

[46] Montgomery's opposition was voiced in a letter
inclosing staff comments on the 17 February memo
cited in note 45. He reversed himself at SCAEF 5th
Mtg, 18 Feb 44. SHAEF SGC file 381 I (Overlord–
Anvil).

[47] Minute, Ismay to Prime Minister, 19 Feb 44.
SHAEF SGS file 381 I (Overlord–Anvil).

fight the critical battle of Italy and to meet "other commitments which might arise in the Mediterranean." [48]

Eisenhower left the meeting at which this discussion took place, feeling that the chances of carrying out ANVIL were slim.[49] Nevertheless he continued to argue for a compromise that would save the southern France assault as long as there was any reasonable prospect that it might be feasible. On 22 February he reached agreement with the British that Italy must have overriding priority over all present and future operations in the Mediterranean, but, subject to that priority, alternative plans would be prepared for amphibious operations to assist OVERLORD, the first alternative being ANVIL on the approximate scale and date originally planned. The Commander in Chief Mediterranean was to release 20 LST's and 21 LCI(L)'s to OVERLORD in exchange for 6 AKA's, the craft to sail for the United Kingdom in April. All these arrangements, finally, would be reviewed on 20 March. If at that time it was decided that ANVIL could not be mounted, the lift in the Mediterranean in excess of that needed for one division would be withdrawn for use in OVERLORD.[50] This compromise was agreed to by the Joint Chiefs of Staff, the President, and the Prime Minister.[51]

The decision held only about long enough to be written down. Eisenhower, more and more convinced that ANVIL would not take place, became equally convinced that it would be dangerous to allow planning for OVERLORD to continue unsettled because of the uncertainty of getting enough landing craft. On 26 February, he considered cabling General Marshall "his view that ANVIL was impossible" in order to force a decision to release ANVIL landing craft for OVERLORD.[52]

Two days later, Generals Wilson and Alexander in the Mediterranean cabled their concern over the difficulties at Anzio, stressed the general shortage of LST's in the theater, and specifically asked that certain proposed transfers of craft to the United Kingdom be held up.[53] The British Chiefs of Staff reacted to the appeal with a blanket recommendation that all LST's then in the Mediterranean be retained there and that 26 LST's (with 26 LCT's as deck loads) scheduled for shipment to the Mediterranean be diverted to the United Kingdom.[54] This proposal was rejected both by General Wilson and by the U.S. Chiefs of Staff.

The debate continued; the uncertainty continued; and the danger of stinting the OVERLORD allocation of landing craft became daily more threatening. General Eisenhower pressed for a decision. Landing craft for OVERLORD were so closely figured that the Supreme Commander

[48] COS (44) 53d Mtg (O), 19 Feb 44.

[49] Cbl, Eisenhower to Marshall, 19 Feb 44. SHAEF SGS file 381 I (Overlord–Anvil).

[50] Cbl, 23 Feb 44, reproduced as CCS 465/11, 24 Feb 44.

[51] Cbl, CCS to SHAEF, 26 Feb 44. SHAEF SGS file 381 I (Overlord–Anvil); cf. CCS 465/11 and CCS 147th Mtg, 27 Feb 44.

[52] SCAEF 6th Mtg, 26 Feb 44. SHAEF SGS file 387/11 (Supreme Commander's Conferences). General Smith demurred despite his previous advocacy that ANVIL be abandoned. Smith said he "felt that there was little necessity for sending this message [suggested by Eisenhower], and feared that it would give the impression of changing our minds too quickly." Cf. below, n. 55.

[53] Cbls in SHAEF SGS file 381 I (Overlord–Anvil).

[54] Cbl, COS to JSM, 29 Feb 44. SHAEF SGS file 381 I (Overlord–Anvil). These were craft which by decision at Cairo were allocated to the Mediterranean from production previously earmarked for the Pacific. See above, Ch. III.

viewed with deep concern the loss of four or five LST's in the United Kingdom and Mediterranean during the first few days of March. He pointed out to General Marshall that SHAEF had not only established minimum landing craft requirements but "went short 15 LST's in the interest of keeping ANVIL alive." Now it had even less than its minimum requirements. "The uncertainty," he added, "is having a marked effect on everyone responsible for planning and executing operation OVERLORD." [55]

To the Joint Chiefs of Staff it became increasingly apparent during March that there would be no break in the battle for Italy that would permit an advance on Rome before the end of the month. ANVIL was dying. Still there seemed sound strategic reasons for trying to keep it alive. General Marshall did not agree with the British that involvement in Italy would necessarily serve the purpose of holding enemy divisions away from the OVERLORD battle. He quoted General Alexander's opinion that the Germans, using only six to eight divisions in the peninsula, could materially delay him. The enemy would still have some ten to fifteen divisions in Italy which he could shift to meet the Allied attack in northern France, "not to mention those [divisions] from Southern France and elsewhere." [56]

On 21 March General Eisenhower recommended the cancellation of ANVIL as an attack timed to coincide with OVERLORD. [57] This recommendation was accepted and the reallocation of landing craft from the Mediterranean was ordered. The Gordian knot, as far as OVERLORD planning was concerned, was cut. OVERLORD was at last assured landing craft in numbers at least adequate for the job to be done, although there would still be few to spare. [58]

The Neptune Plans

The firm decision to expand the assault resulted in the drafting of a new outline plan: the NEPTUNE Initial Joint Plan, published on 1 February 1944 by General Montgomery, Admiral Ramsay, and Air Marshall Leigh-Mallory. The Initial

---

[55] Cbl, Eisenhower to Marshall, 9 Mar 44. SHAEF SGS file 381 I (Overlord–Anvil). He added that the Italian situation was not developing in a way to increase the likelihood of ANVIL and that the demands of OVERLORD on the other hand were making it inevitable to draw on ANVIL resources. "This being the case, I think it is the gravest possible mistake to allow demands for ANVIL to militate against the main effort even in the matter of time and certainty of planning."

[56] Cbl, Marshall to Eisenhower, 16 Mar 44. Eisenhower Personal Files.

[57] Cbl, Eisenhower to Marshall, 21 Mar 44. SHAEF SGS file 381 I (Overlord–Anvil). Eisenhower said nothing in this message about a later mounting of ANVIL. He recommended pressing offensive operations in the Mediterranean "initially in Italy and extending from there into France as rapidly as we can." Specifically he suggested that the Supreme Allied Commander in the Mediterranean theater be directed to assist OVERLORD by containing the maximum number of enemy forces and to do this by "the highest possible tempo of offensive action." Mediterranean plans, he suggested, should include "the mounting of a positive threat against the south of France or the Ligurian coast with provision for taking immediate advantage of RANKIN [enemy collapse] conditions should they occur."

[58] The ANVIL problem, however, was far from settled. The U.S. Chiefs of Staff had yielded only on the timing; they still wanted the assault mounted at a later date. The British were equally insistent on outright cancellation. The debate continued until 1 July when the Prime Minister at last conceded the U.S. argument (though he remained unconvinced). The southern France invasion, scheduled at that time for 15 July, was subsequently postponed and at last mounted on 15 August under the code name DRAGOON. Details of the later ANVIL debate will be found in F. C. Pogue, The Supreme Command, and Major J. D. T. Hamilton, Southern France and Alsace, volumes now under preparation in this series.

Joint Plan called itself an "executive instrument" directing "subordinate planning and its implementation." Extremely detailed at some points and sketchy at others, it reflected its dependence on the original Outline OVERLORD as well as on subsequent planning by lower tactical headquarters for armies and their associated naval task forces and tactical air forces. It threw the whole burden of detailed ground planning to the armies, which were directed to submit outline assault plans before 15 February. These plans were to show regimental frontage with objectives, Ranger (Commando) and airborne tasks, provisional lists of beach defense targets with timing for fire support, and the approximate number of men and vehicles to be landed in each regiment (or brigade) on the first four tides, with the number and types of landing craft required. They were also to furnish lists, by types of units, of the number of men and vehicles to be carried in the initial lift, a forecast of operations and tentative build-up priorities from D plus 1 to D plus 14, and proposals for achieving the airfield construction program.[59]

The First U.S. Army plan, issued on 25 February, and the Second British Army plan, issued on 20 March, together constituted the over-all ground forces plan for OVERLORD, inasmuch as 21 Army Group never drew up an army group plan.[60] Both the naval and air commanders in chief published over-all plans. The naval plan in particular was in exhaustive detail and was subject, of course, to continual amendment as changes occurred at lower levels and as allocations of landing craft and naval vessels were shifted.

Planning proceeded almost simultaneously on all levels. Outline plans for armies, corps, and naval task forces were prepared early and used as a framework for the planning of lower echelons. The lower echelon plans in turn filled in and modified the army, corps, and task force plans, which were generally (though not always) issued in final form as field or operation orders.

In the sections following, no one plan is described. The attempt rather has been to distill out of the scores of relevant documents—plans, memoranda, minutes of meetings, amendments, and similar sources—the salient points of the tactical plan at about army level and to discuss the principal problems that arose in the course of the planning from the time of General Eisenhower's assumption of command. Detailed plans of divisions and lower units will be found in appropriate places in the narrative of operations.

The Enemy [61]

Planning during the winter and early spring proceeded on the assumption that enemy strength and dispositions would remain substantially unchanged before the target date. The assumption was necessary in order to have a firm basis for planning, but actually it was already clear in February that the enemy was busy

---

[59] NEPTUNE Initial Joint Plan by ANCXF, CinC 21 A Gp, and CinC AEAF, pars. 103–104. Pre-Inv file 247.

[60] FUSA Operations Plan NEPTUNE, 25 Feb 44. 12th A Gp file 370.2; Second British Army, Outline Plan, 4 Feb 44. Pre-Inv file 631A.

[61] It should be observed that this whole section represents the enemy dispositions and preparations only as known by Allied commanders. It should be compared with Chapters IV and VII and with the operational chapters, VIII through X. Allied intelligence, on the whole, however, was accurate and complete before the invasion.

strengthening his defenses in the west. It was noted that the rotation of offensive divisions from rest areas in France to the Eastern Front, which had been normal German practice throughout 1943, had now stopped, although the flow of battle-worn divisions into the west from Russia continued. The total German strength in France and the Low Countries was estimated to have climbed from forty to fifty-three divisions by February, and indications were that it might reach sixty by spring. Estimates in May seemed to confirm this prediction.[62] But despite the enemy build-up of divisional units he still had only about twelve reserve divisions, and this was precisely the figure set by COSSAC in July 1943 as the maximum number of offensive divisions that the Allies could safely take on. Thus the estimated addition to Rundstedt's troop list of some twenty divisions between the summer of 1943 and spring of 1944 did not in itself force any revision of Allied plans or cause any grave Allied concern. The May estimates of German capacity to build up against the Allied bridgehead did not greatly exceed COSSAC's maximum figures. COSSAC had set as a condition for the attack that the enemy should not be able to withdraw more than fifteen divisions from Russia. In May it seemed unlikely that any more divisions would be moved from the Eastern Front, at least in the first few months of OVERLORD, or that more than thirteen divisions could be diverted from other fronts. COSSAC's conditions further included a maximum enemy build-up in the invasion area of three divisions on D Day, five

by D plus 2, and nine by D plus 8, in addition to the coastal divisions. Allied intelligence in May reckoned the enemy capable of the same maximum build-up on D Day, of six to seven divisions by D plus 2, and eleven to fourteen divisions by D plus 8. The latter calculations were in equivalent first-class divisions as it was estimated that the majority of the enemy's mobile reserves were neither fully mobile nor up to authorized strength.[63]

More than half the German divisions were known to be static or limited employment—that is, either immobile defense divisions or divisions capable only of limited offensive action.[64] It was considered likely that troops of the static divisions would resist only so long as they could fire from protected positions with minimum risk to themselves.[65] Although in May all divisions were believed in the process of being strengthened for offensive use, it was felt that this upgrading could not be completed in time.[66] Furthermore it was believed that any improvement of the static divisions would be at the expense of at least an equal number of nominal attack divisions which were understrength and underequipped.[67] The conclusion, in short, was that the enemy, suffering from materiel shortages and transportation difficulties, could not

---

[62] See e.g., 4th Div FO 1, Annex 2a, 15 May 44. Division field orders are in the collection of European theater operational records.

[63] JIC (44) 210 (O) (Final), Opposition to OVERLORD, 20 May 44. SHAEF SGS files (JIC Papers).

[64] See Ch. VII for discussion of types of German divisions. "Limited employment" was a G-2 term for which there was no German equivalent. It meant simply a unit which in the opinion of the G-2 had less than full combat value. For classification by the Germans of their own divisions, see below, Ch. VII, n. 66.

[65] Annex I to FUSA plan cited n. 60.

[66] 4th Div FO 1, 15 May 44.

[67] JIC (44) 215 (O), Periodic Review of Conditions in Europe and Scale of Opposition to 'OVERLORD,' 25 May 44.

greatly increase the total offensive striking power of his troops in France although he might choose either to concentrate it or to spread it thin.

The German tactics of all-out defense of the coast line were well known. It was assumed, however, that this did not mean literally a main line of resistance at the water's edge but rather a short stubborn stand in the fortified coastal zone of long enough duration to permit attack divisions in immediate tactical reserve to launch holding counterattacks. These in turn would give time for the massing of armored reserves for a full-scale counterattack designed to drive the Allies back into the sea. If this were the German defense plan, then the location and quality of reserves were the critical factors in any estimate of enemy capabilities.

Reserves available to Rundstedt were estimated at ten panzer and panzer grenadier divisions and fourteen to seventeen attack infantry or parachute divisions.[68] But of these only about three to four panzer and two infantry divisions were considered first quality. It was expected that the enemy would be able to move one panzer and two infantry divisions into the invasion area on D Day to reinforce the defense and mount local counterattacks. Further reinforcements would trickle in during the next two days and would probably be committed piecemeal. By D plus 3 the enemy might have a total of three panzer, two parachute, and four attack infantry divisions in addition to his coastal defense troops. These reinforcements could be organized for large-scale counterattack by D plus 7. Estimates did not agree, however, as to

either the likelihood of such an attack or the probable timing.[69] What was clear was that at any time after D plus 3 considerable enemy pressure in the form either of a large co-ordinated counterattack or of a multiplication of piecemeal attacks could be expected. The Navy was therefore directed to land the maximum number of operational troops before that date.

The German Army in the west awaited attack behind the much-advertised "Atlantic Wall" into which the enemy since 1943 had been pouring a new rumor of impregnability with each bucket of concrete. But despite both rumors and concrete it was clear to Allied planners that the Atlantic Wall had few of the characteristics of a wall and was probably not impregnable, provided a sufficient weight of fire could be directed against it.[70] Of prime concern to the Allies were the coastal batteries. Four batteries of 155-mm. guns were identified in First U.S. Army zone (a total of twenty-two guns), the most formidable of which was the six-gun battery at Pointe du Hoe. The Germans had two heavy (240-mm.) coastal batteries within range of Allied sea lanes and assault areas, one at Le Havre and one (batterie Hamburg)[71] at Fermanville east of Cherbourg. The latter, however, was little cause for concern. In May Allied reconnaissance ascertained that the enemy was busy casemating the Fermanville guns in such a way as to prohibit their being brought to bear against the OVERLORD assault. Last-minute intelli-

---

[68] CCS 454/6, Review of Conditions in Europe (10 May 44), 17 May 44; cf. JIC paper cited n. 67.

[69] See, e.g., CCS 454/5, 14 Apr 44.

[70] Naval Expeditionary Force Planning Memoranda–Section I, 26 Dec 43. SHAEF AG file 045.93–2.

[71] This battery figured in the ground fighting later. See below, Ch. X.

gence reports cheered the enemy on, noting that "construction activity [was] continuing at good pace." [72]

In fixed emplacements it was estimated that the enemy had a maximum total of seventy-three guns that could fire on the American attack. It was believed, however, that he also had mobile artillery behind the coast. Allied intelligence especially warned of the enemy's highly mobile 170-mm. gun, which had a range of 32,370 yards.[73] The gun could be so easily handled that German practice was to fire not more than two rounds from the same position. Frequent displacement would, of course, make effective counterbattery fire almost impossible. All eight of the 170-mm. guns known to be in the U.S. invasion zone were bombed out of positions on the Cotentin during air raids in the middle of May and were thereafter unlocated.[74]

In the early months of 1944, the Germans were observed to be working hard at strengthening their defenses along the invasion coast. On 20 February air photographs for the first time revealed antilanding obstacles below the high-water mark on certain French beaches. The discovery was no surprise but it was a cause for concern. German experimentation with beach obstacles had been reported in the early months of 1943. At about that time the British Combined Operations Headquarters had begun counterexperimentation in clearing such obstacles, chiefly in the expectation that they might be faced in Mediterranean operations. Allied naval planning for OVERLORD in late 1943

gave prominent, if necessarily vague, consideration to the problem. But detailed provisions and training for coping with the obstacles had to wait until their full nature and extent became apparent. Allied reconnaissance watched with special interest the growth of the enemy's works in the tidal flats during the late winter and early spring.[75] The growth was rapid. For example, at Quinéville (east coast of the Cotentin) a double row of tetrahedra or hedgehogs 2,300 yards long, with twenty-six feet between obstacles, was laid in four days.[76]

The enemy began placing his obstacles near the high-water mark and then thickened the bands seaward. There was then some talk among Allied planners of shifting H Hour to coincide with low tide so as to allow engineers as much time as possible to clear the obstacles before the tide covered them.[77] By the middle of May, however, the obstacles on the invasion beaches still did not extend below the eight-foot mark above low water. Planners calculated that, if in the remaining days before D Day they were not set any lower, the planned touchdown time three hours before high water would still permit Allied engineers to deal with the obstacles dry shod. Breaching the obstacles under these conditions was considered feasible, although V Corps had

---

[72] NCWTF Int Bull 2, 29 May 44.

[73] As compared to an estimated maximum range of 25,000 yards for the 155-mm. guns.

[74] NCWTF Int Bull 1, 21 May 44.

[75] COS (44) 393 (O), Clearance of Underwater Obstacles, 3 May 44. SHAEF SGS file 800.8; cf. Ltr, Eisenhower to Marshall, 6 May 44, in which he lists first among the "worst problems of these days" the problem of how to remove underwater obstacles. Eisenhower Personal Files.

[76] FUSA Int Note No. 18, 24 Apr 44. Pre-Inv file 631A.

[77] Memo, Gen Kean (FUSA CofS), for Gen Bradley, 20 Apr 44. Pre-Inv file 631A. H Hour had been fixed in February at about half-flood.

VAUVILLE BEACH, SPRING 1944, *Cotentin Peninsula west coast.*

soberly commented in March that it might be "expensive." [78]

The enemy on the ground, though less formidable than his own propaganda reported, seemed formidable enough. On the sea and in the air there was little question of the Allies' overwhelming superiority. The relatively insignificant German Navy was not expected to risk any of its large surface warships in attacks on Allied convoys in the Channel, though they might attempt diversionary sorties in the Atlantic against Allied shipping there. The enemy's fifty to sixty E-boats (German *S-Boote*) carrying both mines and torpedoes were expected to be the greatest surface menace to the invasion fleet.[79] But even these boats would probably attack only at night. The estimated 130 ocean-going submarines (over 300 tons) based in the Bay of Biscay and the 25 short-range boats in the Baltic had never been used in the Channel. It seemed unlikely that they would take that risk even during the invasion, although they might be concentrated against assemblies of Allied shipping, especially in the western Channel approaches.[80] The enemy was known to be experimenting with midget submarines and human torpedoes. These might be used close to shore against ships carrying the assault troops, but no one could even guess how many of these craft might be available by D Day. On the whole, the Allies predicted that their chief concern at sea would be enemy mines. In any case, they did not anticipate a determined enemy naval attack in the early stages of the assault.

Estimates of the enemy's air strength varied so widely that they might have been drawn from a hat. Certain judgments, however, seem to have been generally accepted. The German Air Force had increased slightly in numbers since the summer of 1943, but the increase, compared to the Allied build-up, was negligible. It was generally believed that the Luftwaffe would be capable of between 1,000 and 1,800 sorties on D Day against OVERLORD, but it was considered unlikely that the enemy would make anything like the maximum air effort in the early stages. Instead, he would probably try to conserve his aircraft for use in close support of the expected large-scale counterattacks at the end of the first week after D Day.[81]

Although Goering was credited with having more than 5,000 aircraft, the effort which that force could exert and sustain would certainly be considerably less than its size alone suggested. The superiority of the Allies would probably prevent the enemy from daylight bombing or would make such bombing ineffective and costly if it were attempted. The difficulties which the Germans were known to be experiencing with replacements in machines and crews would mean that the front-line air forces, however impressive, would have little depth. Allied bombing of airfields, furthermore, was likely to cause drastic curtailment of

---

[78] V Corps Breaching Plan, Underwater and Beach Obstacles, 17 Mar 42, prepared jointly by CG V Corps and Comdr 11th Amph Force. Pre-Inv file 647.

[79] NCWTF Int Bull 1, 21 May 44.

[80] NEPTUNE Monograph, prepared by Comdr Task Force 122, Apr 44. Pre-Inv file 252.

---

[81] For various estimates see AEAF Over-all Air Plan, 15 Apr 44. 12th A Gp file 370.2; JIC (44) 210 (O), 23 May 44; NCWTF Int Bull 1, 21 May 44.

Luftwaffe efficiency. It was deemed unlikely that the enemy would be able to get into the air more than 60 percent of his nominal front-line force.

The German Air Force had been defeated by the Combined Bomber Offensive in the early months of 1944. This victory the Allies were sure of. The knowledge was the most important ingredient in the final decision to go ahead with OVERLORD. It was not certain, however, just how dangerous a death agony the Luftwaffe might still be capable of. Air Marshal Leigh-Mallory said afterward that he was always "confident that the German Air Force would constitute no serious threat to our operations on land, sea or in the air." He did admit, however, the possibility of a major air battle on D Day.[82]

The basic assumption behind all Allied estimates of German military power in the west was that the enemy would make his supreme effort to defeat the invasion, hoping thus to achieve a compromise peace despite his hopeless situation on the Russian front. The principal weakness of the enemy was believed to be the depreciation of his reserves in men and materiel which would prohibit him from a sustained defense. The Allies were of the opinion that the Germans would stake everything on the initial battle of the beach. The decision to go ahead with OVERLORD therefore implied an estimate that the enemy's maximum strength was probably insufficient to win the battle for the beachheads.

Objectives and Terrain

The February revision of the OVERLORD plan did not affect the final objective of the operation in its later phases. The analysis of COSSAC and earlier planners which had led them to select the lodgment area in northwest France bounded by the Seine, Eure, and Loire Rivers was accepted, as well as the general timing and phasing of operations after the capture of Cherbourg. It was the assault phase plan that underwent drastic revision.

The three beaches selected by COSSAC [83] had capacity only for three assault divisions. New beaches were required for the expanded attack. Extension of the front eastward to include the beach between Lion-sur-Mer and Ouistreham was readily accepted. (*Map II*) But the revived proposal to land a fifth division northwest of the Vire estuary met renewed opposition. The debate turned largely on the tactical implications of the topography of the NEPTUNE area.

In the area were five regions with distinguishable topographical characteristics—the north Cotentin (rolling uplands north of Valognes), the south Cotentin (generally flat and well watered), the Bessin (the coastal strip lying between Isigny and Bayeux), the Bocage (hilly wooded country extending south of the Bessin and Cotentin nearly to the base of the Brittany Peninsula), and the relatively open Caen country from Bayeux east and southeast.[84] The three British

[82] "Despatch by Air Chief Marshal Sir Trafford Leigh-Mallory" (submitted to the Supreme Allied Commander in November 1944), *Fourth Supplement to The London Gazette* No. 37838, 31 December 1946, pp. 40–41, cited hereafter as Leigh-Mallory, *Despatch*.

[83] Lion-sur-Mer – Courseulles – Arromanches, and Colleville–Vierville.

[84] The regional nomenclature here, not entirely consistent with current French usage, is derived from NEPTUNE Monograph, pp. 26–31. See n. 80.

beaches all lay in the east portion of the Bessin and in the Caen country. There was no clear demarcation between the Caen country and the Bessin. But whereas the Bessin merged to the south with the Bocage, the Caen country spread southeastward into open arable land suitable for tank maneuver and, more important, for the development of airfields. In both the original COSSAC plan and the "Montgomery" plan, the securing of the Caen country for airfield development was a critical early objective for the assaulting forces. British troops were to take Bayeux and Caen on D Day, and push the bridgehead gradually south and southeast. They would then secure airfield sites and protect the east flank of U.S. forces whose primary mission, in both plans, was the capture of Cherbourg. COSSAC allotted only two British divisions to the initial tasks of taking Bayeux and Caen. For the same tasks the Montgomery plan would land three divisions by sea and in addition put an airborne division (less one brigade) east of the beachheads to secure crossings of the Orne River. In all the planning the vital importance of the "capture and retention" of Caen and neighboring open country was underlined.[85] On the other land no pre-D-Day plans called for exploiting the favorable tank terrain at any phase of the operation for a direct thrust southeast toward Paris. Instead, the British army would push gradually south and east of Caen until its left rested approximately on the Touques River and its right, pivoting on Falaise, swung toward Argentan–Alençon.[86]

In both the COSSAC and Montgomery plans the task of securing the Bessin fell to one U.S. corps, with one division in the assault. Critical topographical feature of the Bessin was the Aure River, which flows out of the Bocage to Bayeux and then turns west to parallel the coast line to Isigny where it joins the Vire near its mouth and empties into the Channel. The Aure in its lower reaches between Trévières and Isigny runs through a broad, flat, marshy valley which can be flooded by damming the river. When flooded, the Aure in effect makes a peninsula of the coastal sector between Port-en-Bessin and Isigny. The "peninsula," varying in width from about a mile and a half at the eastern end to about five miles at the western, is a very gently rolling tableland. Most of it is cut up in the typical Norman pattern of orchards, hedgerow-enclosed meadows, and patches of trees. Only along the coast between Vierville-sur-Mer and St. Laurent is the country relatively open. Through the "peninsula" runs the main lateral road in the invasion area: a section of the principal highway from Paris to Cherbourg. This was the rope which alone could tie the five beachheads into one. Early control of it was essential for the security of the initial lodgment area.

In the COSSAC plan the Bessin–Caen bridgehead would have been expanded south and southwest deep into the Bocage during the first week of the operation. A force would then have broken out northwest to sweep up the Cotentin and capture Cherbourg. Although this was deemed a feasible operation, the low marshy bottom lands of the Douve River

[85] See, for instance, Second Br Army/83 Group, 2d TAF, Plan, 20 Mar 44. Pre-Inv file 631A.

[86] Montgomery, Brief Summary of Operation "OVERLORD" as Affecting the Army, 7 Apr 44. Photo-

static copy with Montgomery's penciled corrections in Hist Div files.

and its tributaries, which stretched nearly across the base of the peninsula, would have made it difficult. Subject to inundation, these almost continuous swamplands, traversed by only three main roads, draw an easily defended moat across about five-sixths of the peninsula. The only dry corridor is on the west coast—a strip 5,000 to 6,000 yards wide between St. Lô–d'Ourville and St. Sauveur de Pierre-Pont, which could easily be held by a small enemy force.

The overriding importance of Cherbourg had therefore led to early consideration of a simultaneous assault in the peninsula itself to establish Allied forces north of the Douve line. Such an attack became practicable only with the decision to employ five divisions in the assault. But even then it had serious disadvantages, chiefly because, in addition to the inundations at the base of the peninsula, there was a flooded coastal strip behind the best landing beach on the east coast. Across this flooded area, which was about two miles wide and extended from the Bancs du Grand Vey to Quinéville, narrow causeways provided the only exits from the beach. Four such exits led from the beach proposed for assault by one U.S. division. Again the terrain favored the defense. Relatively small German forces could hold these causeways, block Allied egress from the beaches, and quite possibly defeat the landing at the coast. The proposed solution was to employ an airborne division to be dropped before H Hour in the vicinity of Ste. Mère–Eglise with primary mission of seizing and holding the causeways in order to permit the seaborne infantry to cross unopposed. Even this solution involved risks which

some planners felt were not justified. The only previous Allied experience with large-scale airborne operations, in Sicily, had not proved a notable success, and these had been launched against an enemy relatively weak and unprepared. More important, it was pointed out that the same water barrier which barred the Cotentin from attack from the south could also be used by the enemy to maintain a wedge between the Allied bridgeheads on either side of the Vire. It was conceivable then that the enemy might defeat the landings in detail. Finally it was argued that the Bessin–Caen attack must be the main Allied effort. If it failed, success on the Cotentin could never be exploited. The fifth division, therefore, should be left in floating reserve to insure the success of the main landing and not committed in the longshot Cotentin gamble.

This argument was presented in a SHAEF planning paper as late as 23 January 1944.[87] A week later, with the publication of the Initial Joint Plan, the decision was made that the risks of the Cotentin assault were worth taking in view of the need to secure the port of Cherbourg as early as possible. First U.S. Army was to assault on both sides of the Vire estuary with one regiment of VII Corps to the north on the beach later called UTAH and two regiments of V Corps between Vierville and Colleville on the beach later called OMAHA.[88] First

---

[87] NEPTUNE–Comparison of Methods of Employment of Additional Resources. SHAEF G–3 files, bundle A–1 (Pre-D-Day Planning Papers).

[88] Beaches UTAH and OMAHA were first designated X and Y respectively. The final code names were published by First Army in Amendment 1 to FUSA plan, 3 Mar 44.

Army's main task would be "to capture Cherbourg as quickly as possible."[89]

For the task of seizing and holding the causeways across the flooded strip behind UTAH Beach, the Initial Joint Plan allotted to First Army one airborne division. Further planning revealed that the force was inadequate and raised the larger problem of how airborne operations could best contribute to the success of OVERLORD.

Airborne Planning

General Morgan, it will be recalled, had been allotted two airborne divisions to be used in the assault but was given only 632 transport aircraft. His plan was to use two-thirds of one division plus seven to nine battalions in the initial drop on D Day to seize Caen and certain river crossings and coastal defenses. But even this force, he calculated, required 372 more planes than he had.[90] The Quebec Conference, considering Outline OVERLORD, increased the allotment of air transport but found that, even counting the problematical availability of four U.S. groups, the total would still fall short of COSSAC's requirements. It appears, however, that the real difficulty as the time for OVERLORD approached was not in finding the necessary aircraft but rather in arriving at a conviction that they were needed. In the last weeks be-

fore the launching of OVERLORD, high-level discussions of the use of airborne troops in the operation turned not so much on the availability of resources as on how, tactically, the forces should be employed.

There was some early skepticism about the capabilities of airborne operations in conjunction with amphibious assault. The Dieppe raid commanders recommended against dependence on parachutists because they felt it would be almost impossible to secure a coincidence of weather and light conditions suitable both for air drops and for landing by sea.[91] The development of navigation aids, however, greatly reduced this objection after 1942. On the other hand, the difficulties encountered in executing the airborne drop in Sicily gave some observers new reason for skepticism. In a report circulated among commanders planning the OVERLORD assault, Combined Operations observers wrote that airborne operations were risky and "undue dependence on airborne effort must only too often lead to disappointment or even disastrous consequences for land forces." [92]

This conclusion was fortunately not shared by either General Eisenhower or General Marshall. In their view the difficulties of the airborne operations in Sicily proved only the error of dispersing the effort. Both wanted greater mass in future drops. Eisenhower recommended that all troops should be landed at once, rather than in successive waves, and that larger forces should be employed. Gen-

---

[89] Amendment 1, 2 March 1944, to NEPTUNE Initial Joint Plan (see n. 59) added as a second priority task the development of the beachhead south toward St. Lô "in conformity with the advance of Second British Army." In the light of Second Army's mission to protect the left flank of First Army, this made a kind of circular relationship which amounted to telling both armies to keep pushing abreast.

[90] COSSAC (43) 36, 28 Jul 43.

---

[91] Combined Rpt, The Dieppe Raid, Sep 42, Part V. SHAEF G–3 files, bundle A, item 9.

[92] CO Rpt, Lessons Learnt in the Mediterranean, 14 Oct 43. Pre-Inv file 661.

eral Marshall agreed and added his opinion: "The value of airborne forces in OVERLORD would be immense, and would enable us to seize quickly and control ports which could not otherwise be used." [93]

Airborne commanders were thinking along much the same lines. The organization of the airborne division under the Army Ground Forces' concept of a light infantry division was ill adapted to its tactical employment in Europe. Maj. Gen. Matthew B. Ridgway (commander of the 82d Airborne Division), from his experience in Sicily, proposed in December 1943 a new Table of Organization which would have added some eight to nine thousand men, roughly doubling the current size of the division.[94] The purpose was to make it capable of sustained ground effort. Although the new organization fitted the developing concept of using airborne forces in mass, it was rejected first by Lt. Gen. Lesley J. McNair, Chief of the Army Ground Forces, and later, on re-examination, by the Joint Staff Planners.[95] These actions postponed formal reorganization, but for European operations they made little practical difference. The two airborne divisions scheduled for use in OVERLORD were in fact swelled to something like the size recommended by General Ridg-

way, by the attachment to each of two separate parachute regiments.

The February revision of the OVERLORD plan struck out COSSAC's use of airborne forces in dispersed packets for a variety of commando objectives. COSSAC's plan to take Caen with airborne troops was also eliminated as unnecessary in view of the additional British division to be landed by sea. On the other hand, expansion of the front to the east raised a new tactical requirement—the need to secure crossings over the Orne River to cover the British left flank. This mission could best be accomplished, it was thought, by dropping parachutists on the east bank of the river. On 7 February General Eisenhower proposed that two divisions be dropped simultaneously in the U.S. and British zones "with such depth of means including trained crews behind the simultaneous lift to enable a third airborne division to be dropped complete 24 hours later." [96] To this the British air staff replied flatly that it was impossible because of the lack of trained crews.[97] Eisenhower for the moment ac-

---

[93] CCS 120th Mtg, 24 Sep 43. Eisenhower's recommendations were made in a letter to Marshall, 17 Jul 43. Eisenhower Personal Files.

[94] Cbl, Marshall to Devers, R 6441, 1 Dec 43. WD Cable log.

[95] App. to CCS 496, 26 Feb 44. The gist of the planners' opinion was simply that it seemed "unwise to make any important changes in our airborne organizations until further tests in actual combat have been made." See Greenfield *et al., Organization of Ground Combat Troops,* p. 349.

[96] COS (44) 140 (O), Airborne Forces for OVERLORD, 7 Feb 44.

[97] *Ibid.* The difficulties of training air crews for airborne operations were discussed in detail in a memorandum by the Chief of Air Staff (COS (44) 135 (O)), 6 Feb 44. An excerpt follows:

"The crew after passing out of the [Operational Training Unit] O.T.U. (3 months' course) and being 'converted' to the handling of heavy aircraft by day and night, require some 30 hours' basic training which consists mainly of map reading from low altitudes. The crew must also receive instruction on the use of radio aids to navigation.

"When proficient as a crew and familiar with their equipment they begin training with troops, first dropping a few parachutists, then full 'sticks' and thence passing on to tugging gliders.

"Finally the very highly organized system of assembly, take-off, manoeuvre and approach has to be learned and practiced. Some idea of the skill and

cepted this verdict because he did not want to risk interference with the intensity of the bomber offensive. During February, however, it became apparent that there would be lift and crews enough for a simultaneous landing of one and two-thirds divisions. It was decided to land the 101st Airborne Division behind UTAH Beach and two British airborne brigades (regiments) of the 6th Airborne Division east of the Orne River.[98] First Army in the meantime had asked for a second airborne division to block the St. Lô–d'Ourville corridor and prevent enemy reinforcement of the Cotentin. This requirement was to be met by dropping the 82d Airborne Division in the vicinity of St. Sauveur-le Vicomte on the night of D Day, using the aircraft returned from the initial operations.

General Marshall, informed of the airborne plans in February, questioned the planners' apparent conservatism. He felt that they still contemplated piecemeal employment, which he regarded just as unsound tactically for airborne as for armor. As an alternative he recommended a bold plan outlined by General Arnold. Arnold's plan briefly called for the establishment on D Day of an airhead in the Evreux–Dreux area which would directly threaten the Seine River cross-

ings and Paris. In recommending this scheme, General Marshall called it a true vertical envelopment involving a major strategic threat which the enemy would have to meet by a major revision in his defense. In effect it would open a new front. He admitted that such an operation had never been done before but added: "Frankly that reaction makes me tired." [99] He was anxious that full advantage be taken of the Allied airborne potential. He therefore sent the plan along to Eisenhower and dispatched a little War Department mission of "young men" to defend its merits in the theater.

Eisenhower studied the plan and rejected it. He agreed to the conception but not to the timing. "Mass in vertical envelopments is sound," he wrote, "but since this kind of an enveloping force is *immobile on the ground,* the collaborating force must be strategically and tactically mobile. So the time for the mass vertical envelopment is *after* the beachhead has been gained and a striking force built up." He went on to draw an analogy between the proposed airhead and the Anzio beachhead. The German, he reflected, had repeatedly shown that he did not fear what used to be called "strategic threat of envelopment." At Anzio "the situation was almost a model for the classical picture of initiating a battle of destruction. But the German decided that the thrust could not be immediately translated into *mobile tactical action,* and himself began attacking." [100] If the Anzio

---

practice required may be gained by realizing that one aircraft with fully loaded glider takes off in the dark from each airfield every 30 seconds; that over 800 aircraft and 440 tows have to arrive at the right place at the right time after a night flight; and that it is intended to land some 440 gliders in 20–30 minutes at their destination.

"All this training after the O.T.U. stage at present takes 2 months and is then dependent on weather. No cut is possible without risking failure."

[98] NEPTUNE Initial Joint Plan, Amendment 1, 2 Mar 44.

---

[99] Ltr, Marshall to Eisenhower, 10 Feb 44. Eisenhower Personal Files.

[100] Ltr, Eisenhower to Marshall, 19 Feb 44. Eisenhower Personal Files.

beachhead could not succeed, though nourished from the sea and opposed by "inconsequential air resistance and only a total of some 19 enemy divisions in the whole of Italy," how much less chance would the isolated Dreux airhead have in the midst of some sixty enemy divisions and dependent on precarious air routes for supply and reinforcement![101]

The fact is that even the decision to land two U.S. airborne divisions in the Cotentin was under severe criticism as unduly risky. The "Air people" anticipated heavy losses which they felt might result in negligible tactical achievement. Toward the end of April, Air Marshal Leigh-Mallory objected so strongly to the risks involved that a substantial revision of plans was made. There was now transport enough for the simultaneous dropping of the parachutists of both U.S. divisions. Leigh-Mallory agreed to this but insisted that most of the glider landings be made at dusk on D Day rather than earlier as first planned. He believed that they would suffer heavy losses by daylight and that large-scale landings early on D Day would force dispersion of the parachutists for defense of the landing zones. His objections were sustained and the changes made.[102]

But this was not the end. Late in May, when Allied intelligence reported that the Germans had moved the *91st Division* into the Cotentin the risks of the air borne drops soared. Planners suggested moving the 82d Division drop zones to the Merderet River, and shifting the 101st zones slightly southward so that both divisions would be committed in the relatively small and easily defensible area between the beaches and the Douve and Merderet Rivers. This proposal had to be modified, however, because the area seemed too small for landings by two divisions. The compromise was to drop the 82d Airborne Division astride the Merderet, two regiments landing west of the river with the mission of securing a bridgehead for exploitation to the west at least as far as the Douve.[103]

Even so, the plan did not look promising. The Sicilian experience had convinced the British air staff that airborne troops should not be routed over heavily defended areas (either enemy or friendly) and that they should not be landed where they would be immediately faced with opposition.[104] The proposed Cotentin drops violated both of these precautions. Air Marshal Leigh-Mallory took an increasingly pessimistic view of what he called "this very speculative operation." On 29 May he told General Eisenhower that it was unwise to risk his carrier force, that casualties were likely to run over 50 percent, and that the results would be so small that the airborne landings could not be depended on to insure the success of the UTAH Beach assault. General Eisenhower replied that he agreed the risks were great but that the airborne landings were essential to the whole operation and that therefore, if the invasion was to go in, the airborne risks must be accepted.[105]

[101] Cbl, Eisenhower to Marshall, 10 Mar 44. Eisenhower Personal Files.

[102] Memo for SAC, 23 Apr 44. SHAEF SGS file 373/2 I; Airborne–Air Planning Committee 9th Mtg, 28 Apr 44. ETO file 337 (Conferences (Secret)), 1 AR–16–Dr 1. See Bibliographical Note.

[103] VII Corps revised FO, 28 May 44.
[104] COS (43) 552 (O), Airborne Forces, 20 Sep 43.
[105] Ltrs, 29 and 30 May. SHAEF SGS file 373/2 I.

Development of the Lodgment

After VII and V Corps secured footholds on either side of the Vire, they were to join up in the ground between the Vire and Taute Rivers. Originally both Carentan and Isigny were listed as D-Day objectives for VII and V Corps respectively.[106] Detailed planning showed this project to be unduly optimistic. Carentan was eliminated, and instead the 101st Airborne Division was ordered simply to seize crossings of the river and canal north and northeast of the city and be prepared to take it "as soon as the tactical situation permits."[107] Plans for the capture of Isigny were ambiguous. Although the city was clearly excluded from the D-Day objectives listed in the 1st Division Field Order of 16 April and from subordinate unit orders issued later, the 29th Division on 29 May published a change to its field order which redrew the D-Day phase line to include Isigny.[108] V Corps always viewed the capture of Isigny as belonging to the first phase of the operations but apparently issued no order that it should be taken on D Day. On 3 June, however, in a command conference on board the Force O headquarters ship, the V Corps commander, Maj. Gen. Leonard T. Gerow, told his subordinate commanders that the 115th Infantry should get to Isigny the first day if possible.[109]

Whether or not Isigny was taken, the principal concern of V Corps initially was to secure the tableland north of the Aure and be prepared to repel enemy counterattacks. It was believed that junction of the two First Army beachheads would actually not require either corps to make a lateral movement in force. Southward advance especially by V Corps, it was thought, would probably force the enemy to pull out of the intercorps zone.[110]

At the same time that the two corps were joining forces between Carentan and Isigny, VII Corps would clear the low rolling country of the south Cotentin as far west as the Douve.[111] The VII Corps line would then be pushed up against the high ground of the north Cotentin, in some places within ten miles of Cherbourg. This line, running just north and northwest of the arc St. Vaast-la Hougue–Valognes–St. Sauveur-le Vicomte, would be reached, it was hoped, by D plus 2. The 4th Division, joined by the 90th and later, if necessary, by the 9th, would then make the final push to the port. This final phase through rugged country and the fortified hills that completely fenced the landward approaches to Cherbourg was first expected to take about a week. But after the Germans had reinforced the Cotentin the

---

[106] NEPTUNE Initial Joint Plan, par. 63.

[107] 101st Abn Div FO 1, 18 May 44.

[108] Change reads that the 116th Infantry will "prepare to defend the D-day objective from La Cambe (excl) west to Isigny (incl) and the eastern banks of the Vire River north thereof." This compared to the second change, 18 May, which gave the 116th Infantry the mission to "prepare to defend the D-day phase line from La Cambe (exclusive) west to Isigny (exclusive) . . . prepare to cross the Aure River west of Isigny for an attack on Isigny from the southeast."

[109] 1st Div G–3 Jnl.

[110] General Gerow, Notes on V Corps Plan, undtd. Pre-Inv file 670.

[111] The revised VII Corps Field Order of 28 May makes no mention of cutting the peninsula, but contemplates an advance to Cherbourg on the Valognes axis with the corps' left flank resting on the Douve River.

date on which the port was expected to fall was set back to D plus 15.[112]

While VII Corps took Cherbourg, V Corps, assisted after D plus 6 by XIX Corps, would push deep into the Bocage country to establish a line roughly including the Lessay–Périers–St. Lô road, the principal lateral communication south of the Carentan–Caen highway. VII Corps would then regroup to attack south and First U.S. Army would advance with three corps abreast to the line Avranches–Domfront, at the base of the Brittany peninsula. (*Map III*) The date set for the completion of this advance was D plus 20. At that point it was expected that the Third U.S. Army would become operational and First U.S. Army Group would take command over it and First Army. The new army group would then clear the Brittany peninsula, using First Army and such forces from Third Army as necessary. Thereafter both armies would face east, Third Army on the right. The Allied forces together would push to the Seine, securing the final lodgment area by about D plus 90 and completing the initial phase of Operation OVERLORD.

The final stages of the operation were conceived and stated in these broad terms. The outlined scheme of maneuver and the timetables were not designed as tactical plans; they were frames of ref-

erence for future planning, set forth primarily so that the men of the beginning should have some idea of the shape of the end, so that their thinking might be large and their preparation adequate.

The Selection of D Day

The general timing of the assault was determined, as noted, by the Combined Chiefs of Staff, in accordance with considerations of weather, availability of resources, and co-ordination with the Russians. The designation of 1 June as the target date meant that the actual assault would take place as soon as possible after that date. Selection of the day would be determined by the conditions required for H Hour. H Hour, in turn, would be chosen to secure an advantageous coincidence of light and tidal conditions. But just what those conditions should be was not easily formulated.

The whole experience of the Mediterranean theater had been with night assaults. A considerable body of Army opinion favored continuing the pattern of surprise landings under cover of darkness in the attack against the Continent. OVERLORD, however, introduced new complications in its unprecedented size and the fact that it would go in against a heavily defended coast. The possibility of achieving tactical surprise seemed slight. Enemy radar would certainly pick up the approach of the Allied armada by day or night. A night assault would impose uncertainty on the enemy as to Allied strength and intentions, but in order to attack at night the convoys would have to make the turn toward the invasion beaches in daylight. Darkness would interfere with the enemy's

---

[112] This was done at the recommendation of General Bradley. See Ltr, Bradley to 21 A Gp, 26 May 44, quoted in Memo for SHAEF G–3, 4 Jun 44, Status of Planning, 21 Army Group. SHAEF G–3 file GCT, Ops A (21 Army Group General). Build-up schedules were then changed to delay the bringing in of port repair and operating units and allow additional combat troops to land in the early phase. The 79th Division was attached from Third Army to VII Corps and was ordered to begin landing on D plus 8. See VII Corps revised FO, 28 May 44.

shooting, reducing risks to the invasion fleet and in particular covering the assaulting troops from observed small arms fire. It was noted, however, that if the enemy chose to use flares extensively this cover might evaporate. Furthermore the obscurity of night was a double-edged weapon—or, better, a twofold shield. It would be quite as effective in preventing the Allies from laying down artillery fires or carrying out aerial bombardment in preparation for the landings. This was, of course, the crux of the decision on daylight or night landing: could the Allies engage successfully in a fire fight with enemy coastal defenders? Should they attempt a landing by a power plan or by stealth?

COSSAC did not decide the question. Although noting that the requirements of the Navy for light in which to maneuver and to deliver observed fire support were likely to be decisive, the July OVERLORD plan did not outline a naval bombardment scheme. There was some doubt whether the ships for adequate fire support would be available. There was still more doubt whether naval fire could neutralize enemy defenses to an extent that would "reasonably assure the success of an assault without the cover of darkness." [115]

Resolution of the problem was to assault soon after first light so that, while maximum use could be made of darkness in covering the approach, the preparatory bombing and naval fire could be delivered in daylight. The argument ultimately accepted in the determination of H Hour in the Initial Joint Plan was admirably set out in an analysis by Lt. Gen. John T. Crocker, Commanding General of the British 1 Corps.[114] The first essential, he said, was the development of "overwhelming fire support from all sources, air, naval and support craft . . . to cover the final stages of the approach and to enable us to close the beaches. This requires daylight." Mediterranean experience, in his view, had shown that the effectiveness of naval fire depended on observation and that it had been much greater than was previously supposed. At least forty-five minutes of daylight, he estimated, would be necessary for full use of fire support, and he concluded that H Hour should be within one hour of first light. This was, in general, accepted. Certain adjustments had to be made, however, to allow for the other more rigid requirements for H Hour: suitable tidal conditions.

The spring tide range on the Normandy Channel coast was about twenty-one feet, the neap tide range about twelve feet. Low tide uncovered at OMAHA Beach a tidal flat of an average width of 300 yards. Assaulting troops attempting to cross this flat would be entirely exposed to enemy small arms, mortar, and artillery fire. The higher the tide, the smaller the tidal flat and the less risk to the assaulting troops. The landings, however, had to take place on a rising tide to permit the vehicle landing craft to ground, unload, and withdraw without having to dry out. The questions then to be answered were: how many vehicles

---

[113] Memo, Col Partridge and Lt Col Bonesteel for Gen Bradley, 15 Dec 43. 12th A Gp file 370.03 (Invasion). Similar doubts had been expressed at the RATTLE Conference, held from 28 June to 2 July to discuss tactics of the assault. See discussion of Mountbatten's Memo on the RATTLE Conference at COS (43) 155th Mtg (O), 12 Jul 43.

[114] Ltr, 14 Dec 43. 12th A Gp file 370.03 (Invasion).

should be landed on the first tide and how much time would that require? There was another difficulty. Outcroppings of rock off the beaches in the British zone would not permit a landing at low tide. But landings on all beaches had to be roughly simultaneous to avoid alerting the enemy before the entire mass of the attack could be applied. The happy mean seemed to be an H Hour three hours before high water. Since there was a two-hour stand of high water, the time thus decided was also only one hour after low tide.[115]

To fix rigid conditions of both light and tide for D Day would have placed the whole invasion unduly at the mercy of the weather. The possibility of a day-to-day postponement in case of bad weather was provided by allowing a certain flexibility in the interval between first light and H Hour. The minimum daylight period was to be thirty minutes; the maximum, an hour and a half. The required conditions of light and tide prevailed during three days each fortnight. An additional requirement of moonlight for the airborne drops further narrowed the choice to three days a month. The first possible D Days after the OVERLORD target date were 5, 6, and 7 June. H Hour on all those dates was to be staggered, varying by about an hour from east to west because of slightly varying tidal and beach conditions.

Organization and Tactics of the Assault Forces

Each of the five assault divisions was to be put ashore by a naval task force or-

ganized not only for the transport of the troops but for their protection in the crossing and their support by naval gunfire before and after the landings. In the U.S. zone Force U would land the 4th Division on UTAH Beach, and Force O, the 1st Division on OMAHA. These, together with Force B carrying the 29th Division, the follow-up for OMAHA Beach, were all under the Western Naval Task Force, commanded by Admiral Kirk. The three British assault divisions, similarly organized, came under the Eastern Naval Task Force commanded by Rear Adm. Philip Vian.

The assaulting infantry were to be carried in transports specially modified for the purpose. The transports would proceed to lowering positions, eleven miles offshore in the U.S. zone and seven miles offshore in the British zone. There the troops would be unloaded into LCVP's or LCA's, each of which carried about thirty men. The small craft were to go in abreast in waves to touch down at regular intervals along the whole length of the beaches to be assaulted.[116]

The basic tactical problem of the assault was to smash through the hard shell of enemy shore defenses. Partial solution could be found in the normal techniques for attack against a fortified position. But amphibious attack introduced a significant and complicating difference. The assaulting infantry would have no room to maneuver. They could not fall back; they could not, except to a very limited degree, outflank enemy strong points. As the Dieppe commanders pointed out, even though "an assault

---

[115] NEPTUNE, Initial Joint Plan, pars. 58–59.

[116] NEPTUNE, Initial Joint Plan, pars. 54–56; cf. [Charles H. Taylor] *Omaha Beachhead* (Washington, 1945), p. 31.

may take place on a flank of the main objective, it is in itself a frontal attack. Thus, once the assault is discovered, there is little room for subtlety. The main necessity is to batter a way through in the shortest possible time." [117] The essential lack of "subtlety" in the first phase might be mitigated by flexibility in the organization of the assault forces. To achieve that, the Dieppe commanders suggested using a minimum assault force on the widest practicable front while holding out a large floating reserve in readiness to exploit soft spots. The reserve, it was suggested, might well constitute half the total force. Instead of staking everything on a power drive, in short, it might be possible to "feel your way in." [118] General Morgan and some of his staff were attracted by this concept, as has been pointed out, but their efforts to apply it were frustrated chiefly by the shortage of landing craft.

In the end, little reliance was placed on probing for weakness and exploiting it through decisive commitment of reserves. The assault was considered as a frontal attack which was unlikely even to have the advantage of tactical surprise. The use of smoke to cover the final run-in to the shore was seriously considered in July 1943,[119] but later experimentation led to its rejection. Trials at the Assault Training Center and in various Allied exercises showed that smoke tended to confuse assault troops as much as the defenders.[120]

The final conclusions were that smoking of the hostile shore could not be sufficiently controlled, that it offered too many opportunities for fatal mistakes, and that by interfering with observed fire it would handicap Allied fire superiority.[121]

An amphibious assault without cover of darkness or smoke, and without the flexibility of a large floating reserve, depended for success on developing a weight behind the initial attack that would not only crumble enemy defenses but would carry the assaulting troops far enough inland so that follow-up troops could be put ashore behind them to consolidate and then exploit the beachhead. The double requirement that the assaulting troops be able to knock out enemy fortifications and push rapidly inland required a careful balancing of striking power and mobility. The first proposal was to organize special assault divisions with one or two Ranger-type battalions, small and lightly equipped for the special task of reducing fortifications. The "Ranger" battalions would land first, followed by normal battalions. The assault division would go in on a broad front and move fast. It would be strong enough, when reinforced by cannon companies and antitank weapons, to hold a beachhead maintenance line. Its task then would be finished and exploitation would be undertaken by normal infantry divisions of the follow-up.[122]

The notion of a specially organized assault division was retained, but planners wished to minimize the structural changes and so facilitate the reconstruction of as-

[117] Dieppe Rpt, cited n. 91.

[118] Address by Maj Gen Roberts (Dieppe Military Force Commander), at Assault Training Center, 7 Jun 43. Adm file 491. See Bibliographical Note.

[119] Proposed revision of Field Manual 31–5, Landings on a Hostile Shore, 1 Jul 43. Adm file 491.

[120] Interv with Brig Gen Paul W. Thompson, cited in Jones, NEPTUNE, I, 204.

[121] Cf. Commentary on Exercise PIRATE, 12 Oct 43. Pre-Inv file 661.

[122] Address by Brig Gen Norman D. Cota at Assault Training Center Conf, 2 Jun 43. Adm file 491.

sault units for normal infantry tasks once they were through the enemy's fortifications. The assault divisions were formed therefore simply by reducing the overhead of a normal infantry division both in men and vehicles and increasing the normal infantry fire power. While the basic divisional structure remained unchanged, the rifle companies were organized in assault teams with special equipment to deal with fortified positions. The platoons of the assault companies were split into two assault sections apiece, each with twenty-nine men and one officer, the size being determined by the capacity of the LCVP. The two assault platoons in each company included rifle teams, a wire-cutting team, a bazooka team, a flame-throwing team, a BAR team, a 60-mm. mortar team, and a demolition team. The third platoon was similarly organized except that it had an 81-mm. instead of a 60-mm. mortar and a heavy machine gun instead of a BAR. After the assault, each platoon was to be reorganized into a normal rifle platoon with two rifle squads and a weapons squad.

The infantry assault troops were to be stripped to the barest combat essentials, but their fist was to be mailed. A tank battalion attached to each of the assault regiments would lead the attack. A portion of the tanks were to be carried in on LCT's to touch down approximately with the first infantry wave. Another portion were modified for amphibious operation and were to be launched about five or six thousand yards off shore and swim in ahead of the assault waves.[123]

The use of tanks in the assault was a subject of prolonged discussion and experimentation. In the end, the decision was to use them not as an armored force but as close-support artillery. Armor's characteristics of shock and mobility were to be disregarded, and no plans were to be made to use the tanks in exploitation from the beaches. Tanks were not the ideal assault artillery but they seemed the best available. Only armored guns had a chance of survival on the beaches. Tests indicated, moreover, that the tank 75-mm. or 76.2-mm. gun could be used effectively in neutralizing or destroying concrete pillboxes by firing into the embrasures. Tank fire so directed would enable the infantry to cut their way through the wire entanglements of the fortification, approach the pillbox with flame throwers and demolition, and destroy it. It was expected that the majority of the tanks would fire from hull down in the water and would not leave the beach at all during the assault phase.[124]

Following closely the beaching of the first tank companies, the leading infantry wave would touch down, clear the beaches, and cover the landing of engineer demolition teams. The task of the engineers—to cut and mark gaps through the belts of shore obstacles before these were covered by the rising tide—was one of the most critical in the operation, and its successful accomplishment demanded meticulous adherence to the time schedule. The engineers were to work with

---

[123] These were M–4 medium tanks equipped with detachable canvas "bloomers"—accordion-pleated screens which when raised were capable of floating the 32-ton tanks by displacement. They had a duplex

drive—twin propellers for swimming and the normal track drive for overland. From the duplex drive came their common name "DD's."

[124] Assault Training Center, Training Memos, ASLT–4, 15 Jan 44 and ASLT–1, 1 Mar 44. Adm file 491.

special naval demolition units and would have the assistance of tankdozers landed at this time.

The succeeding assault waves would consist mostly of infantry and additional engineers to clear the beaches and mine fields inland. The first artillery units would come in about an hour and a half after the first landings. The heavy debarkation of vehicles across the beaches would start about three hours after H Hour. By that time the assaulting infantry was expected to have the beach exits cleared and to have fought their way well inland.[125]

Fire Support

The task of smashing through enemy beach defenses was to be facilitated as far as possible by naval fire support and air bombardment. The early pessimism about what fire support could accomplish was never entirely dissipated. A theoretical study made early in January 1944 concluded that effective neutralization of enemy coastal and beach defenses would require a naval force of a size that was obviously far beyond the range of possibility. The silencing of fifteen enemy coastal batteries, for instance, was estimated to require a force of twenty to twenty-three battleships or cruisers. The drenching of the assault beaches and neutralizing fire on known strong points would take about twenty cruisers and one hundred destroyers, on the basis of three-tenths of a pound of high explosive per square yard of target area, or a total of

3,375 tons of shells.[126] Not only were the ships allotted completely inadequate for the task, but there was considerable doubt whether even the optimum number of bombarding vessels could achieve what was demanded of them. COSSAC's naval staff estimated in the summer of 1943 that it would probably be possible to neutralize (though not destroy) medium and heavy coastal batteries, if they were not too numerous, but that naval fire support could not be relied on to deal with beach defenses or unlocated field batteries or provide effective close support for the assaulting troops.[127] American experience in the landings at Tarawa seemed to confirm this pessimism. A full report of the Tarawa operation was studied in February by Admiral Ramsay, who observed that naval bombardment had apparently been effective against open emplacements but not against concrete. "The heaviest casualties," he noted further, "were caused by the failure to neutralize strong points and dug-outs during the period immediately before and after the touchdown of the assault."[128]

On the other hand, the experience of Dieppe had shown the imperative need for overwhelming fire support in an attack against a fortified coast.[129] One step toward solution of the problem was to increase substantially the naval bombardment forces. Originally these were all to be British according to an agreement made at Cairo. In February Admiral Ramsay assigned one battleship, one monitor, seven cruisers, and sixteen de-

---

[125] For further details of the landing scheme as applied on OMAHA, see Taylor, *Omaha Beachhead*, pp. 30–33.

[126] COS (43) 770 (O), 7 Jan 44.
[127] COS (43) 464 (O), 12 Aug 43.
[128] Ltr, Ramsay to CinC 21 A Gp, Effects of Naval Bombardment of Heavily Defended Beaches, 18 Feb 44. Pre-Inv file 676.
[129] Comb Rpt, The Dieppe Raid, Part V.

stroyers to the Western Naval Task Force to provide escort and fire support for First U.S. Army.[130] It was realized, in the light of the tentative fire plan prepared by First Army, that this allocation was insufficient, but the British Admiralty reported that no additional ships could be found from British resources. Admiral Ramsay in March therefore requested that U.S. warships be assigned to OVERLORD.[131] During April and May, three U.S. battleships, two cruisers, and thirty-four destroyers arrived in the theater and were assigned to Admiral Kirk's command. Certain British ships were detached, but the net result was a substantial increase in the naval forces available to support First Army.[132] Force O was allotted two battleships, three light cruisers, nine destroyers, and three Hunt destroyers (British); Force U was assigned one battleship, one monitor, three heavy cruisers, two light cruisers, eight destroyers, and one gunboat (Dutch). In addition Admiral Kirk was able to set up a reserve fire-support group consisting of one heavy cruiser, one light cruiser, and seventeen destroyers. The reserve group would relieve ships of the other two forces which either were badly damaged or had depleted their ammunition supply.[133]

The fire support plan, in general, emphasized neutralization rather than destruction. It was hoped that, by bringing a continuous heavy volume of fire to bear on enemy defenses, they would be ren-

dered ineffective during the critical stages of the assault. Attacks by air and sea were thus planned in a crescendo up to H Hour. The first targets were the enemy coastal batteries capable of interfering with the sea approach. Second were the beach defenses, the series of enemy resistance nests, which housed infantry weapons designed to check the assaulting troops on the beaches. Finally, naval guns were to furnish heavy artillery support for the infantry advance inland, pending the landing of army long-range artillery.[134]

The project of neutralizing enemy coastal batteries began long before D Day. Allied air forces were assigned missions against them during the preparatory period. At that time only those batteries were to be attacked which had casemates under construction, for the object was not so much to destroy the guns as to arrest or delay work on the protective covering.[135] Actually in the spring nearly all the important batteries in the invasion area were still in the process of being encased in concrete. Attacks against them, however, were severely limited on the one hand by the necessity for concealing from the Germans the selected assault areas and on the other hand by the tactical air forces' heavy prior commitments.[136] Security considerations led to the policy of bombing two coastal batteries outside the assault area for each one bombed inside. Only about 10 percent of the total bomb tonnage dropped during the preparatory phase (from the middle of April to D Day) was

[130] FUSA plan, Annex 21, 25 Feb 44.

[131] Cbl, Eisenhower to Marshall, 20 Mar 44. Eisenhower Personal Files; cf. Cbl, Br Admiralty to Br Adm Div (JSM), 28 Mar 44, Annex IV to COS (44) 295 (O), 29 Mar 44.

[132] Amendment No. 1, 1 May 44 to Operation NEPTUNE, Naval Orders. 12 A Gp files, dr 89.

[133] FUSA plan, Annex 12, 27 May 44.

[134] Ltr, Gerow to CG, FUSA, Prearranged Naval and Air Bombardment Plan, 13 Mar 44. Pre-Inv file 676.

[135] AEAF Overall Air Plan, 15 Apr 44. 12th A Gp file 370.2.

[136] See below, Ch. VI.

PREINVASION BOMBING *of Pointe du Hoe by Ninth Air Force bombers.*

directed against coastal batteries, and only a third of that was expended in the invasion area.[137]

First U.S. Army in a series of plans through May spelled out the details of the counterbattery plan as it affected the U.S. zone. The battery at Pointe du Hoe, consisting of six 155-mm. guns with an estimated range of 25,000 yards, remained top priority in each phase of the counterbattery program. It was capable of firing on lowering positions [138] for both U.S. assault forces and against landings all along the coast from Port-en-Bessin in the British zone to Taret de Ravenoville north of UTAH Beach. In addition to receiving a considerable percentage of Allied bombing and shelling, Pointe du Hoe was singled out for early capture after H Hour by the 2d Ranger Battalion operating under V Corps. Besides Pointe du Hoe, First Army asked for bombardment of four other batteries before the night of D minus 3. They were to be attacked during daylight by medium bombers and at night by heavies of the RAF.[139]

These earliest attacks were naturally enough concentrated against the heaviest-caliber guns in the assault area. Intensification of the attacks on enemy defenses as the hour of assault approached brought in numerous smaller batteries and increased the weight of the effort. If by D minus 1 it was estimated that the enemy was no longer in doubt as to the selected assault area, then 50 percent of the available heavy day bombers would be put on six batteries in the First U.S. Army sector. If it seemed likely that surprise was not

lost, then only half as many bombers would attack.[140] Not until the night of D minus 1 would bombardment be concentrated in the OVERLORD area without regard for deception. Then RAF bombers would attack "with maximum operable strength" ten coastal batteries, including six in the First Army zone.[141] Medium bombers would take up the attack against some of these batteries beginning thirty minutes before H Hour, joined by heavy day bombers from H minus 15 to H minus 5. Four other inland batteries would be attacked by fighter bombers from H Hour to H plus 10. In the meantime naval bombardment forces would have come within range. At first light, battleships and heavy cruisers would open main battery fire on enemy coastal guns.[142]

Coincident with the final phases of the counterbattery fire beach drenching would begin with simultaneous bombardment from sea and air. While heavy bombers of the Eighth Air Force attacked thirteen beach defense targets in the OMAHA area, medium bombers, beginning thirty minutes before H Hour, would attack defenses at UTAH.[143] But the burden of the task of saturating enemy shore defenses to cover the final run-in of the assault forces was assigned to the lighter ships of the naval bombardment forces

---

[137] Calculations are from statistics in Leigh-Mallory, *Despatch*, pp. 46–47.

[138] Also called "transport areas."

[139] FUSA plan, Annex 12 (Fire Support), 2d Rev, 27 May 44.

[140] *Ibid.*

[141] AEAF Overall Air Plan, cited n. 135.

[142] FUSA plan, Annex 12, 27 May 44.

[143] In early planning it was thought that cratering of beaches would be an important tactical by-product of this bombardment, and troops were briefed to expect to find cover in shell and bomb holes. See proposed revision of Field Manual 31–5, 1 Jul 43. Adm file 491. RATTLE Conference, however, assumed cratering to be an "adverse" effect of bombing from the Army point of view. See RATTLE Conf 3d Mtg, 29 Jun 43. SHAEF SGS file 337/6. Actually the only significant cratering that took place was at Pointe du Hoe. See below, Ch. IX.

—especially the destroyers and support craft.[144] Specific beach targets were mostly machine gun positions, many having concrete personnel shelters with some light artillery pieces. It was not expected, however, that specific targets would be destroyed. Ground commanders asked for the destruction of only three targets in the Port-en-Bessin area; all others were to be neutralized.[145] Much reliance was placed on the support craft which could continue to fire up to H Hour after heavy-caliber naval gunfire had to be lifted to targets inland in order to avoid endangering the first waves of troops. Particularly important were the rocket craft, LCT(R)'s, which had performed well in the Mediterranean.[146]

The availability of support craft, however, was always uncertain, and in the end only twenty-three could be assigned to support U.S. landings. U.S. commanders therefore early considered firing divisional artillery from landing craft. Extensive experiments were conducted by the British Combined Operations Headquarters in early 1943. In general those proved that self-propelled 105-mm. howitzers could achieve an acceptable accuracy in direct fire while afloat at ranges from 10,-000 yards.[147] There developed a certain disposition then to think of artillery in the assault as moving landward from suc-

cessive firing positions as it would displace forward in normal land combat.[148] Doctrine of Combined Operations was that self-propelled guns should be capable of direct fire while afloat, and of direct and indirect fire both from beached craft and from hull down in the water. Accepting these theories, U.S. commanders planned to supplement their close-support craft with LCT's modified to take two or three medium tanks apiece in position to fire during the approach to shore, and with normal LCT(5)'s carrying 105-mm. self-propelled howitzers, also in position to fire while afloat.[149]

Final phase of the fire support plan was the arrangement for naval firing in support of the Army's advance inland. To direct this fire, each of the three assault divisions (4th, 29th, and 1st) had nine naval fire support control parties; nine naval gunfire spotting teams were to drop with the 101st Airborne Division.[150] Air observation was to be furnished by forty aircraft of the British Fleet Air Arm, augmented by one RAF squadron and three reconnaissance squadrons, the latter to be relieved not later than noon on D Day for return to normal reconnaissance duties.[151]

[144] Light cruisers also participated and the Force U plan called for the battleship *Nevada* and the heavy cruiser *Quincy* to fire their five-inch batteries at beach targets. See Naval Task Force U, Operations Order, Annex D, 15 May 44.

[145] Norfolk House Mtg, 24 Apr 44, to consider the engagement of beach targets in the U.S. First Army area. ETO 337 (Conferences (Secret)) 1 AR–16–Dr 1.

[146] CO Rpt, Lessons Learnt in the Mediterranean, 14 Oct 43. Pre-Inv file 661.

[147] Address by Col H. F. G. Langley (COHQ), at Assault Training Center Conf, 1 Jun 43; cf. proposed revision of Field Manual 31–5. Both in Adm file 491.

[148] Address by Col M. W. Brewster, Chief, Tactics Subsection, at Assault Training Center Conf, 1 Jun 43. Adm file 491.

[149] Western Naval Task Force had nine LCG (L)'s armored and equipped with multiple rocket projectors; sixteen LCT (A)'s equipped to carry medium tanks; and six LCT (HE)'s, similar to the LCT (A) but with less armor protection. There were also eleven LCF's mounting AA-guns. Two LCT (A)'s or (HE)'s were to carry a platoon of tanks between them. The fifth tank could fire rockets if desired. FUSA plan, Annex 21; cf. Western Naval Task Force, Operation Plan, 21 Apr 44.

[150] Some of the parties assigned to the 29th Division would operate with the 2d and 5th Ranger Battalions. FUSA plan, Annex 21.

[151] AEAF Overall Air Plan, 15 Apr 44.

CHAPTER VI

Preliminary Operations

The French Resistance

When the Germans conquered France in the spring of 1940, they sealed their victory with a symbolic flourish. It was as though by dictating the terms of humiliating armistice in the historic railway carriage at Compiègne they meant to prove not only that France was beaten but that she was helpless even to save her dignity in defeat. So it must have seemed in the railway car and so, too, throughout most of the country. But there were still a few Frenchmen who experienced the fact of defeat and witnessed the symbol of humiliation without accepting the finality of either. In 1940 they could not have seemed very dangerous to the conquerors or, for that matter, very potent to themselves. Their reaction was spontaneous and personal. Yet they were the seeds which, nourished by arms and Allied organizers through four years of occupation, grew into an underground army numbering about 200,000 men—an army that after the Allied landings in June 1944 impressed Allied leaders as having made a substantial contribution to the defeat of the enemy.[1]

During the first two years of the occupation, the Resistance movement developed separately in the occupied and unoccupied zones. When the Germans finally moved into southern France in November 1942, Resistance leaders were faced with the problem of bringing some sort of unity out of the anarchy of rival groups. At that time the northern zone had six independently organized groups; the south had three. Only one organization, the communist *Front National,* which operated through the *Francs Tireurs et Partisans,* extended control over both the northern and southern zones.[2] Between the other groups there was virtually no co-ordination. Their separateness was due not only to the fact that as clandestine organizations they lacked regularized communications; more importantly they were divided by differing shades of political opinion. The French Resistance cannot be viewed as a simple revolt against the enemy, although opposition to the Germans was, of course, always the prime motive. It must be seen also as a movement aimed, at least by its leaders, at eventual national independence. Whoever controlled the underground would evidently be in the strongest position to control the liberated nation.

The chief impetus toward national unification came from General Charles de Gaulle's headquarters in London. General de Gaulle began in 1940 the formation of a special staff, later known as the *Bureau Central de Renseignements et*

[1] Diary of CinC, 17 Jun 44; Rpt, Donovan (OSS) to Marshall, 9 Jul 44. OPD file 336.2, sec. II, cases 29–47.

[2] MS # B–035 (Rogé), A History of the FFI.

HITLER LEAVING RAILWAY CARRIAGE AT COMPIEGNE *where the Germans dictated the 1940 peace terms to the French nation.*

d'Action (*Militaire*) (BCRA), charged with the organization, direction, and supply of the Resistance. Contacts between de Gaulle and the native Resistance were established through agents supplied by the British. The BCRA worked for nearly two years (from the summer of 1941 to the spring of 1943) with Resistance leaders to amalgamate the Resistance groups. Their work culminated in the formation of a National Committee (*le Conseil National de la Résistance*) which met for the first time in Paris on 27 May 1943. The committee under the presidency of Georges Bidault included representatives not only of the main Resistance groups but of the principal political parties as well. Politically the new National Committee recognized General de Gaulle and the London committee as trustees of the interests of the French nation and responsible eventually for founding a French government on democratic principles. De Gaulle's personal representative, Jean Moulin, was selected as political leader of the Resistance. Militarily the committee created an underground army (*l'Armée Secrète*) under the direct command of

General Delestrain (known to the underground as Général Vidal). The Army was elaborately organized on a regional basis and regional commanders selected. Primarily this organization was intended as a framework for the ultimate open co-operation of the French underground with the Allied armies.[3]

Much of the success of this first de Gaullist national organization was illusory, for it is evident that the Gestapo was aware of its progress and waited only for its completion before striking in June 1943 with wholesale arrests. De Gaulle's representative died under torture. General Delestrain was shot. The leadership of the underground army was decimated. The national organization was shattered, and Resistance groups throughout the country suffered heavy losses.[4]

In the widespread catastrophe, however, there were some encouraging facts. By tipping their hand in the summer of 1943, apparently in the expectation that Allied landings were imminent, the Germans revealed the fatal weaknesses of the highly centralized underground organization in time to permit the establishment of a new system of control before D Day. Furthermore, although the underground suffered severe personnel losses both among native resisters and among agents, a surprisingly small percentage of supplies was lost and, on the whole, the supply reception committees were able to

continue operations in most parts of the country.[5]

Despite their losses, the Resistance groups displayed a remarkable resilience, and reorganization began at once. It is impossible in short space to describe the many ramifications of the new organization. In general it may be said that a nominal national unity was retained while sabotage and paramilitary action were controlled regionally. The Germans continued to make periodic arrests of Resistance leaders, but the new decentralization localized the damage to the movement.

Concurrently with the organization of the Resistance for eventual overt activity, both the BCRA and a purely British organization, the SOE (Special Operations Executive), were concerned with encouraging, directing, and supplying immediate and continuing sabotage. The SOE was formed in November 1940 and made the responsibility of the Minister of Economic Warfare—a responsibility that was added to the minister's duties as head of a department. The first mission of the SOE was to investigate the capabilities of the French Resistance, stimulate passive resistance in French industry working for the Germans, and study the possibilities of forming an underground army. As it began to work through agents in the field, the goal of encouraging passive resistance was gradually supplanted by the more ambitious aim of developing French Resistance into a strategic weapon that could be directed by Allied headquarters against military objectives in conformity with the master Allied plan.[6]

---

[3] French Forces of the Interior, MS, pp. 9–40. Hist Div files. This is a 1,500-page history prepared in the European Theater Historical Section, under direction of Colonel S. L. A. Marshall, by United States, French, and British members of the OSS. Cited hereafter as FFI History.

[4] FFI History, p. 40.

[5] Memo, SOE, Present Value and Tempo of Resistance, 9 Oct 43. SHAEF G–3 file 322–7 II, Ops C.

[6] FFI History, pp. 344–45.

The SOE did not attempt to interfere directly in the indigenous organization of the Resistance. The British were content to deal with the groups as established and confine their efforts to setting up and maintaining communications between the Resistance and London. The main task at first was to supply the resisters with arms and sabotage equipment. Later the SOE undertook to direct and co-ordinate Resistance action in accord with the OVERLORD plan.

The first SOE agents parachuted into France in the spring of 1941. Among them was a French radio operator, Begué. Through Begué, contact was made with some of the Resistance groups and arrangements made for the first supply mission flown on the night of 7 July 1941. Containers packed with explosives, small arms, flashlights, and a radio were parachuted to ground organized by members of the Resistance. Location and markings of the grounds had been previously reported to London by Begué's radio. This was the first of many "shipments" of arms to the French underground which would forge out of the will to resist an effective weapon of war. But success was still far in the future. The year 1941 ended for the SOE in failure. Through treachery most of the British agents in the field were arrested, including Begué, and the slender communications link with London was snapped.[7]

The lesson drawn by the SOE from this experience was the impracticability of canalizing control through a central communications channel. Not only was the single communications channel much too vulnerable itself but it required the multiplication of contacts between agents and Resistance groups and thus increased unnecessarily the risk that treachery or indiscretion would compromise a widespread organization. Henceforward the aim of the SOE was to create independent groups with independent communications with London. During 1942, seventeen radio operators, as well as thirty-six other agents, were parachuted into France. As communications became relatively secure and continuous, supply missions were flown in increasing numbers. Additional personnel and materiel were also landed by small boats plying between Gibraltar and the southeast coast. Deliveries by sea were especially important during the winter when bad weather all but prevented air drops. The total amount of supplies sent during the year, however, was very small. In twelve months of operation, for instance, only a little over one ton of explosives was dropped to saboteurs.[8]

SOE efforts to supply the Resistance movements were always handicapped by insufficient air transport. In 1942 and through most of 1943 two squadrons (of approximately twenty aircraft each) were employed to carry out SOE missions. The SOE continually begged for more aircraft, but every plane assigned to it had to be diverted from the bomber offensive and the Resistance seemed like a nebulous kind of operation to feed at the expense of dropping bombs on German industry.[9]

---

[7] *Ibid.*, pp. 347–49.

[8] Materials sent during 1942 were as follows: 2,265 lbs. of explosives; 269 Sten guns; 388 pistols; 856 incendiaries; 3,424 abrasive products; 630 standard charges (clams); 269 cells (food, tobacco, medical equipment, etc.). FFI History, p. 351.

[9] Memo, SIS–SOE/SO Aircraft Requirements, 14 Jan 44. SHAEF SGS file 370.64.

Furthermore, throughout 1943 the SOE program to supply the Balkan guerillas had a higher priority than its operations in western Europe. All this meant that, although from time to time additional planes were available for SOE operations in France, the supply never kept pace with the growing demands from the field.[10]

These demands forced repeated examination of what role the Resistance could be expected to play in the liberation of France and how much reliance could be placed on it. Planners tended to be cautious. First of all, it was difficult to get any accurate assessment of the actual or potential strength of the movement. Second, there was always a danger that the movement might be emasculated by arrests on the eve of invasion. Third, even though much had been done to organize the various patriot groups, it was certain that control of their activities would be difficult and incomplete. COSSAC, in drawing up the original OVERLORD plan, decided to regard Resistance activities as a bonus and to place no reliance on them to accomplish strategic objectives.[11]

In criticizing the plan, the British Chiefs of Staff asked whether a more definite strategic role might not be assigned to the Resistance. A committee representing Army and SOE discussed the question and concluded that COSSAC's appraisal was generally fair but "it erred on the side of caution and did not emphasize the wide strategic possibilities." What the committee was thinking of was a national uprising. It believed that the sabotage of Resistance groups could not be regarded as a strategic weapon unless "backed by a general strike or by a rising on a national scale." Such an uprising, the committee thought, would be desirable from a military standpoint but might be politically objectionable.[12]

Actually there seems little doubt that the concept of a national uprising, which cropped up in discussions of Resistance from time to time, was always unrealistic. A French officer working for the OSS (Office of Strategic Services) commented that the "favorite notion" of mass uprisings "posited the existence of universal courage, whereas courage only inspired a few men—as it has always inspired the few rather than the many. And the idea of mass uprisings implied battling against modern tanks with the stone-throwing catapults of Caesar's time."[13]

The decision apparently was that mass uprisings were at least sufficiently unlikely that no reliance could be placed on them. In February 1944 SHAEF's conclusion was still that Resistance activity must be regarded as a bonus.[14] In view of this conclusion, the project of supplying the Resistance might have languished, but as a matter of fact it received a strong forward impetus. In the beginning of 1943, the Germans put into effect a forced labor draft in France. To escape this draft thousands of young Frenchmen, particularly in central and southern France, broke into open rebellion. They formed maquis bands in hilly and wooded regions and began guerrilla warfare against the Germans and the collaborationist French Militia. SOE sent agents to contact these *maquisards* and began dropping arms

[10] FFI History, pp. 396c–96d.
[11] Outline OVERLORD, Part II, par. 23.

[12] Progress Rpt, Operation OVERLORD, 10 Sep 43. SHAEF G–3 file 322–7 II, Ops C.
[13] Rpt, Analysis of the Resistance Movement, 9 Dec 43. SHAEF G–3 file 370–4–1, Ops C.
[14] Memo, Bull for Morgan, 5 Feb 44. SHAEF SGS file 370.64 I.

and supplies to them.[15] The maquis developed into an important movement by the fall of 1943. The Prime Minister then became interested and in January ordered that an additional thirty-five British aircraft be made available for arming the maquis groups of southeastern France. With this new transport strength, supply drops in February were increased 173 percent.[16] Permanent assignments of aircraft for SOE use rose steadily thereafter. In January, 50 successful sorties were flown; in April, 331; in May, 531; and in June, 866.[17]

The increase in the tempo of supply deliveries reflected also the beginnings of American contributions of aircraft. In 1943 the OSS began operating through agents in France. The London headquarters of SO (Special Operations branch of OSS) collaborated with SOE and gradually amalgamated with the British agency. The amalgamation was completed by January 1944. That month U.S. planes flew their first successful supply mission into France. In late February, however, the chief of Special Operations, Col. Joseph P. Haskell, was still concerned over the small scale of the American contribution. He feared especially the political repercussions on American-French relations of allowing the British to continue carrying the main burden of

supporting the Resistance.[18] The State Department two months later warned the Joint Chiefs of Staff that the impression was gaining ground among the French that, whereas the British were doing everything possible to arm the French patriots, the United States was holding back for political reasons.[19] Thus in May, twenty-five more U.S. aircraft were assigned to Special Operations over the protests of Air Marshal Sir Arthur W. Tedder who, doubting the value of the Resistance movement, considered the increase unjustified.[20]

Air Marshal Tedder's doubts were unquestionably shared by many in the Allied command,[21] and the effectiveness of the Resistance as revealed after D Day was very generally regarded with surprise. There had been signs of the capabilities of the Resistance to undermine the German military power in France, particularly in the monthly reports which SOE and later SOE/SO headquarters submitted to COSSAC and SHAEF from the fall of 1943 when Special Operations was placed under the general control of the OVERLORD command. But the signs were hard to read. Sabotage consisted of a number of more or less un-co-ordinated pinpricks chiefly against various war industries working for the Germans, railroads and canals, and telephone and telegraph

---

[15] The first operation took place on 20 March 1943, but supplies were sent on a very meager scale until the fall of the year. The first agents to the maquis were sent in October. FFI History, pp. 362–63.

[16] Sixth Monthly Progress Report to SHAEF from SOE/SO Hq, London, 7 Mar 44. SHAEF SGS file 319.1/10. The planned increase was 300 percent but bad weather interfered with operations. Of 400 sorties attempted during the month only 166 were successful.

[17] See SOE/SO Rpts in SHAEF SGS file 319.1/10.

[18] Ltr, Haskell to Donovan, 22 Feb 44. SHAEF SGS file 370.64 I.

[19] Cbl, JCS to Eisenhower, 17 Apr 44. SHAEF SGS file 370.64 I.

[20] Memo, Gen Bull for SHAEF CofS, SOE/SO Request for Additional Aircraft, 19 Apr 44; Memo, idem., Allocation of Additional Aircraft for SOE/SO Missions, 28 Apr 44. SHAEF SGS file 370.64 I.

[21] At COS (44) 163d Mtg (O), 18 May 44, General Smith said that "latest reports" had made the Supreme Commander "discount the value of French underground organizations."

systems. It was difficult to add them up and see what they amounted to in terms of damaging the enemy's total defensive capabilities in France.

The most continuous and probably most effective sabotage was that directed against the French railroads. Attacks were made to derail German troop and supply trains, to cut tracks, blow bridges, and damage locomotives. Directed by SOE/SO headquarters, railway sabotage was greatly accelerated in 1944 and tied in to a certain extent with the Allied air offensive against enemy transportation.[22] Damage done by saboteurs compared favorably with that inflicted from the air. In the first three months of 1944 the underground sabotaged 808 locomotives as compared to 387 damaged by air attack. However, in April and May, air attack was stepped up and accounted for the damaging of 1,437 locomotives compared to only 292 put out of action by saboteurs. Between June 1943 and May 1944 a total of 1,822 locomotives was damaged, 200 passenger cars destroyed, 1,500 cars damaged, 2,500 freight cars destroyed and 8,000 damaged.[23] Reliable statistics on other forms of railway sabotage are incomplete. A report by the Vichy police [24] records that during October and November 1943 more than 3,000 attempts were made by patriots to wreck some portion of the railway system. In November, 427 of these were successful major operations which included 132 derailments.

Despite the impressiveness of these figures, there remained some doubt as to the effect of the destruction on German military mobility. Since only a part of the capacity of the French railroads was being utilized directly by the German Army, much of the burden of the interruptions due to sabotage could be and undoubtedly was borne by French civilian traffic.[25] On the other hand, Rundstedt in October 1943 noted with alarm the "rapid increase" in rail sabotage which he attributed to the heavy supply of arms and explosives that the British had parachuted to Resistance groups. He reported that in September there were 534 acts of sabotage against railroads as compared to a monthly average of 130 during the first half of the year. Although he did not assess the effect of this sabotage on his general preparedness for invasion, he made it clear that it was cause for concern, which would become more serious at the time of the Allied assault.[26] A measure of its seriousness was the partial substitution of German uniformed railway workers for employees of the SNCF (Société National des Chemins de Fer). Between February and June 20,000 Ger-

---

[22] See below, section on the Bombing of French Railroads.

[23] Rpt, SNCF, *Les Résultats de l'Action de la Résistance dans la SNCF,* 10 Nov 44, cited in FFI History, pp. 1364ff.

[24] This report, captured by the Resistance, reached London in April 1944. SOE/SO headquarters significantly commented on its statistics as follows: "It was already known that railway sabotage was considerable but no suspicion that it had reached the scale stated by the police has yet reached London." See Rpt, Appreciation of Report by Minister of Interior Vichy, Summary of Acts of Sabotage and Disorder in France 25th October–25th November, 14 Apr 44. SHAEF G–3 file 370–4–1, Ops C.

[25] In the spring of 1944 the directors of the SNCF were apparently unconvinced of the value of rail sabotage which they felt was costing the French more than the Germans. See G–2 Summary of Info, French Railways, 11 Apr 44. SHAEF G–3 file GCT 370–14, Ops C.

[26] Rundstedt Report, 25 Oct 43. See above, Ch. IV, n. 2.

man workers were brought in chiefly to check locomotive sabotage.[27]

As D Day approached, SOE/SO headquarters became more concerned with coordinating rail sabotage to relate directly to forthcoming military operations. It was not expected that Resistance groups could seriously interfere with the movement of local enemy reserves in the bridgehead area. The Germans had in effect quarantined the coastal strip to a depth of about thirty to forty miles inland, and the Normandy Resistance groups, as a result, were weak and scattered. Work on the fortifications was done either by German labor, or by Frenchmen carefully checked for loyalty. Any strangers were immediately suspect and subject to arrest. Such organized groups as did exist were difficult to supply because of the heavy concentration of antiaircraft guns in the coastal zone. Outside the area, however, it was thought the Resistance might operate effectively to delay the movement of strategic reserves into the battle zone. The Resistance was therefore directed to prepare demolitions to be blown on order to cut the main trunk lines leading into the lodgment area.[28]

The plan for cutting the critical military railroads (*Plan Vert*) was supplemented by a plan to interfere with road traffic (*Plan Tortue*). Both were developed by the BCRA under the general direction of SOE/SO headquarters. Approved by SHAEF, these plans were circulated to agents in the field, and saboteurs began placing their demolitions. It soon became apparent that effective road sabotage would require a large amount of heavy equipment which could not be delivered in time. *Plan Tortue* was therefore converted into a project for blocking enemy road movements through guerrilla action.[29] As such, it contributed to the Allied victories after D Day. During the preparation period, however, more emphasis was placed on the rail plan. In May SOE/SO headquarters reported that 571 rail targets were ready for demolition and 30 road cuts were prepared.[30] In addition to accomplishing the specific acts of active sabotage, Resistance leaders hoped to complete the disorganization of the French railroads by planned non-cooperation of the railroad trade union and management.[31] It was estimated that in those ways serious dislocation of rail traffic in France might be maintained for eight to ten days after the Allied landings.

Since the date of the invasion could not be given to the Resistance in advance, arrangements were made to order the execution of sabotage plans by code messages broadcast by the BBC. Organizers were instructed to listen to BBC broadcasts on the 1st, 2d, 15th, and 16th of each month. If the invasion was then imminent, they would hear a preparatory code message. They would then remain on the alert listening for a confirmatory message "B."

---

[27] *OKW/WFSt, KTB Ausarbeitung, Die Entwicklung im Westen vom 1.I.–31.III.44.* See below, n. 115.

[28] The Development of Resistance Groups with Reference to the Land Fighting in "OVERLORD," 15 Feb 44. SHAEF G–3 file 370–14, Ops C; FFI History, pp. 80ff; cf. Ninth Monthly Progress Report to SHAEF from SFHQ, London, May 1944, 10 Jun 44. SHAEF SGS file 319.1/10.

[29] FFI History, p. 83.

[30] Report from SFHQ, cited n. 28. SOE and SO in April were amalgamated into a single headquarters with the title Special Force Headquarters.

[31] See *Plan Vert*, text in FFI History, pp. 175–87. The SNCF was generally disposed to co-operate with the Allies in passive resistance to the Germans. Resistance groups found many recruits among the employees of the railroads.

Forty-eight hours after message "B," code phrases would be broadcast directing that the various sabotage plans be put into effect. Since each of the plans had been drawn on a regional basis and each of the Resistance regions had separate code arrangements, it would have been possible to localize the sabotage activity in direct support of the landings. It was SHAEF's view, however, that it was preferable to obtain the maximum amount of chaos behind the enemy lines at the moment of landing, and therefore the signals actually used set all sabotage plans in motion at once.[32] This decision reflected again the reluctance of Allied headquarters to depend on Resistance activity as a precision weapon to be used against specific objectives related to the general plan.

As a matter of fact, the post-D-Day rail-cutting program of the Resistance was extraordinarily effective. During June a total of 486 rail cuts was reported. On D plus 1 twenty-six trunk lines were unusable, including the main lines between Avranches and St. Lô, between St. Lô and Cherbourg, and between St. Lô and Caen. All were sabotaged with multiple cuts. Road sabotage achieved at least one notable success in delaying the movement of the *2d SS Panzer Division* from the south into the OVERLORD lodgment area.[33]

Plans for employing the Resistance in action against the enemy after the landing included not only sabotage but direct military action. It was hoped that the maquis and possibly other Resistance groups might be able to engage some enemy forces in the interior which would otherwise be employed against the U.S. and British armies. The exact military employment of the underground obviously could not be planned in advance since its strength in any given location could not even be estimated. However, the bonus of having friendly forces behind the enemy's lines was considered sufficiently likely and sufficiently valuable that extensive preparations were made to develop and control it. In March 1944, SHAEF issued a comprehensive directive to the newly designated Special Force Headquarters on the use of Resistance groups in support of OVERLORD.[34] In late May and early June headquarters and staff of the FFI (*Forces Françaises de l'Intérieur*) were established under command of Gen. Joseph Pierre Koenig. Koenig set up a tripartite staff (French, U.S., British) in London and made plans for employing the FFI as one component of the Allied armies under the Supreme Allied Commander.[35]

But although Koenig became a regularly constituted military commander his army remained nebulous. Because of the danger of compromising the security of Allied plans, it was impossible even to attempt to organize the FFI for specific military missions in advance of D Day. Therefore, in order to encourage Resistance groups to organize themselves for military action and to get orders to them, three-man teams (Jedburghs) consisting of one French and one U.S. or British officer and

---

[32] FFI History, p. 388. German agents broke the codes. For German reaction, see below, Ch. VIII.

[33] Tenth Monthly Report to SHAEF from SFHQ, London, June 1944, 10 Jul 44. SHAEF SGS file 319-.1/10; FFI History, p. 1474. See below, Ch. X.

[34] SHAEF (44) 25, Operational Directive to SFHQ, 23 Mar 44. SHAEF G-3 file 322-8, Ops C.

[35] Ltr, Koenig to Gen Smith, *Commandement et Organisation des Forces Françaises de l'Intérieur*, 9 Jan 44. SHAEF SGS file 322 (FFI).

a radio operator were formed to be parachuted in uniform behind enemy lines starting shortly before D Day. The sole assigned function of the Jedburghs was to provide communication links with the FFI command. On occasion, however, they were able to supply useful leadership for the groups to which they were attached. About a hundred Jedburgh teams were organized and eighty-seven of these were operational in France at one time or another.[36]

A major handicap of the Resistance for military action was its inadequate armament, and especially its lack of heavy weapons. Partly to remedy this, both the Americans and the British organized special, heavily armed units to be parachuted behind the lines after operations began. They were to be used either independently on tactical missions or more often to stiffen the local Resistance groups. The American units were called Operational Groups and consisted of four officers and thirty enlisted men, entirely U.S. personnel. Eleven of these groups were sent to France after D Day, five from England and six from North Africa. British equivalent units were much larger. These were the SAS (Special Air Service) troops whose operations were directed by Lt. Gen. F. A. M. Browning, Commander of Airborne Troops. Comprising almost 2,000 men, they included two SAS regiments of British personnel, two French parachute battalions, and a Belgian independent company. The SAS achieved notable success with the well-organized Resistance movement in Brittany, and in addition was able to carry out useful sabotage of railroads leading to the battle areas.[37]

It is impossible to appraise the contribution of the Resistance toward softening the enemy in France before the invasion. Not only was there no systematic recording of the facts of their operations, but there was, in any case, no satisfactory yardstick by which to measure the effectiveness of an irregular force, whose role was strategic rather than tactical. Certainly the Resistance impaired the German military power both materially and morally. A fighter with a bee in his breeches is evidently not at his best. But just how much the bee contributes to his defeat is a question to which statistical method can hardly apply.

The Combined Bomber Offensive

Up to the end of 1942, bombing of German military targets was carried out without any clear-cut directive as to target systems, aims, or timing. Although target priorities had been sketched for the Eighth Air Force by the theater commander, the task of integrating the operations of both U.S. and British air forces according to a combined plan with a combined objective was first attempted at Casablanca in January 1943.[38] The Combined Chiefs of Staff then agreed to order U.S. and British strategic air forces based in the United Kingdom to initiate a "Combined Bomber Offensive" whose object would be "the progressive destruction and dislocation of the German mili-

---

[36] FFI History, pp. 364–65.
[37] *Ibid.*, pp. 365, 544.

[38] Ltr, CofS Eighth AF to CG VIII Bomber Command and VIII Fighter Command, Objectives for Operations Eighth Air Force, 20 Oct 42; Ltr, Eaker to CG ETOUSA, 31 Dec 43, exhibit 2, Report of Lt. Gen. Ira C. Eaker on U.S. Army Air Forces Activities in United Kingdom Covering Period from February 20, 1942 to December 31, 1943 (cited hereafter as Eaker Rpt). AAF file 520.101A.

tary, industrial and economic systems, and
the undermining of the morale of the
German people to a point where their capacity for armed resistance is fatally weakened." [39]

This dual aim recognized the divergent
doctrines of the American and British air
forces. The Americans believed that,
through daylight precision bombing, critical sections of German industry could be
destroyed so effectively as to dislocate
the economic system and paralyze the
German war machine. The British, feeling that daylight bombing would prove
too costly, put their faith in night area
bombing designed to destroy whole critical industrial and military areas. The
Prime Minister tried at Casablanca to get
the Americans to adopt the British view
on the use of air power and persuade
them to use the Eighth Air Force for night
bombing to reinforce directly the operations of the RAF. General Eaker and
General Arnold defeated the suggestions,
and the Casablanca directive recognized
the separate operations of the two air
forces as two different but complementary contributions to a single task.[40]

The primary objectives for both air
forces in the new combined offensive
were: (1) submarine construction yards,
(2) aircraft industry, (3) transportation, (4) oil plants, (5) other enemy war
industry. It was provided that these priorities might be "varied from time to
time according to developments in the
strategical situation." Further flexibility
was provided in that the targets listed

were to be attacked "subject to the exi-
gencies of weather and of tactical feasibility." [41] They might also be supplemented by "other objectives of great
importance either from the political or
military point of view." These "other
objectives" were not defined, but the two
examples given—submarine bases in the
Bay of Biscay, and the city of Berlin—
could have been taken to bracket a wide
range of targets.

The Casablanca directive, though formally initiating the Combined Bomber
Offensive, did not produce any immediate action. The Eighth Air Force, having
depleted its ranks in order to found and
nourish the Twelfth Air Force in the
Mediterranean, remained for about six
months desperately short of planes and
men. It was not until the late spring of
1943 that the air force build-up in the
United Kingdom resumed the tempo interrupted by the development of the
Mediterranean theater, and it was only
then that the Combined Bomber Offensive was implemented by a detailed plan.

The plan had been in the making
since December 1942 when a Committee
of Operations Analysts was appointed by
General Arnold to prepare a report "ana-
lyzing the rate of progressive deterioration that should be anticipated in the
German war effort as a result of . . . increasing air operations . . . against its sustaining sources." [42] The committee on 8
March 1943 reported nineteen enemy

---

[39] CCS 166/1/D, The Bomber Offensive from the
United Kingdom, 21 Jan 43. Approved at CCS 65th
Mtg, 21 Jan 43.

[40] Eaker Rpt, cited n. 38; cf. Craven and Cate, The
Army Air Forces, II, 227, 301.

[41] The principal limitation of "tactical feasibility"
was the short range of all combat planes which, as
long as the air forces were relatively small, largely
prevented bomber sorties deep into Germany.

[42] Ltr, Arnold to ACofS Management Control, Research and Analysis to Fix Earliest Practicable Date
for Invasion of Western Europe, 9 Dec 42. AAF file
3842–2, Tabs for History.

industrial systems vulnerable to air attack.[43] Endorsed by the Eighth Air Force and the British Air Ministry, the committee's findings were embodied in a formal agreed plan which General Eaker submitted to the Joint Chiefs of Staff. From the nineteen target systems listed by the operations analysts, the air forces picked six key enemy industries, including seventy-six precision targets. The systems selected for attack were in order of priority: submarine construction yards and bases, aircraft industry, ball bearings, oil, synthetic rubber and tires, and military transport vehicles. Destruction of the seventy-six targets, it was believed, would result in elimination of 89 percent of the enemy's submarine industry, 43 percent of his fighter aircraft production, 65 percent of his bomber production, 76 percent of the ball bearing industry, 48 percent of his refined oil products, 50 percent of his synthetic rubber, and all of his tire production. "The cumulative effect," said General Eaker, "will 'fatally weaken' the capacity of the German people for armed resistance." [44]

There were initial difficulties, however. General Eaker noted that the air forces' ability to carry out the planned program depended on rendering German fighter defenses ineffective. Actually, despite heavy losses, enemy fighter strength in the spring of 1943 was still increasing rapidly. If the increase continued at that rate, it was expected the Germans would have 3,000 fighter aircraft by January 1944. It was, General Eaker reported,

"quite conceivable" that such an increase "could make our daylight bombing unprofitable and perhaps our night bombing too." [45] The destruction of German fighter aircraft was therefore made an "intermediate objective second to none in priority." [46]

The Joint Chiefs of Staff accepted the plan outlined by General Eaker, and approved his requests for aircraft and personnel to carry it out.[47] The Combined Chiefs endorsed the plan on 18 May 1943 at the Washington Conference.[48] Finally the directive to initiate the planned offensive was issued on 10 June by Air Marshal Portal, British Chief of Air Staff, who had strategic direction over combined air operations.[49] Air Marshal Portal interpreted the new plan to mean an all-out offensive against the German fighter air force and directed the Eighth Air Force to attack air-frame and engine factories and industries associated with them, as well as aircraft repair depots, storage parks, and enemy fighter planes in the air and on the ground. These attacks were declared of primary importance and the order was that nothing should interfere with them. Only when

---

[43] Memo for Gen Arnold, Report of Committee of Operations Analysts with Respect to Economic Targets within the Western Axis, 8 Mar 43. AAF file 3842-2, Tabs for History.

[44] JCS Spec Mtg, 29 Apr 43.

[45] Ibid.

[46] CCS 217, Plan for Combined Bomber Offensive from the United Kingdom, 14 May 43.

[47] JCS 77th Mtg, 4 May 43; JPS 174/1, Plan for Combined Bomber Offensive from the United Kingdom, 2 May 43.

[48] CCS 87th Mtg, 18 May 43.

[49] As by agreement at Casablanca, CCS 65th Mtg; cf. Craven and Cate, The Army Air Forces, II, 304. The RAF was senior in experience and, at this time, preponderant in numbers. "Strategic direction" was never clearly defined nor was Air Marshal Portal ever given any clear-cut directive. In fact, however, he exercised ad hoc command over the strategic air forces as agent of the Combined Chiefs. The directive of 10 June was issued as a letter by Air Vice Marshal N. H. Bottomley to Air Force Commanders. Copy in Eaker Rpt.

"tactical and weather conditions" prevented attacks against enemy fighter plane targets should aircraft be used against what nominally remained the "primary objective"—submarine construction yards and operating bases.

The new offensive was slow in getting started. Between 1 July and 15 November the Eighth Air Force dropped 22,667 tons of bombs, but of these only 1,903 tons hit the enemy aircraft industry despite its overriding priority as a target.[50] In part, this relatively insignificant effort was due to bad weather during the fall and winter months. In part, it was due to the location of most German aircraft plants beyond U.S. fighter range, which made bombing prohibitively costly. Two raids on 17 August against the ball bearing plants at Schweinfurt and the Messerschmitt fighter aircraft factory at Regensburg demonstrated the impracticability at that time of deep penetrations by small forces. Losses on the Schweinfurt raid were 36 planes out of 300, or 12 percent, and on the Regensburg raid 24 planes out of 174, or almost 14 percent. These figures did not include damage. Repetition of the Schweinfurt raid on 14 October resulted in losses of more than a quarter of the attacking aircraft.[51] Although the importance of individual targets might warrant acceptance of such losses, they were prohibitive if applied to any large portion of the routine bombing offensive.

While recognizing the difficulties, General Arnold severely criticized the whole record of accomplishment during the last half of 1943. Not only were the attacks on the enemy aircraft industry disappointingly small, but in general a far greater effort was devoted to secondary targets than to those whose destruction would vitally affect Germany's ability to continue the war. Only four vital industries, he said, were attacked and they were hit with only 20 percent of the total bomb tonnage.[52]

General Eaker believed these strictures were unfair. Reporting in December 1943 on the progress of the Combined Bomber Offensive, Eaker said that, while only 62 percent of the planned forces for the offensive had been allotted, 66 percent of the task was already accomplished.[53] Presumably that meant that 66 percent of the planned targets had been hit. But, since the objective of the offensive was not merely to hit targets but to destroy them and so dislocate German war industry and "fatally weaken" enemy morale, the statistics were neither a reliable measure of accomplishment nor a fair indication of the job remaining to be done. Although it was reasonably certain that the Germans had been hurt by Allied bombing during 1943, it was not true in December that only one-third more bombing on the 1943 scale remained to complete the task outlined by the plan for the Combined Bomber Offensive.

A more accurate measure of achievement was difficult to discover. From intelligence sources, the British Ministry of Economic Warfare and the Air Ministry attempted to estimate the effect of bomb-

[50] Study by ACofAS, The Strategic Aerial Bombardment of Europe, 10 Dec 43. AAF file 2481–2.

[51] Hq Eighth Air Force, Target Priorities of the Eighth Air Force, 15 May 45. AAF file 520.317A.

[52] Foreword by Gen Arnold to Study cited n. 50.

[53] Eaker Rpt.

ing on the total German war potential. They were optimistic. They thought the German war potential had been reduced by about 10 percent and that a "total decline of 20% in overall effort may well be fatal." The job, in other words, was about half done. Still more optimistically the report noted a "very much greater decline in some individual industries (e.g., ball-bearings and rubber), which may be near the point where they could cause the collapse of the whole war machine." [54] Even if it were assumed that the intelligence reports on which that estimate was based were entirely accurate and complete, the significance of the conclusion still remained as dubious as a doctor's pronouncement that his patient was 50 percent dead. Enemy capacity for, and speed in, convalescence was always an unknown factor.

Despite the general optimism in the theater at the end of 1943 over the effects to date of Allied bombing, it was recognized that the future hung in the balance of the still-unsettled battle for air supremacy. By fall, the bombing attacks had forced the enemy to keep about half of his whole force of fighter aircraft in the west. At the same time Eighth Air Force claims of enemy fighters destroyed in combat were estimated at 75 percent of current German production. [55] On the other hand, since relatively few direct attacks were made on fighter production plants, German fighter strength was increasing despite losses. [56] The heavy U.S. losses in the Schweinfurt raid in October demonstrated that, despite attrition of German fighters in combat, Allied air forces still did not have air superiority over more than the fringes of enemy-occupied territory. [57]

General Arnold, commenting on the situation at the end of 1943, said: "It is difficult to appraise the present struggle for air supremacy as representing anything short of a major turning point in the war. What American and Royal Air Force bombers can do to the whole German war machine, once the German fighting force is rendered impotent, needs no comment. The issue hangs now on which side first falters, weakens, and loses its punishing power." [58] Whether victory in the battle for air supremacy was regarded as a prelude to decisive strategic bombing or preparation for OVERLORD, it was accepted as of paramount importance.

With the idea of intensifying the bomber offensive, the Joint Chiefs of Staff in November proposed a revision of the plan to bring it up to date with the changed strategic situation. The relative importance of targets had changed since Casablanca. Submarine construction, for example, was no longer entitled to priority, both because the danger from U-boats had been greatly reduced by measures to combat them at sea and because in general the bombing of factories and

[54] Joint Rpt by Min of Econ Warfare and the Air Min Int Branch, in Rpt by CofAS and CG U.S. Eighth AF on progress made by the RAF and U.S. Eighth AF in Combined Bomber Offensive, 7 Nov 43. AAF file 520.318. Ball bearing output was estimated by the Eighth Air Force A–2 to be down to 75 percent of preattack levels. See Supplement to the Strategic Aerial Bombardment of Europe—Accomplishments and Potentialities, 1 Apr 44. AAF file 2481–1.

[55] ACofAS Study, cited n. 50.

[56] Eaker Rpt.

[57] Target Priorities, 15 May 45, cited n. 51.

[58] Rpt, CG AAF to SW, 4 Jan 44.

pens had hitherto proved ineffective.[59] New air bases had been acquired in Italy on which strategic bombers could be based and a new Mediterranean strategic air force (the Fifteenth) had been established. It thus became necessary to coordinate attacks and target priorities between the United Kingdom and Mediterranean-based air forces. Finally the OVERLORD D Day was approaching and time to establish the prerequisite air supremacy was short.[60]

After some debate between the U.S. and British Chiefs of Staff over the advisability of concentrating on the Axis oil industry, a new directive was issued by the Combined Chiefs on 13 February 1944. The new directive dropped out the sytem of primary, secondary, and intermediate objectives. U.S. and British bomber commands were ordered to accomplish the "depletion of the German air force . . . by all means available." Although other objectives were listed, the order clearly shifted emphasis away from the earlier general aim of dislocating enemy industry to the specific task of destroying the enemy air force.[61]

In October 1943 the U.S. Chiefs of Staff had proposed the establishment of a strategic air force in the Mediterranean. It was observed that the Germans were meeting the air offensive from England by moving critical industries to the southeast and at the same time establishing a strong fighter shield in the northwest.[62] Eighth Air Force losses mounted in October to a point where General Marshall expressed himself as "deeply concerned" over them.[63] It was felt that these losses could be reduced if the enemy were forced to disperse his fighters in order to guard against bombing sorties from the Mediterranean. General Eisenhower was accordingly ordered to regroup the Twelfth Air Force under his command to form the Twelfth Tactical Air Force and the Fifteenth Strategic Air Force. The latter, consisting initially of six heavy bomber groups and two groups of long-range fighters, would be under the general direction of the Combined Chiefs of Staff and would be employed primarily against Combined Bomber Offensive targets.[64] The plan was to build up the Fifteenth Air Force by 31 March 1944 to twenty-one groups of heavy bombers, seven groups of fighters, and one group of reconnaissance aircraft.[65]

---

[59] During 1943, 41.8 percent of the total Eighth Air Force bomb tonnage (21,362 tons) was dropped on enemy submarine yards and bases. General Eaker estimated that the net result of this large expenditure was to prevent 22 out of 200 new submarines from being built. Eaker Rpt. Cf. Memo for CofAS, Evaluation of Results of Strategic Bombardment Against the Western Axis, 27 Jan 44, Tab 56 of Committee of Operations Analysts, COA History, MS. AAF files. COA's conclusion was that though "heavy attacks have been delivered against submarine manufacture and submarine operating bases, the results of these attacks have not been at all proportional to the effort expended."

[60] JCS 563, Modifications of Directive for the Bomber Offensive, 4 Nov 43.

[61] CCS 166/11, Revised Directive for Combined Bomber Offensive, 13 Feb 44.

[62] JCS 524, Plan to Assure the Most Effective Exploitation of the Combined Bomber Offensive, 9 Oct 43.

[63] JCS 125th Mtg, 29 Oct 43. Bomber losses in October amounted to 9.2 percent of the aircraft entering enemy territory. See Statistical Summary of Eighth Air Force Operations—European Theater, 17 Aug 1942–8 May 1945. AAF file 520.308A.

[64] The Mediterranean theater commander was to be allowed to use the units then assigned to the Twelfth Air Force in support of theater operations until the base objective north and east of Rome had been secured.

[65] CCS 217/1, 19 Oct 43.

As soon as the Fifteenth Air Force was formed, doubts occurred as to the effectiveness of the machinery provided for co-ordinating attacks from the Mediterranean and the United Kingdom. Neither the liaison between Fifteenth and Eighth Air Force headquarters nor the "general direction" of the Combined Chiefs was thought adequate for the most effective exploitation of the whole offensive. The Joint Chiefs of Staff therefore proposed a U.S. strategic air command with headquarters in England charged with control of all U.S. strategic air operations in the European–Mediterranean area.[66] Initially directly under the Combined Chiefs, the new headquarters would later be subordinated to the Supreme Allied Commander for OVERLORD. The original conception was that the Strategic Air Forces should command at first only U.S. forces but would, some time before D Day, take in RAF Bomber Command and constitute a strategic air command under the Supreme Allied Commander parallel to the tactical organization of the AEAF.[67] The U.S. proposal, so far as it concerned unification of U.S. air forces, was given to the British Chiefs of Staff for comment at the Cairo conference of November 1943. The British objected chiefly on the grounds that the new setup would destroy the close co-ordination between the Eighth Air Force and RAF through the British Chief of Air Staff. They proposed instead that the authority of Air Marshal Portal should be extended to give him general direction of

the whole bomber offensive against Germany.[68] The British objections could be considered only as advice, however, since Portal freely granted that organization of U.S. forces was the exclusive prerogative of the U.S. Chiefs of Staff. Since the U.S. Chiefs of Staff did not consider the advice sound, they proceeded according to their original proposals and ordered the establishment in England of headquarters of the U.S. Strategic Air Forces in Europe (USSAFE)[69] under command of Lt. Gen. Carl Spaatz. At the same time that USSAFE was established, General Eaker was transferred to command of the U.S. Mediterranean air forces and Lt. Gen. James H. Doolittle took over the Eighth Air Force.[70]

When General Spaatz arrived in England in January the Eighth Air Force was in the midst of its rapid build-up which had begun in the spring of 1943. There were then operating (as of 31 December 1943) twenty-five groups of heavy bombers plus three squadrons (which in March became a training unit) and eleven groups of fighters."[71] Two of the latter groups were equipped with P–38's which, with additional wing gasoline tanks, had a range great enough to accompany bombers deep into Germany. The build-up of long-range fighters increased rapidly in the early months

---

[66] JCS 602, Integrated Command of U.S. Strategic Air Forces in the European–Mediterranean Area, 16 Nov 43.

[67] JCS 601, Strategic Air Force Command in Operations Against Germany, 13 Nov 43.

[68] It was JCS 602 (see n. 66) that was submitted to the British as CCS 400. British reply is CCS 400/1, 26 Nov 43. It may be supposed that British objections were also connected with their previously expressed opposition to subordinating strategic air forces to SAC.

[69] Later redesignated U.S. Strategic Air Forces (USSTAF).

[70] Craven and Cate, The Army Air Forces, II, 749–56.

[71] Statistical Summary of Eighth Air Force Operations, cited n. 63.

of 1944. At the same time belly tanks and wing tanks were added to all types of fighters to permit them to escort bombers at ever extending radii from their United Kingdom bases. By March the Eighth Air Force was strong enough so that bombing missions were deliberately planned to provoke air battles with the Luftwaffe. A series of large-scale raids on Berlin was inaugurated chiefly for this purpose, and though the bomber losses at first were fairly heavy (the maximum was sixty-nine on one raid) enemy resistance was at last crushed, and on the final missions over the German capital enemy fighters no longer flew to the attack.[72] The peak of German fighter defense was reached and passed in February 1944, and even in that month the enemy was not able to inflict losses on U.S. bombers on a scale large enough to deter them from continued operations.[73] By June U.S. bombers had virtually free range of the skies and could bomb strategic targets at will.

While the Eighth Air Force with the RAF Bomber Command achieved mastery of the air over western Europe, the tactical air forces were being built up to exploit this advantage in direct support of OVERLORD. In April 1943 General Eaker drew up plans to expand the Air Support Command of the Eighth Air Force for tactical operations. These plans were studied and revised during the summer. The outcome in the fall was a decision to set up a separate U.S.

tactical air force comprising four major commands: the medium bomber, fighter, air service, and troop carrier commands. Lt. Gen. Lewis H. Brereton, commander of the Ninth Air Force in the Middle East, was ordered to England with his staff but minus his troops and aircraft.[74] On 16 October 1943 the Ninth Air Force was reconstituted in England, absorbing the Tactical Command of the Eighth Air Force. The latter contributed initially four understrength medium bomber groups and several reconnaissance squadrons.[75] The new Ninth Air Force grew rapidly during the first six months of 1944. By 1 June it controlled eighteen groups of fighters, eleven groups of medium bombers, fourteen groups of transports, and two groups of reconnaissance aircraft.[76]

The Ninth Air Force was expressly constituted to support the OVERLORD ground battle and on 15 December 1943, as noted, it came under the operational control of Air Marshal Leigh-Mallory's

---

[72] Study No. 59 by U.S. Strategic Bombing Survey, Military Analysis Division, The Defeat of the German Air Force. AAF file 137.306.

[73] Plan signed by Gen Anderson and transmitted to Eisenhower and Portal, Plan for the Completion of the Combined Bomber Offensive, 5 Mar 44. AAF files; cf. Diary of CinC, 25 Feb 44.

[74] General Brereton, Annapolis graduate in the class of 1911, transferred to the Army after completing the Naval Academy course and, in World War I, saw Air Corps service. In 1941, after heading the Third Air Force in Florida, he was sent to the Philippine Islands as commander of the American Air Forces in the Far East. Early the following year he was appointed head of the Tenth Air Force in India. In June 1942 he was transferred to Egypt and assumed command of the Middle East Air Force, which in November became the Ninth Air Force including all U.S. Army Air Force units in the Middle East. General Brereton was given command of U.S. Army Forces in the Middle East, in addition to his Air Force post, in late January 1943. He held the two commands until he and his staff were ordered to England.

[75] Col William B. Reed (Exec CofS, Ninth AF), The Ninth Air Force in the European Theater of Operations, MS. AAF files.

[76] [Lt Col Robert H. George] Ninth Air Force, April to November 1944 (Army Air Forces Historical Studies: No. 36), MS, p. 81. AAF files.

AEAF. It was provided, however, that long-range fighters under Ninth Air Force command would support the Eighth Air Force bomber offensive until OVERLORD began. At the same time the medium bombers were to reinforce the attack against the Luftwaffe by raiding enemy coastal airfields and so driving enemy fighters inland.[77] Such raids were carried out with particular effectiveness in the spring just before the invasion. But throughout the winter the medium bombers were largely diverted to attack the German V-bomb launching sites, the neutralization of which became for a time the priority mission of the entire AEAF.

Sites for launching pilotless aircraft were observed to be under construction in the summer of 1943, especially in the Pas-de-Calais area. By the middle of December photographic reconnaissance had confirmed the existence of sixty-nine sites.[78] It was then estimated that the enemy might be able to begin a full-scale flying-bomb attack against England in February. The prospective enemy operation was called CROSSBOW.

Instructions were issued to the AEAF to bomb all sites that were more than half completed. In addition, certain sites were assigned to the RAF Bomber Command for night attack. Finally, orders issued on 15 December to the Eighth Air Force assigned "overriding priority" to attacks on CROSSBOW sites whenever weather conditions over northern France were suitable. The decision to divert any portion of the strategic air forces away from the primary mission of defeating the Luftwaffe was a measure of the seriousness with which the Allies viewed the enemy

threat to the security of the British Isles and OVERLORD preparations.[79]

Air attacks against the enemy CROSSBOW launching sites, beginning in December, continued until the last of the sites was captured by the invading forces. Before D Day the tactical and strategic air forces flew more than 30,000 sorties against CROSSBOW installations and estimated that they had succeeded in neutralizing eighty-six out of ninety-seven identified sites. At least seventy-four other sites, however, were not detected by Allied intelligence before the landings. The effectiveness of this program is difficult to estimate. Counterattack against the German rocket certainly postponed its use and reduced the scale of the eventual attack on London in June 1944.[80]

Long before the success of the AEAF air offensive became apparent, however, the seriousness of the CROSSBOW threat was largely discounted. The flurry of alarm in December was within a month replaced by sober estimates which calculated that, on the basis of the most generous assessments of German production capacity, the flying bombs could not be produced in quantity sufficient for a major offensive against London or against staging areas and ports to be used for mounting OVERLORD. For example, intelligence reckoned that the largest conceivable enemy sustained attack on London might mean that the average

---

[77] Reed, The Ninth Air Force, cited n. 75.

[78] COS (43) 760 (O), CROSSBOW, 17 Dec 43.

[79] Ibid.; cf. COS (43) 312th Mtg (O), 22 Dec 43. At this meeting the Chiefs of Staff discussed the possibility of dispersing OVERLORD shipping to minimize the risks from expected CROSSBOW attacks.

[80] "Despatch by Air Chief Marshal Sir Trafford Leigh-Mallory" (submitted to the Supreme Allied Commander in November 1944), Fourth Supplement to The London Gazette, No. 37838, 31 December 1946, pp. 53–54.

V-BOMB OVER LONDON, JUNE 1944. *Most of these pilotless aircraft were launched from the Pas-de-Calais area.*

Londoner would be exposed to a rocket bomb explosion within half a mile of him once a month.[81] Similar calculations applied to possible use of the rockets against an OVERLORD port area resulted in a similar conclusion of probable ineffectiveness.[82] At least by March 1944, it was clear to SHAEF that German aircraft, with or without pilots, were not going to threaten seriously the success of OVERLORD.

The Bombing of French Railroads

With the threat of CROSSBOW waning and the defeat of the Luftwaffe apparently assured, the Allied command could decide how air supremacy might be exploited to insure the success of OVERLORD. Up to the end of 1943, planners had never proposed use of the strategic air forces during the preliminary phase on missions directly connected with the ground battle, although it was suggested that the heavy bombers might be sent in to attack German defenses about two weeks before the landings. Now the unexpectedly early success of the air forces in winning the battle for control of the air opened the possibility of committing them sooner in direct preparation for the assault.

In December an Allied intelligence agency had drawn up a short-term rail-bombing plan designed to block seventeen selected rail routes immediately before D Day. This recommendation was rejected by Leigh-Mallory on the grounds that to be effective it would require a concentrated bombing effort close to D Day which, because of the risk of bad weather and the probable pressure of other commitments at that time, could not be guaranteed. As an alternative, AEAF developed a plan for a three-month bombing attack against thirty-three targets in France and Belgium and thirty-nine in Germany to disrupt rail traffic into the assault area. The new plan drafted in the first half of January drew on an analysis of the Italian rail-bombing experience made by Professor S. Zuckerman, scientific adviser to AEAF. Zuckerman took the view that the Italian rail transport system had been virtually paralyzed through the destruction or isolation of servicing and repair facilities and destruction of locomotives, rolling stock, and track. The paralysis was brought about, he considered, by a total dislocation of the system achieved largely by attacks on marshaling yards where the servicing facilities were concentrated. If similar destruction was to be accomplished in northwest Europe, planners estimated that it would take at least three months of concentrated effort and would involve at least part of the strategic air forces.[83]

Preliminary discussion by the staff of AEAF and representatives of SHAEF brought forth no serious objection to the plan although Maj. Gen. P. G. Whitefoord, SHAEF G–2, expressed his belief

---

[81] COS (44) 25 (O), Probable Scale and Effect of Attack on London by Pilotless Aircraft, 10 Jan 44.

[82] COS (44) 107 (O) (Revised), Progress Report by the ACAS (Ops), 2 Feb 44.

[83] AAF Evaluation Board, Effectiveness of Air Attack Against Rail Transportation in the Battle of France, Jun 45. This is a study prepared after the war by United States air experts in collaboration with the French railroad authorities (cited hereafter as AAF Evaluation Board Study). Copy in AAF file 138.4–37. Cf. Ltr, R. D. Hughes to Maj Gen F. L. Anderson, Report of Conference at Norfolk House, 14 Jan 44. USSTAF files. See Bibliographical Note.

that the first seven or eight enemy divisions brought into the battle area would come in by road and that therefore the rail plan, even if successful, would probably not affect the battle in the early stages. Despite this objection, the meeting decided that the proposed attacks and the principle on which they were based were sound. The number of targets, however, was considered inadequate. AEAF therefore revised the plan to include ninety-three targets, of which fourteen in southern France would be attacked by the Fifteenth Air Force from Mediterranean bases. The German targets were omitted. With these revisions AEAF and SHAEF representatives expressed themselves as satisfied that the plan represented the "only practicable method of dealing with the enemy's rail communications and that it satisfied army requirements." Attacks were to begin at once, but would be regarded as a bonus until operations in support of OVERLORD received precedence over the bomber offensive.[84]

The decision was not as firm as it seemed. The formula with which the meeting concluded was the formula of the COSSAC planning days when plans for air and naval action were drawn up by the independent air and naval commands, submitted through the COSSAC machinery for Army approval and, after such co-ordination, approved. Agreement that the air plan "satisfied army requirements" reflected the habit of mind of regarding decisions as made by co-equal service commanders. SHAEF was

still very new on the scene and the idea of a supreme commander solely responsible for all final decisions affecting the operation he commanded whether they were primarily air, army, or naval matters had still not been absorbed. SHAEF, furthermore, had not yet been given control over the strategic air forces. The result was that, while Leigh-Mallory proceeded on the assumption that his plan was in effect and actually assigned rail targets to the Ninth Air Force in February 1944 as alternatives to its primary missions in support of the Combined Bomber Offensive, SHAEF was only beginning to study the plan. General Whitefoord, the day after the meeting, reported to the operations staff of Supreme Headquarters that the AEAF plan "may well be worth considering."[85]

Quite different was the reaction at General Spaatz's headquarters, USSTAF (United States Strategic Air Forces). The suggestion that any large portion of the strategic air forces should be diverted from the bomber offensive and brought under control of AEAF for tactical purposes was regarded as threatening the completion of the vital primary mission of the strategic air to defeat the Luftwaffe. An intelligence officer, after examining the AEAF plan, concluded that it would fruitlessly dissipate the striking power of the strategic air forces. He pointed out, however, that because of the peculiar command set-up which put Leigh-Mallory directly under Eisenhower the plan would not compete directly for favor with the Combined Bomber Offensive. He suggested that if the strategic air forces did not like the plan they

---

[84] Allied AF Bombing Committee, 6th Mtg, 24 Jan 44. USSTAF files. SHAEF representatives were General Whitefoord and General Napier (Movement and Transportation Officer).

[85] Memo for Bull, West, and McLean, 25 Jan 44. SHAEF SGS file 373.24 I.

would have to devise an alternative for submission to General Eisenhower. He concluded with a recommendation that "a quick and decisive effort be made to prevent the Strategic Air Forces being engulfed in the Zuckerman program." [86]

General Doolittle, new commander of the Eighth Air Force, when asked for an opinion, replied that in no case should the attack on rail targets by strategic bombers be begun until after the German Air Force had been decisively beaten. His operations officer felt that this objective could be accomplished in short order "if we are not prematurely distracted." He believed further that the system of rail targets could be hit within the period D minus 20 to D Day and that this would be the most effective time to undertake the attack. [87]

General Spaatz directed that an alternative plan be prepared "for operations to follow after accomplishment of the primary objective of the Combined Bomber Offensive . . . and for operations of the strategic air forces in the direct support of OVERLORD." [88] USSTAF planners saw no merits at all in the AEAF plan. "Axis European transportation," they said, "cannot be recommended as a target system for strategic attack"; it was too extensive and would require too long to destroy. They estimated that "no military effect would be felt for more than . . . nine months" after the program was completed. As an alternative they

suggested priority attacks on the German oil industry, with emphasis on gasoline, and secondary attacks on fighter aircraft, ball bearing, rubber, and bomber production. Only as a last resort should transportation centers in Germany be attacked when weather conditions forbade precise attacks on the primary targets. [89] This USSTAF proposal, which became known as the "Oil Plan," was submitted to General Eisenhower and Air Marshal Portal on 5 March with request for the Supreme Commander's concurrence.

It will be recalled that, while the tactical air forces had been subordinated to the Supreme Commander at the end of 1943, the Combined Chiefs of Staff had been unable to agree on when and how the strategic air forces should come under Eisenhower's control. Although it was generally conceded that the Supreme Commander should command all forces (including the strategic air) which he needed in the actual battle, the British were opposed to turning over the heavy bombers to him before that battle. On 12 February, General Eisenhower received his directive from the Combined Chiefs of Staff, conspicuously lacking any clause on the control of strategic air. At about the same time the AEAF rail plan was published and General Spaatz's opposition to it developed. All these circumstances served to give urgency to the settling of the command problem. General Eisenhower in the latter part of February 1944 brought the problem to the Prime Minister. Churchill was at first disposed to adhere to his original view that the Bomber Command should remain independent of the Supreme

[86] Ltr, Lt Col Lowell P. Weicker (Dep Dir Int USSTAF) to Dir Int, Future Plan for Employing Air Power in the Support of OVERLORD, 10 Feb 44. USSTAF files.

[87] Ltr, Gen Anderson (A–3, Eighth AF) to CG USSTAF, Force Required Against Railway Targets, 26 Feb 44. AAF Eighth AF files.

[88] Dir, 12 Feb 44.

[89] Plan for the Completion of the Combined Bomber Offensive, 5 Mar 44, cited n. 73.

Commander while co-operating with him in support of OVERLORD. This was substantially the view advanced by the British Chiefs of Staff during the earlier debate with the U.S. Joint Chiefs and was as unacceptable to Eisenhower now as it had been then to General Marshall. Whatever its motive, it seemed to the Supreme Commander like holding back on what had been agreed on as the Allied supreme effort in Europe. If the British insisted on anything less than an all-out commitment to OVERLORD, Eisenhower told the Prime Minister, he would "simply have to go home." [90] Churchill then did not prolong his opposition. He said he would agree to whatever plan Air Marshal Portal and Eisenhower together could work out.

The solution drafted by Portal and Eisenhower was a proposal to give the Supreme Commander "responsibility for supervision of air operations out of England of all the forces engaged in the program" in support of OVERLORD, the responsibility to pass when Portal, "as executive of the Combined Chiefs of Staff for the execution of POINTBLANK [the Combined Bomber Offensive]," and the Supreme Commander jointly approved the plan for air support. The Supreme Commander recognized that his control of air forces assigned to OVERLORD and the Combined Bomber Offensive would be subject to intervention by the Combined Chiefs of Staff. He also announced his intention of designating Air Marshal Tedder, Deputy Supreme Commander, to supervise "all operations under the control of OVERLORD." [91] It was

understood that the requirements of supporting OVERLORD would not absorb the total effort of the strategic air forces and that the use of the balance would be arranged by Portal and Eisenhower in accordance with the existing Combined Chiefs of Staff directive for the Combined Bomber Offensive. Supervision of this part of the air operation would be exercised jointly by Portal and Eisenhower.[92]

This agreement, drawn up on 9 March, was approved on the 17th by the British Chiefs of Staff and forwarded to Washington. The Joint Chiefs accepted all the terms except the word "supervision." They preferred "command" and said so. But, after a "long and complicated" [93] demurral from the British, they compromised on "direction." [94]

Eisenhower would assume control when a plan of air support had been agreed upon. But agreement promised to be difficult. Opposition to the AEAF transportation bombing plan gathered during March. Various intelligence experts examined the problem and came up with unanimous disapproval chiefly on the grounds that German military

---

both the Army and the Royal Flying Corps. In 1938 he began a tour as Director-General of Research and Development, Air Ministry. He was Deputy Commander-in-Chief of the RAF in the Middle East during the Italian phase of African operations and in June 1941 was made Commander-in-Chief, directing air attacks against Rommel's troops and enemy shipping in the Mediterranean. After a short period with the Air Council as Vice-Chief of Air Staff, he returned to the Mediterranean early in 1943 as Commander-in-Chief, Mediterranean Air Command.

[92] Ltr, Portal to Eisenhower, 9 Mar 44. SHAEF SGS file 373/1; cf. CCS 520, Control of Strategic Bombing for "Overlord," 17 Mar 44.

[93] Marshall's words at JCS 154th Mtg, 21 Mar 44.

[94] CCS 520 series. Final agreement is CCS 520/2, 26 Mar 44.

---

[90] Entry 3 Mar 44, Diary of CinC; cf. *ibid.*, Memo under date 22 Mar 44.

[91] Tedder had served during World War I with

traffic required such a small portion of the French rail system that 80 or 90 percent of that system would have to be destroyed before troop and supply movements into the assault area could be affected. They further questioned whether prolonged attack could even sufficiently weaken the system to justify the expenditure of bombs. Air Marshal Portal was persuaded by their findings that the plan was unsuitable. General Brooke agreed and, questioning Zuckerman's interpretation of the Italian experience, suggested that rail bombing in Italy under much more favorable conditions than would prevail in France had actually been of doubtful value.[95]

Despite all this opposition, the AEAF plan won a powerful advocate in Air Marshal Tedder. His advocacy led to fresh examinations. General Spaatz observed to General Arnold that since these examinations had proved adverse to the plan it was hoped by all concerned that "the AEAF plan will be repudiated by Tedder of his own accord, thus avoiding hard feelings."[96] But Tedder did not repudiate the plan, mainly because he did not feel that the alternative oil plan would have effect on OVERLORD in time. At a meeting at the Air Ministry on 25 March presided over by General Eisenhower and attended by all the top airmen concerned in the air support question, Tedder outlined his views. The German Air Force, he felt, should remain the priority target, but the residual effort of all Allied air forces should be devoted to delaying and disorganizing enemy ground movements. It was important, he believed, to concentrate all the air forces

on a single target system. In favor of the transportation plan he pointed out the already strained condition of the French railroads. In view of that, he felt that rail bombing could delay enemy preparations and, more important, it could so canalize rail traffic that it could be more easily disrupted completely after D Day.[97]

As to the first priority of defeating the Luftwaffe there was no argument. Attacks on the German Air Force were interpreted further to include attacks on ball bearing factories. The debate then centered on what rail bombing might accomplish. Tedder did not claim that the proposed rail attacks would prevent all German rail traffic, but he did feel that, even in the light of intelligence estimates, the bombing would have useful military effect. Portal agreed that the efficiency of the enemy rail system could be impaired by bombing but thought that the damage could be absorbed by curtailment of civilian traffic and that the German Army would not be affected. War Office and Economic Ministry representatives in general agreed. Possibly 30 percent of the present efficiency of the enemy railroads could be pared off, they thought, but despite this possibility German military traffic would still get through. A British economic adviser added his belief that, although some food would evidently have to be carried for the civilian population, the Germans would be happy to get along without French industry.

_____

[95] COS (44) 93rd Mtg, 21 Mar 44.
[96] Cbl, Spaatz to Arnold, 16 Mar 44. USSTAF files.

[97] Memo, 24 Mar 44, SHAEF SGS file 373/1. Following account of the meeting is from minutes in AAF files. Mtg, To Discuss the Bombing Policy in the Period Before OVERLORD, 25 May 44, CAS/misc/61 (Final).

General Eisenhower then cut sharply into the core of the question. As he saw it, the first five or six weeks of OVERLORD would be the most critical period, during which it was essential to take every possible step to insure that Allied troops got ashore and stayed ashore. "The greatest contribution that he could imagine the air forces making to this aim was that they should hinder enemy movement." He discounted the arguments that the plan would have less than the effect claimed for it by AEAF. In default of an alternative it was necessary only that the rail bombing have some effect, however small, to justify adopting it.

That the plan would have "some" effect was generally admitted and the discussion turned to whether there was any acceptable alternative. General Spaatz summarized his reasons for preferring the oil plan already outlined by his staff. Strategic attacks on the enemy rail system, he believed, would not affect the course of the initial battle, nor would the attacks be likely to force the German Air Force to fight. The oil plan, on the other hand, would evoke enemy reaction and so lead to attrition of the German fighter air force. It would, furthermore, directly weaken enemy resistance and so hasten the success of OVERLORD. Spaatz's view, in short, was that nothing the strategic air forces could do in the preliminary phase would materially affect the battle of the beaches, and that therefore they should devote their efforts to a plan which would achieve the maximum long-range reduction of German armed strength.

General Eisenhower did not agree. The oil plan, he felt, should be considered as soon as the critical phase of

OVERLORD was passed, but it did not constitute an alternative to the rail plan. The decision of the meeting was that no alternative existed and the rail plan was approved subject only to General Spaatz's examination of whether the Eighth Air Force could carry out its portion of it. The plan was considered not to affect Bomber Command, whose night area bombing could be expected to have only a fortuitous effect on the German transportation system.

At the close of the meeting Portal warned of British Government opposition and asked that the War Cabinet be given an opportunity to consider the implications of killing French civilians in the proposed attacks.

Ever since the plan had been advanced, the War Cabinet had viewed as political dynamite the idea of bombing French and Belgian territory, particularly in attacks on marshaling yards which were generally located close to centers of population. Earlier in March the British Chiefs of Staff had refused Leigh-Mallory blanket clearance of his rail targets without Cabinet approval. Even after General Eisenhower had declared the plan essential to the military success of OVERLORD, Cabinet approval was still withheld. Estimates of civilian casualties likely to be caused ran as high as 160,000, of which it was thought a quarter might be killed.[98] The Joint Intelligence Committee was invited to prepare an appreciation of French reaction.[99] Pending its report, certain targets in relatively unpopulated areas were to be cleared in-

[98] COS (44) 273 (O), Attacks on Rail Targets in Enemy Occupied Territory, 19 Mar 44.

[99] Issued as JIC (44) 147 (O) (Final), Bombing Targets in France and the Low Countries in Relation to Overlord, 15 May 44.

dividually. For about two weeks the Cabinet earnestly debated the question.[100] Their opposition was at last overcome largely by the firm stand which the British Chiefs of Staff took that the program was a military necessity.[101] On 18 April the Cabinet had cleared all rail targets except two in the Paris area.[102] The Prime Minister however, continued to urge General Eisenhower to consider alternative targets the bombing of which would not kill more than a hundred Frenchmen per target. Only if study proved all other schemes militarily inferior could he concur that military considerations must override the political.[103] At the end of April General Eisenhower directed the suspension of attacks on twenty-seven targets in heavily populated districts, including seventeen of the twenty-four targets originally assigned to Bomber Command.[104] With modifications such as this and a system of warning the civilian population, casualties were kept down below the most optimistic estimates. On 16 May the Prime Minister had become reconciled to the program and, vetoing a proposal to call in French railway experts to assess the psychological effects of the bombing, he said, "I suggest

that the matter should be dropped." [105] As a practical matter it, of course, had been dropped and the transportation bombing program at that point was nearing completion.

On 14 April General Eisenhower took over direction of the strategic air forces in support of OVERLORD and three days later issued his directive for the transportation bombing. The over-all mission of destruction of the German military and economic system remained unchanged. The particular mission of the strategic air forces was first to deplete the German Air Force and destroy the facilities serving it, and second, "to destroy and disrupt the enemy's rail communications, particularly those affecting the enemy's movements towards the 'OVERLORD' lodgment area." [106] Targets in eastern France and part of Belgium were allocated to the Eighth Air Force; Bomber Command was to hit western France and the area around Paris while the AEAF concentrated its efforts on northern France and Belgium. Although German targets were not included in the plan as approved in April, the Eighth Air Force before D Day dropped about 5,000 tons on railroad centers in the Reich and along the Franco-German border.[107] Eisenhower also personally gave Spaatz permission to try out a series of heavy attacks on the German oil industry; these were initiated in March and continued along with the rail bombing. Attacks against oil targets began to assume the proportions of an all-out offen-

---

[100] COS (44) 190th Mtg (O), 4 Apr 44. For the discussion on bombing of French railroads see, in addition, COS (44) 258 (O), 10 Mar 44; COS (44) 273 (O), 19 Mar; and COS (44) 93rd and 95th Mtgs, 21 and 23 Mar respectively. Entries in Diary of CinC, under dates of 5, 13, and 20 Apr 44, summarize the salient points accurately.

[101] Cbl, Smith to Marshall, 17 May 44; Ismay, Minute to Prime Minister, 29 Mar 44. SHAEF SGS file 373.24 I.

[102] Transportation Targets Committee (SHAEF) 2d Mtg, 18 Apr 44. SHAEF SGS file 334, bundle N.

[103] Ltr to Eisenhower, 29 Apr 44. SHAEF SGS file 373.24 I.

[104] Dir to USTAF. Bomber Command, and AEAF, 29 Apr 44. SHAEF SGS file 373.24 I.

[105] Minute, annexed to COS (44) 158th Mtg (O), 16 May 44.

[106] Dir to USSTAF and Bomber Command, 17 Apr 44. SHAEF SGS file 373/1.

[107] AAF Evaluation Board Study.

sive about the middle of May, and on 8 June General Spaatz announced the destruction of German oil resources as the primary strategic aim of the U.S. Strategic Air Forces.[108]

Bombing of enemy railroads in France and Belgium was carried out by all three air forces, and before D Day nearly all assigned targets had been hit. AEAF reported good results. But outside the AEAF the program was carried on with general skepticism. A representative of 21 Army Group referred to it as "pinpricking on rail communications." [109] The attacks were continued because they were believed to constitute the best that could be devised and because it was hoped they would have some effect. The hope, however, according to intelligence reports, was sheer delusion. A week before D Day the SHAEF G–2 reported that the whole rail bombing operation had accomplished nothing of importance. It had failed "so [to] reduce the railway operating facilities as to impair the enemy's ability to move up reinforcements and maintain his forces in the West." Although the attacks had probably imposed some slight delays and had laid some groundwork for effective tactical thrusts after the assault, it was still estimated that the enemy had three times the rail capacity needed for military traffic, four times the required number of cars, eight times the required locomotives, and ten times the required servicing facilities.[110]

Seldom have intelligence estimates been so wrong. They were wrong primarily because the method of statistical evaluation took no account of either cumulative or critical damage. A machine only 10 percent worn out may still be incapable of functioning. Similarly, destruction of a single cotter pin, an infinitesimal portion of a machine by weight, nevertheless may precipitate the shattering of the whole mechanism. By D Day the Allied air forces, ably assisted by saboteurs of the French Resistance, had knocked cotter pins out of the railroads all over France, and the transportation system was on the point of total collapse.

The Germans had long anticipated that the Allies would preface their invasion of the Continent with a widespread attack on the Continental rail system. Rundstedt realized further that without an air force of his own he would be virtually helpless before such an attack. Interference with troop movement and supply was certain to be serious. Lacking sufficient motor transport even for its combat troops, Rundstedt's army was dependent almost entirely on the railroads for supply.

Certain measures might have been taken, both to lessen that dependence (by decentralization of the supply system, for instance) and to protect the railroads. Actually, little was done. The Commander in Chief West had to face the twin facts that France had been used for three years as a grazing ground for the rest of the German military establishment and that by the time Hitler recognized the imperative need for strong defensive measures in the west there were

---

[108] Msg, Spaatz to Doolittle, U–63552, 8 Jun 44, in Eighth Air Force, Dir Vol 3. AAF files.

[109] AEAF Mtg to discuss bombing targets, 6 May 44. AAF file 505.25–5.

[110] SHAEF G–2, Evaluation of Rail Centre Attacks, 20 May 44. AAF file 505.26–38. These conclusions were repeated in the report of 31 May.

no longer any resources with which to carry them out.

The French railroads had already been weakened before the war by a series of financial crises which resulted in economizing on repair facilities and renewal and maintenance expenditures. The campaign of 1940 destroyed 500 way structures and 1,200 railroad buildings. But this loss was nothing compared to that caused by the depredations of the Germans during the occupation. Out of the 18,000 locomotives in France, 4,000 were removed to Germany, including a large percentage of the heavier .types. More than a third of the rolling stock, which before the war amounted to 31,000 passenger cars and 480,000 freight cars, was also "loaned" to Germany. Personnel of the SNCF was reduced 20 percent and the quality diluted by calling back retired employees and increasing the proportion of unskilled workers.[111]

Before Allied bombs began to fall, the SNCF was severely strained and lacked the usual reserve of excess capacity. Under constant pressure to increase loading, hampered by shortages perhaps most crucial in personnel and facilities for repair, burdened with a cumbersome mixed German-French management, and plagued with active sabotage and passive resistance on the part of a large number of workers and the French management, the French railroads were peculiarly sensitive to attack.

In anticipation of transportation difficulties to come, OB WEST on 3 January ordered the establishment of a strict priority system restricting rail shipments to the most important military supplies.

Seventh Army had worked out and put into effect this system for Normandy and Brittany by the end of February.[112] Up to that time no difficulties more serious than local delays were experienced through spasmodic Allied air attacks and sabotage. But in March the co-ordinated attacks began and the strained transportation system showed immediate signs of breakdown. Despite the regulation of nonessential traffic, 1,600 trains by the end of April were backlogged in France, including 600 carrying army supplies. In addition, valuable army supplies had been destroyed in attacks on marshaling yards; other supplies ready for shipment were held up in warehouses awaiting freight cars.[113] Seventh Army, during the month, got a taste of things to come. In its sector, two major attacks on le Mans resulted in considerable losses of locomotives and cars and put the yards out of operation for several weeks. Since the beginning of 1944 railroads in the army area had suffered twenty-five air attacks and fifty-six reported cases of sabotage. The cumulative effect was to increase the backlog of trains feeding Normandy and Brittany from 30 at the beginning of the month to 228 at the end.[114]

The five to six hundred locomotives destroyed in the OB WEST sector during March was nearly double the figure for February. But the acceleration of the tempo of attacks had only begun. OKW noted that in March the majority of Allied

---

[111] AAF Evaluation Board Study.

[112] Seventh Army, KTB; Taetigkeitsbericht des Bevollmaechtigten Transport Offiziers beim A.O.K.7 (referred to hereafter as Seventh Army, Trans. O.), KTB 1.I.–30.VI.44.

[113] OB WEST, Oberquartiermeister West (referred to hereafter as OB WEST, O.Qu.), KTB 1.I.–17. VIII.44.

[114] Seventh Army, Trans. O., KTB 1.I.–30.VI.44.

BOMBARDMENT OF MARSHALING YARDS *at Busigny in northern France.*

air attacks in France were still hitting Luftwaffe installations. In April the concentration shifted dramatically to railroads: there were 249 reported attacks as against 93 in March. Sabotage cases at the same time increased from 460 to 500.[115] The first serious military effect was the curtailment of supplies for the construction of the Atlantic Wall. In April the naval commander in Normandy was already complaining about the lack of steel and concrete due to the destruction of rail centers. Construction delays, he added, would be inevitable.[116]

Countermeasures were discussed in a conference on 15 April between Field Marshal Keitel, Chief of OKW, and the Reich Minister for Rail and Road Communications (*Reichsverkehrsminister*) but no really effective measures were possible. Fighter protection could not be increased, since Allied bombing of vital targets in Germany continued unabated while Luftwaffe fighter strength

deteriorated. Military leaves were suspended throughout the west on 25 April to relieve the pressure on the railroads.[117] Additional restriction of nonmilitary traffic, which achieved a sharp curtailment of rail operations in France, brought a temporary improvement. *Seventh Army* noted that its backlog of trains had been reduced from 228 at the end of March to 120 at the end of April.[118] Reduction in total traffic further cut the losses of equipment. But the statistical improvement indicated no solution to the problem.

Allied attacks were stepped up in May. *Seventh Army* reported "important destruction" during the first week and predicted that in case of a landing the enemy would be able to disrupt rail traffic completely, as he had done in Italy. The same conclusion had already led *OB WEST* to order the formation of truck companies under centralized control that would pool all available motor transport for supply in accordance with the critical tactical needs. The order was not easy to implement in view of critical shortages of motor transport. On 7 May *Seventh Army* had worked out the details of a scheme to motorize portions of certain infantry divisions in reserve as well as Kampfgruppen of the coastal defense divisions so that they could be employed in mobile fighting. The remainder of all units were to give up all transportation for the formation of motor companies under corps control—each company with a capacity of 120 tons. Units in the forward positions would bring their weaponing up to 75 percent of authorized allotments and secure three days' supply of all material needed to make them self-sufficient in combat. It

---

[115] *OKW/WFSt, KTB Ausarbeitung, Der Westen 1.IV.–16.XII.44,* cited hereafter as *Der Westen*. This draft War Diary (KTB), like that cited in n. 27, was written by Major Percy Schramm, OKW historian, from records and daily notes made at OKW headquarters. Until the end of 1943 the Diary was kept chronologically and supplemented by information from participants in the operations. After 1943 the diary was written up at intervals of three months or more in the form of separate narratives on the various fronts and the special problems faced by OKW. Besides official' documents, Schramm made use of a *Merkbuch* in which he recorded informal notes on the situation meetings he attended and special interviews he held with the Deputy Chief of WFSt, General Warlimont. In view of the destruction of OKW records ordered in 1945 by General Scherff, the copies of Schramm's *Ausarbeitungen* for 1944 represent unique source material for OKW history.

[116] *Marine Gruppenkommando West, Kriegstagebuch* (referred to hereafter as *Navy Group West, KTB*), *16.IV–30.IV.44.* Navy Dept files, Tambach Collection.

[117] *Der Westen.*

[118] *Seventh Army, Trans.O., KTB 1.I.–30.VI.44.*

was reckoned that it would take three days for resupply through the centralized transport system.[119]

One German answer to Allied bombings, in short, was an attempt to reduce dependence on the railroads. The other was an attempt to keep the railroads in repair. Repair of bomb damage on rail lines and marshaling yards was generally not a difficult or time-consuming process. Even after very heavy raids on marshaling yards, traffic could almost always be resumed in a day or two. Evidently, however, widespread and constant air attacks could involve a very heavy total expenditure of man-hours for repair. The cumulative strain spread across theater boundaries. By the middle of January, for example, all the rail lines in Italy were broken and the supply situation became so serious that two more railway engineer battalions were requisitioned, one from Russia and one from the west. At the end of March Rundstedt was called on to send another battalion to Italy. Although the French railroad system was then already beginning to suffer from Allied attacks the Italian situation was thought to be still worse.[120] Rundstedt at the end of March was thus left with about three railway engineer battalions to supervise repair work on French railroads for military use. Laborers were drawn at first from the SNCF and from the civilian population as a whole. But when the coordinated bombings began to take effect in the spring extraordinary measures became necessary. Immediately 18,000 men

of Organization Todt were taken off construction work on the Atlantic Wall to try to keep the railroads running. On 8 May OKW approved the withdrawal of an additional 10,000 men.[121] Two weeks later Reich Minister Albert Speer noted after a conference with Hitler that the latter approved his view "that in the west, even though building operations on the Atlantic Wall should be possible, the main duties of the O.T. [Organization Todt] should lie in the elimination of difficulties in transport, including those in the interior of France."[122]

But repairs could not keep pace. To the systematic attacks on marshaling yards, the Allied tactical air forces in May added new damaging attacks on bridges over the Seine, Oise, and Meuse Rivers. These attacks, begun suddenly on 7 May, had not been included in the original transportation bombing plan because it was believed on the basis of experience in Italy that the weight of bombs required to knock out a bridge was out of all proportion to the military value of success. The first attacks were undertaken experimentally at the urging of 21 Army Group, which had little faith in the efficacy of general attacks on rail centers.[123] Success was spectacular. Bridges were toppled along the whole length of the Seine from Rouen to Mantes-Gassicourt before D Day at a cost of only 220 tons of bombs to a bridge. On 26 May, all routes over the Seine north of Paris were closed to rail traffic and they remained closed for the next thirty days despite German efforts to repair one or

---

[119] Order, *Seventh Army* to subordinate corps and divisions, *Beweglichmachung und Bildung zusaetzlichen Transportraumes*, 7 May 44. *Seventh Army, KTB Anlagen 1.I.–30.VI.44.*

[120] *OKW/WFSt, KTB Ausarbeitung, Die Entwicklung im Westen vom 1.I.–31.III.44.*

[121] *Der Westen.*

[122] Notes by Reich Minister Albert Speer on Conference with Hitler on 22, 23 May 44, MS (trans). AAF files.

[123] AEAF Mtg, 6 May 44. AAF file 505.25–5.

RESULTS OF AIR ATTACKS *on railroad bridges and rolling stock. Bridge over the Seine at Port du Graviers (above), and wreckage of military train after aerial strafing attack (below).*

two of the less completely damaged structures. German repair operations were kept under observation and whenever a bridge seemed on the point of becoming usable again it was reattacked.[124] The success of the first bridge bombings led to the development of a plan to close off the lodgment area. The first line of interdiction was set at the line of the Seine and Loire Rivers and a gap section between the rivers. The second line included bridges over a number of rivers on a general line from Etaples to Fismes to Clamecy and thence along the upper Loire to Orléans. Bridges on the Loire were not to be hit until after D Day to avoid defining the assault area. (*Map IV*)

On 21 May, known to the air forces as "Chattanooga Day," fighter-bombers opened attack on line targets, bombing open track and small stations and strafing trains and rail facilities. *Seventh Army* on that day recorded 50 locomotives destroyed in its sector.[125] French records

show 113 locomotives damaged during the day throughout France.[126] Generaloberst Friedrich Dollmann, commander of *Seventh Army*, told Rommel the new attacks would bring a grave deterioration of the already strained transportation system and asked increasing use of motor transport.[127] Before D Day 2,700 sorties were flown against line targets.

Transportation bombing before D Day had a far more profound effect on the ability of the German Army in the west to resist invasion than the Allies realized. Statistics were misleading. The number of locomotives destroyed by air attack was actually less than the number awaiting repair from normal deterioration; the physical destruction done to rail and servicing facilities was small; rail cuts were repaired quickly on the important military lines. But despite all these facts, which mathematically added up to negligible destruction, rail traffic in France actually declined 60 percent between 1 March and 6 June. More significantly, in the area most heavily bombed, the *Région Nord*, three-quarters of the normal traffic was knocked off the rails. In the *Région Ouest* (generally in the invasion zone), which was bombed relatively lightly in order to preserve security, traffic declined by only 30 percent, but immediately after the assault it dropped even lower than in the *Région Nord*. These results were to prove critical in the battle for Normandy.[128]

---

[124] For example, two bridges south of Oisel were attacked and damaged on 10 May. The Germans decided to repair one for emergency use. On 6 June the railway engineers announced that it was operating. On that day it was bombed but suffered only light damage. The next day Allied planes returned to finish the job. The attack caused heavy damage, but the German engineers nevertheless set to work to repair the bridge and estimated that they could have it in shape again by 2 July. Allied air forces kept watch and on 29 June when the repairs were almost finished flew again to the attack. That attack at last finished the agony as three superstructures fell into the river and the Germans abandoned all thoughts of repair. See Rpts of the 6th Ry Eng Regt, May–Jun 1944, in *OKH Chef des Transportwesens, General der Eisenbahntruppen, Lagemeldungen (Ausschnitte) Frankreich, Band 1a, 1943–44.*

[125] *Seventh Army, Trans.O., KTB 1.I.–30.VI.44.*

[126] AAF Evaluation Board Study.

[127] *Seventh Army, KTB 1.I.–30.VI.44,* 23 May 44.

[128] AAF Evaluation Board Study. Normal traffic calculated as that of 1943.

CHAPTER VII

German Defense Measures, 1944

OKW Policy in 1944

German strategy for 1944 rested on the realization that decisive offensives could no longer be mounted in the east and that the growing strength of the Western Allies made almost certain a major invasion attempt before the end of the year. The prospective invasion of western Europe presented both the gravest danger to the Reich and the most hopeful opportunity for turning defeat into victory. If the Allies were not stopped at the landings, their attack would carry at once into the heart of Germany; if they were stopped and their beachheads annihilated, it was unlikely that a new attempt could be made for a long time to come, and as many as fifty German divisions might thereby be freed for the struggle against the Soviet Union.[1]

Recognizing the superiority of the Allied military potential, the Germans knew that their one chance for defeating the invasion was to defeat it quickly. It was therefore vital that the maximum German force be on the spot to fight the decisive battle as soon as the Allies attacked. To stake everything on a battle whose place and timing would be entirely of the enemy's choosing was to put an all but impossible burden on the defense, demanding of it a mobility it did not have and a sure knowledge of enemy intentions it had no means of acquiring. It was one thing to decide—as Hitler did with the issuance of his Directive No. 51—to prepare the west for the critical battle to come; it was another to find the means to carry out those preparations.

Regardless of how critical the defense of the west was declared, there could be no question of withdrawing forces from the hard-pressed eastern armies to reinforce it. The best that could be hoped for was to hold on to forces already in the various occupied territories outside of Russia and devote to the west the bulk of the new resources in men and equipment that became available in the months remaining before the Allies attacked. After Hitler's November order, OKW drew up a plan providing in detail for the shift of troops to meet a major Allied invasion of any one of the western theaters of operations. If the invasion hit France—the most likely possibility—OKW planned to move three infantry divisions from Norway and Denmark, one infantry division, a *Werfer* regiment and a corps headquarters from Italy, and four mobile infantry or *Jaeger* divisions and some minor units from the Balkans.[2] Although these

---

[1] *OKW/WFSt, KTB Ausarbeitung, Die OKW Kriegsschauplaetze im Rahmen der Gesamtkriegsfuehrung 1.I.–31.III.44.* Cited hereafter as *Die OKW Kriegsschauplaetze.* See above, Ch. VI, n. 115. Cf. Fuehrer Directive No. 51, 3 Nov 43. Translation in App. D, below.

[2] *Die OKW Kriegsschauplaetze. Werfer* regiments were equipped with either heavy mortars or rocket projectors. *Jaeger* divisions were light infantry divisions.

troop shifts would not amount to evacuation of any occupied area, they would mean a considerable concentration of force.

Such concentration was based on the assumption that the Allies would make one main attack. In January OKW began to wonder whether the assumption was justified. All signs still pointed to an attack across the Channel, probably at its narrowest point, but there were also indications that such an attack might be preceded or accompanied by other major thrusts. OKW noticed the "astonishing" emphasis in Allied quarters on preparations for a "second front" and reasoned that these might be designed to conceal another "main blow" that would not strike across the Channel. The "other place" selected might be Portugal or the Balkans, but the choice of the latter had particular plausibility.[3] It seemed unlikely that the large Allied forces in the Mediterranean would be committed in the slow and costly attempt to push all the way up the Italian peninsula.[4] The Balkan area offered greater strategic prizes and was conveniently at hand.

Whatever area was threatened OKW viewed the twin facts of accumulated Allied power in the Mediterranean and comparative stalemate in Italy as a kind of strategic unbalance which might be solved by another sudden major assault. German jitteriness on this score was not calmed by a report at about this time from agents in England that the ratio of Allied seagoing landing ships to landing craft for Channel use was ten times as great as the Doenitz staff had previously estimated.[5] This discovery seemed to confirm the guess that the Allies were planning an expedition outside the Channel.

All these fears seemed to be further confirmed by the Allied landings at Anzio on 22 January. The Anzio beachhead, in the German view, had only a slim tactical connection with the main Italian front. General Jodl, Chief of the Armed Forces Operations Staff, considering it to be an independent, self-sustaining operation, argued that it might well be the first of a series of attacks on the periphery of the Continent with the purpose of forcing dispersion of German reserves in preparation for a thrust across the Channel.[6] This interpretation drew support from the fact (which the Germans found "surprising") that the Allies instead of at once pushing inland from the Anzio beaches paused for about a week to consolidate a beachhead, as though the object were not to gain tactical objectives but to attract German forces. Reasoning thus, Jodl told Hitler that they now had to reckon with a peripheral Allied strategy which would probably entail attacks on Portugal, on the west and south coasts of France, or in the Aegean, before the assault on the *Kanalkueste*. With regard to France, it was thought that the most likely Allied peripheral operations would be simultaneous landings on the Mediterranean and Biscay coasts to pinch off the Iberian Peninsula. This threat was taken seriously enough that during February two new infantry divisions then being formed were attached to *Nineteenth Army* for defense

---

[3] Summary, dtd 4 Jan 44, of impressions of senior naval member of the Armed Forces Operations Staff in *Seekriegsleitung/1.Abt., KTB 1.–31.I.44*, 15 Jan 44; *Die OKW Kriegsschauplaetze.*

[4] *OKW/WFSt, KTB 1.IX.–31.XII.43*, 28 Dec 43.

[5] *Seekriegsleitung/1.Abt., KTB 1.–31.I.44*, 16 Jan 44.

[6] *Die OKW Kriegsschauplaetze.*

of the south coast and the *9th SS Panzer Division* was released from *OB WEST* and moved south into the Avignon area as army reserve. One new division went to *First Army* for defense of the Biscay coast and Spanish border.[7]

The most important effect of the new appreciation, however, was to unsettle German plans for the defense. If the Allies were going to pursue a policy of many simultaneous or successive assaults, the Germans could not afford to weaken sectors not immediately under attack in order to concentrate on one main invasion. It would, in fact, be very difficult to discover which of many attacks constituted the major threat. Partly for this reason, and partly because the military situation both in the Mediterranean area and in Russia was shifting so rapidly during the early months of 1944 that any plans for the future were subject to almost daily changes, OKW in March canceled its comprehensive defense plans. Instead, theater commanders were advised that troop movements would be ordered in detail only at the time they were needed, presumably *after* a given Allied attack had developed into a major action. In addition, a new plan was drawn providing for a shift of certain units from the Replacement Army in Germany to any OKW front under heavy attack. *OB WEST* by this plan might get one corps headquarters, two reinforced panzer grenadier regiments, one reinforced infantry demonstration regiment, Kampfgruppen of three infantry regiments which were cadre for new divisions, a motorized artillery demonstration regiment, five *Landesschuetzen* battalions, and one *Nebel-*

werfer demonstration battalion.[8] These miscellaneous, partly green units were hardly a substitute for the eight divisions (reinforced) which would have gone to *OB WEST* under the old plan. Although OKW did not formally abandon the intention of drawing additional reinforcements from occupied areas not under attack, as a practical matter the possibility of such reinforcement had by March become negligible. With the high command admitting the possibility of not one but several landings, strategic uncertainty would evidently delay any possible concentration.[9]

By March 1944, the German western defense had thus been weakened by a growing confusion as to Allied intentions. This confusion, however, was a relatively small element in the difficulties that multiplied for the Germans after the end of 1943. Not threats but immediate dangers in both the south and east were the principal preoccupations of the German high command. For three months after Hitler issued his order that the west was no longer to be weakened in favor of the Eastern Front, the Germans succeeded generally in holding the manpower dikes despite ominous cracks, and rising tides of Soviet victories. Just before Christmas, 1943, the Russians launched an offensive on the Kiev front which in a few days drove nearly two hundred miles west; in January, Leningrad was relieved by successful attack against the German *Army Group North;* at the end of the month,

---

[7] *OKW/WFSt, KTB Ausarbeitung, Die Entwicklung im Westen 1.I.–31.III.44.*

[8] *Die OKW Kriegsschauplaetze. Landesschuetzen* battalions were security units. *Nebelwerfer* were rocket projectors or chemical mortars.

[9] In fact only one division was moved from other OKW theaters to *OB WEST* in the first month of the invasion. This was the *89th Division* from Norway, and it was committed on the *Kanalkueste.*

much of the German *Eighth Army* was encircled near Cherkassy; in February, the Russians attacked the German *Sixth Army* in the Ukraine in a general offensive to clear the Dnepr bend. The temptation again to corral idle divisions from the west was very great. But only one infantry division was taken from Norway, and it was replaced by a unit which, though not completely formed, was roughly equivalent in combat strength. The west suffered only minor depredations. In February, three reinforced regiments being formed in Germany and earmarked for OKW reserve for the west went east. During the same month 3,000 Russian-front soldiers who were suffering from frostbite were exchanged for a like number of troops in the west.[10] Signs of the mounting pressure of the Russian war, these borrowings still did not constitute important weakening of the west.

But at the end of January the Anzio landings had opened another small crack. The Germans reacted to the Anzio attack in force, not only because they believed it to be the first of a series of major Allied amphibious assaults, but because they saw the possibility of gaining political prestige by wiping out at least one Allied beachhead. In accordance with plans for meeting a large-scale landing in the southwest, the fully motorized *715th Division* was ordered out of France. By 4 February, however, it was seen that this reinforcement was not enough to crush the Anzio beachhead and General Jodl asked Hitler for permission to move in the *9th SS Panzer Division,* the only fully combat-ready armored division in France. Hitler refused. With an eye on the large Allied

reserve forces in North Africa, he feared an attack against the Mediterranean coast of France. He doubted, furthermore, whether the *9th SS Panzer Division,* even if eventually returned to France, could make up its losses in Italy, particularly in equipment. *OB WEST* thus survived that crisis. But the loss of the *715th Division,* which because of its unusual mobility had been included with the reserve armored force, was serious enough.[11]

Much worse was to come. In March, the manpower dikes broke wide open as the Soviet Union launched a new offensive, and at the same time fears increased that Hungary was getting ready to pull out of the war. These circumstances forced temporary abandonment of the principles of Hitler's Directive No. 51. The bulk of the troops for the occupation of Hungary (carried out in the latter part of the month) were to be furnished by the Commander in Chief Southeast from the Balkans, and by the Replacement Army, but *OB WEST* had to send the *Panzer Lehr Division,* a corps headquarters, some aircraft, and a few minor units. The plan was to return all these units as soon as Hungary was firmly in German hands. In fact, the occupation took place rapidly and smoothly and the bulk of the Hungarian Army remained under arms and continued to fight for the Germans. The *Panzer Lehr Division* thus was actually able to come back to France in May. But two divisions from the Replacement Army and two of the divisions contributed by the Commander in Chief Southeast were shuttled on to the Russian front and a third was saved only by a last-minute appeal to Hitler. The loss indirectly

---

[10] *Die OKW Kriegsschauplaetze; OKW/WFSt, KTB Ausarbeitung, Osten 1.I.–31.III.44.*

[11] *OKW/WFSt, KTB Ausarbeitung, Die Kaempfe um den Brueckenkopf Nettuno 22.1.–31.III.44.*

affected the west in that it further reduced the reserves available to meet the invasion.

With the Russian armies again on the move and threatening to collapse the whole southern wing of the German defense, the danger of invasion in the west for a time dimmed by comparison. The Russians attacked on 4 March. On the 9th Uman fell; the Germans evacuated Kherson and Gayvoron on the 14th. Still the Russian armies suffered no check. Before the end of the month they crossed the Bug, Dnestr, and Pruth Rivers. In Galicia they temporarily encircled the German *First Panzer Army*. The crisis for the Germans was too desperate to permit consideration of long-range plans. Reinforcements were needed at once and they had to be taken wherever they could be found. On 10 March the *361st Division* was ordered out of Denmark, and replaced with a division of much lower combat value. Two weeks later a similar exchange removed the *349th Division* from France and brought as a substitute a new weak division, the *331st,* from the Replacement Army. At about the same time four divisions under *OB WEST* (the *326th, 346th, 348th,* and *19th Luftwaffe Field*) were ordered to give up all their assault guns, initially to strengthen Românian forces and later to be distributed to various divisions along the whole Eastern Front. The big ax fell on 26 March when the whole *II SS Panzer Corps* with the *9th* and *10th SS Panzer Divisions* received marching orders to leave France and go to the assistance of the *First Panzer Army*.[12]

The departure of the *II SS Panzer Corps* left *OB WEST* with only one fully mobile division (the *21st Panzer*). The OKW historian has suggested that, had the Allies invaded at that time, Rundstedt could have offered no effective resistance.[13] This may be an exaggeration, but it is true that the end of March 1944 marked one of the low points of preparedness in the west and that during the next six weeks, with the Russian front relatively stabilized, the west did much to recoup its losses. By the middle of May four panzer divisions were ready for combat (despite deficiencies of equipment) and four more were being built up. Toward the end of the month *Panzer Lehr Division* returned from Hungary and the *1st SS Panzer Division* from the Eastern Front was attached to *OB WEST* for rebuilding. At the same time the *XLVII Panzer Corps* under General der Panzertruppen Hans Freiherr von Funck, one of the oldest and most experienced armored commanders in the German Army, was brought from the east to serve under Rundstedt.

Actually the recuperative powers of the west under the severe and continuing strain of supplying transfusions to the east were remarkable. Between November 1943 and June 1944, the total of combat divisions under Rundstedt's command increased from forty-six to fifty-eight. The increase was accounted for in part by the transfer of fought-out units from Russia but in larger part by the formation of new units. In the fall of 1942 the German Army, already sorepressed for manpower, adopted the policy of combining training with occupation duties. The old combined recruiting and training units were split, and the recruit henceforth after induction into a recruit-

---

[12] *Die OKW Kriegsschauplaetze.*

[13] *Ibid.*

ing unit near his home was sent to an affiliated training unit in the field. In 1943 about two-thirds of these training units were located in France, the Low Countries, Denmark, Poland, Lithuania, the Soviet Union, and northern Italy. The infantry and panzer units were organized into reserve divisions of which twenty-six (including four panzer) were formed during 1942 and 1943. Half of these were stationed in the OB WEST sector. Though they remained under the commander of the Replacement Army and theoretically retained their primary function of training replacements, in reality they came to be regarded as low-grade field divisions. Their time was increasingly devoted to garrison duty and on occasion to fighting Resistance forces. In order to carry out these duties, they received administrative attachments from the regular field army. As their operational responsibilities expanded and they began to occupy a permanent place on OB WEST's order of battle, it became impossible for them to give up personnel for filler replacements to regular units. In short they became themselves an integral part of the field army. In recognition of this fact, most of them were eventually redesignated as infantry or armored divisions. Six of OB WEST's reserve divisions, including all three reserve panzer divisions, had thus been upgraded before the invasion. Five of the remaining seven were similarly converted in the summer of 1944; the other two were disbanded.[14]

Besides converting reserve divisions, the Commander in Chief West enlarged his army by rehabilitating German units

from the east as already noted, and by activating new divisions out of miscellaneous personnel drawn in part from his own resources and in part from the Replacement Army. The effect of all this on the organization and character of the west army must be described in some detail, but in summary it may be said that the steady drain of the Eastern Front left to Rundstedt on the eve of his great battle two kinds of units: old divisions which had lost much of their best personnel and equipment, and new divisions, some of excellent combat value, some only partially equipped and partially trained. The majority of the new divisions were formed according to streamlined tables of organization designed generally to use the fewest possible men to produce the maximum fire power.

Organization for Combat

Between 1939 and 1943 the German standard infantry division contained three regiments with a total of nine rifle battalions. Each of the infantry regiments had, besides its twelve rifle and heavy weapons companies, a 13th (infantry howitzer) and 14th (antitank) company. The division had also an antitank and a reconnaissance battalion. Organic artillery consisted of one regiment of one medium (150-mm. howitzer) and three light (105-mm. howitzer or gun) battalions with a total armament of forty-eight pieces. German division artillery was thus roughly equal to that of a U.S. division. Chiefly because of the antitank and reconnaissance units, on the other hand, the division with 17,200 men was substantially larger than its U.S. counterpart.

---

[14] WD TM–E #30–451; Military Intelligence Division, The German Replacement Army (Ersatzheer).

It was also substantially larger than could be supported by the dwindling supply of manpower after four years of war. In October 1943 the division was drastically overhauled to reduce its size while maintaining its fire power. Organization charts of the new-style division (with 13,656 men) comprising three regiments of two battalions each had only just been published when further slashes were ordered. The problem (set in January 1944 by Hitler) was to trim the personnel to something like 11,000 without affecting the combat strength. Army planners rejected this sleight of hand as impossible and contented themselves with a further cut from 13,656 to 12,769. Reductions were made chiefly in supply and overhead, and the proportion of combat to service troops was thereby raised to 75–80 percent. The result was the so-called 1944-type infantry division.[15]

The reduction from nine infantry battalions to six was partly alleviated by the substitution of a *Fuesilier* battalion for the old reconnaissance unit. The *Fuesilier* battalion, still charged with reconnaissance duties, was organized like a rifle battalion except that one company was equipped with bicycles and the unit had slightly more horse-drawn vehicles and some motor transport. In practice the *Fuesilier* battalion came to be reckoned as a seventh rifle battalion.

Besides lopping off three battalions, the new division pruned out the rifle squad and company while at the same time increasing the proportion of automatic weapons.[16] The basic unit, the rifle com-

pany, was cut to 140 enlisted men and 2 officers, as compared with the U.S. company of 187 enlisted men and 6 officers. Rifle strength in the German division was about 1,200 less than in the American but the total division fire power was superior. About equal in artillery, the German division enjoyed a slight preponderance in infantry howitzers, and a heavy superiority in automatic weapons.[17]

The 1944 infantry division was set up as the basic type for new divisions as well as for the reorganization of certain old formations, as for instance, the Luftwaffe field divisions.[18] The division which included the bulk of Rundstedt's infantry, however, the static (*bodenstaendige*) division, was exempted from reorganization unless specifically so ordered. The static divisions were formed at the request of Rundstedt in 1942 in order that he would have a nucleus of divisions not subject to transfer to the east. Though triangular with nine rifle battalions, they were substantially weaker than the normal old-type infantry division. They lacked the reconnaissance battalion and had only three battalions of artillery.[19]

Although the static divisions were expressly designed as permanent garrison troops for the west, they were by no means safe from the periodic troop collections

---

emphasized small infantry units equipped with maximum automatic fire power.

[17] See App. F, Comparative Fire Power of the U.S. and German 1944-type Infantry Divisions.

[18] These divisions, of which there were twenty, are not separately discussed since they played no part in the fighting described in this book. They were formed of Luftwaffe personnel, remained at first administratively under the Luftwaffe, and then were integrated into the Army.

[19] *OKH/Org.Abt., KTB 1.I.–31.VII.42*, 31 Jul 42; *Organisation des Heeres, Band 10* in *Befehlshaber des Ersatzheeres. Allgemeines Heeresamt.*

---

[15] *OKH/Org.Abt., KTB Anlagen, 1944.*

[16] It should be noted that this process, while forced by the shortage of manpower, also followed the direction of German tactical doctrine which always

for the east. Actually, by the end of 1943, most of the divisions had lost their third regiments. Attempts in 1943 and early 1944 to rehabilitate the units and fill their ranks chiefly with *Ost* battalions resulted in virtual abandonment of tables of organization in favor of improvisation that reflected both the particular nature of the coastal assignments and the vicissitudes of the long struggle for manpower and equipment. In total strength and number and variety of combat units the static divisions bore little resemblance to one another. While the *716th Division,* for instance, had six battalions and only one regimental headquarters under its control on D Day,[20] the *709th,* occupying two and a half times as long a coast line, had eleven battalions under three regiments.

Even after the 1944-type division had been standardized, experimentation continued. Certain divisions (notably the *77th* and *91st* in *Seventh Army* area) organized their six rifle battalions in two regiments. They lacked the fuesilier battalion and had three instead of four artillery battalions.[21] In the case of the *77th Division* this organic lack was partly made up by the attachment of an *Ost* battery and a Volga-Tatar rifle battalion. The *91st Division* went into combat with an attached parachute regiment. The two-regiment infantry division therefore did not operate in T/O form in the invasion area, and for the German Army as a whole it may be regarded as experimental and eccentric, designed further to conserve

manpower but not accepted as a generally satisfactory solution.

The best infantry units in the 1944 German Army were the parachute divisions, administratively under the Luftwaffe but tactically always subordinated to Army command. Until the fall of 1943 German airborne forces comprised only one corps with two parachute divisions. At that time Goering proposed and Hitler approved a program intended to produce by the end of 1944 two parachute armies with a total strength of about 100,000 men. They were to be an elite arm and were put on an equal status with the SS units in recruiting, armament, equipment, and training.[22]

Of the new parachute units created during the early months of 1944, *OB WEST* received the *3d* and *5th Divisions* and the *6th Parachute Regiment* (from the *2d Parachute Division*).[23] Only the separate regiment and the *3d Division* were encountered during the fighting described in this volume. Both were first-rate fighting units.

The *3d Parachute Division* comprised three regiments of three battalions each and in addition had in each regiment a 13th (mortar) company, 14th (antitank) company, and 15th (engineer) company. The mortar company in the *6th Parachute Regiment* actually contained the nine heavy (120-mm.) mortars which the tables of organization called for, but in the *3d Parachute Division* weaponing

[20] Its second regiment was attached to the *352d Division.* See below, Ch. VIII.

[21] Tables of Organization show an antitank company instead of the normal battalion. The *77th Division,* however, had a two-company antitank battalion with 24 guns (75-mm. and 50-mm.).

[22] MS # B–839 (von der Heydte).

[23] When its parent *2d Parachute Division* was sent to Russia in November 1943, the *6th Parachute Regiment* was left in Germany to provide cadre for the *3d Parachute Division.* The regiment, while still formally organic to the *2d Parachute Division,* was reconstituted under the direct command of the *First Parachute Army.*

was miscellaneous, including 100-mm. mortars and 105-mm. *Nebelwerfer*.[24] The parachute division had only one battalion of light artillery (twelve 70-mm. howitzers). An order of 12 May 1944 to substitute an artillery regiment with two light battalions and one medium was not carried out before the division entered combat. The same order called for formation of a heavy mortar battalion (with thirty-six 120-mm. mortars) but this, too, was apparently not complied with. During April and May the division was able to constitute its antiaircraft battalion which had, besides light antiaircraft artillery, twelve 88-mm. guns. The total ration strength of the division as of 22 May was 17,420. The strength of the *6th Parachute Regiment* with fifteen companies was 3,457. Both were thus considerably larger than the normal corresponding infantry units. They were superior not only in numbers but in quality. Entirely formed from volunteers, they were composed principally of young men whose fighting morale was excellent.[25]

The average age of the enlisted men of the *6th Parachute Regiment* was 17½. The parachute units were also much better armed than corresponding army units. The rifle companies of the *6th Parachute Regiment* had twice as many light machine guns as the infantry division rifle companies. The heavy weapons companies with twelve heavy machine guns and six medium mortars each were also superior in fire power to army units. Chief weakness of the parachute troops was one they shared with the rest of Rundstedt's army—their lack of motor transport. The *6th Parachute Regiment,* for instance, had only seventy trucks and these comprised fifty different models.[26]

Theoretically, about on a par with the parachute divisions were the panzer grenadier divisions which, by American standards, were infantry divisions with organic tank battalions, some armored personnel carriers, and some self-propelled artillery. The only such division in the west during the invasion period was the *17th SS Panzer Grenadier Division (Goetz von Berlichingen)*. Like all SS divisions it was substantially stronger than the corresponding army division. On the other hand, like so many west divisions, its combat strength in fact was much less than it appeared on paper. Its six rifle battalions were organized in two regiments which were supposed to be motorized; one battalion was supposed to be armored. In reality four of the battalions had improvised motor transport (partly Italian), two being equipped with bicycles. The "tank" battalion had thirty-seven assault guns, five less than authorized. The division had no tanks. Intended

---

[24] *Kriegsgliederung*, 18 May 44. *Seventh Army, KTB Anlagen 1.I.–30.VI.44;* cf. MS # B–839 (von der Heydte). Weaponing of the *6th Parachute Regiment* is as given in *Seventh Army* organization charts. Von der Heydte's report differs slightly. He says the regiment originally had twelve 105-mm. *Nebelwerfer,* but as the manufacture of these was discontinued they were gradually replaced, partly by 81-mm. mortars and partly by 120-mm. mortars.

[25] MS # B–839 (von der Heydte). The *6th Parachute Regiment* was fully trained in jumping. Each man had made at least nine jumps, including three night descents. About three-quarters of the men of the *3d Parachute Division* had some jump training but this was because the division received trained paratroopers as cadre. The division itself did not carry out jump training. MS # B–401 (General der Fallschirmtruppen Eugen Meindl, CG *II Parachute Corps*). Apparently neither of the parachute divisions in France was equipped with parachutes. See MS # B–283 (Blumentritt).

[26] MS # B–839 (von der Heydte).

personnel strength was 18,354, of which on 1 June the division actually mustered 17,321. The antitank battalion, supposed to consist of three companies of self-pro-pelled guns, had actually only one com-pany, equipped with nine 75-mm. and three 76.2-mm. guns. The division had a full armored reconnaissance battalion of six companies, and an antiaircraft bat-talion. The latter contained twelve towed 88-mm. guns as well as guns of smaller calibers, but lacked almost a fifth of its personnel.[27]

To meet the invasion in June, OB WEST had six army and three SS panzer divisions. Their strength and organiza-tion varied so widely that it is impossible to talk of a type. Personnel strength of the army divisions ranged from 12,768 (9th Panzer) to 16,466 (2d Panzer).[28] The SS divisions, which had six instead of four infantry battalions, varied from 17,590 (9th SS Panzer)[29] to 21,386 (1st SS Panzer). All the panzer divisions were thus much larger than their American counterparts, the 1st SS being more than twice as large. On the other hand they all had fewer tanks. Here again individual variations were enormous. The type or-ganizational tables for both army and SS divisions called for a tank regiment with one battalion of Mark IV and one bat-

talion of Mark V tanks. Each battalion was supposed to have four companies each with twenty-two tanks. The fact was quite different. Even the 2d Panzer Divi-sion, the best prepared of the armored divisions on D Day, had less than its au-thorized number of the heavier Mark V's.[30] Each of the divisions had a separate and slightly different organization which in no case conformed to the type. The 1st SS Panzer Division, for instance, was sup-posed to have 45 assault guns, 21 Mark III, 101 Mark IV, and 81 Mark V tanks. It had in fact the full complement of as-sault guns but only 88 tanks in all, includ-ing 50 IV's and 38 V's. The table of or-ganization for the 2d SS Panzer Division, on the other hand, called for 75 assault guns of which 33 were on hand on 1 June; 7 Mark III tanks, none on hand; 57 Mark IV tanks, 44 on hand; and 99 Mark V's, 25 on hand.[31]

The army panzer divisions included, in addition to the two regiments (four bat-talions) of infantry and one tank regi-ment, a self-propelled antitank battalion (armed more often with assault guns), an armored reconnaissance battalion, a towed antiaircraft battalion and an artil-lery regiment with one light self-pro-pelled battalion, one light towed battal-ion, and one medium towed battalion. SS divisions had an additional towed light battalion.

The miscellaneous tank armament of the panzer divisions was typical of the weaponing of nearly all units in the west and reflected the long drain on the Ger-

---

[27] Status Report, 17th SS Panzer Grenadier Divi-sion "Goetz von Berlichingen," 1 Jun 44. General-inspekteur der Panzertruppen, Zustandsberichte, SS-Verbaende VIII.43–VII.44. Substitution of assault guns (generally 75-mm. guns without turrets, on self-propelled chassis) for tanks became quite usual in the panzer grenadier division.

[28] Overstrength of 296 apparently accounted for by an attached "tank" battalion, armed with assault guns.

[29] The 9th SS Panzer Division was brought back to France during June. See below, Ch. X. The three SS panzer divisions under OB WEST on 6 June were the 1st, 2d and 12th.

[30] It had 94 Mark IV's and 67 Mark V's.

[31] Status Reports, 1st SS Panzer Division "Leib-standarte Adolf Hitler," and 2d SS Panzer Division "Das Reich," 1 Jun 44. Generalinspekteur der Panzer-truppen, Zustandsberichte, SS-Verbaende VIII.43–VII.44.

man war economy of the Russian war and the increasing production difficulties imposed by the accelerating Allied air offensive. As long as the Russian front was the main theater of war and the west was not immediately threatened, it was natural to ship the bulk of the best materiel to the east and arm the west as well as possible with what was left. The policy of equipping west divisions primarily with captured materiel was laid down in December 1941 when ten divisions were ordered so equipped.[32] The east continued to enjoy priority on new equipment until the end of 1943, and although German-made tanks and assault guns were shipped to *OB WEST* during that time the deliveries were often more than outweighed by the transfer of armored units. First-class armored equipment remained a comparative rarity in divisions assigned to *OB WEST* until 1944. At the end of October 1943, for instance, there were in the west 703 tanks, assault guns, and self-propelled 88-mm. antitank guns (called "Hornets"). At the end of December the number had risen only to 823, the increase being largely in the lighter Mark IV tank. All the Hornets and Tiger (Mark VI) tanks had been shipped out to the Russian front, and the stock of assault guns was considerably decreased. The total of 823, moreover, compared to a planned build-up of 1,226.[33] The new year brought a change. January showed only a slight increase, but thereafter the deliveries to the west were speeded up. Although most

new Tiger tanks continued to go to the east, deliveries to *OB WEST* of the powerful Panther (Mark V) tank were notably increased. At the end of April *OB WEST* had 1,608 German-made tanks and assault guns of which 674 were Mark IV tanks and 514 Mark V's. The planned total for the end of May was 1,994.[34]

Against the background of disintegrating German war economy, the tank build-up in the west was a notable achievement that strikingly revealed the importance assigned to the forthcoming struggle with the Western Allies. Exponents of the theories of Blitzkrieg, like Generaloberst Heinz Guderian, the Inspector General of Panzer Troops, believed that without a large armored striking force Germany could not hope to return to offensive operations essential for ultimate victory. In late 1943, therefore, Guderian proposed and Hitler approved a scheme to form a ten-division strategic armored reserve while at the same time trying to bring all armored divisions up to strength in equipment. The need, in short, was for new tanks in large numbers. But the combined pressure of the Allied air offensive and Russian ground attack was rapidly creating an economic quagmire in which the harder the enemy struggled the deeper he sank. Russian armies were destroying existing tanks while Allied bombers were making it increasingly difficult to produce new ones. The Germans tried to find an answer in diverting additional men, materials, and factory space into the manufacture of tanks. One result was to curtail the production of prime movers and parts. But without prime movers in adequate numbers the German armies in

---

[32] Memo, *OKH/Org.Abt.* for *OKH/Op.Abt., Umbewaffnung von Westdivisionen auf Beutewaffen,* 6 Dec 41. *OKH/Op.Abt., Kraefte Westen, Allgemein, Band II, 13.X.41–25.VII.42.*

[33] This and the following material on tanks is from *Generalinspekteur der Panzertruppen, Fuehrervortragsnotizen, Band I, 3.IV.43–1.VI.44.*

[34] In addition, units in the west still had a considerable number of French and Russian tanks.

Russia were unable to withdraw their heavy guns or retrieve tanks that were damaged or out of fuel. Between October and December 1943, 979 Mark III and IV tanks and 444 assault guns were lost, in large part because they had to be abandoned in retreat. Similarly between July and December 2,235 artillery pieces and 1,692 antitank guns were captured or destroyed. General Guderian at last pointed out that there was little sense in producing more tanks and guns if they were to be thus recklessly sacrificed.

A still more important by-product of concentrating on tank manufacture at the expense of a balanced production program was the increasingly serious lack of spare parts. In June 1943 the Germans had 2,569 operational tanks with 463 in process of repair. In February 1944, only 1,519 tanks remained operational while 1,534 were under repair. During February, moreover, only 145 damaged tanks were actually returned to the front. On the first of the month, Guderian estimated that the tanks and assault guns awaiting repair equaled about nine months' new production. At the end of March, the situation had not improved; the number of operational tanks was still decreasing despite accelerated deliveries of new machines.

Although the German Army in the west on the eve of its great test was considerably weaker than planned in equipment, quality, and numbers, it was nevertheless a force strong enough to hope for victory in a battle in which Allied materiel superiority would be partly counteracted by the natural advantages of a coast line defense. (Map V) Under Rundstedt's command on 1 June 1944 were 58 combat divisions of which 33

were either static or reserve, suitable only for limited defense employment. There were 24 divisions classified as fit for duty in the east by reason of their relative mobility and high-grade personnel. They included 13 infantry divisions, 2 parachute divisions, 5 army panzer divisions, and 4 SS panzer and panzer grenadier divisions. One panzer division (the 21st), being still equipped in part with captured materiel, was not considered suitable for service in Russia, although in other respects it was ready for offensive use, and in fact had exceptional strength in heavy weapons.[35]

All the infantry divisions were committed on or directly behind the coast under the command of one of the four armies or the German *Armed Forces Commander Netherlands*.[36] The four armies were the *First* holding the Atlantic coast of France, the *Seventh* occupying Brittany and most of Normandy, the *Fifteenth* along the *Kanalkueste,* and the *Nineteenth* defending the French Mediterranean coast. The *Seventh Army,* which was to meet the actual invasion, had fourteen infantry (including static) divisions under the control of four corps.[37]

Command and Tactics

It may be that the most serious weakness of the German defense in the west

---

[35] MS # B–441 (Generalleutnant Edgar Feuchtinger, CG *21st Panzer Division*).

[36] *Wehrmachtbefehlshaber Niederlande.* Equivalent in size to a corps command.

[37] *Seventh Army (LXXXIV Corps)* also had responsibility for defense of the Channel Islands and commanded the *319th Division* stationed there. But, since this division never figured in any of the fighting and because of Hitler's orders could not even be considered as a reserve, it will not be included in any calculations of *Seventh Army's* strength.

was not the shortage of men and materiel but the lack of a unified command. While Rundstedt was charged with the entire responsibility for the defense of France and the Low Countries, his powers were far from commensurate with that responsibility. He had, in the first place, no command over air and naval units. The four air corps that comprised the fighter and bomber aircraft stationed in the west were under command of the *Third Air Force* (Generalfeldmarschall Hugo Sperrle), which in turn was directly subordinate to OKL. Similarly *Navy Group West,* which under Admiral Theodor Krancke commanded the destroyers, torpedo boats, and smaller naval vessels based in the ports within Rundstedt's jurisdiction, was responsible directly to OKM. Rundstedt could issue no orders to either Sperrle or Krancke; he could only request their co-operation. (*Charts 2, 3, 4*)

Air and naval forces were too small to have decisive effect on the battle. From Rundstedt's point of view the more important limitation of his power was the fragmentation of the command over the ground forces. Some of this fragmentation was normal and universal in the German military establishment. The *Third Air Force* had, for instance, besides command of the flying units, administrative control over parachute troops and the antiaircraft units that were under the *III Flak Corps.*[38] *Navy Group West* controlled through regional commanders not only ships and shore installations but most of the coastal artillery, although command of the latter was

mixed. The Navy had complete jurisdiction before operations on land had begun. Afterward, firing on sea targets remained a naval responsibility, but at the moment of enemy landing, in most cases, command of the batteries in the beachhead area was to pass to the Army. Virtually the whole burden of tying in the important naval batteries to the coastal defense was thus shifted to the initiative of local commanders.

A similar division of command affected the employment of the security troops which as instruments of the occupation were normally under the two military governors (*Militaerbefehlshaber*), France and Northern France (including Belgium). The military governors were directly subordinated to OKH, but for purposes of repelling invasion their security troops might be tactically under *OB WEST.* In preparation against invasion, the Commander in Chief West could only direct that the military governors co-operate with the army groups in matters affecting the latter's authority and undertake to settle any differences that might arise between them. Even this control was limited. Employment of security troops could only be ordered by the Commander in Chief West "in matters outside the scope of security."[39]

During 1944 *OB WEST*'s authority was abridged in special ways. In November 1943, it will be recalled, Field Marshal Rommel had taken command of the *Army Group for Special Employment,* which was charged at first with in-

---

[38] Tactically and for purposes of supply *III Flak Corps* was under the *Luftgaukommando Westfrankreich.*

[39] *Grundlegender Befehl des Oberbefehlshabers West Nr. 38, Neuregelung der Befehlsgliederung im Ob. West-Bereich,* 7 May 44, cited hereafter as *OB WEST Grundlegender Befehl Nr. 38. OKW/- WFSt, Op. (H.), Grundlegende Befehle West 28.IV.42– 7.V.44.*

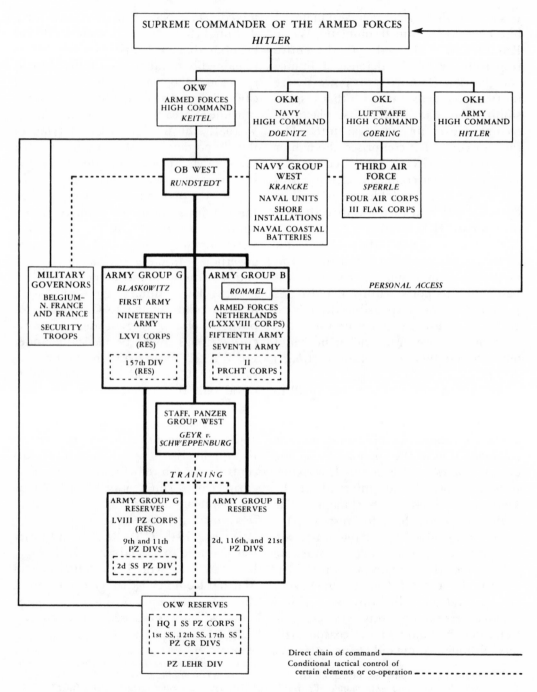

CHART 2.—GERMAN CHAIN OF COMMAND IN THE WEST, MAY 1944

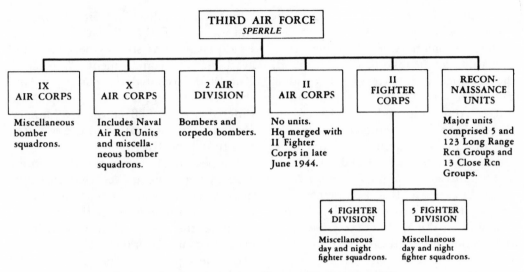

CHART 3.—LUFTWAFFE COMMAND IN THE WEST

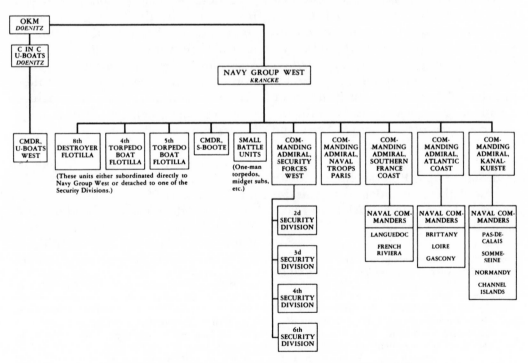

CHART 4.—GERMAN NAVAL COMMAND IN THE WEST

spection of the western defenses and the preparation of plans for counterattack against the main Allied landings wherever these might take place. Ultimately the Rommel headquarters was to conduct the main battle against the invading forces. About the middle of December, Rommel, having completed the first of his tasks, the inspection of the coastal defenses of Denmark, arrived in France and began a survey of the *Fifteenth Army* sector. Both he and Rundstedt recognized at once that it was neither logical nor practical for the *Special Army Group* to remain outside the theater chain of command.[40] Its independence could only be a source of friction and inefficiency. On 30 December Rundstedt recommended that it be subordinated to *OB WEST* as *Army Group B* with command of the *Seventh* and *Fifteenth Armies* and of the *German Armed Forces of the Netherlands*. Whether the initial suggestion for this change came first from Rommel or from Rundstedt, it was clearly in the beginning agreeable to both.[41] Since the main Allied invasion was likely to strike somewhere along the Channel coast, it made sense to put Rommel in immediate command there in order to familiarize him with his task and allow him to take such steps as he found necessary to

strengthen the defense. Hitler approved but warned *OB WEST* that the Rommel headquarters was still to be considered available for commitment elsewhere.[42] Rundstedt accepted the condition, and the reconstitution of *Army Group B* was ordered to take effect on 15 January. Rommel's subordination to OKW was at this time canceled.[43]

His position, however, remained anomalous: whereas he had less than full command over the armies attached to him, he enjoyed an influence over the whole defense of the west which was in some measure commensurate with Rundstedt's. His orders provided that he was to be solely responsible for the conduct of operations *(Kampffuehrung)*, but that in matters not directly affecting this tactical command *OB WEST* would continue to deal directly with the armies. Thus on questions of defense, training, organization and equipment, supply, artillery matters, communications, and engineer problems, the command channel might bypass the new army group.[44] Rommel continued to be the coastal inspector for the whole of the west, and although his reports henceforth were forwarded through *OB WEST* his ability to influence coastal defense policies and practices did much to blur his subordination to Rundstedt. Moreover the binding of the Rommel staff to a geographical sec-

---

[40] Ltr, Rundstedt to Salmuth, 27 Dec 43. *Fifteenth Army, KTB Anlagen, Chefsachen 26.X.–27.XII.43;* MS # A–982 (Vizeadmiral Friedrich Ruge, Navy liaison officer with *Army Group B*); MS # C–069b (Ruge); MS # C–069c (Buttlar-Brandenfels); MS # C–069e (Warlimont); MS # C–069f (Rundstedt).

[41] The change was logical and there is nothing in the rather fragmentary contemporary record to confirm the thesis of the *OB WEST* history (MS # T–121) that Rommel was forced on *OB WEST* from above and was unwanted. Cf. MS # C–069a (Blumentritt); MS # C–069d (Zimmermann); MS # C–069e (Warlimont); MS # C–069f (Rundstedt).

[42] Rad, 1 Jan 44, *OKW/WFSt, Op. (H.), to OKH/-Gen.St.d.H., OB WEST,* and *Army Group B. OKH/-Org.Abt., Bd. Chefsache 7.V.43–4.II.44.* Commitment was specifically contemplated in Denmark and Hungary. In fact, neither contingency materialized. For Hungary operation see above, p. 234.

[43] Rad, 1 Jan 44, cited n. 42; Order, 12 Jan 44, *OB WEST, (Ia Nr. 246/44). OKH/Op.Abt., Gliederung West, Chefsachen, Band VIII, 2.Teil, 8.I.–21.–II.44.*

[44] Order, 12 Jan 44, cited n. 43.

tor was only tentative; the headquarters was thought of still as a reserve command and as such the recommendations of its commander carried special if informal weight.[45] Finally, and most importantly, Rommel in common with all German field marshals enjoyed at all times the right of appeal directly to Hitler.[46] That privilege was especially important for the west because of the personalities involved. The evidence indicates that Rommel had an energy and strength of conviction that often enabled him to secure Hitler's backing, whereas Rundstedt, who was disposed whenever possible to compromise and allow arguments to go by default, seems to have relaxed command prerogatives that undoubtedly remained formally his. It is possible, of course, that he too came under Rommel's influence and failed to press acceptance of his own ideas because he was content to allow Rommel to assume the main burden of responsibility. In any case the clear fact is that after January 1944 Rommel was the dominant personality in the west with an influence disproportionate to his formal command authority.

Rommel's position, however, was not unchallenged. In November 1943 Rundstedt, thinking in terms of a large-scale counterattack against the main Allied landings, created a special staff to control armored units in that attack. The staff, designated *Panzer Group West,* was headed by General der Panzertruppen Leo Freiherr Geyr von Schweppenburg, and was directed to take over at once the formation and training of all armored units in the west and to advise the Com-

mander in Chief West in the employment of armor. Geyr was ordered to co-operate with and respect the wishes of army group commanders.[47] Actually, however, Geyr's ideas on the proper employment of armor were so completely at variance with Rommel's that co-operation was impossible.

In March 1944, at a meeting of the senior commanders in the west with Hitler, Rommel asked for an extension of his own authority that to all intents would have eliminated Geyr and Rundstedt as well from effective command of the defense forces. Specifically he requested that all armored and motorized units and all GHQ artillery in the west be put directly under his command and that he also be given some control over the *First* and *Nineteenth Armies.* The latter two armies, defending the Atlantic and Mediterranean coasts of France respectively, were at this time still subordinated immediately to *OB WEST.* In one sense, Rommel's request logically arose from his mission. Assigned responsibility for countering the major Allied invasion attempt, he required control over all the forces that might be used in the defense. It was plausible furthermore that such control should be turned over to him before the battle so that he could properly prepare and dispose the troops to fight the kind of battle he would order. Making a strong bid to unify defense policies, he asked that the Humpty-Dumpty command in the west be put together again under him. Although the method of repair naturally did not please Rundstedt, his objections

---

[45] *OKW/WFSt, KTB Ausarbeitung, Der Westen, 1.IV.–16.XII.44,* cited hereafter as *Der Westen.*
[46] MS # C–047 (Halder).

[47] Order, 19 Nov 43, *OB WEST (Ia Nr. 681/43). Seventh Army, KTB Anlagen, Chefsachen 2.III.43– 1.VIII.44;* Order, 12 Jan 44, cited n. 43.

were unheeded at the March meeting and Hitler approved the expansion of Rommel's command. Only after a study by the operations staff of OKW had supported Rundstedt's later written protest did Hitler reverse himself. Even then the reversal was not complete. Three panzer divisions (the *2d, 21st,* and *116th*) were assigned to Rommel as *Army Group B* reserves, over which he was to have full tactical control while Geyr remained responsible for their training and organization.[48] The patchwork solution solved nothing.

At the same time four other panzer-type divisions in *OB WEST*'s sector (the *1st SS Panzer, 12th SS Panzer, 17th SS Panzer Grenadier,* and *Panzer Lehr*) were set aside as a central mobile reserve under the direct command of OKW. The two decisions smacked of a compromise tending to preserve something of both Rommel's and Rundstedt's tactical ideas.[49] The main effect, however, was to deprive the Commander in Chief West of the means to influence the battle directly without transferring those means to Rommel. Thus, even such inclusive authority as was possible in the German military establishment was scrupulously withheld from both high commanders in the west.

The final command change before the invasion was made in May when Rundstedt ordered the formation of a second army group headquarters to take command of the *First* and *Nineteenth Armies. Army Group G,* formed under Generaloberst Johannes Blaskowitz, took over, besides the two armies, the remaining three panzer divisions in France (the *9th, 11th,* and *2d SS*).[50] The reorganization provided a counterbalance for Rommel and somewhat simplified the command channels. It probably also expressed final recognition of the impracticability of the reserve high command concept.

With the establishment of Blaskowitz's headquarters, Rundstedt undertook to define his own position. He outlined for himself what amounted to an over-all ground command in his theater, subject to the restrictions already discussed. He announced his intention of granting his army group commanders the maximum freedom of action in their own sectors. He would intervene only when he fundamentally disagreed with their policies or when decisions had to be made affecting the theater as a whole. He promised to confine his directives to passing on Hitler's orders and to specifying policies that ought to be uniformly carried out by all commands.[51]

In fact, during the critical preparatory months of 1944, general directives were few either from Rundstedt or Hitler. Hitler, far away at his headquarters in

---

[48] *Der Westen.*

[49] Rundstedt apparently considered the attachment of these reserves to OKW purely formal and made plans to use them under Geyr. Compare, however, what happened on D Day (Ch. VIII). Control of the three SS divisions had a triple twist: trained and organized under *Panzer Group West,* tactically subordinated to OKW, they were for administrative purposes under the *SS-Fuehrungshauptamt.*

[50] *OB WEST Grundlegender Befehl Nr. 38,* 7 May 44. Blaskowitz's command was given inferior status as an *Armeegruppe* instead of the usual *Heeresgruppe,* in part because of lack of personnel and perhaps also in part as a mark of the relative disfavor in which Blaskowitz was held by Hitler. *Oberkommando Armeegruppe G, KTB Nr. 1, 26.-IV.-30.VI.44; Der Westen;* MS # T–121 (Zimmermann *et al.*). See Chart 2, p. 244.

[51] *OB WEST Grundlegender Befehl Nr. 38,* 7 May 44.

East Prussia, was so preoccupied with the Russian war that he did not even visit the west until after the invasion. Furthermore he seems not to have had any clear and consistent view of tactics himself, and his interventions in the western scene resulted more often in decisions of detail than in definitions of policy. The failure of Hitler to provide consistent guidance together with the vague demarcation of authority between Rommel and Rundstedt left the west with a vacillating leadership. Defense preparations in 1944 were increasingly scarred by compromise as the Commander in Chief West and the commander of *Army Group B* made detailed decisions in accordance with divergent aims.

The perspective from which Rommel viewed his task derived in part from his experience with desert warfare in North Africa and in part from the circumstances of his new assignment. It is important to bear in mind that Rommel came to the west only at the point when the battle was about to be fought there, and that he was assigned responsibility specifically for the conduct of that battle. He had not endured the long waiting period with its periodic alarms. He had not spent months making plans, calculating actual but shifting deficiencies against ideal needs, outlining defense systems and struggling to find the means to carry them out. The theoretical approach to tactics—the drafting of the abstractly best plan first, the search for resources second—was ruled out by the nature of his mission as well as by the limited time at his disposal. He was appointed coastal inspector and told to assess defensive capacities and make his plans accordingly. Whatever he chose to do had to be com-

pleted in three or four months. He was bound therefore to start by examining his limitations.

The experience in North Africa had convinced Rommel of the folly of trying to use massed armor as long as the enemy enjoyed air superiority. In Africa Rommel commanded some of the best trained and equipped troops that Germany produced. In France he was to command an army that was already crippled in part by inadequate training, inferior human material, and lack of mobility. Furthermore, there was still less hope in 1944 than in 1942 that the Luftwaffe could challenge the supremacy of the Allies in the air. To Rommel that meant that mobile operations were impossible in fact however desirable they might be in theory. If the German Army could not hope to maneuver on anything like terms of equality with the Allies, its only chance for a defensive success was to fight from the strongest possible natural positions. The pillboxes, entrenchments, wire, and mines of the Atlantic Wall and the waters of the Channel, in short, seemed to Rommel to offer not only the best but the only means to offset Allied superiority in mass and mobility.[52]

Rommel therefore was led to place an exclusive dependence on fortifications that Rundstedt never advocated and that even Hitler had not contemplated in his directive of November. The battle for the west, Rommel believed, would be decided at the water's edge, and the decision would come literally within the first forty-eight hours of the Allied landings.[53] In accord with that diagnosis, his first aim was to create a defensive belt around

[52] MS # A–982 (Ruge).
[53] *Ibid.*

the entire coast (with special concentration on the *Fifteenth Army* sector) extending five or six kilometers inland. Within this belt all infantry, artillery, headquarters staffs, and reserves up to division level were to be located in a series of resistance nests.[54] Between the resistance nests mines and obstacles were to be laid so thickly as to prevent enemy penetration. Because of limited time, labor, and materials, Rommel concentrated on many simple, field-type defenses rather than on a few complex fortifications. He stressed in particular the laying of mines. He introduced, further, a defense device new to the Atlantic Wall: underwater obstacles designed to wreck landing craft.[55] In Normandy, hedgehogs and tetrahedra located inland as tank obstacles were moved to the beaches suitable for enemy landings. They were supplemented by Belgian Gates and stakes slanting seaward. The intention was to cover every possible landing beach between high- and low-water marks with obstacles staggered to leave no free channel for even a flat-bottomed boat to reach shore. Obstacles as far as possible were to be mined. As it was considered most likely that the Allies would land at flood tide to reduce the amount of open beach to be crossed under fire, laying of the obstacles began at the high-water line and was extended in belts seaward as materials and labor became available.[56]

To complete his hedgehog fortress,

Rommel undertook to stake all fields suitable for glider landings behind the coastal zone. The stakes were to be placed close enough together so that gliders could not come down between them. They, too, were to be mined. The German estimate was that Allied airborne troops would be used in diversionary and subsidiary operations, for which Brittany and Normandy were considered the most likely target areas. Rommel therefore concentrated the erection of antiairlanding obstacles in these areas.[57]

The general scheme of obstacle defense of the Continent was further to be extended by mine fields in the Channel. Sixteen fields, each about five miles long, were put down in the Channel between Boulogne and Cherbourg from August 1943 to January 1944. These were to be kept renewed as far as possible, but it was not believed that they would have much effect on Allied shipping. They were therefore to be supplemented by hasty mine fields laid down by all available vessels immediately before the invasion was expected. These fields would be planted without keeping open any marked lanes for German vessels. From Zeebrugge to Granville thirty-six mine fields were planned. It was also planned, when invasion seemed imminent, to sow mines from the air in British harbors. Finally along the French coast shallow-water mines were to be laid and a special seventy-kilogram concrete mine was developed for the purpose.[58] In all these

---

[54] See below, Ch. VIII, n. 68, for a description of various types of German fortifications.

[55] MS # A–982 (Ruge). Underwater obstacles of this type were first used in 1943 by the Germans in the west, when preparing the defense of the Danish coast against an attack from the sea. For description of obstacles mentioned in the text, see Glossary.

[56] MS # A–982 (Ruge).

---

[57] *Bericht ueber die Reise des Herrn Oberbefehlshabers am 17. und 18. Mai 44. Seventh Army, KTB Anlagen 1.I.–30.VI.44.*

[58] ONI, *Fuehrer Conferences, 1944; Marinegruppenkommando West, KTB 16.I.–31.I.44.*

ANTILANDING OBSTACLES *under construction on a French beach (above). Lower picture shows Belgian Gate.*

ways Rommel sought to make the expected invasion physically impossible. The Allied force entangled in the spider web of obstacles would be given the paralyzing sting by the German Army waiting at the water's edge.

Rommel's construction and mine-laying program called for a very large expenditure of labor, and labor was scarce. It has already been pointed out that Organization Todt was employed chiefly in the major port fortress areas, on V-weapon sites, and, in the spring of 1944, on railroad maintenance. In the apportionment of the remaining labor supply among the armies, *Fifteenth Army* continued to receive priority. *Seventh Army* thus had special difficulty in completing its defense works. The *LXXXIV Corps* was assigned three engineer battalions in January, two for fortress building and one for mine laying. In addition, 2,850 men of the former French Labor Service were set to work on a secondary defense line immediately behind the belt of coastal resistance points. Pleas for more construction hands were answered by attachment of two *Ost* battalions.[59]

The only other available labor source was the combat troops. Increasingly during 1944 infantrymen were employed in work details on the Atlantic Wall with consequent serious reduction of combat training. The reserve battalion of the *709th Division,* for instance, devoted three days a week exclusively to labor duty. The time for training in the rest of the week was further reduced by transport and guard details. During the first two weeks in May the battalion was employed full time on the coastal defense

in the Barfleur sector.[60] The *709th* was an old division, but its personnel constantly shifted. The lack of continuous adequate training meant that the total combat fitness of the division steadily deteriorated through the accretion of untrained recruits.

Still worse was the effect on the new and reorganized divisions that represented a large proportion of the German striking force in the west. In *Seventh Army* all but one of the nonstatic infantry divisions were organized during 1944. New divisions accounted for six of the fourteen divisions under the army's command. All of these units were burdened with construction duties. In February Rommel ordered that infantry be used to lay mines and obstacles. On 25 May *Seventh Army* reported to OKH that all its units were engaged in construction projects and that consequently the necessary training was not being carried out.[61]

The only units specially exempted from work on the fortifications were the two parachute divisions. The *3d Parachute Division* was brought into Brittany in March and stationed east of Brest. Its mission was to complete its organization and at the same time train for defense against airborne attack. The *5th Parachute Division* moved into the Rennes area between 5 and 14 May with a similar mission. Both divisions in May were put under command of the *II Parachute Corps* which, though subordinated tactically to *Seventh Army*, was administratively and for training purposes under the *Third Air Force*. Since the Luftwaffe was thus responsible for parachute unit

[59] *Seventh Army, KTB 1.I.–30.VI.44,* 5, 6, 8, and 16 Jan 44.

[60] Hoffmann Report. *Seventh Army, KTB Anlagen 1.I.–30.VI.44.*
[61] *Seventh Army, KTB 1.I.–30.VI.44,* 25 May 44.

training and, on the other hand, was not responsible to army commands anywhere in the hierarchy, Reich Marshal Goering ordered that the parachute divisions not be used for construction work except in providing local security for themselves against airborne attack.[62] The *5th Parachute Division* had scarcely more than begun to fill out its ranks when invasion struck; but the *3d* proved one of the best prepared of the new units in *Seventh Army.*

The general stinting of training under the circumstances seems to have been inevitable and apparently did not arouse any serious protests at the time.[63] Where Rommel's program met really effective opposition was in his efforts to concentrate reserves within the coastal zone. If it was true that the Germans had to fight on a fortified line, if they could not hope to maneuver freely, and if the crisis of the battle against the invaders would come within the first forty-eight hours, then it followed that all forces would be wasted which were not near enough to the coast to be committed at once against the first landings. This deduction was the final extension of the doctrine of static defense implicit in the original decision to build the Atlantic Wall. At least one high German commander had predicted the development and had warned against it in caustic tones. Sodenstern, commanding the *Nineteenth Army,* wrote privately in the summer of 1943 of his fear that German generalship would

exhaust itself in the construction of huge masses of concrete. "As no man in his senses," he argued, "would put his head on an anvil over which the smith's hammer is swung, so no general should mass his troops at the point where the enemy is certain to bring the first powerful blow of his superior materiel." [64] Rommel's answer, in all likelihood, would have been, first, that there was no practical alternative, second, that the first Allied blow at the point of the landings would not be the most powerful but the weakest since only a small portion of Allied fire power could then be effective, and, third, that the German general in massing his troops in fortified positions was at least giving their heads some protection against the smith's hammer.

The difference of opinion was essentially a difference in judgment of what was possible. Rommel's chief of staff has testified that Rommel would have preferred a battle of maneuver had he seen any chance of its succeeding.[65] Rundstedt, like Sodenstern, was clearly more optimistic, perhaps because he had not had firsthand experience with the air power of the Western Allies. In any case, he did not accept Rommel's thesis and the influence of *OB WEST* was exerted spasmodically in resisting Rommel's efforts to shift the weight of the army forward to the coast, and in trying instead to free as many units as possible from bondage to the rigid defense system.

In practice any plan to introduce flexibility into the defense depended primarily on whether units could be made

---

[62] *Ibid.,* 20 Feb 44.

[63] Various commanders since the war have underscored this lack of training as one of the most serious weaknesses of the defense. The evidence, however, is inconclusive. See MS # B–234 (Pemsel); MS # B–466 (Geyr); MS # B–784 (Oberstleutnant Friedrich von Criegern, CofS *LXXXIV Corps*).

[64] Notes written in August 1943, appended to MS # B–276 (Sodenstern).

[65] MSS # B–720 and # C–017 (Speidel).

mobile and whether they could be organized and equipped to support themselves in combat. Through the early months of 1944 Rundstedt struggled to strengthen and provide some transport for the coastal divisions. In the *Seventh Army* area he succeeded in forming mobile Kampfgruppen (of reinforced regiments) from four of the infantry divisions (the *265th, 266th, 275th*, and *353d*) defending the Brittany coast. In case of a major invasion of Normandy, *Seventh Army* had plans to move these Kampfgruppen into the combat zone. In the Cotentin, the *243d Division* was converted from a static into a nominal attack infantry division.[66] It was reorganized according to the 1944 type with six infantry battalions. Four battalions were to be equipped with bicycles. The artillery regiment, supply troops, and antitank battalion were to be motorized. Reorganization took place in late 1943, but the motorization planned to begin in May 1944 could be carried out only in very limited degree.[67]

It should be observed in this connection that German notions of mobility in the west in 1944 hardly corresponded to American concepts of a motorized army. A mobile infantry unit in general was one equipped with bicycles, with horse-drawn artillery, and a modicum of horse and motor transport for supply purposes. It was called mobile more because of its ability to maintain itself in the field than

because of its ability to move rapidly from one place to another.

For the most part the Germans lacked resources even to provide that limited mobility for the west army. Rundstedt's efforts to restore mobility to his static divisions on the whole failed. A beginning, for instance, was made to upgrade the *709th Division*, but the vehicles allotted in March had to be withdrawn in May when, as a result of the Allies' successful rail bombing attacks, *Seventh Army* began to scrape together everything on wheels to form corps transport companies.[68]

Rundstedt's efforts to put wheels under his army were at least partly offset by Rommel's concurrent labors to dig in every available soldier and gun along the coast line. After an inspection trip in the *LXXXIV Corps* sector in February, Rommel concluded that reserves were held in too great strength too far from the coast. In particular, he felt that the *352d Division*, located near St. Lô, and the *243d Division*, near la Haye du Puits, should be regrouped so that they could be committed in the first hours after an enemy landing. *Seventh Army* therefore ordered that the divisional reserves of the *709th* and *716th Divisions* (the *795th Georgian Battalion* and *642d Ost Battalion* respectively) should be committed at the coast, that the *243d* and *352d Divisions* should move slightly northward,[69] and that the *352d Artillery Regiment* of the latter division should be emplaced in the coastal zone under the control of the

---

[66] The Germans classified divisions in four categories, depending on whether they were capable of full attack, limited attack, full defense, or limited defense missions. In these categories the degree of mobility was one of the most important factors. All static divisions were in the third or fourth categories.

[67] *Karteiblatt, 243d Infantry Division. OKH/Org.-Abt., Karteiblaetter 1943–1945.*

[68] Hoffmann Report. *Seventh Army, KTB Anlagen 1.I.–30.VI.44.*

[69] New assembly areas were: for the *243d Division*, Carentan–Montebourg–Bricquebec–Lessay; for the *352d Division*, Bayeux–Trévières–Isigny–St. Lô.

GERMAN MOBILE INFANTRY *equipped with bicycles (above), and animal transport (below).*

CAPTURED GERMAN ARMOR. *U.S. troops inspecting Panther (Mark V) tank (above) and 75-mm. assault gun (below) mounted on Mark IV chassis.*

716th Division.[70] Similar reshuffling in Brittany put the artillery of the *275th* and *353d Divisions* into static defense positions.[71] The shift forward of the *352d Division* meant in effect that it was no longer in reserve. On 14 March *Seventh Army* therefore proposed that the division actually take over responsibility for the left half of the *716th Division* sector. On *OB WEST*'s approval, this change was accomplished by 19 March. With the doubling of the troops on the coast, the former battalion sectors of the *716th Division* became regimental sectors. The *726th Regiment* of the *716th* was attached to the *352d,* less the *2d Battalion* which became division reserve for the *716th.* One regiment of the *352d* plus the *Fuesilier Battalion* was held in corps reserve in the vicinity of Bayeux.[72]

Hitler, whose ideas, possibly under Rommel's influence, had undergone some change since Directive 51, wondered at this time whether all units of limited mobility which were located immediately behind the coast should not as a matter of policy be incorporated in the main line of resistance (MLR), leaving only fully mobile forces as attack reserves. General Jodl of the OKW pointed out that, except for three divisions, units were already far enough forward for their artillery to bear on the invasion beaches. To shift all troops into the coastal fortifications would be dangerous since concrete shelters were limited and field work might be destroyed by Allied bombing. In Brittany and the Cotentin, moreover, it was necessary to preserve some depth of defense in order to resist probable airborne landings.[73]

Commitment of all forces at the MLR was thus not accepted as a principle. But in practice Rommel continued to shift the weight of his army forward. In April the *21st Panzer Division* was moved from Rennes to Caen where its battalions were split on either side of the Orne River and its artillery committed on the coast. The disposition to all intents removed the *21st Panzer Division* as a unit from the pool of mobile reserves.[74] The other two panzer divisions directly under Rommel's command were placed in position to reinforce the *Fifteenth Army,* one between Rouen and Paris, the other near Amiens. In May, another inspection tour convinced Rommel that movement of units from right to left into the invasion area would be impossible. He therefore requested that the four divisions in OKW reserve be assembled nearer the coast. Rundstedt entered an immediate protest with OKW, contending that the move was tantamount to committing the reserves before the battle. OKW agreed, and Rommel's proposal was turned down.[75]

---

[70] Two battalions of the *352d Artillery Regiment* were already ordered committed on the coast on 26 January 1944. See *Seventh Army, KTB 1.I.–30.VI.44,* 26 Jan 44.

[71] The *353d Division* was the sister division of the *352d,* formed at the same time and according to the same tables of organization. As an attack infantry division, it was scheduled for full offensive employment. The *275th Division,* a static division, upgraded in part, would give up a mobile Kampfgruppe if needed for employment outside Brittany.

[72] *Seventh Army, KTB 1.I.–30.VI.44,* 14, 19 Mar 44. The reserve regiment was rotated. After 20 May, it was the *915th.*

[73] *Der Westen.*

[74] The *21st Panzer Division* replaced the *77th Division* in the Caen area. The *77th* was shifted to St. Malo–St. Brieuc where in turn it replaced the *346th Division.* The *346th* had been taken out of static coastal defense positions in the latter part of 1943, made mobile, and in January 1944 transferred to *Fifteenth Army.*

[75] *Der Westen.*

These four divisions (three panzer and one panzer grenadier) thus saved by OKW's intervention were the only mobile units in the west on the eve of invasion which could properly be designated strategic reserves. Three were located within easy marching distance of Normandy (easy, that is, if the Allied air forces were discounted); the fourth was far away on the Belgium–Netherlands border.

In summary, the conflict between Rommel's and Rundstedt's theories of defense was never resolved definitely in favor of one or the other and led to compromise troop dispositions which on D Day were not suitable for the practice of either theory. The pool of mobile reserves had been cut down below what would be needed for an effective counterattack in mass; it had been removed from *OB WEST*'s control, and, as though to insure finally that it would not be employed in force, it had been divided among three commands. While the possibility of seeking a decision by counterattack had thus been whittled away, considerable forces were still held far enough from the coast so that, if Rommel's theories were correct, they would be unable to reach the battlefield in time to influence the action. In short, operational flexibility had been curtailed without achieving a decisive thickening of the coastal defense.

The Defense on the Eve of Invasion

The scheduled completion date for the winter construction program and all troop preparations for meeting the expected invasion was 30 April.[76] Up to that

time the Germans made all arrangements to repel a major attack against the *Kanalkueste*. At the end of 1943 Hitler ordered the assembly of all available forces behind the front of the *Fifteenth Army* and the right wing of *Seventh Army,* but the latter sector was to be considered much less in peril. *OB WEST* was to release four divisions from coastal sectors of the *Seventh, First,* and *Nineteenth Armies*. Of these, the *243d Division,* released from *Seventh Army,* was to remain as a reserve division in the army area. The other three were all attached to *Fifteenth Army*. Similarly, of four reinforced regiments obtained at this time from the Replacement Army, three went to *Fifteenth Army*; one was attached to the *709th Division*. The latter attachment was made because the coastal defenses of the *709th Division* were thin and enemy attack there was "possible." [77]

That possibility, however, was not taken very seriously until the end of April. Since the German intelligence system had been supplying very little reliable information, estimates of Allied intentions continued to be based more on logical inference than on fact. Air reconnaissance was severely restricted by Allied air supremacy. Reconnaissance by sea could never be depended on. German agents in England steadily dwindled and the work of those remaining was made almost fruitless by the closing off of the English coastal areas in April 1944. News filtering through neutral countries, especially from Portugal and Switzerland, was abundant but confusing.[78] The difficulty

[76] *Grundlegender Befehl des Oberbefehlshabers West Nr. 33, Neuregelung des Bauwesens in den besetzten Westgebieten,* 3 Nov 43. *OKW/WFSt, Op. (H.), Grundlegende Befehle West 28.IV.42–7.V.44.*

[77] *OKH/Op.Abt., Gliederung West, Chefsachen, Band VIII, 1.Teil, 11.XII.42–2.I.44,* and *2.Teil, 8.I.–21.II.44.*

[78] MS # B–234 (Pemsel).

was not that no reliable reports got through, but that they were too few and too spasmodic to allow the formation of a convincing picture of Allied intentions, particularly since such a picture had to compete for acceptance with various preconceptions.

The best guess was Hitler's, though how he arrived at it the records do not show. While military leaders were nearly unanimous in predicting invasion in the Pas-de-Calais area, Hitler in March suddenly decided that the Allies were likely to land on the Cotentin and Brittany peninsulas. He believed they would be tempted by the ease with which defensible bridgeheads could be established there, but he apparently did not undertake any analysis of the possible military advantages.[79]

The supposition of a special threat to Normandy and Brittany received some support a few weeks later from the Navy. On 26 April Admiral Krancke, Commander of *Navy Group West*, observed that recent air photographs showed no activity in the ports of southeast England or the mouth of the Thames, and concluded that Cap Gris Nez and the coast northeast were not threatened by Allied landings. The conclusion was reinforced by the facts that Allied air attacks against coastal

batteries and radar installations were concentrated between Boulogne and Cherbourg, that Allied mine sweeping and mine laying generally blocked off the same area, and that the bombing of railroads had interrupted traffic to the Channel coast but had not affected communications with the Atlantic area. In short, Admiral Krancke felt that all signs pointed to an invasion between Boulogne and Cherbourg, probably with the main effort against the Cotentin, the mouth of the Seine, or the mouth of the Somme.[80] This appreciation differed from previous estimates only in lopping off the Pas-de-Calais sector between Boulogne and Dunkerque as a possible landing area. The resulting difference in emphasis, however, was striking, particularly in the singling out of the Cotentin as threatened by a possible major attack. Later reports by Admiral Krancke further emphasized this threat, particularly from Allied airborne attack.[81] Krancke's view, developed chiefly during May, was that Le Havre and Cherbourg seemed likely prime objectives for the Allied invasion forces. This conviction grew as it was seen that Cherbourg and Le Havre alone of the major French ports had been spared from heavy air attack.

Whether Hitler saw and reacted to these naval estimates or whether he had access to other information, in late April his interest in Normandy increased and he began to insist strongly on the need to reinforce the defense there.[82] On 6 May

---

[79] *Seekriegsleitung/1.Abt., KTB 1.–31.III.44*, 4 Mar 44, and *KTB 1.–31.V.44*, 3 May 44; *Der Westen*. German generals, commenting after the war on their experiences, were unanimous in giving Hitler the credit for first pointing to the danger of invasion in Normandy. In the light of the German Army's general reluctance to admit that Hitler had shown any military perspicacity at all, the testimony is fairly convincing. The generals, who were then unable to see the military advantages of a Cotentin assault as compared to an attack against the *Kanalkueste*, alleged that Hitler's choice was sheer intuition. The records at least do not contradict that interpretation.

[80] *Marinegruppenkommando West, KTB 16.–30.-IV.44*, 26 Apr 44; cf. in same *KTB Lageuebersicht des Marinegruppenkommandos West, Fuehrungsstab, Rueckblick Monat April 1944.*

[81] *Seekriegsleitung/1.Abt., KTB 1.–31.V.44*, 15 May 44.

[82] *Der Westen.*

Seventh Army was notified by Rommel of Hitler's concern, and the army ordered the deployment of one parachute regiment and two separate battalions in the immediate vicinity of Cherbourg. The parachute regiment selected was the 6th and it was to be placed in the general area of Lessay–Périers. The 206th Panzer Battalion, a separate tank battalion equipped with a miscellany of Russian, French, and German light tanks, was ordered to dig in between Cap de la Hague and Cap de Carteret. The Seventh Army Sturm Battalion was sent to la Haye du Puits and later shifted to le Vast, southeast of Cherbourg. Decision was made at the same time to divert to the Cotentin the 91st Division, which was then on its way from Germany to Nantes. Orders were issued the next day switching the trains to the vicinity of la Haye du Puits. The 91st Division was told that on arrival it would take over command of the 6th Parachute Regiment. This movement was completed on 14 May. On 9 May Rommel ordered that the 101st Stellungswerfer Regiment, released from OB WEST reserve, be committed in the Cotentin, split between the east and west coasts. On the day that this move was completed, 12 May, the 17th Machine Gun Battalion (a well-trained unit of young men) also completed relief of the 795th Georgian Battalion on Cap de la Hague and the latter battalion, under command of the 709th Division, was moved on 17 May south to Brucheville northeast of Carentan. Mission of all the major units, the 91st Division, 6th Parachute Regiment, and Seventh Army Sturm Battalion, was defense against airborne landings. The 100th Panzer Replacement Battalion

south of Carentan at the same time was instructed to be prepared for action against airborne troops.[83]

The Cotentin was thus substantially reinforced and fully alerted a month before the two U.S. airborne divisions were dropped there. While expecting airborne assault on the Cotentin, however, neither Rommel nor Rundstedt reckoned that such assault would form part of the main Allied effort. Having reinforced the actual garrison in the peninsula, therefore, they took no further steps to cope with a major landing in the area. On the contrary, a Seventh Army proposal on 5 May to shift the whole of the LXXIV Corps from Brittany to Normandy in case of large-scale landings in the LXXXIV Corps sector was rejected by Field Marshal Rommel.[84] No reserves were moved nearer the Cotentin, and no plans were made to move them in mass in case of attack.

As for the Navy, having called its opponent's trumps it relaxed under the curious delusion that the Allies might not play at all. Krancke's thesis seems to have been that unless the invasion were preceded by large and devastating attacks on

[83] Seventh Army, KTB 1.I.–30.VI.44, 6, 7, 9, 12 May 44; Seventh Army, Trans.0., KTB 1.I.–30.VI.44, 8 May 44, and Anlage 15. The Sturm Battalion was an irregular Army unit for shock employment. It contained about 1,100 men in four companies armed as infantry and had four light field howitzers. The 101st Stellungswerfer Regiment was organized in the west in January 1944. It consisted of three mobile rocket launcher battalions armed either with 210-mm. rocket launchers or 280-mm./320-mm. launchers. The 100th Panzer Replacement Battalion, equipped with a handful of French and Russian light tanks, had very slight combat value. Half of the 243d Division which occupied inland ports was also charged with antiairborne defense. See MS # B–845 (Schlieben).

[84] Seventh Army KTB 1.I.–30.VI.44, 2, 5, May 44.

the coastal batteries it could not succeed.[85] He noted on 31 May that such attacks had indeed increased, but they were, he thought, still too limited to insure the success of landings. Actually, from his point of view, he was right. Despite his prognostications about the threat to the Cotentin he continued to believe that large-scale landings would strike the Pas-de-Calais. Here the coastal batteries were formidable. The Allied air attacks had hit them more often than they had hit any other sector of the coast, and yet the attacks up to the eve of D Day had eliminated only eight guns. In the Seine–Somme sector five had been destroyed, and three in Normandy.[86] The Navy thus remained confident that its artillery could still knock the Allied invasion fleet out of the water —provided of course it sailed where it was expected. That confidence was further nourished by the fact that, despite heavy air attacks on radar stations, the radar warning system remained virtually intact as of 31 May. In fine, reviewing the situation on 4 June Admiral Krancke was driven to the conclusion that not only was attack not imminent but there was a good chance that observed Allied preparations were part of a huge hoax. The mixture of bluff and preparation for a later invasion would keep up, the naval chief thought, until German forces were so weakened in the west that landings could be attempted without great risk.[87]

The contrast between Krancke's optimism about enemy intentions and his sober accounting of the helplessness of his own forces in the face of enemy overwhelming superiority was the most striking aspect of his last report before the invasion. His fleet of combat ships was so small that it could scarcely be talked about in terms of a naval force and even what he did have was for the most part bottled up in the ports by what he called "regular and almost incessant" Allied air sorties. His main offensive units in June were a flotilla of destroyers (which on 1 April had two ships operational),[88] two torpedo boats,[89] and five flotillas of small motor torpedo boats (S-Boote) with thirty-one boats operational. In addition he had a few mine sweepers and patrol craft. Fifteen of the smaller submarines based in French Atlantic ports, though not under Krancke's control, were scheduled to take part in resisting the invasion. Midget submarines and remote-controlled torpedoes were being developed but they never got into the fight.[90] Even this tiny fleet could not operate. Krancke reported thirty Allied air attacks on his naval forces during

[85] Marinegruppenkommando West, KTB 16.–31.V.44, 22 May 44.

[86] Rpt, 12 Jun 44, Admiral Kanalkueste. Seekriegsleitung/1.Abt., KTB Anlagen 1.–30.VI.44. This, however, does not take into account total interference with the effectiveness of the coastal batteries through destruction of communications and damage to auxiliary facilities. Air attacks in Seventh Army area at least were a serious enough threat to uncasemated batteries that General Dollmann ordered alternate and dummy positions prepared.

[87] Lageuebersicht des Marinegruppenkommandos West, Fuehrungsstab, Rueckblick Monat Mai 1944 in Marinegruppenkommando West, KTB 16.–31.V.44, cited hereafter as Navy Group West, Rueckblick Monat Mai 1944. Blumentritt, CofS, OB WEST, also believed the invasion would not come. See MS # T–121 (Zimmermann et al.).

[88] Figures not available for a later date. In any case, however, the destroyers were not used against the invasion fleet in the landings.

[89] He had seven on 1 April, lost three in a brush with Allied destroyers in April and two more in May. Marinegruppenkommando West, KTB 1.–15.IV.44, KTB 16.–30.IV.44, KTB 1.–15.V.44, and KTB 16.–31.V.44.

[90] Conf, 29 Jun 44, ONI, Fuehrer Conferences, 1944.

May and added that even in dark nights his units got no relief. He predicted an enforced reduction of effort and heavy losses in the future.[91] In the meantime he found himself unable to carry out his plan for blocking off the invasion coast with mine fields. Delivery of all types of mines had been delayed chiefly by transportation difficulties. Up to the end of April there were on hand only enough concrete shallow-water mines to put in two mine fields in the Dieppe area.

In May, more mines became available. But in the meantime the mine-laying fleet had been depleted by Allied attacks, and increased Allied air surveillance of the sea lanes made all German naval activity difficult.

The anticipated mining operations [Kranke reported on 4 June] to renew the flanking mine fields in the Channel have not been carried out. On the way to the rendezvous at Le Havre T–24 fell behind because of damage from [a] mine, "Greif" was sunk by bombs, "Kondor" and "Falke" were damaged by mines, the former seriously. The 6th MS-Flotilla [mine layers] likewise on its way to Le Havre to carry out KMA [coastal mine] operations reached port with only one of its six boats, one having been sunk by torpedoes and the other four having fallen out through mine damage, air attack or sea damage. The laying of KMA mines out of Le Havre therefore could not be carried out.[92]

In fact during the month only three more coastal mine fields could be laid and all these were put down off the Kanal-kueste. The essential mining of waters around the Cotentin could scarcely be begun. Naval defense preparations were

actually losing ground. The program of replacing the 1943 mine fields in mid-Channel finally had to be abandoned in March 1944 because of lack of mines and because of Allied radar observation. Krancke estimated that the deepwater fields would all be obsolete by mid-June. Some hasty mine fields were laid in the Bay of the Seine during April but their estimated effective life was only five weeks. The dearth of materials and adequate mine layers continued to disrupt German plans. Krancke's conclusion on the eve of invasion was that mining activity of E-boats could only provide a "nonessential" contribution to the German defenses.[93]

If Admiral Krancke's forces were helpless in naval action, they were scarcely more effective on land, where their assigned task of casemating coastal batteries dragged along past the completion date with no end in sight. Hitler had ordered in January that all batteries and antitank guns were to be casemated by 30 April.[94] On that date Admiral Krancke reported that of 547 coastal guns 299 had been casemated, 145 were under construction; remaining concrete works had not been begun. Like all other defense preparations, this effort had been concentrated along the Kanalkuesie. In the Pas-de-Calais and Seine–Somme sectors, 93 of the 132 guns had been casemated. Normandy had 47 guns, 27 of which were under concrete at the end of April. As for the fixed antitank positions, 16 of the 82 guns had

---

[91] Navy Group West, Rueckblick Monat Mai 1944.
[92] Ibid. All ships mentioned in the report were torpedo boats.

[93] Navy Group West, Rueckblick Monat Mai 1944. Mines swept by the Allies during the crossing on 6 June were presumably among those counted obsolete by the Germans. Some fresh mines were laid in the assault area during the night of 6–7 June. See MS # D–333 (Krancke) and MS # D–334 (Ruge).
[94] Seventh Army, KTB 1.I.–30.VI.44, 17 Jan 44.

been covered in the *Fifteenth Army* area. The nine guns in the *Seventh Army* sector were all open.[95]

The Army's construction program, of course, suffered along with the Navy's and was far from completion on D Day. Shortage of materials, particularly cement and mines, due both to production and to transportation difficulties affected all fortification work. The shortage of cement, critical even at the outset of the winter construction program, was greatly intensified by the Allies' all-out rail bombing offensive. Late in May *LXXXIV Corps*, for example, received 47 carloads of cement in three days against a minimum daily need of 240 carloads. Two days after this report was made, the flow of cement to the *Seventh Army* area stopped altogether as trains had to be diverted to carrying more urgently needed ordinary freight. During May the cement works in Cherbourg were forced to shut down for lack of coal. Plans were then made to bring up cement by canal to Rouen and ship by sea to the *Seventh Army* area, but this was a last-minute solution and could never be tried out.[96]

On 15 May *Seventh Army* reported that its defense preparations were to be considered complete, its beach obstacles and antiairlanding obstacles set, and its troop dispositions made. This was, to say the least, an exaggeration, analagous to a claim that a bombing program was complete as soon as all targets had been hit. In fact, a week later *LXXXIV Corps* estimated that the construction program was

only half complete.[97] The corps was particularly concerned that not even the fortification of the immediate MLR along the water's edge nor the naval and army coastal batteries were finished. The so-called *Zweite Stellung,* which Rundstedt in late 1943 ordered to be built a few kilometers in from the coast line in order to get some depth of defense, had progressed still more slowly, even though, being largely a system of prepared field positions constructed by the French, it took relatively few priority materials or labor. In March *LXXXIV Corps* reported the position 65 percent finished, but the more critical fact was that only thirty-one of the planned eighty-eight resistance nests and strong points were actually fully ready for defense. In the sector of the *709th Division,* defending the vital east coast of the Cotentin, only one of forty-two planned positions was fully prepared. Rommel decided in April that the *Zweite Stellung* was wasting time and effort that were vitally needed for reinforcing the main line of resistance. He therefore ordered all work discontinued except where the *Zweite Stellung* lay close to the coast and could be considered part of the primary defense.[98] Thus the last chance to secure some depth of defense was lost.

But the sacrifice of depth did not result in solidity for the main line. Despite *Seventh Army*'s report that obstacles on the shore line and in fields suitable for airborne landings were complete by the middle of May and needed only deepening, it was precisely that deepening which alone could have made them effective. Rommel's inspection of the antiairlanding obstacles on 18 May convinced him

[95] Status Report, *Stand der Verschartungen, Stichtag 30.IV.44,* in *Marinegruppenkommando West, KTB 16.–30.IV.44.*

[96] *Seventh Army, Trans.0., KTB 1.I.–30.VI.44,* 25, 28 May 44, and *Anlage 8; Seventh Army KTB 1.I.–30.VI.44,* 23 May 44.

[97] *Seventh Army KTB 1.I.–30.VI.44,* 15, 22 May 44.
[98] *Ibid.,* 13 Apr 44.

that, far from being complete, they had only just been begun. Few were mined and his goal was to have them all mined. For that purpose he required 13,000 shells for Normandy alone.[99] As for the shore obstacles, they had been completed only along the high-water mark and a few yards seaward. Admiral Krancke warned against continued acceptance of earlier estimates that the Allies would land at high tide.[100] If landings were made near low tide they would not be materially hindered by the obstacles already in place. This was true but increasing their number was inevitably a slow process. A measure of the difficulties faced by the German Army was the experience of the *352d Division,* which had to cut stakes for obstacles by hand in the Forêt de Cerisy some ten or twelve miles inland, haul the wood by cart to the beach, and drive the stakes, again by hand, into the tidal flats.[101]

Mining of the coastal zone had made considerable progress but was still far short of the goal. In the first six months of 1944 Rommel succeeded in tripling the number of mines in the coast defense zone. But the five or six million mines laid by D Day contrasted with Rommel's own minimum estimate of fifty million needed for continuous defense belts. For the *352d Division* sector alone ten million were needed to cover a thirty-mile front to a depth of three miles. The division

actually received about ten thousand anti-personnel mines during 1944 and no Teller mines at all.[102]

Similar incompleteness marked the fortifications on D Day. On the east coast of the Cotentin, strong points and resistance nests were spaced about 875 yards apart; between the Orne and Vire Rivers they were 1,312 yards apart.[103] Most of them were field fortifications, sometimes with concreted troop shelters and sometimes embodying concrete gun casemates. Of the installations in the *352d Division* sector only 15 percent were bombproof; the remainder were virtually unprotected against air attack.[104] The fortifications had no depth whatsoever. According to the commander of the *716th Division* the forty to fifty fortified resistance centers in his sector were beaded along the coast like a string of pearls.[105] Generalmajor Horst Freiherr Treusch von Buttlar-Brandenfels, OKW operations staff officer, had warned after his inspection trip of Normandy defenses in January that if the enemy broke through one strong point there would be a gap of three or four kilometers into which he could advance unhindered.[106] The abandonment of the *Zweite Stellung* meant that to a large degree this condition still prevailed in June.

Rommel's inability to complete the Atlantic Wall undoubtedly contributed to the general ineffectiveness of German resistance to the Allied landings on 6 June. A stronger wall would have meant a

---

[99] *Bericht ueber die Reise des Herrn Oberbefehlshabers am 17. und 18. Mai 44. Seventh Army, KTB Anlagen 1.I.–30.VI.44.* For lack of sufficient mines, the artillery shells were to be provided with trip wires and attached to the antiairlanding stakes.

[100] An important element in this changed estimate was the observation of British landing exercises in May. *Seekriegsleitung/1.Abt., KTB 1.–31.V.44,* 7 May 44.

[101] MS # B–432 (Oberstleutnant Fritz Ziegelmann, G–3, *352d Division*).

[102] *Ibid.;* MS # A–982 (Ruge).

[103] MS # B–234 (Pemsel).

[104] MS # B–432 (Ziegelmann).

[105] MS # B–621 (Richter). Generalleutnant Richter commanded the *716th Division* at the time of the invasion.

[106] MS # B–672 (Buttlar-Brandenfels).

harder crust, and in cracking it the Allies would unquestionably have suffered heavier losses. But it also seems likely that such a difference would not have proved decisive. The critical weakness, as Rommel had seen, was the German inability to maneuver. And the most important cause of that was the unchallenged supremacy of the Allies in the air. The Luftwaffe had not only been beaten before D Day; it had been all but annihilated.

The story of what happened to Goering's air force, which four years before had been the world-famed spearhead of blitzkrieg, cannot here be told in detail. Among the causes of its decline there was at least an element of bad judgment. Through 1942 Hitler persisted in believing that the end of the war was just around the corner of the next campaign; at the same time he refused to recognize the tremendous productive capacity of the Western Allies, particularly the United States.[107] Although in 1940 the Germans had pioneered in the use of specially developed attack aircraft for support of ground operations, after the end of the French campaign they neglected to develop the tactics further. They turned instead first to creating a bomber fleet to knock out England and later to producing fighter forces to protect the homeland. Their efforts on both scores were inadequate. In the meantime the development of an Air Force to co-operate with the Army went by the board. In 1944 the

Luftwaffe depended for the most part on two fighter types: the Focke-Wulf 190 and the Messerschmitt 109. The attack plane, the twin-engined Junkers 88, was available in such small quantities that the tactical air commands were equipped mainly with the standard interceptor aircraft. Not only did this mean less offensive power in land warfare but, more important, it entailed competition between the demands for air support and the demands for the defense of Germany against the ever intensified Combined Bomber Offensive. Thus the Germans faced the same dilemma in the allocation of air forces that they did in the division of their ground troops between the west and east. In both cases the compromise effected between the rival claims resulted only in establishing inferiority to the enemy on all fronts. And this, in turn, produced a spiral of attrition and increasing inferiority, spinning inevitably to disaster.

In the beginning of 1944, when it was already too late, Reich Minister Albert Speer tried to halt the spiral by concentrating on fighter production. Under the impetus of the Speer program monthly production of fighters rose steadily in 1944 despite all the Allied air forces could do to destroy aircraft and ball bearing factories. In the three months before D Day between seven and eight thousand fighters were produced. Since losses continued to mount, the net gain was only about a thousand planes. But even this gain was not reflected in a stronger air force. Increase in the number of available aircraft only emphasized the critical shortage of qualified pilots. This in turn resulted primarily from a lack of gasoline which compelled a progressive shortening of the pilot-training period from about 260

---

[107] Von Rohden, *Development and planning in the German Air Force*, Parts 1–3. Von Rohden Collection at the Air University, Maxwell Field, Alabama. A microfilm of the material in this collection is in the Library of Congress, Washington, D. C. General-major Hans-Detleff Herhudt von Rohden was the director of the Historical Section of the Luftwaffe High Command during the final years of the war.

hours in 1942 to 110 and even in some cases to 50 in 1944.[108] The green pilots accelerated the deterioration of the Luftwaffe as a whole, since their inexperience increased their own losses and the losses of their planes. Moreover the planes themselves, mass produced in haste, were inferior. During 1943 an average of 500 aircraft a month had been lost or damaged because of mechanical or pilot failures. In February 1944 the losses from these causes soared to 1,300, accounting, in short, for about half the month's new production. This was unusual, but losses through accidents continued to be as important as losses through enemy action. In May, for instance, 712 aircraft were destroyed or damaged by the Allies, while 656 were lost in flying accidents.[109]

On D Day there were about 400 fighter planes in the west under *Third Air Force*.[110] But only about half of these were available to oppose Allied air forces supporting the invasion. The 400 planes were grouped under *II Fighter Corps* and divided between two subordinate commands, the *4th Fighter Division* with headquarters at Metz and the *5th Fighter Division* located near Paris. The mission of the *4th Division* was to intercept Allied heavy bombers entering or leaving Germany. Thus tactically its planes belonged to the Reich defensive system. In case of invasion they were to be diverted to intercept Allied planes over the invasion area, but with bases so far from the scene of operations they were unlikely to be very effective, and would not be on hand on D Day.[111]

Despite the accepted thesis that the first hours of the landings would be the critical period for the defense of France, the Luftwaffe made no comprehensive plans to be on hand in strength during those hours, mostly because with its limited supply of planes and pilots it could not afford to hoard reserves in idleness while waiting for the Allies to strike. In December 1943 the *II Air Corps* was transferred to France from Italy to take over control of all the fighter aircraft to be used in support of the German Army. On D Day, however, the *II Air Corps* was still only a headquarters without any planes. In case of invasion, it was to get ten wings (*Geschwader*) from Germany. Actually only about six wings arrived, and these trickled in with the result that they could never be employed in a concentrated effort. None were on hand on 6 June. The wings earmarked for *II Air Corps* were then just being refitted in Germany. The majority of the pilots were new graduates of the accelerated training programs. Not only did they have no battle experience; they were barely able to handle their planes. Most of them were not familiar with France and did not know how to read maps. The commander of the *II Air Corps*, Generalleutnant Alfred Buelowius, aware of their inexperience, proposed that he send

---

[108] *Luftwaffe Historical Section, Beurteilung des Krieges,* 14 Aug 44. Von Rohden Collection. This report was based on observations of a Lt. Col. Alewyn who visited the west between 15 and 30 July 1944.

[109] Notes for a study on *Strength and Losses of the GAF* in the Von Rohden Collection.

[110] Notes by Von Rohden from *Lagekarten, Third Air Force,* in Von Rohden Collection; *Beurteilung des Krieges,* 14 Aug 44. Cf. German Air Force Order of Battle charts, 31 May and 10 June 1944, prepared by the Air Historical Branch of the Air Ministry, London, from German documents in their possession, MS. Hist Div files. British figures for 10 June are just over 400. On 31 May the number of operational fighter planes is given as 278. See Chart 3, p. 245.

[111] MS # B–013 (Hentschel). Generalmajor Karl A. F. Hentschel was commanding general of the *5th Fighter Division.*

planes out to guide the reinforcements into the flying fields prepared for them. Responsibility for the movement, however, rested with the German Home Air Command (*Luftflotte Reich*) and Buelowius was not consulted. The result was that on D Day the units were scattered and lost on their flights from Germany and many were forced to make emergency landings. Few arrived at their assigned bases.[112]

Thus for one reason or another the planes that should have been in France on 6 June to shield Rundstedt's army against intolerable Allied air supremacy were not

there. The 50 to 150 planes that did fly to the attack in the critical hours of the defense could achieve nothing, and the German Army faced the massed blows of Allied combined arms alone.[113]

---

[112] MS # B-620 (Buelowius).

---

[113] Again reports of the number of planes vary. CofS *II Fighter Corps* estimated he had only fifty planes. See Survey, 18 Nov 44, Some Aspects of the German fighter effort during the initial stages of the invasion of North-West Europe, Translation No. VII/19 by Air Historical Branch, London. Hist Div files. Von Rohden's calculations all come out nearer 150, based on Luftwaffe Historical Section reports, especially *Ueberblick ueber den Luftkrieg*, Karlsbad, 1944. See notes for a study of *Strength and Losses of the GAF* in the Von Rohden Collection. About 1,000 planes were brought into France between 6 June and 7 July but the net gain was only about 250. See *Beurteilung des Krieges*, 14 Aug 44.

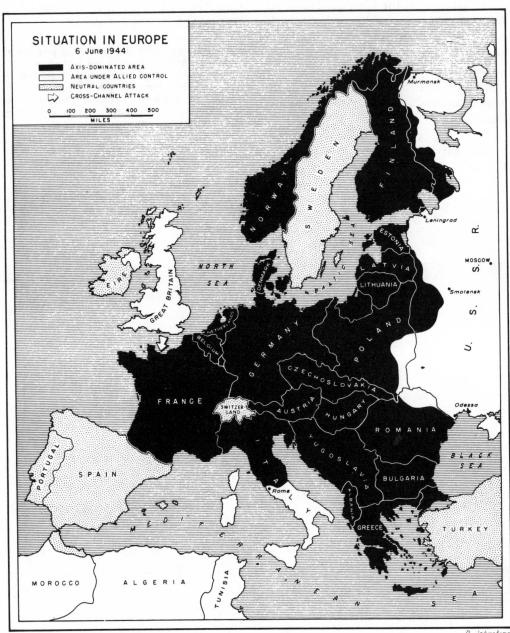

SITUATION IN EUROPE
6 June 1944

AXIS-DOMINATED AREA
AREA UNDER ALLIED CONTROL
NEUTRAL COUNTRIES
CROSS-CHANNEL ATTACK

0   100 200 300 400 500
MILES

R. Johnstone

MAP 1

CHAPTER VIII

The Sixth of June

The Invasion Is Launched

On 8 May General Eisenhower set D Day for Y plus 4, or 5 June. The plans were made (though changes would be introduced up to the last minute), the troops were trained, the preparatory softening up of the enemy was well under way. What remained was to get the men on ships and give the order to go. The vastly complicated process of organizing and equipping the assault units for embarkation began in April. It followed in general the pattern worked out in British exercises in the fall of 1943 which broke down the mounting into a series of movements bringing the troops successively nearer embarkation and at the same time providing for their equipment and assault organization. Unless the troops were already stationed near the south coast of England, they were moved first to concentration areas where they received special equipment, waterproofed their vehicles, and lost certain administrative overhead considered unessential during the assault. The second move brought them to marshaling areas located close to the embarkation points. There, final supplies were issued for the voyage, maps distributed, briefing for the operation accomplished, and the units broken down into boatloads to await the final move down to the ships.[1]

Force U (seaborne units of the VII Corps) was marshaled in the Tor Bay area and east of Plymouth; Force O (1st Division), in the area of Dorchester; Force B (29th Division), near Plymouth and Falmouth; and the early build-up divisions, the 9th Infantry and 2d Armored Divisions, near Southampton. Marshaling areas for the airborne units were as follows: glider troops in the central counties between London and the Severn River; paratroopers of the 101st Division in the Newbury–Exeter area; paratroopers of the 82d Division in the eastern half of England, north of London.[2] (*Map VI*)

About 54,000 men, including the temporary housekeeping services of the entire 5th Armored Division, were required to establish and maintain installations for mounting the seaborne assault forces alone, and to perform services necessary to make them ready for sailing. To cook their meals, more than 4,500 new army cooks were trained during the first three months of 1944. To transport them and haul their supplies, over 3,800 trucks were operated by the Southern Base Section.

Through the first five months of 1944 individual and group assault training had continued, supplemented from January on by large-scale exercises designed to test not only assault techniques but co-ordination between the joint armies, smoothness of staff work in all phases of the operation, and techniques of mounting, mar-

---

[1] Information on mounting and training from [Clifford Jones] NEPTUNE: Training, Mounting, The Artificial Ports (The Administrative and Logistical History of the ETO: Part IV), MS, pp. 275ff. Hist Div files.

[2] The latter was the principal area of Eighth AF installations.

shaling, loading, and unloading. These exercises culminated in two dress rehearsals for the invasion: exercise TIGER for Force U (VII Corps units) held at the end of April; the series of exercises, FABIUS, for Force O (1st Division), Force B (29th Division), and British assault and follow-up forces conducted in the early part of May.

The assault exercises were held at Slapton Sands on the coast of Devon southwest of Dartmouth under conditions simulating as closely as possible those expected in the actual operations. As a result of the exercises certain minor technical improvements were made, but the basic organization and the techniques as worked out at the Assault Training Center were unchanged.

Amid all the simulation there came one serious note of war. One of the convoys of exercise TIGER was attacked by two German E-boat flotillas totaling nine boats.[3] Losses were heavier than those suffered by Force U during the actual invasion. Two LST's were sunk and one damaged. About 700 men lost their lives.[4] The loss of three LST's to the OVERLORD assault lift was particularly critical in view of the general shortage of landing craft. General Eisenhower reported to the Combined Chiefs of Staff that the sinkings reduced the reserve of LST's

to nothing.[5] The Germans realized that they had sunk landing craft but guessed that the craft had been participating in an exercise.[6] The incident passed without repercussions.

After the TIGER and FABIUS rehearsals the assault troops returned to the marshaling areas to complete their last-minute preparations and to wait. Troops of Force U had almost a month of waiting. It was a trying time for the men and a dangerous time for the fate of the invasion. Although troops were not briefed on operation OVERLORD until the last week in May, the fact that they were concentrated and ready to go and that they had just practiced the invasion maneuver with the organization actually to be used would have been sufficient information in the hands of enemy agents to jeopardize the operation. All troops were therefore sealed in the marshaling areas behind barbed wire and with a host of some 2,000 Counter Intelligence Corps men guarding them closely. The whole coastal area had been closed to visitors since April. Now, in addition, the camps themselves were isolated from all contact with the surrounding countryside. Camouflage discipline was more severely enforced during these weeks than at any time subsequently during actual operations. The German Air Force, though weak, was believed capable of damaging raids against troop concentrations and port areas. Actually, only one raid of any consequence did occur, when on the night of 30 May bombs were dropped in

---

[3] *Marinegruppenkommando West, KTB 16.–30.IV. 44*, 27 Apr 44.

[4] Jones, NEPTUNE, p. 258. Navy figures were 638 killed and 89 wounded. See *Report by Allied Naval Commander-in-Chief Expeditionary Force on Operation NEPTUNE* (London, 1944), I, 33, cited hereafter as ANCXF *Report*. Jones, historian for engineer units that were chiefly involved in the disaster, gives 749 killed, and bases his calculations on after action reports of the units and detailed casualty breakdowns. Even so, he feels his figures may be incomplete.

[5] Diary of CinC, 28 Apr 44.

[6] *Marinegruppenkommando West, KTB 16.–30.-IV.44*, 28 Apr 44. On the basis of a German broadcast, the ANCXF *Report* erroneously stated that the Germans were unaware of the nature of their success. ANCXF *Report*, I, 33.

PREINVASION SCENES. *Soldiers in mess line (above) in one of the marshaling camps in southern England, and (below) men and equipment being loaded on LST's at Brixham.*

a camp near Falmouth, causing a few casualties to an ordnance battalion. The enemy continued to miss his opportunities to disrupt the final preparations.

Loading of Force U, Force O, and Force B began on 30 May, 31 May, and 1 June, respectively, and all troops were aboard by 3 June. Force U craft were loaded mostly at Plymouth, Dartmouth, Tor Bay, Torquay, Poole, Salcombe, Brixham, and Yarmouth. They were divided into twelve convoys for the cross-Channel movement depending on their missions, assembly points, and speed. Force O was split into five convoys and the craft loaded in a relatively concentrated area including the ports of Portland, Weymouth, and Poole.[7]

Operation OVERLORD was ready.

On 29 May the senior meteorologist for SHAEF, Group Captain J. M. Stagg of the RAF, had drawn an optimistic long-range forecast of the weather to be expected in the first week of June. On the basis of that forecast all preparations had been made. General Eisenhower cabled General Marshall on Saturday, 3 June: "We have almost an even chance of having pretty fair conditions . . . only marked deterioration . . . would discourage our plans."[8] But marked deterioration was already in the cards. That Saturday evening Group Captain Stagg again came before the Supreme Commander and his commanders in chief who were meeting at Southwick House north of Portsmouth, the headquarters of Admiral Ramsay. Group Captain Stagg had bad news. Not only would the

weather on 5 June be overcast and stormy with high winds and a cloud base of 500 feet to zero, but the weather was of such a nature that forecasting more than twenty-four hours in advance was highly undependable. The long period of settled conditions was breaking up. It was decided, after discussion, to postpone decision for seven hours and in the meantime let Force U and part of Force O sail on schedule for their rendezvous for the 5 June D Day.

At 0430 Sunday morning a second meeting was held at which it was predicted that the sea conditions would be slightly better than anticipated but that overcast would still not permit use of the air force. Although General Montgomery then expressed his willingness to go ahead with the operation as scheduled, General Eisenhower decided to postpone it for twenty-four hours. He felt that OVERLORD was going in with a very slim margin of ground superiority and that only the Allied supremacy in the air made it a sound operation of war. If the air could not operate, the landings should not be risked. A prearranged signal was sent out to the invasion fleet, many of whose convoys were already at sea.[9] The ships turned back and prepared to rendezvous twenty-four hours later.

On Sunday night, 4 June, at 2130 the high command met again in the library of Southwick House. Group Captain Stagg reported a marked change in the weather. A rain front over the assault area was expected to clear in two or three hours and the clearing would last until Tuesday morning. Winds then of 25 to

---

[7] ANCXF *Report*, Vol. III, Rpt, Comdr Assault Force O, p. 5; *Ibid.*, Rpt, Comdr Assault Force U, pp. 13–14.

[8] Cbl. Eisenhower Personal Files.

[9] The first ships actually sailed on 31 May. They were 54 "Corncobs" (Blockships) for the artificial harbors which weighed anchor from Oban.

ALLIED INVASION CHIEFS. *Left to right: General Bradley, Admiral Ramsey, Air Chief Marshal Tedder, General Eisenhower, General Montgomery, Air Chief Marshal Leigh-Mallory, General Smith. This photograph was taken during a conference in early 1944.*

31 knots velocity would moderate. Cloud conditions would permit heavy bombing during Monday night and Tuesday morning although there would be considerable cloudiness Tuesday. The cloud base at H Hour might be just high enough to permit spotting for naval gunfire.

All this was good news, but it indicated weather that might be barely tolerable rather than ideal for the assault. After listening to the forecast Admiral Ramsay reminded the commanders that there was only half an hour to make a decision, and that if Admiral Kirk's forces were ordered to sail for a D Day on Tuesday, 6 June, and were later recalled they would not be able to sail again for a Wednesday rendezvous, the last day for two weeks on which light and tidal conditions would be suitable for the assault.

Both Eisenhower and General Smith welcomed the break and felt the decision should be made to go in on Tuesday. The gamble that worried Smith was the possibility of not being able to spot naval fire but he thought it was still the best gamble to take. To call off the invasion now meant to wait until 19 June before it could be tried again. Troops would have to be disembarked with great risk to security, as well as to morale. The 19 June date would mean acceptance of moonless conditions for the airborne drops. Finally, the longer the postponement, the shorter the period of good campaigning weather on the Continent.

Still Air Chief Marshal Leigh-Mallory was skeptical of the ability of the air force to operate effectively in the overcast predicted. Air Chief Marshal Tedder agreed that the operations of heavies and mediums were going to be "chancey."

General Eisenhower refused the pessimistic view. "We have a great force of fighter-bombers," he said, and then turning to General Montgomery he asked, "Do you see any reason for not going Tuesday"?

"I would say—Go!" Montgomery replied.

"The question," Eisenhower pointed out, "[is] just how long can you hang this operation on the end of a limb and let it hang there."

The discussion continued a few more minutes.

At 2145 Eisenhower announced his decision. "I'm quite positive we must give the order. . . . I don't like it, but there it is. . . . I don't see how we can possibly do anything else." [10]

There remained still a possibility that the weather might become so much worse that the decision would have to be reversed. A final meeting was held shortly after midnight. Weather charts were studied again, but nothing had changed. The invasion was launched and through the choppy waters of the Channel the 5,000 ships and craft of the largest fleet ever assembled held to their carefully plotted courses toward the transport areas off the enemy coast.

When General Eisenhower left Southwick House before dawn of 5 June, he had made the last of a long series of planning and command decisions which through three and a half years had translated the idea of the cross-Channel attack into an operation of war. The war leaders, the high commanders, the planners with whom we have been so long concerned had no choice now but to sit back and wait. They had done what they could to insure that the men who crossed the Channel on 5 June 1944 should have the greatest possible chance of success at a cost as low as careful planning could set it. Long before the armada sailed, the Combined Chiefs of Staff had focused their attention far ahead of the battle of the beaches. The SHAEF staff similarly had long been working on plans for the later phases of the operation. The nearer H Hour approached, the more heavily and exclusively the responsibility for the invasion settled on the lower commanders.

In the narrative to follow, the great names drop out. Even Eisenhower and Montgomery appear but seldom. In their place will be the corps and division commanders, the colonels, the lieutenants, and the privates. For the few will be substituted the many, as the battlefield, so long seen as a single conceptual problem, becomes a confused and disparate fact—a maze of unrelated orchards and strange roads, hedgerows, villages, streams and woods, each temporarily bounding for the soldier the whole horizon of the war.

One may say of almost any successful operation that it carried out the plan, but this is to say little of how or why it succeeded. The Normandy assault was perhaps as thoroughly planned as any battle in the history of war. Nevertheless the fighting men went in trained to improvise battlefield solutions to the immediate problems facing them—how to take out an unseen machine gun in the hedgerows, how to outflank an enemy holed

---

[10] Account of the meeting from notes made by Air Vice Marshal James M. Robb, SHAEF CofS for Air. Direct quotes are as given by Robb in sgd rpt, Mon A.M., 5 Jun 44. Hist Div files.

up in a stone farmhouse. The fighting in these terms proceeded not according to plan but according to the trial and error of battle. It is to the narrative of this testing that we now turn.

While the Allied invasion force steamed across the Channel, the Germans in France, so long schooled for this moment, had no direct knowledge that it was at hand. The enemy was all but blind. There had been no air reconnaissance during the first five days of June. Naval patrols scheduled for the night of 5–6 June, along with the mine-laying operations for that date, were canceled because of bad weather.

The stages of alert among the various commands in the west varied, reflecting both the nebulous character of such intelligence as was available and the lack of command unity. On 1 and 2 June German agents who had penetrated Resistance groups picked up twenty-eight of the BBC prearranged signals ordering the Resistance to stand by for the code messages that would direct the execution of sabotage plans. The central SS intelligence agency in Berlin reported these intercepts on 3 June to Admiral Doenitz and warned that invasion could be considered possible within the next fortnight. At the admiral's headquarters they were not taken too seriously. It was thought that perhaps an exercise was in progress.[11]

On the evening of 5 June *OB WEST* and *Fifteenth Army* independently intercepted the "B" messages which at this time *Fifteenth Army* at least understood to be warnings of invasion within forty-eight hours.[12] This was at 2215,[13] precisely the hour at which the transport planes carrying troops of the U.S. 101st Airborne Division began taking off from airfields in England. What happened next is not altogether clear. While *Fifteenth Army* put its troops on the highest alert, *Army Group B* apparently took no action. On the basis of past experience Rommel's staff considered it unlikely that the intercepts warned of an imminent invasion. Rommel himself was in Herrlingen at his home, on his way to visit Hitler at Obersalzburg; he was not immediately called back. *Army Group B* did not alert *Seventh Army*. In fact the routine daily orders from *Seventh Army* headquarters to subordinate corps on the evening of 5 June actually canceled a planned alert for that night.[14] Perhaps the chief reason for the cancellation was that a map exercise, to which a number of division and lower commanders in *Seventh Army* had been invited, was scheduled for the morning of 6 June at Rennes. Whatever the reason, it is apparent that General Dollmann believed on the night of 5 June that there was less cause for alarm than on many a previous night in May when his troops had been alerted.

The net effect on German preparedness of the intercepted warnings to the Resistance was therefore slight. *Seventh Army* was alerted only in the sense that it was in the same state of "defensive

---

[11] *Seekriegsleitung/1.Abt., KTB 1.–30.VI.44,* 3 Jun 44.

[12] *Fifteenth Army, KTB 1.I.–30.VI.44,* 5 Jun 44.

[13] Double British Summer Time. German clocks, set by Central European time, showed 2115. All times given in text are DBST.

[14] Rad, 5 Jun 44, *Seventh Army* to *XXV, LXXIV,* and *LXXXIV Corps. Seventh Army, KTB Anlagen 1.V.–5.VI.44.*

readiness" that it had been in all through the spring. The Resistance messages of the evening of 5 June may have persuaded *OB WEST* that invasion was imminent, although there is evidence that Rundstedt's intelligence officer at least rejected the warning on grounds that it would be absurd for the Allies to announce their invasion in advance over the BBC.[15] In any case, a last-minute alert of the supreme headquarters in such vague terms was of little value for the command. It gave no indication of where or precisely when the Allies would strike; reconnaissance, moreover, could not be put out in time to answer these questions.

As for the Navy, it was, on 5 June, thoroughly complacent. German naval experts had calculated that Allied landings would be possible only in seas of less than intensity 4,[16] with a wind force up to 24 knots and a visibility of at least three sea miles. These conditions were not being met on 5 June.[17] Lacking weather-reporting stations to the west whence most of the Channel weather came, the German meteorologists were unable to make reliable predictions.[18] Weather planes flew out over the North Sea daily to points west of Ireland, but the data provided by their observations were of limited usefulness. The Germans could not have forecast the break in the weather which Group Captain Stagg reported to General Eisenhower.[19] Although there is no evidence that meteorologists advised German commanders that invasion on 6 June was impossible, it is clear that the generally unfavorable wind and sea conditions contributed to reducing the enemy's alertness.[20]

This was particularly true of the naval command. Lulled into a sense of security by the weather and the judgment that the Allies had not yet completed essential preparatory bombardment of the coastal fortifications, Admiral Krancke received reports of the SOE intercepts on 5 June without alarm. Notice of the BBC affair was faithfully transcribed in his war diary for 6 June together with his assurances that nothing was likely to happen—all under the general heading: "Large-scale enemy landing in the Seine Bay." [21]

---

[15] *Marinegruppenkommando West, KTB 1.–7.VI.-44*, 6 Jun 44.

[16] Wave heights between five and eight feet.

[17] *Seventh* and *Fifteenth Army* commanders thought the weather was not too adverse for invasion, but it is not clear what standards they applied. See the *KTB*'s for the respective armies. The almost complete lack of co-ordination between Army, Navy, and Air Force headquarters makes generalization on German preparedness extremely difficult.

[18] One German meteorologist commented that commanders were virtually reduced to looking at the morning skies for their weather forecasts. See Interv with Maj Heinz Lettau, 5 Oct 49. Hist Div files.

[19] It is likely, however, that they would not have considered that the break made invasion possible, since weather conditions were still unsettled and the German Navy view was that at least five consecutive days of favorable weather would be necessary for the success of the landings. Rpt, *Beitraege zur Frage der Landemoeglichkeiten an der Kueste des Kanals*, 1 Jan 44. *Seekriegsleitung/1.Abt., KTB Anlagen 1.I.–30.VI.44.*

[20] The story told by Captain Harry C. Butcher, *My Three Years with Eisenhower* (New York, 1946), pp. 646–47, concerning German weather predictions is erroneous. Major Lettau, far from being "the chief German meteorologist," was in fact attached to an antiaircraft outfit and had nothing to do with forecasting invasion weather. He was with the *155th Flak Regiment*, stationed in Amiens, and his job was to analyze flying conditions over England from data collected by radio sound stations. See interv cited n. 18.

[21] *Marinegruppenkommando West, KTB 1.–7.VI.-44*, 6 Jun 44.

GERMAN FIELD COMMANDERS. *Upper left, General von Schlieben; upper right, General Marcks; lower left, General Geyr von Schweppenburg; lower right, General Dollmann.*

The Airborne Assault

The time and place at least of the "large-scale landing" caught the Germans wholly by surprise. *Seventh Army*'s first knowledge that anything was afoot was a series of reports in the early morning hours of 6 June that Allied paratroopers were dropping from the skies over Normandy. At 0130 Lt. Col. Hoffmann, commander of the *3d Battalion, 919th Regiment* of the *709th Division,* was at his headquarters in St. Floxel east of Montebourg. (*Map VII*) He heard aircraft approaching. The sound indicated great numbers, and, as he listened during the next hour, it seemed to him to swell louder and louder. At 0200 six airplanes flying, he thought, at about 500 feet approached the headquarters shelter and released parachutists in front of and above it. In a few minutes Hoffmann's staff and security guards were heavily engaged with paratroopers of the 101st Airborne Division in one of the opening skirmishes of the battle for Normandy.[22]

News of the landings spread fast. At 0215 *Seventh Army* ordered the highest state of alarm through the *LXXXIV Corps* sector. The alarm was passed at once by wire to all Army, Navy and Air Force units in the corps area. At 0220 *Naval Commander Normandy* (Konteradmiral Walther Hennecke)[23] reported paratroopers near the Marcouf battery. During the next five minutes additional reports came in of landings in the sector of the *716th* and *711th Divisions.* Before

three o'clock *LXXXIV Corps* had taken its first prisoner. The situation was still obscure, but, as reports piled in, something of the extent and scale of the operation became visible. Generalmajor Max Pemsel, *Seventh Army* chief of staff, had already (by 0300) concluded that the long-heralded major invasion had begun, and had correctly located the points of main effort near Carentan and Caen.[24] His judgment, however, was at this time a minority report. Field Marshals Rundstedt and Sperrle and Admiral Krancke as well as Rommel's chief of staff, Generalleutnant Hans Speidel, all thought they were probably experiencing the diversionary operation which had been expected in the *Seventh Army* area while the Allies prepared to strike the main blow against *Fifteenth Army.* But, whatever the larger estimate of the situation, local measures could be and were promptly taken. The *91st Division* in reserve in the Cotentin was released to *Seventh Army,* attached to *LXXXIV Corps,* and, together with the *709th Division,* was ordered to counterattack. There was actually little else to be done. All units in the Cotentin had been briefed to expect airborne operations. The meeting engagement was inevitably the individual problem of these units.

The situation on the American side was similar. The first actions of all airborne units in the Cotentin on D Day were attempts by small groups of men to carry out in the fog of the battlefield their own small portions of the assigned plan. There could be little over-all direction from above. And, in fact, little in-

---

[22] Hoffmann Report. *Seventh Army, KTB Anlagen 1.I.–30.VI.44.*

[23] Naval district commander for the Normandy coast, under *Admiral Kanalkueste* who had the whole Channel coast command. See naval command chart, p. 245.

[24] He reversed himself later in the day to agree with higher command estimates. Tel Msgs. *Seventh Army, KTB Anlagen 1.I.–30.VI.44.*

PARACHUTE TROOPS *marching onto airfield on evening of 5 June.*

formation got through to corps and army as to what was happening.[25]

By the revised VII Corps field order of 28 May both U.S. airborne divisions were to land in the eastern half of the peninsula between Ste. Mère-Eglise and Carentan, establishing a beachhead from which the corps would push west and north to the capture of Cherbourg. The six parachute regiments of the two divisions, which together with organic supporting units numbered over 13,000 men, were loaded in 822 transport planes at nine airfields in England. They began taking off before midnight to fly routes calculated to bring the first serials in from the west side of the Cotentin Peninsula and over the designated drop zones between 0115 and 0130. The main flights were preceded by pathfinder planes that were

to land paratroopers to mark the drop zones. Glider reinforcements would be brought in at dawn and again at dusk on landing zones that the paratroopers were expected to have cleared of the enemy. The whole airborne operation was by far the largest and most hazardous ever undertaken, and thousands of American lives depended on its success.[26]

---

[25] See First Army G-3 Jnl.

[26] Allied airborne operations required 1,087 transport aircraft including lift for the pathfinders but excluding aircraft used to tow gliders. See AEAF Memo, Operation "NEPTUNE," Employment of British and American Airborne Forces, 27 May 44. SHAEF G-3 file 24533/Ops (Future Operations). Pathfinders of the 101st Airborne Division began dropping at 0015; the first serial of combat troops was scheduled to drop at 0119. See Leonard Rapport and Arthur Norwood, Jr., *Rendezvous with Destiny* (Washington, 1948), pp. 73, 94.

Records of airborne operations in the Cotentin are very sketchy; those of the 101st Airborne Division in particular are all but useless. The narrative following is based on a set of comprehensive interviews

The primary mission of the 101st Airborne Division was to seize the western edge of the flooded area back of the beach between St. Martin-de-Varreville and Pouppeville. Its secondary mission was to protect the southern flank of VII Corps and be prepared to exploit southward through Carentan. The latter task was to be carried out by destroying two bridges on the main Carentan highway and the railroad bridge west of it, by seizing and holding the la Barquette lock, and finally by establishing a bridgehead over the Douve River northeast of Carentan.

Two parachute regiments less one battalion, the 502d and the 506th (—), were assigned the primary mission. The 502d Parachute Infantry, with the 377th Parachute Field Artillery Battalion attached, was to drop near St. Martin-de-Varreville, destroy the enemy coastal battery there, secure the two northern beach exits, and establish a defensive line tying in the division's north flank with the 82d Airborne Division to the west. The 506th Infantry would seize the two southern exits.

The four battalion serials of the 502d Infantry came in ten minutes apart led by the 2d Battalion and regimental headquarters. The leading planes, scattered by clouds and flak, dropped the majority

of the 2d Battalion outside their assigned zone. (*Map VIII*) The battalion as a result spent most of the day assembling and, as a unit, took no part in the D-Day fighting. The regiment's planned artillery support did not materialize. Only one of the six howitzers of the 377th Field Artillery Battalion was recovered after the drop, and the fifty men of the battalion who assembled during the day fought as infantry in scattered actions.[27]

The commander of the 3d Battalion, 502d, Lt. Col. Robert G. Cole, dropped east of Ste. Mère-Eglise. (*See Map VII.*) He began then to make his way toward St. Martin-de-Varreville. Out of the darkness, toy "crickets" snapped as paratroopers identified themselves and began assembling in groups. The groups were generally miscellaneous at first. The men looked only for company and leadership. Seventy-five men, including some paratroopers from the 82d Airborne Division, gathered in this way under Colonel Cole and moved steadily toward the coast. Except for an encounter with a small enemy convoy on the way, in which some Germans were killed and ten taken prisoner, the group had no trouble reaching its objective. Discovering that the guns of the St. Martin coastal battery had been removed and that the position was deserted, Cole went on to Audouville-la-Hubert where his men established themselves at the western end of the causeway without a fight.[28] About

conducted during July 1944 by Col. S. L. A. Marshall with officers and men of the airborne units. Colonel Marshall, subsequently European Theater Historian, developed the information thus secured in a number of battalion and regimental studies which in mimeographed form are in the Historical Division files. The airborne material is exploited in greater detail than here in [R. G. Ruppenthal] *Utah Beach to Cherbourg* (Washington, 1948), to which the author is generally indebted for the bulk of the story of U.S. VII Corps operations during June 1944. See Bibliographical Note.

[27] 377th FA Bn AAR.

[28] Bombing had not injured the six Russian 122-mm. guns at the St. Martin emplacement but had so damaged the fire control setup that the guns were moved before the invasion. See MS # B–260 (Generalmajor Gerhard Triepel, gen. Schulze). Triepel during the first half of June commanded the *1261st Army Coastal Artillery Regiment;* in the latter half, he was artillery commander of *LXXXIV Corps.*

two hours later, at 0930, the enemy began retreating across the causeway from the beach. The paratroopers, lying in wait, shot down fifty to seventy-five and at 1300 made contact with the 8th Infantry (4th Division). They had suffered no casualties. Cole, having completed his mission, remained in the area to collect and organize his battalion. By the end of the day he had about 250 men. With this group he was ordered into regimental reserve near Blosville for the next day's operations.

The 1st Battalion, 502d Parachute Infantry (Lt. Col. Patrick J. Cassidy), had a much harder fight for its objectives. Colonel Cassidy, landing about in the center of the battalion zone near St. Germain-de-Varreville, collected a small force mostly of his own men and moved toward the stone buildings on the eastern edge of Mésières which were thought to be occupied by the German unit manning the St. Martin coastal battery. Without opposition the battalion secured the crossroads west of St. Martin near which the building stood. Taking stock of his position there, Colonel Cassidy found that both the northern exits for which the regiment was responsible were clear. He then made contact with a group of forty-five men of the battalion who had assembled north of his own position and ordered them to establish a defensive line at Foucarville. The situation to the west of St. Martin, however, remained obscure. Colonel Cassidy decided to keep a portion of his force (nominally a company) in reserve to block any enemy attempt to break through from the west to the beaches. A group of about fifteen men was sent to clean out the buildings on the eastern edge of Mésières. This

fight was conducted almost singlehandedly by S/Sgt. Harrison Summers. Summers rushed the buildings one by one, kicked in the doors, and sprayed the interiors with his Tommy gun. On occasion he had the assistance of another man, but it was his drive and initiative that kept the attack going. When the last building was cleared in the afternoon, about 150 Germans had been killed or captured.[29]

Near the close of this action Lt. Col. John H. Michaelis, regimental commander, arrived in the area with 200 men. Cassidy was thus free to complete his D-Day mission to cover the north flank of the regiment and tie in with the 82d Airborne Division on the left. While the fight near Mésières was in progress the men of the 1st Battalion whom Colonel Cassidy had sent to Foucarville in the morning had succeeded in establishing four road blocks in and around the town and had trapped and largely destroyed a four-vehicle enemy troop convoy. Despite this early success the road blocks were threatened all day with being overrun by a superior enemy force that occupied prepared positions on a hill to the northwest.

The American situation was not immediately improved by Cassidy's move north, since he came up west of Foucarville in order to carry out the plan of tying in at Beuzeville-au-Plain with the 82d Airborne Division. He ran into trouble there. The company ordered to Beuzeville-au-Plain mistook the hamlet of le Fournel for its objective and there became involved in three separate pla-

---

[29] Summers was awarded the DSC. Details of the action from interviews by Col. S. L. A. Marshall. Hist Div files.

toon fights which proceeded in some confusion until dark. The troops then withdrew to the south where they remained under enemy pressure during the night. Since contact was not made with the 82d Airborne Division, Cassidy committed the reserve company on the left and moved up some spare riflemen to fill the gap between le Fournel and the road blocks around Foucarville. Even so the whole line remained very weak, and the regimental commander, having already decided to pass the 2d Battalion through the 1st on the following day, ordered Colonel Cassidy to pull back and dig in.

During the night the Germans facing the battalion's right flank at Foucarville unexpectedly decided to surrender, apparently because the increasing volume of American machine gun and mortar fire led them to overestimate the battalion's strength. Eighty-seven Germans were taken prisoner and about fifty more shot down as they attempted to escape.

Here as elsewhere in the 101st Airborne Division's early contacts with the enemy, it seems that the German dispersion of units in small packets to garrison villages and strong points took no account of the splintering effect of airborne landings in their midst, even though the enemy command expected just such landings. The isolated German units, apparently out of contact with their parent outfits, ignorant of what was occurring as well as of what German countermeasures were in the making, were prone to fancy themselves about to be overwhelmed whenever American fire was brought to bear on them with any persistence. The attackers at least had the psychological advantage of knowing the large things that had been planned, even though they seldom knew what was actually happening beyond the field or village in which they found themselves.

The two beach exits south of the zone of the 502d Infantry were the responsibility of the 506th Parachute Infantry Regiment (Col. Robert F. Sink). The 506th (less the 3d Battalion) was to land between Hiesville and Ste. Marie-du-Mont and seize the western edge of the inundated area between Audouville-la-Hubert and Pouppeville. The 3d Battalion, dropping just south of Vierville and charged with defending the Douve River line in the regiment's sector, was to seize two bridges at le Port and establish a bridgehead there for subsequent exploitation southward.

Like the 502d, the 506th experienced a badly scattered drop, but had rather better luck in assembling rapidly. Within two hours of landing, about ninety men of regimental headquarters and fifty men of the 1st Battalion (Lt. Col. William L. Turner) had assembled in the regimental zone. Colonel Sink established his command post at Culoville. At the same time the 2d Battalion (Lt. Col. Robert L. Strayer), despite a landing completely out of its zone in the sector of the 502d Parachute Infantry to the north, succeeded in assembling rapidly about 200 of its men. Strayer had the principal regimental mission of securing the southern beach exits at Houdienville and Pouppeville. Before dawn his men headed south toward their objectives. They ran into opposition on the same road over which the 1st Battalion, 502d Parachute Infantry, had passed shortly before. Delayed all morning by enemy machine guns, they did not reach their first objective, Houdienville, until early afternoon, after the seaborne troops were already through the exit and proceeding inland.

Meanwhile Colonel Sink, at Culoville, knowing nothing of the 2d Battalion's movements, decided to send his reserve, the 1st Battalion under Colonel Turner, to carry out a part of the mission. Turner's "battalion" of fifty men was ordered to Pouppeville. Again relatively light enemy opposition succeeded in harassing the march and delaying for several hours Turner's arrival on his objective.

In the course of the delay a third unit was sent on the same mission by the division commander, Maj. Gen. Maxwell Taylor,[30] who had no knowledge of the two previous moves. The 3d Battalion, 501st Parachute Infantry (Lt. Col. Julian Ewell), had been designated to land as division reserve with the additional task of protecting the glider landing zone northwest of Hiesville. Although three planes of the 3d Battalion serial were shot down with the loss of three-quarters of their personnel and other planes were scattered by fog and flak, enough carried out their scheduled drops so that about 300 men of the battalion and of the division headquarters were able to assemble quickly and establish the division command post as planned near Hiesville. From there Colonel Ewell, with a group of about forty men from the line companies and some miscellaneous head-

quarters personnel, was sent at 0600 to clear the Pouppeville beach exit.

At about 0800 Ewell's men reached Pouppeville and attacked to clean it out. The enemy force of approximately sixty to seventy men of the *1058th Regiment (91st Division)* [31] did not offer determined resistance, but it was nevertheless a slow task for the numerically inferior Americans to fight them house to house. It was noon before the local German commander surrendered. The Americans had suffered eighteen casualties, while inflicting twenty-five on the enemy and taking thirty-eight prisoners. The rest of the enemy in Pouppeville retreated toward the beach where they were caught by the advancing U.S. seaborne forces, and at last surrendered to the 8th Infantry. The first contact between seaborne and airborne forces was made at Pouppeville between Colonel Ewell's men and the 2d Battalion, 8th Infantry (Lt. Col. Carlton O. MacNeely).

Throughout D Day Colonel Sink at the 506th regimental headquarters felt wholly isolated and almost alone on the Cotentin Peninsula. Most of the time he was out of touch with his own battalions and with the division; he had little information about the enemy, and his headquarters was involved in scattered fights for its own security. The regiment unknowingly had set up in the midst of a small hornet's nest. In the Ste. Marie-du-Mont area was the entire *2d Battalion of the 191st Artillery Regiment* which had been committed to coastal defense in the *709th Division* sector.[32] The battalion headquarters was in Ste. Marie

---

[30] General Taylor, commissioned in the Corps of Engineers from West Point in 1922, transferred to the Field Artillery in 1926. As chief of staff of the 82d Division in 1942 he assisted in organizing the first airborne divisions. In 1943 he went overseas as artillery commander of the reorganized 82d Airborne Division. After serving through the Sicilian and Italian campaigns he received command of the 101st Airborne Division in March 1944.

[31] Probably of the *3d Battalion*, whose headquarters was at St. Côme-du-Mont.

[32] MS # D–330 (Blumentritt).

and the three batteries, each with four 105–mm. howitzers, were all in the immediate vicinity. Four of the pieces were captured near Holdy by groups of the 1st Battalion, 506th Infantry. The enemy battalion headquarters was overrun by combined action of the 506th Infantry and elements of the 4th Division later in the day.[33] For the most part, however, Colonel Sink had no men to spare either to clear the enemy from his immediate vicinity or even to reconnoiter to make contact with other friendly units. He believed it necessary to keep together his handful of men to protect the rear of the units engaged in clearing the causeways and to provide a nucleus for concentration of the regiment. The group maintained itself, fighting off enemy riflemen who twice during the day closed in among the surrounding hedgerows. In the evening, with forces of the 1st and 2d Battalions, Colonel Sink controlled about 650 men.

The hedgerows, which bottled up Colonel Sink's men in apparent isolation despite the nearness of friendly units, were to become the most important single preoccupation of American fighting men during their next two months in Normandy and would remain as their most vivid memory of the land. These hedgerows, ubiquitous throughout the Cotentin and the *bocage* country, were earth dikes averaging about four feet in height and covered with tangled hedges, bushes, and even trees. Throughout the entire country they boxed in fields and orchards of varying sizes and shapes, few larger than football fields and many much smaller. Each hedgerow was a po-

tential earthwork into which the defenders cut often-elaborate foxholes, trenches, and individual firing pits. The dense bushes atop the hedgerows provided ample concealment for rifle and machine gun positions, which could subject the attacker to devastating hidden fire from three sides. Observation for artillery and mortar fire was generally limited to a single field, particularly in the relatively flat ground of the beachhead areas. Each field thus became a separate battlefield which, when defended with determination, had to be taken by slow costly advances of riflemen hugging the hedgerows to close with the enemy with rifle and grenade. Both Americans and Germans complained that the hedgerows favored the other side and made their own operations difficult. In fact, the country was ideal for static defense and all but impossible for large co-ordinated attacks or counterattacks. The chief burden of the fighting remained with the individual soldier and the advance of his unit depended substantially on his own courage and resourcefulness, and above all on his willingness to move through machine gun and mortar fire to root the enemy out of his holes.

The 101st Airborne Division within a relatively few hours of landing had secured the western edge of the inundated area west of UTAH Beach. The task was accomplished, not quite according to plan, but on time and with much smaller cost than anyone had thought possible before the operation.[34] The remaining

---

[33] Another of the batteries was captured still later by the 8th Infantry. See below, p. 329.

[34] Total D-Day casualties calculated in August 1944 amounted to 1,240 including 182 known killed and 501 missing and presumed captured or killed. See 32d MRU Rpt, Analysis of Battle Casualty Reports Received from 101st Airborne Division, 13 Aug 44. FUSA file CC 21, dr 4, item 704.

HEDGEROW COUNTRY. *Aerial view (above) of typical hedgerow terrain in Normandy; and (below) infantry crouching behind the bushes atop hedgerow.*

part of the division's D-Day task was to seize and occupy the line of the Douve River on either side of Carentan, initially to protect the southern flank of VII Corps and later to drive southward through Carentan to weld together the VII and V Corps beachheads.

The 3d Battalion, 506th Parachute Infantry, was to drop south of Vierville, seize two bridges over the Douve at le Port, and establish a bridgehead on the south bank of the river. Its mission came perilously near failure at the outset. The enemy, fully alerted before the drop, not only put up a heavy antiaircraft barrage but illuminated the drop zone by setting fire to an oil-soaked building near by. Paratroopers that landed in the area were greeted by a concentration of machine gun bullets and mortar shells. Others, experiencing delayed drops, came down in or near the swamplands east of the drop zone.

The battalion S–3, Capt. Charles G. Shettle, landing near Angoville-au-Plain, collected two officers and twelve men and then proceeded at once across the flat marshy river plain toward his objective. By the time he reached the bridge at Brevands at 0430 he had picked up a total of thirty-three men, and was there reinforced by twenty more a little later and by another forty during the night of 6–7 June. Shettle's group established themselves first on the southeast bank of the river but could not hold the position in the face of increasing enemy machine gun fire. They therefore withdrew across the river and dug in on the northwest bank. During the day the enemy did not counterattack; in the middle of the night he made only a half-hearted push toward the bridge, from

which he readily backed off when the Americans opened fire. The situation at Brevands on D Day paralleled that on the northern flank where the 502d Parachute Infantry was also holding a tenuous line facing superior enemy forces. Both defenses succeeded chiefly by grace of the enemy's reluctance to leave his prepared positions and attack, and his confusion as to American strength and intentions. It is worth observing, however, that the Carentan canal was the boundary between the *709th* and *352d Divisions*. The latter, located to the south, would not attack across the canal without orders from corps. Corps, in fact, had ordered the reserve unit, the *6th Parachute Regiment*, to make such an attack from the south but it did not at once come into action.[35]

Completion of the 101st Division's defense of the Douve River line west to St. Côme-du-Mont was the task of the 501st Parachute Infantry (Col. Howard R. Johnson) less the 3d Battalion. The regiment's missions in detail were to seize the lock at la Barquette, blow the bridges on the St. Côme-du-Mont–Carentan road, take St. Côme-du-Mont if possible, and destroy the railroad bridge to the west. Of these objectives the lock at la Barquette had a special importance for the planners.

The purpose of the lock was to permit the controlled flow ot the tide up the river channel so as to maintain a depth sufficient for barge navigation as far upstream as St. Sauveur-le Vicomte. If the lock were destroyed the swamplands of the Douve and Merderet would suffer erratic tidal flooding. On the other

---

[35] See below, pp. 293 ff.

hand, partial obstruction of the lock would permit controlled flooding of the same area by backing up the river flow. The latter kind of inundation had been effected by the Germans before D Day. Capture of the lock, it was believed, was tactically important in order that VII Corps might control the Douve and Merderet inundations, which together constituted a barrier to military movement across the whole eastern half of the base of the peninsula. The importance was stressed even though it was recognized that flooding and draining of the area were slow processes and that the natural swamps and flat bottomlands, crisscrossed with drainage ditches, in themselves formed a convincing obstacle to vehicle movement and a grave hindrance to infantry maneuver.

Just before D Day the drop zone for the 501st Parachute Infantry (and the 3d Battalion, 506th) had been shifted about a mile and a half southeast—from the vicinity of Beaumont to east and south of Angoville-au-Plain—in order to bring the paratroopers down nearer their objective and avoid the antiairlanding obstacles which last-minute reconnaissance had discovered on the original drop zone. The change does not seem to have been responsible for the inaccuracy of the drop. The scattering of the 1st Battalion planes resulted from the same conditions of fog and enemy antiaircraft fire which had affected all the other airborne units and was certainly no more serious. What was serious, however, was the loss in the drop of the entire battalion command. The commanding officer was killed; the staff and all the company commanders were missing from the first critical battles.

Colonel Johnson, the regimental commander, by good fortune landed about where he was supposed to and, in the process of moving southward toward la Barquette, managed to collect some 150 men of miscellaneous units with whom he set out to accomplish his mission. The first step went well. Before the enemy had been fully alerted, a portion of the force crossed the lock and dug in on the far side. They seemed relatively secure there as the enemy made no attempt to press in on them. Colonel Johnson therefore decided to try to get the Douve bridges to the west. With fifty men he first went north to Basse Addeville, where he had ascertained that a considerable number of paratroopers had assembled under Maj. Richard J. Allen, the regimental S–3. Although Allen's men were already in contact with the enemy to the north and west, it proved possible to assemble about fifty of them in the early afternoon to return with Colonel Johnson to la Barquette. Met by intense enemy artillery, mortar, and small arms fire, chiefly from the rear, the force called for naval fire support through a naval shore fire control officer who had initially joined Major Allen's unit at Addeville. Salvos from the 8-inch guns of the *Quincy* adjusted on enemy positions around St. Côme-du-Mont caused almost immediate slackening of the enemy fire. At about 1500 Major Allen was ordered to bring the rest of his force to the lock and he joined Colonel Johnson an hour or two later.[36]

---

[36] The account here follows that of Col. S. L. A. Marshall, who interviewed a number of the officers and men, including Colonel Johnson, soon after the action. See Marshall's account in The Fight at the Lock, mimeo MS. Hist Div files. Some doubt has subsequently arisen as to whether Johnson reached

Even with this support, however, it proved impossible to advance westward to the Douve bridges. The *3d Battalion* of the *1058th Regiment* held St. Côme-du-Mont and the surrounding ground in force and strongly resisted with fire every move in that direction. The opposition here in the sector of the *91st Division* and immediately to the south where the *6th Parachute Regiment* held Carentan and the road and rail bridges was much more determined than anywhere in the coastal sector held by the *709th Division*.

The unexpected strength of the enemy in the Carentan–St. Côme-du-Mont area had been discovered by the 2d Battalion, 501st Parachute Infantry (Lt. Col. Robert A. Ballard), shortly before Colonel Johnson tried unsuccessfully to move westward. Colonel Ballard had assembled parts of his lettered companies and his battalion staff between Angoville-au-Plain and les Droueries. Since his assigned mission was the destruction of the Douve bridges above Carentan, he began at once an attack toward St. Côme-du-Mont. The companies, of about thirty men each, ran into strong opposition in the hamlet of les Droueries, which they had attacked frontally in the belief that not more than an enemy platoon faced them. After they were turned back initially, a renewed flanking attack was meeting some success when Colonel Bal-

lard was ordered by Colonel Johnson to move to la Barquette to participate in the drive from that point toward the Carentan highway. The 2d Battalion disengaged but, in attempting to move south through Addeville, was stopped almost immediately by heavy fire from the same enemy force that had opposed the attack on les Droueries. Ballard's men remained during the night in close contact with the enemy. In the meantime, Colonel Johnson, abandoning for the time the attempt to get to the Douve bridges, consolidated the position at la Barquette, deepening the southern bridgehead, pushing out his flanks, and maintaining contact with the 3d Battalion, 506th Parachute Infantry, on the east. Patrols during the night of 6–7 June were sent out to try to find the 506th Regiment and division headquarters, but they did not succeed and the southern line remained isolated and precariously held by groups equivalent to about three companies instead of three battalions as planned.

By the end of D Day the 101st Airborne Division had assembled only about 2,500 of the 6,600 men who had dropped during the early morning hours.[37] They were distributed in mixed units of varying size. But despite the handicaps of scattered landings and heavy losses in both men and equipment the division had carried out the most important of its D-Day tasks. Above all, the paratroopers had succeeded in clearing the way for the move of the seaborne forces inland. This was the task which had been considered so vital to the whole Allied invasion plan as to warrant the extraordinary

---

the lock during the morning *before* he made contact with Major Allen. See Lawrence Critchell, *Four Stars of Hell* (New York, 1947), pp. 52–54. In view of Colonel Johnson's death, the issue cannot be finally settled. The evidence for Critchell's version does not seem conclusive. See Leonard Rapport and Arthur Norwood, Jr., *Rendezvous with Destiny* (Washington, 1948), p. 111. Rapport tried unsuccessfully to resolve the difficulty through extensive correspondence with survivors.

[37] See above, n. 34.

risk of airborne landings in heavily defended enemy territory. If the division's defensive line north and south was weak, that weakness was for the moment balanced by the enemy's failure to organize concerted counterattacks.

The position of the 82d Airborne Division (Maj. Gen. Matthew B. Ridgway) [38] on the west was cause for far greater concern both to General Ridgway and to the Allied command. Landing on the edge of the assembly area of the German *91st Division*, it met more determined opposition in the early stages. It suffered more seriously also from scattered drops which left two of its regiments unable to assemble in sufficient force to carry out their missions.

By the revised plan of 28 May, Ridgway's division was ordered to drop astride the Merderet River, clear the western portion of the beachhead area between the sea and the Merderet and from the Douve River north to Ste. Mère-Eglise, and establish a bridgehead on the west bank of the Merderet. One parachute regiment (the 505th) was to capture Ste. Mère-Eglise, secure crossings of the Merderet near la Fière and Chef-du-Pont, and establish a defensive line north from Neuville-au-Plain to Beuzeville-au-Plain to tie in with the 502d Parachute Infantry of the 101st Airborne Division. The other two regiments (507th and 508th), drop-

ping west of the river, were to consolidate the two 505th bridgeheads and push out a defensive line about three miles westward, anchored on the south at the crossroads just west of Pont l'Abbé and thence extending north in an arc through Beauvais. The 507th Parachute Infantry would defend the line of the Douve, destroying bridges at Pont l'Abbé and Beuzeville-la-Bastille. Both regiments would be prepared to attack west in the direction of St. Sauveur-le Vicomte.

Only one of the 82d Airborne Division's missions was carried out according to plan: the capture of Ste. Mère-Eglise. Success at Ste. Mère-Eglise was due in part to the exceptionally good drop of the 505th Parachute Infantry northwest of the city. (*Map IX*) Most of the regiment's planes, though initially scattered like the others, were able to circle back and release the paratroopers over the drop zone which pathfinders had clearly marked. In addition the regiment had the good fortune to come down in an area devoid of enemy. The 3d Battalion (Lt. Col. Edward C. Krause), which was to take the town of Ste. Mère-Eglise, rapidly assembled about a quarter of its men and moved out in the early morning hours. Counting on speed and surprise, Colonel Krause ordered his men to enter the town without a house-to-house search and to use only knives, bayonets, and grenades while it was still dark so that enemy gunfire could be spotted. The enemy was caught off balance and before dawn the town had fallen—the first prize for American arms in the liberation of France. Resistance had been slight: when Ste. Mère-Eglise was cleared Krause's men counted only ten enemy dead and about thirty prisoners. The battalion cut the main Cher-

---

[38] General Ridgway, a 1917 graduate of the U.S. Military Academy, served with the War Plans Division of the War Department from 1939 to 1942. He then became assistant division commander of the 82d Division at its activation in March 1942 and commander three months later. When that division was reorganized as the 82d Airborne Division he continued to command and led it in the Sicilian and Italian campaigns.

bourg communications cable and established a perimeter defense of the town.

The 2d Battalion, 505th Parachute Infantry (Lt. Col. Benjamin H. Vandervoort), in the meantime had assembled half of its men and was moving northward to establish the regimental defense line through Neuville-au-Plain and Bandienville. (See Map VII.) At 0930 the enemy counterattacked Ste. Mère-Eglise from the south and the regimental commander, Col. William E. Ekman, ordered his 2d Battalion back to aid in the defense. Before turning back Colonel Vandervoort detached a platoon under Lt. Turner B. Turnbull and sent it to organize a defense at Neuville which was reported to be lightly held by the enemy. Turnbull moved through the town without opposition and deployed his men on the high ground north of the town. He was hardly in position before the enemy attacked with a force outnumbering the defenders about five to one. The platoon fought stubbornly and for eight hours held its ground. The small action had a significance which Turnbull did not realize at the time. The fight at Neuville kept the enemy in the north at arm's length while the defenders of Ste. Mère-Eglise beat off the simultaneous enemy attack from the south. The cost of the platoon's gallant stand was heavy. Only sixteen of the forty-two men who had gone to Neuville-au-Plain survived to be withdrawn late in the afternoon to rejoin their battalion.

In Ste. Mère-Eglise the 2d Battalion of the 505th on its arrival at about 1000 took over the northern half of the perimeter defense, permitting the 3d Battalion to strengthen its position on the south. Two companies were held in reserve inside the town. By agreement between the bat-

talion commanders, Colonel Krause took charge of the defense. The first enemy thrust up the Carentan road, made in strength of about two companies supported by some armor, was repulsed. Krause then ordered a counterattack. Company I with eighty men was instructed to move out south, turn east, and hit the flank of the enemy, whose main positions were astride the highway. The attack, however, hit only a single enemy convoy moving southward. Having destroyed the convoy with grenades, Company I returned to Ste. Mère-Eglise. The enemy made no further serious effort during the day to dislodge the Americans.[39]

The prompt occupation of Ste. Mère-Eglise and its defense were a boon for which the 82d Airborne Division had increasing reason to be grateful as the day's actions along the Merderet River developed. The establishment of bridgeheads over the Merderet was the mission of the 1st Battalion of the 505th Parachute Infantry, attacking from the regiment's drop zone east of the river. Ultimate success in this mission, however, depended on the ability of the 507th and 508th Parachute Infantry Regiments to occupy the west bank of the river in force. The 507th and 508th drop zones lay in the triangle at the confluence of the Douve and Merderet Rivers—an area of about twelve square miles—and along the outer perimeter of the VII Corps planned beachhead. Presence of the enemy in the scheduled drop zones prevented the pathfinders from marking them, and the pilots of the two regimental serials, looking in vain for the markers, in most cases delayed

---

[39] For extraordinary heroism in the capture and defense of Ste. Mère-Eglise Colonels Krause and Vandervoort were awarded the DSC.

flashing the jump lights until they had overshot the zones. Both regiments were thus widely dispersed and many paratroopers, heavily laden with equipment, dropped in the swamplands along the river.

Absorbed naturally with the basic problem of assembling, these paratroopers tended to collect along the embankment of the main railroad from Cherbourg to Carentan, both because it was high dry ground and because it was a recognizable terrain feature. By following this embankment south, they crossed the river and arrived in the vicinity of la Fière with the river between them and their objectives. The only large group which, under command of Brig. Gen. James A. Gavin, Assistant Division Commander, tried to push down along the edge of the swamps on the west bank of the river was delayed in starting until dawn by vain efforts to recover equipment from the swamps. With daylight, enemy fire west of the river became intense. Gavin therefore had to give up the attempt and moved his men on down the embankment to join the others west of Ste. Mère-Eglise.[40]

By the middle of the morning 500 to 600 men of miscellaneous units had gathered at la Fière, which was one of the two known crossings of the Merderet in the 82d Airborne Division zone. The la Fière crossing was an exposed narrow causeway raised a few feet above the river flats and extending 400 to 500 yards from the bridge over the main river channel to the gently rising hedgerow country of the west shore.

Two of the first groups on the scene, portions of Company A of the 505th and a group mostly of the 507th Parachute Infantry under Lt. John H. Wisner, had tried to rush the bridge in the early morning but were repulsed by machine gun fire. When General Gavin arrived, he decided to split the la Fière force and sent seventy-five men south to reconnoiter another crossing. Later, receiving word that the bridge at Chef-du-Pont was undefended, he took another seventy-five men himself to try to get across there. The groups remaining at la Fière made ·no progress for several hours. Then General Ridgway, who had landed by parachute with the 505th, ordered Col. Roy Lindquist, the commanding officer of the 508th Parachute Infantry, to organize the miscellaneous groups and take the bridge.[41]

In the meantime west of the river about fifty men of the 2d Battalion, 507th Parachute Infantry, had collected under the battalion commander, Lt. Col. Charles J. Timmes. Shortly after the drop, Timmes had passed through Cauquigny, the tiny village at the west end of the la Fière causeway. But he did not stay. Hearing firing in the direction of Amfreville, he reckoned that paratroopers were attacking the village from the north and decided to support the attack by advance from the east. His estimate proved wrong; the enemy firing was actually directed against his own group. Unable to proceed toward the village Timmes withdrew his men to a

---

[40] General Gavin, a graduate of West Point in 1929, took command of the 505th Parachute Infantry in July 1942 and led that regiment into combat in Sicily a year later. He commanded the same regiment in the parachute landing on Salerno Bay in September 1943 and the following month became assistant division commander.

[41] By the original plan Ridgway was supposed to come in by glider just before dawn, but this was changed a few days before D Day. See Ltr, Ridgway to Maj Gen Harry J. Malony, 12 Nov 48. Hist Div files.

position along the river east of Amfreville and began to dig in. When the position was organized about midmorning, he sent a patrol of ten men back to Cauquigny to establish a fire position to dominate the west end of the la Fière causeway. The patrol set up a machine gun in the Cauquigny church, and awaited developments.[42]

At noon the forces around la Fière gathered for a co-ordinated three-company attack. In two hours one company under Capt. F. V. Schwarzwalder succeeded in carrying the attack across the causeway, and established contact with Timmes' patrol. The way was then open to consolidating the bridgehead and completing one of the most important of the 82d Airborne Division's missions. The initial success, however, was not followed up. Probably because it was difficult in the hedgerow country for any unit to tell quickly what was going on beyond its immediate limited observation, the first crossing by about seventy-five men was not immediately reinforced. Furthermore Schwarzwalder's company, instead of holding on the west bank, decided to proceed on to Amfreville to join the 2d Battalion, 507th Parachute Infantry, to which most of the men belonged. As Schwarzwalder moved out, the enemy began to react to the initial American attack with artillery, small arms fire, and at last a tank sally.[43] It was in the middle of this counterattack that belated American reinforcements arrived on the west bank and were immediately disorganized and

beaten back. The bridge was lost. Colonel Timmes' group east of Amfreville reinforced by Schwarzwalder's company was isolated under heavy and continuing enemy pressure which effectively prevented it for the next two days from any further active attempts at accomplishing the division's mission. The enemy tried to follow up his advantage with attacks across the causeway. These netted him only temporary footholds on the east bank but during the day compelled the Americans to bring back most of the troops sent earlier to probe out crossings of the river to the south.

While the la Fière bridge was won and lost, the attempt to cross at Chef-du-Pont about two miles south had reached a temporary deadlock, as a relatively small number of Germans dug in along the causeway tenaciously resisted all efforts to dislodge them.[44] Late in the afternoon, after most of the paratroopers had been recalled to strengthen the la Fière position, the understrength platoon left at Chef-du-Pont under Capt. Roy E. Creek was threatened with annihilation by an enemy counterattack. Under heavy direct fire from a field piece on the opposite bank and threatened by German infantry forming for attack on the south, Creek's position seemed desperate. At that moment a glider bearing an antitank gun landed fortuitously in the area. With this gun the enemy was held off while about a hundred paratroopers, in response to Creek's plea for reinforcements, came down from la Fière. The reinforcements gave Creek strength enough to beat off

---

[42] See S. L. A. Marshall, La Fière Bridgehead, mimeo MS. Hist Div files. The account in Ruppenthal, *Utah Beach*, p. 38, differs slightly.

[43] Undoubtedly units of the *100th Panzer Replacement Battalion* equipped with light Russian and French tanks.

[44] Their tenacity may in part have been caused by the shooting on two occasions of enemy soldiers who stood up apparently with the idea of surrendering. See Marshall, La Fière Bridgehead.

the Germans, clear the east bank, and finally cross the river and dig in. This position, however, did not amount to a bridgehead and Creek's tenuous hold on the west end of the causeway would have meant little but for the action of the 508th Parachute Infantry west of the river.

Elements of the 508th, amounting to about two companies of men under command of Lt. Col. Thomas J. B. Shanley, commanding officer of the 2d Battalion, were the most important of at least four groups of paratroopers who assembled west of the Merderet but who for the most part, being forced to fight for survival, could contribute little toward carrying out planned missions. Dropped near Picauville, Colonel Shanley gathered a small force of paratroopers—too small to proceed with his mission of destroying the Douve bridge at Pont l'Abbé. He tried during the day to join other groups in the vicinity with whom he had radio contact, but under constant enemy pressure he was unable to effect a junction until late in the day. It had then become apparent to him that he was engaged with an enemy force of at least battalion strength, and he decided to withdraw to the battalion assembly area on Hill 30. In fact, the Germans, elements of the *1057th Regiment,* had been pushing eastward in this area most of the day under orders to counterattack in order to wipe out American parachutists west of the Merderet. Colonel Shanley's resistance undoubtedly helped save the forces at la Fière and Chef-du-Pont. Once he was firmly established on Hill 30, he formed a valuable outpost against continuing German attacks and a few days later would be in position to contribute substantially to establishing the Merderet bridgehead. For Colonel

Shanley's success three enlisted men have received a large share of the credit. They were Cpl. Ernest T. Roberts, Pvt. Otto K. Zwingman, and Pvt. John A. Lockwood who, while on outpost duty in buildings at Haut Gueutteville, observed the forming of a German counterattack by an estimated battalion of infantry with tank support. They stayed at their posts holding off the enemy attack for two hours and allowing the main body of Shanley's force to establish an all-around defense at Hill 30.[45]

As reports of the airborne landings came in to the German *Seventh Army* headquarters and the extent of the landings became apparent, General Dollmann ordered a series of moves designed to seal off the airhead and destroy it. (*Map 2*) The *709th Division* with the *1058th Regiment* (*91st Division*) attached was ordered to clear the area east of the Merderet.[46] At the same time the *91st Division* counterattacked from the west using the *1057th Regiment* and the *100th Panzer Replacement Battalion* in an attempt to wipe out paratroopers who had landed west of the inundated area. The *6th Parachute Regiment* under control of the *91st Division* was to attack through Carentan from the south.[47] Finally at the end of the

---

[45] All three were captured. Pvt Zwingman was killed in December 1944 while still a prisoner. The three men were awarded DSC's.

[46] *Seventh Army KTB 1.I.–30.VI.44,* 6 Jun 44. Schlieben denies that the *1058th Regiment* was attached to his division and in fact the regiment's action on D Day does not seem to have been directed at first by the *709th Division.* MS # B–845 (Schlieben).

[47] Again the subordination ordered by *Seventh Army* was apparently not effected. Von der Heydte directed the operations of his regiment without any orders from the *91st Division.* MS # B–839 (von der Heydte).

MERDERET RIVER CROSSING *at Chef-du-Pont. Village of les Merieux is in lower right-hand corner of picture.*

MAP 2

GERMAN COUNTERATTACK IN THE COTENTIN.   *Reproduction of a cap-tured OB WEST map dated 6–7 June 1944.*

day the *Seventh Army Sturm Battalion* was ordered to move against the American bridgehead from the vicinity of Cherbourg, attacking in the direction of Ste. Mère-Eglise. A regiment of the *243d Division* was ordered to move by night to Montebourg.[48] By means of these moves and concentric counterattacks Dollmann was sure at first that he could cope with the Cotentin landings without moving in any additional forces. It was only in the evening that his optimism waned, as the *91st Division* reported that its counterattack was making very slow progress because of the difficulties of maneuvering in the hedgerow country. In fact the attack had scarcely materialized at all except in local actions along the Merderet.

Similarly the *1058th Regiment,* apparently harassed by scattered American paratroopers, could not get moving in its attack toward Ste. Mère-Eglise. By evening its advance elements were still north of Neuville-au-Plain. Generalleutnant Karl-Wilhelm von Schlieben, commander of the *709th Division,* ordered it to resume the attack on Ste. Mère-Eglise the next morning. He attached to it two motorized heavy artillery battalions, the *456th* and *457th* (each with two 150-mm. guns and a battery of Russian 122-mm. guns), and the company of self-propelled guns of the *709th Antitank Battalion.*[49]

For the general sluggishness of German reaction in the Cotentin, there seem to be several explanations. In the first place two of the three division commanders, von Schlieben and Generalleutnant Wilhelm

Falley (of the *91st Division*), together with some of the subordinate commanders, were at Rennes attending a war game when the invasion struck. Schlieben did not get back to his headquarters near Valognes until noon. Falley on his return was killed by paratroopers. To the uncertainty caused by the commanders' absence was added the confusion of disrupted communications. Von Schlieben, for instance, during the day had no contact with two of his battalions in the thick of the fighting, the *1st Battalion, 919th Regiment,* in the UTAH Beach area, and the *795th Georgian Battalion* near Turqueville. In attempting counterattacks against scattered U.S. riflemen the Germans experienced the same difficulties with the hedgerow country that the Americans did. Finally the *LXXXIV Corps* headquarters, far away in St. Lô, could not exercise effective control and co-ordinate the action of the three divisions in the peninsula. On the other hand communications were not set up to enable the division commanders to effect their own co-ordination.[50]

The experience of the *6th Parachute Regiment* illustrates in striking fashion the confusion and lack of co-ordination in the initial German reactions and throws a strange half-light on the D-Day battles in the Cotentin. The commander of the regiment, Major Friedrich-August Freiherr von der Heydte, was at his command post north of Périers when the Allied landings began. But telephone lines to the *91st Division* and to *LXXXIV Corps* were broken during the night by open action of the French Resistance. It was not until about 0600 that von der

---

[48] The regiment, nominally the *922d,* contained a battalion of the *922d,* a battalion of the *920th,* and the division's *Engineer Battalion.* MS # B–845 (Schlieben).

[49] MS # B–845 (Schlieben); MS # B–260 (Triepel).

[50] MS # B–845 (Schlieben).

Heydte was able to reach General Marcks at *LXXXIV Corps* headquarters by a private line and get his orders, which were to attack with his regiment through Carentan and clean out the rear area of the *709th Division* between Carentan and Ste. Mère-Eglise. Von der Heydte arrived in Carentan in the morning and found no Allied troops and very few Germans. He got in touch with his battalions and ordered them to assemble southwest of Carentan. He then climbed the church steeple in St. Côme and looked around. The picture before him was, he said, overwhelming. He could see the Channel and the armada of Allied ships, covering the water to the horizon. He could see hundreds of small landing craft plying to the shore unloading men and tanks and equipment. Yet, for all that, he got no impression of a great battle in progress. It was then about noon. The sun was shining. Except for a few rifle shots now and then it was singularly quiet. He could see no Allied troops. The whole scene reminded him of a summer's day on the Wannsee.[51]

It was apparently his impression that no seaborne U.S. troops had come inland in the direction of St. Côme. In accordance with that impression he made his dispositions. He ordered his battalions to come up to St. Côme; the *2d Battalion* was then instructed to proceed to Ste. Mère-Eglise and attack and destroy any enemy encountered. The *1st Battalion* was to move to the high ground near Ste. Marie-du-Mont and protect the regiment from any enemy thrusts inland from the

sea. The *3d Battalion* was to return to Carentan to provide the regiment with a defense in depth, and the attached *3d Battalion, 1058th Regiment*, was to remain with von der Heydte in St. Côme-du-Mont. The *1st* and *2d Battalions* moved out at about 1900. By midnight the *1st Battalion* had marched apparently without serious trouble through the territory occupied by the 101st Airborne Division and reached the vicinity of Ste. Marie-du-Mont. The *2d Battalion* moved north and possibly reached the vicinity of Fauville. Both battalions sent a number of American prisoners back to the regimental headquarters.

During the night the landing of U.S. glider reinforcements impressed von der Heydte as new large-scale airborne landings. They cut off the *2d Battalion* from the regiment and from the *1st Battalion*. (In reality, both battalions were already cut off by the advance of the 8th Infantry inland, but this development was apparently unknown to von der Heydte.) He ordered the battalions to maintain contact with each other and pull back to form a crescent defense of St. Côme. Only the *2d Battalion* acknowledged receipt of the order and reported that it was not in touch with the *1st Battalion*. As for the *1st Battalion*, it set out on the morning of 7 June to rejoin the regiment, moving south toward Carentan. It never got there, for at the Douve River it ran into the 101st Airborne Division units and surrendered almost to a man.[52]

The experience of the *6th Parachute Regiment* was typical of the inability of the German forces to concentrate against the landings, even when, as in the case of

---

[51] This paragraph and the following two are from von der Heydte's report, MS # B–839. The Wannsee is a lake near Berlin, a favorite place for Berliners to spend a Sunday.

[52] See below, Ch. IX.

CROSSING THE CHANNEL. *Columns of LCI (L)'s (above) heading for the French coast, and troops on deck of LCI (L) (below) on D-Day morning.*

the 82d Airborne Division, they were scattered and relatively weak. Thanks to this failure, the 82d was able to maintain itself while it gradually built back its strength. At the end of D Day, the division was strongly ensconced in the vicinity of Ste. Mère-Eglise but was precariously situated outside the main VII Corps beachhead. It had no contact with the 101st Airborne or 4th Infantry Divisions. It had assembled only a fraction of its own men. Planned seaborne reinforcements had not arrived. The bulk of the glider reinforcements (the 325th Glider Infantry) were not due until the next morning. At the end of the day, the division reported that it controlled only 40 percent of its combat infantry and 10 percent of its artillery.[53] The first estimate sent on to VII Corps indicated total casualties of about four thousand.[54] The bulk of these, however, were the missing paratroopers scattered far and wide in enemy territory. Revised calculations in August 1944 showed D-Day losses of 1,259 including 156 known killed and 756 missing, presumed captured or killed.[55]

Hitting the Beaches

While U.S. airborne troops dropped on the Cotentin and British paratroopers landed near Caen, the invasion fleet was bringing the main body of the Allied armies to the shores of Normandy. The assault convoys, after turning back for the day's postponement, reassembled during the morning of 5 June and sailed again for the transport areas 22,000 to 23,000 yards off the French coast in the Bay of the Seine. Behind mine sweepers which cleared and marked ten lanes through old enemy mine fields in the Channel, the huge convoys, under constant air umbrella of fighter squadrons flying at 3,000 to 5,000 feet, made an uneventful voyage unmolested by the enemy either by air or sea.[56] H Hour for U. S. beaches was 0630.

The weather was still cause for concern. During the passage a gusty wind blowing from the west at fifteen to twenty knots produced a moderately choppy sea with waves in mid-Channel of from five to six feet in height. This was a heavy sea for the small craft, which had some difficulty in making way. Even in the assault area it was rough for shallow-draft vessels, though there the wind did not exceed fifteen knots and the waves averaged about three feet. Visibility was eight miles with ceiling at 10,000 to 12,000 feet. Scattered clouds from 3,000 to 7,000 feet covered about half the sky over the Channel at H Hour becoming denser farther inland. Conditions in short were difficult though tolerable for both naval and air forces.[57]

Most serious were the limitations on air operations. Heavy bombers assigned to hit the coastal fortifications at OMAHA Beach had to bomb by instruments through the overcast. With concurrence of General Eisenhower the Eighth Air Force ordered a deliberate delay of several seconds in its release of bombs in order to insure that they were not dropped among the assault craft. The result was that the 13,000

---

[53] 82d Div AAR. At noon, 8 June, the division reported still only 2,100 effectives—or less than a third of its combat strength.

[54] See Phantom Intercept in 21 A Gp Sitrep 4. SHAEF G–1 file 704/6, 21 A Gp Casualty Rpts, Vol. I.

[55] 32d MRU Rpt, Analysis of Battle Casualty Reports received from 82d Airborne Division, 13 Aug 44. FUSA file CC 21, dr 4, item 704.

[56] ANCXF *Report*, Vol. III, Annex D, p. 44.

[57] Prov Eng Spec Brig AAR.

bombs dropped by 329 B–24 bombers did not hit the enemy beach and coast defenses at all but were scattered as far as three miles inland. Medium bombers visually bombing UTAH Beach defenses from a lower altitude had slightly better results, although about a third of all bombs fell seaward of the high-water mark and many of the selected targets were not located by pilots. Of 360 bombers dispatched by IX Bomber Command, 293 attacked UTAH Beach defenses and 67 failed to release their bombs because of the overcast. On the whole the bombing achieved little in neutralizing the coastal fortifications.

At about 0230 the *Bayfield*, headquarters ship for Task Force U (Rear Adm. Don P. Moon) and VII Corps (Maj. Gen. J. Lawton Collins), dropped anchor in the transport area off UTAH Beach. Twenty minutes later the *Ancon*, flagship of Admiral Hall and headquarters ship for Task Force O and V Corps, reached the OMAHA Beach transport area. Unloading of assault troops into the LCVP's that would take them to the beaches began.

Up to this point there had been virtually no enemy reaction. The German radar stations still in operation had failed to pick up either the air or the sea approach. Because of bad weather Admiral Krancke had no patrol boats in the Channel during the night, nor did he order them out after he heard of the airborne landings. Tidal conditions would not permit them to leave the harbors before daylight and, besides, Krancke was still not sure that a major attack was in progress. Shortly after three o'clock, however, *Naval Commander Normandy* reported sighting ten large craft lying some seven miles off the coast north of Port-en-Bes-

sin. This news, in conjunction with an increasingly sharp definition of the extent of the airborne landings, at last convinced Admiral Krancke that he was confronting a large-scale landing. He gave such orders as he could. The *Western Defense Forces* were to patrol the coastal waters; the *Landwirt* submarines were to be alerted; the *8th Destroyer Flotilla* was to move up from Royan to Brest; the *5th Torpedo Boat Flotilla* was to reconnoiter the Orne estuary area; and the *9th Torpedo Boat Flotilla* was to patrol off Cap de la Hague. The torpedo boats of the *5th Flotilla* left Le Havre at 0430, but an hour out of port they met six Allied warships escorted by 15 to 20 destroyers. After firing torpedoes at the Allied vessels, the small German boats were attacked from the air. They succeeded in driving off the attackers with antiaircraft fire, but then had to return to Le Havre to replenish their load of torpedoes and ammunition. Two torpedo boat flotillas reconnoitering out of Cherbourg were forced by heavy seas to return to port at dawn. This virtually concluded German naval activity for the day. Admiral Krancke wrote in his diary: "It was only to be expected that no effective blow could be struck at such a superior enemy force." [58] He made plans, however, to attack the Allied fleet that night.

German coastal batteries began sporadic firing at 0535, or only fifteen minutes before Allied naval bombardment opened prearranged counterbattery fire. Projectiles from Allied battleships and cruisers and destroyers continued to thunder over the heads of the troops making the final run-in to shore until a few minutes before the touchdown. Beach drench-

---

[58] *Marinegruppenkommando West, KTB 1.–7.VI.-44*, 6 Jun 44.

ing was then taken up by the close-support craft. Although the time schedule went generally according to plan on both American beaches, the volume of fire laid down on vital targets was considerably less at OMAHA than expected. Most enemy coastal defenses were sited to cover the beaches rather than the sea approaches. They were therefore well concealed from observation from the sea and were correspondingly difficult to hit. The beach drenching seems generally to have missed its targets; a large percentage of the rockets overshot their marks.[59]

Naval gunfire coupled with the air bombardment, however, had one important effect at OMAHA Beach which was not at first apparent to the assaulting troops. The Germans credit the Allied bombardment with having detonated large mine field areas on which they counted heavily to bar the attackers from penetrating inland between the infantry strong points. Preparatory fire seems also to have knocked out many of the defending rocket pits. But it was supporting naval gunfire after H Hour which made the substantial contribution to the battle, in neutralizing key strong points, breaking up counterattacks, wearing down the defenders, and dominating the assault area.

In the VII Corps zone the 4th Division (Maj. Gen. Raymond O. Barton)[60] planned to land in column of regiments on a two-battalion front of about 2,200

yards. The 8th Infantry (Col. James A. Van Fleet), with the 3d Battalion of the 22d Infantry attached, would make the initial assault. It would first occupy the high ground along the road between Ste. Marie-du-Mont and les Forges and would be prepared to move with the bulk of its force thereafter westward across the Merderet River in the zone of the 82d Airborne Division. One battalion would be left in the area west of St. Martin to protect the division's north flank until the arrival of the 22d Infantry. The 22d Infantry (Col. Hervey A. Tribolet), next infantry unit to land, beginning at H plus 85 minutes, would turn north from the beaches to seize the causeway across the inundations at les Dunes de Varreville. Continuing the push northwest, the regiment would capture Quinéville and occupy the high ground at Quinéville and Fontenay-sur-Mer. In the center of the beachhead the 12th Infantry (Col. Russell P. Reeder), landing after H plus 4 hours, would advance with two battalions abreast to seize the high ground between Emondeville and the Merderet River. One battalion of the regiment was at first designated as division reserve to pass to division control in the vicinity of Turqueville. By the late May change of plan, following the alteration of the airborne missions, the battalion was instead released to regimental control and the 12th Infantry was assigned the additional mission of seizing a crossing over the Merderet at le Port Brehay just southwest of the regiment's main objective area. One regiment (the 359th Infantry) of the 90th Division, the first follow-up division, was attached to the 4th Division to begin landing on D Day.[61] It would assemble in re-

---

[59] Notes by Col B. B. Talley, Asst CofS, V Corps. Hist Div files. Talley also says the rocket-carrying LST's did not come up on line and consequently did not fire their rockets simultaneously as planned.

[60] General Barton had been chief of staff at headquarters of the 4th Division in 1940. In June 1942 he took command of the 4th Motorized Division, which subsequently became the 4th Infantry Division, and in January of 1944 arrived with his unit in the European theater.

[61] 4th Div FO 1, 12 May 44.

TROOPS ON UTAH BEACH. *The troops wading ashore (above) were photographed shortly after H Hour. Note DD tanks on beach. Soldiers (below) take shelter behind sea wall while awaiting orders to move inland.*

serve near Foucarville. In May, enemy activity was observed on the St. Marcouf Islands flanking UTAH Beach on the north. It was therefore decided to land detachments of the 4th and 24th Cavalry Squadrons two hours before H Hour to clean out what was suspected to be an enemy observation post or mine field control point.

The airborne troops had done their job well and the 4th Division therefore had little difficulty getting ashore. The cavalry detachments (132 men) found the St. Marcouf Islands unoccupied though heavily mined. From mines and a concentration of enemy artillery that hit the islands in the afternoon the cavalry units lost two men killed and seventeen wounded.[62] The small craft (LCVP's) carrying the first waves of the 1st and 2d Battalions of the 8th Infantry were launched in relatively sheltered water and had no serious trouble with the wind and surf. At H Hour there was no enemy opposition. The thirty-two DD tanks supposed to land in the first wave were delayed by the loss of a control vessel that struck a mine. All but four, which were lost when the LCT carrying them hit a mine, were beached approximately fifteen minutes late. But, as it turned out, the assault troops had no immediate need for them.

Leading elements of the two assault battalions touched down approximately on time but almost 2,000 yards south of where they were supposed to land. The error was probably caused in part by the obscuring of landmarks by smoke and dust raised by the naval bombardment and in part by the southeast coastal cur-

rent. In any case it turned out to be fortunate since it brought troops in on beaches much less heavily defended than those designated in the plan. Although the mislanding meant that the tasks assigned to each assault section could not be carried out as planned, the lack of serious enemy opposition permitted reconnaissance and speedy reorganization for improvised maneuver.[63] After company-size task forces had reduced the very lightly defended field fortifications covering the two middle beach exits, both assault battalions began their advance across the flooded area. The 1st crossed toward Audouville-la-Hubert; the 2d turned south to pick up the Pouppeville road. (*Map 3*)

The first infantry wave was followed by engineer and naval demolition parties to clear the underwater obstacles. The obstacles were all dealt with dryshod and were so much sparser than expected that the original plan of blowing fifty-foot gaps was abandoned in favor of clearing the entire beach on the first tide. The job was completed in an hour. Engineers then proceeded to their next tasks of blowing gaps in the sea wall behind the beach and clearing mine fields. Enemy opposition consisted only of intermittent shelling.

While engineers worked on the beach, the 3d Battalion, 8th Infantry, supported by tanks of the 70th Tank Battalion, and the 3d Battalion, 22d Infantry, were landing and moving out. Well before H plus 3 hours the beach area had been cleared and landings were virtually routine, harassed only by sporadic enemy artillery fire.

---

[62] 4th Cav Gp AAR.

[63] Brig. Gen. Theodore Roosevelt, assistant division commander, who went ashore with the first wave and helped organize the attack inland, was awarded the Medal of Honor for gallantry displayed in his leadership under fire.

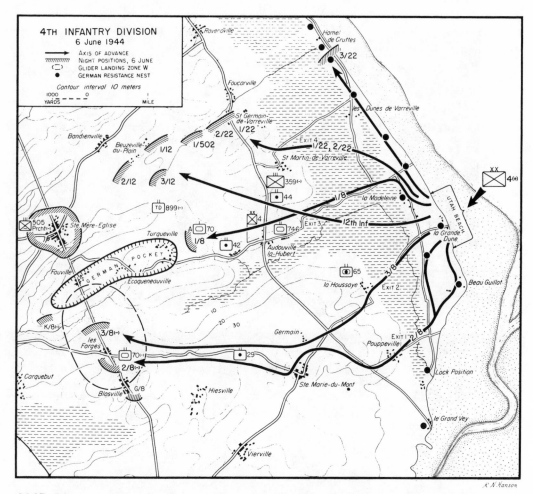

MAP 3

Early success and extraordinarily light casualties on UTAH Beach contrasted sharply with the difficulties experienced during those first critical three hours at OMAHA. The German *LXXXIV Corps* and *Seventh Army* believed through most of D Day that the OMAHA assault had been stopped at the water's edge. It was late in the morning before General Bradley aboard the *Augusta* could have contra-

dicted that view and much longer before the Allied command could feel secure about the V Corps beachhead.[64]

Leading the attack of General Gerow's V Corps was the 1st Division (Maj. Gen. Clarence R. Huebner) assaulting with two regiments abreast, the 116th Infantry (attached from the 29th Division) on the

---

[64] First Army G–3 Jnl.

AERIAL VIEW OF UTAH BEACH ON D-DAY MORNING.

right, the 16th Infantry on the left.[65] Each regiment was to land two battalion landing teams at H Hour with initial missions to clear the beach defenses and seize and secure that portion of the beachhead maintenance line in their respective zones. (*Map X*) The beachhead maintenance line roughly followed the ridge of high ground parallel to the main coastal road and was in most places from two to three miles inland. From this line the assault regiments, supported by the 18th Infantry landing after H plus 3 hours and the 26th Infantry landing on order of the Commanding General, V Corps, would punch out toward the D-Day phase line. Occupation of that phase line would mean securing a coastal strip five or six miles deep astride the Bayeux highway.

The 116th Infantry was responsible for capturing the Pointe du Hoe coastal battery. On the assumption that the six partially casemated 155-mm. guns would not have been destroyed by pre-D-Day bom-

bardment and the heavy naval fire directed on them just before H Hour, two Ranger battalions were attached to the 116th Infantry with the special H-Hour mission of taking out the guns. Three companies of Rangers from the 2d Ranger Battalion were to land at the foot of the cliff which the fortified battery surmounted, scale the cliff by means of rope ladders, and attack the German position. Another company, landing on the 116th Infantry main beaches to the east, would attack the fortifications at Pointe et Raz de la Percée and then continue westward to cover the flank of the Ranger force at Pointe du Hoe. The rest of the Rangers would land at Pointe du Hoe, provided the initial landings succeeded; otherwise they would come in on the 116th beaches and assist the right battalion of the 116th in attacking westward.

The whole right flank of the V Corps assault forces would thus swing due west almost immediately on landing while the left battalion of the 116th and the 16th Infantry pushed south. It was hoped to clear the coast as far as Isigny by the end of D Day. It even seemed possible that Isigny itself might fall either to the 116th or to the 115th Infantry.[66] The latter regiment, landing on corps order, would initially leapfrog the 116th to organize the high ground around Longueville.

Perhaps the most important job assigned to the first assault waves was the reduction of enemy positions defending the roads leading from the beach inland. The gently sloping sand of OMAHA Beach was backed by an embankment of loose stones, or shingle, in places as much as fifteen yards wide. In the Vierville sector the

---

[65] Maj. Gen. Leonard T. Gerow was graduated from the Virginia Military Institute in 1911. Between 1920 and 1940 he was on four separate occasions assigned to War Department staff duty: in the War Plans and Organization Section (1923–24), in the office of the Assistant Secretary of War (1926–29), in the War Plans Division (1935–39), and as Assistant Chief of Staff with duty in the War Plans Division (1940–41). He commanded the 29th Division in 1942 and took command of V Corps in July 1943.

General Huebner enlisted in 1910 and was commissioned in the infantry in 1916. He went overseas as commander of a company of the 28th Infantry in 1917 and served with the 1st Division at Lunéville, Beaumont, Cantigny, and in the Aisne–Marne, St. Mihiel and Meuse–Argonne offensives. He was twice wounded and received the DSC with cluster, the DSM, and Silver Star. In 1940 he was chief of the Training Branch of the Operations and Training Division of the War Department and in 1942 Director of the Training Division, Headquarters SOS. In August 1943 he took command of the 1st Division in North Africa.

[66] See above, p. 187.

shingle piled up against a part-masonry, part-wood sea wall. On the rest of the beach there was no wall, but the shingle lay against a sand embankment or dune line. Both the shingle and the dune line were impassable for vehicles. Behind the beach rose scrub-covered bluffs 100 to 170 feet high of varying steepness and merging east and west with the cliffs, which at Pointe et Raz de la Percée and east of Colleville marked the extremities of the 7,000-yard crescent beach. The bluffs were cut by five draws. Through four of these ran unimproved roads, one connecting with the main coastal highway at Vierville-sur-Mer, two at St. Laurent, and one at Colleville.[67] The fifth draw northeast of Colleville was steep and contained only a trail, but it was considered capable of development as a vehicle exit. The plan assumed these exits would be open to traffic at least by H plus 2 hours when the heavy flow of vehicular reinforcements was scheduled to begin. The importance of the beach exits was, of course, as obvious to the Germans as to the Allies and local coastal defenses were grouped to deny their use to the attackers.[68] On the

other hand, the 1st Division had precise information on the location of these defenses and every provision was made to give the assaulting infantry the heavy fire support needed to knock them out. (*Map XI*)

At H minus 50 minutes, two companies of DD tanks (741st Tank Battalion) destined for the 16th Infantry beaches were launched 6,000 yards offshore and almost immediately began to founder. Of the thirty-two tanks launched only five reached shore.[69] These were the first of the casualties to the weather. There were others. The assaulting infantry was transferred from transports to LCVP's ten to eleven miles offshore. At least ten of the ferrying craft were swamped on the way in. More serious for the operation was the sinking of much of the artillery. The attempt to ferry guns ashore in DUKW's through the heavy seas proved disastrous. All but one of the 105-mm. howitzers of the 111th Field Artillery Battalion were

---

[67] The road that passes through les Moulins will be called hereafter the les Moulins Exit. The St. Laurent Exit will refer to the road immediately east which leads up the valley of the Ruguet River. Note that the towns of Vierville, St. Laurent, and Colleville in this sector all bear the suffixes "sur-Mer." Only in the case of Vierville will the suffix be retained in order not to confuse it with the other Vierville in the UTAH Beach sector.

[68] German coastal defense works were of four classes depending on size and complexity. The smallest and most usual was the resistance nest (*Widerstandsnest*), a single self-contained defensive position manned by one or two squads sometimes though not necessarily with heavy weapons. When several resistance nests were combined for co-ordinated defense of a larger sector the defense was called a strong point (*Stuetzpunkt*). Strong points in general were manned by at least a platoon of infantry with

heavy weapons and a local reserve. Strong points might be grouped in a *Stuetzpunktgruppe* either for command unity or for defense of a small fortified area. None of these strong point groups existed in the invasion area. Finally, certain strategically important places like ports, submarine pens, and mouths of large rivers were organized into defensive areas (*Verteidigungsbereiche*) garrisoned by units whose size was conditioned by the size and importance of the area and the forces available. All had both local reserves within the defensive area and reserves in general support stationed outside. See *Grundlegender Befehl des Oberbefehlshabers West Nr. 7, Begriffsbestimmungen in der Kuestenverteidigung,* 28 May 42. OKW/WFSt, Op. (H.), *Grundlegende Befehle West 28.IV.42–7.V.44.*

[69] Three of the five were beached by an LCT which could not lower its ramp at sea. For details of the difficulties in the initial landings at OMAHA see [Charles H. Taylor] *Omaha Beachhead* (Washington, 1945). The narrative of U.S. V Corps operations is largely based on Taylor's study. See Bibliographical Note.

AERIAL VIEW OF OMAHA BEACH ON D PLUS 1.
Note the five draws leading up from the beach.

TERRAIN ON OMAHA BEACH. *Bluffs west of Vierville Draw (top). In distance is Pointe et Raz de la Percée. Concrete casemate in bluff is sited to cover beach. Hamel au Prêtre (center) as seen from Vierville Draw. Les Moulins area (bottom) as seen from the east.*

sunk. Six of the 105's belonging to the 7th Field Artillery Battalion suffered the same fate. Five of the six howitzers of the 16th Infantry Cannon Company were also swamped. In addition to these wholesale losses the 58th Armored Field Artillery Battalion, whose guns were mounted on LCT's and had taken part in the initial beach drenching, lost three of its pieces when the craft carrying them hit mines. In short, the artillery that was planned to support the infantry attack particularly in the advance inland did not reach the shore.

The weather contributed also to navigational difficulties. Mist mixed with the smoke and dust raised by the naval bombardment obscured landmarks on the coast; in addition a lateral current of from two to three knots tended to carry craft eastward of their touchdown points. The actual errors in landing caused thereby were considerably less than at UTAH, in most cases amounting to not more than a few hundred yards. On the other hand, they proved much more serious for the tactical situation, partly because the errors were not constant, with the result that units became scattered on the final approach. Since the men had been briefed only for their particular areas, they were confused by the changed picture. The difficulties were compounded by the heavier enemy opposition which had the effect of isolating boat sections only a few hundred yards apart and at first made reassembly and reorganization for improvised missions almost impossible.

Naval gunfire had temporarily neutralized some of the enemy batteries and fortifications but most of them were still able to fire at the incoming troops as soon as the bombardment was forced to lift in-

land. The 1st Division men in the first LCVP's could hear machine gun bullets splatter against the steel ramps of their craft before they grounded. Debarking in water sometimes up to their necks, the troops on some sectors of the beach were met with a hail of bullets that drove some to seek shelter under the surf, others to scramble over the sides of the craft. Control of boat sections was thus often lost before the men were even started in to the beach. The troops, overladen with heavy clothing and equipment, waded slowly through the surf and through fire that increased as they approached the beach. Some stopped to rest or seek shelter behind obstacles. Some lay at the water's edge and were able eventually to crawl in with the tide. But casualties generally were heavier among those who delayed in getting up onto the beach. Many of the wounded were drowned in the rising tide.

The first wave should have landed nine companies evenly spaced along the beach. Because of withering enemy fire and mislandings, however, the right wing all but disintegrated; two companies bunched in front of les Moulins, and the remainder of the landings (elements of four companies) clustered in the Colleville sector. One company was carried so far to the east that it landed an hour and a half late.

The two right-flank companies (Company C of the 2d Ranger Battalion, and Company A of the 116th Infantry) landed as scheduled in front of the Vierville draw. One craft foundered and one was hit four times by mortar fire. Men from the remaining craft struggled to shore. Intense small arms fire took toll of about two-thirds of Company A and more than half of the Ranger company before any reached the comparative shelter of the sea

ASSAULT LANDINGS, OMAHA BEACH. *LCVP's unloading infantry in the surf (above), and (below) men of the 1st Division, loaded with equipment, heading for the shore.*

wall or the base of the cliff. Of the six-teen tanks scheduled to land in this sector just ahead of the infantry, only eight survived enemy artillery to reach the shore. All had been brought in on LCT's as 116th Infantry officers decided the sea was too rough to launch the DD's.

In the eastern part of the 116th Infantry zone the initial landings had not gone much better. A 1,000-yard gap separated the troops who touched down there from the remnants of the two companies on the right. The two companies of tanks that landed first were brought in on LCT's without losses. This initial success was not shared by the infantry. Only two of the three companies of the 2d Battalion, 116th Infantry, landed within the regimental zone. One of these companies lost a quarter of its men to enemy fire during the forty-five minutes which it took them to cross the beach to the protection of the shingle bank. The remainder had better luck in landing in front and just west of les Moulins where the bluff was obscured by smoke fires and enemy fire was sporadic and inaccurate. Even these men were somewhat disorganized and the officers who survived with them were confused by the knowledge that they had landed east of their designated beaches.

The experience of the 16th Infantry on the left flank of the division duplicated that of the 116th, as scattered landings and heavy casualties left the first boat sections incapable of undertaking their primary assault missions. In the 16th's zone, however, one soft spot was discovered. Four boat sections of the 2d Battalion, 16th Infantry, landing between the St. Laurent and Colleville exits, crossed the beach with only two casualties from enemy fire. The local defense of this sector

of the beach was the Colleville strong point, which was planned as three mutually supporting resistance nests. Of these the field fortified position atop the bluff midway between the two draws was unoccupied in February 1944 and seemingly remained unoccupied on D Day.[70] Apparent German negligence that left the beach northwest of Colleville without immediate defense was balanced at first by Allied ill fortune in landing so few men there. Except for those four boat sections of the 2d Battalion the first wave of the 16th Infantry (Companies E and F) touched down immediately in front, or east, of the occupied fortifications of the Colleville strong point and was there caught in machine gun fire as intense as that which decimated the 116th Infantry. Many of the men of Company E, hard hit and exhausted in their efforts to wade ashore, flopped on the sand and crawled in ahead of the tide; nearly half of them did not survive. Because of the swamping of most of the DD tanks and immediate enemy destruction of five of the company of mediums beached from LCT's, the 16th Infantry had initially only a third of the planned armor support. Those tanks available went into action on the beach between the St. Laurent and Colleville exits.

The heavy losses and disorganization of the first wave had repercussions on each succeeding wave through the morning of D Day. The first serious effect of the failure to neutralize enemy beach defenses was the inability of the 6th Special Engineer Brigade and naval demolition parties to blow gaps in the beach obstacles as

[70] Ltr, *OB WEST*, O.Qu. to *OKH/Generalquartiermeister*, 4 Feb 44. *OKH/Generalquartiermeister, Stuetzpunktbevorratung an der Atlantik- und Kanalkueste.*

FIRST AID ON THE BEACH. *Soldiers of the 16th Infantry (above) being treated for injuries, and wounded soldier (below) receiving plasma.*

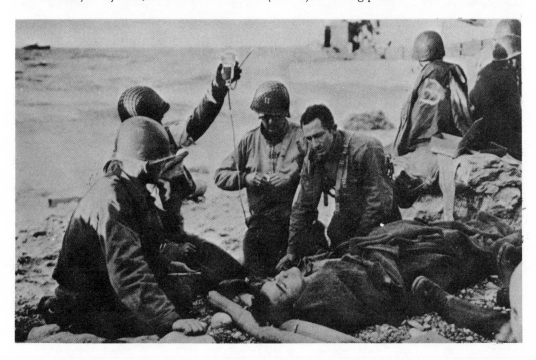

planned. Weather conditions also played a hand in hindering the engineers from accomplishing their mission. Half the demolition teams were delayed in landing and only a third of them touched down on their appointed sectors. Since the rest were carried eastward by the coastal current, the 116th Infantry zone received substantially less than the scheduled effort. But enemy fire also took a heavy toll of both men and equipment. Of sixteen bulldozers only three could be put into operation on the beach, and one of these was prevented from maneuvering freely by riflemen who sheltered behind it. So many of the marking buoys and poles were lost that only one of the six gaps blown by 0700 could be marked. Casualties to the engineers amounted to about 40 percent for the day and were certainly very much higher for the first groups ashore. In half an hour after H Hour the tide, rising at the rate of about four feet an hour, had covered the obstacles to an extent that made further clearance impossible;[71] remnants of the engineers joined the infantry behind the shingle to wait for the next tide. Fifteen officers and men of the demolition parties from private to colonel were awarded the Distinguished Service Cross for carrying out their missions under incredible difficulties: a colonel had his craft come close to shore and directed it under heavy fire up and down along the beach so that he could observe what had to be done, then came ashore, issued new orders to expedite the clearance, and supervised the work under fire; a lieutenant, though wounded in the legs while coming ashore, refused evacuation, directed his team in demolishing the obstacles until the tide covered them, and returned to the job when the tide permitted and was again wounded; an enlisted man operated a tankdozer until it was knocked out of action and then crossed the fire-swept beach to mount a deserted bulldozer and continue his job.[72]

The second group of assault waves, consisting of five separately timed landings, was to complete the build-up of the two assault regiments by H plus 1 hour and bring in the 81st Chemical Battalion, two combat engineer battalions whose principal task would be to clear mine fields for the advance inland, naval shore fire control parties, and advance elements of artillery, medical, and antiaircraft units. In the zone of the 116th Infantry, the remaining three companies of the 1st Battalion were to come in behind Company A on the right. On the left the heavy weapons company of the 2d Battalion would land to complete that unit and would be followed by the 3d Battalion.

The right flank, however, continued to be an area of particular misfortune. Only scattered sections of the reinforcing units managed to land there and they were hit by the same destructive fire that had virtually knocked Company A out of the battle. The battalion headquarters company, including the beachmaster for the 1st Battalion sector, landed at the base of the cliff west of the rifle companies and under such severe enemy small arms fire that it was unable to move most of the day. The heavy weapons company, scattered and hard hit on the approach, took two hours to assemble survivors. It salvaged only three mortars, three machine guns,

---

[71] About 80 yards of sand would be covered each hour.

[72] For a complete list of the DSC winners, see App. I, below.

and a few rounds of ammunition. Only one company of the 1st Battalion survived as an organized group capable of pursuing its assault missions. This was Company C, which mislanded 1,000 yards east of its planned beach within the area of the bluffs covered by the smoke of a brush fire. With few casualties and equipment virtually intact, the company waded in on a front of not more than a hundred yards and reorganized in the shelter of the sea wall.

Next to land in the 116th zone were the Rangers. The 5th Ranger Battalion together with two companies of the 2d Rangers had waited offshore for news of the assault on Pointe du Hoe, which would determine whether they landed there or came in on the 116th Infantry zone. The Pointe du Hoe assault, however, had been delayed forty minutes by the eastward drifting of the craft carrying the Rangers. There was therefore no news at all, and the Ranger reinforcements, concluding that the assault must have failed, proceeded with the alternative plan. The 5th Ranger Battalion followed Company C, 116th Infantry, and shared the relatively easy assault in landing too far east. But the two companies of the 2d Ranger Battalion came in about where planned on the fire-swept right flank behind elements of Companies A and B. Only between a third and a half of the two 65-man companies survived to take shelter at the head of the beach.

In the 2d Battalion zone, the second wave brought in the heavy weapons company and battalion headquarters. Company H suffered such losses and disorganization that it could be of little immediate help in supplying mortar or machine gun support. The battalion commander, Maj.

Sidney V. Bingham, Jr., coming ashore near les Moulins, organized a few sections of Company F which had landed in the first wave and attempted an assault on the enemy positions in the draw.[73] The attempt made with only a handful of men was unsuccessful, but in the meantime the 3d Battalion was landing bunched up astride the regimental boundary just east of les Moulins. It was somewhat disorganized by the intermingling of units but suffered little from enemy fire in crossing the beach.

At the end of the first hour the 116th Infantry had at least a nucleus of force which could be organized for attack against the enemy's beach positions. Most hopeful was the situation roughly in the center of the regimental zone just west of les Moulins where enemy fire masked by smoke was light and ineffective, and where shortly after 0730, by great good fortune, the regimental command group with Col. Charles D. W. Canham and Brig. Gen. Norman D. Cota, the assistant division commander, came ashore.

The experience of the 16th Infantry's later waves was similar to that of the 116th. Losses were lighter but the confusion and intermingling of units on the beaches became more serious. The two remaining companies (G and H) of the 2d Battalion followed by the 1st Battalion landed about where planned, due north of Colleville. The 3d Battalion completed landing on the left shortly after 0800. The 3d Battalion headquarters, however, landed to the west and could not join its troops for several hours. The 16th Infantry suffered another misfortune when the regimental executive officer, coming in with the first

---

[73] Major Bingham was awarded the DSC.

section of the headquarters, was killed together with thirty-five of his men. The commander, Col. George A. Taylor, did not arrive until 0815 with the second headquarters section.

Command was generally one of the gravest problems faced by assault units, not only because officer casualties were high and mislanding of command groups had left many units leaderless, but also because of extreme difficulties of communication. Three-quarters of the 116th Infantry's radios were destroyed or useless.[74] Furthermore, in the confusion of the mixed units, which were under heavy fire in some places, their men huddled along the shingle embankment or sea wall and generally shaken by the shock of the first few minutes of severe action, it would have been impossible for any commander to exercise control over more than a small group of men on a relatively narrow sector of the front.

In these first few hours on OMAHA Beach, the OVERLORD operation faced its gravest crisis. Deprived of the expected air support by accident of weather and preceded by a generally ineffective beach drenching, the 1st Division had gone in against the one sector of the Normandy coast that had anything like the kind of cordon defense which Field Marshal Rommel counted on to hold and smash the Allies on the beaches. Instead of attacking in the sector of one regiment of

an overextended static division as expected, General Huebner's troops hit on the front of a full attack infantry division, the *352d*, whose presence in the coastal zone had been missed by Allied intelligence even though it had been in place for almost three months.[75]

To the German officer in command of the fortifications at Pointe et Raz de la Percée it looked in these first hours as though the invasion had been stopped on the beaches. He noted that the Americans were lying on the shore seeking cover be-

---

[74] Carrying heavy communications equipment through the surf under enemy fire was a formidable task that took many lives. Five men of the 16th Infantry were decorated for their heroic work in struggling ashore with vital radios and wire despite serious wounds. T/5 John J. Pinder, Jr., received a posthumous award of the Medal of Honor for his intrepidity in recovering two radios and other equipment, while suffering two severe wounds. On his third trip into the fire-swept surf he was killed.

[75] Reasons for this failure remain one of the more interesting mysteries of the war. Allied intelligence had otherwise a remarkably detailed and accurate picture of the German defenses and troop dispositions. It was unquestionably difficult to get reliable information from agents in the coastal zone since all persons whom the Germans allowed to remain in these areas were carefully screened. In this connection the short distance of the move of the *352d Division* from St. Lô to the coast may have contributed to concealing it, although a similar inching forward of the *21st Panzer Division* was found out. Another interesting surmise is suggested by the fact that one agent known to be active in the zone of the *352d Division* as late as May was working in the Grandcamp area which happened to be the sector of the *3d Battalion* of the *726th Regiment* of the *716th Division*. That the *726th Regiment* had been attached to a new division could easily have been unknown to him. In May the Germans shot down a carrier pigeon carrying a message from this agent. The message was a report of the location of the *3d Battalion* of the *1716th Artillery Regiment*, also in the Grandcamp area and also a *716th Division* unit, attached to the *352d*. See MS # B–022 (Ziegelmann). Brigadier Williams, G–2 of 21 A Gp, has said since the war that just before the invasion he did find out about the *352d's* presence on the coast but was unable to inform the troops. See Interv, Pogue with Williams, London, 31 May 47. This is partially confirmed by 21 Army Group Weekly Neptune Review 17 of 4 June which warned: "It should not be surprising if we discovered that it (the *716th Division*) had two regiments in the line and one in reserve while on its left *352d Division* had one regiment up and two to play. . . ." The fact remains noteworthy that for almost two and a half months the Allies were unaware of the true position of the *352d Division*.

hind the obstacles, that ten tanks and a "great many other vehicles" were burning. The fire of his own positions and the artillery, he thought, had been excellent, causing heavy losses. He could see the wounded and dead lying on the sand.[76]

Sketchy reports to V Corps and First Army must have painted very much the same picture for the American command. From a DUKW cruising 500 to 1,000 yards offshore, Col. Benjamin B. Talley, the assistant chief of staff of V Corps, radioed General Gerow what he could observe of the progress of the landings. Observation was difficult, and on the whole Colonel Talley refrained from reporting mere pessimism. However, he had to report something of the evident disorganization. He could see that the beaches were jammed with infantrymen and that enemy artillery and machine gun fire was still effective. He sent a message to that effect about 0930. What particularly concerned him was the fact that reinforcing waves were being held up by the continued enemy opposition and the LCT's were milling around offshore like "a stampeded herd of cattle," although some of the more daring commanders took their craft into the hail of enemy fire and beached them. This situation seemed to Talley to continue without alleviation until midmorning, and it was the situation conveyed to Generals Gerow and Bradley.[77]

[76] MS # B-432 (Ziegelmann).

[77] Talley Notes, cited n. 59. The milling of the landing craft offshore was actually caused at least as much by an order from the 7th Naval Beach Battalion at about 0830 to suspend the landing of vehicles pending clearance of some beach exits. This fact seems to have been unknown to Talley. See below, next section. Cf. Taylor, *Omaha Beachhead*, p. 79. Talley was awarded the DSC for his liaison work on 6 June.

Already, however, as Talley sent forward his discouraging reports, the crisis was bit by bit dissolving. Among the groups of scared, tired riflemen huddled along the beach were a few intrepid leaders—officers, noncoms, and privates on whose individual backs the big responsibility at the moment lay. They began by example and exhortation to prod the men to get up, leave such poor shelter as they had found, and walk or crawl across the beach flat and up the hills where the enemy was dug in with rifles, mortars, and machine guns. From the larger perspective the combined weight of Allied arms was gradually wearing down the defenders. The *916th Regiment* in the center of the *352d Division* sector, while reporting that the landings had been frustrated, added that its own casualties were mounting chiefly from the heavy Allied naval fire and that consequently reinforcements were needed. Reinforcements, however, could not immediately be spared since they were much more urgently needed elsewhere.

The gravest immediate threat for the Germans arose to the east of V Corps where the British assault cracked through the coast defenses in some places during the first few hours. (*Map XII*) The British Second Army attacked with three divisions abreast under control of 1 and 30 Corps. Immediately on the flank of the American attack, the British 50th Division landed two infantry brigades supported by tanks of the 8th Armoured Brigade and assault teams of the 79th Armoured Division and the 47th Royal Marine Commando. The troops touched down approximately on time at 0725.

Opposition was heavy at certain points, but on the whole it was much less determined than at OMAHA. In the 50th Division zone le Hamel, strongly defended by the *1st Battalion, 916th Regiment,* resisted until late in the day. To the east, however, the British division's left brigade struck a soft spot in the German defenses. The strong point at la Rivière held out only a few hours and when it fell at about 1000 its defenders, the *441st Ost Battalion,* attached to the *716th Division,* broke and pulled out, leaving the road to Bayeux open. This development, however, was not known to the British. Opposition continued to be reported south of Buhot, at Ryes, St. Sulpice, and Summervieu. It was always difficult in the early stages of the assault properly to distinguish enemy delaying action from major opposition or to discover where the holes were in the German defense. The 50th Division, moreover, still had only its assault forces ashore. Rising tide had prevented effective clearance of underwater obstacles. Enemy opposition and mines delayed the opening of beach exits. Caught in the resulting congestion, the two follow-up brigades of the 50th Division were two hours late in landing. When they did arrive, they found their assembly areas still not entirely cleared of enemy. Elements of the *352d Division,* in fact, were still on the Meuvaines ridge after midday.[78]

From the German point of view the crumbling of the *441st Ost Battalion* was immediately critical. The gap had to be plugged at once. The *915th Regiment* reinforced (*LXXXIV Corps* reserve) had been stationed near Bayeux and had often practiced just the maneuver now required—counterthrust, toward Crépon.

But earlier in the morning (at 0400) the *915th* had been ordered to the Carentan— Isigny area to attack reported large-scale enemy airborne landings between the Vire and Douve Rivers. The report was discovered to be unfounded at just about the time the hole in the *716th Division* opened up. Threatened with having his whole right flank rolled up, Generalleutnant Dietrich Kraiss, the commanding general of the *352d Division,* secured corps approval for the return of the *915th Regiment.* But an hour was consumed trying to reach the regiment. Then it had to countermarch almost twenty miles from a point nearly five miles west of the Forêt de Cerisy. The march was made partly on foot, partly by bicycle and French motor vehicles which suffered numerous mechanical breakdowns. Another three hours passed before even a portion of the unit was in position to attack. That delay proved crucial, for in those hours much happened to change the situation on OMAHA completely.[79]

The D-Day Beachhead

First Army's assault plans provided that the initial task of clearing the beaches be carried out by assault sections organized by boatloads. Troops were then to proceed inland to various assembly areas where they would be reorganized in battalions and regiments to carry out their subsequent D-Day missions of securing and consolidating the corps beachheads.

On OMAHA Beach the troops of V Corps in order to reach their assembly areas had to cross a beach flat, varying in width from a few yards at each end to about 200 yards in the center, and climb steep bluffs be-

[78] Facts on British action furnished by the British Cabinet Office Hist Sec.

[79] MS # B-432 (Ziegelmann).

hind. (*See Map XI.*) Although the beach flat offered only patches of tall marsh grass for concealment, the bluffs had irregularities that could provide cover for individual riflemen. The plan called for clearing five exit roads from the beach and an advance inland generally along the axis of these roads. But despite naval bombardment and tank fire from the beach on enemy positions defending these roads all remained active during the first two hours of the assault. Movement off the beach, in consequence, at first took place between the exits. It began before 0800 in a number of independent actions by groups of men, never more than of company size and often much smaller. Some of the attacks had tank fire support; others were materially aided by the bold action of destroyers which came within a few hundred yards of the beach and delivered direct fire wherever they could observe enemy activity.[80]

Certainly the first troops to move inland were the Ranger companies at Pointe du Hoe, though their action was independent of the main landings at OMAHA and was, in fact, part of the fire support plan rather than of the assault proper. Forty minutes late, the three companies of the 2d Ranger Battalion under command of Lt. Col. James E. Rudder [81] made landfall under close-in supporting fire of the U.S. destroyer *Satterlee* and the British destroyer *Talybont*. The *Satterlee,* having delivered effective prelimi-

nary fire, stayed in the area near shore and watched over the Ranger action most of the day. By 1730 it had expended 70 percent of its ammunition in missions in aid of the Rangers and was relieved by the *Barton* and *Thompson.* The *Satterlee's* fire was particularly effective during the first moments of the assault when it forced the enemy to take cover while the Rangers scaled the cliff with ropes and ladders.[82] Enemy fire, reduced by the naval shellings, remained light after the Rangers reached the top of the cliff and began moving inland in groups of three or four across a desert cratered by concentrated aerial and naval bombardment. In disparate and confused actions the Rangers speedily carried out their primary mission. Patrols found the 155-mm. gun emplacements deserted. The guns themselves were discovered farther inland in a camouflaged field position. They were, curiously enough, unmanned and unguarded. The handful of Rangers who stumbled on them were therefore able to destroy them easily. Thus far the Rangers, despite thirty to forty casualties in the landings, had not had a hard fight. Their difficulties began later in the day with the first of a series of counterattacks by the *1st Battalion, 914th Regiment,* that would keep them in a state of siege for two days, and reduce their combat effectives to about ninety.[83]

---

[80] Admiral Hall, commander of Task Force O, paid special tribute to U.S. destroyers *Carmick, Doyle, McCook, Thompson, Frankford, Harding, Emmons,* and *Baldwin,* and British Hunt class destroyers *Melbreak, Talybont,* and *Tanatside.* ANCXF *Report,* Vol. III, Rpt, Comdr Assault Force O, p. 56.

[81] Colonel Rudder was awarded the DSC for extraordinary heroism in continuing to lead his battalion despite being twice wounded.

[82] The *352d Division,* anticipating commando assaults on the cliffs, had laid 240-mm. shells hooked to trip wires, along the crest at 100-yard intervals. They were designed to roll down and explode over the water with an effective radius of about 650 yards. These shells caused no difficulty for the Rangers although they hindered beach clearance parties later on. See Talley Notes, cited n. 59; MS # B-432 (Ziegelmann).

[83] For a detailed account of the Ranger action, see Charles H. Taylor, "Pointe du Hoe," *Small Unit Actions* (Washington, 1946).

RANGERS SCALING THE CLIFFS AT POINTE DU HOE

Apart from the Ranger movements at Pointe du Hoe, the principal areas of penetration inland were four, two in each regimental zone. The 116th Infantry with the 5th Ranger Battalion made successful independent attacks inland on both sides of the les Moulins draw. On the west side Company C, urged on by Colonel Canham and General Cota, left the protection of the sea wall and, after blowing a gap in the concertina wire along the beach road, crossed the 150 yards of beach flat to the bluffs.[84] Men were lost to machine gun fire in this initial attack but, once they gained the hillside, smoke concealed their moves and small folds in the ground gave them good protection from enemy bullets. They found no Germans atop the bluff and proceeded a couple of hundred yards inland before fire from the flanks caused them to halt. Company C was closely followed by the 5th Ranger Battalion which sent its men forward by platoons as they landed. The command group of General Cota was established shortly after 0830 near the crest of the hill and began the task of reorganizing disordered units.

At approximately the same time the 3d Battalion, 116th Infantry, in a series of simultaneous, independent advances by straggling columns of twenty to thirty men, left the beaches east of les Moulins and arrived by various routes on the high ground. Meeting no resistance on the crest, the sections, coagulating haphazardly into larger groups, began moving southwest generally toward St. Laurent and their designated assembly area beyond.

[84] Both General Cota and Colonel Canham were awarded the DSC for extraordinary heroism shown during their D-Day leadership under fire.

Penetrations in the 16th Infantry zone were made between the St. Laurent and Colleville exits and up the draw on the extreme eastern flank of the beach. The former breach was opened up by two companies of the 2d Battalion, 16th Infantry. Company G and a section of Company E made separate attacks at about the same time and only a few yards apart. After blowing gaps through the wire beyond the shingle embankment the two groups crossed the flats and converged on the lower slopes of the bluff. But despite some effort to co-ordinate the advance the "companies" continued independently, threading their way through mine fields that took some casualties and slowed the advance. Company G, covered by the fire of their 60-mm. mortars and light machine guns emplaced on the beach, gained the top of the bluff against only light enemy opposition and pushed inland. Company E (consisting of twenty-three men under 2d Lt. John M. Spalding) on reaching the top of the hill turned west and attacked the rear of the enemy fortifications defending the east side of the St. Laurent exit. It was a typical coastal position including pillboxes and a maze of communicating trenches. The garrison, men of the *916th Regiment,* caught by surprise and demoralized by naval fire hitting just below the top of the bluff, fought a confused battle for about two hours before an officer was cornered and forced with a group of about twenty men to surrender. Although Lieutenant Spalding had too few men to mop up the area, his action was the first step in clearing a vehicle exit from the beach. In the meantime most of the 2d and 1st Battalions of the 16th Infantry had followed Company G's route up the bluffs, on order of Colonel Taylor, regimental commander, who on his arrival on the beach at 0815 had begun organizing his men and pushing them forward.

The 3d Battalion, 16th Infantry, at the same time had opened its own path inland at the draw northeast of Colleville. Under covering fire from tanks on the beach and naval guns, 3d Battalion units made a direct attack on the enemy strong point defending this draw and by 0900 had, with surprisingly small losses, succeeded in subduing it.[85]

Improvisation and courageous personal leadership in the first hours had taken considerable numbers of troops off the beach where for a time it had looked as though they might be stopped. However, the initial successes were limited by the fact that the infantry had very few heavy weapons, no supporting artillery, and, since the beach exits had not been cleared, little prospect of getting tank support or large-scale supplies or reinforcements. The beaches themselves remained under heavy enemy fire and on most sectors no gaps had been blown through the obstacles. The obstacles submerged by the rising tide materially increased the difficulties of approaching the beach. Landing craft became more and more congested offshore. When shortly after 1000 the 18th Infantry began landing in column of battalions in the 16th Infantry zone, it must have looked to them as though little progress of any kind had been made in the assault. The enemy apparently still had control of the high ground above the beach; American troops still seemed pinned behind the shingle

embankment and vehicles were piled up along the narrow strip of beach.

In breaking this deadlock during the next hour, naval intervention played an important part. At about 1030 two landing craft, LCT 30 and LCI (L) 544, steamed full ahead through the obstacles off the Colleville beaches, firing all weapons at enemy strong points guarding the Colleville draw. The craft continued to fire after beaching. Not only did their action prove that the obstacles could be breached by ramming, but their fire, though failing to neutralize German positions in the Colleville draw, had at least a heartening effect on the assault troops. At about the same time two destroyers approached to within 1,000 yards of the beach and shelled enemy positions from les Moulins eastward. Under cover of this fire engineers of the 37th and 146th Engineer Combat Battalions [86] bulldozed two gaps through the dune line on either side of the St. Laurent exit, filled the antitank ditch, and cleared the mine fields. The resistance east of this draw had already been neutralized by the 16th Infantry. While the engineers worked, heavy weapons of the 3d Battalion, 116th Infantry, contained other enemy defenses still in action. A pillbox west of the draw was reduced by skillfully directed destroyer fire at about 1130. The Germans in this last organized defense at the St. Laurent draw surrendered to the 2d Battalion of the 18th Infantry, which had begun landing at about 1000. Thus, in little over an hour, concerted bold action had wrought the most substantial improvement on the beach since H Hour. Reinforcements were coming ashore, and most

---

[85] American losses were one killed and five wounded. Thirty-one German prisoners were taken at the strong point. See Combat Interv, 16th Inf.

[86] Not the 149th, as given in Taylor, Omaha Beachhead, p. 82.

important of all a road was at last open to move vehicles inland.

In the meantime the battles inland were already being joined. The troops who gained the top of the bluffs by mid-morning were scattered groups, a small percentage of the assault battalions, who were incapable of carrying out the D-Day advances as planned. Their objectives at first were simply to reach the various battalion assembly areas. Because of their small numbers and the difficulty of control in the hedgerow country their actions were fragmented, and because they completely lacked both armored and artillery support their movements could be, and constantly were, checked by small enemy prepared positions seldom held in even as much as company strength.

Under the circumstances, this scattered resistance by small enemy groups constituted in sum a considerable obstacle to American advance. Furthermore, sporadic and un-co-ordinated as it seemed, it was in general the kind, though not quite the scale, of defense that the Germans had planned. Determined resistance in coastal positions, even though isolated or bypassed, did succeed at first in splintering the attacking forces so that only weak, disorganized elements could penetrate the hinterland. Continued, though relatively feeble, nodal defense inland during the day had the further effect of hindering reorganization and co-ordinated American action. So far the theory of coastal defense seemed justified in practice. That nothing came of this initial success was due, first, to the Germans' lack of reserves with which to counterattack the relatively weak penetrations, and, second, to the fact that, while the American ground attack had locally and temporarily been splintered, the vast supporting naval and air power was practically unopposed. By dominating the battlefield, planes and naval guns smashed such German reserves as could be gathered for a counterthrust and so gave the fragmented V Corps infantry a chance to recover, rebuild, and again become a ground army superior in numbers and equipment to anything that the Germans could thereafter muster to meet them.

Action during the remainder of D Day inland from OMAHA Beach took place in three general areas, Vierville-sur-Mer, St. Laurent, and Colleville. The three actions were generally unconnected and un-co-ordinated.

Attacks on Vierville-sur-Mer were made by elements of the 1st and 2d Battalions of the 116th Infantry and the 5th Ranger Battalion—something more than 600 men altogether. These units were reorganized near the edge of the bluff and started inland between 1000 and 1100. The plan was for the Rangers to bypass the town and attack from the south while the 116th advanced along the exit road. The Rangers reached the coastal highway but found further advance across the fields checked by enemy machine gun positions concealed among the hedgerows. After four hours of trying in vain to get around the enemy guns, they turned and entered Vierville in the early afternoon. The town had already been captured by the 116th, which met little opposition in its frontal attack. At 1100 Vierville was clear, and Colonel Canham then tried to push the attack westward to make juncture with the Ranger force at Pointe du Hoe. His men, however, encountered the same kind of nettling opposition that had stopped the Rangers. Lacking heavy weapons to support the attack, Colonel Canham decided to call it off and return to the defense of Vierville. He had few men to spare from that task since few reinforcements had landed in the area and the beach exit was not opened until evening. Although enemy beach defenses opposite Vierville had been largely neutralized by naval fire early in the afternoon, the engineers responsible for clearing the exit had scattered in the landing, losing three-quarters of their equipment and many of their men.

East of the les Moulins draw, the 3d Battalion, 116th Infantry, and scattered sections of the 2d Battalion fought inland toward St. Laurent and the 3d Battalion assembly area southwest. During the day confused and inconclusive fighting by small groups of men took place in country which, though relatively open, still provided the enemy with sufficient cover that the American troops could seldom locate their positions. The 116th Infantry was stopped short of St. Laurent.

In the meantime northeast of the town another attack, by the 115th Infantry, was in progress. The 115th had been brought ashore ahead of schedule. Original plans had called for the rifle and heavy weapons companies of this regiment to be held as V Corps floating reserve to be employed on order of General Gerow. If all went according to plan in the initial assault, the 115th Infantry would be committed in the zone of the 116th to organize the high ground near Longueville and be prepared to capture Isigny. Alternative plans were made to have the 115th take over missions of the 116th in case any units of the latter regiment should fail in the assault.[87] Ini-

tially the 115th Infantry was to be on call between the first and second tides. But Maj. Gen. Charles H. Gerhardt, commanding the 29th Division, contended that this plan meant leaving the 116th Infantry without reinforcements for a dangerously long time.[88] At the last minute, therefore, General Gerow decided to commit the 115th Infantry immediately in support of the 116th. At H Hour Admiral Hall on General Gerow's request gave the order to land the 115th beginning at H plus 4 hours.

Like so many units, the 115th Infantry drifted eastward, and instead of coming in where scheduled on the beaches in the left portion of the 116th zone it landed on top of the 18th Infantry east of St. Laurent. The confusion on the crowded beaches and intermingling of 18th and 115th units delayed the movement inland of both regiments. It was early afternoon when, under orders to carry out the primary mission in the Longueville area, the battalions of the 115th Infantry started for their assembly areas southwest of St. Laurent. The 2d Battalion attacked St. Laurent, estimated to be held by about a company of Germans, but could make no headway. At dusk the attack was halted and the battalion withdrawn to join the 1st, which had bypassed St. Laurent to the east and moved a few hundred yards south of the town. The 3d Battalion, on the regiment's left flank, had in the

---

[87] Notes on V Corps Plan, 17 May 44. Pre-Inv file 670. Compare this use of a floating reserve with that proposed by British Commanders following the Dieppe raid. See above, p. 191.

[88] Ltr. Gerhardt to Gen Malony, 2 Jan 47. Hist Div files. General Gerhardt was commissioned in the cavalry from West Point in 1917. He served with the 89th Division in the St. Mihiel and Meuse–Argonne offensives in 1918. In May 1942 he became commander of the 91st Division and in July took command of the 29th Division in England.

meantime made even slower progress and drew up at dark still north of the St. Laurent–Colleville road.

Between St. Laurent and Colleville a whole series of confused and generally un-co-ordinated actions were taking place during the remainder of D Day as parts of two battalions of the 16th Infantry, supported during the afternoon by the 18th Infantry, attempted to maneuver south to positions along the beachhead maintenance line. Company G, the first unit to move inland in this area, at first made rapid progress, but an attack against Colleville drew an enemy counterattack that put the company on the defensive for the rest of the day. Elements of the 1st Battalion fought separate actions in the same general area attempting to clean up isolated enemy riflemen and machine gun positions.

As the 18th Infantry landed, Brig. Gen. Willard G. Wyman, the assistant division commander and senior army commander ashore, had diverted all three battalions to take over the missions of the 16th Infantry. The 2d Battalion, going to the assistance of the 2d Battalion, 16th Infantry, at Colleville, passed to the west of Company G and at dark halted just south and southeast of the town. The 3d Battalion, at first ordered to capture Formigny and Surrain, was held up so long by small arms harassing fire that its orders were changed and it was sent to the high ground south of the highway to tie in with 16th Infantry on the left and the 115th on the right. The 1st Battalion was directed into the same general area with orders to attack Surrain, but at dark was still north of the St. Laurent–Colleville road.[89]

The St. Laurent–Colleville sector was still considered weak. When the 26th Infantry, the first of the follow-up forces, landed in the evening, two battalions were ordered to take defensive positions southeast of St. Laurent ready to attack toward Formigny. The remaining battalion backed up the left flank where the 3d Battalion, 16th Infantry, with about one hundred men had managed to occupy le Grand Hameau. To help hold the position during the night seventeen tanks were moved up from the beach.

While V Corps units struggled to find secure defenses for the night in their shallow lodgment VII Corps was pouring ashore almost unhindered. (*See Map 3.*) As the 8th Infantry battalions moved inland to their objectives they had only minor engagements with an enemy who, on the whole, showed little inclination to fight. The 3d Battalion was held up briefly north of Ste. Marie-du-Mont where it overran another of the batteries of the German *191st Artillery Regiment*—the unit which earlier in the day had caused the 506th Parachute Infantry so much trouble. The battalion then went on to the les Forges crossroads where it bivouacked for the night and where it was joined in the evening by the 2d Battalion. The 1st Battalion had moved almost due west from the beaches and reached Turqueville by nightfall.

The 8th Infantry, when it halted for the night, was confronted by an enemy salient which cut the Valognes–Carentan highway between Ste. Mère-Eglise and les Forges, extending northeast as far as Turqueville. It was enemy from this salient that had attacked Ste. Mère-Eglise during the morning. The 505th Para-

[89] 18th Inf S–1 Jnl, 6 Jun 44.

chute Infantry counterattack had caused only a slight enemy withdrawal southward. The Germans were able thereafter to consolidate on high ground at Fauville where they formed a strong barrier between the 8th Infantry and the 82d Airborne Division.

Late in the afternoon a task force of infantry and tanks, belonging to the 82d Airborne Division and under command of Col. Edson D. Raff, landed by sea with the mission of reinforcing their division in the Ste. Mère-Eglise area. Raff's men, including ninety men of the 325th Glider Infantry and a company of tanks of the 746th Tank Battalion, followed the 3d Battalion, 8th Infantry, into the les Forges position. The infantry battalion had already decided not to attack northward that evening. Raff, however, was concerned not only with getting his tanks through to his division, but also with clearing the area north of les Forges. The meadows in this area were the division's glider landing zone. Here at dusk artillery units were to land. Raff's tanks and infantry made several jabs at the enemy to try to discover his dispositions but, after three tanks were lost to enemy high-velocity fire, the attempt to get through was abandoned. The enemy remained at full strength and still well concealed when, on schedule at 2100, about sixty gliders came in low over the area and cut loose for landings. The Germans reacted with intense automatic fire. Many of the gliders crashed, others came down within the enemy lines. Casualties were heavy. Remnants of the glider force including the pilots were collected by Colonel Raff and formed into a makeshift defense for the night.

In the northern portion of the 4th Division zone neither the 12th nor the 22d Infantry Regiment reached its D-Day objective. Delays were caused not by enemy opposition but by the difficulties of moving up through the marshes. The 22d was halted in the general area from Hamel de Cruttes on the coast to St. Germain-de-Varreville. The 12th came up on the left of the 502d Parachute Infantry, which was holding the 101st Division north flank near Beuzeville-au-Plain.

General Bradley's right corps on UTAH Beach had its weaknesses at the end of D Day, but on the whole it was in a sound position, smaller than planned but better organized and stronger than might have been expected. The beach, though still under intermittent enemy artillery fire, was cleared and prepared for the orderly reception of reinforcements. The 4th Division was present in the beachhead virtually intact, organized and equipped for offensive action. Its casualties for the day were less than 200. If the position of the 82d Airborne Division caused some concern, the force was at hand to consolidate it.

The situation on the left at OMAHA was quite different. The main V Corps position at the end of the day was the narrow sector between St. Laurent and Colleville, a toehold on the enemy-shore nowhere more than a mile and a half deep. The right flank at Vierville-sur-Mer, held by elements of the 116th Infantry and the Rangers, was isolated from the main body although the beach exit was open and reinforcements thus could be brought in. All units were lacking vehicles, supplies, ammunition, artillery, and armored support necessary for further advance inland.

No artillery could be landed during the morning. The elements of five battalions which beached in the afternoon all suffered heavy losses of equipment, including a total of twenty-six guns. Two antiaircraft gun battalions scheduled to arrive on D Day could not come in until the following day. Only one artillery mission was fired on 6 June. The V Corps losses for the day were about 2,000 killed, wounded, and missing.[90]

The failure of the Germans to exploit the weakness of V Corps was the result quite simply of their own greater weakness. During the first few hours it looked as though the OMAHA assault had been stopped, and the chief concern of the *352d Division* was with its right flank which was threatened by the British penetration near Meuvaines. (*See Map XII.*) To meet this the *LXXXIV Corps* reserve, the reinforced *915th Regiment* (*Kampfgruppe Meyer*) had been ordered to attack in the direction of Crépon. By 1100 the division commander, General Kraiss, began to consider the situation in his center more serious in the light of

additional information on the whole invasion front. The *709th Division* opposing U.S. VII Corps was reporting strong armored reinforcements landed from the sea. At the same time the British were building up their beachhead. A concentration of shipping observed off St. Laurent was thought to indicate Allied intention to reinforce what had heretofore been considered minor penetrations in the St. Laurent area.[91] General Kraiss concluded (apparently for the first time) that the Allies were planning a two-pronged attack on Bayeux from bridgeheads at St. Laurent and Meuvaines. The *2d Battalion* of the *915th Regiment* was therefore split off from the force on its way toward Crépon and together with one antitank company (with twelve self-propelled 75-mm. antitank guns) was attached to the *916th Regiment* in the center of the division sector. The infantry reinforcements moved into the Colleville area in the early afternoon but reported that their counterattack had been stopped by firm American resistance and that they had suffered heavy losses.

The body of *Kampfgruppe Meyer*[92] in the meantime advanced toward the area Bazenville–Villiers-le-Sec whence it planned to attack to Crépon. By the time it reached its assembly area at about 1730 it found the British already in possession. The units on the right were able to with-

[90] This is frankly a guess, based on a number of estimates of various dates and various headquarters, none of which agree. Under the Army's present casualty reporting system, it is unlikely that accurate figures of D-Day losses by unit will ever be available. The *V Corps History* gives D-Day losses as 2,374, of which the 1st Division lost 1,190, the 29th Division 743, and corps troops 441. The after action report of the 1st Division and the 29th Division history both scale down their own losses slightly. See Joseph H. Ewing, *29, Let's Go* (Washington, 1948), p. 306. Source for the 1st Division report is its own G–1 report of daily casualties; source for the 29th Division figures is not given. On 8 June the 1st Division G–1 issued a "corrected" casualty report for D Day and D plus 1 which reduced total losses reported for the two days from 1,870 to 1,036. See V Corps G–3 Jnl. Neither the original report nor the corrected one conforms to the division G–1's accounting in his monthly report of operations. See study of First Army casualties during June 1944, prepared by Royce L. Thompson, MS. Hist Div files.

[91] It is possible that the Germans were interpreting as concentration of force what was actually only congestion of landing craft backlogged by the difficulties of beaching them. See above, n. 77.

[92] Consisting of the *1st Battalion, 915th Regiment,* the *352d Fuesilier Battalion,* and one company of the *352d Antitank Battalion* (the *1352d Assault Gun Company*) equipped with ten assault guns. MS # B–432. Ziegelmann's reference to the *1352d Assault Gun Battalion* is an error. Cf. *Kriegsgliederung,* 18 May 44. *Seventh Army, KTB Anlagen 1.I.–30.VI.44.*

NINAction-K.H AIR FORCE B–26 OVER BRITISH BEACHHEAD *at Lion-sur-Mer. Note markings on plane. All Allied aircraft, except 4-engine bombers, in support of the invasion were painted thus for purposes of identification. Two black and three white stripes were painted on wings and around the fuselages.*

draw to St. Gabriel where they were joined by the ten assault guns of the Kampfgruppe. But the infantry battalion under direct command of Colonel Meyer on the left brushed with British forces near Bazenville. Meyer was killed and the battalion lost contact with other German units for several hours. It seems clear that Meyer's forces made no concerted attack, but were chewed up in small defensive actions. The assault guns scored the only success of the day in knocking out four British tanks near Brécy. On the other hand four of the guns were themselves lost, possibly to British naval fire. Out of the entire Kampfgruppe only about ninety men escaped. In the evening these remnants

were attached to the *726th Regiment,* which was ordered to establish a defensive line: Coulombs–St. Gabriel–the Seulles River west to Esquay-sur-Seulles–Hill 64 (west of Bazenville)–the Gronde River to Asnelles-sur-Mer. The plan for 7 June on this front was simply to muster all available troops including artillery units in Kampfgruppen to prevent a British break-through into Bayeux.[93]

---

[93] This story has been pieced together from the telephone diary of the *352d Division* and from reports of British action supplied to the author by the British Cabinet Office Hist Sec. The account (MS # B–432) written after the war by Lt. Col. Ziegelmann, G–3 of the *352d Division,* telling of a counterattack smashed by Allied fighter bomber interception and overrun by British tanks seems considerably exaggerated.

In the meantime the commander of the British 50th Division had decided to halt on a line north and northeast of the city roughly between Vaux-sur-Orne and Vaux-sur-Seulles. He had been advancing against very slight opposition, but because of the delays in getting started he feared that he could not occupy Bayeux and organize a proper defense before dark. He ordered the attack to be resumed at daylight.[94]

Most of the countermeasures initiated by *OB WEST* and *Army Group B* on D Day were directed against the British. Because the British had established the most extensive beachhead, their landings seemed to constitute the main Allied effort. Matching the success of the 50th Division immediately on the flank of U.S. V Corps, the 3d Canadian Division, landing on beaches near Courseulles, had advanced from three to six miles and had sent armored patrols as far as Bretteville l'Orgueilleuse some ten miles from the beach. On its left the 3d British Division advanced beyond Biéville to within about two miles of Caen. East of the Orne River the two parachute brigades of the 6th Airborne Division had successfully accomplished their missions of seizing bridges at Bénouville and destroying the enemy coastal battery at Merville. Although the advances of all British units fell short of their objectives (particularly in the failure to take either Caen or Bayeux), they nevertheless represented the widest and deepest penetration on the Allied front. Besides, they broke through what the Germans considered an especially vital portion of the

---

[94] From information furnished by British Cabinet Office Hist Sec.

defense. Caen was the gateway to the open country constituting the best tank route to Paris. In German eyes it was therefore the key to their whole position in France.

At 0500 *Army Group B* released the *21st Panzer Division* (Generalleutnant Edgar Feuchtinger) to *Seventh Army* control in order to counterattack British airborne landings east of the Orne River. For the attack the division lacked half of its infantry, one artillery battalion, and the antiaircraft and antitank battalions. These units, located on both sides of the Orne River, had been attached to the *716th Division* after the seaborne landings began. General Feuchtinger organized the remainder of his troops and started them northward. But, while still on the approach march, at about noon he was ordered to cross the Orne and make his attack west of the river to counter directly the threat to Caen. Delayed in passing through Caen where only one bridge over the Orne was still usable, Feuchtinger could not jump off until 1600. Then, with his troops organized in two regimental combat teams, he attacked the British 3d Division from about the line St. Contest–Hérouville. The attack was heavily resisted and made little progress along the Orne. But to the west one battalion struck through to Cresserons and sent elements to the coast. A few stragglers got into a Luftwaffe communications bunker near Douvres where they held out until 17 June, but the bulk of the battalion after being badly mauled pulled out. Before dark Feuchtinger halted the attack all along the line and ordered his units to dig in only a few hundred yards north of the line of departure. He tied in with infantry units of the division fighting east of the Orne.[95]

Feuchtinger's attack, stopped before it had achieved anything, was the only large-scale counterattack on D Day. That no more decisive moves were taken was due at least in part to the muddled German command system. Rundstedt had reacted to the first news of the airborne landings with a quick decision to commit at once all operational reserves within striking distance. (Map XIII) He took this decision, despite uncertainty as to the extent of the Allied landings, on the grounds that whether the landings were major or subsidiary it was still imperative to repel them at once. It was between 0330 and 0400, two hours before the seaborne landings, that he ordered the 12th SS Panzer Division to move immediately toward Caen and the Panzer Lehr Division to prepare for similar movement.[96] He estimated that the reported airborne landings were on such a large scale that they could not be a mere deception maneuver and they therefore would have to be reinforced from the sea. The only feasible area for such reinforcement was the east coast of the Cotentin and the beaches between the Vire and Orne Rivers. From observation of Allied assault exercises, the Germans were sure the assault on the coast would take place at dawn. Rundstedt wanted to have armor at hand to counterattack in the first hours. There was therefore

no time to debate contingencies. He reasoned further that, even if the Normandy assault were planned by the Allies as a secondary effort, it was probable that they would exploit whatever success it achieved. The attack, whatever its character, should therefore be met with all available force. Rundstedt's reasoning was clear and his action decisive. But the two panzer divisions which he ordered to move were not under his command. They were in OKW reserve. To save precious time Rundstedt issued his orders first and then notified OKW of the action, requesting approval. OKW did not approve. At about 0730 Jodl informed Rundstedt that the two divisions would not be committed until orders were received from Hitler. The 12th SS Panzer Division was to hold up at Lisieux; Panzer Lehr would not move at all. In contrast to his earlier decisiveness, Rundstedt apparently accepted this critical intervention by Hitler's staff without argument. He made no effort to reach Hitler himself.[97] The two panzer divisions waited, far from the beachheads, all during the morning hours of heavy overcast that might have permitted them to move without serious interference from Allied aircraft. They waited until 1600 when Hitler at last gave the word to move both divisions into battle. But by then cloud cover had broken up. Allied fighters and bombers ranged the skies smashing at everything that moved. It was necessary to delay the move further until dark.

Although scattered infantry elements of the 12th SS Panzer Division arrived

[95] MS # B-441 (Feuchtinger).

[96] This timing is given in MS # T-121 (Zimmermann et al.). See also Rad, 0445 (0545 DBST), OB WEST to OKW/WFSt, 6 Jun 44. OKH/Op.Abt., Lagemeldungen OB WEST 1.IV.–8.VI.44; cf. Fifteenth Army, KTB 1.I.–30.VI.44, 6 Jun 44. Rundstedt's reasoning detailed in the remainder of the paragraph is as reported in MS # T-121.

[97] Under the German command system it would have been perfectly proper for Rundstedt to have appealed directly to Hitler, since OKW itself did not have command authority except as it spoke in Hitler's name.

during the afternoon at forward assembly areas in the zone of the *21st Panzer Division,* it was actually not until 8 June that the bulk of the two reserve divisions could be committed. The plan for their use, developed on D Day, was to place both the *12th SS* and *Panzer Lehr Divisions* under *I SS Panzer Corps* along with the *21st Panzer* and *716th Infantry Divisions* (the latter consisting at the end of the day of little more than one German battalion and about twelve artillery pieces).[98] The massed armor was to counterattack on the right wing of *LXXXIV Corps.* The new corps boundary was to be the former boundary between the *716th* and *352d Divisions.*

The commitment of another corps in the Caen area would mean an indirect strengthening of General Marcks' (*LXXXIV Corps*) position by relieving him of responsibility for the Bayeux–Orne sector. More direct support was on the way. The *30th Mobile Brigade* was moving by bicycle from Coutances toward the invasion area, but it would not arrive until the morning of 7 June. In addition *Seventh Army* had taken the first steps to shift its weight into Normandy. In the morning the army commander, General Dollmann, ordered the *XXV Corps* in Brittany to prepare the mobile Kampfgruppen of the *275th* and *265th Infantry Divisions* for immediate movement to the invasion area. General Dollmann also wanted to move the Kampfgruppe of the *266th Division* and the entire *77th Division* from Brittany into Normandy, but Rommel considered the move premature in view of certain reports that Brittany itself might be

threatened with airborne landings. When Dollmann repeated his request that night as the *352d Division* front seemed to be rapidly reaching a breaking point, Rommel yielded so far as to alert the units involved.[99]

While waiting for these reinforcements, the *352d Division* had to depend wholly on its dwindling resources. Its last reserve, the engineer battalion, was moved from the vicinity of St. Martin-de-Blagny and attached in the evening to the *916th Regiment* in the expectation of heavy Allied attacks on 7 June to exploit the Colleville–St. Laurent beachhead.

At midnight General Kraiss reported his situation to General Marcks at corps. He was not sanguine. He thought his present forces might be sufficient to hold off enemy attacks on 7 June but his losses were so heavy that he would need reinforcements for the following day's fighting. In the coastal positions, he said, he had suffered a total loss of men and equipment. His casualties for the day were about 1,200, or nearly one-fifth of his combat effectives. General Marcks replied that the reserves which could be spared to the *352d Division* had already been sent forward. Kraiss would simply have to hold on as tenaciously as possible with what he had.[100]

Actually there was reason for the German outlook to be considerably darker than it was. All of the reinforcements ordered up on D Day would arrive late and many would take severe losses from Allied air attack on the approach march. Although all German commanders had long realized that their mobility would

---

[98] MS # B–621 (Richter).

[99] *Seventh Army, KTB 1.I.–30.VI.44,* 6 Jun 44.
[100] MS # B–432 (Ziegelmann).

be severely restricted by Allied air supremacy, the full tactical significance of that fact was not yet apparent. General Dollmann, at his most pessimistic, could not have foreseen that the so-called mobile Kampfgruppen ordered out of Brittany would take ten days to reach the battle area.

The immediate effect of Allied air power on the battle for the beaches was discouraging enough for the Germans. The *352d Division* observed that not a single German plane had appeared over its sector during the day. All of the 250 sorties flown by *II Air Corps* on 6 June were against shipping. The rest of the German air effort, which did not exceed 500 sorties altogether, consisted largely of fighter interventions, a good part of which occurred far inland. Some of these were planned interventions; many were chance encounters by planes sent on support missions and jumped by Allied aircraft before they could reach the battle area.[101] The 500 sorties of the Luftwaffe were in striking contrast to the almost 3,000 sorties by the Ninth Air Force fighters and bombers alone, flying chiefly tactical missions in the U.S. zone.[102]

---

[101] MS # B–620 (Buelowius).

[102] [Lt Col Robert H. George] Ninth Air Force, April to November 1944 (Army Air Forces Historical Studies: No. 36), MS, p. 81. AAF files.

CHAPTER IX

The V Corps Lodgment
(7–18 June)

Securing the Beachheads

Supreme in the air, the Allies began on D Day to build up a similarly crushing superiority on the ground. By the end of 6 June 1944 First Army had succeeded in landing most of eight and a third infantry regiments—only a little less than planned. For operations on 7 June five divisions were ashore and operational (although one, the 29th, lacked one of its regiments until later in the day). All of these divisions were seriously deficient in transport, tank support, artillery, and above all supplies. The worst situation was in the V Corps zone where, of 2,400 tons of supplies planned to be unloaded during D Day, only about 100 tons actually came in. Ammunition shortage was grave. Both beaches on D plus 1 were still under enemy artillery fire. On OMAHA pockets of enemy riflemen still held out at various points along the coast; beach obstacles, even after work by the engineers during low tide of the afternoon of D Day, were still only about a third cleared; beach exits had not been opened as scheduled nor vehicle parks established inland on the scale contemplated.

Nowhere in First Army zone had initial objectives been fully achieved. In the V Corps zone not only had the two assault regiments stopped far short of their objectives along the beachhead

maintenance line, but they were so badly chewed up and disorganized by the hard fighting that they were scarcely capable of continuing the attack as planned. Units of VII Corps had been more successful in staking out a beachhead large enough to remove the beaches from direct enemy fire and to provide sufficient space for maneuver and build-up. The 4th Division had taken only light casualties and was in relatively good condition for subsequent attacks. Nevertheless the area was considerably smaller than desired and the initial efforts to push it out westward across the Merderet and southward toward a junction with V Corps were barred by the hard-fighting *91st Division*.

The operations in the two days following the landings were a continuation of the assault phase as all units sought to reach their D-Day objectives.[1] The exhaustion of the 16th and 116th Infantry Regiments in the V Corps zone required some reshuffling of regimental and battalion missions, and, in the VII Corps zone, missions of the 4th Division had to be tempered to conform to the realities of enemy opposition.

In effect, the V Corps attack continued on 7 June with two divisions abreast although the regiments of the 29th Divi-

---

[1] See below, however, for shift in operational priorities to insure early junction of V and VII Corps beachheads.

sion did not formally come under command of Maj. Gen. Charles H. Gerhardt, the division commander, until 1700. Gerhardt had landed on the evening of D Day and with General Cota planned and directed the operations of the 115th and 116th Infantry Regiments during D plus 1. (*MapXIV*) The third regiment of the division, the 175th Infantry, began landing at 1230 on 7 June, two hours later than scheduled, and was ashore by 1630. The 29th Division operated generally west of a line through St. Laurent and Formigny; the 1st Division, with all three of its regiments in line, operated generally to the east.

The principal 1st Division attack on 7 June was the 18th Infantry's drive southward toward its D-Day objectives: the high ground north of Trévières and the Mandeville–Mosles area south of the Aure River. For this attack the 3d Battalion, 26th Infantry, was attached. The other tasks confronting the 1st Division were to make contact with the British and to clean out the Colleville area. To accomplish the first, two battalions (the 1st of the 26th Infantry and the 3d of the 16th Infantry) under control of the 16th attacked southeastward with the mission of taking the high ground west and southwest of Port-en-Bessin, including Mt. Cauvin. The clean-up job was assigned to the 1st and 2d Battalions of the 16th Infantry. The 2d Battalion, 26th Infantry, was held in division reserve.

Despite wide dispersion of the attacking battalions and scanty artillery and tank support, all units made good progress against slight and sporadic resistance. A marked degree of enemy disorganization had been observed beginning on the afternoon of D Day. Expected counterattacks had not materialized and the enemy's morale seemed low. The 1st Division realized that it was through the coastal crust and at the moment had to deal only with remnants of the *352d Division*. It was thought, however, that an armored counterattack might be in the making.[2]

On the right, Huppain and the forward slopes of the ridge line 1,000 yards north of Mt. Cauvin were occupied. But the enemy, strongly opposing simultaneous British attacks from the east, continued to hold a narrow wedge between American and British beachheads through Port-en-Bessin and south along the valley of the Drôme River. In the center the 18th Infantry made two crossings of the Aure, the 2d Battalion occupying Mosles and the 3d, Mandeville. The 1st Battalion, effectively supported by five tanks of the 741st Tank Battalion, captured the high ground at Engranville after a fight with something less than a company of German infantry which lasted most of the afternoon.

The success of the 18th Infantry attack was somewhat qualified by the inability of the 3d Battalion, 26th Infantry, on the division's right to take Formigny. Although opposition by exhausted elements of the *916th Regiment* was not heavy, the battalion was unable to get moving.[8]

---

[2] 1st Div G–2 Per Rpt 1.

[8] The 26th Infantry casualties for the day were only 15 killed and missing and 30 wounded. The G–3 of the German *352d Division* in reporting on this action cited the Formigny assault as an example of the sluggishness of American infantry attack over open terrain, which he found in strong contrast to the determined fighting by individual American riflemen in the towns. See MS # B–433 (Ziegelmann).

It was not until the next morning that the enemy was driven out of Formigny by a company of 18th Infantry and some tanks attacking from the Engranville position.

On the German side the *352d Division* at the end of D Day had been chiefly concerned with its open flank where the British were driving into the hole opened by the collapse of the left wing of the *716th Division.* Throughout 7 June there was little General Kraiss could do to repair the damage, for his last organic reserves had had to be committed in the center where the *916th Regiment* was strained to the breaking point. At noon he requested and secured the attachment of the *30th Mobile Brigade.* The brigade, which came up from Coutances on bicycles, arrived only late in the afternoon, its young, inexperienced recruits tired in body and spirit from constant attacks by low-flying planes along the route. One battalion (the *513th*) was committed in the vicinity of Formigny to strengthen the *916th Regiment.*

The brigade, less this battalion, assembled northwest of Bayeux and was attached to the *726th Regiment* with orders to attack the flank of British forces advancing on Bayeux. (*See Map XII*.) Action of German units in the Bayeux area during 7 June was so confused that no coherent story can be told in detail. The whole flank of the *352d Division* from the Drôme River to the division boundary east of St. Léger was falling apart. The disintegration, furthermore, was so rapid that reports reaching division headquarters were late and scattered. As evidence of the confusion, it is worth contrasting the German command picture of the action with what actually happened.[4]

In the early afternoon following the commitment of the *30th Mobile Brigade*, General Kraiss's headquarters believed that the *352d Division* held a thin defensive arc north and northeast of Bayeux from about Vaux-sur-Aure to Sommervieu. From left to right the units engaged were the *30th Mobile Brigade* (−), elements of the *2d Battalion, 916th Regiment*, and elements of the *3d Battalion, 1352d Artillery Regiment*. Having expended their last rounds, these units had destroyed their guns and fought as infantry. South of this line there were only scratch forces, the most important of which were remnants of *Kampfgruppe Meyer* (*2d Battalion, 915th Regiment* and the *Fuesilier Battalion, 352d Division*), thought to be defending weakly northeast and north of Tilly-sur-Seulles. The Bayeux defense was believed to have held during the day, despite penetrations by British armor and a British thrust through Sommervieu which was reported to have split the *2d Battalion, 916th,* from the artillery unit. At midnight, the *352d Division* and *Seventh Army* supposed that the main British advance had been checked short of Bayeux and that countermeasures were in process to avert the fall of the city. While the *352d Division* commander, General Kraiss, seriously doubted that those measures would succeed in view of the depletion of his own forces and their exhaustion after constant pounding by Allied aircraft and

---

[4] See MS # B–433 and MS # B–434 (both by Ziegelmann); *Seventh Army, KTB 1.I.–30.VI.44,* 6 and 7 Jun 44; information from British Cabinet Office Hist Sec. Hist Div files.

naval artillery, he still did not know the true extent of the collapse on his right.[5]

The collapse was, in fact, almost complete. In the morning of 7 June, before the arrival of the *30th Mobile Brigade* on the Drôme River, two battalions of the British 56th Infantry Brigade (50th Division) entered Bayeux and by noon had cleared the city. The British then pushed out along the southwest road to occupy the high ground at Monunirel. The third battalion of the brigade in the meantime advanced about two miles southwest from Vaux-sur-Aure. On the coast, the 47th Royal Marine Commando captured Port-en-Bessin in a stiff fight beginning about 1600, 7 June, and not ending until the early morning hours of 8 June. East of Bayeux, if there were still German forces at nightfall on 7 June, they were no more than remnants with insufficient coherence even to form a resistance pocket within British lines. Two brigades of the 50th Division were south of the Bayeux–Caen highway. On their left and astride that highway was one brigade of the 3d Canadian Division.

The converging moves of the British 50th Division and the U.S. 1st Division on 7 June had squeezed the German *30th Mobile Brigade* and elements of the *726th Regiment* into a narrow corridor along the Drôme River north to its junction with the Aure. (*See Map XIV.*) On 8 June the Allied vise was tightened in an effort to destroy the enemy forces separating the British and American beachheads. On the American side, the mission of attacking to effect a junction with

the British was assigned to the 26th Infantry. The attack, however, never gathered momentum, partly because of the difficulty of assembling the widely dispersed battalions, and partly because of heavy enemy resistance.

The 2d Battalion, 26th Infantry, released from division reserve at 1745, 7 June, had moved during the night from the vicinity of Etreham to the crossroads between Mosles and Tour-en-Bessin which they occupied about dawn. There they awaited the rest of the regiment throughout 8 June. The 1st Battalion, meanwhile, bogged down on 8 June at the Aure River crossing at Etreham, where the enemy fought stubbornly to hold one side of the Drôme corridor. The 3d Battalion remained at Formigny during the morning until it could be relieved by a battalion of the 115th Infantry. In the early afternoon it began a march down the Bayeux highway. At 1800 it attacked through the 2d Battalion positions, and through Tour-en-Bessin to Ste. Anne which it reached shortly after midnight. During the night a violent and confused action took place at Ste. Anne as the Germans, now in process of withdrawing from the corridor, fought to keep the escape route open.

The 1st Division thus failed to trap the enemy. The British were similarly checked east of the Drôme. Elements of the 50th Division attacked and cleared Sully during 8 June but were unable to hold a bridgehead over the Drôme. Other elements of the division pressed in the northern end of the enemy corridor by clearing the château at Fosse Soucy. But, in the face of threatened enemy counterattacks, the British withdrew to high ground near Escures.

---

[5] Losses of the *352d Division* during the day were virtually made up by the attachment of the *30th Mobile Brigade* but the combat value of the latter was inferior. See MS # B–433 (Ziegelmann).

Thanks to these actions, the German *726th Regiment* during the night of 8–9 June was able to extricate the bulk of its forces. This was perhaps the first German withdrawal from coastal positions accomplished on orders from division and corps. In direct disobedience of Hitler's command to hold every inch of ground to the last bullet, the decision reflected the seriousness of the German position. During the morning of 8 June the *352d Division* was out of touch with the *726th Regiment.* At about 1500, however, contact was established with the regimental commander (possibly just west of Sully). He was ordered to resist stubbornly with all available forces until nightfall and then break out to the southwest and form a defensive line from Blay east to Haley and thence south to Agy. Shortly after General Kraiss had given this order, the corps commander, General Marcks, came into the *352d Division* command post. Marcks was asked to approve the decision on the grounds that, if the troops in the Bayeux salient were sacrificed, the division would have nothing with which to repair the rip in its right flank and the way would be open for unopposed Allied marches to the south. "After a long pause, the Commanding General [Marcks] agreed. . . ." [6]

While the U.S. 1st Division and the British converged on Bayeux the 29th Division on D plus 1 still found itself entangled in the enemy's coastal defenses and spent most of the day cleaning up the fragments of enemy units that were shattered but not destroyed by the initial shock of the landings. In some areas small arms fire from groups of enemy

riflemen or isolated strong points was almost continuous; American troops gradually became used to moving under the constant crack of bullets.

D Day had left the units of the 115th and 116th Infantry Regiments and a large part of the two Ranger battalions in the sliver of coast between Vierville and St. Laurent, where they were still meeting scattered opposition. The 175th Infantry was still afloat. A precondition for the division's pursuit of D-Day objectives was to expand this toehold and clear room for maneuver. The 115th Infantry, after mopping up around St. Laurent, attacked generally southwest toward Louvières and Montigny, while the 116th Infantry with Ranger units undertook to clear the bluffs and go to the relief of the three Ranger companies isolated on Pointe du Hoe.

The 115th Infantry made slow progress. Moving on a broad front, the regiment found communication difficult. Furthermore, since the regiment still had no transport, ammunition and heavy weapons had to be hand-carried. Near the end of the day Col. Eugene N. Slappey requested the immediate establishment of army supply points as an urgent prerequisite for further advance.[7]

Colonel Canham's 116th Infantry, on the other hand, advanced rapidly. The regiment moved in column down the coastal road with ten tanks rolling between files of infantry. Tank fire was employed to neutralize small enemy positions and the main body of the regiment pushed on past them. Before noon Canham was only 1,000 yards from Pointe du Hoe. The Rangers awaiting relief

---

[6] MS # B–433 (Ziegelmann).

[7] 29th Div G–3 Jnl.

there then numbered less than 100 effectives. Their position had seriously deteriorated during the night of 6–7 June as a result of a counterattack by the *914th Regiment* which overran their outpost line and pinned the force to a strip of the headland only about 200 yards deep. While destroyer fire and the Rangers' two mortars kept the enemy at bay, the situation remained desperate until the afternoon when two LCVP's landed water, food, and ammunition and about thirty reinforcements. At the same time a series of attacks by the relieving force from the vicinity of St. Pierre-du-Mont, although frustrated by well-placed enemy artillery fire, at least eased the pressure.

By 1630 on 7 June the 175th Infantry (Col. Paul R. Goode) had come ashore and was placed in the line in the vicinity of Gruchy. Additional landings of artillery units swelled the 29th Division's artillery support to a total of twenty-nine guns belonging to five battalions. Although the achievements of the division on D plus 1 seemed slight measured in yards or vital objectives taken, in reality the crust of enemy defenses was broken and the division was set for a full-scale attack on the morrow.

The fighting in the VII Corps zone on D plus 1, like that in V Corps, aimed first at clearing the beachhead already staked out and second at pushing on toward D-Day objectives. *(Map XV)*

The only substantial advances of 7 June were made on the north flank where the two regiments of the 4th Division pushed the enemy back two miles to his strongly fortified positions at Azeville and Crisbecq. The 12th Infantry, attacking on the left from the vicinity of Beuze-ville-au-Plain, reached the forward slope of hills between Azeville and le Bisson where, faced with stiffened resistance, it halted for the night to reorganize. The 22d Infantry on the right advanced directly on Crisbecq. It moved rapidly to a point between Azeville and de Dodainville where it began getting fire from the forts.

Both the Crisbecq and Azeville fortifications were permanent coastal artillery positions thoroughly organized for defense from land attack. Crisbecq was a naval battery with 210-mm. guns.[8] Azeville contained the four French 105-mm. guns of the *2d Battery* of the *1261st Artillery Regiment* (army coastal artillery). At both positions massive concrete blockhouses with underground ammunition storage and interconnecting trenches constituted the core of the fortifications and were ringed with barbed wire and defended by automatic weapons. At Azeville the main positions were outposted with concrete sentry boxes.

Attacks were launched on both forts in battalion strength and were driven back. The task at Crisbecq was especially difficult because approach to the fort was canalized along a narrow hedged trail. Open fields lay on the west, and on the east were either swamplands or steep slopes. The battalion advancing along this trail was counterattacked on the left flank and fell back in considerable confusion to re-establish a line 300 yards south of Bas Village de Dodainville. The Germans, trying to press their advantage with renewed attacks after dark, were routed by naval fire.

In the meantime, along the beach, the

---

[8] In German documents it is called the *Batterie Marcouf.*

3d Battalion of the 22d Infantry had been advancing northward with the mission of reducing the beach fortifications. Progress was slow and costly as troops came under small arms fire from the beach resistance points as well as artillery fire from inland batteries. About 2,000 yards were made during the day and two enemy resistance nests cleared. In the evening the battalion was brought inland as regimental reserve to guard against further counterattacks from the Azeville–Crisbecq positions. During the night the bulk of the battalion returned to the beach to receive the surrender of the enemy at Taret de Ravenoville who had been discouraged from continued resistance chiefly by naval shelling.

In the center of the VII Corps beachhead the day was occupied chiefly with eliminating the enemy forces south of Ste. Mère-Eglise who on D Day had prevented firm junction between the 8th Infantry on the south and the 82d Airborne Division. A patrol of the 82d Airborne Division got through to General Barton during the night and plans were then co-ordinated for the next day's operations. In the morning the 8th Infantry, on General Barton's order, attacked the Turqueville salient. Turqueville itself, held by the *795th Georgian Battalion,* was hit by the 1st Battalion from the east. After a hard fight the Russian unit was talked into surrender by a Russian-speaking American captive. At the same time the 2d and 3d Battalions struck north from their positions near les Forges. The 1st and 2d Battalions were supported by two companies of the 70th Tank Battalion.[9] The 3d Battalion on the

left, advancing astride the main highway, was stopped hard at the Fauville–Ecoqueneauville ridge by machine gun and artillery fire. These troops were shaken loose, however, by the 2d Battalion's capture of Ecoqueneauville, and both units continued the advance. When they reached Ste. Mère-Eglise they found a German counterattack in progress, although they apparently did not recognize it as such.

This counterattack, which lasted most of the day, actually represented General von Schlieben's supreme effort to drive in the Cotentin beachhead from the north. It will be recalled that the *1058th Regiment* (less one battalion) had been ordered to attack St. Mère-Eglise on D Day. Lacking artillery, it had spent all day working through the hedgerows against spasmodic paratroop opposition and only reached Neuville by nightfall. At dawn on D plus 1 the attack was resumed. For it the *1058th* now received attachments of the *456th* and *457th Artillery Battalions,* the *3d Battalion* of the *243d Artillery Regiment* (less one battery), the *Seventh Army Sturm Battalion,* and one company of the *709th Antitank Battalion* with ten self-propelled 75-mm. guns.[10]

After preparatory fire the *Sturm Battalion* began the attack astride the main highway, initially to make contact with elements of the *1058th Regiment* which had been cut off in action during D Day. When contact was made, the attack was reorganized and the *Sturm Battalion* struck down the west side of the highway, with the *1058th* on the east. It is apparent that the *1058th Regiment,* de-

---

[9] 70th Tk Bn AAR.

[10] MS # B–845 (Schlieben).

TROOPS ON UTAH BEACH UNDER ARTILLERY FIRE

moralized in the fighting of the day before, made little progress. The *Sturm Battalion,* however, supported by the *709th Division* assault guns, which the Americans mistook for tanks, carried the attack to the outskirts of Ste. Mère-Eglise.

To the American command the situation looked gravely threatening. Ste. Mère-Eglise, besides being important as a communications hub, was the core of the 82d Airborne Division's position, which elsewhere was still tenuous. General Ridgway, thinking that a German armored thrust was building up, called for assistance. A staff officer met Maj. Gen. J. Lawton Collins, VII Corps commander, at the 4th Division command post near Audouville-la-Hubert.[11] Collins ordered a task force of the 746th Tank Battalion, which had been in 4th Division reserve near Reuville, to proceed at once to Ste. Mère-Eglise. The task force, commanded by Lt. Col. C. G. Hupfer and consisting of Company B, the assault gun platoon, and three headquarters tanks, drove into Ste. Mère-Eglise in the early afternoon and turned north along the Montebourg highway. A few hundred yards out of town the leading tanks came under heavy enemy artillery fire and about the same time spotted the German assault guns in column along the road. A fire fight began which, because of the column formation on each side, was inconclusive. Colonel Hupfer in the meantime reconnoitered a trail east of the main highway leading north into Neuville. Some of the 746th Battalion tanks took this route, entered

Neuville, destroyed two enemy assault guns, occupied the town, and took about sixty prisoners as well as releasing nineteen captured U.S. paratroopers.[12]

More significantly this armored slice northward cut the German forces attacking Ste. Mère-Eglise and began a panic on the German side. For the first time in the early beachhead battles the Americans were confronting the Germans with something like massed armor in a relatively small sector. When the 8th Infantry (−) arrived north of Ste. Mère-Eglise with two companies of the 70th Tank Battalion in support, about sixty American tanks were deployed in the area. While some of the tanks of the 746th Tank Battalion were moving on Neuville, Colonel MacNeely's 2d Battalion, 8th Infantry, joined Colonel Vandervoort's 2d Battalion, 505th Parachute Infantry, in an infantry-tank attack to clear the enemy in the vicinity of Sigeville. Vandervoort, with the commander of the 70th Tank Battalion, Lt. Col. John C. Welborn, directing tank operations from a jeep, advanced up the highway north of Ste. Mère-Eglise, while MacNeely swept in from the west.[13] In the envelopment 300 of the enemy were captured or killed.

The *1058th Regiment,* thus splintered by two separate American attacks and demoralized by the presence of so many American tanks, broke and pulled out in disorder. The *Sturm Battalion* west of the highway and out of contact with the main force also withdrew. The retreat was checked only late in the day by intervention of General Schlieben. The division

---

[11] Collins had commanded the 25th Division in the Pacific theater in 1942 and 1943, achieving a notable combat record in the Guadalcanal and New Georgia campaigns. In December 1943 he was transferred to the European theater, assuming command of the VII Corps the following February.

[12] Hist Div Combat Interv with S–3, 746th Tk Bn.

[13] First Army GO 35. Colonel Welborn was awarded the DSC, with citation covering both this action and action of 6 June.

commander rallied his panicky troops and began putting them into a defensive line about 1,300 yards north of Neuville. Convinced after the failure of the Ste. Mère attack that he no longer had the strength needed for a successful counterattack to reduce the American bridgehead, Schlieben determined that his policy must be simply to contain it and prevent a breakthrough to Cherbourg. He concentrated therefore on building a strong defensive line. He brought into the line a battalion of the *919th Regiment* as well as the *922d Regiment* (*243d Division*), which had arrived during the morning of 7 June. All these elements were formed into a Kampfgruppe under command of Oberst Helmuth Rohrbach, commander of the *729th Regiment*. Further to concentrate his strength, Schlieben ordered the withdrawal of the bulk of the troops from defenses along the east coast which were not under attack. In succeeding days this defense was to be still further reinforced until it constituted a strong barrier to the attempts of the 4th Division to push north.[14]

After the 8th Infantry had pushed north from les Forges, the 325th Glider Infantry began landing in the area in two serials as scheduled. Although somewhat scattered and hit by ground fire, the majority of the gliders came in where planned and rapid assembly was effected. The regiment originally intended as 82d Airborne Division reserve was actually split: one battalion was committed in the la Fière area to strengthen attacks to force a crossing there; and one battalion was attached to the 505th Parachute Infantry for operations to the north of Ste. Mère-Eglise.

[14] MS # B–845 (Schlieben).

While the 82d Airborne Division had thus consolidated its base, its principal D-Day assignment—the establishing of bridgeheads across the Merderet—came no nearer accomplishment. On the contrary, during the morning of 7 June it was touch and go whether a determined enemy counterattack might not break the division's hold on the east bank of the river. At about 0800 the attack of elements of the enemy *1057th Regiment* began to form against the American la Fière position. Mortar and machine gun fire ranged in, chiefly on Company A, 505th Parachute Infantry, which was dug in to the right of the bridge. An hour or so later four Renault tanks led a German infantry advance across the bridge. The lead tank was disabled by either bazooka fire or a shell from a 57-mm. antitank gun that was supporting Company A. Although this checked the advance, the German infantry took advantage of the cover furnished by the knocked-out tank and some burned-out vehicles, which the American defenders had pulled onto the causeway during the night, to open a critical fire fight at close range. At the same time German mortar shells fell in increasing numbers among Company A's foxholes. The American platoon immediately to the right of the bridge was especially hard hit and eventually reduced to but fifteen men. These men, however, encouraged by the heroic leadership of Sgt. William D. Owens and by the presence in the thick of the fighting of division officers, including General Ridgway, held their line. The fight was halted at last by a German request for a half-hour's truce to remove the wounded. When the half hour expired, the enemy did not return to the attack. A count of Company A revealed that

PLANES AND GLIDERS CIRCLING LES FORGES *on the morning of 7 June. Dust is raised by gliders landing in fields at upper left. Wrecked gliders in foreground are some of those that landed on the evening of 6 June.*

almost half of its combat effectives had fallen in the defense, either killed or seriously wounded.[15]

South of the 82d Division the 101st Division with small forces of the 3d Battalion, 506th Parachute Infantry, and the 501st Parachute Infantry still held precarious positions on the north bank of the Douve. Isolated and short of ammunition, these troops were unable to go on the offensive on 7 June. They nevertheless scored a notable success during the day when together they killed or captured the whole *1st Battalion* of the *6th Parachute Regiment*. This battalion had advanced on regimental order to Ste. Marie-du-Mont on D Day and then had been cut off. Patrols sent out by von der Heydte on 7 June from St. Côme-du-Mont became involved in fighting a few hundred yards east of the town and could not get through. The isolated battalion in the meantime was already moving south. About the middle of the afternoon paratroopers at le Port and la Barquette observed the Germans (about 800 in all) advancing through the open fields and marshes north of the river and east of the Carentan highway. In independent actions the men under Captain Shettle and those under Colonel Johnson opened fire. Caught by surprise and bluffed by demonstrations designed to impress them with overwhelming American strength, the majority of the Germans surrendered. About 250 were taken by Captain Shettle's men at le Port, about 350 by Colonel Johnson at la Barquette.[16] More than half the remainder were killed in the fire fight preceding surrender. Only twenty-five men escaped to Carentan.[17]

During D Day no news of the actions along the Douve had reached the 101st Division headquarters. Since capture of the Douve bridges was one of the most important of the division's missions, on which depended the immediate security of VII Corps on the south and ultimate junction with V Corps, General Taylor decided on the afternoon of D Day to send the 506th Parachute Infantry (less the 3d Battalion) south on a reconnaissance in force. The reconnaissance, which in fact became an attack, led off on the morning of 7 June in column down the road from Culoville. Though harassed by scattered rifle fire, the 506th reached Vierville without undue delay, cleared the town, and then split, with the 1st Battalion heading down the highway to Beaumont and the 2d diverging cross country to the left toward Angoville-au-Plain. Halted just beyond Vierville by heavy small arms fire, the attacks broke loose only after a platoon of medium tanks had been brought up and attached to the 2d Battalion. The 1st Battalion fought its way down astride the highway to Beaumont where it was stopped by two enemy counterattacks.[18] The 2d Battalion medium tanks together with a platoon of light tanks were then sent to its support and they advanced another 1,000 yards to just east of St. Côme-du-Mont.

---

[15] Details from S. L. A. Marshall, Regimental Study 5, MS. Hist Div files. Marshall's full account was based on group and individual interviews which he collected.

[16] Colonel Johnson was awarded the DSC.

[17] MS # B–839 (von der Heydte).

[18] These "counterattacks" may have been only the probing patrol actions by which von der Heydte was trying to regain contact with his *1st Battalion*. Von der Heydte reports no counterattacks in this area. Lacking two of his four battalions, he was much more concerned at the moment with maintaining his position than with aggressive action. See MS # B–839.

At the same time that the 506th Infantry was attacking south, the 2d Battalion of the 501st Infantry, which on D Day had fought an isolated and inconclusive action around les Droueries, continued its attempt to push westward into St. Côme-du-Mont, still held in some force by two battalions under von der Heydte's command. This attack, co-ordinated in early afternoon with Colonel Sink, commanding the 506th Infantry, and supported by six medium tanks of the 746th Tank Battalion and the guns of the 65th Armored Field Artillery Battalion, made substantial headway. But it was a typical Normandy battle—cleaning out dug-in enemy riflemen and machine gun positions from the hedgerows field by field. The battalion did not get far enough west to tie in with the 1st Battalion, 506th Infantry. The latter was therefore ordered to withdraw to Beaumont and all units held during the night, reorganizing for resumption of the attack the next day.

The small American gains of 7 June encouraged the Germans to feel that they had at least frustrated the Allied time schedule.[19] On the other hand, their own countermeasures planned for the day had also been checked, and, in general, it was clear that the invasion had succeeded in gaining a foothold. The build-up race was on.

On the Caen front the *21st Panzer Division* had called off its counterattack on the evening of D Day short of its objectives. (*See Map XII.*) Throughout 7 June the division remained on the defensive except for small unsuccessful attacks east of the Orne against the British airborne forces. The *12th SS Panzer Division* began arriv-

ing in assembly areas between Caen and Bronay during the day and *Panzer Lehr Division* formed to its left rear, north and northeast of Tilly-sur-Seulles. In the afternoon the reconnaissance battalion of the *12th SS Panzer Division* was committed to reconnoiter the wide gap between the *21st Panzer* and the *352d Divisions.*[20] But air attacks had so delayed the assembly of *I SS Panzer Corps* and caused such heavy casualties that the corps postponed until the morning of 8 June the scheduled two-division counterattack to recapture Courseulles. Rundstedt on 7 June had decided to put his own armored staff, *Panzer Group West* under General Geyr, in charge of the attack. Geyr was attached to *Seventh Army* and ordered to take over the sector on both sides of the Orne River and west as far as Tilly-sur-Seulles, seal off the penetrations at Caen and in the *352d* Division sector, and counterattack the Allies who had broken through southeast of Bayeux. But Geyr did not arrive to take over until the night of 8–9 June. In the meantime *I SS Panzer Corps* had decided to make only a limited-objective attack with the *12th SS* and *21st Panzer Divisions* and a Kampfgruppe of *Panzer Lehr Division,* pending the arrival of the tanks of the latter division. The attack of 8 June to gain a line of departure for the later planned three-division attack made little progress and before evening both

[19] *Tagesmeldung,* 7 Jun 44. *Seventh Army, KTB Anlagen 6.–30.VI.44;* MS # B–433 (Ziegelmann).

[20] Apparently this reconnaissance unit tangled with the 3d Canadian Division near Authie and an engagement resulted heavy enough to give the Canadians the impression of an enemy counterattack. See notes by British Cabinet Office Hist Sec. Hist Div files. The German *Seventh Army* war diary is, however, emphatic on the point that no attack by *I SS Panzer Corps* took place on 7 June. The narrative (MS # C–024) of General Kraemer, chief of staff of the corps, confirms this.

divisions had gone over to the defensive.[21] The *12th SS* was holding positions astride the Caen–Bayeux road between Authie and Carpiquet. The *21st Panzer Division,* also on the defensive, was split on either side of the Orne. *Panzer Lehr* remained in assembly areas near Thury-Harcourt, southwest of Caen. As the attack failed to materialize on 8 June and Allied pressure continued to build up, the plan for a bold strike to the coast with two armored divisions abreast was abandoned. *Seventh Army,* concerned over the loss of Bayeux, decided to maneuver to recapture it. *I SS Panzer Corps* intended, therefore, to hold north and west of Caen while directing *Panzer Lehr* and portions of the *12th SS Panzer Division* on Bayeux. Thus, as General Geyr commented later, the fist was unclenched just as it was ready to strike.[22]

While *Seventh Army* indulged fatal second thoughts concerning its critical right flank, Field Marshal Rommel began to focus attention on the threat to Cherbourg. Reports of large-scale Allied airborne and glider landings in the Coutances–Lessay area caused him on the morning of 7 June to order the immediate move of both the *17th SS Panzer Grenadier Division* and the *77th Division* to meet the threat. He believed that the Coutances landings were part of an Allied move to cut off Cherbourg and the whole Cotentin Peninsula and that it was therefore an "unconditional necessity" to counter with all available forces. The risk of weakening Brittany by the transfer of the *77th Division* could be accepted, he

thought, since it looked as though the Allies were fully committed in Normandy.[23]

Later in the morning *Seventh Army* assigned the task of cleaning up the west coast of the Cotentin to the *II Parachute Corps* then in Brittany. In addition to the *77th Division* and the *17th SS Panzer Grenadier Division,* already under orders to move, the corps was to command the *3d Parachute Division.* The latter received marching orders to move by motor to assembly areas near those planned for the *17th SS* northeast of Avranches.

The *77th Division,* which received orders to move by foot at 1015, actually began moving out at 1500. By 2000, advance elements of the *17th SS Panzer Grenadier Division* had crossed the Loire. But traffic thereafter was interrupted by Allied air attacks on the Loire bridges which lasted for an hour and a half and scored twenty-four hits on a railroad bridge that the division had been using. With requisitioned vehicles the *3d Parachute Division* formed an advanced motorized group consisting of one battalion from each of the regiments, two engineer companies, two artillery batteries, and the antiaircraft and signal battalions. This group moved out, surprisingly, without opposition from the air. But *Seventh Army* reported that movement of the remainder of the division was dependent on motor transport space from the two corps remaining in Brittany and requested an additional 2,000 tons from *OB WEST* and other reserves. On the morning of 8 June after General der Fallschirmtruppen Eugen Meindl, commanding *II Parachute Corps,* had personally

---

[21] See special Hist Div questionnaires on this action answered by Kraemer (CofS, *I SS Panzer Corps*) and Bayerlein (CG, *Panzer Lehr Division*) , MS # B–814. See also MS # C–024 (Kraemer) .

[22] MS # B–466 (Geyr) .

[23] *Seventh Army, KTB 1.I.–30.VI.44,* 7 Jun 44.

confirmed that the reports of airborne landings in the Coutances area were without foundation, the *II Parachute Corps* with two divisions was diverted to St. Lô.[24]

Concern over the defense of Cherbourg again faded before the greater urgency of holding at Caen. This reaction was not due to ignorance of the true situation. On the contrary, on the evening of 6 June a copy of the VII Corps field order had been picked up by the *914th Regiment* from a boat that drifted ashore in the mouth of the Vire River. The next evening a copy of the V Corps order was taken from the body of an American officer killed at Vierville-sur-Mer. The Germans thus had in their hands the entire scheme of maneuver and order of battle for American units in the first phase of the invasion.[25]

The fact that possession of these plans had no effect on the German conduct of operations throws considerable light on the tactical and strategic problems facing the enemy command. From the plans, *Seventh Army* and *OB WEST* learned that the major immediate objectives of Bradley's forces were Cherbourg and St. Lô. But this news, after the first day, was hardly a revelation. The plans were confined to outlines of the initial phase and did not reveal American intentions beyond the establishment of a lodgment including Cherbourg and St. Lô. Even if they had revealed the planned American push into Brittany, however, the Germans could not have profited materially from the knowledge. Rommel was not free to shift the weight of his defense to the American flank to block either the assault on Cherbourg or Bradley's planned move southward toward Brittany. The major operational threat, from his point of view, remained the possibility of a British breakout at Caen and a sweep to Paris. Without British plans, the Germans could not be sure that such a move had not been calculated. Even if it had not, a German collapse on that sector would undoubtedly be exploited to turn the flank of *Seventh Army*. In short, complete knowledge of American intentions could not have altered the logic of the battle dictated by terrain, the disposition of forces, and the location of the strategic objectives.[26]

One fact might have been deduced from the plans: that they envisaged such a large commitment of force as to rule out a second major landing attempt. General Dollmann drew this conclusion. Field Marshal Rundstedt was inclined to agree. But OKW and Hitler figured the evidence was inconclusive. Again the fact that British plans were missing left a large realm for speculation and, according to German intelligence estimates, a large uncommitted military force.

As of 1 June, the Germans had estimated that the Allies had combat forces in the United Kingdom equivalent to eighty-five divisions including eight airborne divisions.[27] The Allied high com-

---

[24] *Ibid.*, 8 June; cf. MS # B–401 (Meindl). The two divisions at first ordered to St. Lô were the *17th SS Panzer Grenadier* and the *77th Division*. The *77th*, however, was later ordered to Montebourg (see below, p. 370) and the *3d Parachute Division* actually came into the St. Lô area.

[25] See MS # B–656 (Pemsel); MS # B–637 (Blumentritt); MS # B–636 (Ziegelmann).

[26] *Ibid.*

[27] MS # B–782 (Oberst Anton Staubwasser, G–2, *Army Group B*). Cf. MS # B–901 in which Zimmermann (G–3 of *OB WEST*) says that the large number of Allied units estimated to be still in England after the Normandy assault made it impossible for the Germans to rule out the probability of a second landing.

mand, aware that the enemy was overestimating British and American strength, made every effort to sustain the illusion. In addition, the Allies made use of the high regard in which General Patton was held by the Germans to persuade them that an army group under his command still remained in England after 6 June. The existence of this large reserve force was easy for the Germans to believe since it fitted with their preconceptions that a second major landing would strike the *Kanalkueste*. The Allies fostered this belief by various ruses so successfully that not until July did OKW finally appreciate that no second landing would take place. In the meantime the *Fifteenth Army* remained tied to the *Kanalkueste*.

Tactically, German knowledge of American plans might have made some difference by enabling the Germans to mass reserves and stage counterattacks at points along the planned axes of the American advance. Such a concentration of reserves was actually carried out by *Seventh Army* in and around St. Lô, but even without knowledge of American intentions the Germans would probably still have chosen to defend St. Lô because of its importance as a road junction and the terrain configurations that made it defensively strong. For the rest, the Germans could never maneuver with enough freedom to exploit any tactical situation. Instead of being able to mass reserves in accordance with plan, General Dollmann picked up the reserve companies and battalions as they straggled in, delayed and decimated by air attacks, and put them in to plug gaps in his lines wherever the immediate danger seemed gravest. The policy of maintaining an intact defense, whether wise or not, meant that German

tactical commanders in disposing their reserves were continually confronted with emergencies and never with tactical choices. Absorbed, therefore, in sealing off today's penetrations, they had no resources with which to face tomorrow's threat.

Junction between V and VII Corps

The failure of both V and VII Corps to make any substantial progress toward the vital joining of the beachheads, together with the general slowness of the advances on D-Day objectives, had become a matter of concern to General Eisenhower, General Montgomery, General Bradley, and both corps commanders. The American build-up was far behind schedule, particularly in the landing of supplies. At the end of D plus 1 not more than a quarter of the planned 14,500 tons were ashore. The troop build-up, planned at about 107,000 for the first two days, was 20,000 short. Scarcely more than half the 14,000 vehicles had been disembarked.[28] Delayed build-up was in part due to technical difficulties of unloading and in part to the slow advance inland. Rapid expansion of the beachhead was vital to permit the massing of supplies and reinforcements. Both expansion and reinforcement were necessary to defend the lodgment against the expected full-scale enemy counterattacks which, it was thought,

---

[28] Unloading figures for the first two days are estimates. Figures for UTAH have been taken from ANCXF, *Report*, Vol. III, Rpt by Comdr Assault Force U, pp. 33–34. OMAHA figures, not available from naval sources, are taken from the Provisional Engineer Special Brigade and OMAHA Beach Command situation reports as cited in [Clifford Jones] NEPTUNE, Training, Mounting, the Artificial Ports (The Administrative and Logistical History of the ETO: Part VI), MS, II, 175ff. Hist Div files.

U.S. COMMANDERS. *Left to right: Generals Bradley, Gerow, Eisenhower, and Collins.*

might come any time after D plus 3 and would almost certainly come during the first week.

General Eisenhower toured the assault area by mine layer with Admiral Ramsay on 7 June and ordered that the immediate tactical plan be altered to give priority to a concerted drive by both corps to link up through Isigny and Carentan. General Bradley gave orders accordingly during the afternoon of 7 June. For VII Corps the changed priority resulted in assigning to the 101st Airborne Division the sole task of capturing Carentan with reinforcements to be provided if necessary. V Corps gave the 29th Division the primary mission of seizing Isigny while the 1st Division continued the push east to join with the British and south to expand the beachhead.[29]

Plans for the employment of the 29th Division were discussed that evening at General Gerhardt's command post in a rock quarry just off OMAHA Beach. (*See Map XIV.*) The mission of taking Isigny was given to the 175th Infantry; it was to drive between the 116th and the 115th straight for its objective while the other two regiments cleared either flank of the advance. The 747th Tank Battalion (less Company B) was attached to the 175th Infantry and the attack jumped off that night. Advancing along the Longueville–Isigny road with tanks leading the columns of infantry, the regiment captured la Cambe before daylight and met its first real resistance about three miles west of that town. Antitank guns knocked out

[29] Cbl, Eisenhower to Marshall, 8 Jun 44. Eisenhower Personal Files.

one tank in front of the town and artillery fire disabled six more to the west. However, isolated enemy resistance, here and in other villages north and south of the Isigny road, was overrun, in some cases with the aid of naval fire. There was no organized resistance in Isigny itself, and it was entered and cleaned out during the night of 8–9 June. The town was partially gutted and burning from heavy naval bombardment.

The speed of the 175th Infantry's advance collapsed the left flank of the *352d Division* and opened a hole in German lines comparable to the disintegration at Bayeux. The sector overrun was the responsibility of the *914th Regiment* and had contained, in addition to the remnants of that regiment, a battalion of the *352d Artillery Regiment* and the *439th Ost Battalion*. In the Grandcamp area, where the 116th Infantry was attacking, were additional units of the *914th Regiment* and the *3d Battalion* of the *1716th Artillery Regiment* which manned fixed coastal artillery positions there. General Kraiss recognized that in view of the increasing pressure on his center and right he could not expect to hold with his left. At about the same time that he ordered the *30th Mobile Brigade* and *726th Regiment* to pull out of the Drôme corridor, he gave similar orders to the *914th Regiment*. They were to fight to hold all positions during the day but withdraw the bulk of their forces at night south of the Aure. A small bridgehead was to be held at all cost northeast of Isigny. The isolation of the various units in the Grandcamp–Isigny area as well as the presence of valuable artillery pieces there complicated the problem of withdrawal. It required time to organize and carry out. No

time was granted. The *914th Regiment* found itself unable to offer effective resistance on the road to Isigny. The battalion of the *352d Artillery Regiment* had to pull out in such a hurry that its guns were abandoned, thus reducing division artillery for the fighting on 9 June to fourteen guns. The *Ost* battalion which was supposed to blow the bridge at Isigny across the Aure retreated without doing so.

The fall of Isigny meant that the *352d Division* could no longer block the corridor between the American bridgeheads. The *914th Regiment* was ordered to organize a defense south of the Aure in the vicinity of Hill 35 near la Madeleine to prevent the division's left flank from being rolled up. Kraiss counted on the Aure inundations to cover the gap in his lines between Isigny and Trévières.[30]

While the main 29th Division attack gathered momentum that carried it without pause to its objective, both the 115th and 116th Infantry Regiments had cracked resistance in the coastal area, and virtually completed the seizure of the whole of the high ground north of the Aure River by the end of the day. The troops of the 115th met almost no resistance, although lack of transport brought them tired and without rations to their objectives overlooking the river. The 116th Infantry, reinforced with Rangers and two companies of tanks, and supported by destroyer fire, achieved the relief of the Rangers on Pointe du Hoe before noon and then proceeded to Grandcamp where, because of a canalized approach over a flooded area, it ran into a nasty fight lasting until dark. One battal-

---

[30] MS # B–434 (Ziegelmann).

TO VALOGNES   ST. COME-DU-MONT   TO CARENTAN

ST. COME-DU-MONT AREA

ion of the 116th had been detached to sweep south of the main regimental advance toward Maisy. The Maisy position was taken on 9 June and the rest of the area mopped up to the Vire River.

With dispatch V Corps had completed its part of the drive to join the American beachheads. The 101st Airborne Division had a much harder time. (*Map XVI*) After the failure of the 506th Parachute Infantry (Colonel Sink) on 7 June to wrest St. Côme-du-Mont from the *6th Parachute Regiment,* a much larger attack was mounted the following day. The 1st and 2d Battalions of the 506th were reinforced with the 3d Battalion, 327th Glider Infantry,[31] the 3d Battalion, 501st Parachute Infantry, eight light tanks, and the 65th Armored Field Artillery Battalion. The glider battalion, commanded by Lt. Col. Ray C. Allen, on the left wing of the attack was to pass to the east of St. Côme-du-Mont, proceed down the main highway, and blow the bridges on the Carentan causeway. Colonel Ewell's battalion of the 501st was to attack to the south of St. Côme to cut the highway there while Colonel Sink's two battalions (506th) drove in column directly into the town. Behind effective artillery prepara-

tory fire followed by a rolling barrage, the attack jumped off at about 0500.[32] The glider battalion bogged down in the hedgerows. But Colonel Ewell's men, despite considerable confusion and intermingling of units, reached their objectives south of St. Côme within three hours. In the meantime the battalions of the 506th pressed against the town from the east and artillery continued to fall heavily on the German defenders. In the first hour and a half, the 65th Armored Field Artillery Battalion fired about 2,500 rounds of 105-mm. high explosive.

The brunt of the U.S. attack was borne by the *3d Battalion, 1058th Regiment,* which on 7 June had been reinforced by two companies of the *3d Battalion, 6th Parachute Regiment,* from Carentan. Early in the morning, the *1058th* men under heavy artillery fire began to show signs of cracking. Von der Heydte, still in charge of the defense, had no more reserves to bring up. Observing that men of the *1058th* were beginning to straggle in retreat westward and having lost contact with the *1058th* battalion headquarters, von der Heydte decided to pull out his own units and such troops of the *1058th* as he could contact. The withdrawal involved some severe fighting with Ewell's battalion posted south of the town, but eventually the majority of the Germans got out to the west and retreated on Carentan following generally the axis of railroad embankment.

This route was also taken during the day by the *2d Battalion, 6th Parachute*

---

[31] The 327th Glider Infantry, like all glider regiments at the time, had only two organic rifle battalions. In the informal reorganization of the airborne division between the Sicily experience and the Normandy D Day, a third rifle battalion was added to the glider regiments of both the 82d and 101st Airborne Divisions by splitting another regiment, the 401st, between them. Thus the 1st Battalion, 401st Glider Infantry, while retaining its formal status as an independent unit, normally functioned as the 3d Battalion of the 327th; the 2d Battalion, 401st, similarly constituted the 3d Battalion, 325th Glider Infantry, 82d Airborne Division. To avoid confusion the attached battalions will be referred to as the 3d Battalions of the respective foster regiments.

[32] For details of this action see S. L. A. Marshall's account based on his interviews with personnel of the 101st Airborne Division. MS in Hist Div files. The story is also told in detail in Rapport and Norwood, *Rendezvous with Destiny,* pp. 153–59.

Regiment, pulling back from north of St. Côme. With surprising ease the *2d Battalion* disengaged and streamed southward. Most of the men swam the Douve and arrived in Carentan with few losses. There von der Heydte with the bulk of two battalions plus elements of the *1058th Regiment* organized his defense. Late on 8 June he had learned that Isigny had fallen and, primarily concerned with possible attack against Carentan from the east, he at first placed the whole *2d Battalion* on that side of the city.[33]

The U.S. 101st Airborne Division, meanwhile, with the occupation of St. Côme-du-Mont, completed the clearing of the enemy north of the Douve and east of the Merderet. Preparations began at once for an all-out attack on Carentan from the north. In preparation for that attack, the 101st Airborne Division, by the night of 8 June, had grouped three regiments along the Douve with a fourth regiment assembled in reserve near Vierville. The 502d Parachute Infantry was placed in line on the right flank from the junction of the Douve and Merderet Rivers to Houesville. The 506th Parachute Infantry was assembled astride the Carentan highway, and the 327th Glider Infantry, which had come in by sea, relieved elements of the 506th and 501st Parachute Infantry Regiments at la Barquette and le Port. The 501st Parachute Infantry was in reserve.

The scheme of this attack had been worked out by the division in England. It appeared then that the only feasible route of attack was across the river flats in the vicinity of Brevands. Accordingly VII Corps on 8 June ordered attack in this

zone. On 9 June, however, Colonel Sink led a patrol across the causeway toward Carentan. He was fired on and returned before reaching the city. The reports he sent back were apparently misinterpreted to indicate that Carentan was only lightly held. It was therefore considered possible to make a two-pronged attack across the causeway and through Brevands to envelop the city.[34]

The final plan was for the 327th Glider Infantry to make the main effort on the left, crossing the Douve near Brevands to clear the area between Carentan and Isigny and join with V Corps near the highway bridge over the Vire. Since the key to possession of this objective area was Carentan, the 327th planned to use the bulk of its force in an attack on the city from the east. At the same time the 502d Parachute Infantry, relieved of its defensive mission on the right flank by the 501st, would cross the causeway over the Douve River northwest of Carentan, bypass the city on the west, and seize Hill 30. To secure Carentan after its capture, the 101st Airborne Division had the additional mission of occupying the high ground along the railway west of the city as far as the Prairies Marécageuses.

The causeway over which the 502d Parachute Infantry was to attack was banked six to nine feet above the marshlands of the Douve and crossed four bridges over branches of the river and canals. One of the bridges was destroyed by the Germans. Difficulties in repairing this under fire forced postponement of the right wing of the division attack, first sched-

[33] MS # B–839 (von der Heydte).

[34] Account based on correspondence conducted by Lt. Leonard Rapport, 101st Division Historian, with General Taylor and other 101st commanders. Other patrols were sent out by the 327th Glider Infantry.

CARENTAN CAUSEWAY. *In foreground is northwestern tip of Carentan. Circles indicate position of bridges.*

uled for the night of 9–10 June. It was the middle of the afternoon of 10 June before the 3d Battalion, 502d Parachute Infantry (Lt. Col. Robert G. Cole) advanced over the causeway single file. The men moved in a low crouch or crawled, and it took three hours for the point to cross three of the bridges. Then the enemy opened fire from a farmhouse and hedgerows, methodically searching the ditches with machine guns. At the fourth bridge a Belgian Gate had been drawn so far across the road that only one man at a time could squeeze by it. Under cover of artillery fire, which all afternoon worked on enemy positions, this maneuver was tried. Six men made it; the seventh was hit, and the attempt was abandoned in favor of building up additional fire. Mortars were brought forward. The stalemate, however, lasted until midnight while enemy fire and a bombing and strafing attack after dark took heavy toll of the thin battalion line stretched across the causeway. After midnight, resistance slackened and three companies were able to filter men through the bottleneck and across the last bridge where they could deploy on either side of the highway.

The nub of the opposition seemed to be a large farmhouse to the west of the road on ground that rose sharply from the marshes. In the morning of 11 June after attempts to knock this out with artillery had failed, Colonel Cole, battalion commander, ordered a charge which he and his executive officer, Lt. Col. John P. Stopka, led. Followed at first by only a quarter of their 250 men, Cole and Stopka ran through enemy fire. The charge gathered momentum as more men got up and ran forward. The farmhouse was not occupied but the Germans had rifle pits and machine gun emplacements in hedgerows to the west. These were overrun and the Germans killed with grenades and bayonets.[35]

The heavy casualties and disorganization of the battalion prevented Cole from following up his advantage. Instead he sent word back to have the 1st Battalion of the regiment pass through and continue the attack south. The 1st Battalion, which was near the fourth causeway bridge when request came to move forward, reached Colonel Cole's position through heavy fire. But since it was as hard hit and disorganized as the 3d Battalion it was in no better condition to move on. Both battalions set up a defensive line and held on during 11 June against determined German counterattacks, which on one occasion threatened to break through. The 2d Battalion took over the line during the night, but the 502d Parachute Infantry was too exhausted to renew the attack and the 506th Parachute Infantry was sent to its relief.

While the bitter battle of the Carentan causeway was being fought, the left wing of the 101st Airborne Division attack had carried south and made tenuous contact with V Corps units east of Carentan. In the early morning hours of 10 June all three battalions of the 327th Glider Infantry were across the Douve near Brevands. One company, reconnoitering to Auville-sur-le Vey, met the 29th Reconnaissance Troop and Company K of the 175th Infantry. The 175th Infantry (29th Division) had followed up the capture of Isigny by sending Company K to take the

---

[35] For exceptional bravery in this action Colonel Cole was awarded the Medal of Honor. The award was made after Cole's death in the Holland airborne operation in September 1944.

Vire bridge at Auville-sur-le Vey while the main body of the regiment moved toward objectives in the Lison–la Fotelaie area to the south. The bridge was found to have been destroyed and the company, reinforced with the reconnaissance troop and a platoon of tanks, fought most of the day of 9 June to force a crossing. They forded the river late in the afternoon, seized Auville-sur-le Vey, and held it during the night while engineers built the bridge behind them. Contact with the airborne unit the next day was only the beginning of the link between the corps. A savage fight remained for the possession of Carentan as well as some confused and costly maneuvering to clear the ground to the east.

The Germans meanwhile made plans to reinforce the city, whose defense Field Marshal Rommel considered vital not only to prevent the junction of the American beachheads but to forestall any attempt by General Bradley to cut the Cotentin by a drive southwest across the Vire toward Lessay and Périers. As immediate stopgap measures *LXXXIV Corps* sent von der Heydte two *Ost* battalions and remnants of the defenders of Isigny. He placed these troops, of limited combat value, on the east side of the city and concentrated the two battalions of his own regiment on the north. But this was still admittedly a weak defense for such a critical objective. Late on 9 June Rommel decided to commit the *II Parachute Corps* (Meindl), which was on its way up from Brittany, to counter this threat.[36] Under Meindl's corps, the *17th SS Panzer Grena-*

dier Division (Generalmajor der Waffen-SS Werner Ostendorff) was assigned the primary mission of blocking an Allied westward thrust. Ostendorff's orders were to move to positions southwest of Carentan prepared to counterattack south of the city.

These plans were frustrated by the difficulty of getting the units into position. On 8 June the move of Meindl's troops was reported greatly delayed by air attack and sabotage. Ostendorff's division had been forced by continued severe air attacks on the railroads to make most of its march northward by road. Shortage of gasoline then further delayed the move. By the end of 11 June only Ostendorff's forward elements had reached their assembly areas southwest of Carentan.[37]

While awaiting reinforcements and holding off the concentric attacks of the 101st Airborne Division, von der Heydte in Carentan was running desperately short of ammunition. It was impossible to bring up resupplies by truck in view of the shortage of motor transport and gas and Allied air interdiction of the roads. *OB WEST* at last considered the need so critical that an air supply mission was flown during the night of 11–12 June and eighteen tons of infantry ammunition and 88-mm. shells were dropped to von der Heydte on a field south of Raids, some seven miles southwest of Carentan.[38] This, the first air supply mission attempted by the Germans in Normandy, came too late to save Carentan.

On 10 June the bulk of the 327th Glider Infantry pressed in on Carentan from the northeast. Its initial objective

---

[36] The corps actually controlled only the *17th SS Panzer Grenadier Division*. The *77th Division* had been diverted to Montebourg. See below, pp. 371, 395

[37] *Seventh Army, KTB 1.I.–30.VI.44*, 11 Jun 44.
[38] *Oberquartiermeister West, KTB 1.I.–17.VIII.44*, 11 Jun 44.

was to seize the highway and railroad bridges over the Vire–Taute Canal and so seal off the city from the east. The regiment advanced rapidly until at 1800 it came within five hundred yards of its objective. Stopped by enemy fire from the east bank, it reorganized and resumed the drive with two battalions abreast on either side of the Carentan–Isigny highway. The men fought until midnight through those last five hundred yards and succeeded at last in clearing the enemy from the east bank and digging in along the hedgerows beside the canal.

Col. Joseph H. Harper, who had taken command of the 327th Glider Infantry that afternoon, now decided against any attempt to rush the bridge in favor of moving a portion of his force north to cross on a partly demolished footbridge and approach Carentan through the wooded area along the Bassin à Flot. Most of the regiment would hold positions along the canal and support the attack by firing into the city. After a patrol had repaired the footbridge, three companies crossed under enemy mortar fire during the morning of 11 June, but were unable to advance more than a few hundred yards before they were stopped by enemy fire from the outskirts of Carentan.

In the evening of 11 June, First Army decided to commit another regiment and co-ordinate the two wings of the attack by forming all units into a single task force under command of Brig. Gen. Anthony McAuliffe, artillery commander of the 101st Airborne Division. The 506th Parachute Infantry was to take over from the 502d the attack on the west toward Hill 30. Colonel Harper would continue to hold east of Carentan while attacking with a battalion plus one company along

the Bassin à Flot. The 501st Parachute Infantry was to be taken from defensive positions north of the Douve and committed through the Brevands bridgehead. It was to drive east of the 327th Glider Infantry in a wider envelopment of Carentan designed to link with the 506th Infantry south of the city at Hill 30.

Gerow's corps was drawn only slightly into this new effort. The bulk of V Corps continued the drive south to expand the beachhead. But inasmuch as the 101st Airborne Division task force was now wholly absorbed with the envelopment of Carentan it became necessary to use V Corps units to protect the east flank in the area between the Douve and Vire Rivers. The bridgehead at Auville-sur-le Vey was reinforced on 11 June by the 3d Battalion, 41st Armored Infantry Regiment of the 2d Armored Division, which had begun landing on 9 June. In addition, on 12 June, the 175th Infantry was ordered to reconnoiter in force in the region of Montmartin-en-Graignes and seize two bridges over the Vire–Taute Canal, to secure the still insubstantial link between the corps from German counterattack from the south.

The city of Carentan blazed during the night under concentrations of naval fire, artillery, mortars, and tank destroyer guns. The attack of the 506th Parachute Infantry got started at 0200, 12 June, and advanced rapidly against slight resistance. On his objective, Hill 30, Colonel Sink at 0500 ordered the 2d Battalion to attack into Carentan. Despite interdictory artillery fire and some spasmodic machine gun fire the battalion entered the city within a few hours. At the same time the 327th Glider Infantry on the northwest attacked out of the woods at Bassin à Flot and

CARENTAN AND HILL 30 AREA

drove rapidly into the center of town. The two units met at about 0730. Only enemy stragglers remained to contest possession of the city. While the concentric attack squeezed into the city, the wider envelopment made equally rapid progress as the 501st Parachute Infantry swept down east of Carentan and made contact with the 506th half an hour after the entry into the city.[39]

The closing of the trap had captured the objective, but few enemy prisoners were caught. The fact is that von der Heydte had pulled out of the city before dark on 11 June without being observed and had set up a defense line to the southwest.[40] This new resistance line was discovered in the afternoon (12 June) when General Taylor attempted to push the attack to the southwest. His objective was to establish a deep defense of Carentan hooked up on the right with the 82d Airborne Division, which was driving south across the Merderet in the direction of Baupte.[41] The 506th Parachute Regiment thrust out on the axis of the Baupte road while the 501st attacked along the Périers road. But both bogged down and by the end of the day had reached out only a few hundred yards from the line of departure near Hill 30.

The simultaneous effort to secure the ground east of Carentan on 12 June proved just as inconclusive as the push

westward. In the morning a task force consisting of two companies of the 175th Infantry, reinforced by mortars and heavy machine guns, crossed the Vire. Enemy outposts of the newly arrived mobile Kampfgruppe of the *275th Division* [42] observed the crossings but made no serious attempts to interfere with them. Not far from Montmartin, however, the Germans ambushed and badly cut up one company on a hedgerow-lined road. Remnants of the company withdrew north of Montmartin to re-form and there joined with the remainder of the task force. Into this position in the afternoon came the 1st Battalion, 327th Glider Infantry, which with the 2d Battalion had attacked south early in the afternoon after the capture of Carentan. The combined force then secured high ground south of Montmartin. The 2d Battalion in the meantime had been checked at Deville to the northeast. During the night Colonel Goode, 175th commander, took a company across the Vire to attempt to reinforce General Cota but stumbled into a German bivouac. Colonel Goode was captured. Remnants of his force straggled back across the Vire.[43]

The fighting southeast of Carentan had been on a very small scale and was not in itself important, but, in the course of it, reports came in to General Bradley's headquarters of a strong concentration of German forces in the area, including the *17th SS Panzer Grenadier Division*. Signs pointed to a possible enemy build-up of three divisions with the probable mission of counterattacking in force between Car-

---

[39] See Ruppenthal, *Utah Beach to Cherbourg,* pp. 78–93, for further details.

[40] The withdrawal was a blunder for which von der Heydte reportedly escaped court martial only on the basis of his past record. See Pemsel, CofS *Seventh Army,* commentary on von der Heydte's account. Von der Heydte explained his action rather weakly on the grounds that he did not know that the *17th SS Panzer Grenadier Division* was on its way up. MS # B–839 (von der Heydte).

[41] See below, Ch. X.

[42] For the move of this unit from Brittany, see below, pp. 378–79.

[43] The account of the Montmartin action in Taylor, *Omaha Beachhead,* pp. 157–59, was checked with General Cota and as a result is here slightly modified.

entan and Isigny where, General Bradley pointed out, "we are very weak." [44] As communications were temporarily out between First Army and V Corps, Bradley sent a letter by courier to Gerow ordering him to move a battalion of tanks and a battalion of armored infantry from the 2d Armored Division into the Montmartin-en-Graignes area "prepared for action to the south." The movement was to be completed by daylight and co-ordinated with the 327th Glider Infantry. In addition Bradley ordered that the 116th Infantry be held in reserve for possible commitment on the right of the 175th. By 0630 of 13 June the 2d Battalion, 66th Armored Regiment, in accordance with these orders had joined the 3d Battalion, 41st Armored Infantry, already west of the Vire, and the task force was ready to move south. The move, however, did not take place, for by morning Carentan was being threatened from the southwest rather than the southeast and the armored task force was diverted to go to the support of the 506th Parachute Infantry.

After the fall of Carentan, the Germans planned to counterattack with the *17th SS Panzer Grenadier Division* to retake it. But the attack was delayed on 12 June because the battalion of assault guns, which moved north by train, was held up in the assembly areas by air attacks. With the guns in position on the morning of 13 June, Ostendorff attacked. The attack hit both the 506th and 501st Parachute Infantry Regiments at about 0630 and during the morning drove them back to within 500 yards of Carentan. (*Map 4*) The 502d Parachute Infantry was

brought down to Carentan to reinforce the defense of the 506th. At 1030 the armored task force arrived and in the early afternoon the 101st Airborne Division resumed the initiative. The 502d drove through the 506th, and the 501st continued on its mission of the day before. With close support from the 14th Armored Field Artillery Battalion the enemy was thrown back with estimated losses of 500 men. A defensive position was secured along the road from Baupte to the Carentan–Périers highway.

On the east the company of the 175th Infantry beleaguered at Montmartin was pulled out and Colonel Harper established a line north of the main railroad linked with the 29th Division to the east. Now V and VII Corps were securely joined, although the strip between them still lacked depth for adequate communications and defense. First Army, however, now had resources to deepen it and on 13 June the mission was assigned to XIX Corps, which became operational the next day.

Operations to fuse the two First Army beachheads have been traced through to their conclusion because they form a single story with few direct contacts with what was going on elsewhere in Normandy. The actions described were considered by the high command as of first importance. They did not, however, constitute a main effort by the First Army. Larger forces were being used simultaneously to expand the beachhead westward and southward. Virtually the whole of V Corps during the week of 8–14 June was pushing south through the *bocage* country making rapid progress against a disintegrated German defense.

---

[44] Ltr, Bradley to Gerow, 13 Jun 44. V Corps G–3 Jnl.

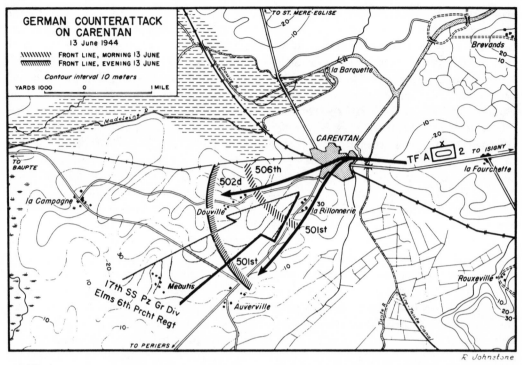

GERMAN COUNTERATTACK
ON CARENTAN
13 June 1944
\\\\\\\\\\ FRONT LINE, MORNING 13 JUNE
\\\\\\\\\\ FRONT LINE, EVENING 13 JUNE
Contour interval 10 meters
YARDS 1000   0   1 MILE

R. Johnstone

MAP 4

The Caumont Gap

From its D-Day objectives reached on 8 June, V Corps ordered a three-division attack designed simply to push out the lodgment area in conformity with the advance of the British on the left. The 2d Division (Maj. Gen. Walter M. Robertson),[45] which had begun landing the evening of 7 June, had enough units ashore by midday of the 9th to be operational and it took over 5,000 yards of the 1st Division front north of Trévières. (*Map XVII*) Here the main effort of the corps was to be made with the final objective

of seizing the Forêt de Cerisy, high ground which always figured prominently in V Corps plans as a possible assembly area for enemy counterattack forces and as ground dominating the whole corps beachhead. The 1st Division on the east was to put its main effort on its right and advance to seize three towns: Agy, la Commune, and Vaubadon, on high ground along the St. Lô–Bayeux highway. The 29th Division, on the other flank, would seize the north bank of the Elle River from la Communette west to the Vire. A portion of its forces, as already noted, would operate west of the Vire to establish contact with VII Corps. Each division was to attack with two regiments abreast and each was to leave all or part of the third regiment prepared to defend

[45] General Robertson was graduated from West Point in 1912. Assigned to duty with the 2d Division in 1940, he became commanding officer of the 9th Infantry in 1941 and took command of the division in May 1942.

the D-Day positions. Positions gained by the attack would be organized for defense in depth. Both latter measures were insurance against enemy counterattack in strength, a contingency that continued to figure prominently in Allied calculations.

Enemy resistance broke first on either flank of the attack and then disintegrated all through the corps zone. Despite this collapse, however, certain units had hard fighting on 9 June. The 29th Division, after clearing Isigny in the morning, pushed south with the 175th Infantry on the right, the 115th on the left.[46] The 175th Infantry, having smashed the *914th Regiment* in its rapid seizure of Isigny, advanced southward against only scattered opposition. Near la Forêt, *352d Division* stragglers defending a supply dump held off the American advance long enough to permit the evecuation of the bulk of the supplies. This action cost the Germans an estimated 125 killed. The 175th Infantry then moved on down to its objectives in the Lison–la Fotelaie area before nightfall.

The 115th Infantry, during the night preceding the attack, reconnoitered crossings of the Aure River. The crossing promised to be difficult since the river flats were flooded to a width of half a mile to two miles. Although nowhere deep under water they were marshy and crisscrossed by drainage ditches. During the night 2d Lt. Kermit C. Miller of Company E took a platoon across south of Canchy. Entering Colombières on the south bank, which had been hard hit by American artillery, Miller's patrol caught a considerable force of Germans by surprise, cut down about forty of them, and took a dozen prisoners. Thanks to this action the regiment's crossing the next day was unopposed, for Colombières turned out to have been the only defended locality on the south bank of the river within range of the Canchy crossing. The lack of opposition was extremely fortunate, for the physical difficulties of crossing the swampy flats made progress very slow and exposed the troops for several hours as they struggled through the mud and waited for improvised bridges to span the few impassable streams. Two battalions were across by 1100. The third followed after enemy fire frustrated an attempt to cross a narrower portion of the river valley farther east. Once across, the 1st Battalion moved to Bricqueville and the 3d Battalion farther south to la Folie. Neither had met serious opposition. But the 2d Battalion ran into trouble from the start. Turning west to clean out the Bois de Calette, from which enemy riflemen were harassing bridging operations at the la Cambe–Douet causeway, the battalion brushed with enemy bicycle troops near Vouilly. Although the wood was not occupied in force the battalion took three hours to flush snipers from the thick brush. Then heading south for le Carrefour it took a wrong turning that added three miles to the six-mile march to its objective. Thoroughly exhausted the troops reached their initial objective at 0230, 10 June. Leading units moved off the road. Reconnaissance to establish a temporary defensive position was difficult in view of the condition of the men and the dark night. Most of the men simply dropped to the ground and were almost at once asleep.

---

[46] The 116th Infantry with the 2d and 5th Ranger Battalions attached spent 9 and 10 June mopping up.

While the rear of the column still waited on the road to move into the bivouac area, an enemy infantry and armored vehicle column blundered down the road in retreat from the Aure valley fighting. A machine pistol was fired. American rifle shots replied. The enemy swung into action, sprayed the road with machine gun fire, and sent armored vehicles (probably self-propelled 88-mm. guns) down the road, firing into hedgerows and fields. The 2d Battalion men, scattered, confused, and disorganized, could offer no effective resistance. One man had presence of mind to take a bazooka and attack the enemy guns, knocking out two of them. But the greater part of the battalion—its commander, Lt. Col. William E. Warfield, killed—dispersed in small groups and retreated north and west during the night. In the melee 150 men were lost, including 11 officers. The next day the battalion was reorganized with 110 replacements, moved back into the line, and the 115th Infantry proceeded to its objectives on the Elle River without opposition.

On the opposite flank of the corps attack the left wing of the 1st Division drove forward against rapidly collapsing resistance. The 26th Infantry reached its objectives, Agy and Dodigny, at night. The 18th Infantry, held up initially by a single enemy strong point, at length bypassed it leaving it to be cleared by the reserve battalion. Thereafter moving rapidly, with strong artillery support on known enemy positions, possible assembly areas, and roads, it continued to advance through the night. It met no enemy after midnight and arrived by morning abreast of the 26th Infantry. During 10 June it moved down to its

objectives on the St. Lô–Bayeux highway. Only the 3d Battalion at the edge of the Forêt de Cerisy met resistance.[47]

In the center of the corps zone the newly landed 2d Division had a harder time, in part because it hit the center of the *352d Division,* which despite the collapse of both wings continued to hold out during 9 June in strong defenses about Trévières, and in part because it lacked most of its artillery, transportation, communications (wire and radios), machine guns and mortars, as well as a large part of its supporting troops.[48] For the attack of 9 June, one company of tank destroyers and one company of tanks were attached.

While the 38th Infantry attacked Trévières from the north, the 9th Infantry struck to the east to cut the Trévières–Rubercy road. The 9th Infantry had relieved the 18th Infantry at Mandeville and Engranville. The line of departure for its attack was due east of Trévières, but the 2d Battalion was at Engranville north of the Aure at 1100 when it received orders to jump off. It spent the whole day fighting to the line of departure, unable without heavy weapons to overcome enemy flanking fire from the direction of Trévières. By midnight, however, it reached the initial objective, Rubercy. The 3d Battalion, starting from the Mandeville area, fought down the road toward

---

[47] Here S/Sgt Arthur F. DeFranzo was killed in a heroic action in which he destroyed an enemy position with grenades despite five wounds that finally felled him a few yards in front of the enemy. He was awarded the Medal of Honor.

[48] Since it had not been anticipated that the division would be sent into action immediately on landing, the weapons and equipment had been preloaded in vehicles scheduled to land on 10 June. Ltr, Col Walter Elliott (CO, 38th Inf) to author, 4 Feb 48. Hist Div files.

Rubercy but made very slow progress and was still short of the objective by dark. A gap of at least 4,000 yards separated the battalion from the 1st Division on the left. This was covered only by patrols of the 18th Infantry.

The attack on Trévières by the 38th Infantry ran into difficulties aggravated by its total lack of mortars and machine guns, the hedgerow terrain, and a stubborn though not numerous enemy. The Aure River had been selected as the line of departure, but both the 2d and 3d Battalions ran into opposition before reaching it. Progress was slow. The men were continually pinned down by enemy fire difficult to locate among the hedgerows and still more difficult to neutralize with only light infantry weapons. The attacking troops were given direct support by accurate fire from two batteries of the 38th Field Artillery Battalion. But the attack was kept moving chiefly by bold leadership. The success of the 3d Battalion in crossing the Aure under heavy German machine gun fire was due at least in part to the intrepidity of Capt. Omery C. Weathers of Company K who led his men through the fire at the cost of his own life.[49] Col. Walter A. Elliott, the regimental commander, unable to depend on communications in the typically fragmental maneuver of groups of men through the fields and orchards, spent most of the day moving between his battalions pushing the attack forward. Late in the afternoon the regiment, still short of its objective, was ordered by General Robertson to continue the attack to take Trévières that night. By midnight the 2d Battalion had

occupied the town except for a small strong point on the southern edge which was cleaned out the following morning.[50]

The Germans' abandonment of Trévières, however, was not due primarily to the efforts of the 38th Infantry. The *352d Division* with both flanks torn open had at last decided to pull out of an untenable position. At about 1900, 9 June, General Kraiss reported his hopeless situation to General Marcks at *LXXXIV Corps* and received orders to withdraw far to the south to establish a defense along the Elle River from Berigny to Airel. The withdrawal was to take place during darkness and to be completed by 0600, 10 June. For the defense of this new line of about ten miles, General Kraiss had 2,500 men, 14 artillery pieces, 16 antiaircraft guns, and 5 tanks.[51]

The withdrawal of the *352d Division* allowed the 2d Division on 10 June to march to its objectives west and south of the Forêt de Cerisy. About ninety enemy stragglers were rounded up during the advance. Both the 1st and 2d Divisions spent the day of 11 June virtually out of contact with the enemy, reorganizing the ground won and preparing for a new attack. The 1st Division units had made no advances since noon on 10 June. The only fighting on 11 June took place at the southern tip of the Forêt de Cerisy where the 1st Battalion, 38th Infantry, fought to dislodge a stubborn group of enemy well dug in at the Haute-Littée crossroads. Even patrols probing far in

---

[49] Captain Weathers was awarded the DSC posthumously.

[50] Ltr cited n. 48.

[51] MS # B–435 and MS # B–436 (both by Ziegelmann). Kraiss estimated that he was lucky to escape with any of his division since he felt that, had the 29th Division driven east after crossing the Aure, it would have rolled up his flank and trapped the bulk of the *916th Regiment* in the Trévières area.

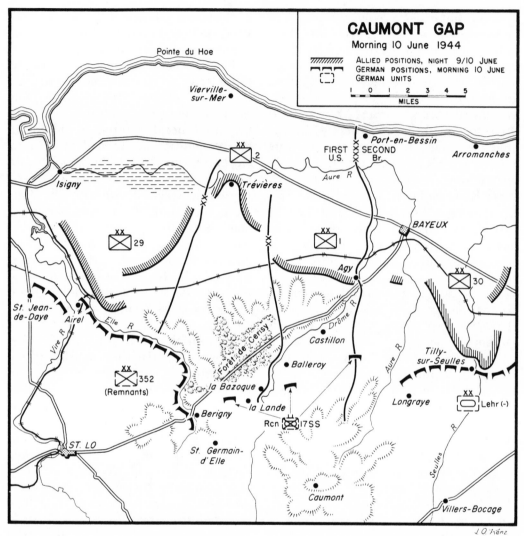

MAP 5

the south met no large forces and on the entire 2d Division front during the day only twice was enemy artillery fire reported.

The 1st and 2d Divisions on 10 and 11 June were in fact facing a gaping hole in the German lines more than ten miles broad from Berigny due east to Longraye where the *Panzer Lehr Division* was attacking. (*Map 5*) This hole grew directly out of the D-Day collapse of the left wing of the *716th Division* followed by the capture of Bayeux and the smashing of the *352d* left flank. The ten-mile-wide corridor opened the way through Caumont to the high wooded terrain in the vicinity of the Bois du Homme and le Bény-Bocage. Occupation of that high ground would have placed V Corps in a deep southern wedge in *Seventh Army* lines which the Germans feared could be gradually reinforced and then exploited either to outflank Caen or more decisively to drive westward toward Avranches.[52] General Dollmann foresaw this development on the morning of 9 June, but the *LXXXIV Corps* no longer had any troops to plug the gap. Dollmann therefore proposed that the *II Parachute Corps* be assembled south of Balleroy for attack northward in conjunction with the *I SS Panzer Corps.* Although the order for this maneuver was given to General Meindl, Dollmann was doubtful whether it could be accomplished since it was not known when the *II Parachute Corps* units would arrive. It was probable that they would straggle into the battle area and would not be available for a concerted counterattack.[53]

Of the units originally attached to Meindl's corps, the *77th Division* had already been diverted to the Cotentin. The increasing urgency of blocking a threatened penetration at Montebourg made it imperative that the *77th* continue on that mission.[54] Meindl was thus left with only two fresh divisions, the *17th SS Panzer Grenadier* and the *3d Parachute.* By the evening of 9 June the bulk of *3d Parachute Division* had only reached Brécey, east of Avranches. The *37th SS Panzer Grenadier Regiment* of the *17th SS Division* was in the same general area; the *38th SS Panzer Grenadier Regiment* was east of Laval. The tracked vehicles of Ostendorff's division were being transported

by train and on 9 June were strung out between la Flèche and Saumur. Because of rail breaks due to air attack the last two trains had to be unloaded south of the Loire. Only advance elements of the division had reached Balleroy, including the reconnaissance battalion equipped with amphibious *Volkswagen.* Reconnaissance north and northeast of Balleroy was begun on 10 June preparatory to commitment of the division in that sector.

In the meantime, however, plans were changed. Rommel considered that German weakness in the Carentan area was more dangerous than the hole on the right of *LXXXIV Corps. II Parachute Corps* was diverted to block the sector between Carentan and St. Lô, and this task was given priority over support of the *352d Division* despite the desperate condition of the latter. The *3d Parachute Division* was still to come into the St. Lô area with the tentative mission of occupying the north edge of the Forêt de Cerisy. The *353d Division,* the last mobile unit in Brittany, was also ordered to St. Lô to come under Meindl's corps. But the chief concern was along the Vire. Most of the *17th SS Panzer Grenadier Division* was sent southwest of Carentan. *Kampfgruppe Heintz* (mobile combat group of the *275th Division*) was to move on arrival into the St. Jean-de-Daye area.[55]

The only immediate step to plug the Caumont gap on 10 June was the decision to leave Ostendorff's reconnaissance battalion in the vicinity of Balleroy. Although the move does not seem to have been intended as deception, it had that effect. The 1st Division immediately took prisoners and located forward positions

---

[52] See MS # B–204 (General der Panzertruppen Heinrich Freiherr von Luettwitz, CG, *2d Panzer Division*) .

[53] *Seventh Army, KTB 1.I.–30.VI.44,* 9 Jun 44.

[54] See below, Ch. X.

[55] *Seventh Army, KTB 1.I.–30.VI.44,* 9 and 10 Jun 44.

of elements of the *17th SS Panzer Grenadier Division* south of Balleroy east to St. Paul-de-Verney.[56] Unidentified medium tanks were also reported on the afternoon of 10 June in the vicinity of la Londe.[57] The light mixed units actually in contact were recognized to be incapable of major counterattack, but from prisoner interrogations V Corps deduced that the *17th SS Panzer Grenadier Division* might be in position to attack, probably from the direction of the Forêt de Cerisy by daylight of 11 June.[58] The G–2 further warned of a long-range contingency. The *11th Panzer* and *1st SS Panzer Divisions* were reported on the move from the south and northeast respectively. It was thought that one of them might be used against V Corps, although when either would arrive could not even be guessed at.

The possibility of enemy armored counterattacks was in the forefront of most American commanders' minds. This was D plus 3, when according to all planning calculations the enemy could begin to exert heavy pressure against the beachheads.[59] Signs that the Germans had actually succeeded in concentrating reserves for counterattack were, to be sure, scanty. They consisted chiefly in the identification of elements of *Panzer Lehr Division* in the British sector, of the *17th SS Panzer Grenadier Division* in front of the 1st Division, and a curious multiplication of

rumors from prisoners and civilians that there were large enemy concentrations in the Forêt de Cerisy. First Army G–2 wrote at the end of 9 June: "No surprise should be occasioned should this cover produce an armored or motorized division." [60] The whole tone of the intelligence estimates of this date was dominated by conviction that the enemy was preparing to strike a major blow. In summing up the fighting of 9 June, First Army reported: "Enemy forces pursued their delaying tactics pending the arrival of armored counterattack forces." [61] There was no appreciation of the havoc that had been wrought in the German defenses by Allied success in smashing the coastal crust. On 10 June First Army observed that the *17th SS Panzer Grenadier Division* had come into the area south of Carentan and that no new identifications had been made on V Corps front. The enemy units in contact were still only the *352d Division* and elements of the *716th*. First Army G–2 believed that in the fighting of 10 June German forces had withdrawn south along the Vire and their eastern flank had been forced back to the northern edge of the Forêt de Cerisy.[62] In reality, not only had the German forces been south of the forest for at least twelve hours, but at the time the intelligence report was issued troops of the U.S. 2d Division were also south of the forest.[63]

The Caumont gap was literally held by the reconnaissance battalion of the *17th*

---

[56] 1st Div AAR.

[57] V Corps G–2 Jnl. Corps located the *17th SS Panzer Grenadier Division* chiefly by prisoner reports. The bulk of the division was thought to be moving up opposite the 2d Division. The latter, however, had made no identifications through 11 June. See 2d Div G–2 Jnl.

[58] G–2 believed that the division had both a tank and an assault gun battalion. Actually Ostendorff had no tanks and his guns were far to the south.

[59] See above, p. 176.

[60] First Army G–2 Per Rpt.

[61] *Ibid.*

[62] First Army Int Sum as of 2400, 10 Jun.

[63] See above, p. 370. Despite concern over the Forêt de Cerisy as a possible enemy assembly area, apparently no special report came to the First Army G–2 when the 2d Division found the forest clear. It seems that the intelligence summary as of 2400, 10 June, was prepared on information probably twelve

SS Panzer Grenadier Division during 10 June. Plans were made that day to bring the *XLVII Panzer Corps* (General Funck) into the gap with the *2d Panzer Division* (Generalleutnant Heinrich Freiherr von Luettwitz). The *2d Panzer Division* had in fact begun its move from Amiens to the battle area during the night of 9–10 June. Advance units had reached Paris, but the movements under air attack during the day were slow and costly. On the evening of 10 June while wheeled elements were near Alençon the tanks had just begun to move from Amiens by train. With the example of the ineffective piecemeal commitment of the *12th SS, 21st,* and *Panzer Lehr Divisions,* Funck wanted to delay commitment of the *2d Panzer* until it had completed assembly with its tanks. This was expected by 13 June. In the meantime, on the strong urging of General Luettwitz, the reconnaissance battalion was committed at Caumont with the mission of holding the high ground there.

During the day one reinforced regiment of the *3d Parachute Division* arrived in the vicinity of St. Georges-d'Elle. The division commander, Generalleutnant Richard Schimpf, wanted to take positions according to plan in the Forêt de Cerisy area along with Ostendorff's reconnaissance units.[64] But Meindl (*II Parachute Corps*), to whom the regiment was attached, believed that the more urgent need was to strengthen the *352d Division* defenses along the Elle. The regiment therefore went into line from Berigny to St. Germain-d'Elle. *II Parachute Corps*

thus refused its right flank at the gap to establish an arc defense north and northeast of St. Lô. The gap was slightly narrowed but it remained open.

While attempting to fill the gap, the Germans on 10 June had also made a final effort to mount a counterattack in the Caen sector against the British. Inasmuch as *Panzer Lehr* was fully engaged in defensive fighting south of Bayeux, General Geyr (*Panzer Group West*), who took over command in the Caen sector on 9 June, planned to use half of the *12th SS* and half of the *21st Panzer Divisions* in a limited-objective attack due north of Caen. The objective was the Anisy–Anguerny area. Both Geyr and Rommel would have preferred to attack more to the northwest of Caen, but Geyr did not want to spend another twenty-four hours maneuvering into position. He felt that what was needed was aggressive action even if its immediate purposes were relatively inconsequential. Rommel agreed, and the attack was ordered for the evening.[65]

Even this attack could not be carried out. In the afternoon British pressure mounted against the right of *Panzer Lehr* and the left of *12th SS Panzer Division* where the British 30 Corps had committed the 7th Armoured Division to drive through Tilly-sur-Seulles, toward Villers-Bocage. Knowing that *Panzer Lehr* was already dangerously weakened Geyr called off the attack.

Less than an hour later his headquarters was hit by fighter-bombers that wiped out his entire staff. All personnel in the operations section were killed, as well as

---

hours old. The G-2 report of 11 June covers the error by saying that the *352d Division* "was forced back from the line Moon-sur-Elle–la Gouesmerie *and from the Forêt de Cerisy* . . ." Italics are the author's.

[64] MS # B–541 (Schimpf) .

[65] MS # B–466 (Geyr) . Geyr believed that, against enemy air superiority and heavy naval artillery fire, no daylight attack would have a chance.

most of the officers of the forward echelon. The bulk of the signal equipment was destroyed. With Geyr physically unable to exercise command, the sector reverted to the control of *I SS Panzer Corps* and *Seventh Army. Seventh Army* henceforth abandoned the idea of a decisive armored counterattack and bent all its efforts to solidifying its defense.[66]

After the rest and reorganization of 11 June, V Corps mounted a new attack, this time with the deepest southward penetration planned on the left flank in the 1st Division zone. (*See Map XVII.*) This was designed primarily to assist the British Second Army attempt to outflank Caen. The *Panzer Lehr Division,* despite heavy losses, had checked the British 7th Armoured Division on 10–11 June at Tilly-sur-Seulles. On the other hand the U.S. First Army advance had evidently struck a weak spot in the enemy lines. Although the true extent and significance of the gap were unknown, it was planned to take advantage of obvious German weakness in the area to thrust the British 7th Armoured Division south close to the inter-army boundary and hook past the *Panzer Lehr* to capture Villers-Bocage on the Caen–Avranches highway. The 1st Division advance to the high ground at Caumont would protect the right flank of this maneuver. In conformity with the drive to Caumont the 2d and 29th Divisions would continue to push south, but with objectives echeloned to the right rear so that the advance called for on the Vire River flank was relatively small. Besides achieving specific tactical objectives, the renewed V Corps attack, it was hoped,

would help take pressure off VII Corps, which was making the main army effort aimed at the capture of Cherbourg.

The 1st Division estimated that, although the enemy was capable of offering only scattered opposition to the advance, there was a chance that weak elements of *Panzer Lehr* might penetrate the division left boundary and that the *17th SS Panzer Grenadier Division* might attack the right flank of the advance. General Huebner's plan provided strict control of the attack. Regiments were to move by bounds and prepare to defend successive phase lines. They would report arrival at the phase lines and, except for pushing out aggressive reconnaissance, would continue the advance only on division order.[67]

The attacks of 12 June on either side of the army boundary at first seemed to promise rapid and spectacular success. The 1st Division, jumping off at 0800 with the 18th and 26th Infantry Regiments on a 3,000-yard front behind a screen of two troops of the 102d Cavalry Squadron, moved rapidly against light enemy forces which readily gave way. The 18th Infantry had reached the Caumont–St. Lô highway by evening and sent patrols into Caumont. The 26th Infantry at the same time got one battalion to the edge of Caumont but there ran into determined resistance from an estimated two companies of Germans who belonged to the reconnaissance battalion of the *2d Panzer Division.* The town was not cleared until the following morning.[68] On

---

[66] MS # B–466 (Geyr) and *Panzer-Armeeoberkommando 5* (referred to hereafter as *Fifth Panzer Army*), *KTB 10.VI.–8.VIII.44*, 10 Jun 44.

[67] 1st Div FO 37, 11 Jun 44.

[68] The enemy patrolled strongly during 13 June, giving the Americans the impression at some points that counterattacks were in progress. Actions, however, though sometimes sharp were all local and involved few troops.

the 1st Division right the 9th Infantry of the 2d Division occupied the Litteau ridge south of the Forêt de Cerisy. Not until it reached the objective did it make firm contact with the enemy.

The 7th Armoured Division in the British 30 Corps zone, starting its attack in the afternoon, at first made similarly rapid progress. By 1745 leading elements had passed through Livry three miles northeast of Caumont. At dark the point of the attack was south of the divisional objective and the armor began to wheel east. Villers-Bocage was entered the following morning. This initial success, however, was qualified by the failure of the British 50th Division on the northeast to make any progress in direct attacks against the *Panzer Lehr Division* west of Tilly-sur-Seulles. On 13 June the *2d Panzer Division* (with two infantry regiments supported by two battalions of artillery but no tanks) strongly counterattacked between Cahagnes and Villers-Bocage. The Germans drove up almost to the Caumont–Villers-Bocage road. The 7th Armoured Division, with its forward movement stopped, found itself in a dangerously exposed thin salient. In the afternoon it withdrew to high ground some two miles west of the town where it tied in with the 1st Division at Caumont. During the afternoon of 14 June, renewed enemy attacks induced a further withdrawal of about five miles north to the Parfouru–L'Eclin area on the Aure River and Caumont–Caen road. The *2d Panzer Division* attacks were broken up in large measure by artillery concentrations in which batteries of the V Corps, which had observation of the enemy from the Caumont heights, took an important part.

Positions on high ground covering Villers-Bocage remained for about six weeks in enemy hands. The Caumont gap remained open between the *2d Panzer* and *3d Parachute Divisions,* but in view of the strong enemy opposition to British advance the 1st Division was ordered to hold at Caumont while Gerow continued to push with his right against the *352d* and *3d Parachute Divisions* in front of St. Lô.

The push was to net few gains during the next week. Two regiments of the 2d Division and the whole of the 29th Division had run into a new kind of enemy resistance, based in part on stubborn defense of positions prepared in depth and in part on small counterthrusts against the flanks of advancing American forces. The *3d Parachute Division,* moreover, turned out to have some of the best and toughest infantrymen in Rundstedt's armies.

On 12 June the attacks of the 2d Division in the center of the corps zone were split by the Forêt de Cerisy. While the 9th Infantry on the left advanced in conformity with the 1st Division and against only slight opposition, the 23d Infantry directed its attack southwest toward St. Lô in an operation linked with the advance of the 29th Division on its right. Principal objective of the 23d Infantry was Hill 192—a dominating hill mass north of the main Bayeux–St. Lô road—the key to St. Lô because it provided observation of all approaches to the city for miles to the north and east. The regiment, attacking with two battalions, was stopped at the Elle River. This stream, only ten feet wide and no military obstacle in itself, marked the enemy's main line of resistance. It was clear, too, that the enemy was making effective use of the observation afforded by Hill 192. But neither American fighter-bomber missions shortly before dark nor repeated artillery concentrations on enemy positions there achieved any effective results.

On 13 June the 2d Division renewed the attack and the 38th Infantry, with heavy artillery support (more than 6,500 rounds were fired), advanced about two miles south of the Elle. As enemy resistance thickened, the American troops were stopped by division order and directed together with the 23d Infantry to organize their present positions for defense. The difference in enemy opposition east and west of the Forêt de Cerisy can be seen from comparative casualties. While the 1st Division lost 92 men in the two-day attack, the 2d Division lost 540, most of them from the two regiments that had struggled toward Hill 192.

The 29th Division attacked on 12 June with one regiment, the 115th, while the 175th Infantry held north of the Elle protecting the corps west flank and the 116th remained in corps reserve as precaution against an enemy counterattack west of the Vire.[69] The 747th Tank Battalion was held in division reserve also against the contingency of counterattack. The 115th Infantry, despite direct support by three battalions of artillery, had hard going. The 1st Battalion was stopped at the river bank mostly by small arms fire. The 3d Battalion succeeded in crossing and advanced south about 3,000 yards. Enemy forces built up in the hedgerows, and by the end of the morning the battalion was not only stopped but was fighting to avoid being cut off. After taking severe losses it withdrew to its original line of departure.[70] In the afternoon two platoons of tanks were put in with the 1st Battalion to try to outflank the enemy holding the river crossing southeast of Ste. Marguerite-d'Elle. After three tanks were lost, the attempt was abandoned. In the evening the 116th Infantry was passed through the 115th and not only succeeded in crossing but by daylight had approached its objectives, against resistance reported to be light. Continuing under generous supporting artillery fires the regiment entered St. Clair-sur-Elle and Couvains. Casualties to the 29th Division for the two days were 547.

At the end of 13 June the V Corps attack toward St. Lô was halted by order of General Bradley. The Carentan–Isigny link between his two corps was still thin and weak, and despite success in beating off the attack of the *17th SS Panzer Grenadier Division* it still seemed possible that the enemy might try again. Furthermore XIX Corps was just becoming operational in this area and it was necessary to adjust troop assignments between the corps. The 29th Division passed to the control of the new corps and the 30th Division was brought into the zone between the Vire and Taute Rivers. Supporting troops were reshuffled.

In calling off the southward push, General Bradley was also influenced by the desire to avoid a general engagement of V Corps which might absorb resources needed for First Army's main effort—the VII Corps attack to cut the peninsula and take Cherbourg.[71] Finally, since the British seemed to be stopped north of Tilly-sur-Seulles, any advance by V Corps

---

[69] See above, section on Junction Between V and VII Corps.

[70] 115th Regt S-3 Jnl.

[71] Ltr, Lt Gen C. R. Huebner to author, 17 Oct 47. Hist Div files.

would expose both flanks to possible enemy armored attack. There seemed a real danger of that in the afternoon, when the *2d Panzer Division* was identified on the left of the 1st Division, and the warning was issued to both 1st and 2d Divisions to dig in when they reached suitable defensive positions.

For the time being the mission of V Corps became to hold its present positions while First Army devoted its main effort to the capture of Cherbourg and, as a precondition for that, strengthened the Vire–Taute corridor. The corps' divisions, however, were given a certain latitude to improve their defensive positions and were ordered to conduct aggressive patrolling "so as to deny the enemy any opportunity to abandon this front with impunity" and to give the impression of continued major offensive action.[72]

Toward St. Lô

When V Corps halted on 13 June, the whole First Army line on the south was echeloned to the right from Caumont held by the 1st Division to the Carentan area in the zone of the 101st Airborne Division. The 1st Division held a salient in the Caumont area substantially in advance of the 2d Division on its right. The 2d and 29th Divisions were deployed on a northwest–southeast line generally from Cormolain to Airel on the Vire River. They confronted the right wing of *II Parachute Corps,* temporarily subordinated to *LXXXIV Corps,* which defended St. Lô on an arc along the high ground north and northeast of the city. The 1st and 2d Divisions remained under V Corps, which had also the 2d Armored Division (less

Combat Command A)[73] in reserve. The XIX Corps (Maj. Gen. Charles H. Corlett)[74] became operational on 13 June, with the 30th Division (Maj. Gen. Leland Hobbs) attached, and on the next day took over from V Corps control of the 29th Division.

In anticipation of renewing the drive south, both V and XIX Corps on 14 June issued warning orders marking out objectives and schemes of maneuver. Following the outlines of these orders all forward divisions except the 1st made limited-objective attacks during the next week primarily to secure better defensive positions, although commanders hoped that larger rewards might be reaped.

The series of limited-objective attacks began on 15 June with a thrust by XIX Corps aimed at securing the high ground on the line St. Georges de Bohon (three miles southwest of Carentan)–le Hommet d'Arthenay (three miles northwest of Pont Hébert)–St. Lô–la Barre de Semilly. The 30th Division, which had not yet landed all its troops, attacked initially with only one regiment. The attack made very slow progress even though the estimated enemy opposition consisted of only one platoon of riflemen and a section of the machine guns. At the end of the day the 120th Infantry occupied Montmartin-en-Graignes and the high ground north of the Vire–Taute Canal.[75] The day's op-

---

[72] V Corps FO 5, 13 Jun 44.

[73] CCA was still attached to the 101st Airborne Division.

[74] General Corlett had come to the European theater after serving in the Pacific. He had taken command of the 7th Division in September 1943, and led it in combat on Kwajalein. He was transferred to Europe to take over XIX Corps in April 1944.

[75] Although Montmartin had been entered on 12 June, troops had pulled back to a defensive line along the high ground north of the town.

erations cost it less than twenty casualties.

Again the fighting between the Vire and Taute Rivers had proceeded on a very small scale, as the attitude on both sides remained defensive and the opposing forces almost equally weak. Curiously enough, each opponent viewing his own weakness expected the other to attack. Though the narrow zone between the rivers cut by the open muddy depression at the Vire–Taute Canal would have made any attack difficult, the rewards of success might have tempted either of the respective commanders to accept the risks. The Americans expected the Germans to strike for the sea and split the First Army; the Germans expected the Americans to drive for Périers and split the *Seventh Army*. The fact was that neither opponent had the strength to do anything but hold on.

Weakness on the German side resulted mainly from the nearly incredible difficulties of moving troops into the line— difficulties that had constantly disrupted *Seventh Army* offensive plans and jeopardized its defensive positions everywhere in Normandy. The story of how *Kampfgruppe Heintz* struggled up to Montmartin-en-Graignes where it fought against the 120th Infantry is worth the telling for it shows how completely the battlefield was sealed off by Allied air forces. (*Map XVIII*)

Kampfgruppe Heintz consisted of the *984th Regiment* of the *275th Division*, reinforced by the division *Fuesilier* battalion, a three-battery artillery battalion, the engineer battalion, and a Flak battery.[76] It had been ordered on the morn-

ing of 6 June to begin immediate priority movement to the battle area. The division headquarters then at Redon in Brittany was less than 120 miles by rail from St. Lô. A day or two should have been ample for the movement. But Allied aircraft, sovereign in the skies, ruled otherwise.

The Kampfgruppe took only about ten hours to assemble but was delayed in entraining by air attacks which blocked tracks, damaged locomotives, and generally interfered with the assembling of cars. These delays continued through the night, and by 0800 the following morning only three sections of the Kampfgruppe had been loaded. In the afternoon five trains were under way; three were still being loaded. The lead train made good progress to Avranches, where at 1400 it was held up by undetermined trouble ahead. While this was being cleared up, the rails behind it were cut. Late in the afternoon the train passed through Avranches and reached Foligny a few miles to the north. At Foligny, however, air attack destroyed it with total loss of vehicles and equipment and very heavy casualties. The second train in the meantime reached Pontorson but was there halted by rail cuts to the east. Under heavy air attack which took severe toll of the men and equipment of the engineer unit aboard, the train was unloaded and the troops ordered to continue on foot.[77]

---

[76] It also took over command of the *Angers Engineer Battalion*, an alarm unit, which consisted of the school troops and students of the *Seventh Army Engineer School* at Angers. On 6 June the battalion

consisted of a headquarters and headquarters company, a heavy weapons company, and two infantry companies, which were committed west of the Vire on 10 June when the *17th SS Panzer Grenadier Division* was delayed in moving into its sector south of Carentan. *Seventh Army, KTB 1.I.–30.VI.44,* 27 Jan and 6–9 Jun 44.

[77] The account of the move of *Kampfgruppe Heintz* is from the *Seventh Army, Trans. O., KTB 1.I.–30.VI.44.*

All other trains en route on 7 June had been attacked and so delayed that at 1800 they were still all south of Rennes. At that time it was reported that bombs had cut the rails in three places between Rennes and Dol and the whole movement was ordered rerouted via la Brohinière–Dinan–Dol. Scarcely had this decision been made when it was discovered that between Dinan and Dol the tracks were broken in no fewer than nineteen places. All during 8 June seven trains languished on the rails south of Rennes. Two other trains meanwhile were struggling to load artillery units of the Kampfgruppe and were being continually interrupted by air attacks. It was 1915 on 8 June before the last train got under way. Since no progress had been made to clear the route beyond Rennes on 7 June, it had been decided to reroute the trains through Fougères. On 9 June the Fougères line was cut. The transportation officers then gave up. The troops of *Kampfgruppe Heintz* were all unloaded and ordered to proceed by truck or foot. The bulk of the unit had thus in two days and three nights traveled less than thirty miles. Three to five more days were consumed in the road march to the final assembly areas where the Kampfgruppe was attached to the *17th SS Panzer Grenadier Division* and put at once into the line southeast of Carentan.[78]

The experience of *Kampfgruppe Heintz* in trying to move under unrestricted Allied air attacks was by no means exceptional. On the contrary the difficulties of a unit of the *265th Division* ordered out of Brittany at the same time were even worse. Original orders to move the whole *265th* unit by train were canceled on 7 June in order to save trains for the use of *Kampfgruppe Heintz*. The bulk of the troops thus turned out on the road arrived in about five days in the battle area. But the so-called immobile portions deemed essential to move by rail entrained at Quimperle and took seven days to reach Rennes about one hundred miles away. From that point they had to walk.

Discouraged by these and similar experiences, on 13 June *Seventh Army* decided that rail movements between Brittany and Normandy were impossible and that there was little hope that the situation would improve. Dollmann therefore closed the branch rail office under *LXXIV Corps* which had been established on D Day.[79]

By the attack of 15 June XIX Corps secured a defensive position fronting the depression of the Vire–Taute Canal. In this position the 30th Division continued to build up. It did not seem feasible to continue the push south through the bottleneck of the St. Lô highway across the lowlands. The decision was made to wait for additional troops with which to force a crossing of the river in attack westward. General Corlett therefore ordered the 30th Division to defend the line of the canal while the 29th Division and the

---

[78] It was attached to the *352d Division* for supply. The *2d Battalion, 984th Regiment,* and the *Fuesilier Battalion* came up on bicycles in the evening of 11 June. The *1st Battalion* arrived on the 13th. Order, 13 Jun 44, *Kampfgruppe Heintz.* Miscellaneous orders in *275th Division* files, 1944; cf. *XXV Corps, KTB and Anlagen 6.–30.VI.44; Seventh Army, Trans. O., KTB 1.I.–30.VI.44.*

[79] *Seventh Army, Trans.O., KTB 1.I.–30.VI.44.* German supply by road and rail was similarly disorganized. See below, pp. 410–11.

2d Division of V Corps renewed the attack toward St. Lô.[80] (*Map XIX*)

The critical objective of the new attack was again Hill 192. The hill itself was the assigned objective of the 38th Infantry on the right flank of the 2d Division. To assist in taking it the 29th Division, attacking with two regiments abreast, was to put its main effort on the left. There the 116th Infantry, with the 3d Battalion of the 115th Infantry attached, was to drive for St. André-de-l'Epine and Hill 150 at the northeastern end of the Martinville ridge (later one of the bloodiest of the St. Lô battlefields). The 175th Infantry, attacking with its right on the Vire River, would advance to Hills 90 and 97 northwest of St. Lô. The 2d Division, besides taking Hill 192 with the 38th Infantry, would seize the high ground astride the St. Lô highway near la Croix Rouge with the 23d Infantry and the heights west of St. Germain-d'Elle and northwest of Montrabot with the 9th Infantry. The 1st Division was alerted by V Corps to advance later to a line roughly from la Lande-sur-Drôme to Cahagnes, but the attack would wait for the completion of the 2d Division advance.

Enemy positions had been discovered on 15 June, in and around St. Germain-d'Elle, by patrols of the 102d Cavalry Squadron which probed as far south as Vidouville. The cavalry also identified German paratroopers at Montrabot. Since the arrival on 10 June of advance elements of the *3d Parachute Division* to take up defensive positions on the right flank of the *352d Division,* other march groups of the division had straggled in to extend the line southeast and gradually

fill the Caumont gap. Although the final assembly of all three regiments of the division was not complete until the night of 17 June, the line was already strong by the 16th. Unlike most German units moved to the front during June, the regiments of the *3d Parachute Division* arrived almost intact. By marching only at night, avoiding the main roads, and maintaining strict march and camouflage discipline, they had almost wholly escaped air attack.[81]

The U.S. 2d Division in the attack of 16 June, which began for all three regiments at 0800, pushed both wings forward slightly but was unable to advance in the center. All along the line, heavy fighting netted advances measured only in yards, as the enemy put up a skillful and stubborn defense in position that made maximum use of the tangled hedgerow country. The experience of one platoon of the 9th Infantry on the left was typical. The platoon advancing through open fields was hit by fire from eight machine guns emplaced in the network of hedgerows: its leader was lost as well as a third of its men. With observation from high ground west of St. Germain-d'Elle, the enemy repeatedly permitted the attackers to reach exposed positions and then opened withering fire. At the end of the day the 9th Infantry had lost 140 men—twenty of them killed—and had advanced only a few hundred yards. St. Germain-d'Elle remained in enemy hands.[82]

The most important advance of the day occurred on the 2d Division right, where the 3d Battalion of the 38th Infantry pushed up Hill 192 to within 700 yards of the crest. The value of the success, how-

---

[80] Ltr, Gen Corlett to author, 14 Oct 48. Hist Div files.

[81] MS # B–541 (Schimpf).

[82] Regimental S–3 Jnls.

ever, was limited by the failure of units on the right and left to keep up. The 23d Infantry in the center of the division zone fought hard all day, losing 11 officers and 162 men. But the end of the day found it still virtually at the line of departure.

Despite the exposed position of the battalion on Hill 192, it was decided to leave it in place and the 2d Engineer Battalion was ordered up to double for infantry and reinforce its lines. The hill salient was held throughout the rest of June, as the 2d Division by corps order passed to the defensive.

The attack of the 29th Division on 16 June at first seemed to go well. Colonel Canham planned to advance his 116th Infantry by bounds. The 1st Battalion leading off at 0800 would pass through the 3d Battalion to take the plateau between the Bois du Bretel and la Blotrie. There it would reorganize and be prepared to advance to capture Hills 147 and 150 on the Martinville ridge. The 3d Battalion, 115th Infantry, attached for this operation, would advance southwest to cut the St. Lô–Isigny highway near la Fossardière and organize the high ground there for all-around defense. The 2d Battalion, 116th Infantry, then in contact with the enemy at St. Clair-sur-l'Elle, would break contact and assemble in the vicinity of Couvains prepared to strike through the other two battalions to take Hill 115 and the stretch of highway near la Luzerne. The two battalions that led the attack (Canham's 1st and the 3d of the 115th) each had eight tanks attached. The order emphasized the organization of all objectives for defense against enemy counterattack. The 115th Infantry, less the 3d Battalion, was held in corps reserve near Ste. Marguerite-d'Elle.

All units got off on time and at 0930 the lead battalions were both making good progress against slight opposition. About noon, however, the 3d Battalion, 115th, reported meeting two companies of enemy infantry with two tanks. By mid-afternoon two of its own tanks were knocked out and forward progress was virtually halted east of les Foulons. At the same time the 1st Battalion, 116th Infantry, was far to the south, only about 1,000 yards short of St. André-de-l'Epine. Here it was stopped by artillery fire and an enemy counterattack. The 2d Battalion, committed about noon to attack toward la Luzerne, was held up just west of the highway near Villiers-Fossard where the enemy was dug in on a nose of high ground. Supporting artillery fire failed to shake the battalion loose. The 3d Battalion, 115th Infantry, in the meantime was withdrawn 1,000 yards to the rear. By 1800 General Corlett at corps had given up the idea of reaching final objectives before dark and all forward battalions dug in to hold for the night and resume the attack the next day.[83]

Enemy resistance from commanding ground and hedgerows had been stubborn, but Colonel Canham was nevertheless not satisfied with the effort his regiment had made. He admonished his subordinate commanders that night to take up the attack the next day with new vigor. They should advance their units on a broad front, he said, and "get around the sniper and machine gunner and wipe him out. . . . If you allow your unit to bunch up behind a hedgerow and wait for hours you are only playing into Jerry's hand. He will move around where he can enfilade

[83] 29th Div G–3 Jnl; 115th and 116th Inf Regts S–3 Jnls.

you or drop artillery or mortar fire on you. . . . It is time to get over the jitters and fight like hell." [84]

The 175th Infantry (Lt. Col. Alexander George) [85] during the day met much lighter resistance as it attacked with its right on the Vire River. The 1st and 3d Battalions, north of the Elle River, were relieved during the night of 15–16 June by elements of the 119th Infantry and crossed the river to gain a line of departure along the ridge line on the south bank. The move was made without opposition, but the next morning both battalions ran into some enemy machine gun, mortar, and artillery fire as they pushed south to reach Amy and les Buteaux. One company of the 119th Infantry followed the 3d Battalion, stationing patrols along the river to guard possible crossing sites against an eruption of the enemy into the regiment's open flank.

The comparatively rapid advance of the 175th Infantry led the 29th Division command to believe that enemy opposition in this zone had cracked.[86] As late as 1400 on 17 June General Gerhardt told General Corlett, "I feel we'll be getting to St. Lô before long." But he added, "It's hard to tell." [87]

Actually, in the fighting of 17 June there appeared indications of stalemate. The 116th Infantry, renewing the attack at 0400, ran into strong enemy machine gun and mortar fire. The worst spot was in the gap of about 1,000 yards developed in the previous day's attack between the 116th and 175th. There in the vicinity of

Villiers-Fossard the enemy was strongly entrenched. General Gerhardt observed that it was "a devil of a place. Every time they go forward they are driven back." [88] Attempts to smash through with artillery or 4.2-inch mortar support foundered on the difficulties of observation. Sources of enemy fire could be located generally but seldom pinpointed.[89]

This was true everywhere on the front. It was also noted that preparatory artillery fire did little good since the Germans made a practice of thinly outposting their front lines and moving the bulk of their forces forward to meet the infantry attack after the artillery lifted. The attack of the 115th Infantry (less the 2d Battalion) got off at 1840, 17 June. Leading the attack, the 1st Battalion lost direction and was caught by machine gun fire in an orchard not far from the line of departure. The 3d Battalion remained in the assembly area and dug in for the night.

Under the attacks of the 29th Division on 16 and 17 June the German *352d Division,* already only a Kampfgruppe of about regimental strength, lost about 500 men. On the other hand withdrawal southward coupled with the build-up of the *3d Parachute Division* had resulted in a substantial shortening of Kraiss's lines. His right rested on high ground west of St. André-de-l'Epine, his left on the Vire. The division, furthermore, was strengthened on the evening of 16 June when *Kampfgruppe Boehm* of the *353d Division* arrived from Brittany. Boehm, who was commander of the *943d Regiment,* brought up two infantry battalions and a few supporting troops on bicycles. Pending the arrival of the rest of the divi-

---

[84] 116th Inf S–3 Jnl.

[85] George replaced Colonel Goode, who had been captured 13 June. See above, section on Junction Between V and VII Corps.

[86] So estimated in 29th Div FO 9.

[87] 29th Div G–9 Jnl.

[88] *Ibid.*

[89] See, for instance, 115th S–3 Jnl, 18 Jun.

sion (still south of Avranches) he was attached to the *352d* and ordered into the area of la Luzerne. It was chiefly Boehm's fresh infantry that fought in the Villiers-Fossard salient during 17 June.[90]

In the 175th Infantry zone only the 1st Battalion attacked on 17 June. On Hill 108 it ran into heavy enemy artillery and machine gun fire and at 1440 reported that it was unable to advance. About the same time the 2d Battalion, which had held in position just northwest of the 1st, reported a counterattack that seemed designed by the Germans to cut off the 1st Battalion. Although the enemy made no significant penetrations of the 175th Infantry's lines, the advance southward was effectively halted.

For the third day's attack (on 18 June) General Gerhardt got eight battalions of artillery, six of which were to mass fires in front of the 115th and 116th Infantry Regiments. A seven-minute artillery concentration before the jump-off had little effect in softening enemy defenses. At noon the 115th reported that the general advance had been stopped. The troops were getting mortar, 88-mm., 105-mm., and 20-mm. explosive fire and found it impossible to determine the exact location of the enemy in the immediate area. As for the 116th, it was exhausted by the attacks of the first two days. The 1st Battalion commander reported that he could not attack as he had "hardly anyone left." His executive officer added that "everyone is done out physically. No leaders left. No reorganization possible." [91]

A similar situation developed in the 175th zone. The 3d Battalion, after being

relieved at Méauffe about midnight by the 119th Infantry, attacked south the morning of 18 June and reached le Carillon without meeting much opposition. But the 1st Battalion was getting badly battered on Hill 108. To relieve it, the 3d Battalion was first diverted at 1400 to attack southeast toward Hill 102; later it was ordered to disengage and go directly to the assistance of the 1st Battalion.

Positions occupied by V Corps units on 18 June were held for the next two weeks. Less than five miles from the key city of St. Lô, the 29th Division would not enter it for almost a month and then at the cost of some of the most difficult and expensive fighting of the war. A foretaste of the struggle had already come in the last three days of the June attacks as V Corps mired in the hedgerow country. One of the prime difficulties faced by the Americans in this terrain was in co-ordinating tanks and infantry. The enemy skillfully established defenses combining antitank guns and automatic weapons well concealed in hedges. Tanks could not go forward to knock out the machine guns, nor could infantry spearhead the advance to take out the antitank guns. The effect was graphically described in the account by the 747th Tank Battalion of a limited-objective attack on 20 June to reduce the Villiers-Fossard salient:[92]

At 0600 Company B moved forward, with the engineers blowing gaps in hedgerows and the infantry following. The infantry was pinned down and tanks could not move further forward. But they were on part of their objective. Tanks were forced to withdraw due to heavy antitank fire and bazooka fire. One tank was knocked out and the crew of five men were wounded. The tanks kept try-

---

[90] MS # A–983 (Generalleutnant Paul Mahlmann, CG, *353d Division*).

[91] 116th S–3 Jnl, 18 Jun.

[92] 747th Tk Bn AAR, with supporting documents.

ing to move forward, but got stuck. And the infantry stayed pinned down. Another tank was hit. On order of the regimental commander four tanks forced their way through fire to the objective. No infantry followed. Two tanks returned; one was knocked out by antitank guns. The other was stuck so that [the] crew had to abandon [the] tanks as no help could reach them. The infantry withdrew 900 yards and took up defensive positions. The tanks covered the withdrawal. . . .

One answer was the development of small infantry–tank teams which could advance together. To make this possible hedgerow cutters were devised and welded to the fronts of the tanks to allow them to bull through the earth banks. Technicians wrestled with difficult problems of direct communication between infantry and tanks. All during the rest of June training took place in the V Corps zone to perfect tank–infantry tactics which could set the attack rolling once more toward St. Lô when the time came.[93]

---

[93] During the remainder of the month the whole V Corps front was static, except for a limited objective attack in the Villiers-Fossard area on 29 June. See below, p. 444.

TANK EQUIPPED WITH HEDGEROW CUTTER

CHAPTER X

The Capture of Cherbourg
(8 June–1 July)

Securing the North Flank

On 18 June, when V Corps went on the defensive in front of St. Lô, VII Corps on First Army's right had just completed a brilliant victory—the cutting of the Cotentin—which split the German *Seventh Army* and sealed the fate of Cherbourg. The victory, swift and dramatic in the final stage, was preceded by ten days of hard slugging in order to break out the ring which the Germans pressed around the D-Day beachhead.

Some of the hardest fighting during the first week of the invasion took place on the north flank of VII Corps where the 4th Division, together with the 505th Parachute Infantry (82d Airborne Division) on its left, fought to take the corps D-Day objective: the ridge line, Quinéville–Montebourg–le Ham, from the coast to the Merderet River. (*Map XX*) The enemy in this area had the advantage of defending higher ground which rises gradually northward to the Quinéville–Montebourg ridge. Field fortifications were prepared throughout the area making maximum use of the network of hedgerows. In addition, the fully developed fortified areas at Azeville, Crisbecq, Ozeville, and along the beach as far as Quinéville provided strong nodes of defense. It will be remembered that the 4th Division had

butted up against the southernmost defenses on 7 June but had been unable to subdue them.

After the D-Day lodgment area had been cleaned out on D plus 1, VII Corps organized a full-scale attack to the north. It was essential to reach the Quinéville–Montebourg line in order to knock out enemy batteries which kept the UTAH landing beaches under artillery fire as well as to widen the base of attack for a drive westward across the peninsula.

Four regiments attacked abreast on 8 June: the 505th Parachute Infantry and 8th Infantry west of the Montebourg highway with objectives between the Merderet River and Montebourg, and the 12th and 22d Infantry Regiments in the zone east to the coast with final objectives along the Quinéville–Montebourg ridge.

The 8th Infantry and 505th Parachute Infantry made slow but steady progress under harassing opposition during 8 June to reach a line generally from the Montebourg highway through Magneville to the Merderet. Probing attacks farther north before dark revealed what seemed to be a prepared defense along the tributary of the Merderet just north of Magneville. Centers of resistance were apparent at the Magneville hangar and at Ecausseville. Along the creek bank machine guns were dug in and artillery was registered on all routes of approach.[1]

These positions were actually part of the defense set up by General von Schlieben after the unsuccessful counterattack on Ste. Mère-Eglise on 8 June. The main German defensive line, however, was to the north along the railroad from le Ham to Montebourg and thence northeast following the main highway to Quinéville. Between 9 and 12 June troops were gathered to man this line from miscellaneous units of the *709th, 243d,* and *91st Divisions* and the *Seventh Army Sturm Battalion* and formed into three Kampfgruppen of nominally regimental size. The east wing of the line rested securely on the high ground at Quinéville extending to the sea, but the west flank was open. It was planned that the *77th Division* would tie in on the west as soon as that unit, still moving up slowly from the south, should arrive.[2] The chief strength of the German defense in the meantime was its unusually strong artillery support. In addition to the artillery that von Schlieben had on 8 June (a battalion of the *243d Artillery Regiment* and two heavy motorized battalions, the *456th* and *457th*), on about 9 June two Russian 122-mm. guns were moved from Carteret on the west coast of the Cotentin to northwest of Quinéville. At the same time the six French 155-mm. guns of the *3d Battalion, 1261st Artillery Regiment,* were shifted from Fontenay to positions about half a mile west of Lestre. In addition the guns of two fixed coastal battalions at Videcosville and Morsalines (about four miles north of Quinéville ridge) were removed from their bases and mounted on carriages so that they could be used in the land fighting—the job being done by ordnance personnel working day and night under almost constant American fire. The effectiveness of this comparatively large aggregation of guns in support of the German defense was qualified, however, by a shortage of ammunition and by the fact that the crews were submitted to almost constant Allied naval bombardment and air attacks.[3]

Co-ordinated American attacks on 9 June had varying success. The 8th Infantry at the cost of hard fighting and heavy losses made significant gains in overcoming some of the points of heaviest German resistance. Company L took the hangar positions at Magneville by charging across open fields in the face of heavy grazing fire and at the cost of many lives. In the meantime the 2d Battalion, assaulting Ecausseville, which was reported to be lightly held, had its leading company chewed by enemy artillery, mortar, and machine gun fire that caught it in a hedgerowed trail. The 1st Battalion, however, took up the fight late in the day and fared better. With two platoons of tanks in the lead the 1st Battalion moved up the road east of Ecausseville. At the crossroads east of the town, tanks shot up a group of houses from the rear and enabled the infantry to move in and take 100 prisoners. Ecausseville itself held out as enemy 88-mm. guns prevented the tanks from enter-

---

[1] Combat intervs, 82d Abn and 4th Inf Divs. For treatment in greater detail of this action and others on the road to Cherbourg see Ruppenthal, *Utah Beach,* pp. 95ff.

[2] MS # B–845 (Schlieben); cf. Hoffmann Report. *Seventh Army, KTB Anlagen 1.I.–30.VI.44.* The Kampfgruppen formed were: *Kampfgruppe Hoffmann* from the le Ham railroad station to Montebourg; *Kampfgruppe Keil* from Montebourg to the vicinity of les Landes; and *Kampfgruppe Mueller* from les Landes to Quinéville.

[3] MS # B–260 (Triepel).

ing. But the outflanking maneuver was successful, and during the night the Germans withdrew to their main defensive positions.

The 8th Infantry then advanced rapidly and by the night of 10 June all three battalions had reached objectives along the le Ham–Montebourg highway. But attacks toward the le Ham–Montebourg railroad line were met with very heavy enemy fire. The entire regiment therefore dug in east of the highway and established a defensive line which it was to hold until the beginning of the major drive north to Cherbourg on 19 June.

The simultaneous attack on 10 June of the 505th Parachute Infantry on the left proved more difficult, largely because of the nature of the tactical problem. The regiment was to take the Montebourg Station and le Ham. The latter town was the western anchor of the German defense line and was situated on the Merderet between two small tributaries. The plan of attack was for one battalion to seize the Station and defend to the north while the 2d came up behind and then swung west between the creeks to le Ham.

The first part went well. Under heavy artillery rolling ahead of the attack, the 1st Battalion reached its objective within six hours of the jump-off. The 2d Battalion, following the 1st slightly farther north than intended in order to avoid flanking fire from the left, turned to attack le Ham along the axis of the Montebourg road. The enemy troops at le Ham, some of whom had retreated there from the Station, fought stubbornly as they were pressed into their last stronghold. The attack was halted at dark still about a thousand yards from its objective.

On the morning of 11 June Colonel Ekman, regimental commander, ordered the 2d Battalion to employ a holding attack on the north of le Ham while the 2d Battalion, 325th Glider Infantry, thrust at the enemy from the east. The attack of the latter battalion, though prepared by a fifteen-minute artillery concentration and covered by smoke, nevertheless cost heavy casualties as troops struggled through open fields and swamps. The battalion was halted short of its objective, weakened by casualties and low in ammunition. Then the enemy began to withdraw. A new attack was mounted and the battalion, widely deployed, moved in against a badly shaken covering force. Passing abandoned German field pieces the Americans entered le Ham to find it deserted. The bridge over the Merderet west of le Ham was secured, and during the rest of the day the whole position was organized for defense. On the morning of 13 June the 505th Parachute Infantry was relieved by a battalion of the 359th Infantry of the 90th Division.

The attacks of the 8th and 505th Infantry Regiments, which have been traced through to their conclusion, were only part of the general advance of the 4th Division northward which in four days pushed back the enemy into his last prepared defensive positions south of the Cherbourg *Landfront* (landward fortifications of the port). In the center of the division zone Colonel Reeder's 12th Infantry, after losing 300 men in a violent fight around Emondeville during 8 June, broke loose and moved up to Joganville where it destroyed a German resistance point. Reeder then advanced another 2,000 yards. The next day his 3d

FONTENAY   FORTIFIED AREA   DANGUEVILLE   CRISBECQ

CRISBECQ FORTIFICATION. *In foreground is village of St. Marcouf. Inset: One of the forts.*

Battalion sped north to just short of the regimental objective, 1,500 yards northeast of Montebourg, and far in advance of all other 4th Division units.

On the division's right the attack of 8 June against the Crisbecq and Azeville fortifications repeated the experience of the day before. Two companies of the 1st Battalion, 22d Infantry, led the assault on Crisbecq after a twenty-minute preparation of naval fire, together with field artillery and mortar concentrations. Advancing then under a rolling barrage which the infantry followed at about 200 yards, and under indirect fire from heavy machine guns, the two companies reached the edge of the fortified area with few losses. The third company was then passed through to blow the concrete emplacements with pole charges. The assault sections, however, used all their explosives without materially damaging the concrete and then became involved in small arms fights with Germans in the communicating trenches. A counterattack on the left at last forced the battalion to withdraw to its starting point north of Bas Village de Dodainville. Action of the 2d Battalion before Azeville was similar, and similarly unsuccessful.

Twice turned back, Colonel Tribolet, commander of the 22d Infantry, on 9 June revised his tactics. He temporarily abandoned the assault on Crisbecq and concentrated on Azeville. The 3d Battalion (less one company engaged in attacking beach defenses) was brought up to take over the mission of assaulting that position. While naval and artillery fire neutralized the Crisbecq guns, two companies circled to the west of the four Azeville blockhouses whose southern approaches had been rendered almost impenetrable by mine fields, barbed wire, and concrete one-man shelters. Although there were mines and wire on the west, too, the Germans here had not cleared fields of fire and apparently had made no preparations to cover this approach. The assaulting troops were thus able to cut their way through the wire and pick paths through the mines without removing them. Bazookas and one tank that managed to get through the mine fields opened fire on the nearest of the blockhouses but without effect. A demolition team then made three separate attempts to blow up the blockhouse. All three failed. It looked as though once more the attackers might run out of explosives and have to pull back. Then happened one of those minor miracles that may turn the course of battle. On orders of his company commander, Pvt. Ralph G. Riley took the last available flame thrower to "give it a few more squirts." Reaching the blockhouse after running through enemy fire, Private Riley lighted his flame thrower with a match, as the firing mechanism failed, and trained the stream of blazing oil on the threshold of the door. The fire should have had no more effect than previous squirts. But it did. It hit some ammunition inside. Explosions followed. Within minutes a white flag emerged. When the firing ceased the German commander stepped out and surrendered the whole of the Azeville fortifications with their garrison of 169 men. Riley received the Silver Star.

The capture of Azeville opened the way for continuing the attack north toward Quinéville. Even though Crisbecq and other known German prepared positions remained in action, General Bar-

AZEVILLE FORTS *are located at upper left of photo on both sides of road. Inset: One of the forts.*

ton, in view of success all along his front, decided to bypass them and send a task force straight through to Quinéville.

But although each of the regiments of the 4th Division at the end of 9 June had succeeded in cracking determined enemy resistance no holes had been punched in the enemy's main defenses. A task force of the 22d Infantry [4] under command of Brig. Gen. Harry A. Barber found that it was not at liberty to move through the Azeville gap for direct attack on the Quinéville positions. Germans held out in strength all along the right side of the proposed advance— at Crisbecq, Dangueville, Château de Fontenay, and Fontenay-sur-Mer. On the left, the enemy had scattered positions in the mile-and-a-half gap between the 22d and 12th Infantry Regiments. Too weak to contain the enemy on its flanks and at the same time push ahead, and plagued by bad weather which prevented air support, Task Force Barber made little headway for the next three days.

On 12 June General Collins, VII Corps commander, decided to commit another regiment on the right to clear the fortified beach and coastal area and so free General Barber for his main mission of advancing to capture the Quinéville ridge. Collins was also anxious to take out the coastal batteries whose harassing fire on UTAH Beach threatened to slow down the unloading of supplies. Accordingly the 39th Infantry of the 9th Division, which had landed on 11 June, was committed in the zone roughly from the Fontenay-sur-Mer–St. Marcouf road

where it relieved the 1st Battalion, 22d Infantry.

The 39th Infantry (Col. Harry A. Flint) in part profited from the hard fighting of the three previous days which had seemed to batter unsuccessfully against the enemy's fortifications. The 2d Battalion found Crisbecq unoccupied, and pushed on to take Dangueville in the afternoon. Advances elsewhere were more heavily contested. The 1st Battalion cleared the beach between Taret de Ravenoville and Fort St. Marcouf, while the 3d Battalion captured Fontenay-sur-Mer in a hard fight against an enemy whose resistance grew more stubborn as he was forced back against his main line on the Quinéville ridge.

Freed now for the attack north, Task Force Barber devoted its entire strength to the reduction of the Ozeville fortifications. Two battalions took up flanking positions from which they could deliver mortar, tank, and cannon fire on the enemy defenses while the 3d Battalion, with a company of chemical mortars and a platoon of tanks, advanced behind artillery concentrations from two battalions. At the same time naval fire neutralized German guns at Quinéville. Bad weather again prevented the use of air, but the concentrated volume of fire was decisive. Ozeville in short order hung out the white flag. The close of the fight, however, was not to be capitulation. An American officer trying to stop the firing in order to receive the signaled surrender was shot down. Infuriated, the assault company rushed the enemy emplacements with bayonets and grenades and all but exterminated the garrison.

Capture of Ozeville was the signal for the 12th Infantry on the left to advance

---

[4] With the 899th Tank Battalion and the bulk of the 746th Tank Battalion attached.

to its objective on the Montebourg end of the Quinéville–Montebourg ridge. The 12th Infantry had actually reached this objective on the morning of 11 June but it was then far ahead of units on both flanks. It was therefore ordered back behind the Montebourg–St. Floxel road where it remained on the defensive until the attack on Ozeville seemed assured of success. Late in the afternoon of 12 June it reoccupied the heights of les Fieffes Dancel.[5]

The enemy from the Merderet to Montebourg had thus been forced back to the line of the railroad by the night of 12 June. Montebourg itself remained in enemy hands. Until 12 June General Barton felt that the limited forces at his disposal would not warrant involving any considerable numbers of them in street fighting. On that day, after reports that Montebourg was lightly held, he at last ordered Colonel Van Fleet to take the city, if it could be done cheaply.

Actually the Germans were prepared to defend Montebourg strongly as a key to the defense of Cherbourg. Located in the angle between the German line defending south under von Schlieben and the line of the *91st Division* defending west, the city was ordered to be held with every available means. On 8 and 9 June twenty-five light French tanks and the *3d Battalion* of the *919th Regiment* had moved in to the defense.[6]

When the 8th Infantry task force discovered the strength of the Montebourg garrison, the attack was called off and a mixed force of infantry and armor of somewhat less than battalion size was

formed to contain the city. The right-wing units of the 4th Division then set about completing their D-Day tasks. What remained was the capture of the Quinéville ridge. The 12th Infantry, which already occupied the western end of the ridge, was to hold there and protect the 22d Infantry's left flank while the 22d advanced north and then east along the ridge toward Quinéville. At the same time Colonel Flint with the 39th Infantry would attack north along the beach and west edge of the inundations.

Progress of the attack during 13 June was disappointingly slow. The 39th Infantry made only small gains while Colonel Tribolet's 22d Infantry was able only to maneuver into position for attack in column of battalions down the ridge to Quinéville. On 14 June the attack was resumed. Tribolet's three battalions fought their way to the nose of the ridge and captured two hills just west of Quinéville. The 3d Battalion of the 39th Infantry in the meantime came up from the south and, when abreast of the 22d Infantry, turned east. The plan then was for it to continue the advance on the town of Quinéville with the 3d Battalion, 22d Infantry. Instead, Colonel Flint with permission of the division attacked alone, after a bombardment of Quinéville by thirty-six A–20's.

Company K of the 39th led off the attack and at first moved rapidly. Supported by mortar fire the company entered Quinéville but at once ran into stiff opposition from Germans defending the beach positions east of the town. There was little room for maneuver and it was impossible to employ the other two companies without exposing them in open fields barred by wire entanglements.

---

[5] Colonel Reeder was wounded on 11 June and Lt. Col. James S. Luckett took command of the regiment.

[6] MS # C–018 (Keil); MS # B–845 (Schlieben).

QUINEVILLE. *Village is in foreground. At top of photograph along beach is Quinéville Bains.*

Tanks could not advance because of an antitank gun on the beach and heavy enemy mortar fire. The answer was smoke. A concentration fell squarely on enemy positions and permitted Company K to push the attack to the beach fortifications. The enemy's situation was then hopeless and he promptly surrendered. While the capture of Quinéville was accomplished, the 1st Battalion of the 39th Infantry, despite severe casualties from mines, had completed the clearing of the beach with the capture of Fort St. Marcouf.

The northern flank of VII Corps anchored on the Quinéville ridge was now secure. In the ensuing lull in the fighting the enemy would be allowed to build up slightly opposite the 4th Division but his attitude remained purely defensive. Actually, after the initial attempt to counterattack on 6 June, the Germans never could muster enough strength on this front to take the offensive. On the contrary, from 9 June they became increasingly concerned over their ability to hold and prevent a clean breakthrough to Cherbourg. On the 9th the *77th Division* received orders to proceed to Valognes and at the same time General Marcks, the corps commander, secured the immediate release of two battalions from the Cherbourg *Landfront*.[7] He also asked for air support, saying that the fate of his troops, pressed hard between Montebourg and Marcouf, depended on it. *Third Air Force* replied that bad weather made it momentarily impossible.[8] Actually with all airfields in the vicinity of the coast unusable, Luftwaffe fighters were never able to intervene in the Cotentin battles.

While awaiting ground reinforcements, Marcks tried to straighten out the command situation in the Cotentin. Troops had been rushed hurriedly into battle and committed promptly on arrival to plug the defense wherever the weakness seemed most critical at the time. Reorganization became necessary. Marcks named Generalleutnant Heinz Hellmich of the *243d Division* to command a Kampfgruppe of these miscellaneous units along the Montebourg–Quinéville line. The formation of *Kampfgruppe Hellmich* simplified the chain of command, but at the lower levels it is probable that the mixed Kampfgruppe had considerably less cohesion in defense than regular units would have had.

On 10 June the advance elements of the *77th Division*, consisting of about a battalion, arrived in the vicinity of Valognes. Two days later the bulk of the division was in position on both sides of the Merderet. General Dollmann expressed himself as satisfied that the situation was restored to balance on this portion of the front.[9] Units of the new division relieved *Kampfgruppe Hoffmann*, which had been holding the western wing of the Montebourg line.[10] But the restored balance was short-lived. Again success in the defense of one sector was almost immediately nullified by breaks in the line elsewhere. The Ger-

---

[7] *Seventh Army, KTB 1.I.–30.VI.44,* 9 Jun 44; *Kriegsgliederung,* 18 May 44. *Seventh Army, KTB Anlagen 1.I.–30.VI.44;* MS # B–845 (Schlieben). The battalions released were the *2d Battalion, 921st Regiment,* and *1st Battalion, 922d Regiment* (both of the *243d Division*).

[8] *Seventh Army, KTB 1.I.–30.VI.44,* 9 Jun 44.
[9] *Ibid.,* 11 Jun 44.
[10] Hoffmann Report. *Seventh Army, KTB Anlagen 1.I.–30.VI.44.*

mans' Montebourg line could hold only so long as their position on the west remained firm. U.S. VII Corps troops in the week following D Day hammered this position into crumbled ruins.

Attack to Cut the Peninsula

The drive north had reached only a little beyond D-Day objectives in a week of hard fighting. The delay had been caused chiefly by German success in bringing up considerable reinforcements to hold a line which the enemy command deemed vital to the defense of Cherbourg. On the VII Corps west flank on the Merderet River a similar delay of about a week in reaching D-Day objectives was caused principally by the original accidents that befell the airborne drops and by terrain difficulties in subsequent attempts to force the river crossing. Although the *91st Division* was ordered to counterattack the American bridgehead from the west, the Germans were never able to concentrate in the Merderet area. The parachute drops in their midst caused heavy losses and disorganization, including the death of the division commander, General Falley, and effectively stifled the planned attacks.[11]

Even against relatively small enemy forces, the problem of seizing a bridgehead over the Merderet remained difficult. At the end of 7 June, there were at la Fière some 600 men of the 507th and

508th Parachute Infantry Regiments, together with some tanks and artillery and the 1st Battalion of the 325th Glider Infantry which had moved up with the 8th Infantry after landing by sea. West of the river were three organized but isolated groups, ranging from company to battalion size. After the failure of the attempt to establish a bridgehead at la Fière on D Day, the 82d Airborne Division had been under violent counterattack. While elements of the division held the bridge, other units cleared the east bank of the river and established firm contact with American forces to the north and south.[12]

Late on 8 June two men from Colonel Timmes' force west of the Merderet discovered a submerged but passable road across the swamps north of la Fière, crossed without incident, and reported to division headquarters. The discovery opened up a promising route to reach Colonel Timmes' and Col. George V. Millett's groups, isolated on the west bank, and then attack south in force to clear the enemy defending the la Fière causeway. The plan was for the 1st Battalion, 325th Glider Infantry (Maj. Teddy H. Sanford), to cross the swamp road after dark while Colonel Millett's force near Amfreville thrust southeast to join with Colonel Timmes. Sanford's battalion negotiated the crossing successfully and made contact with Timmes. (*Map 6*) But in the meantime Millett's attack failed as his column, fired on in the dark, fell apart. Millett and some of his men were captured; the remainder withdrew northeast toward the river and took no further part in the fighting until 10 June. Lack-

[11] Memo, Dollmann for *Army Group B*, 10 Jun 44. *Seventh Army, KTB Anlagen 1.I.–30.VI.44. Seventh Army* considered the Allied mass use of airborne troops in an occupied area a brand new tactic comparable to the British introduction of the tank in World War I. Cf. von der Heydte's discussion of the difficulties of assembling his widely scattered troops to concentrate for attack. MS # B–839.

[12] See above, p. 346.

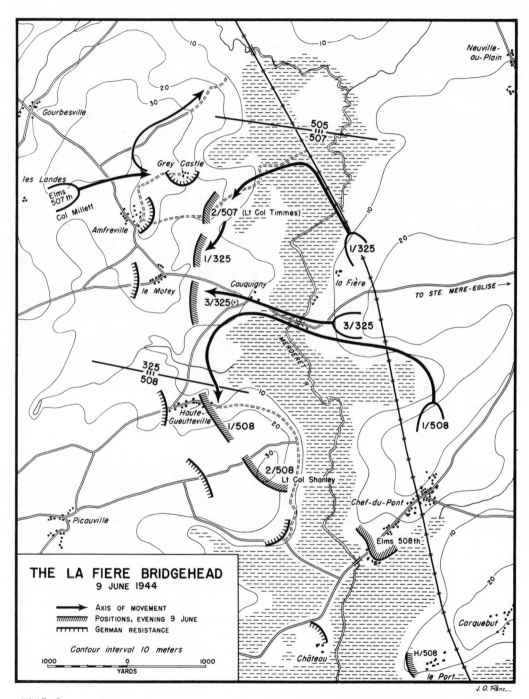

MAP 6

THE LA FIERE BRIDGEHEAD
9 JUNE 1944

AXIS OF MOVEMENT
POSITIONS, EVENING 9 JUNE
GERMAN RESISTANCE

Contour interval 10 meters

1000   0   1000
YARDS

ing Millett's support, Sanford organized his men and headed for the western end of the causeway. They had not gone far when the enemy opened heavy fire. The Americans were thrown back with severe losses to Colonel Timmes' position along the river east of Amfreville.

When Colonel Lewis, commander of the 325th Glider Infantry, reported the failure of the attack, General Ridgway, the division commander, decided to renew the attempt to force the causeway at la Fière. The mission was given to the 3d Battalion, 325th Glider Infantry, which was to move up under cover of smoke from positions at Chef-du-Pont. A fifteen-minute artillery and tank fire preparation was arranged and a reinforced company of the 507th Parachute Infantry was to follow up the causeway attack if it faltered. General Gavin, the assistant division commander, was directed to co-ordinate the attack.

Although the smoke screen proved too thin and the troops of the 325th Glider Infantry came under enemy machine gun fire before they reached the line of departure, the men were able to creep up along a stone wall to the jump-off point. At 1045 the attack was signaled and the men left their shelter under orders to sprint the 500 yards across the exposed causeway. Everything depended on the first dash. But it proved too much for most of the men. Under mortar and artillery fire, all but a handful yielded to the overpowering instinct to seek shelter, and though there was no shelter they threw themselves down along the roadside. Some were casualties, and later arrivals, seeing them, lost the spirit needed to carry them across. The causeway became congested with the dead, the wounded,

and the disheartened. Congestion which threatened to abort the attack was made worse by a tank that got out on the causeway and hit an uncleared American mine field. An enemy tank destroyed in earlier action already blocked the road in part. The double constriction increased the difficulty of crossing and added to the casualties. Despite all this, men encouraged by Generals Ridgway and Gavin and Colonel Lewis did succeed in reaching the opposite bank and parts of two companies were able to proceed with their missions. Company E cleared Cauquigny with comparative ease as the Germans under heavy fire from the east bank were disposed to surrender.[13] Company G, deploying southward, made slower progress. The delayed crossings meant that when the support company, Company F, crossed under orders to mop up the bridgehead it found no bridgehead. On the initiative of the commander, therefore, it attacked west along the main road.

In the meantime, General Gavin, lacking reports of progress in pushing out the bridgehead from the west bank and worried about the increasing congestion of the causeway, committed the company of the 507th under Capt. R. D. Rae with orders to sweep the causeway stragglers across with him. A part of Captain Rae's company pushed westward with Company F and entered le Motey. Another part broke off to the south to seek contact with Company G. At the same time a platoon of Company E in Cauquigny was sent north to join the 1st Battalion, 325th Glider Infantry, held up near Amfreville. This platoon was pulled back

---

[13] See above, Ch. IX, n. 31, for glider regiment organization.

LA FIERE CAUSEWAY. *Merderet River is in foreground.*

later when a patrol reached Major Sanford's position and discovered that enemy pressure had so far eased that Sanford was actually freed to move as he wished. While the north flank of the new bridgehead was thus secured, fighting continued in the center and on the south, complicated by confused small unit maneuvers extremely difficult to control among the hedgerows.

The gravest threat to the new bridgehead developed during the day at le Motey. Le Motey, sited on a slight rise, afforded ideal ground for defense of the la Fière causeway. By the same token, its commanding position and the cover of its buildings provided a good assembly point for German forces to form for a counterattack. It was the intention of Company F and the company of the 507th to clean out and secure the village.

While they were proceeding to this task, however, General Gavin on the east bank of the river, unaware that the American push had already carried into le Motey and fearing a German assembly there, ordered the supporting artillery to pull back its fire and hold it on the village. One or two shells fell on American troops. Few casualties were suffered but commanders on the spot tried in vain to get word back to have the fire lifted. Company F was therefore forced to withdraw to poorer defense positions on the lower ground. In its new position the company found both its flanks open, and the commander therefore requested that Company E move up on his left.

That move was accomplished, but only after a considerable delay during which Company F, apprehensive of being surrounded, again withdrew a few fields to

the east. When Company E moved up, it in effect exchanged positions with F, neither group having observed the other's move. Company E, coming into line where it expected to find American troops, was greeted only by enemy fire from the flanks. With a sense of isolation and under the impression of being counterattacked, it pulled out in disorder.

The retreat was checked by officers on the west bank of the river before it acquired the momentum of a general panic, and fortunately the enemy made no move. The bridgehead was saved and the line was redressed. The four companies that had crossed from la Fière were securely tied in on the north with the 1st Battalion, 325th Glider Infantry, plus Colonel Timmes' force. On the south, contact was made with the 2d Battalion, 508th Parachute Infantry, under command of Colonel Shanley.

For Shanley the la Fière bridgehead served as a long-overdue relief. He had fought for three days in a virtual state of siege on Hill 30. Although he had a relatively large force occupying strategic ground that might have provided a basis for developing a bridgehead at Chef-du-Pont, he attracted such heavy enemy pressure that he had to fight hard and ingeniously just to maintain his position. As far as the command on the east bank of the river was concerned, Shanley's men were isolated and apparently the only thought was to rescue them. One such attempt made on 9 June failed. Not until the bridgehead was established at la Fière and tied in with Hill 30 did Shanley's real contribution to the division's battle become clear. In denying to the enemy control of the west bank of the Merderet and in absorbing a large measure of the enemy's striking force which might otherwise have been pointed more sharply at la Fière, he had done much to assist the ultimate establishment of a bridgehead.[14]

Late in the afternoon of 8 June the Merderet bridgehead was consolidated as the 1st Battalion, 508th, was moved in between Colonel Shanley and the 325th. With all units west of the Merderet at last brought within a single bridgehead, the crossing was ready for exploitation in the first step of the major corps effort to cut westward across the peninsula.

This mission was given to the 90th Division (Brig. Gen. Jay W. MacKelvie), which had begun landing on D Day, and verbal orders were issued by General Collins on 9 June.[15] The 359th Infantry had been attached to the 4th Division to assist the latter in the attack north in accordance with the original operational plan that contemplated committing the entire 90th Division on the 4th Division right for a co-ordinated advance on Cherbourg. Despite the change in plan, the 359th Infantry was to remain at first with the 4th Division while MacKelvie operated west of the Merderet with his remaining two regiments, the 357th and 358th. The initial divisional objective was the line of the Douve where the river flows south between Terre-de-Beauval and St. Sauveur-le Vicomte. (Map XXI) The northern part of this objective was assigned to the 357th Infantry attacking through the lines of the

82d Division just west of la Fière. The 358th Infantry would cross at Chef-du-Pont attacking toward Picauville, Pont l'Abbé, and St. Sauveur-le Vicomte. When the 82d Airborne Division had been relieved by the 90th's attack, it would first hold the line of the Merderet River and then, following the 90th Division, would take over the security of the VII Corps south flank along the Douve.

The attack of the 90th Division jumping off early in the morning of 10 June went badly from the start. The 357th Infantry (Col. Philip H. Ginder) scarcely advanced beyond the perimeter of the 9 June bridgehead. Just beyond le Motey the regiment ran into strongly entrenched troops of the *1057th Regiment* (*91st Division*). The 2d Battalion in the lead recoiled under its first experience with heavy enemy fire and was relieved in the afternoon by the 1st Battalion. But the latter, attacking toward Amfreville, made virtually no progress. Since the 325th Glider Infantry had stayed in position after being passed through, the bridgehead, though scarcely enlarged, remained secure. Ginder lost ninety-nine men in the action.

On the left, the 358th Infantry (Col. James V. Thompson) advanced a few hundred yards west of Picauville before meeting serious resistance. It then halted on Thompson's order and the forward companies dug in. Thompson felt that his position was insecure. Germans still held out in a château to the rear which had been bypassed in the advance, and an engineer-infantry detachment ordered to blow the Beuzeville-la Bastille bridge over the Douve had been deterred from its mission by heavy enemy fire from across the river. When the regiment

---

[14] For details of Shanley's action see Col. S. L. A. Marshall, "Affair at Hill 30," *The Marine Corps Gazette*, February 1948, pp. 8–15, and March 1948, pp. 20–25.

[15] VII Corps Opns Memo No. 10, 11 Jun 44, contains the commanding general's verbal order of 9 June.

tried later in the afternoon to resume the attack westward, it was unable to move. Both the 1st and 3d Battalions dug in on the forward line. The bulk of the 129 casualties of the 1st Battalion, 358th Infantry, during the first day of action appear to have been from mortar and artillery fire.

On 11 June both regiments continued the attack, but nightfall found them still short of the D-Day objective line set for the 82d Airborne Division by the original plan. The 357th Infantry was still fighting in the vicinity of les Landes, and the 358th had encircled but not captured Pont l'Abbé. Next day the 359th Infantry, released from attachment to the 4th Division, was committed between Ginder and Thompson on a 1,000-yard front and assigned objectives along the Douve in the center of the division zone.

South of the 90th Division zone the 508th Parachute Infantry, reinforced and under command of Brig. Gen. G. P. Howell,[16] was ordered to attack across the Douve on 12 June to seize the area between the river and the Prairies Marécageuses and join with the 101st Airborne Division at Baupte. By the same order the 325th Glider Infantry was given the mission of defending the north bank of the Douve westward as the 90th Division advanced.[17] After a night crossing of the river at Beuzeville-la Bastille, Howell marched to his objective without a fight worth mentioning and reached Baupte by 0800. What happened was that

the *100th Panzer Replacement Battalion,* which was holding this sector with a large number of foreign personnel and makeshift equipment, broke at first contact with the Americans and pulled out. The debacle not only opened a new hole in the German lines but resulted in exaggerated reports of the strength of the American penetration. German countermeasures were taken in the belief that American armor had broken through in strength.[18] The Kampfgruppe of the *265th Division,* which was just arriving, was diverted to hold the Baupte–les Moitiers sector and was ordered reinforced by one battalion of the *1049th Regiment* of the *77th Division* to be brought down from the Cherbourg *Landfront.*[19]

While the 508th Parachute Infantry drove unexpectedly into a hole in the enemy lines, the 90th Division continued its sticky movement through defended hedgerow country. By 13 June it had struggled to its initial objectives roughly on a line from Gourbesville to Pont l'Abbé. The latter town was captured by the 358th Infantry after bombing and artillery concentration had leveled it, leaving, as the regimental commander remarked, only two rabbits alive. Criticizing its own failures in the four-day attack, the 90th Division afterward pointed out that training lessons had not been properly applied, particularly the doctrine of fire and maneuver and the precept of closely following artillery.[20] In the hedgerow country the normal difficulties of any division green to combat were greatly intensified. In a country

---

[16] Howell was commander of the 2d Airborne Brigade, a headquarters that originally controlled the 507th and 508th Parachute Regiments, which were not organic to the 82d Airborne Division. In combat Howell was attached to the division headquarters and assigned special missions.

[17] 82d Abn Div Opns Memo, FO 6.

[18] Actually TF Howell had no tank support.

[19] *Seventh Army, KTB 1.I.–30.VI.44,* 13 Jun 44.

[20] 90th Div Opns Memo No. 2, 19 Jun 44; 358th Inf Jnl, 15 Jun 44.

where each field constituted a separate battlefield and where there was no chance of seeing what was happening on either side control was at times impossible. To the shock of experiencing hostile fire for the first time was added the demoralizing invisibility of an enemy entrenched in natural earthworks and concealed in the thick vegetation that luxuriated on their tops. These conditions were, of course, pretty general throughout the Normandy fighting and each division had to work out a solution. General Eisenhower believed that the 90th Division's special difficulties were due to the fact that the division had not been "properly brought up." [21] On 13 June General MacKelvie, who had commanded the division since 19 January 1944, was relieved without prejudice and replaced by Maj. Gen. Eugene M. Landrum.[22] Two regimental commanders were relieved at the same time.

The division was left in the line, but General Collins decided to reorganize completely his attack scheme. The main attack west was to be taken over on 14 June by the 9th Division (Maj. Gen. Manton Eddy) and the 82d Airborne Division.[23] Detailed verbal orders for the attack were issued by General Collins on 13 June. The 82d Airborne Division was assigned the southern part of the 90th Division's original attack zone with an axis of advance along the Pont l'Abbé–St. Sauveur-le Vicomte road; the 9th Division in the northern half of the zone would attack toward Ste. Colombe. The 90th Division, when passed through, would wheel north to take objectives along a line from le Ham to Terre-de-Beauval covering the north flank of the westward drive. On General Collins' request, General Bradley assigned the 79th Division to VII Corps as a replacement for the 90th, but as it turned out the 79th was not used in the attack.

Attack on 14 June began in the south where the 358th Infantry advanced 1,000 yards west of Pont l'Abbé. General Ridgway committed his regiments about noon, the 325th Glider Infantry and the 507th Parachute Infantry abreast, left and right of the highway respectively. Despite an evening counterattack which forced back the right flank of the 507th, the division by night had pushed forward about a mile. While the 358th Infantry was relieved, the 359th began a pivot northward toward its new objectives, opening a gap in the lines near Gottot. Here the 9th Division's 60th Infantry (Col. Frederick J. de Rohan) was committed, attacking through the narrow zone in column of battalions. Under enemy mortar and artillery fire, the lead companies advanced slowly to reach the Valognes–Pont l'Abbé highway by dark.

---

[21] Ltr to Marshall, 5 Jul 44. OPD file 319.1, sec. I, cases 1–80.

[22] General Landrum enlisted in 1910 and was commissioned in 1916. He served with the American Expeditionary Forces in Siberia in 1918–19. Assigned to the Alaskan Defense Command in 1942–43, he commanded U.S. troops in the occupation of Attu. In October 1943 he took command of the 87th Division.

[23] Each division put only two regiments into the attack. The 39th Infantry of the 9th Division was still engaged on the 4th Division right flank. The 505th Parachute Infantry was released from attachment to the 4th Division on the morning of 13 June. The 508th Parachute Infantry had a defensive role in the Baupte bridgehead. The 9th Division, a battle-tested unit like the 82d, had been commanded by

General Eddy since 1942. Eddy, who had served with a machine gun detachment and been wounded in World War I, led his troops in 1942 and 1943 through the campaigns of North Africa and Sicily before entering the Normandy operations.

Virtual paralysis of the 90th Division, however, continued and the 359th and 357th Infantry Regiments made little progress. Two full days of fighting were required for the 357th to take Gourbesville, while the 359th inched forward and a battalion of the 358th committed on 15 June on the division right flank achieved little.

Whatever may be the full explanation of the 90th Division's continued slow progress, there is no question that the German defense on the north and northwest was substantially stronger than on the west. While Landrum faced elements of the recently arrived *77th Division,* opposition to the drive due west was still only the *91st Division,* now beaten down to a battle-weary Kampfgruppe. The bringing up of the Kampfgruppe of the *265th Division* did not reinforce the *91st,* since the bulk of the new unit was committed in the Pretot area south of the Douve where the Germans thought a large-scale break-through threatened. General der Artillerie Wilhelm Fahrmbacher, who replaced Marcks as commander of *LXXXIV Corps* after the latter's death in an air attack on 12 June, reported to *Seventh Army* on 14 June that a, large-scale American attack westward could not be held because of the splitting and mixing of units, the fatigue of the troops, and the lack of sufficient ammunition.[24]

He was right. On 15 June the 82d Airborne Division accelerated its advance against decreasing opposition. The

[24] *Seventh Army, KTB 1.I.–30.VI.44,* 12 and 14 Jun 44, and MS # B–784 (Criegern). Fahrmbacher, former commanding general of the *XXV Corps* in Brittany, took command of *LXXXIV Corps* on the evening of 12 June.

325th Glider Infantry got within 1,000 yards of St. Sauveur-le Vicomte while the 505th Parachute Infantry, after relieving the 507th, established its night line just south of Reigneville. The 60th Infantry on the other hand was hit shortly after the jump-off by a strong counterattack supported by tanks which drove it back to its line of departure. Fighting through the remainder of the day succeeded in recovering only about half the lost ground. Resistance here turned out to be the enemy's last stand east of the Douve.

Colonel de Rohan's direction of attack had been shifted slightly to point more nearly due west, increasing the divergence between his advance and that of the 359th on the right. This permitted another regiment to be committed between them. The 47th Infantry (Col. George W. Smythe) was brought in to attack shortly after noon for the high ground west of Orglandes. Colonel Smythe's advance was rapid, though he was bothered by the exposure of his north flank which was harassed by enemy fire from the vicinity of Orglandes. Despite this the regiment reached its objective by dark.

In planning the continuation of the attack on 16 June, General Collins decided to drive to the Douve with his southernmost regiment (the 325th) regardless of whether commensurate advances could be made on the rest of the front. The whole attack would thus be echeloned to the right rear, as each regiment refused its right to tie in with the regiment to the north of it. Speed in reaching the Douve seemed essential in order to forestall enemy reinforcement. Although the only enemy opposition con-

TANK ENTERING ST. SAUVEUR-LE VICOMTE. *Company A of the 746th Tank Battalion supported the 325th Glider Infantry in the advance on St. Sauveur.*

sisted of small groups fighting delaying action, it seemed possible that, given time, the Germans might be able to organize a co-ordinated defense along the Douve. The main effort of the corps, General Collins announced on 15 June, would now be to cut the peninsula. To give more weight and cohesion to the attack the 39th Infantry was returned to the 9th Division, and in addition the 359th Infantry was attached, with the result that the division resumed the attack with four regiments in line. The 90th Division committed only the 358th Infantry in its zone. The 82d Airborne Division employed the 325th Glider Infantry and the 505th Parachute Infantry in the attack while the 507th relieved the 508th in the Baupte sector and the latter regiment passed to reserve in the vicinity of Pont l'Abbé.

The attack of the 82d Airborne Division again made rapid progress on 16 June, and before noon both the 325th Glider Infantry and 505th Parachute Infantry had reached the line of the Douve opposite St. Sauveur-le Vicomte. They were joined here by the 508th, released from reserve. General Ridgway, observing the enemy withdrawing from St. Sauveur, asked and received corps permission to continue his advance. The city was occupied easily as artillery interdicted the escape routes north, south, and west. The 505th and 508th together established a bridgehead 2,000 to 3,000 yards in depth.

Actually the Germans had been pulling out through St. Sauveur all during the night and it looked as though they were in general retreat. General Collins therefore decided to accelerate his attack. Before noon he called General Eddy of

the 9th Division and directed that, instead of stopping at the limited objectives (Reigneville, Hautteville-Bocage, Orglandes) assigned in the original order, Eddy should push his leading regiments, the 47th and 60th, all the way to the Douve line, while the 39th swung around to protect the north flank. Eddy ordered Colonel de Rohan to advance the whole 60th Infantry to the river. Colonel Smythe was assigned objectives for the 47th Infantry on the high ground just east of Ste. Colombe. Smythe had a hard fight in the area of Hautteville-Bocage and Biniville on the last high ground east of the Douve, but pushed on to the main highway west of Biniville.

While this advance was going on, the 2d Battalion of the 60th Infantry under Lt. Col. Michael B. Kauffman, with the support of a company of tanks of the 746th Tank Battalion, made a cross-country sweep, avoiding enemy contact except for a brush with some machine gunners, and entered Ste. Colombe. Scarcely pausing there, Kauffman's lead company began crossing the river without any preparatory fire. The Douve at this point splits into three small streams and the road traversing the river flat runs for almost 1,000 yards between Ste. Colombe and Néhou on the west bank. Both towns are built on the hills rising from the river valley, but the slopes are gradual and observation restricted by the ubiquitous hedgerows. With tanks in the vanguard, the crossing of the first two bridges proceeded uneventfully. But the third bridge was out and the tanks turned back. Enemy artillery fire began to range in on all three rifle companies. Company E reached the west bank and dug in before Néhou, under increasing enemy artillery and di-

DOUVE RIVER   NEHOU   STE. COLOMBE

STE. COLOMBE–NEHOU AREA. *Circles indicate position of bridges.*

rect large-caliber fire. The other two companies, disorganized by enemy fire, either dug in between the bridges or withdrew to Ste. Colombe. Company G was at last moved up to support Company E on the west bank and during the night the 3d Battalion was brought up to bolster the shaky line.

Hitler Intervenes

By the end of 16 June, the 9th and 82d Divisions together had broken the last enemy defenses east of the Douve in their zones and had given impetus to what looked like a precipitate German withdrawal that might be followed rapidly to the sea. As a matter of fact the way *was* open, and the withdrawal was actually the retreat of disorganized remnants; the *91st Division* had been smashed beyond repair.

For the Germans, the threatened splitting of their Cotentin forces was serious enough in itself. But the crumbling of the *91st Division* was not a unique or merely local failure; it took place against a background of developing crisis in the whole German defense of the west—a crisis that in the view of OKW demanded not tactical doctoring but far-reaching revision of policy.

During the first week of operations there remained a chance that German armor in the beachhead might be able to seize the initiative at least locally and that, by so doing, might so far check the Allies as to allow the Germans to restore a balance of forces. Whether or not that was ever a real chance, by the end of the week it was becoming increasingly illusory. On 12 June General Marcks, the *LXXXIV Corps* commander, who was re-

spected throughout the German west army as an inspired leader, was killed. His death coincided roughly with the loss of Carentan, the capture of the Quinéville ridge, which strained von Schlieben's Montebourg line to the breaking point, another postponement of offensive action against Caen by the *I SS Panzer Corps,* and a discouraging survey by *Seventh Army* of the resources remaining in Brittany to reinforce the Normandy front. This survey turned up only a handful of mobile battalions suitable for transport to the battle area.[25] In Normandy *Seventh Army* had no closed front, no prepared positions behind the front, and no possibility of even making up the losses in front-line units, much less of building up a striking reserve.

Still worse was the situation in the rear areas, where Allied air power assisted by saboteurs of the French Resistance had so effectively sealed off the battlefields that supplies and replacements could not hope to keep up with the need. Before 6 June Leigh-Mallory's tactical air forces had knocked out all the bridges across the Seine River between Mantes-Gassicourt and the sea. (*See Map IV.*) Between 6 and 15 June at least eight bridges over the Loire were destroyed and all were severely damaged.[26] The *Seventh Army* quartermaster noted on 13 June that rail traffic since the invasion had been 90 percent paralyzed. No transport at all had come into the army area from the east.[27] One bridge over the Loire at Tours had been repaired on 17 June to the extent

---

[25] *Seventh Army, KTB 1.I.–30.VI.44,* 12 Jun 44.

[26] AAF Evaluation Board, Effectiveness of Air Attack Against Rail Transportation in the Battle of France, Jun 45. AAF file 138.4–37.

[27] Report of Railroad Situation, 13 Jun 44. *Seventh Army, O.Qu., KTB Anlagen 1.–30.VI.44.*

SEINE RIVER BRIDGE AT MANTES-GASSICOURT UNDER BOMBARD-
MENT *by aircraft of Ninth Air Force.*

that it was possible to push cars across it, although it could not support the weight of a locomotive. An officer from army headquarters was assigned to make sure that five trains a day were moved across.[28]

Interdiction at the river lines was reinforced by air attacks on the rail centers of the Région Ouest and by continual strafing attacks which made the Germans refrain from risking rail movements that would otherwise have been possible. For example, although some rail lines remained passable between Paris and Orléans traffic along them was negligible. In the week ending mid-June only four trains came through; in the three succeeding weeks, none at all.[29] Within the *Seventh Army* area, the routes between Normandy and Brittany had been mostly destroyed by bombing and sabotage. Engineers worked night and day repairing the lines, but they could not keep up with the rate of destruction. Finally, even on the undestroyed routes, few undamaged locomotives could be found to move the trains.[30]

The total effect of constant air attacks, dispersed over main and secondary lines and small wayside stations, was much greater than the reduction in rail capacity statistically computed. In the first place, because losses of equipment and personnel through line attacks became insupportable in view of already grave shortages, the Germans were forced to ban nearly all daylight movements, thus cutting two-thirds of their capacity. In addition, cumulative disorganization caused

by the unpredictability of rail movements resulted in an increasing paralysis that made impossible even traffic which was not physically blocked. Finally, once the rate of attack outstripped the rate of repair, attacks causing only minor damage had the same effect as destruction of large portions of the rail system.

Examples of the effect of interdiction on troop movement have already been noted. The effect on supply was at least as serious. During the first ten days of the battle *Seventh Army* received from *OB WEST* supply depots a little over one million gallons of gasoline against estimated requirements of almost four million. To make up part of the deficit, about a third of the 900,000 gallons in army stock piles was consumed. In the same period ammunition requirements were 6,700 metric tons.[31] Against actual consumption of about 5,000 tons, deliveries amounted only to 3,000, leaving again a deficit to be made up out of local reserves. Against ten days' ration requirements of 5,250 tons, only 200 tons were delivered.[32]

By the middle of June, rail supply had become impracticable. For supply by road *Seventh Army* was allocated 1,300 tons of transport space, of which only about one-quarter was serviceable because of unreliable French drivers and the disrepair of the vehicles.[33] With this truckage *Seventh Army* needed to bring up daily 3,200 tons

---

[28] *Seventh Army, Trans.O., KTB 1.I.–30.VI.44,* 17 Jun 44.

[29] AAF Evaluation Board study, cited n. 26.

[30] Report of Railroad Situation, cited n. 27.

[31] A metric ton equals 2,204 pounds and thus compares roughly to a U.S. long ton (2,240 pounds).

[32] Supply Requisition and Consumption Figures for *Seventh Army, 6.–15.VI.44,* 15 Jun 44. *OB WEST, O.Qu., KTB Anlagen 1.I.–17.VIII.44.*

[33] Report of the Supply Situation, 14 Jun 44. *OB WEST, O.Qu., KTB Anlagen 1.I.–17.VIII.44.* German *Transportraum* (transport space) means total capacity of vehicles fully loaded.

of ammunition, gasoline, and rations for a defensive action or 4,500 tons for attack. Although the army had substantial stores of ammunition on hand, most of it was captured material and most of it was in Brittany. Dollmann estimated a minimum need for 3,000 more tons of transport space and a daily arrival of eight to nine trains carrying gas, ammunition, rations, and vehicles and equipment.[34] He looked with envy at the vehicles with a capacity of 15,000 tons which were being held for the support of *Fifteenth Army*. But requests for transfer of trucks from *Fifteenth Army* were rejected by Rundstedt and OKW who, in view of the estimates that large Allied forces still remained in England, held to their belief that the *Kanalkueste* was threatened by a second landing. Allocation of more trucking might have eased the shortages, but it was perfectly clear to General Dollmann that there was only one real solution. He wrote on 11 June that it was absolutely essential that the German Luftwaffe be committed in strength to eliminate the unbearable enemy air superiority.[35] Supplies must be able to move by day if the army was to be nourished for offensive action. Armor must be rendered mobile, not only by sufficient deliveries of gasoline, but by protection from direct attack both in the battle zone and on the approach marches. Rail movement of troops and supplies could be resumed only if one line was protected with all available forces, engineers, Flak, and

fighter planes.[36] Without such air support, the transport situation would certainly get progressively worse. The German Army would continue to have its strength drained away far behind the battle lines.

Hitler's solution to this dilemma was to exhort the dying man to fight harder. On 12 June *Seventh Army* received word that every strong point and resistance nest surrounded by the enemy must fight to the last man and the last bullet in order to prepare for the counterattack which would strike through to the coast. Hitler bluntly ordered *Seventh Army* to wipe out the Allied beachhead between the Vire and Orne Rivers.[37] What Dollmann would use to counterattack with was not immediately clear. Hitler had taken one constructive step in canceling a planned attack at Kowel on the Eastern Front so that the *II SS Panzer Corps* with the *9th SS* and the *10th SS Panzer Divisions* could be released for employment in the west.[38] But the move of these reinforcements would consume many days. Furthermore, it was the opinion of Keitel and Jodl in OKW that the time had passed when the situation could be patched up. Only a bold revision of strategy could hope to meet the crisis.

Keitel and Jodl believed that the situation was very serious. If the Allies once fought their way out of the beachhead and gained freedom of action for mobile warfare, then all of France would be lost. The

---

[34] Report of *Seventh Army* Supply Situation, 21 Jun 44. *Seventh Army, O.Qu., KTB Anlagen 1.–30.-VI.44.* Ammunition stocks on 21 June amounted to 16,000 tons.

[35] *Seventh Army, KTB 1.I.–30.VI.44,* 11 Jun 44.

[36] *Seventh Army, Trans.O., KTB 1.I.–30.VI.44.*

[37] *Seventh Army, KTB 1.I.–30.VI.44,* 12 Jun 44; cf. *Fifteenth Army, KTB Anlagen 1.I.–30.VI.44,* 12 Jun 44.

[38] *OKW/WFSt, KTB Ausarbeitung, Der Westen, 1.IV.–16.XII.44,* cited hereafter as *Der Westen.* For nature of the document, see above, Ch. VI, n. 115.

best hope of avoiding that defeat, they felt, lay in an unsuccessful Allied landing attempt at some other point. But they questioned whether the Allies would make such an attempt unless they could be compelled to by the long-range rocket bombardment of London soon to begin. If there were no second landing, a chance still remained of isolating the Normandy beachhead. To that end, they thought, German efforts should be directed with all possible means.[39] On 13 June Jodl recommended to Hitler that the risks of landings on other fronts now be accepted and the maximum forces moved into the critical fight for France.[40]

Three days later Hitler sent an order to Rundstedt which conformed in tone to the recommendations of OKW but in substance amounted to no more than another attempt to patch up the front without altering the basic strategy.[41] The order told Rundstedt to concentrate his forces, taking the risk of weakening all fronts except that of *Fifteenth Army*. Specifically, one infantry corps (the *LXXXVI*) was to be moved up from *First Army*. The *12th SS Panzer, Panzer Lehr,* and *2d Panzer Divisions* were to be relieved by infantry divisions to be transferred from Holland and the *Fifteenth* and *Nineteenth Armies*. But the *Fifteenth Army* in return was to get *two* new divisions from Norway and Denmark, and the *Nineteenth Army*'s loss would be made up by transfer of one division from

Germany and by naval alarm units. Preparations were to be made for a mass armored counterattack using the three panzer divisions relieved from the line and the four panzer divisions that were on their way to the battle area (the *2d SS* from southern France, the *1st SS* from the Netherlands–Belgium border, and the *9th SS* and *10th SS* from the east).

The plan looked good on paper. Without really weakening any front—the *Fifteenth Army* would actually be strengthened—seven armored divisions would be freed for offensive action. What the plan failed to take into account was simply the sum of the military realities of the battle developing in Normandy. To discuss the future conduct of operations in more realistic terms, Rundstedt had asked that either Jodl or Warlimont come to France. On 16 June Hitler decided to come himself. Accordingly he flew from Berchtesgaden to Metz and then drove to a spot near Soissons where he met Rundstedt and Rommel on the morning of the 17th. There was an irony in the meeting place. Hitler, the field marshals, and their aides gathered in a concrete bunker that had been designed and built in 1940 at the height of Hitler's success to serve as his headquarters for the invasion of England. It had never been used until this mid-June meeting called to discuss measures to check the swelling flood of military disasters. The pall of defeat hung over the meeting.

He [Hitler] looked sick and tired out. Nervously he played with his spectacles and with colored pencils which he held between his fingers. He sat bent forward on a high stool while the field marshals remained standing. His old personal magnetism seemed to have gone. After brief and cool

---

[39] Conf, 12 Jun 44, ONI, *Fuehrer Conferences, 1944.* The first ten V–1 rockets were launched on the night of 12–13 June. See Rad, *OB WEST to OKW,* 13 Jun 44. *OB WEST, KTB Anlagen 1.I –30.VI.44.*

[40] *Der Westen;* cf. MS # B–672 (Buttlar-Brandenfels).

[41] *Der Westen; Seekriegsleitung/1.Abt., KTB 1.–30.VI.44,* 16 Jun 44.

greetings, Hitler, raising his voice, first expressed sharp dissatisfaction with the successful Allied landings, found fault with the local commanders, and then ordered that fortress Cherbourg be held at any cost.[42]

The field marshals sought in vain to impress Hitler with the need for comprehensive revision of the conduct of operations in the west. What they wanted above all was freedom of action, including permission to draw reserves at will from coastal areas not immediately threatened by invasion. They deplored the dependence on fixed defense of fortified areas and recommended certain withdrawals in order to shorten their lines and mass their forces. They predicted the fall of Cherbourg and asked that future plans be made accordingly.[43]

To Hitler any proposal to withdraw, whatever its motive, was evidence of defeatism. He made no direct reply but talked instead of how the tide would soon be turned by the V-weapons. The meeting ended without decision, but Rommel and Rundstedt could not have been left in any doubt that Hitler would continue to demand an absolutely rigid defense of every inch of ground. His decision on the Cotentin crisis was characteristic.

On 14 June it had been clear to Rommel that he must reckon with an American break-through at St. Sauveur that might cut the peninsula. He decided accordingly that two divisions (the *709th* and the *243d*) were sufficient for the defense of Cherbourg and that the *77th Division* should be moved to defend against the Americans' westward push. *Seventh Army* issued orders accordingly and provided that, if the peninsula were cut or a break-through threatened in the Valognes sector, the *709th, 243d,* and remnants of the *91st Division* should fall back on Cherbourg.[44] Against this contingency, *LXXXIV Corps* divided the Cotentin forces into two groups: *Group von Schlieben,* to be charged with the defense of Cherbourg and comprising chiefly the troops on the Montebourg line (except the *77th Division*); and *Group Hellmich,* which with the *77th Division* and all troops south and west of the Merderet would have the mission of building a defensive line along the Prairies Marécageuses north of la Haye du Puits.[45]

The *77th Division* apparently had trouble disengaging on the north front,[46] and no major moves were made on 15 June. On the morning of the 16th General Fahrmbacher of *LXXXIV Corps* telephoned army that the planned division of forces must be carried out at once. *Group Hellmich* was already completely cut off from supplies and fought out; it could only hold for a matter of hours. Only two companies of the *91st Division* and scattered elements of the *243d Division* remained between the Americans and the west coast. Fifteen minutes after Fahrmbacher had made his report and urgent request for immediate action, *Sev-*

[42] MS # C–017 (Speidel). Speidel, Rommel's chief of staff, was present in the bunker during the meeting and took notes which he later expanded. See MS # B–718 (Speidel).

[43] MS # C–017 (Speidel). Rundstedt recalled after the war that he had proposed at the meeting the evacuation of southern France and withdrawal from Normandy in order to establish a defensive line along the Seine River to the Swiss border with *Army Group B* on the right, *Army Group G* on the left. See MS # B–633 (Rundstedt) and MS # B–308 (Zimmermann).

[44] *Seventh Army, KTB 1.I.–30.VI.44,* 14 Jun 44.

[45] MS # B–784 (Criegern).

[46] Tel msg, CofS *Seventh Army* to CofS *Army Group B,* 15 Jun 44. *Seventh Army, KTB Anlagen 1.I.–30.VI.44.*

enth Army was informed by *Army Group B* that Hitler had forbidden the planned withdrawal of *Group von Schlieben* on Cherbourg.[47] This meant that it would be impossible to shift the *77th Division* from von Schlieben's right flank, that nothing therefore could be done to prevent the cutting of the peninsula, and that the *77th Division* would be sacrificed in a bitter-end fight to hold Cherbourg. The sacrifice furthermore promised to weaken rather than strengthen the defense of Cherbourg. With limited supplies in the fortress and little possibility of bringing in more, an increase in the number of defenders would simply reduce their endurance.

Rommel was at *LXXXIV Corps* headquarters when the Hitler order reached him late in the afternoon. In an effort to make the best of an impossible situation, Rommel then decided that the *77th Division* without giving ground should send weak elements to the south. After Rommel had left the command post, Fahrmbacher called *Seventh Army* to say that he had decided to shift the whole *77th Division* to the vicinity of St. Sauveur. "The Chief of Staff [Pemsel] reminded him of the Fuehrer order and asked whether he had permission of Field Marshal Rommel for this move. . . . General Fahrmbacher replied that Rommel had not given his specific approval but that they had talked about these measures only in that sense."[48] Army thereupon forbade the move. The orders earlier given to the *77th Division* to disengage and move south were countermanded.[49] During the

night of 16–17 June command in the Cotentin remained paralyzed, letting slip what was in the judgment of both corps and army commanders their last chance to rescue the *77th Division* from the closing trap.

Thus the time for action passed. The following day witnessed only anticlimax. On the morning of 17 June Hitler at Soissons issued a new order. He still did not authorize the *77th Division* to pull out to the south. Instead he directed Rommel to defend Cherbourg under all circumstances as long as possible; Schlieben was permitted to withdraw, but only under pressure. This decision ignored the fact that, after the American break-through to the coast, the country to the north would be undefended between Valognes and the west coast, and that Schlieben's whole position could thus be bypassed. Interpreting rather freely this relaxation of the original stand-fast order, *Seventh Army* at once ordered the *77th Division* to move south to assembly areas near la Haye du Puits.[50] In the afternoon through OKW came a second order scarcely more realistic. Schlieben, instead of pulling back into the more or less prepared positions of the Cherbourg *Landfront,* was now instructed to establish a line between St. Vaast-la Hougue and Vauville which he was to hold to the last.

---

[47] Tel msgs, 16 Jun 44. *Seventh Army, KTB Anlagen 1.I.–30.VI.44.*

[48] *Ibid.*

[49] Captured German orders in VII Corps G–2 Jnl.

[50] Later, in response to a questionnaire from Hitler, *Seventh Army* denied that it ever gave such an order and that the withdrawal which actually took place was done on the initiative of a regimental commander. The available evidence, including a written *77th Division* field order signed by General Stegmann, argues strongly against this version of the affair. See also the account by the *LXXXIV Corps* chief of staff which leaves no doubt that at least *Seventh Army* approved all the moves taken. MS # B–784 (Criegern).

Both the delay in making these decisions and the unworkable compromise that they entailed resulted in disastrous confusion which sacrificed the bulk of the *77th Division* without profit. Still more disastrous for the Germans than the tactical blunder was the principle that underlay it. The crisis of the *Seventh Army*, strained beyond endurance in its attempt to seal off the Allied beachhead, was to be met by pretending that it did not exist. The renewed determination to hold everything meant that in the end nothing could be held. The principle that withdrawals should be undertaken only after enemy penetrations had made them impossible to organize in orderly fashion meant gaining a few hours for the defense today at the cost of the battle tomorrow.

While the Germans were paralyzed in the Cotentin, General Collins on 16 June prepared the final coup to strike to the coast, and at the same time alerted both the 4th and 79th Divisions for the next step—the drive north. The 4th Division was ordered to prepare for attack on Valognes; the 79th Division was to get one regimental combat team ready for movement on four hours' notice. The intention was to pass the 79th through the 90th Division as soon as the latter had reached its objective line from le Ham to Terre-de-Beauval. (*See Map XXI.*) Concurrently, in anticipation of an early completion of the drive to the west coast, the southern flank was being organized to hold while VII Corps turned north toward Cherbourg. On 15 June VIII Corps (Maj. Gen. Troy H. Middleton) had become operational with the attachment of the 101st Airborne Division. The mission of VIII Corps was the organization of defensive positions from Carentan

west across the peninsula. The 82d Airborne Division would come under its control and, in preparation for this, was ordered to attack south on 17 June to establish a bridgehead south of Pont l'Abbé about a mile and a half deep. The 9th Division would extend its zone south, attacking with one regiment westward through the St. Sauveur bridgehead. The main effort of the 9th Division on 17 June was to be made by the 60th Infantry, attacking through Néhou to capture Hills 145 and 133 dominating the west coast in the 9th Division zone. The 47th Infantry, attacking from St. Sauveur toward St. Lô-d'Ourville, would protect its left flank. The 39th Infantry would seize and hold the ground between Hautteville-Bocage and Ste. Colombe until the 90th Division reached its objective.

The attack drove ahead so fast against nothing more than straggler units of a completely disorganized enemy that original objectives were changed and battalions of both the 60th and 47th Infantry regiments were pushed up to cut the coastal road at Grande Huanville and Barneville-sur-Mer. Escape routes to the south were effectively blocked when, during the night and the following morning (18 June), elements of the *77th Division* attempted to carry out the ordered withdrawal to la Haye du Puits. West of Hill 145 on the morning of 18 June, an enemy column, largely of artillery vehicles, was caught on the road and methodically destroyed by the guns of the 60th Field Artillery Battalion, abetted by infantry and antitank fire. This column and others destroyed near Barneville and north of le Valdecie presumably included much of the *77th Division* artillery, which was wholly lost in the attempt to evacuate it to the south. On the other hand, the *3d Battalion, 243d Artillery Regiment,* successfully passed through the Americans at Barneville during the night.[51] In the meantime a bitter night fight developed around St. Jacques-de-Néhou where the 1st Battalion, 39th Infantry, attached as reserve to the 60th Infantry, occupied positions astride a north–south road. Elements of the *77th Division* trying to move south attacked here before daylight on 18 June. Riflemen fought at close quarters, without artillery support, for the 60th Field Artillery Battalion was forced to displace by the attack. Mortars at ranges of as little as 250 yards fired some 900 rounds. A limited withdrawal was at length directed and carried out in orderly fashion. After daylight, as enemy pressure let up, the battalion prepared for a counterattack. After a heavy artillery preparation reinforced by 81-mm. mortars which fired their entire basic load, the battalion pushed back to its original positions, taking 60 prisoners and counting about 250 enemy dead. Among the Germans who fell here was the *77th Division* commander, Generalmajor Rudolf Stegmann, fatally wounded by a fighter-bomber attack.

The 9th Division lines were not penetrated on 18 June by any substantial enemy force. But the next day, after the 357th Infantry (90th Division) had relieved the 47th Infantry near St. Lô-d'Ourville, a battalion of the *1050th Grenadier Regiment (77th Division)* captured a bridge over the Ollande River along with more than a hundred Americans and enabled Oberst Rudolf Bacherer

(commanding the *77th Division* after the death of General Stegmann) to lead about 1,400 men through to the south.

Relief of the 47th Infantry by the 357th Infantry of the 90th Division was the beginning of the new phase of corps operations. Control of the 90th and of the 82d Airborne Division passed on 19 June to VIII Corps, charged with responsibility for the security of VII Corps' south flank. The 9th Division, relieved of defense of the ground it had won in the drive across the peninsula, began to regroup for the attack on Cherbourg in conjunction with the 79th and 4th Divisions.

Advance to the Cherbourg Landfront

Plans for the final drive on Cherbourg were developed during 18 June by General Collins in consultation with General Bradley and some of the division commanders. The original plan to attack with the 4th and 90th Divisions, while the 9th Division blocked the St. Lô-d'Ourville corridor on the west coast, was changed in favor of a stronger attack designed to move fast and take maximum advantage of German disintegration. A fresh division, the 79th, was to replace the 90th, which would take over the 9th Division responsibility for blocking along the west coast. Three divisions, the 9th, 79th, and 4th, would then jump off abreast. (*Map XXII*) On the right, the 4th Division was to bypass the coast defenses in order to advance directly on Cherbourg as rapidly as possible. To screen its right flank the 24th Cavalry Squadron was committed. The 4th Cavalry Squadron under 4th Cavalry Group control was also to be put in line to attack between the 9th and 79th Divisions. Thus

---

[51] During all the fighting since D Day and the withdrawal on 17 June the battalion lost only four guns.

VII Corps would commit its full combat strength in the attack.

Through capture by the 9th Division of field orders of the German *LXXXIV Corps* and the *77th Division,* VII Corps had a pretty accurate picture of the state of German defenses in the peninsula. General Collins knew of the splitting of German forces and of the order to General Schlieben to withdraw on the fortress Cherbourg. The last-minute attempt of the *77th Division* to pull south of the 9th Division lines had been cut off, and it could be assumed that disorganization existed in the western half of the German lines. By attacking fast and hard VII Corps might exploit the disorganization as well as push General Schlieben's planned withdrawal into a rout. The VII Corps G–2 estimated that the enemy would fight delaying actions and would stand for a defense of Cherbourg on the line of hills ringing it to a depth of about five miles. Fixed defenses in this position had been reconnoitered and plotted accurately long before D Day. Although the exact number of German troops at General Schlieben's disposal for the defense of Cherbourg could only be guessed at, it was known that all his major combat units (the *709th, 243d, 91st* and *77th Divisions*) existed only in fragments. The total enemy force locked in the peninsula was variously estimated at between twenty-five and forty thousand including Flak and naval personnel and Organization Todt workers.

The estimate of enemy capabilities proved substantially correct. The 9th Division, beginning its attack at 0550, 19 June, found nothing in front of it, and the 60th and 39th Infantry Regiments marched rapidly to their desig-nated objectives between Rauville-la Bigot and St. Germain-le Gaillard before noon. The 4th Cavalry Squadron kept pace until it reached Rocheville. There it was delayed by enemy resistance and at noon the squadron lagged slightly behind the 9th Division.

To keep the 9th Division attack going, it was necessary to protect its right flank. A battalion of the 359th Infantry (90th Division) was brought up to hold the Rocheville area. The 4th Cavalry Squadron was attached to the 9th Division and its zone extended northward. These arrangements completed by the middle of the afternoon, General Eddy ordered resumption of the attack. Still without opposition, the 39th Infantry reached Couville and St. Christophe-du-Foc while the 60th Infantry, bypassing les Pieux, put leading elements into Helleville. The cavalry, delayed briefly by enemy artillery and small arms fire near Rauville-la Bigot, nevertheless kept abreast and entered St. Martin-le Gréard that night. From Rocheville east the corps attack met increasing opposition. The 79th Division (Maj. Gen. Ira T. Wyche)[52] attacked from the line Golleville–Urville, the objective of the 90th Division in its week-long push north from the Merderet bridgehead. The 313th Infantry (Col. Sterling A. Wood) on the left reached its objective, the Bois de la Brique, west of Valognes against only slight resistance. But the 315th Infantry (Col. Porter B. Wiggins), which was supposed to bypass Valognes to

---

[52] General Wyche was graduated from West Point in 1911. Commissioned in the infantry he transferred in 1917 to the field artillery. In the 1930's he commanded various artillery units and in 1941 became commander of the 74th Field Artillery Brigade. In May 1942 he took command of the 79th Division.

the west and cut the Cherbourg highway northwest of the city, was held up by fire from Urville and a counterattack at Lieusaint. At night it was still southwest of Valognes. General Wyche then decided to leave Wiggins there in position to contain the city, move Wood's regiment to the right of the division zone, and commit the 314th on its left. The 314th Infantry (Col. Warren A. Robinson) moved out during the night and came up abreast of Wood about dawn.

In all the VII Corps zone, only the 4th Division encountered organized resistance. Since General Barton had held the line from Quinéville to Montebourg Station for four days, the enemy had had ample time to prepare defenses against the anticipated thrust to Cherbourg. Barton ordered the 8th and 12th Infantry Regiments to attack abreast on a northwest axis on either side of Montebourg. The 24th Cavalry Squadron screened the right flank while the 22d Infantry was held in reserve. Through probing by patrols during the division's four days in place, it was known that elements of the *Seventh Army Sturm Battalion* and the *729th Regiment* (estimated at 1,000–1,500 men) were dug in generally along the spur railroad that runs from the main Cherbourg line just north of Montebourg. The plan was to strike through this prepared line before daylight, and both regiments jumped off at 0300. Fighting all along the line was similar. None of the forward battalions were able to break the German defenses in the dark although at least one company walked right through the line without being fired on. Where the enemy fought, however, he was in deep entrenchments and difficult to dislodge. Control of the

attacking troops was tenuous and some units got lost. It was not until daylight that the attack could start moving with tank support. Then both regiments broke the German line. Schlieben began to withdraw. The 8th Infantry at nightfall was just south and east of Valognes; the 12th Infantry was on its right. The 3d Battalion of the 22d Infantry entered Montebourg at 1800 and found it deserted. Later in the evening the 22d Infantry was concentrated on the division right flank to take part in a three-regiment attack the next day.

The resistance in front of the 4th Division on 19 June was actually little more than a gesture by General Schlieben at carrying out his orders to fight his way slowly back to fortress Cherbourg. The orders could scarcely have been carried out. On his west flank, General Schlieben had no positions to hold and only disorganized troops who would have been needlessly sacrificed if they had attempted a stand. The plunge forward of the 9th and 79th Divisions during 19 June rendered defense of the sector opposite the 4th Division useless and dangerous. During the night, therefore, General Schlieben ordered a general disengagement on this front and drew all his force back to the fortress ring immediately defending Cherbourg. Delaying actions were ordered, but the battle-weary troops did not stop to fight them.[53]

---

[53] Hoffmann Report. *Seventh Army, KTB Anlagen 1.I.–30.VI.44.* Hoffmann pointed out that the Americans were apparently unaware of the gap in the German lines west of Valognes where the Kampfgruppe of the *77th Division* had pulled out to head south. An attack through this gap, Hoffmann believed, either would have turned Schlieben's flank and prevented his withdrawal to Cherbourg or would at least have made that withdrawal more precipitate and disorganized.

When the 4th Division resumed the attack on 20 June, it found open country ahead. At first the troops advanced cautiously. They paused to investigate Valognes. The city was choked with rubble but no enemy were in sight. By noon it was clear that the enemy had broken all contact and the regiment took route march formations on the roads and walked north. In this way all arrived by nightfall on their objectives in a line from le Theil to the Bois de Roudou. This line was just in front of the main enemy defenses of Cherbourg, and as the leading companies approached they brushed with enemy outposts and in some cases came under severe hostile artillery fire.

The experience of the 79th Division on 20 June was similar. Both the 313th and 314th Infantry Regiments advanced to the road running roughly east-west between the Bois de Roudou and St. Martin-le Gréard. On that line both met resistance which clearly indicated that they had hit outposts of the Cherbourg defenses. Eloquent of the haste with which the Germans had withdrawn was the capture intact at one point of four light tanks and an 88-mm. gun and at another of eight tanks. The 315th Infantry during the day cleared stragglers from the Valognes area and then moved into reserve positions behind the lead regiments.

The 9th Division, which on 19 June had already come up against the outer veil of the main enemy defenses, had quite a different experience on 20 June. On wings of optimism in the course of the rapid unopposed advance of 19 June, VII Corps had given General Eddy objectives deep inside fortress Cherbourg: Flottemanville-Hague, Octeville, and positions athwart the Cherbourg–Cap de la Hague road.

The plan outlined on the afternoon of the 19th was complicated by the dual mission of the division: to breach the Cherbourg fortress by capture of what were thought to be its two main defenses in the 9th Division zone, Flottemanville and the Bois du Mont du Roc; and to block the Cap de la Hague where it was known the enemy had prepared defenses to which he might fall back for a prolonged last stand. The latter mission was given Colonel de Rohan's 60th Infantry with orders to drive straight north to seize positions from Hill 170 through Branville to the sea. Colonel Flint with the 39th Infantry would initially contain the enemy to the east while the 47th Infantry followed behind de Rohan as far as Vasteville, then turned east in front of Flint's positions to attack the Bois du Mont du Roc. Colonel Flint would support this attack with fire, then move on north across the rear of the 47th Infantry to attack Flottemanville.

The advance of the 60th Infantry, paralleling the main enemy defenses, was rapid until about noon when it reached high ground a few hundred yards from its initial objective, Hill 170. It was slowed then by increasing enemy artillery fire. Delay here, however, was not serious, for sufficient advance had been made to permit the 47th Infantry following to come up west of its objectives and make the turn east. The 1st and 2d Battalions attacked abreast north and south of the Bois de Nerest. Both were stopped not far from their line of departure as the enemy suddenly uncovered a stiff and carefully prepared defense. The experience of the 2d Battalion was typical of what happened all along the front as VII Corps pressed in on the enemy's last bastion. Fired on by German outposts in houses at a crossroads southeast of Acqueville, the battalion was first checked. Then from the main enemy positions on hills to the east came withering direct and indirect fire from 88-mm., 20-mm., and machine guns. The command group of the battalion was hit by a shellburst, the commander, Lt. Col. James D. Johnston, mortally wounded, and a number of his officers injured. Unable to push forward, the battalion had to withdraw out of the area of concentrated fire.

Since, with the 47th Infantry stopped, the 39th would be unable to advance past it toward objectives to the north, General Eddy promptly altered the division plan. Objectives at Flottemanville were assigned to the 1st and 2d Battalions of the 60th Infantry while the 3d Battalion was directed to carry out a portion of the regiment's original blocking mission by taking positions on the crossroads formed by the junction of the les Pieux and Cherbourg roads into Cap de la Hague. Again the advance north proved relatively easy and the 3d Battalion came within 1,000 yards of its objectives. But the two battalions that attempted to turn east were stopped virtually in their tracks in front of Gourbesville. The 9th Division ground to a halt. Road marches were over; hard fighting lay ahead.

The German defenses now faced by VII Corps consisted of a belt of concrete and field fortifications disposed in a semicircle four to six miles from Cherbourg. Placed in commanding ground along the collar of steep hills, the German positions covered every approach route into the city. Advantage was taken of steep-sided stream beds for antitank obstacles, and these were supplemented by ditches where necessary. Included within the ring of defense were antiaircraft batteries sited for both air and ground defense. Although most of the fixed defenses had long been known to the Americans and were overprinted on maps issued to all commanders, extensive reconnaissance of the positions was ordered on 21 June in order to discover whether certain sectors might not be weakly held.

During 20 June, after Schlieben's retreat from the Montebourg line, the Germans had reorganized the Cherbourg *Landfront* as far as possible to put regimental commanders in sectors familiar to them and their own troops under them. Foreign and miscellaneous units drawn back from the fighting in the peninsula or already present in the port were distributed throughout the regimental sectors. Four regimental Kampfgruppen were formed. On the west a group under Oberstleutnant Franz Mueller, commander of the *922d Regiment,* comprised the remnants of the *243d Division* in the sector between Vauville and Ste. Croix-Hague. The *Landfront* fortified line from there to the Bricquebec–Cherbourg road was taken over by the *919th Regiment* and the *17th Machine Gun Battalion* under Oberstleutnant Guenther Keil. Oberst Walter Koehn with the *739th Regiment* occupied the line eastward to just south of Mesnil au Val, and on the east was Oberst Helmuth Rohrbach's *729th Regiment.* The combat efficiency of all the troops now asked to make a last stand before the port was extremely low. Those who had fought on the northern front against the 4th Division were fought out and the "battalions" contained not more than 180 effectives.[54] The miscellaneous troops from naval and air force security units and headquarters staffs were all green. Schlieben reported to *Seventh Army* that he was especially worried about these troops. "Good treatment of prisoners on the part of the enemy," he reported, "is very dangerous." [55] On the other hand he was not concerned about supply. Ammunition was generally sufficient for immediate needs and, except for a shortage of machine gun cartridges, stocks were maintained at adequate levels during the defense by air drops and U- and E-boat deliveries.[56]

The 9th and 79th Divisions devoted the day of 21 June to patrolling and reorganization while the 4th Division, still a little short of the enemy's ring of prepared defenses, continued the attack to reach the objectives of the day before and develop the German main line of resistance. The 9th Division readjusted its front to put its full weight in position to drive into Cherbourg. The 4th Cavalry Squadron was relieved on the right by the 39th Infantry and took over screening of the left flank from the 60th

---

[54] Hoffmann (in report cited n. 53) estimated that a worth-while defense of the port would have required three full divisions with armored support, and insurance of regular resupply. Such a force, he believed, might have held out for several weeks, but even they would have to have been relieved by a successful attack from the south. Cf. Schlieben's estimate, MS # B–845.

[55] *Seekriegsleitung/1.Abt., KTB 1.–30.VI.44,* 21 Jun 44.

[56] Air drops were modest. Between 20 and 30 June only 107 transport planes were used and they dropped a total of 188 tons of supplies. *Luftwaffe Historical Section, Beurteilung des Krieges,* 14 Aug 44. AAF files.

Infantry, which was thus enabled to use all three of its battalions for the attack against Flottemanville. The reserve battalion of the 47th was committed between the other two. In short, all three regiments of the division were concentrated in line and the 60th and 47th, which would carry the brunt of the attack, had all their rifle battalions forward. The 79th Division similarly concentrated its weight for the attack by bringing up its reserve regiment, the 315th Infantry, into the St. Martin-le Gréard area on the left flank, where it took over from the 9th Division. Patrols of both divisions probing into the enemy lines during the day found the enemy very sensitive. Attempts to move up brought storms of artillery and small arms fire all along the line and yielded only the negative information that the enemy would apparently fight hard everywhere.

The attack of the 4th Division completed the development of the German main line of resistance. The 22d Infantry, ordered to thrust straight north to cut the main road from Cherbourg east to St. Pierre-Eglise, put the 3d Battalion on its objective, Hill 158, which was on the Cherbourg road and just southwest of the heavily defended Maupertus airfield. The advance was resisted, however, and the 1st Battalion was held up 500 yards short of the hill. Both battalions, moreover, found large though apparently unorganized German forces to their rear near Gonneville, and for four days supply trains had to fight their way up with tank escort.

The 8th and 12th Infantry Regiments during 21 June attacked northwest into the main Cherbourg defenses. The 8th

Infantry's objective was high ground 800 yards northwest of the Bois de Roudou. The attack plan called for the advance of the 1st and 3d battalions north through the woods while the 2d Battalion attacked northwest and west from Rufosses. Enemy structures suspected to be V-weapon sites had been observed in the corridor between the Bois de Roudou and the Bois du Coudray; the regiment's first mission was to clean these out. The 1st and 3d battalions fought their way out of the woods, meeting heavy fire from unfinished concrete shelters at the northwest tip. The 3d Battalion fought through to the edge of its objective. Attack by the 2d Battalion from the east succeeded in forcing the German position at Bourdonnerie crossroads. A platoon of tanks deployed in line was closely followed by a company of infantry. Despite limited maneuver room, the attack carried as the tanks, unhindered by the low hedgerows, moved easily cross country. After the 2d Battalion had passed through to the base of its objective, Germans came back into the crossroads position and had to be cleaned out during the night and the next morning. In all, 300 prisoners were flushed out of the area by heavy concentrations of mortar and cannon fire.

The 12th Infantry, attacking through the Bois du Coudray, at first met little opposition. It arrived at the northwest edge of the woods on the banks of the Saire River before heavy enemy fire and a blown bridge stopped the advance. At the edge of the principal enemy defenses, Col. James S. Luckett, the regimental commander, decided not to push the attack further that day.

On the evening of 21 June, VII Corps, with all three divisions drawn up tight against the Cherbourg fortress, was ready for the final assault.

The Fall of Cherbourg

The early capture of Cherbourg was given dramatic urgency by a four-day storm over the English Channel which struck without warning on 19 June. It struck just as the machinery for delivering supplies across the beaches had begun to work smoothly and at full capacity. Initially considerable delay in the planned build-up had been caused by the stubborn German opposition to V Corps. It had been four days before the advance of V Corps inland had established the planned beachhead maintenance area. During those four days engineers, working to organize the beach to receive reinforcements and supplies, were hampered by artillery and sniper fire. On the other hand enemy air activity was much lighter than had been expected and damage from the sporadic raids was negligible throughout the month. The peak of enemy air activity, as a matter of fact, coincided with the onset of the storm when, on the night of 19–20 June, 116 German aircraft were over the beaches and shipping lanes.

The first V Corps dumps opened during the night of 6–7 June despite chaotic conditions on the beach. On 7 June engineers finished the marking of the beaches. On the same day construction of the artificial port off OMAHA began on schedule with the sinking of the first blockships to form the outer breakwater. No artificial port was planned for UTAH, but a line of blockships to provide sheltered water was towed in beginning on 8

June. Two of these ships were sunk by German coastal batteries approximately in their proper position. The American Navy sank the rest and the work was completed on 13 June.

The immediate success of the landings at UTAH made beach organization there much easier than at OMAHA. However, the unexpectedly stiff resistance which held up the 4th Division's push northward meant that the maintenance area which was planned to be extended to Quinéville had to be confined to the original landing beaches together with a third beach opened later on D Day. Sporadic enemy artillery fire continued to harass supply operations until after the capture of the Quinéville ridge on 14 June.

Unloading thus fell behind schedule on both American beaches. Beginning on D plus 2 on OMAHA and D plus 3 on UTAH, it was greatly speeded up by drying out LST's. This process of grounding the craft on a falling tide and unloading directly to the shore had been rejected in the planning period for fear that the beached LST's might break their backs. Tried from necessity, it proved so successful that it became standard practice, eliminating the time-consuming transshipment of supplies by ferry craft.[57]

Between 8 and 12 June inland dumps replaced the beach dumps, and the supply system was integrated on the 13th under First Army control. Beach maintenance began to be supplemented about the middle of June with the opening of three minor ports: Grandcamp-les Bains and Isigny and Port-en-Bessin. The lat-

ter, which could be used by coasters drawing up to twelve feet, was jointly operated by Americans and British.

On 18 June the build-up of men and supplies, though still slightly less than planned, was approaching the target figures. The deficiency, moreover, was balanced by smaller combat losses and lower matériel consumption than expected. At the end of 18 June about 116,000 tons of supplies, 41,000 vehicles, and 314,514 troops had come ashore in the U.S. zone.[58] The British had at the same time landed approximately 102,000 tons of supplies, 54,000 vehicles, and 314,547 troops.[59]

On the morning of 19 June strong winds began to blow from the northeast. Before noon ferrying operations were suspended on both beaches and antiaircraft personnel had to be taken off the outer breakwater of the port of OMAHA because of the heavy seas. In the evening the wind velocities increased to 25–32 knots. Scores of small craft were driven ashore. Some were tossed so high above normal high-water mark by the combination of storm and spring tides that, though undamaged, they could not be refloated for ten days. Others were destroyed against the sea walls and rocks. On 20 June the storm continued; the artificial port showed signs of breaking up. The floating breakwater of bombardons broke its moorings, casting all twenty-four bombardons adrift.[60] Some piled into the pier; others washed up on

---

[57] [Clifford Jones] NEPTUNE: Training, Mounting, the Artificial Ports (The Administrative and Logistical History of the ETO: Part VI), MS, II, 72–73. Hist Div files.

[58] *Ibid.*, II, 175ff.

[59] Figures as of afternoon 18 June. Cosintrep 36, 20 Jun 44. SHAEF AG file 370.2/11.

[60] Bombardons were huge air-filled cylindrical floats, constructed of rubberized canvas and reinforced concrete. Each was 200 feet long and had a 12-foot beam and 13-foot draft.

UTAH BEACH DURING THE BUILD-UP. *Scene (above) at a beach head-quarters, and (below) aerial view of beach showing breakwater of sunken ships.*

OMAHA BEACH DURING THE BUILD-UP. *Reinforcements of men and equipment moving inland (above), and (below) unloading directly to the shore from LST's grounded on the beach.*

land. Strenuous efforts were made to bring at least ammunition ashore, but the only ships that could unload were a few small coasters that beached at low tide. On the night of 21 June the artificial port's pierheads were carried away and the bridging connecting the piers with the shore was twisted. Landing craft were piled on the beaches. Winds began to moderate the next day but still not enough to permit resumption of operations. Unloading did not begin until 23 June when DUKW's were able to navigate.

Damage caused by the storm is impossible to assess accurately. On OMAHA alone 90 ferrying craft were lost plus indeterminate numbers of larger craft. Some 800 craft were stranded on U.S. and British beaches. The artificial port was a total loss. OMAHA Beach, littered with wreckage, had few open spots where new landings could take place when the seas abated. Opposite one of the OMAHA exits, an eyewitness at noon of 22 June counted 35 LCM's, 11 LCT's, 9 Rhino ferries, 3 LCI's, and more than twenty other craft chaotically piled up. UTAH suffered less both in craft losses and in beach wreckage. In the afternoon of 23 June unloading was resumed there at full scale, and such congestion of beached craft as there was caused little difficulty since landings could be extended northward.[61]

The naval commander at OMAHA, Admiral Hall, concluded that the artificial port had proved impractical and should not be reconstructed.[62] On the other hand, he felt that the outer breakwaters should be reinforced, for, despite the fact that they could not survive northerly gales, they provided the only possible means of getting sheltered water for small craft. Materials for the repair of the artificial port were diverted to the port in the British sector near Arromanches which had not been so badly damaged. The most important factors in the decision to abandon the artificial port project, on which so much dependence had been placed during the planning period, were, first, the discovery that LST's could be dried out, which meant faster build-up during favorable weather, and, second, the belief that Cherbourg would soon be opened and would replace OMAHA as the supply entry in the American zone.[63]

Before the storm ended, General Collins on 21 June issued orders for the resumption of the attack on Cherbourg. He called attention to the new urgency of the objective and the fact that the attack was "the major effort of the American army." [64]

---

[61] ANCXF, *Report*, Vol. III, Rpt of Comdr Assault Force O, p. 11; Jones, NEPTUNE, II, 124–27. There are no reliable figures on ship casualties in the storm. The British estimate that they lost 250 ferrying craft. See Ltr, Col Warhurst (British Cabinet Office Hist Sec) to author, 7 Sep 48. The U.S. Navy Department could supply no estimates of American losses.

[62] A naval investigator, studying the effect of the storm, concluded that it had proved the total impracticability of the artificial port. He pointed out that the so-called storm had been only a "half-gale" and that, in fact, the wind had seldom exceeded force 6. (Force 6—up to 30 miles an hour—is referred to by seamen as a "strong breeze.") See Memo, Capt Robert C. Lee for Gen Crawford (SHAEF G–4) *et al.*, 26 Jun 44. SHAEF G–4 file 825.1 (Piers).

[63] Actually OMAHA continued to overshadow Cherbourg as a port of entry until the fall of the year and handled far more tonnage than anticipated in the most optimistic estimates before the invasion. Jones, NEPTUNE, II, 109 and 134ff.

[64] VII Corps G–3 Jnl, 21 Jun 44.

ARTIFICIAL PORT AT OMAHA BEACH. *Unloading equipment (above) on pier off Vierville Draw. Pier on right is under construction. Both were destroyed during the storm on 21 June. Breakwater of sunken ships (below). At upper left is les Moulins draw.*

Collins requested "air pulverization" of some twenty square miles before the jump-off, more to demoralize the Germans and force surrender than as direct preparation for the ground advance.[65] The air strike would employ the entire IX Bomber Command (medium bombers) as well as large numbers of U.S. and British fighter-bombers. The plan was developed under great difficulties not only because time was short but because all the units of the Ninth Air Force participating in the attack were based in England. Although Maj. Gen. Elwood R. Quesada, commander of the IX Tactical Air Command, was able to consult with Generals Bradley and Collins, the final plan was made in England with no First Army representatives present. It was flown to the Continent on the morning of 22 June.

All air preparation was to be concentrated in the zones of the 79th and 9th Divisions south and southwest of Cherbourg. (*Map XXIII*) Starting 80 minutes before H Hour, four squadrons of Typhoons of the 2d Tactical Air Force (RAF) were to attack with rockets throughout the northern portion of the attack zone concentrating on enemy antiaircraft positions. Following them, six squadrons of Mustangs also belonging to the British tactical air forces would strafe throughout the area. From H minus 60 minutes twelve groups of U.S. Ninth Air Force fighter-bombers would bomb and strafe enemy strong points in front of the American lines, attacking in waves at five-minute intervals. As ground troops moved out, all eleven groups of the IX Bomber Command were to bomb

eleven defended localities in a pattern bombing designed to constitute a kind of rolling barrage in front of the ground attack. Despite the large number of aircraft involved, the bombs to be dropped amounted to only about 1,100 tons over a wide area. The attack was not intended as a "carpet" bombing of the type later used at Caen and in the St. Lô breakout. The idea was to achieve the maximum demoralization of an enemy who, because he was already in a state of hopeless siege, might be expected to have an already weakened morale.

The hopelessness of the German position was pointed out to the Cherbourg garrison in a multilingual broadcast (German, Russian, Polish, and French) on the night of 21 June when General Collins demanded the immediate surrender of Cherbourg. General Schlieben was given until 0900 the following morning to capitulate. But the ultimatum expired without answer from General Schlieben. Preparations were therefore completed for the assault.

Attack into Cherbourg itself was to be made by the 9th and 79th Divisions while the 4th Division sealed off the city from the east. The 9th Division, making its main effort on its right, would seize Octeville while the 79th Division captured the nose of high ground which terminated in Fort du Roule overlooking Cherbourg from the south. This would bring both divisions up on the high ground immediately ringing the port. The 4th Division on the right was to capture Tourlaville and send patrols from there to the sea. H Hour was set for 1400.

Bombing began according to plan at 1240, 22 June. From the testimony of

---

[65] Rpt by XIX Corps observers: Watson–Hickey Notes, 18 Jun, in XIX Corps G–3 Jnl.

prisoners, it appears that the air attacks were successful in their main purpose of weakening German will to resist, though the results were not apparent during the first day's action. For twenty minutes hundreds of fighters dived, strafed, and skip-bombed from altitudes as low as 300 feet. Twenty-four were lost to enemy flak. The attacks were entirely unopposed by any German planes, and there was no cover anywhere from which the enemy could not be flushed by the ubiquitous fire from the skies. The end of the nerve-wracking attack signaled only the beginning of an hour of relentless bombing —wave after wave (375 planes in all) flying out of the west and loosing their bombs methodically on or near the six principal targets: Flottemanville-Hague, Martinvast, les Chevres, la Mare à Canards, Fort du Roule, and a defended locality just west of Octeville. At the same time, artillery shelled enemy anti-aircraft batteries, with particular effectiveness in the 9th Division zone, and then, after troops began to move, fired on enemy defenses.

All three divisions made slow advances during the afternoon. The 9th Division attacked with the 60th Infantry on the left and the 47th Infantry (backed by the 39th Infantry) on the right. The axis of advance remained the same: the 60th pointed toward Flottemanville, the 47th toward the Bois du Mont du Roc. The 39th Infantry was assembled near Helleville. The 60th Infantry, attacking with battalions echeloned to the left to guard its open flank, at first moved rapidly and captured Acqueville within half an hour of the jump-off. The 47th similarly moved past Crossroads 114 where it had been held up on 21 June and pushed one

battalion beyond Beaudienville. But the latter advance was made by bypassing the enemy at the crossroads and it had to be halted in the early evening to permit mopping up. At the end of 22 June, forward battalions were dug in on the slopes of Hill 171 just west of the Bois du Mont du Roc. The 60th Infantry pressed the attack to the edge of enemy fortifications at Flottemanville but could not penetrate the position before dark.

The 79th Division, attacking with three regiments abreast, came up against similarly stubborn enemy resistance. The 313th Infantry, making the division's main effort along the Valognes–Cherbourg highway, was first stopped by the les Chevres strong point which straddled the road. The German line was broken by the 3d Battalion on the left and rolled up while the 1st Battalion attacked frontally. After reorganization, the regiment pushed on against lighter resistance to reach a point just south of its next major obstacle—the fortified antiaircraft position at la Mare à Canards. The 315th Infantry meanwhile spent the day fighting to clear the Hardinvast area. The 314th Infantry fought in the draws east of Tollevast until after dark, when one battalion slipped around the enemy positions and made contact with the 313th Infantry west of Crossroads 177. At this point the 314th was only a few hundred yards from a communications bunker which contained the switchboard for the entire Cherbourg *Landfront*. The bunker was not discovered and remained to function for a day or so behind the American lines, reporting to Schlieben some details of American movements.[66]

---

[66] Hoffmann Report. *Seventh Army, KTB Anlagen 1.I.–30.VI.44.*

The three regiments of the 4th Division experienced hard, confused fighting on 22 June which netted only small gains. The main effort was made by the 12th Infantry attacking northwest from the northern tip of the Bois du Coudray with the mission of seizing Tourlaville. But in confused fighting, during which the enemy continually filtered to the rear of the forward battalions, the regiment was able to advance only a few hundred yards. On its right the 22d Infantry, which was to have attacked from positions near Gonneville to take Digosville and so support the effort of the 12th Infantry, found itself surrounded by the enemy and spent the whole day trying to clear its own rear areas to keep its supply routes open. The 8th Infantry on the division left flank had the mission of capturing high ground east of la Glacerie in the triangle between the Trotebec and its principal tributary, where it would be pinched out by the northwest advance of the 12th Infantry on Tourlaville. Attacking from the north edge of the Bois de Roudou, the regiment made little progress. One of its battalions, attempting to envelop the enemy line, was caught by delayed enemy fire from prepared hedgerow positions and by tree burst artillery fire; it lost thirty-one killed and ninety-two wounded.

Although the day of 22 June ended with slight gains for VII Corps achieved against desperate enemy resistance all along the line, there were nevertheless signs that continued pressure might soon crumble the Cherbourg defenses. Everywhere troops met loosely organized Kampfgruppen containing not only fragments of infantry units but labor troops, military police, and naval and coast artillery personnel.

That the final stand was hopeless and could not last long was perfectly clear to General Schlieben. On 22 June he had received from Hitler full authority for the entire defense of the port together with a ringing admonition to do his duty. "Even if worst comes to worst," said Hitler, "it is your duty to defend the last bunker and leave to the enemy not a harbor but a field of ruins. . . . The German people and the whole world are watching your fight; on it depends the conduct and result of operations to smash the beachheads, and the honor of the German Army and of your own name." [67]

To this rhetoric General Schlieben replied with a few facts. He told Rommel that his own troops were exhausted in body and spirit, that the port garrison was over-age, untrained, and suffering from "bunker paralysis" (verbunkert), and that the leaderless remnants of the 243d and 77th Divisions were more of a burden than a support. "Reinforcement," he concluded, "is absolutely necessary." [68]

Reinforcement was briefly contemplated the next day as the 15th Parachute Regiment in Brittany was alerted for movement by sea to Cherbourg. A few hours later, reports of the complete destruction and closing of the Cherbourg harbor caused cancellation. Dropping of parachute troops was considered but no planes were available.

Fighting on 23 June was still heavy, but all three divisions made significant penetrations into the main German de-

[67] Seekriegsleitung/1.Abt., KTB 1.–30.VI.44, 22 Jun 44.
[68] Ibid.

fenses. In the 9th Division zone, the 39th Infantry cleared fortified positions northwest of Beaudienville, which had been bypassed. The 47th Infantry completed the reduction of enemy defenses on Hill 171, capturing 400 prisoners during the day's fighting. The two regiments thus established themselves firmly astride the ridge leading to Cherbourg inside the outer ring of enemy defenses. The 60th Infantry, after a long-delayed air bombardment and artillery concentrations on the Flottemanville area, moved in to occupy its objective with comparative ease in the evening.

The 79th Division was troubled at first by enemy infiltrations behind the forward regiments. While these were cleared up, the 314th Infantry attacked the enemy positions at la Mare à Canards. The attack failed to achieve its objective, but one company worked around to the northwest and was able to hold there while the remainder of the regiment was withdrawn a little to await air bombardment.

The 4th Division, though unable to reach its principal objective, Tourlaville, made good progress on 23 June as the attack of the 12th Infantry with tank support began to gather momentum. Tanks had not been used in the previous day's attack because the infantry had been unable to find suitable routes to bring them up. A route was discovered during the night. Two tanks attached to each of the forward companies of the lead battalion moved generally along the roads firing in support of the infantry and, on occasion, turning into the fields to steamroller enemy riflemen. The tanks apparently broke the back of German

resistance and the advance became easier as it neared the objective. In the evening behind a rolling artillery barrage laid close to their front, the troops marched up a hill that commanded the approaches to Cherbourg and dug in for the night, ready for the final assault in Tourlaville. The 22d Infantry again on 23 June was occupied mainly with clearing enemy from its own sector. One battalion, eventually released for attack northwest, was stopped at once by heavy German fire. The 8th Infantry, while scoring only minor advances during the day, had one notable success when the 3d Battalion launched an attack at the very moment when the enemy was forming for counterattack. Finding the Germans lying head to heel along some hedgerows, the battalion opened rifle and tank fire and routed them with heavy losses.

With the penetrations of 23 June into the outer ring of the Cherbourg fortress, the battle for the port entered its final phase. General Schlieben reported on the morning of the 24th that he had no more reserves and that he had given orders to his troops to defend to the last cartridge. The fall of Cherbourg, he said, is inevitable. "The only question is whether it is possible to postpone it for a few days." [69]

On 24 June VII Corps closed in on the city. The 9th Division overran three defended Luftwaffe installations as the 47th and 39th Infantry Regiments attacked along the ridge northeast into Octeville while the 60th Infantry held and cleared the north flank. Enemy fire was often heavy but, when the American

---

[69] *Ibid.*, 24 Jun 44.

infantry closed in, the defense crumbled. The 39th Infantry in the evening halted and established positions in front of Octeville under corps orders not to become involved in the city that day. The 47th Infantry, after assisting the 39th in the capture of an antiaircraft emplacement, turned north toward the old French fort of Equeurdreville, the German coastal battery north of it, and the Redoute des Fourches. With the coming of darkness, however, attack on these positions was postponed.

In the 79th Division zone the 314th Infantry, supported by dive-bombing P–47's of the Ninth Air Force, cleared la Mare à Canards and pushed on to within sight of Fort du Roule. Three attempts to break through to the fort were frustrated by fire from the direction of Octeville on the division's dangling left flank. The 315th Infantry on the left was far behind, still engaged at Hardinvast. The 313th Infantry, on the other flank, kept pace, veering slightly eastward to reduce resistance west of la Glacerie and at Hameau Gringor. At the latter position 320 prisoners and several artillery pieces were taken.

The whole Cherbourg defense was collapsing and nowhere more completely than on the east. But the collapse was preceded by some bitter last stands that exacted heavy toll of some of the attacking units. The 8th Infantry making its last attack before being pinched out between the 12th Infantry and 79th Division, hit determined resistance east of la Glacerie. The Germans here, defending with light artillery, antiaircraft guns, mortars, and machine guns, threw back the first American attack. The second attempt made with tank support got around to the east of the enemy position and the Germans pulled out. The cost of the day's fighting to the 8th Infantry was thirty-seven killed, including Lt. Col. Conrad Simmons, the 1st Battalion commander. The 12th Infantry, again making the main divisional effort, now with one battalion of the 22d Infantry attached, by evening had occupied the last high ground before Tourlaville, from which the city of Cherbourg was visible. In the attack Lt. Col. John W. Merrill, who had taken command of the 1st Battalion the day before, was killed. One of the hardest fights in the area was fought at Digosville where the enemy stood to defend an artillery position. The position was overrun by one company with tank support, after a dive-bombing attack by twelve P–47's. The enemy, in withdrawing, left six field pieces. Tourlaville was occupied that night without a fight. In the day's advance the 12th Infantry took 800 prisoners.

General Schlieben in the evening reported: "Concentrated enemy fire and bombing attacks have split the front. Numerous batteries have been put out of action or have worn out. Combat efficiency has fallen off considerably. The troops squeezed into a small area will hardly be able to withstand an attack on the 25th." [70]

American matériel superiority would be still further increased on 25 June by naval bombardment of the Cherbourg batteries arranged by General Bradley to coincide with the final ground assault. The bombardment was to be carried out by a task force of three battleships, four cruisers, and screening destroyers.

---

[70] *Ibid.*

AMERICAN ARTILLERY IN ACTION AGAINST CHERBOURG. *This is a 155-mm. howitzer of the 79th Division.*

Meanwhile VII Corps closed in. On the right, the 12th Infantry scarcely paused on reaching its objective of 24 June. Continuing the attack through the night and into the day of the 25th, Colonel Luckett pushed hard to accelerate the enemy collapse. The 1st Battalion had a sharp fight to capture the coastal battery north of Tourlaville, but in early afternoon the enemy garrison of 400 finally surrendered, abandoning, among other things, three 8-inch guns. The other two battalions patrolled to the coast. In position blocking the eastern approaches to Cherbourg, the regiment and the division had completed their original mission. Early in the afternoon of 25 June, however, General Collins altered the division boundary so that the 4th Division could

share in the capture of the city. All three battalions of the 12th Infantry entered Cherbourg during the evening. Two battalions cleared the city streets in the eastern portion as far as the limit of the division's zone, hampered only by scattered fire and mines. The 1st Battalion fought all night to reduce pillboxes of beach fortifications east of the Fort des Flamands, but it was not until early the next morning when tanks were brought up that 350 Germans finally decided to surrender. Then at last the 4th Division's part in the capture of Cherbourg was complete.

On the opposite side of the city, the 47th Infantry of the 9th Division was fighting in the suburbs during 25 June. After pushing down the ridge toward Octeville with the 39th Infantry, the 47th had turned north in the evening of 24 June to attack Equeurdreville and had pushed one battalion to within 500 yards of the German fort there. The fort was a formidable-appearing position on top of a hill surrounded by a dry moat like a medieval fortress. It was used, however, only as an observation post for the coastal battery on the reverse slope and was not well defended from the south. In the morning of 25 June the fort was shelled and one company of the 2d Battalion attacked after a mortar barrage. In fifteen minutes the German garrison surrendered. Two companies then pushed rapidly into Equeurdreville and a platoon got to the beach, but it was withdrawn for the night. At the same time the 3d Battalion reduced the Redoute des Fourches with heavy artillery support. The enemy's right had now collapsed as thoroughly as his left on the day before, although a node of resistance in Octeville held up the 39th Infantry. The 9th Division took more than 1,000 prisoners in the day's fighting.

Schlieben radioed: "Loss of the city shortly is unavoidable. . . . 2,000 wounded [are] without a possibility of being moved. Is the destruction of the remaining troops necessary as part of the general picture in view of the failure of effective counterattacks? Directive urgently requested."

In the early afternoon, Schlieben noted the opening of the naval bombardment. "In addition to superiority in matériel and artillery, air force and tanks," he reported, "heavy fire from the sea has started, directed by spotter planes." Actually the weight of the bombardment on the Cherbourg defenses was much less than planned, for the Allied warships were forced to engage in counterbattery fire with enemy shore batteries on Cap de la Hague. Nevertheless the added pressure on the German defenses was intolerable. "I must state in the line of duty," Schlieben concluded, "that further sacrifices cannot alter anything."

To this Rommel replied by radio: "You will continue to fight until the last cartridge in accordance with the order from the Fuehrer." [71]

In the 79th Division zone, just such a fanatic defense was in progress where the garrison of Fort du Roule south of Cherbourg chose to fight it out. This fort, principal objective of the 79th Division, was one of the most formidable of the Cherbourg bastions. It was built into the face of a rocky promontory above the city and housed coastal guns commanding the entire harbor area. The guns were in lower levels under the edge of the cliff. In the upper level were mortars and machine guns in concrete pillboxes defending the fort from landward attack. On the southeast was an antitank ditch.

Fort du Roule was attacked on the morning of 25 June by the 2d and 3d Battalions of the 314th Infantry, after a bombardment by a squadron of P–47's which largely missed its mark and did no appreciable damage. While the guns of the 311th Field Artillery Battalion laid fire on the fort, the 3d Battalion led off the attack, but was halted at a draw 700 yards from the fort. Here it was greeted with a hail of small arms fire from enemy dug in on the forward slope. Lacking artillery (which was fully engaged in neutralizing Fort du Roule) the 3d and 2d Battalions massed their machine gun fire on

---

[71] *Ibid.*, 25 Jun 44.

FORT DU ROULE *with Cherbourg in background.*

the German line. Most of the defenders were killed and the few survivors retreated to the fort. The 2d Battalion then took over the attack under the covering fire of the 3d Battalion. The attackers came under heavy machine gun fire from pillboxes as well as shelling from the direction of Octeville.

Reduction of the positions now became a matter largely of the courage and initiative of individuals and small groups. Cpl. John D. Kelly's platoon of Company E was hugging the ground immobilized by German machine gun fire from a pillbox. Kelly took a ten-foot pole charge, crawled up the slope through enemy fire, and fixed the charge, but the explosion was ineffective. He returned with another charge and this time blew off the ends of the German machine guns. A third time Kelly climbed the slope, blew open the rear door of the pillbox, and hurled hand grenades inside until the enemy survivors came out and surrendered. In the 3d Battalion zone, Company K was stopped by 88-mm. and machine gun fire. Here 1st Lt. Carlos C. Ogden, who had just taken over the company from its wounded commander, armed himself with rifle and hand grenades and advanced alone under fire toward the enemy emplacements. Despite a head wound, Ogden continued up the slope until from a place of vantage he fired a rifle grenade that destroyed the 88-mm gun. With hand grenades he then knocked out the machine guns, receiving a second wound but enabling his company to resume the advance.[72] Through these acts and others, portions of the German garrison began to surrender. By mid-

night the 314th Infantry was in possession of the upper defenses of the fort.

The 313th Infantry in the meantime attacked from Hameau Gringor into the flats southeast of Cherbourg. Troops entered the outskirts of the city but could not penetrate in strength because they came under fire from guns in the lower levels of Fort du Roule, still uncaptured. The fort was finally reduced on 26 June by lowering demolitions from the top levels, by antitank fire from guns in the city, and by assault of a demolition team under S/Sgt. Paul A. Hurst around the precipitous west side of the cliff. Both the 313th and 314th Infantry Regiments cleared the city in their zones during the day. Street fighting was only sporadic. The heaviest resistance fell on the left flank of the 314th Infantry, left open by the slower, more difficult progress of the 9th Division in the western half of the city.

The attempt of the 47th Infantry to clear the northwest section of the city was checked by the Germans' stubborn daylong defense of a thick-walled arsenal on whose parapets were emplaced antitank, antiaircraft, and machine guns. Artillery support was rendered difficult by the bad weather and smoke and dust of enemy port demolitions. Assault of the arsenal was postponed until the morning of 27 June when an elaborately supported three-battalion attack was planned. Before it took place, however, a psychological warfare unit broadcast an ultimatum; shortly thereafter white flags were flown and Generalmajor Robert Sattler, deputy commander of the Cherbourg fortress, surrendered the 400 men under his immediate control to Colonel Smythe, commander of the 47th Infantry.

---

[72] Both Kelly and Ogden were awarded the Medal of Honor. Kelly died of wounds in a subsequent action.

HOUSE-TO-HOUSE SEARCH IN CHERBOURG

A more dramatic surrender had occurred on 26 June when the 39th Infantry advancing on Octeville learned from a prisoner that General Schlieben was in an underground shelter at St. Sauveur on the southern outskirts of Cherbourg. Fighting in the vicinity of Schlieben's command post had taken place during 25 June and Schlieben had directed it until he was driven underground by American artillery fire. He stayed on there for about twenty-four hours, isolated and helpless. At 1506, 26 June, he got through a final radio message to *Seventh Army:* "Documents burned, codes destroyed." [73] After that, communications were broken off.

The two companies of the 39th Infantry sent to take him advanced through enemy artillery and *Nebelwerfer* fire from Octeville to the St. Sauveur tunnel entrance. A prisoner was sent into the shelter to demand surrender, but the demand was refused. Tank destroyers were then brought up to fire into two of the three tunnel entrances while preparations were made to blow up the stronghold. A few rounds were sufficient to bring the enemy out. Some 800 Germans in all, including both General Schlieben and Admiral Hennecke, *Naval Commander Normandy,* capitulated to General Eddy. General Schlieben, however, still concerned with gaining time, declined to make a general surrender of the Cherbourg fortress.[74] The 39th Infantry therefore pushed its attack northward to the coast. In the city it received another surrender of about 400 troops that had for-

tified themselves in the city hall. They gave up when convinced of General Schlieben's capture and after being promised protection from French snipers. With the surrender of General Schlieben on 26 June and of his deputy, General Sattler, the following day, all organized resistance in Cherbourg ceased. The primary objective of First Army in the assault phase of OVERLORD had been achieved.

But this was not the end. Cherbourg had fallen, but some fighting continued. General Schlieben had surrendered, but some 6,000 of his men remained to fight on in the Cap de la Hague. The anticlimax was often as bitter as the main event and men died making secure what they and their comrades had captured. There was no doubt of the eventual outcome of that afterfight—what the operations reports call "mopping up"—but it still had to be fought.

End of a Phase

On both sides of the captured port the enemy held prepared defenses. On the east the defense ran from Gonneville, through the Maupertus airfield, to Cap Lévy; on the west the main line of resistance cut the Cap de la Hague from Gruchy to Vauville with advance positions from Querqueville to Vauville. (*See Map XXII.*) While the bulk of VII Corps' three divisions threw their weight against Cherbourg, the 22d Infantry and the 24th Cavalry Squadron screened the east flank and the 60th Infantry with the 4th Cavalry Group (—) blocked off Cap de la Hague on the west.

On the east the 22d Infantry had been continuously engaged, containing the

[73] *Seventh Army, KTB 1.I.–30.VI.44,* 26 Jun 44. *Seekriegsleitung/1.Abt., KTB* reports the same message under date of 25 June (evidently an error). See Schlieben's account, MS # B–845.

[74] MS # B–845 (Schlieben).

AMERICAN INFANTRY CAPTAIN WITH CHERBOURG PRISONERS

enemy in the Maupertus area and mopping up the supply routes to the rear. On 25 June when Cherbourg was tightly ringed and units had penetrated its suburbs, the 22d Infantry was ordered to attack to clear the Maupertus airfield. The attack jumped off at 1100, 26 June, with all three battalions abreast and a troop of cavalry on each flank. The Americans fought all day against determined enemy resistance and did not occupy the airport until the 27th. Thereafter the regiment pivoted north and speedily overran the last fortified positions to the coast. *Batterie Hamburg,* a naval coastal battery with four 240-mm. guns, was silenced by fire from the 44th Field Artillery Battalion and surrendered 990 troops. With that, organized resistance northeast of Cherbourg collapsed. Cavalry reconnoitering east to Barfleur found the area unoccupied.

The clearing of Cap de la Hague was expected to be more difficult, for it was estimated that about 3,000 enemy troops still held out there. The corps reorganized. The 79th Division moved south on 28 June to reorganize under VIII Corps for the coming drive southward out of the Cotentin. The 4th Division took over the security of Cherbourg, and the 9th Division was relieved to undertake the sweep of Cap de la Hague.[75] General Eddy prepared for the attack during 27 and 28 June; the 47th Infantry assembled in the Henneville area and the 39th west of Octeville, joining the 60th which was in position near Ste. Croix-Hague. Patrols re-

connoitered to the northwest. The regrouping took place under more or less continuous shelling from enemy batteries in the cape. Neither air strikes by fighter-bombers and mediums against known German batteries nor counterbattery artillery fire reduced the enemy fire.

The 9th Division attacked on the morning of 29 June with the 47th Infantry advancing up the north coast, the 60th Infantry in the center attacking astride the main cape highway, and the 4th Cavalry Group (—) advancing in a narrow zone on the left. Very little resistance was met anywhere until troops reached the line just southeast of Beaumont-Hague. The 47th Infantry swept through fortified but unoccupied positions to seize the ridge at Nicolle by midafternoon and then attacked across a stream to a known fortified area which was thought to be an outpost of the main German defensive line running from Gruchy across the cape to Vauville. Under heavy preparatory fire from two battalions, two companies assaulted the position and in a two-hour fight captured 250 prisoners. The 60th Infantry meanwhile reached the main road junction southeast of Beaumont-Hague before suffering check. There the enemy had taken a stand behind an antitank ditch defended by antitank guns and emplaced machine guns which in a singularly barren terrain had clear fields of fire. The 1st Battalion was stopped, but the 3d Battalion with tank destroyer and tank support smashed through the north end of the line just south of Fleury. It came within about 1,000 yards of Beaumont-Hague but did not attempt to go farther inasmuch as the Germans still held at the road junction.

---

[75] The 4th Division was in turn relieved by the 101st Airborne Division, and on 30 June it, too, had started moving south for the new offensive. 4th Div AAR.

The road junction was overrun the next day (30 June) by the 2d Battalion. Just beyond it Capt. Stephen W. Sprindis led his Company E in a classic infantry charge over open ground with all three platoons advancing in a line of skirmishers firing as they charged. Despite the lack of artillery support the men kept going against enemy machine gun and mortar fire. At the same time Company F on the right advanced with tanks up the main road. Both attacks gathered momentum against an enemy whose zeal for fighting was easily dampened in these last days, and the two companies drove into Beaumont-Hague.

While the 60th's attack broke the center of the main German defense line, the 47th Infantry smashed through Gruchy, coastal anchor of the line, and Gréville to the southwest. Gréville was entered by the 2d Battalion, after a heavy artillery concentration, while tank fire neutralized some pillboxes. Enemy entrenched near the town had to be routed out with hand grenades, but the strong point actually fell with unexpected ease. The 2d Battalion had more trouble at Gruchy where the Germans were dug in along a ridge line to the west and south and brought considerable mortar fire to bear on the attackers. However, a two-battalion concentration of artillery in the early afternoon discouraged the defense here, too, and the thoroughly beaten enemy came out of his holes to relinquish his last chance for a co-ordinated defense of any part of the Cherbourg peninsula. The drive up the cape continued but little remained except to clear out a few isolated strong points and round up thousands of prisoners. The senior German commander, Colonel Keil, was captured about midnight on 30 June. The mop-up, netting about 6,000 prisoners, or twice the number estimated to be in the cape, was completed by that afternoon.

The last harbor forts in the Cherbourg area, after enduring heavy tank destroyer fire and dive-bombing attacks, at last surrendered on 29 June. Before that, engineers and naval personnel had begun detailed reconnaissance of the extent of the damage to the port. What they found was not encouraging. Col. Alvin G. Viney, who prepared the original engineer plan for port rehabilitation, wrote: "The demolition of the port of Cherbourg is a masterful job, beyond a doubt the most complete, intensive, and best-planned demolition in history." [76] The harbor was strewn with a variety of different types of mines. All basins in the military and commercial port were blocked with sunken ships. The Gare Maritime, containing the electrical control system and heating plant for the port, was demolished and 20,000 cubic yards of masonry were blown into the large deep basin that had been used in peacetime for docking Atlantic liners. The entrance of this basin was completely blocked by two large ships. Quay walls were severely damaged. Cranes were demolished in all areas. The left breakwater for the inner harbor was cratered so that the sea poured through. The whole port was as nearly a wreck as demolitions could make it. For this work of destruction Hitler awarded the Knight's Cross to Admiral Hennecke the day after his capture by VII Corps troops,

---

[76] Cited in [Herbert E. French, Morton Yarman, and Henry G. Elliott] Cherbourg—Gateway to France, MS, Ch. I, p. 13. Hist Div files.

calling the job "a feat unprecedented in the annals of coastal defense." [77]

Planning estimates based on experience at Naples had calculated that Cherbourg could begin operations three days after its capture. In reality it was almost three weeks before the port was opened at all and months before it began to handle cargo in quantity. The mine sweeping of the western portion of the harbor was not completed until 14 July, and not until the end of September were all the obstructions cleared from the harbor. The work of reconstructing port facilities began before the last forts had surrendered. The advance party of the 1056th Engineer Port Construction and Repair Group arrived in Cherbourg on 27 June.[78] The first task was the clearing of a beach area (the Nouvelle Plage), a fashionable bathing beach in peacetime, now designed by the engineers for use by DUKW's. But the first cargo was landed by DUKW over this beach only on 16 July.[79]

The capture of Cherbourg completed a distinct phase of operations. The final-

ity was marked as well on other fronts. While VII Corps advanced on the port, the Germans made their last plans for decisive offensive action in Normandy. On 20 June OKW ordered Rundstedt to prepare a co-ordinated counterattack with six panzer divisions to annihilate American forces in the vicinity of Balleroy, and drive north generally along the Allied interarmy boundary toward Bayeux.[80] (*Map XXIV*) The six divisions included three that had not yet arrived (the *1st SS, 9th SS,* and *10th SS Panzer Divisions*), one that was assembled immediately behind the front (the *2d SS*),[81] and two that were already in the line (*Panzer Lehr* and the *12th SS*). The latter two were to be relieved as soon as possible by two infantry divisions (the *276th* and *277th*) being brought up from southern France. The main attack was to be preceded by an attack to wipe out the British beachhead east of the Orne which would remove the potentially most dangerous threat of deep penetration in the direction of Paris.

The scheme of 20 June was ambitious far beyond German capabilities. Because of the time required to move troops into position, it was out of the question to launch successive major attacks. The thrusts at Balleroy and east of the Orne, therefore, would have to be made simultaneously, which meant that neither attack could have adequate artillery support. There were guns enough but too few shells. Estimated to be available were 150 pieces of GHQ artillery (including

---

[77] Destruction had begun as early as 7 June and was carried on methodically by naval personnel until the final surrender. The *KTB* of Navy Group West has a daily account of the progress of demolitions. The only comfort for the Americans was the surprisingly small damage to the city itself and the fact that the rail network of the port could be repaired with relative ease.

[78] Reconstruction was supervised by the 4th Port Hq.

[79] Little by little the port capacity was increased until in November Cherbourg handled more than half of all the cargo landed in France for the American armies, discharging 433,201 tons, or an average of about 14,500 tons a day. This compared with a pre-D-day planning estimate of 8,500 tons a day. Most dramatically it contrasted to a total peacetime cargo handling for the entire year of 1937 of only 325,150 tons. For details of port reconstruction see French, Yarman, and Elliott, *Cherbourg—Gateway to France,* Ch. III.

[80] *Der Westen.*

[81] *Seventh Army, KTB 1.I.–30.VI.44,* 18 Jun 44. The *2d SS Panzer Division* was considerably delayed in its march from near Toulon by harassing attacks by the French maquis. It closed at last in assembly areas near Torigni-sur-Vire about 18 June, when it passed to *Seventh Army* reserve.

twelve heavy battalions) and 487 division artillery pieces. But the requirement of ammunition for sustained offensive action was calculated at 14,000 tons.[82] In view of the fact that ammunition on hand was already insufficient for defensive missions, the additional requirement was fantastically outside the realm of possibility.

Even if this problem could have been solved, it remained doubtful whether the Allies would sit still long enough to enable the Germans to relieve the armor in the line. Rundstedt therefore viewed the plan without much hope. Nevertheless preparations were got under way. All available armor was to be brought again under the unified command of General Geyr, who with his reconstituted staff of *Panzer Group West* would take over the entire section between the Seine and Drôme Rivers with four corps, *XLVII Panzer Corps, I SS Panzer Corps, II SS Panzer Corps,* and *LXXXVI Infantry Corps* (east of the Orne). *Seventh Army* with two corps (*LXXXIV Infantry* and *II Parachute*) would have a purely defensive mission from St. Lô to the west coast.[83]

In the next few days the rapid collapse of General Schlieben's forces in the Cotentin caused Hitler to flirt with the notion of a relieving attack up the west coast. Rundstedt, ordered to study the possibility, replied that he had no forces available for such an attack, that he would not have

any for several days at least. In any case, he thought it unwise to shift his weight from the Caen front. On the other hand, fearing that the American capture of Cherbourg would lead to a considerable strengthening of the Allied west flank, Rundstedt wanted to build a strong defense from Portbail along the south edge of the Prairies Marécageuses and along the Vire to St. Lô in order to hold Bradley while preparing his own counterattack toward Bayeux. Although such a temporary diversion of force to the defense would delay the counterattack, Rundstedt counted it well worth while to be able to operate without interruption from a series of emergencies that would continue to nibble away his striking power.

The decision was so made, but it could not be carried out, for an emergency was already in the making in the British zone. On 18 June General Montgomery, in his first written directive since the beginning of operations on the Continent, signaled his intention of stepping up his attack. He pointed out: "After the very great intensity of the initial few days, we had to slow down the tempo of the operation" to get a sound position against possible enemy counterattack and build up strength to push on. "All this is good," he continued, "but we are now ready to pass on to other things, and reap the harvest." The harvest he had in mind included Cherbourg (which General Collins was well on the way to capturing) and Caen as the "first step in the full development of our plans." He therefore ordered the attack by Second British Army to begin at once to take Caen, which he regarded as "really the key to Cherbourg." Its capture, he added, "will release forces which are now locked up in ensuring that our left

---

[82] *Army Group B*, Munition estimate, 21 Jun 44. *Seventh Army, KTB Anlagen, Chefsachen 1.I.–30.-VI.44.*

[83] German information here and following is from *Der Westen; Seventh Army, KTB Anlagen 1.I.–30.VI.44*; MS # T–121 (Zimmermann *et al.*); MS # B–466 (Geyr); MS # B–633 (Rundstedt); and MS # B–672 (Buttlar-Brandenfels).

flank holds secure."[84] But the Caen attack could not be begun at once. On 19 June, Montgomery changed the scheme of maneuver and scheduled the jump-off for 22–23 June. Weather then intervened to delay the landing of 8 Corps troops. On the morning of 25 June, 30 Corps at last began a preliminary thrust east of Tilly-sur-Seulles. The main attack was to be made the following day when 8 Corps with one armored and two infantry divisions would pass through the 3d Canadian Division and advance on the axis St. Mauvieu–Esquay–Amaye-sur-Orne to establish itself southeast of Caen in the Vimont–Bourguebus–Bretteville-sur-Laize area.[85] The push of 25 June resulted in only small gains for 30 Corps but alarmed the Germans, because it pressed hard against the already worn-down *Panzer Lehr* and *12th SS Panzer Divisions.* As the *I SS Panzer Corps,* holding this sector, had no reserves, *Seventh Army* attached to it the advance battalion of the *1st SS Panzer Division* just beginning to close in forward areas.[86]

The opening of the British 8 Corps attack the next day forced *Seventh Army* to scramble further for reinforcements. Two battalions of the *2d SS Panzer Division,* which had been in reserve behind the *II Parachute Corps,* one tank battalion of the *2d Panzer Division,* portions of the *21st Panzer Division* relieved from the bridgehead east of the Orne, the *7th Werfer Brigade,* and one artillery battalion were ordered brought up at once.

In addition Rommel ordered the *II SS Panzer Corps* to speed its assembly in areas north and northeast of Vire. The *2d SS Panzer Division* was to be attached and the entire corps would attack at once the flank of the British penetration generally along the axis of the Villers-Bocage–Caen highway. The emergency requiring immediate piecemeal commitment of the *II SS Panzer Corps* was considered so urgent that for two nights (25 and 26 June) all supply movements were ruled off the roads so that the armor could move forward. But even with this priority the corps could not get in position to attack until 29 June.[87]

On that day came another emergency. General Gerow launched a limited-objective attack with the recently arrived 3d Armored Division at Villiers-Fossard. The purpose was simply to wipe out an enemy salient in the 29th Division lines and so secure a more favorable line of departure for the forthcoming resumption of the 29th Division's drive toward St. Lô. *Seventh Army,* however, continually worried over the weakness of the *II Parachute Corps,* demanded that the Kampfgruppe of the *2d SS Panzer Division* attached to *II SS Panzer Corps* be returned to reserve positions behind the St. Lô front. The crisis at St. Lô passed when the 3d Armored Division, having achieved its main objectives on 30 June, halted.

But the German plans for counterattack on the east had already been hopelessly compromised. On 28 June General Geyr took command of the sector between the Seine and the Drôme Rivers but under circumstances which, instead of giving him a free hand, forced him to continue

---

[84] In First Army file, Directives 21 A Gp. See Pogue, The Supreme Command, a volume in preparation in this series, for discussion in detail of Montgomery's operations and intentions in the Caen area.
[85] Information supplied by the British Cabinet Office Hist Sec.
[86] *Seventh Army, KTB 1.I.–30.VI.44,* 25 Jun 44.

[87] *Ibid.*

the piecemeal measures already started. General Dollmann died that day of a heart attack. Generaloberst der Waffen-SS Paul Hausser, commander of *II SS Panzer Corps,* replaced him and temporarily took command of the entire front including *Panzer Group West.* This arrangement was made pending more far-reaching reshuffling, which Rommel and Rundstedt had been summoned to Berchtesgaden to discuss. In their absence no radical decisions could be made. In consequence, therefore, Geyr had no recourse but to order *II SS Panzer Corps* to attack with the *9th SS* and *10th SS Panzer Divisions* as planned against the west flank of the deep British penetration.[88] The attack began the afternoon of 29 June and had largely spent itself by nightfall. Although it made some temporary gains in reducing the British bridgehead over the Odon, the two divisions exhausted themselves in generally indecisive struggles for local objectives. On the 30th the *II SS Panzer Corps* was ordered on the defensive.[89]

General Montgomery, after identification of the concentration of German armored units on his front, had already made a similar decision. Orders to Second British Army were to continue offensive tactics and "develop operations for the capture of CAEN as opportunity offers— and the sooner the better." But the army's mission was to "hold the main enemy forces in the area between CAEN and VILLIERS BOCAGE" and "to have no set-backs." General Montgomery also warned of the possibility of "a full-blooded enemy counterattack" between Caen and Villiers-Bocage and to meet this threat directed that the 7th Armoured Division be pulled out of line and held in army reserve.[90]

In the meantime Rommel and Rundstedt journeyed to Berchtesgaden. Rundstedt had to make the entire trip by car. When he arrived, Hitler kept him waiting six hours. Tired and angry, Rundstedt remarked to Keitel that it should cause no surprise "upstairs" if an old and sick man like himself should fall dead some day like General Dollmann.[91] It was an inauspicious beginning for a meeting which did nothing to reconcile the tactical thinking of Hitler and that of his field marshals or to restore the shattered confidence on either side.

The meeting was long and private; only Hitler, Rommel, Rundstedt, Keitel, and Jodl were present.[92] When it was over Hitler made an announcement for the record in which he simply restated the stand-fast tactics he had always advocated for the west. "The overpowering air superiority of the enemy," he said, "and his very effective naval artillery limit the possibilities of a large-scale attack on our part. . . . We must not allow mobile warfare to develop, since the enemy surpasses us by far in mobility due to his air superiority and his superabundance of motor vehicles and fuel. Therefore everything depends on our confining him to his bridgehead by building up a front to block it off, and then on fighting a war of

---

[88] Geyr angrily told army that "by this order the panzer group is already sold out." Tel msg, 28 Jun 44, Geyr to CofS *Seventh Army. Seventh Army, KTB Anlagen 1.I.–30.VI.44.*

[89] MS # B–466 (Geyr).

[90] Dir, 21 A Gp, 30 Jun 44. First Army file, Directives 21 A Gp.

[91] MS # B–633 (Rundstedt).

[92] Conf, 29 Jun–1 Jul 44, ONI, *Fuehrer Conferences, 1944.*

attrition to wear him down and force him back, using every method of guerrilla warfare. . . ." [93] It is clear that Rommel and Rundstedt argued in the meeting against this conception, perhaps with some heat since they were convinced of the desperateness of the situation in France. But what they said has not been recorded.

On the following day an order went out from OKW giving effect to Hitler's roping-off policy.[94] It canceled the attack planned on the west flank to drive toward Cherbourg; it declared that an attack to split the British and U.S. bridgeheads was no longer possible because the necessary troops could not be disengaged in the face of Allied pressure; it recognized that the *LXXXIV Corps* was not in condition to attack; and, finally, it admitted that an attack east of the Orne was contingent on the arrival of the *16th Luftwaffe Field Division* and the withdrawal of Allied naval forces. Having thus abandoned all thought of offensive action, OKW told *Seventh Army* that its principal mission was to avoid being pushed back into open country. For that purpose it was initially to hold the *2d SS Panzer Division* in reserve for flank attacks against any Allied drive south. The time had not yet come, OKW continued, to weaken the *Kanalkueste* defense, but preparations for the transfer of troops from *Fifteenth Army* to the Normandy battle front should be made.

In effect the order said: Hold on—go on doing what you have been doing. But the high commanders in the west by the end of June had become convinced that the tactics so far pursued offered no hope for

victory and meant only the inexorable and profitless wearing-down of the German strength. Probably Rommel and Rundstedt made that point to Hitler in the 29 June meeting. On their return to France they put it clearly on the record. In their absence, General Geyr of *Panzer Group West* and General Hausser, the new commander of *Seventh Army*, had prepared estimates of the situation, substantially along the same lines, calling for an evacuation of the Caen pocket, the establishment of a shorter line (Orne River–Bully–Avenay–Villers-Bocage–vicinity of Caumont) outside the range of naval artillery, and the relief and refreshment of the armored divisions to re-create a counterattack force.[95] To these estimates, so completely at variance with Hitler's newest order, Rommel gave his complete approval and sent them on to *OB WEST*. There was a notable air of haste about the proceedings. The documents left Rommel's headquarters at about midnight, 30 June. A few minutes later *Army Group B* approved the beginning of the evacuation of Caen.[96] At 0200, 1 July, Rommel's proposals arrived at *OB WEST* and an hour and a half later Rundstedt had endorsed and forwarded them to OKW, adding a request for a free hand in carrying out the planned evacuation of the Caen pocket.[97] They arrived at OKW at 0700. OKW recommended their rejection, commenting that they were

---

[93] *Ibid.*

[94] *Der Westen;* cf. *Seekriegsleitung/1.Abt., KTB 1.–30.VI.44,* 30 Jun 44.

[95] Tel msg, 30 Jun 44, Geyr to CofS *Seventh Army,* 30 Jun 44. *Seventh Army, KTB Anlagen 1.I.–30.VI.44.* For text of estimates see Rad, *Army Group B* to *OB WEST,* 30 Jun 44. *Army Group B, Ia Operations Befehle 9.VI.–31.VIII.44.*

[96] Rad, *Army Group B* to *Seventh Army,* 1 Jul 44. *Army Group B, Ia Operations Befehle 9.VI.–31.VIII.-44.*

[97] *OB WEST, KTB 1.–31.VII.44,* 1 Jul 44.

tantamount to a decision to pull out of France and that the question was simply whether to retreat to the West Wall or to fight it out in place to the last man. Hitler wanted to fight it out. His decision reached Rundstedt at 1740. *OB WEST* was ordered to hold every position then occupied and halt every threatened breakthrough by stubborn defense in place or local counterattack.[98]

The decision certainly came as no surprise. Why, then, was it so elaborately called for? Were the generals in the west concerned only with setting the record straight, believing they could no longer hope to make their ideas prevail, and unwilling therefore to accept responsibility without power? Did they feel, rather, that Hitler, confronted with the unanimous opinion of the military leaders in France, might at the last moment defer to their judgment? Whatever the reason back of the *démarche* of 1 July, it had the effect of marking an irreconcilable opposition between *OB WEST* and Hitler. The aftermath was swift. On 2 July Hitler's adjutant entered the *OB WEST* command post and, in the Fuehrer's name, presented to Rundstedt the oak leaf to the Knight's Cross together with a polite handwritten note from Hitler relieving the field marshal of his command on grounds of age and health.[99] An order was delivered at the same time relieving General Geyr as commander of *Panzer Group West*. When Rommel heard of these changes, he is reputed to have said, "I will be next." [100] Rundstedt turned over his command to Generalfeldmarschall Guen-

ther von Kluge on 3 July. The following morning Geyr was relieved by General der Panzertruppen Heinrich Eberbach.

Operations in France were then entering a new phase. General Bradley had already launched his first full-scale attack south in an attempt to push out the lodgment. The Second British Army would shortly resume its attack for Caen. Hitler's decision to attempt a permanent roping-off of the Allied beachheads was to be put to the test.

The Allied armies were ready for the test. Since D Day 929,000 men, 586,000 tons of supplies, and 177,000 vehicles had been landed.[101] American and British build-ups were roughly equal. General Bradley had four corps with eleven infantry and two armored divisions.[102] For the new attack under Second British Army were four corps (three in the line), ten infantry divisions, and three armored divisions.

Allied armies, however, occupied a lodgment considerably smaller than planned. Shortly after mid-June when it became apparent that neither the U.S. V Corps nor the British Second Army could push fast to the south, General Montgomery asked for a shift in build-up priorities to get a higher proportion of combat troops ashore. This was done in both British and American sectors. First Army got the 83d Division about a week sooner than planned, and combat units of XV Corps (borrowed from Third Army) were put ashore a few days ahead of the original schedule. Correspondingly the build-up

---

[98] *Der Westen.*

[99] *OB WEST, KTB 1.–31.VII.44,* 2 Jul 44; MS # B–633 (Rundstedt).

[100] MS # B–466 (Geyr).

[101] SHAEF G–3 War Room Daily Summary as of D plus 27, 5 Jul 44.

[102] Including the 82d Airborne Division which was used in the initial attack, but excluding the 101st Airborne Division on guard duty in Cherbourg, awaiting return to England.

of service and supporting troops was reduced. The result was at the end of June an increasing disproportion of combat and service elements. The disproportion could be borne because the shallowness of the bridgehead meant reduced requirements for supply and administrative overhead. It involved, however, a considerable risk. As long as Allied armies advanced slowly, administration and supply constituted no special problem. If the increasing pressure of Eisenhower's forces cracked the German front and war of movement suddenly developed, the undermanned supply lines would be severely taxed. This possibility at the end of June was a source of some concern to the SHAEF command, but in view of the limited lodgment the risk had to be accepted.[103]

The slow advance southward, and especially the failure to push out into open country south and southeast of Caen, also meant a reduction in the planned program of airfield construction. This was, however, much less serious than planners had anticipated. By dint of improvisation Ninth Air Force engineers were able to lay out fields in country that planners had considered unsuitable for air strips. In early July about one-third of the Ninth Air Force fighters and fighter-bombers were based on the Continent. It was true, however, that the available space for airfields in Normandy was virtually taken up at that time and that the fields constructed on a temporary basis were requiring an ever increasing proportion of engineer labor to maintain them. In short, from an air force point of view, the lodgment secured at the end of June was

relatively satisfactory for the moment but would not long remain so.[104]

The failure to make anticipated territorial gains was the only major respect in which the OVERLORD operation had fallen short of planning calculations. For the rest, the success achieved by Allied combined arms outstripped the plan. While the planners had always held their breath over the risks of the UTAH Beach assault, the airborne landings had in fact achieved such complete tactical success that the seaborne infantry had had little to do but walk ashore. Only at OMAHA had the fortified coast line proved to be the hard crust that planners had counted on finding everywhere. There the planners' worries about the capacity of naval guns and support craft to deal with concrete defenses proved justified. On the other hand, the effectiveness of naval and air power in hindering the forming of German reserves for counterattack exceeded expectations. Throughout the beachhead battles the confused German command, and in some cases the inferior quality of green or non-German enemy troops, provided a bonus for the Allies which did not figure in the planning. Perhaps the biggest and most important surprise was the proved ability of the combined air forces and French saboteurs to cripple the enemy's transportation system. It would be difficult to overestimate the handicaps imposed on the enemy by his lack of mobility. It was the primary reason why the big counterattack that figured in all Allied estimates never materialized.

There was reason on 1 July for the Allies to be satisfied with their achieve-

---

[103] Memo, Gen Bull for SAC, Jun 44. SHAEF G-3 file (Complete Planning for OVERLORD Buildup).

[104] Air force logistics on the Continent will be covered in the seventh volume of *Army Air Forces in World War II.*

ment to date, but there was no time to indulge that satisfaction. The problems of the next step were all-absorbing. The next step was to break out of Normandy. Scarcely an Allied soldier from Eisenhower down was not eager to see his last hedgerow and unleash the tanks in open country. But before that could happen some of the bloodiest battles of Normandy still had be fought. The beginning had been good; it had carried out the plan at least in the essentials that counted. But it was only the beginning; still in the incalculable future lay the final objective of operation OVERLORD—the thrust into the heart of Hitler's Germany.

Appendix A

DIGEST OF OPERATION "OVERLORD"

Object.

1. The object of Operation "Overlord" is to mount and carry out an operation, with forces and equipment established in the United Kingdom, and with target date the 1st May, 1944, to secure a lodgement on the Continent from which further offensive operations can be developed. The lodgement area must contain sufficient port facilities to maintain a force of some twenty-six to thirty divisions, and enable that force to be augmented by follow-up shipments from the United States or elsewhere of additional divisions and supporting units at the rate of three to five divisions per month.

Selection of a Lodgement Area.

2. In order to provide sufficient port facilities to maintain these large forces, it will be necessary to select a lodgement area which includes a group of major ports. We must plan on the assumption that ports, on capture, will be seriously damaged and probably blocked. It will take some time to restore normal facilities. We shall thus be forced to rely on maintenance over beaches for an extended period.

3. A study of the beaches on the Belgian and Channel coasts shows that the beaches with the highest capacity for passing vehicles and stores inland are those in the Pas de Calais,* and the Caen †—Cotentin ‡ area. Of these, the Caen beaches are the most favourable, as they are, unlike the others, sheltered from the prevailing winds. Naval and air considerations point to the area between the Pas de Calais and the Cotentin as the most suitable for the initial landing, air factors of optimum air support and rapid provision of airfields indicating the Pas de Calais as the best choice, with Caen as an acceptable alternative.

4. Thus, taking beach capacity and air and naval considerations together, it appears that either the Pas de Calais area or the Caen–Cotentin area is the most suitable for the initial main landing.

5. As the area for the initial landing, the Pas de Calais has many obvious advantages such that good air support and quick turn round for our shipping can be achieved. On the other hand, it is a focal point of the enemy fighters disposed for defence, and maximum enemy air activity can be brought to bear over this area with the minimum movement of his air forces. Moreover, the Pas de Calais is the most strongly defended area on the whole French coast. The defences would require very heavy and sustained bombardment from sea and air: penetration would be slow, and the result of the bombardment

---

* "Pas de Calais area" has been assumed as the area between Gravelines and the River Somme.

† "Caen area" is taken as that between the River Orne and the base of the Cotentin Peninsula.

‡ The "Cotentin" Peninsula is the peninsula in which Cherbourg is situated.

of beach exits would severely limit the rate of build-up. Further, this area does not offer good opportunities for expansion. It would be necessary to develop the bridgehead to include either the Belgian ports as far as Antwerp or the Channel ports Westwards to include Havre and Rouen. But both an advance to Antwerp across the numerous water obstacles, and a long flank march of some 120 miles to the Seine ports must be considered unsound operations of war unless the German forces are in a state not far short of final collapse.

6. In the Caen–Cotentin area it would be possible to make our initial landing either partly on the Cotentin Peninsula and partly on the Caen beaches, wholly in the Cotentin or wholly on the Caen beaches. An attack with part of our forces in the Cotentin and part on the Caen beaches, is, however, considered to be unsound. It would entail dividing our limited forces by the low-lying marshy ground and intricate river system at the neck of the Cotentin Peninsula; thus exposing them to defeat in detail.

7. An attack against the Cotentin Peninsula, on the other hand, has a reasonable chance of success, and would ensure the early capture of the port of Cherbourg. Unfortunately, very few airfields exist in the Cotentin, and that area is not suitable for rapid airfield development. Furthermore, the narrow neck of the Peninsula would give the Germans an easy task in preventing us from breaking out and expanding our initial bridgehead. Moreover, during the period of our consolidation in the Cotentin the Germans would have time to reinforce their coastal troops in the Caen area, rendering a subsequent amphibious assault in that area much more difficult.

8. There remains the attack on the Caen beaches. The Caen sector is weakly held; the defences are relatively light and the beaches are of high capacity and sheltered from the prevailing winds. Inland the terrain is suitable for airfield development and for the consolidation of the initial bridgehead; and much of it is unfavourable for counter-attacks by panzer divisions. Maximum enemy air opposition can only be brought to bear at the expense of the enemy air defence screen covering the approaches to Germany; and the limited number of enemy airfields within range of the Caen area facilitates local neutralisation of the German fighter force. The sector suffers from the disadvantage that considerable effort will be required to provide adequate air support to our assault forces and some time must elapse before the capture of a major port.

After a landing in the Caen sector it would be necessary to seize either the Seine group of ports or the Brittany group of ports. To seize the Seine ports would entail forcing a crossing of the Seine, which is likely to require greater forces than we can build up through the Caen beaches and the port of Cherbourg. It should, however, be possible to seize the Brittany ports between Cherbourg and Nantes and on them build up sufficient forces for our final advance Eastwards.

Provided that the necessary air situation can first be achieved, the chances of a successful attack and of rapid subsequent development are so much greater in this sector than in any other that it is considered that the advantages far outweigh the disadvantages.

The Lodgement Area Selected.

9. In the light of these factors, it is considered that our initial landing on the Continent should be effected in the Caen area, with a view to the eventual seizure of a lodgement area comprising the Cherbourg–Brittany group of ports (from Cherbourg to Nantes).

Opening Phase up to the Capture of Cherbourg.

10. The opening phase in the seizing of this lodgement area would be the effecting of a landing in the Caen sector with a view to the early capture and development of airfield sites in the Caen area, and of the port of Cherbourg.

11. The main limiting factors affecting such an operation are the possibility of attaining the necessary air situation; the number of offensive divisions which the enemy can make available for counter attack in the Caen area; the availability of landing ships and craft and of transport aircraft; and the capacity of the beaches and ports in the sector.

12. Although the strength of the G.A.F. available in 1944 on the Western front cannot be forecast at this stage, we can confidently expect that we shall have a vast numerical superiority in bomber forces. The first-line strength of the German fighter force is, however, showing a steady increase and although it is unlikely to equal the size of the force at our disposal, there is no doubt that our fighters will have a very large commitment entailing dispersal and operations at maximum intensity. Our fighters will also be operating under serious tactical disadvantages in the early stages, which will largely offset their numerical superiority. Before the assault takes place, therefore, it will be necessary to reduce the effectiveness of the G.A.F., particularly that part which can be brought to bear against the Caen area.

13. The necessary air situation to ensure a reasonable chance of success will therefore require that the maximum number of German fighter forces are contained in the Low Countries and North-West Germany, that the effectiveness of the fighter defence in the Caen area is reduced and that air reinforcements are prevented from arriving in the early stages from the Mediterranean. Above all, it will be necessary to reduce the overall strength of the German fighter force between now and the date of the operation by destruction of the sources of supply, by the infliction of casualties by bringing on air battles, and, immediately prior to the assault, by the disorganization of G.A.F. installations and control system in the Caen area.

14. As it is impossible to forecast with any accuracy the number and location of German formations in reserve in 1944, while, on the other hand, the forces available to us have been laid down, an attempt has been made in this paper to determine the wisest employment of our own forces and then to determine the maximum number of German formations which they can reasonably overcome. Apart from the air situation, which is an over-riding factor, the practicability of this plan will depend principally on the number, effectiveness, and availability of German divisions present in France and the Low Countries in relation to our own capabilities. This consideration is discussed below (paragraph 35).

15. A maximum of thirty and a minimum of twenty-six equivalent divisions are likely to be available in the United Kingdom for cross-Channel operations on the 1st May 1944. Further build-up can be at the rate of three to five divisions per month.

16. Landing ships and craft have been provided to lift the equivalent of three assault divisions and two follow-up divisions, without "overheads," and it has been assumed that the equivalent of an additional two divisions can be afloat in ships.

17. Airborne forces amounting to two airborne divisions and some five or six parachute regiments will be available, but, largely owing to shortage of transport aircraft, it is only possible to lift the equivalent of two-thirds of one airborne division simultaneously, on the basis of present forecasts.

18. Even if additional landing ships and craft could be made available, the beaches in the Caen area would preclude the landing of forces greater than the equivalent of the three assault and two follow-up divisions, for which craft have already been provided. Nevertheless, an all-round increase of at least 10 per cent. in landing ships and craft is highly desirable in order to provide a greater margin for contingencies within the framework of the existing plan. Futhermore, sufficient lift for a further assault division could most usefully be employed in an additional landing on other beaches.

19. There is no port of any capacity within the sector although there are a number of small ports of limited value. Maintenance will, therefore, of necessity be largely over the beaches until it is possible to capture and open up the port of Cherbourg. In view of the possibilities of interruption by bad weather it will be essential to provide early some form of improvised sheltered waters.

20. Assuming optimum weather conditions, it should be possible to build up the force over the beaches to a total by D plus 6 of the equivalent of some eleven divisions and five tank brigades and thereafter to land one division a day until about D plus 24.

Proposed Plan.

Preliminary Phase.

21. During the preliminary phase, which must start forthwith, all possible means including air and sea action, propaganda, political and economic pressure, and sabotage, must be integrated into a combined offensive aimed at softening the German resistance. In particular, air action should be directed towards the reduction of the German air forces on the Western front, the progressive destruction of the German economic system and the undermining of German morale.

22. In order to contain the maximum German forces away from the Caen area diversionary operations should be staged against other areas such as the Pas de Calais and the Mediterranean Coast of France.

Preparatory Phase.

23. During this phase air action will be intensified against the G.A.F., particularly in North-West France, with a view to reducing the effectiveness of the G.A.F. in that area, and will be extended to include attacks against communications more directly associated with move-

ment of German reserves which might affect the Caen area. Three naval assault forces will be assembled with the naval escorts and loaded at ports along the South Coast of England. Two naval assault forces carrying the follow-up forces will also be assembled and loaded, one in the Thames Estuary and one on the West Coast.

The Assault.

24. After a very short air bombardment of the beach defences three assault divisions will be landed simultaneously on the Caen beaches, followed up on D Day by the equivalent of two tank brigades (United States regiments) and a brigade group (United States regimental combat team). At the same time, airborne forces will be used to seize the town of Caen; and subsidiary operations by commandos and possibly by airborne forces will be undertaken to neutralize certain coast defences and seize certain important river crossings. The object of the assault forces will be to seize the general line Grandcamp–Bayeux–Caen.

Follow-up and Build-up Phase.

25. Subsequent action will take the form of a strong thrust Southwards and South-Westwards with a view to destroying enemy forces, acquiring sites for airfields, and gaining depth for a turning movement into the Cotentin Peninsula directed on Cherbourg. When sufficient depth has been gained a force will advance into the Cotentin and seize Cherbourg. At the same time a thrust will be made to deepen the bridgehead South-Eastwards in order to cover the construc-

tion and operation of additional airfields in the area South-East of Caen.

26. It is considered that, within fourteen days of the initial assault, Cherbourg should be captured and the bridgehead extended to include the general line Trouville–Alençon–Mont St. Michel. By this date, moreover, it should have been possible to land some eighteen divisions and to have in operation about fourteen airfields from which twenty-eight to thirty-three fighter-type squadrons should be operating.

Further Developments after Capture of Cherbourg.

27. After the capture of Cherbourg the Supreme Allied Commander will have to decide whether to initiate operations to seize the Seine ports or whether he must content himself with first occupying the Brittany ports. In this decision he will have to be guided largely by the situation of the enemy forces. If the German resistance is sufficiently weak, an immediate advance could be made to seize Havre and Rouen. On the other hand, the more probable situation is that the Germans will have retired with the bulk of their forces to hold Paris and the line of the Seine, where they can best be covered by their air forces from North-East France and where they may possibly be reinforced by formations from Russia. Elsewhere they may move a few divisions from Southern France to hold the crossings of the Loire and will leave the existing defensive divisions in Brittany.

It will therefore most probably be necessary for us to seize the Brittany ports first, in order to build up sufficient forces with which we can eventually force the passage of the Seine.

28. Under these circumstances, the most suitable plan would appear to be to secure first the left flank and to gain sufficient airfields for subsequent operations. This would be done by extending the bridgehead to the line of the River Eure from Dreux to Rouen and thence along the line of the Seine to the sea, seizing at the same time Chartres, Orleans and Tours.

29. Under cover of these operations a force would be employed in capturing the Brittany ports; the first step being a thrust Southwards to seize Nantes and St. Nazaire, followed by subsidiary operations to capture Brest and the various small ports of the Brittany Peninsula.

30. This action would complete the occupation of our initial lodgement area and would secure sufficient major ports for the maintenance of at least thirty divisions. As soon as the organization of the L. of C. in this lodgement area allowed, and sufficient air forces had been established, operations would then be begun to force the line of the Seine, and to capture Paris and the Seine ports. As opportunity offered, subsidiary action would also be taken to clear the Germans from the Biscay ports to facilitate the entry of additional American troops and the feeding of the French population.

Command and Control.

31. In carrying out Operation "Overlord" administrative control would be greatly simplified if the principle were adopted that the United States forces were normally on the right of the line and the British and Canadian forces on the left.

Major Conditions Affecting Success of the Operation.

32. It will be seen that the plan for the initial landing is based on two main principles—concentration of force and tactical surprise. Concentration of the assault forces is considered essential if we are to ensure adequate air support and if our limited assault forces are to avoid defeat in detail. An attempt has been made to obtain tactical surprise by landing in a lightly defended area—presumably lightly defended as, due to its distance from a major port, the Germans consider a landing there unlikely to be successful. This action, of course, presupposes that we can offset the absence of a port in the initial stages by the provision of improvised sheltered waters. It is believed that this can be accomplished.

33. The operation calls for a much higher standard of performance on the part of the naval assault forces than any previous operation. This will depend upon their being formed in sufficient time to permit of adequate training.

34. Above all, it is essential that there should be an over-all reduction in the German fighter force between now and the time of the surface assault. From now onwards every practical method of achieving this end must be employed. This condition, above all others, will dictate the date by which the amphibious assault can be launched.

35. The next condition is that the number of German offensive divisions in

reserve must not exceed a certain figure on the target date if the operation is to have a reasonable chance of success. The German reserves in France and the Low Countries as a whole, excluding divisions holding the coast, G.A.F. divisions and training divisions, should not exceed on the day of the assault twelve full-strength first-quality divisions. In addition, the Germans should not be able to transfer more than fifteen first-quality divisions from Russia during the first two months. Moreover, on the target date the divisions in reserve should be so located that the number of first-quality divisions which the Germans could deploy in the Caen area to support the divisions holding the coast should not exceed three divisions on D Day, five divisions on D plus 2, or nine divisions by D plus 8.

During the preliminary period, therefore, every effort must be made to dissipate and divert German formations, lower their fighting efficiency and disrupt communications.

36. Finally, there is the question of maintenance. Maintenance will have to be carried out over beaches for a period of some three months for a number of formations, varying from a maximum of eighteen divisions in the first month to twelve divisions in the second month, rapidly diminishing to nil in the third month. Unless adequate measures are taken to provide sheltered waters by artificial means, the operation will be at the mercy of the weather. Moreover, special facilities and equipment will be required to prevent undue damage to craft during this extended period. Immediate action for the provision of the necessary requirements is essential.

37. Given these conditions—a reduced G.A.F., a limitation in the number or effectiveness of German offensive formations in France, and adequate arrangements to provide improvised sheltered waters—it is considered that Operation "Overlord" has a reasonable prospect of success. To ensure these conditions being attained by the 1st May, 1944, action must start *now* and every possible effort made by all means in our power to soften German resistance and to speed up our own preparations.

Offices of the War Cabinet, S.W. 1,
30th July, 1943

Appendix B

DIRECTIVE TO SUPREME COMMANDER, ALLIED EXPEDITIONARY FORCE

1. You are hereby designated as Supreme Allied Commander of the forces placed under your orders for operations for liberation of Europe from Germans. Your title will be Supreme Commander Allied Expeditionary Force.

2. *Task.* You will enter the continent of Europe and, in conjunction with the other United Nations, undertake operations aimed at the heart of Germany and the destruction of her armed forces. The date for entering the Continent is the month of May, 1944. After adequate channel ports have been secured, exploitation will be directed towards securing an area that will facilitate both ground and air operations against the enemy.

3. Notwithstanding the target date above you will be prepared at any time to take immediate advantage of favorable circumstances, such as withdrawal by the enemy on your front, to effect a reentry into the Continent with such forces as you have available at the time; a general plan for this operation when approved will be furnished for your assistance.

4. *Command.* You are responsible to the Combined Chiefs of Staff and will exercise command generally in accordance with the diagram at Appendix. Direct communication with the United States and British Chiefs of Staff is authorized in the interest of facilitating your operations and for arranging necessary logistic support.

5. *Logistics.* In the United Kingdom the responsibility for logistics organization, concentration, movement and supply of forces to meet the requirements of your plan will rest with British Service Ministries so far as British Forces are concerned. So far as United States Forces are concerned, this responsibility will rest with the United States War and Navy Departments. You will be responsible for the coordination of logistical arrangements on the continent. You will also be responsible for coordinating the requirements of British and United States forces under your command.

6. *Coordination of operations of other Forces and Agencies.* In preparation for your assault on enemy occupied Europe, Sea and Air Forces agencies of sabotage, subversion and propaganda, acting under a variety of authorities are now in action. You may recommend any variation in these activities which may seem to you desirable.

7. *Relationship to United Nations Forces in other areas.* Responsibility will rest with the Combined Chiefs of Staff for supplying information relating to operations of the Forces of the U. S. S. R. for your guidance in timing your operations. It is understood that the Soviet Forces will launch an offensive at about the

same time as OVERLORD with the object of preventing the German forces from transferring from the Eastern to the Western front. The Allied Commander in Chief, Mediterranean Theater, will conduct operations designed to assist your operation, including the launching of an attack against the south of France at about the same time as OVERLORD. The scope and timing of his operations will be decided by the Combined Chiefs of Staff. You will establish contact with him and submit to the Combined Chiefs of Staff your views and recommendations regarding operations from the Mediterranean in support of your attack from the United Kingdom. The Combined Chiefs of Staff will place under your command the forces operating in Southern France as soon as you are in a position to assume such command. You will submit timely recommendations compatible with this regard.

8. *Relationship with Allied Governments—the re-establishment of Civil Governments and Liberated Allied Territories and the administration of enemy territories.* Further instructions will be issued to you on these subjects at a later date.

Appendix C

Fuehrer Headquarters
23 March 1942

Top Secret

The Fuehrer
and Supreme Commander of the Armed Forces

25 Copies
Copy No. . . .

OKW/WFSt/Op.Nr.: 001031/42 g.Kdos.

D i r e c t i v e No. 40

Subj: Command Organization on the Coasts

I.) General Situation:

In the days to come the coasts of Europe will be seriously exposed to the danger of enemy landings.

The enemy's choice of time and place for landing operations will not be based solely on strategic considerations. Reverses in other theaters of operations, obligations toward his allies, and political motives may prompt the enemy to arrive at decisions that would be unlikely to result from purely military deliberations.

Even enemy landing operations with limited objectives will—insofar as the enemy does establish himself on the coast at all—seriously affect our own plans in any case. They will disrupt our coastwise shipping and tie down strong Army and Luftwaffe forces which thereby would become unavailable for commitment at critical points. Particularly grave dangers will arise if the enemy succeeds in taking our airfields, or in establishing airbases in the territory that he has captured.

Moreover, our military installations and war industries that are in many instances located along or close to the coast, and which in part have valuable equipment, invite local raids by the enemy.

Special attention must be paid to British preparations for landings on the open coast, for which numerous armored landing craft suitable for the transportation of combat vehicles and heavy weapons are available. Large-scale parachute and glider operations are likewise to be expected.

II.) General Tactical Instructions for Coastal Defense:

1.) Coastal defense is a task for the Armed Forces, and requires particularly close and complete co-operation of all the services.

2.) Timely recognition of the preparations, assembly, and approach of the enemy for a landing operation must be the goal of the intelligence service as well as that of continual reconnaissance by Navy and Luftwaffe.

Embarkation operations or transport fleets at sea must subsequently be the target for the concentration of all suitable air and naval forces, with the object of destroying the enemy as far off our coast as possible.

However, because the enemy may employ skillful deception and take advantage of poor visibility, thereby catching us completely by surprise, all troops that might be exposed to such surprise operations must always be fully prepared for defensive action.

Counteracting the well-known tendency of the troops to relax their alertness as time goes on will be one of the most important command functions.

3.) Recent battle experiences have taught us that in fighting for the beaches—which include coastal waters within the range of medium coastal artillery—responsibility for the preparation and execution of defensive operations must unequivocally and unreservedly be concentrated in the hands of one man.

All available forces and equipment of the several services, the organizations and formations outside of the armed forces, as well as the German civil agencies in the zone of operations will be committed by the responsible commander for the destruction of enemy transport facilities and invasion forces. That commitment must lead to the collapse of the enemy attack before, if possible, but at the latest upon the actual landing.

An immediate counterattack must annihilate landed enemy forces, or throw them back into the sea. All instruments of warfare—regardless of the service, or the formation outside of the armed forces to which they might belong—are to be jointly committed toward that end. Nevertheless, shore-based Navy supply establishments must not be hampered in their essential functions, nor Luftwaffe ground organizations and Flak protection of airfields impaired in their efficiency, unless they have become directly affected by ground combat operations.

No headquarters and no unit may initiate a retrograde movement in such a situation. Wherever Germans are committed on or near the coast, they must be armed and trained for active combat.

The enemy must be kept from establishing himself on any island which in enemy hands would constitute a threat to the mainland or coastwise shipping.

4.) Disposition of forces and improvement of fortifications are to be so made that the main defensive effort lies in those coastal sectors that are the most probable sites for enemy landings (fortified areas).

Those remaining coastal sectors that are vulnerable to coups de main of even small units must be protected by means of a strongpoint type of defense, utilizing, if possible, the support of shore batteries. All installations of military and military-economic importance will be included in that strongpoint defense system.

The same rules apply to offshore islands. Coastal sectors that are less endangered will be patrolled.

5.) The several services will establish a uniform definition of coastal sectors, if necessary on the basis of a final decision on the part of the responsible commander named in III.) 1.) below.

6.) By means of proportionate allocation of forces, improvement of positions (perimeter defense), and stockpiling of supplies, the fortified areas and strongpoints must be enabled to hold out even against superior enemy forces for extended periods of time.

Fortified areas and strongpoints are to be held to the last. They must never be forced to surrender because of a shortage of ammunition, rations, or water.

7.)   The commander responsible according to III.) 1.) below, issues orders for coastal security, and assures a speedy evaluation, collation, and dissemination to authorized headquarters and civil agencies of intelligence procured by all the services.

Upon the first indication of an imminent enemy operation, that commander is authorized to issue the necessary orders for unified and complementary reconnaissance by sea and air.

8.)   All elements stationed in the vicinity of the coast, whether headquarters or units of the Armed Forces, or organizations or formations outside of the Armed Forces, will forego the niceties of peacetime protocol. Their quarters, security measures, equipment, state of alert, and utilization of local resources will be governed solely by the necessity of countering every enemy raid with the utmost speed and force. Wherever the military situation demands, the civilian population will be evacuated at once.

III.)   Command:

1.)   The following authorities are responsible for the preparation and conduct of defense on coasts under German control:

a) in the Eastern Theater of Operations (excluding Finland), the army commanders designated by OKH;

b) in the coastal sector under the control of Army Lapland, the Commanding General of Army Lapland;

c) in Norway, the Armed Forces Commander, Norway;

d) in Denmark, the Commander of German Troops in Denmark;

e) in the occupied West (including the Netherlands), the Commander in Chief West;

In matters pertaining to coastal defense, the commanders mentioned in categories d) and e) above are under the direct control of OKW.

f) in the Balkans (including the occupied islands), the Armed Forces Commander Southeast;

g) in the Baltic and the Ukraine, the Armed Forces Commanders Baltic and Ukraine;

h) in the Zone of Interior, the commanding admirals.

2.)   Within the framework of coastal defense missions, the commanders designated in III.) 1.) above, will have command authority over tactical headquarters of the services, the German civil authorities as well as units and organizations outside of the armed forces that are located within their respective areas. In exercising that authority, the commanders will issue tactical, organizational, and supply orders necessary for coastal defense, and insure their execution. They will influence training to whatever extent is necessary for preparing their forces for ground operations. The required data will be put at their disposal.

3.) Orders and measures implementing this directive will give priority to the following:

a) inclusion within fortified areas or strongpoints of all installations important militarily or to the war economy, particularly those of the Navy (submarine bases) and the Luftwaffe;

b) unified direction of coastal surveillance;

c) infantry defenses of fortified areas and strongpoints;

d) infantry defenses of isolated installations outside of fortified areas and strongpoints, such as coastal patrol and aircraft warning stations;

e) artillery defenses against ground targets (in installing new shore batteries and displacing those in position, the requirements of naval warfare will receive priority);

f) defense preparedness of fortified establishments, their structural improvement, and the stockpiling of reserve supplies, as well as defensive preparedness and stockpiling of supplies in isolated installations outside of those establishments (including supply with all weapons necessary for defense, mines, hand grenades, flame throwers, obstacle material, and similar items);

g) signal communications;

h) tests of the state of alert as well as infantry and artillery training within the framework of the defensive missions.

4.) Similar authority will be vested in the commanders of local headquarters down to sector commands, insofar as they have been made responsible for the defense of coastal sectors.

The commanders enumerated in III.) 1.) above, will generally confer such responsibilities on commanding generals of army divisions that are committed for coastal defense, and in Crete, on the Fortress Commander Crete.

In individual sectors and subsectors, and particularly in establishments that have definitely been designated as air or naval bases, the local Luftwaffe or Navy commanders are to be put in charge of the entire defense, insofar as their other missions permit them to assume those responsibilities.

5.) Naval and strategic air forces are subject to the control of the Navy or Luftwaffe, respectively. However, in case of enemy attacks on the coast they are— within the framework of their tactical capabilities—bound to comply with requests from the commanders responsible for defensive operations. For that reason they must be included in the exchange of military intelligence, in preparation for their future employment. Close contact must be maintained with their respective higher headquarters.

IV.) Special missions of the several services within the framework of coastal defense:

1.) Navy:

a) organization and protection of coastwise shipping;

   b) training and commitment of the entire coastal artillery against sea targets;

   c) commitment of naval forces.

   2.) Luftwaffe:

   a) air defense in the coastal areas.

   This mission does not affect the right of local defense commanders to direct the assembly of Flak artillery suited and available for commitment against enemy invasion forces.

   b) improvement of the Luftwaffe ground organization and its protection against air and surprise ground attacks on airfields that have not been sufficiently protected by their inclusion in the coastal defense system.

   c) commitment of strategic air forces.

   Instances of overlapping control resulting from those special missions must be accepted as unavoidable.

V.) As of 1 April 1942, all instructions and orders not in agreement with the present directive are rescinded.

   New combat directives issued by the responsible commander pursuant to my directive will be submitted to me through OKW.

                                                    signed: Adolf Hitler

Appendix D

Fuehrer Headquarters
3 November 1943

Top Secret

The Fuehrer
OKW/WFSt/Op.No. 662656/43 g.K. Chefs

27 Copies
Copy No. ...

Directive No. 51

For the last two and one-half years the bitter and costly struggle against Bolshevism has made the utmost demands upon the bulk of our military resources and energies. This commitment was in keeping with the seriousness of the danger, and the over-all situation. The situation has since changed. The threat from the East remains, but an even greater danger looms in the West: the Anglo-American landing! In the East, the vastness of the space will, as a last resort, permit a loss of territory even on a major scale, without suffering a mortal blow to Germany's chance for survival.

Not so in the West! If the enemy here succeeds in penetrating our defenses on a wide front, consequences of staggering proportions will follow within a short time. All signs point to an offensive against the Western Front of Europe no later than spring, and perhaps earlier.

For that reason, I can no longer justify the further weakening of the West in favor of other theaters of war. I have therefore decided to strengthen the defenses in the West, particularly at places from which we shall launch our long-range war against England. For those are the very points at which the enemy must and will attack; there—unless all indications are misleading—will be fought the decisive invasion battle.

Holding attacks and diversions on other fronts are to be expected. Not even the possibility of a large-scale offensive against Denmark may be excluded. It would pose greater nautical problems and could be less effectively supported from the air, but would nevertheless produce the greatest political and strategic impact if it were to succeed.

During the opening phase of the battle, the entire striking power of the enemy will of necessity be directed against our forces manning the coast. Only an all-out effort in the construction of fortifications, an unsurpassed effort that will enlist all available manpower and physical resources of Germany and the occupied areas, will be able to strengthen our defenses along the coasts within the short time that still appears to be left to us.

Stationary weapons (heavy AT guns, immobile tanks to be dug-in, coast artillery, shore-defense guns, mines, etc.) arriving in Denmark and the occupied

West within the near future will be heavily concentrated in points of main defensive effort at the most vulnerable coastal sectors. At the same time, we must take the calculated risk that for the present we may be unable to improve our defenses in less threatened sectors.

Should the enemy nevertheless force a landing by concentrating his armed might, he must be hit by the full fury of our counterattack. For this mission ample and speedy reinforcements of men and materiel, as well as intensive training must transform available larger units into first-rate, fully mobile general reserves suitable for offensive operations. The counterattack of these units will prevent the enlargement of the beachhead, and throw the enemy back into the sea.

In addition, well-planned emergency measures, prepared down to the last detail, must enable us instantly to throw against the invader every fit man and machine from coastal sectors not under attack and from the home front.

The anticipated strong attacks by air and sea must be relentlessly countered by Air Force and Navy with all their available resources. I therefore order the following:

A) Army:

1.) The Chief of the Army General Staff and the Inspector General of Panzer Troops will submit to me as soon as possible a schedule covering arms, tanks, assault guns, motor vehicles, and ammunition to be allocated to the Western Front and Denmark within the next three months. That schedule will conform to the new situation. The following considerations will be basic:

a) Sufficient mobility for all panzer and panzer grenadier divisions in the West, and equipment of each of those units by December 1943 with 93 Mark IV tanks or assault guns, as well as large numbers of antitank weapons.

Accelerated reorganization of the 20 Luftwaffe Field Divisions into an effective mobile reserve force by the end of 1943. This reorganization is to include the issue of assault guns.

Accelerated issue of all authorized weapons to the SS Panzer Grenadier Division Hitler Jugend,* the 21st Panzer Division, and the infantry and reserve divisions stationed in Jutland.

b) Additional shipments of Mark IV tanks, assault guns, and heavy AT guns to the reserve panzer divisions stationed in the West and in Denmark, as well as to the Assault Gun Training Battalion in Denmark.

c) In November and December, monthly allotments of 100 heavy AT guns models 40 and 43 (half of these to be mobile) in addition to those required for newly activated units in the West and in Denmark.

d) Allotment of large numbers of weapons (including about 1,000 machine guns) for augmenting the armament of those static divisions that are committed for coastal defense in the West and in Denmark, and for standardizing the equipment of elements that are to be withdrawn from sectors not under attack.

---

* In this month (November 1943) this division was converted to a Panzer division *(12th SS)*.

e) Ample supply of close-combat AT weapons to units in vulnerable sectors.

f) Improvement of artillery and AT defenses in units stationed in Denmark, as well as those committed for coastal protection in the occupied West. Strengthening of GHQ artillery.

2.) The units and elements stationed in the West or in Denmark, as well as panzer, assault gun, and AT units to be activated in the West, must not be transferred to other fronts without my permission. The Chief of the Army General Staff, or the Inspector General of Panzer Troops will submit to me a report through the Armed Forces Operations Staff as soon as the issue of equipment to the panzer and assault gun battalions, as well as to the AT battalions and companies, has been completed.

3.) Beyond similar measures taken in the past, the Commander in Chief West will establish timetables for, and conduct maneuvers and command post exercises on, the procedure for bringing up units from sectors not under attack. These units will be made capable of performing offensive missions, however limited. In that connection I demand that sectors not threatened by the enemy be ruthlessly stripped of all forces except small guard detachments. For sectors from which reserves are withdrawn, security and guard detachments must be set aside from security and alarm units. Labor forces drawn largely from the native population must likewise be organized in those sectors, in order to keep open whatever roads might be destroyed by the enemy air force.

4.) The Commander of German Troops in Denmark will take measures in the area under his control in compliance with paragraph 3 above.

5.) Pursuant to separate orders, the Chief of Army Equipment and Commander of the Replacement Army will form Kampfgruppen in regimental strength, security battalions, and engineer construction battalions from training cadres, trainees, schools, and instruction and convalescent units in the Zone of the Interior. These troops must be ready for shipment on 48 hours' notice.

Furthermore, other available personnel are to be organized into battalions of replacements and equipped with the available weapons, so that the anticipated heavy losses can quickly be replaced.

B) Luftwaffe:

The offensive and defensive effectiveness of Luftwaffe units in the West and in Denmark will be increased to meet the changed situation. To that end, preparations will be made for the release of units suited for commitment in the anti-invasion effort, that is, all flying units and mobile Flak artillery that can be spared from the air defenses of the home front, and from schools and training units in the Zone of the Interior. All those units are to be earmarked for the West and possibly Denmark.

The Luftwaffe ground organization in southern Norway, Denmark, northwestern Germany, and the West will be expanded and supplied in a way that will —by the most far-reaching decentralization of own forces—deny targets to the enemy bombers, and split the enemy's offensive effort in case of large-scale operations. Particularly important in that connection will be our fighter forces. Possibilities for their commitment must be increased by the establishment of numerous advance landing fields. Special emphasis is to be placed on good camouflage. I expect also that the Luftwaffe will unstintingly furnish all available forces, by stripping them from less threatened areas.

C) Navy:

The Navy will prepare the strongest possible forces suitable for attacking the enemy landing fleets. Coastal defense installations in the process of construction will be completed with the utmost speed. The emplacing of additional coastal batteries and the possibility of laying further flanking mine fields should be investigated.

All school, training, and other shore-based personnel fit for ground combat must be prepared for commitment so that, without undue delay, they can at least be employed as security forces within the zone of the enemy landing operations.

While preparing the reinforcement of the defenses in the West, the Navy must keep in mind that it might be called upon to repulse simultaneous enemy landings in Norway and Denmark. In that connection, I attach particular importance to the assembly of numerous U-boats in the northern area. A temporary weakening of U-boat forces in the Atlantic must be risked.

D) SS:

The Reichsfuehrer-SS will determine what Waffen-SS and police forces he can release for combat, security, and guard duty. He is to prepare to organize effective combat and security forces from training, replacement, and convalescent units, as well as schools and other home-front establishments.

E) The commanders in chief of the services, the Reichsfuehrer-SS, the Chief of the Army General Staff, the Commander in Chief West, the Chief of Army Equipment and Commander of the Replacement Army, the Inspector General of Panzer Troops, as well as the Commander of German Troops in Denmark will report to me by 15 November all measures taken or planned.

I expect that all agencies will make a supreme effort toward utilizing every moment of the remaining time in preparing for the decisive battle in the West.

All authorities will guard against wasting time and energy in useless jurisdictional squabbles, and will direct all their efforts toward strengthening our defensive and offensive power.

signed: Adolf Hitler

Appendix E

CHRONOLOGY OF MAIN PLANNING PAPERS FROM 1 JANUARY 1944

Date	Hq	Paper
31 Jan	FUSA	Planning Directive for OVERLORD
1 Feb	Joint Commanders	NEPTUNE, Initial Joint Plan
4 Feb	Second Army (Br)	Outline Plan
10 Feb	TF 122, FUSA	Joint Agreement for Amphibious Operations
12 Feb	V Corps	Preliminary 'OVERLORD' Plan
25 Feb	FUSA	Operations Plan NEPTUNE
28 Feb	V Corps	Planning Guide, Operation "OVERLORD"
28 Feb	ANCXF	Operation "NEPTUNE"—Naval Plan*
7 Mar	21 A Gp	Directive to FUSAG
10 Mar	SHAEF	Directive to 21 A Gp, AEAF, ANCXF
20 Mar	Second Army, 83 Group (2d TAF)	Joint Plan
26 Mar	V Corps	NEPTUNE Plan
27 Mar	VII Corps	Plan of Operation, NEPTUNE
8 Apr	21 A Gp, ANCXF	NEPTUNE Joint Fire Plan
10 Apr	ANCXF	Operation NEPTUNE—Naval Orders (ON)
15 Apr	AEAF	Operation NEPTUNE—Overall Air Plan
16 Apr	1st Div	Field Order No. 35
21 Apr	WNTF	Operation Plan No. 2–44 (ONWEST 2)†
24 Apr	War Office	Movement Plan
28 Apr	21 A Gp	Amended Directive to FUSAG
1 May	ANCXF	Amendment No. 1 to ON
2 May	Ninth AF	IX Tactical Air Command Plan for Operation NEPTUNE
6 May	82d Abn Div	Field Order No. 6
8 May	FUSAG, 9th AF, WNTF	Joint Operations Plan, U.S. Forces for Operation OVERLORD (Revised)
9 May	VII Corps	Field Order No. 1
12 May	4th Div	Field Order No. 1
15 May	Assault Force U	Operation Order No. 3–44— (ONWEST/U–3)‡

* Superseded by Operation NEPTUNE—Naval Orders (ON). All copies ordered destroyed.
† Changes of 4, 10, and 22 May and addenda of 29–31 May.
‡ Changes of 30 May and 1 June.

18 May	V Corps	Letter of Instruction, Amending NEP-TUNE Plan
18 May	101st Abn Div	Field Order No. 1
20 May	Assault Force O	Operation Order No. BB–44 (ON-WEST/O)
27 May	FUSA	Revision No. 2 to Annex 12 (Fire Support)
28 May	82d Abn Div	Revision of Field Order No. 6
28 May	VII Corps	Field Order No. 1 (Corrected Copy)

Appendix F

COMPARATIVE FIRE POWER OF THE U.S. AND GERMAN 1944-TYPE INFANTRY DIVISIONS

	U.S.	German 1944
Strength (officers and enlisted men)	14,037	12,769
Rifles–carbines	11,507	9,069
Pistols	1,228	1,981
Submachine guns	295	1,503
Light MG's and automatic rifles	539	566
Heavy MG's	90	90
60-mm. mortars	90	—
81-mm. mortars	54	48
120-mm. mortars	—	28
Bazookas	558*	108†
Flame throwers	—	20
U.S. .50-cal. MG's; German 20-mm. AA guns	237	12
37-mm. AT guns	13	—
57-mm. AT guns	57	—
75-mm. AT guns	—	35
75-mm. infantry howitzers	—	18
105-mm. howitzers	54‡	36
U.S. 155-mm. howitzers; German 150-mm. howitzers	12	18§

*Also had 2,131 rifle grenade launchers.
†Either bazookas or antitank rifles.
‡Eighteen were found in the cannon companies of the infantry regiments.
§Six were infantry howitzers, two in an infantry howitzer company assigned to each infantry regiment. Each howitzer company had, in addition, six 75-mm. howitzers.

Appendix G

Theater	Inf type	Pz type	Misc
Denmark	2	1+ 2 Brig	3
Norway	11		
Finland	10		
Eastern Front	122	25+ 1 Brig	17+ 1 Brig
OB SUEDOST (Balkans)	20	2	3
OB SUEDWEST (Italy)	17+ 1 Brig	7	1
OB WEST (France and Low Countries)	41+ 1 Rgt	11	9
Zone of Interior	3+ 1 Brig	1+ 2 Brig	4+ 2 Brig
TOTAL GERMAN DIVISIONS	226+ 2 Brig 1 Rgt	47+ 5 Brig	37+ 3 Brig
AXIS SATELLITES			
Finnish, Eastern Front and Finland	14+ 8 Brig	1	1 Brig
Românian, Eastern Front and România	17+ 5 Brig	1	2
Hungarian, Eastern Front and Hungary	9+ 3 Brig	2	5
Bulgarian, Occupation Duty in Balkans and Bulgaria	11		
Italian, In Zone of Interior	4		
TOTAL AXIS SATELLITE DIVISIONS	55+ 16 Brig	4	7+ 1 Brig

Appendix H
Table of Equivalent Ranks

U.S. Army	German Army and Air Force	German Waffen–SS
None	Reichsmarschall	None
General of the Army	Generalfeldmarschall	Reichsfuehrer-SS
General	Generaloberst	Oberstgruppenfuehrer
Lieutenant General	General der Infanterie	Obergruppenfuehrer
	Artillerie	
	Gebirgstruppen	
	Kavallerie	
	Nachrichtentruppen	
	Panzertruppen	
	Pioniere	
	Luftwaffe	
	Flieger	
	Fallschirmtruppen	
	Flakartillerie	
	Luftnachrichtentruppen	
Major General	Generalleutnant	Gruppenfuehrer
Brigadier General	Generalmajor	Brigadefuehrer
None	None	Oberfuehrer
Colonel	Oberst	Standartenfuehrer
Lieutenant Colonel	Oberstleutnant	Obersturmbannfuehrer
Major	Major	Sturmbannfuehrer
Captain	Hauptmann	Hauptsturmfuehrer
Captain (Cavalry)	Rittmeister	
First Lieutenant	Oberleutnant	Obersturmfuehrer
Second Lieutenant	Leutnant	Untersturmfuehrer

Appendix I

Recipients of the Distinguished Service Cross

All pertinent Army records have been scrutinized in the endeavor to include in the following list the name of every soldier that received the DSC for his part in the operations recounted in this volume. Inasmuch as no complete listing of DSC awards is maintained in any single Army file, it is possible that some names may inadvertently have been omitted. (P) indicates a posthumous award.

Alexander, S/Sgt. Paul E. (P)
Amerman, 2d Lt. Walter G.
Anderson, 2d Lt. William A.
Anker, 2d Lt. Leonard A.
Appleby, T/4 Stanley P.
Armellino, Capt. John R.
Armstrong, T/Sgt. L. M.
Arnold, Capt. Edgar L.
Atchley, Pvt. John E.
Atwell, T/4 Daniel E.
Bailey, Maj. Woodrow W.
Baker, Pvt. Odell
Barba, Cpl. James N.
Barber, Pfc. Alexander W.
Barcellona, 2d Lt. Gaetano R.
Beavers, 1st Lt. Harold R.
Beitler, Capt. Kenneth E.
Belcher, Sgt. Julius W.
Benn, T/Sgt. William R., Jr.
Bennet, Lt. Col. Donald V.
Benton, S/Sgt. John L.
Berkowitz, Pfc. Henry
Bingham, Maj. Sidney V.
Bleau, 2d Lt. Kenneth (P)
Bolderson, Pfc. John D.
Bowen, Pfc. George H.
Briggs, Capt. Victor H.
Brooks, 1st Lt. Elton E.
Burgin, Pfc. James F.

Buschlen, Sgt. Arthur B. (P)
Canham, Col. Charles D. W.
Cassidy, Sgt. O'Dell K.
Cassidy, Lt. Col. Patrick F.
Cavalierre, Pvt. Peter
Chase, S/Sgt. Donald L.
Chesnut, 1st Lt. Webb W.
Clark, S/Sgt. Philip C.
Clarke, Pvt. James A.
Clayman, Lt. Col. Donald C.
Coffman, S/Sgt. Ralph S.
Colson, Sgt. Clarence
Colwell, S/Sgt. Curtis
Cordes, Pvt. Herman J. (P)
Cota, Brig. Gen. Norman D.
Cotter, Capt. John J.
Courtney, Sgt. William J.
Curtis, T/Sgt. Earl R.
Cutler, 1st Lt. Robert R.
Danforth, Cpl. Vergial E.
Dawson, 1st Lt. Francis W.
Dawson, Capt. Joseph T.
Deery, T/5 John F.
Dickinson, Pfc. Byron B.
Dillon, 1st Lt. William T.
Ditullio, Pfc. Dominick
Dock, T/4 Lowell L.
Dove, Pvt. Vinton W.
Dowdy, Lt. Col. John (P)
Dreher, Pfc. William E., Jr.
Dulin, Lt. Col. Thaddeus R. (P)
Earl, Sgt. Thomas R.
Eberle, 1st Lt. George M.
Eddy, Maj. Gen. Manton S.
Elder, Pfc. Leonard P.
Elder, Capt. Ned S.
Ellis, T/Sgt. Calvin L.
Ernest, Capt. Charles A., III
Evans, 2d Lt. William M. (P)
Fair, 1st Lt. DeWitt C., Sr.
Ferguson, 2d Lt. Forest K.

Fitzsimmons, 1st Sgt. Lawrence
Fleishman, Pfc. Ward D. (P)
Fournier, Pfc. Edgar L.
Fryer, Pvt. Gibson
Gallagher, Pfc. Richard J.
Ganabrant, Capt. John R. (P)
Gandara, Pvt. Joe
Gavin, Brig. Gen. James M.
Gearing, 1st Lt. Edward N.
George, Capt. Malcolm L. (P)
Gettman, T/5 John
Gibbs, Lt. Col. George W.
Giles, 1st Lt. Carl K.
Glider, 2d Lt. Joseph
Goranson, Capt. Ralph E.
Gowdy, 1st Lt. George H.
Graff, 1st Lt. Elmer W.
Griffin, Pfc. Harry E.
Griffin, Pfc. John V.
Habib, Sgt. George A.
Haley, Capt. James W.
Hall, Pfc. Henry H. (P)
Hannum, 1st Lt. Craig B. (P)
Harbauga, Pvt. Francis L.
Hargrove, 1st Lt. Robert C.
Harris, 1st Lt. Ernest O. (P)
Harrison, Sgt. Bailey
Harrison, Maj. Willard E.
Hartman, T/5 Harry
Heenan, Pfc. John R.
Heim, Pvt. Marcus
Henderson, T/Sgt. Gerald M. (P)
Henshan, 1st Lt. Robert E.
Hicks, Lt. Col. Herbert C.
Horan, 2d Lt. Roger J.
Houston, Sgt. Robert J.
Isley, Lt. Col. Carl J.
Jackson, Lt. Col. Charles L.
Jenkins, S/Sgt. Floyd M.
Jewett, Maj. Milton A.
Johnson, Sgt. Denziel O.
Johnson, Col. Howard R. (P)
Jones, Pfc. Aaron B.
Jones, 1st Lt. Charles H. (P)
Jones, 1st Lt. Henry W.
Katsoulakos, Pvt. William (P)
Kehaly, 1st Lt. William J.
Kelly, Cpl. John D. (P)
Kerchner, 2d Lt. George F.
Kidwell, Pvt. Kenneth P.
Kirby, T/5 Varsel (P)

Kolodziek, Pfc. Frank S. (P)
Krause, Lt. Col. Edward C.
Kulp, Capt. John A.
Lacy, 1st Lt. Joseph R.
Langen, T/4 Robert F.
Lanterman, 1st Lt. Raymond E.
Larson, T/Sgt. Donald W.
Lee, Capt. Gail B.
Leino, Pvt. Loyd J.
Lillyman, Capt. Frank
Lockwood, Pvt. John A.
Lomell, 1st Sgt. Leonard G.
Lovell, Sgt. Warden F.
Lutz, Pvt. Frederick P.
Mabry, Capt. George L., Jr.
MacConchie, 1st Lt. Howard P.
MacNeely, Lt. Col. Carlton O.
Mager, 2d Lt. Irvin A. (P)
Maloney, Lt. Col. Arthur A.
Maloney, Capt. John S.
Mansfield, S/Sgt. Paul F.
Marez, Pvt. Joe M.
Masny, Capt. Otto
Mayor, Pvt. Arthur C.
McElyea, 2d Lt. Atwood M.
McKissick, T/5 Howard D.
McLaren, Pvt. Donald B.
Meredith, S/Sgt. Iral (P)
Merendino, Capt. Thomas N.
Millener, Lt. Col. Raymond D.
Miller, 1st Lt. Jesse R.
Miller, Pfc. Milan M. (P)
Mitman, T/Sgt. Erwin F.
Montilio, Cpl. George
Moody, 1st Lt. William D. (P)
Moody, Sgt. Willie W.
Morse, 1st Lt. Verne V.
Mullins, Lt. Col. Thornton L. (P)
Murrin, S/Sgt. Richard C.
Nash, Pfc. Freeman J.
Nicoli, Sgt. Raymond E.
Nothel, Sgt. Henry V.
O'Brien, Capt. Thomas F.
Odom, 1st Sgt. Hubert
O'Donnell, Sgt. Francis C.
Ogden, 1st Lt. Carlos C.
O'Neill, Lt. Col. John T.
Orndorff, Sgt. Douglas
Ostberg, Lt. Col. Edwin J.
Panas, 1st Lt. James P.
Paolini, Pfc. Camillus J.

Parke, Pvt. Joseph P.
Parker, 1st Lt. Charles H.
Patch, Capt. Lloyd E.
Patterson, S/Sgt. Lyman K.
Pellarine, 2d Lt. John J. (P)
Pence, Capt. James L.
Perehinec, S/Sgt. Joseph P. (P)
Perry, Capt. Edwin R.
Peterson, S/Sgt. Gerard B.
Peterson, Sgt. Kenneth F.
Peterson, Pfc. Lenold C.
Peterson, Pfc. Victor E. (P)
Philips, Capt. Vodra C.
Porter, Pvt. Benton L.
Pressley, 1st Sgt. William M.
Profit, T/Sgt. Carl D.
Pryne, Pfc. Gordon
Purvis, S/Sgt. Darvin D.
Radford, S/Sgt. David N.
Rae, Capt. Robert D.
Ralston, Capt. Emerald M.
Rebarchek, 1st Lt. John C.
Reckford, Capt. John G. (P)
Reed, 2d Lt. Richard N.
Reeder, Col. Russell P., Jr.
Richards, Maj. William A. (P)
Richmond, Capt. Kimball R.
Riggs, Pfc. William C.
Ridgway, Maj. Gen. Matthew B.
Ritter, T/Sgt. Ozias C.
Roach, T/Sgt. John A.
Roberts, Cpl. Ernest T.
Roberts, 2d Lt. Eskoll F.
Robinson, T/4 Earl A.
Robinson, 1st Lt. James L. (P)
Rogers, T/Sgt. Howard W.
Rogers, Pfc. Lee N.
Rosemond, Capt. St. Julien P.
Rosen, Pfc. Sanford
Ross, 1st Lt. Robert P.
Ross, 2d Lt. Wesley R.
Ruby, 2d Lt. Clarence T.
Rudd, T/5 Jack L.
Rudder, Lt. Col. James E.
Samuels, Maj. Joseph T.
Santarsiero, 2d Lt. Charles J.
Savino, T/5 Felice J.
Schneider, S/Sgt. George
Schneider, Lt. Col. Max F.
Scoroposki, 1st Sgt. Felix
Sefchick, S/Sgt. Joseph F.

Settineri, Capt. John
Shaffer, T/5 Edward
Shelby, 1st Lt. John D.
Shindle, T/4 Elmer G.
Shoemaker, Pvt. William J.
Shorter, S/Sgt. Paul R.
Skaggs, Lt. Col. Robert N.
Smith, Pvt. Gerald E. (P)
Smulik, T/4 Bolick
Soliz, S/Sgt. Marcelo M.
Songer, 1st Lt. Francis E.
Sosnack, Pvt. Andrew
Spaulding, 2d Lt. John M.
Sprecher, 1st Sgt. Kenneth N.
Sproul, Capt. Archibald
Steiner, Lt. Col. Fred A. (P)
Stephens, Pfc. Otto K.
Stockwell, S/Sgt. Leeward W.
Streczyk, Sgt. Phillip
Strojny, S/Sgt. Raymond F.
Sullivan, Maj. Richard P.
Summers, S/Sgt. Harrison C.
Sweeney, Pfc. Lawrence G.
Synowsky, 1st Lt. John
Talley, Col. Benjamin B.
Taylor, Col. George A.
Taylor, Maj. Gen. Maxwell D.
Teague, Lt. Col. Arthur S. T.
Tegtmeyer, Maj. Charles E.
Thompson, Col. Paul W.
Townsend, 2d Lt. John N.
Tubbs, 1st Sgt. Herbert A.
Tucker, Pvt. Albert J.
Turner, Lt. Col. William L. (P)
Upham, Lt. Col. John S., Jr.
Urish, Sgt. Joseph W.
Vandervoort, Lt. Col. Benjamin H.
Van De Voort, Ist Lt. Leo D.
Van Fleet, Col. James A.
Van Valkenburg, Pvt. John J.
Wade, S/Sgt. John E. (P)
Washington, Maj. William R.
Weathers, Capt. Omery C. (P)
Welborn, Lt. Col. John C.
Wells, S/Sgt. James A.
Werner, 1st Lt. Carlton G. (P)
Wetherholt, Pfc. Lee, Jr.
White, T/Sgt. John W.
Whittington, Capt. George P.
Wilk, Pfc. Theodore T.

Williams, 1st Lt. Alfred H., Jr.
Winters, 1st Lt. Richard D.
Woelfel, Pfc. Earl L.
Woodward, Capt. Robert W.
Woodward, Pfc. Russell H.
Wozenski, Capt. Edward F.

Wray, 1st Lt. Waverley W.
Wyman, Brig. Gen. Willard G.
Zahn, Sgt. Donald E.
Zantow, Capt. Forrest
Zeigler, 1st Lt. Harvey J.
Zwingman, Pvt. Otto K.

Appendix J

Basic Military Map Symbols*

Symbols within a rectangle indicate a military unit, within a triangle an observation post, and within a circle a supply point.

Military Units—Identification

Antiaircraft Artillery . . . .

Armored Command . . . .

Army Air Forces . . . .

Artillery, except Antiaircraft and Coast Artillery . . . .

Cavalry, Horse . . . .

Cavalry, Mechanized . . . .

Chemical Warfare Service . . . .

Coast Artillery . . . .

Engineers . . . .

Infantry . . . .

Medical Corps . . . .

Ordnance Department . . . .

Quartermaster Corps . . . .

Signal Corps . . . .

Tank Destroyer . . . .

Transportation Corps . . . .

Veterinary Corps . . . .

Airborne units are designated by combining a gull wing symbol with the arm or service symbol:

Airborne Artillery . . . .

Airborne Infantry . . . .

*For complete listing of symbols see FM 21–30, from which these are taken.

Size Symbols

The following symbols placed either in boundary lines or above the rectangle, triangle, or circle inclosing the identifying arm or service symbol indicate the size of military organization:

Squad . . . . •

Section . . . . ••

Platoon . . . . •••

Company, troop, battery, Air Force flight I

Battalion, cavalry squadron, or Air Force squadron II

Regiment or group; combat team (with abbreviation CT following identifying numeral) III

Brigade, Combat Command of Armored Division, or Air Force Wing . X

Division or Command of an Air Force XX

Corps or Air Force XXX

Army XXXX

Group of Armies XXXXX

EXAMPLES

The letter or number to the left of the symbol indicates the unit designation; that to the right, the designation of the parent unit to which it belongs. Letters or numbers above or below boundary lines designate the units separated by the lines:

Company A, 137th Infantry . . . . A⊠137

8th Field Artillery Battalion . . . . ⊡8

Combat Command A, 1st Armored Division . . . . A⬭1

Observation Post, 23d Infantry . . . . △23

Command Post, 5th Infantry Division . . . . ⊠5

Boundary between 137th and 138th Infantry . . . . . —|||— 137/138

Weapons

Machine gun . . . . →

Gun . . . . •

Gun battery . . . . ⊔⊔⊔

Howitzer or Mortar . . . . ◆

Tank . . . . ◇

Self-propelled gun . . . . ◨

Glossary

A–2	Intelligence section of air staff
AAF	Army Air Forces
AAR	After action report
ABDA area	American-British-Dutch-Australian theater of war covering area from Bay of Bengal to Australasia
Abn	Airborne
AC	Air Corps
ACofAS	Assistant Chief of Air Staff
Admiral Kanalkueste	Admiral commanding Channel coast naval district
AF	Air Force
AEAF	Allied Expeditionary Air Force
AFHQ	Allied Force Headquarters
AGWAR	Adjutant General, War Department
A Gp	Army group
AKA	Cargo Ship, Attack
Amph	Amphibious
ANCXF	Allied Naval Commander Expeditionary Force
ANFA	Hotel at Casablanca at which plenary meetings were held in January 1943
Anlage	Appendix or annex
APA	Transport Ship, Attack
l'Armée Secrète	Secret army formed by officers and men of the French Regular Army
ASW	Assistant Secretary of War
BAR	Browning Automatic Rifle
Bazooka	Rocket launcher, hand-carried
BCRA	*Bureau Central de Renseignements et d'Action* (Central Intelligence and Operations Bureau)
Belgian Gate	Barricade-like gates used as underwater obstacles
Bn	Battalion
bodenstaendig	Static (division)
Br	British; branch
Bull	Bulletin
CC	Combined Commanders
CCA	Combat Command A
CCS	Combined Chiefs of Staff
CG	Commanding General
CinC	Commander in Chief

CO	Commanding Officer
COA	Committee of Operations Analysts
CofS	Chief of Staff
COHQ	Combined Operations Headquarters
Comdr	Commander
Commandos	Specially trained British assault troops
Concertina wire	Cylindrical portable barbed wire entanglement
le Conseil National de la Résistance	National Council of Resistance
Corncobs	Blockships
COS	British Chiefs of Staff
Cosintrep	Combined situation and intelligence report
COSSAC	Chief of Staff to the Supreme Allied Commander (Designate)
CPS	Combined Planning Staff
DBST	Double British Summer Time
DD	Duplex Drive amphibious tank
D Day	The first day of any military operation, specifically the day OVERLORD was launched
DSC	Distinguished Service Cross
DSO	Distinguished Service Order
DUKW	2½-ton, 6x6 amphibious truck
E-boat	Small German torpedo boat (German *S-Boot*)
Ersatzheer	German Replacement Army
ETO	European Theater of Operations
ETOUSA	European Theater of Operations, United States Army
FA	Field Artillery
FFI	*Forces Françaises de l'Intérieur* (French Forces of the Interior)
Flak	Antiaircraft
FO	Field Order
Francs Tireurs et Partisans	French communist resistance group
Freiwillige	Volunteers
Fuesilier battalion	Separate infantry and reconnaissance battalion in the German 1944-type division
FUSA	First United States Army
FUSAG	First United States Army Group
G–1	Personnel section of divisional or higher staff
G–2	Intelligence section
G–3	Operations section
G–4	Supply section
Geschwader	Luftwaffe wing

GHQ	General headquarters
Gkdo.	*Generalkommando* (German corps-type headquarters)
GO	General Order
Grossadmiral	Grand-Admiral
Hedgehog	Portable obstacle, made of three crossed angle irons
Hilfswillige	Volunteer Auxiliaries (non-German)
Hornets	88-mm. self-propelled antitank guns
Int sum	Intelligence summary
Jaeger (division or other unit)	Light infantry (division or other unit)
JB	Joint Board
JCS	Joint Chiefs of Staff
Jedburgh teams	Three-man inter-Allied teams, parachuted into French territory to act as liaison between the maquis groups and SHAEF
JIC	Joint Intelligence Committee
JPS	Joint Planning Staff
JSM	Joint Staff Mission
JSSC	Joint Strategic Survey Committee
JWPC	Joint War Plans Committee
Kampffuehrung	Conduct of operations
Kampfgruppe	A term loosely assigned to improvised combat units of various sizes, named usually after their commanders
KMA	German coastal mine
KTB	*Kriegstagebuch* (war diary)
Landesschuetzen battalion	Home Guard battalion sometimes employed outside Germany
Landfront	Landward fortifications of Cherbourg
Landwirt submarines	Submarines of *"Group Landwirt,"* a special anti-invasion force of thirty-six small U-boats
LCA	Landing Craft, Assault
LCG	Landing Craft, Gun
LCI	Landing Craft, Infantry
LCM	Landing Craft, Mechanized
LCT	Landing Craft, Tank
LCT (R)	Landing Craft, Tank (Rocket)
LCVP	Landing Craft, Vehicle and Personnel
LSH	Landing Ship, Headquarters
LST	Landing Ship, Tank
Luftflotte Reich	German Home Air Command
Luftgaukommando Westfrankreich	Headquarters of the Luftwaffe administrative and supply organization in western France
Luftwaffe	German Air Force
Maquisards	Men of the maquis

Mark III, IV	German medium tanks
Mark V	German medium tank with heavy armor and high-velocity gun
Merkbuch	Notebook
Militaerbefehlshaber	Military governor
MLR	Main Line of Resistance
MRU	Machine Records Unit
MS-Flotilla	German mine sweepers
Nebelwerfer	Rocket projector or chemical mortar
OB SUED	*Oberbefehlshaber Sued,* German theater headquarters in Italy
OB WEST	*Oberbefehlshaber West,* Highest German ground headquarters of the Western Front
OKH	*Oberkommando des Heeres* (Army High Command)
OKL	*Oberkommando der Luftwaffe* (Luftwaffe High Command)
OKM	*Oberkommando der Kriegsmarine* (Navy High Command)
OKW	*Oberkommando der Wehrmacht* (Armed Forces High Command)
ONI	Office of Naval Intelligence
OPD	Operations Division, War Department General Staff
Opns	Operations
Org. Abt.	*Organisations Abteilung* (Staff subdivision in charge of organization)
Organization Todt	Paramilitary construction organization of the Nazi party, auxiliary to the Wehrmacht. Named after its founder, Dr. Todt.
OSS	Office of Strategic Services
Ost	East
Osttruppen	Non-German volunteer troops from east-European countries
Panther	German Mark V tank
Per Rpt	Periodic report
Plan Tortue	Resistance plan to block road traffic
Plan Vert	Resistance plan to cut railroads
POD	Plans and Operations Division
RAF	Royal Air Force
Rangers	Specially trained American assault troops
Rhino ferry	Barge constructed of ponton units
RN	Royal Navy
S–1	Personnel section of regimental or lower staff
SAC	Supreme Allied Commander
SAS	Special Air Service

S-Boot	E-boat
SCAEF	Supreme Commander, Allied Expeditionary Force
SF	Special Force
SFHQ	Special Force Headquarters
SGS	Secretary General Staff
SHAEF	Supreme Headquarters, Allied Expeditionary Force
SIS	Special Intelligence Service
Sitrep	Situation report
SNCF	*Société Nationale des Chemins de Fer* (National French railroad system)
SO	Special Operations
SOE	Special Operations Executive
SPOBS	Special Observers
SS	*Schutzstaffel* (Elite Guard)
Stuetzpunkt	Strong point
Teller mines	German antitank mines
Tetrahedra	Pyramid-shaped steel antitank obstacles
TF	Task Force
Tiger	German Mark VI tank
Tk Bn	Tank Battalion
TM	Technical Manual
T/O	Table of Organization
UK	United Kingdom
USA	United States Army
USAFBI	United States Army Forces in the British Isles
USN	United States Navy
USSAFE	United States Strategic Air Forces in Europe
USSTAF	United States Strategic Air Forces
Vergeltung	Vengeance
Verteidigungsbereich	Defensive areas
Volksdeutche	Citizens of a country other than Germany who were considered Germans racially
Volkswagen	German jeep
Waffen-SS	Combat arm of the SS, in effect a partial duplication of the German Army
WD	War Department
WDCSA	War Department Chief of Staff, U.S. Army
Wehrmachtbefehlshaber Niederlande	Armed Forces Commander Netherlands
Wehrmachtfuehrungsstab	Armed Forces Operations Staff
Werfer	Mortars; rocket launchers
WFSt	*Wehrmachtfuehrungsstab* (Armed Forces Operations Staff)
Widerstandsnest	Resistance nest
WP	War Plans

XAP	Merchant cargo ship
Y Day	Target date for any military operation, specifically target date for OVERLORD
Zweite Stellung	German secondary defense position

Code Names

ABC–1	Agreements reached at Washington Conference, January–March 1941
ANVIL	The planned 1944 Allied invasion of Southern France in the Toulon–Marseille area
ARCADIA	U.S.–British staff conference at Washington, December 1941–January 1942
BOLERO	The build-up of troops and supplies in the United Kingdom in preparation for a cross-Channel attack
BUCCANEER	Operation planned against the Andaman Islands, Bay of Bengal, 21 June–15 November 1943
COCKADE	Diversionary operations in 1943 to pin down German forces in the west
CROSSBOW	The anticipated enemy pilotless aircraft offensive against England in 1944
DRAGOON	Allied invasion of southern coast of France, 15 August 1944, planned under the code name ANVIL
ECLIPSE	Plan for the initial phase of military occupation of Germany
EUREKA	The Tehran Conference, 26 November–2 December 1943
FABIUS	Amphibious landing exercises of all assault forces except Force U, early May 1944
FORTITUDE	Threat operation in 1944 directed against the Pas-de-Calais area
GYMNAST	1941 plan for invasion of North Africa
HARLEQUIN	Loading exercise in connection with operation COCKADE, September 1943
JUPITER	Plan to attack Norway
MAGNET	1942 build-up of U.S. forces in Northern Ireland
MULBERRIES	Artificial harbors for OVERLORD
NEPTUNE	Actual 1944 operations within OVERLORD. This code name was used for security reasons after September 1943 on all OVERLORD planning papers which referred to the target area and date.
OMAHA	Beach assaulted by troops of U.S. V Corps, 6 June 1944
OVERLORD	Plan for the invasion of northwest Europe, spring 1944
PIRATE	1943 exercise by Force J (British and Canadian)
POINTBLANK	The Combined Bomber Offensive from the United Kingdom against Germany
QUADRANT	The first Quebec Conference, August 1943

RANKIN	Plan for return to the Continent in the event of German deterioration
RATTLE	Conference held by the Combined Operations Head-quarters in 1943 to discuss amphibious tactics and techniques
ROUNDHAMMER	Code name used at the Washington Conference in May 1943 to designate a modified ROUNDUP invasion
ROUNDUP	Various 1941–43 plans for a cross-Channel attack in the final phases of the war
SEELOEWE (SEA LION)	The German planned invasion of England in 1940–41
SEXTANT	The Cairo Conference, 22–26 November 1943
SKYSCRAPER	A cross-Channel attack plan drawn by the Combined Commanders in spring of 1943
SLEDGEHAMMER	Plan for limited-objective attack across the Channel in 1942 designed either to take advantage of a crack in German morale or as "sacrifice" operation to aid Russians
STARKEY	Threat directed in 1943 against the Pas-de-Calais
TIGER	Invasion exercise of Force U (VII Corps)
TINDALL	Threat directed against Norway in 1943
TORCH	Allied invasion of North and Northwest Africa, 1942
TRIDENT	Washington Conference, May 1943
UTAH	Beach assaulted by troops of U.S. VII Corps, 6 June 1944
WADHAM	Threat directed against the Cotentin in 1943
ZITADELLE	German offensive in Russia, spring 1943

Bibliographical Note

Cross-Channel Attack is based almost entirely on documents now in the custody of the Department of the Army. These range from the official records of the Combined Chiefs of Staff to the operational journals of combat battalions; they include all the records of the German Army which have not been destroyed or sent to the USSR. Quantitatively the archives containing material relevant to this book are measured literally in scores of tons. Evidently no one researcher could have examined the whole record. In the past five years, however, the combined researches of Department of the Army historians have sifted through the bulk of it. While the author cannot claim a definitive exploitation of all the sources, he can at least reasonably hope that the available documents of major interest have not escaped his attention. Free access was had to all relevant material regardless of classification.

Primary Sources

I

The formal record of the wartime proceedings of the U.S. Joint Chiefs of Staff and the Combined Chiefs of Staff consists of minutes of their meetings together with papers embodying all the proposals which they formally considered. This record includes minutes of the plenary conferences presided over by President Roosevelt and Prime Minister Churchill.

Rounding out the Joint and Combined record are the thousands of cables between Roosevelt and Churchill, between the War Department and the theater, be-tween the British Chiefs of Staff and their military mission in Washington, and between various commanders and planners. Light is thrown on many of the official ambiguities by the personal letters and cables between General Marshall and General Eisenhower.

The heart of the material for the present volume is the very large collection of SHAEF documents. Again cables, letters, memoranda, and minutes of both routine and special staff meetings recording the day-to-day work of the headquarters comprise the bulk of the collection. Besides these, however, SHAEF collected extracts from memoranda by the British Chiefs of Staff and their affiliated planning bodies as well as minutes of those British Chiefs of Staff meetings at which OVERLORD matters were discussed. Finally SHAEF inherited most of the records of its predecessors, COSSAC and the Combined Commanders. In supplementing the written record a series of interviews conducted by Forrest C. Pogue of the ETO Section of the Historical Division in 1946 with British commanders and planners proved very useful particularly in filling in background to important decisions. The author has interviewed and corresponded with a number of American commanders.

The bulk of the narrative of operations is based on preliminary studies by War Department historians (see below), but these were checked and supplemented by reference to the primary sources. The latter consist of unit journals, after action reports, and interviews conducted by historical officers with participants in most cases immediately after the battle. The unit journals contain most of the contemporaneous incoming and outgoing messages of the headquarters involved together with overlays of troop dispositions, reports, intelligence estimates, and other supporting documents. These constitute the principal primary sources for the history of operations during June 1944 except for the action of the two airborne divisions. No contemporary record of any value for the historian was kept by the airborne units. This lack was fortunately remedied in good part by the extensive interviews conducted by Colonel S. L. A. Marshall with airborne officers and men during June and July 1944.

The much abbreviated accounts of British operations are largely based on information supplied by the British Cabinet Office Historical Section.

II

Information on German preparations and combat comes from original records of the German Army and from manuscript histories prepared after the war by more than two hundred German general and general staff officers working under direction of Col. Harold E. Potter, USA. Original documents include army headquarters war diaries (*KTB*'s) and their supporting papers, special orders, reports, telegrams, and conference minutes. Although a large number of documents were destroyed by German order or by Allied looters, and a considerable number were sent to the Soviet Union, the collection remaining available to the Western historian is still relatively rich for the pre-D-Day story of the German Army in France. In contrast, few original records of German operations in Normandy sur-

vided the annihilation of von Schlieben's force in the Cotentin and the later August collapse of the *Seventh Army*. The principal extant source is the *Seventh Army KTB*. This is supplemented by the postwar accounts of various unit commanders and staff officers. The War Diary of *Army Group B* has been lost and only a few of the supporting documents remain. The *OB WEST* diary has been preserved only from 1 July 1944.

Some use was made of German naval and air force records. The U.S. Navy Department has duplicates and microfilms of original German Navy documents held by the British Admiralty. Especially useful for the present work were the war diaries of Admiral Doenitz and of Admiral Krancke, Naval Commander in the West. Luftwaffe records are particularly spotty. Most useful were those preserved by the Luftwaffe Historical Section in the Von Rohden Collection, now at the Air University, Maxwell Field (microfilms in the Library of Congress).

III

Following is a guide to some of the principal documents and document collections.

AAF files. Army Air Force files containing operational records of the Eighth and Ninth Air Forces. Now at the Air University, Maxwell Field, Montgomery, Alabama.

Adm. file. Administrative file; contains miscellaneous papers mostly from nonoperational headquarters in the period before D Day. Like the Pre-Invasion file (q.v.) it includes chiefly documents which were rescued from destruction or dispersion by historians in the European theaters.

Barker papers. Personal papers, chiefly correspondence, of Maj. Gen. Ray W. Barker (ret.) specially made available by him to War Department historians.

CC. Combined Commanders' papers filed in SHAEF SGS files (q.v.). A duplicate collection is in the Pre-Invasion file (q.v.).

CCS. Combined Chiefs of Staff papers and minutes of meetings. These are all contained in the OPD files (q.v.). CCS papers are memoranda, reports, reprints of cables, etc., prepared by the U.S. or British Chiefs of Staff or by their subordinate agencies and submitted for combined discussion. Minutes of the meetings are not stenographic. Notes were kept by U.S. and British secretaries. The minutes in final form were specifically and individually approved by each of the Combined Chiefs.

COS. British Chiefs of Staff papers and minutes of meetings. Selections of memoranda and excerpts of minutes relating to matters of interest to SHAEF are bound and separately filed with the SHAEF SGS collection (q.v.). The few COS papers preserved in other special SHAEF files are so cited in the footnotes.

COSSAC. Designates papers officially issued by General Morgan's headquarters and the minutes of COSSAC staff meetings. All such documents are to be found separately bound in the SHAEF SGS files (q.v.).

C/S file. Contains documents filed during the war in the Office of the Chief of Staff. Now held as a separate collection by Historical Records Section, Departmental Record Branch, AGO.

Dep C/S file. A small collection of documents which during the war were filed in the office of the Deputy Chief of Staff. Now held in a separate collection by Historical Record Section, AGO.

Diary of CinC. MS diary of the Office of the Commander in Chief, kept for General Eisenhower by his naval aide, Capt. Harry C. Butcher. It was begun in July 1942 just before Eisenhower became commander in chief of the Mediterranean Theater of Operations. Edited excerpts have been printed by Butcher in *My Three Years with Eisenhower* (New York, 1946).

Eisenhower Personal Files. Contains communications between General Eisenhower and General Marshall including both personal letters and cables which had limited distribution and were not sent to regular operational files.

ETO file. Files of the European theater headquarters now held by the Organization Records Branch, Records Administration Center, AGO.

FUSA file. Administrative and pre-D-Day planning papers of First U.S. Army now held by the Organization Records Branch, AGO.

Hist Div files. A miscellaneous collection of documents chiefly comprising material prepared or collected by War Department historians. It includes interviews, responses to special questionnaires, manuscript histories, and certain British documents not found in U.S. operational files.

JCS. Joint (U.S.) Chiefs of Staff papers and minutes of meetings. Copies of all JCS documents cited can be found in OPD files (q.v.). The JCS papers include memoranda by the Joint Chiefs as a body, by individual members, and by subordinate agencies. Minutes of the meetings were not stenographic. Cf. note under CCS.

JIC. Joint Intelligence Committee (British) estimates found, unless otherwise noted, in SHAEF SGS files (q.v.) in separately bound collection of JIC papers.

JPS. Joint Planning Staff (U.S.) papers and minutes of meetings. Copies of JPS documents are in OPD ABC files, which include in most cases not only the final planners' memoranda, but OPD drafts, discussions, and working notes.

JWPC. Joint War Planning Committee (U.S.) papers, many of which were reissued as JPS or JCS documents. All cited are in OPD files. Cf. note under JPS.

Navy Dept files. The manuscript studies of U.S. operations and the occasional documents cited are in the Office of Naval Record. German documents are in the so-called Tambach collection which contains carbon duplicates and microfilms of German originals held by the British Admiralty office.

OPD files. Collection of the Operations Division of the War Department. They include the central files bearing the OPD decimal classification, and two separate collections: one kept by the Strategy and Policy Group within OPD which is identified by the initials ABC, and one kept by the Executive Group identified as the Exec file.

Pre-Inv file. The Pre-Invasion files contain miscellaneous papers on planning and strategy originating with or collected by various headquarters in the European theater before the invasion. The documents were turned over to War Department historians in the theater during 1944, and are now held by the Historical Records Section, AGO.

SHAEF files. Files of the Supreme Headquarters, Allied Expeditionary Force. This is a very large collection of all the working papers of the staff sections of General Eisenhower's headquarters together with records of COSSAC, the Combined Commanders, and the British Chiefs of Staff. Files of each of the five general staff sections and of the Secretary of the General Staff (SGS) and the Adjutant General (AG) are separate, each containing the papers of chief concern to the respective section. For the present work the richest files are those of SGS, G–3, and AG. The SGS section actually contains the bulk of the important cables, memos, minutes, and planning papers with which SHAEF was concerned. Files are held by the Historical Records Section, AGO.

12th A Gp file. Operational files of the 12th Army Group with certain planning papers from the preinvasion period when the headquarters was designated 1st Army Group. Files now separately held by the Historical Records Section, AGO.

USSTAF file. Comprises documents specially collected by the chief USSTAF historian. Formerly in the Air Force Historical Section office, some of these papers have been transferred to the Spaatz file in the Library of Congress. Others can be found in AAF files at the Air University, Maxwell Field, Montgomery, Alabama.

WD Cable log. The large collection of cables which cleared through the War Department Message Center, filed by date in incoming and outgoing books.

Secondary Sources

I

Unpublished preliminary historical studies by Army, Navy, and Air Force historians greatly facilitated the task of research into subjects peripheral to the main narrative. Especially useful was the series, The Administrative and Logistical History of the European Theater of Operations. The eleven volumes of special studies on such matters as training, manpower, planning, and supply were written by Army historians in the European Theater of Operations under the direction of Maj. Roland G. Ruppenthal, assistant theater historian, USFET. The Administrative History, U.S. Naval Forces in Europe, on file in the Historical Division, contains material on naval organization for the assault. Other manuscript studies of naval administrative history, on file in the Navy Department, were consulted chiefly for aspects of the submarine war and landing craft procurement. Of some help were two manuscript histories of the Ninth Air Force, one by Lt. Col. Robert H. George and one by Col. William B. Reed, both in Air Force files. The 1500-page history of the French Forces of the Interior, prepared by Capt. Lucien Galimand, Capt. Marcel Vigneras, and Maj. R. A. Bourne-Paterson, is an important compilation of information on the French Resistance, drafted in 1945 from documents that have since been widely scattered. From interview material, Col. S. L. A. Marshall made a series of small-unit studies of airborne operations in Normandy. These manuscripts in Historical Division files are often brilliantly illuminating as to the nature of the fighting in the Cotentin.

II

Published sources include official reports and dispatches of commanders, special studies generally for limited distribution, official histories, unofficial histories, and memoirs.

Of the dispatches and reports, most of which are not very useful for historical purposes, special mention need be made only of "Despatch of Air Chief Marshal Sir Trafford Leigh-Mallory," *Fourth Supplement to the London Gazette No. 37838*, 31 December 1946; and *Report by Allied Naval Commander-in-Chief Expeditionary Force on Operation* NEPTUNE (London, 1944), 3 vols. Both of these reports are exceptionally full. A pertinent special study particularly valuable for the OVERLORD story is George E. Mowry, *Landing Craft and the WPB (Civilian Production Administration, Historical Reports on War Administration: WPB Special Study No. 11)* (Washington, 1946).

The Historical Division of the Department of the Army has published in the AMERICAN FORCES IN ACTION series, two preliminary narratives of U.S. operations in Normandy in June 1944 which cover most of the fighting described in *Cross-Channel Attack*. These narratives are [Charles H. Taylor] *Omaha Beachhead* (Washington, 1945) and [R. G. Ruppenthal] *Utah Beach to Cherbourg* (Washington, 1947). Fully documented manuscripts of both studies are on file in the Historical Division. This documentation has not been repeated in the present volume. Official histories of the U.S. Navy and Air Forces are just beginning to appear and for the most part those so far published do not cover the period with which this volume is chiefly concerned. However, some use has been made of the first two volumes of Wesley F. Craven and James L. Cate (eds.), *The Army Air Forces in World War II* (Chicago, 1947 and 1948). In addition, portions of that work still in manuscript have been made available to the author by the Air Force Historical Section. The published volumes of the semiofficial naval history, Samuel E. Morison, *The Battle of the Atlantic* (Boston, 1948), and *idem, Operations in North African Waters* (Boston, 1947), bear only indirectly on the subjects of this volume. Col. C. P. Stacey, *The Canadian Army, 1939–1945 (An Official Historical Summary)* (Ottawa, 1948), a preliminary work, is the only official account of British or Dominion forces to appear so far.

Semiofficial histories exist for most U.S. combat units but few go beyond the bare outlines of after action reports colored by accounts of individual exploits. A noteworthy exception is the history of the 101st Airborne Division: Leonard Rapport and Arthur Norwood, Jr., *Rendezvous With Destiny* (Washington, 1948).

Of the unofficial histories touching OVERLORD far the best now in print is Robert E. Sherwood, *Roosevelt and Hopkins:* *An Intimate History* (New York, 1948). A revised edition with supplementary material was published in 1950. Henry L. Stimson and McGeorge Bundy, *On Active Service in Peace and War* (New York, 1948) is a fine volume of memoirs and a valuable contribution to the strategy story at the highest level. Some use has been made of Dwight D. Eisenhower, *Crusade in Europe* (New York, 1948) and Lt. Gen. Frederick E. Morgan, *Overture to Overlord* (New York, 1950), although these books deal with subjects abundantly covered by the primary sources consulted. Captain Harry C. Butcher, *My Three Years With Eisenhower* (New York, 1948) is not the "personal diary" of Captain Butcher as advertised but a collection of excerpts from the personal and official diary of General Eisenhower kept for him by Captain Butcher. Winston S. Churchill, *The Grand Alliance* (New York, 1950) touches only on the very beginnings of the OVERLORD story.

UNITED STATES ARMY IN WORLD WAR II

The following volumes have been published or are in press:

The War Department
  Chief of Staff: Prewar Plans and Preparations
  Washington Command Post: The Operations Division
  Strategic Planning for Coalition Warfare: 1941-1942
  Strategic Planning for Coalition Warfare: 1943-1944
  Global Logistics and Strategy: 1940-1943
  Global Logistics and Strategy: 1943-1945
  The Army and Economic Mobilization
  The Army and Industrial Manpower
The Army Ground Forces
  The Organization of Ground Combat Troops
  The Procurement and Training of Ground Combat Troops
The Army Service Forces
  The Organization and Role of the Army Service Forces
The Western Hemisphere
  The Framework of Hemisphere Defense
  Guarding the United States and Its Outposts
The War in the Pacific
  The Fall of the Philippines
  Guadalcanal: The First Offensive
  Victory in Papua
  CARTWHEEL: The Reduction of Rabaul
  Seizure of the Gilberts and Marshalls
  Campaign in the Marianas
  The Approach to the Philippines
  Leyte: The Return to the Philippines
  Triumph in the Philippines
  Okinawa: The Last Battle
  Strategy and Command: The First Two Years
The Mediterranean Theater of Operations
  Northwest Africa: Seizing the Initiative in the West
  Sicily and the Surrender of Italy
  Salerno to Cassino
  Cassino to the Alps
The European Theater of Operations
  Cross-Channel Attack
  Breakout and Pursuit
  The Lorraine Campaign
  The Siegfried Line Campaign
  The Ardennes: Battle of the Bulge
  The Last Offensive

Index